Praise for *Mere Christian Hermeneutics*

I select one highlight among many luminous points in this book: *Mere Christian Hermeneutics* offers a reformed catholic paradigm for reading divinely inspired, canonical Scripture in the context of the one, holy, catholic, and apostolic church and within a christological, historically attuned, and eschatologically oriented Protestant framework. And this is only one theme it rehearses. Could this be Kevin Vanhoozer's most brilliant book yet? *Tolle, lege, crede*!

—Gregg R. Allison, professor of Christian theology, Southern Baptist Theological Seminary

This is a state-of-the-art work in Christian theological hermeneutics. Vanhoozer not only clarifies a whole range of contested issues but also offers careful analysis, penetrating insights, and a constructive way forward. *Mere Christian Hermeneutics* is a creative yet biblically disciplined proposal worthy of close engagement by everyone who is serious about reading Scripture as the Word of God. This is a stellar contribution to Vanhoozer's promising "mere Christian" theological project. Highly recommended!

—Uche Anizor, professor of theology, Talbot School of Theology, Biola University

Kevin Vanhoozer once more draws deep connections between reading practices old and new, theological confessions catholic and reformed, and hermeneutical insights literary and "literal." The result: literal + figural = transfiguring interpretation. This theological *tour de force* is generously marked throughout by a wonderful wisdom and lyrical largesse. Case studies on light in Scripture raise, as it were, "literally fascinating" questions. This book will not resolve all the church's fractured interpretive debates, but may it illuminate her pilgrimage through the ongoing struggles of biblical interpretation in our time.

—Richard S. Briggs, principal, Lindisfarne College of Theology

In *Mere Christian Hermeneutics*, Kevin Vanhoozer constructs a bridge across the modern divide between exegesis and theology. He suggests a rapprochement that presses for engagement with both literal and spiritual ("transfigural") readings. With his characteristic engagement and facility with ancient and modern interpreters of Scripture, Vanhoozer problematizes disinterested readings and seeks to demonstrate the existential stake all readers have in biblical interpretation. A bold clarion call from an eminent scholar for Scriptural reading as a spiritual endeavor.

—Jeannine K. Brown, David Price Professor of Biblical and Theological Foundations, Bethel Seminary

For nearly three decades Kevin Vanhoozer has been the leading evangelical scholar of Christian theological interpretation of Scripture. With this volume he finally delivers what so many of us have been waiting for: the mature fruit of his long labors. Vanhoozer understands that church, theology, and hermeneutics all need each other as fellow creatures and servants of God's living word. In this "reformed catholic" proposal, we see all the puzzle pieces brought together by a lover and lifelong student of Christ's powerful speech. It is a fitting completion of Vanhoozer's "mere Christian" trilogy; it will immediately become a touchstone for pastors, theologians, and biblical scholars. Above all, it directs readers' gaze to the face of Christ, shining with the Spirit's light. The glory that once shone on Tabor through the human flesh of Jesus is one and the same as the glory that shines even now through the human words of Scripture. Vanhoozer helps us to see what was true all along: namely, that transfiguration encapsulates our life with God through his word—whether spoken aloud, written in ink, or incarnate in flesh and blood.

—Brad East, associate professor of theology, Abilene Christian University

Mere Christian Hermeneutics puts theological interpretation on the offensive side of the ball. The various critical approaches spawned by the historicist hegemony of the last two centuries come with their methods and variegated vis-à-vis. The temptation is to situate theological interpretation within this scholarly fray, maneuvering it in conversation with or over against these competing options. Vanhoozer doesn't play by these rules because the stakes are too high. If God is the authorizing agent of all Scripture, Old and New Testaments, then everything changes. This confession of faith places all methods and approaches in service of this organon of Scripture's nature. From Vanhoozer's vantage point, Holy Scripture remains on the short side of the Mount of Transfiguration if readers are canonically unaware and redemptively irresponsible. *Mere Christian Hermeneutics* calls on its readers to ascend the mount of a transfigured text, to see Jesus just as he is. The church and its members—and academics too!—would do well to go hiking with Professor Vanhoozer up this mountain. Who knows? Perhaps we will be transfigured as well. I certainly hope so.

—Mark Gignilliat, professor of divinity, Beeson Divinity School, Samford University

With so many of us concerned that we are facing a crisis in the formation of disciples today, Kevin Vanhoozer's rich and beautiful offering could not be more timely or important. Mining the robust biblical imagery of transfiguration, Vanhoozer offers a vision of biblical engagement in which we ourselves are transfigured and conformed to the image of Christ when we rightly read Scripture. At heart, Vanhoozer is issuing a much-needed call to churches and seminaries to do all we can to become theological reading cultures in which Christians are formed through Scripture to be literate citizens of the gospel who bear witness to the light of Christ in the world as they are transfigured into the likeness of Christ. This clarion call is a must-read for pastors, seminary professors and administrators, and all who care about deep Christian formation.

—Kristen Deede Johnson, dean and vice present of academic affairs, G. W. and Edna Haworth Professor of Educational Ministries and Leadership, Western Theological Seminary

Kevin Vanhoozer, a leading and generational pastor-theologian, invites us to consider how the transfiguration of Christ, an experiential-learning fieldtrip taken by Jesus' inner three disciples, serves as a novel and meaningful symbol for Christian hermeneutics. While these disciples were in many ways blindsided, this significant textbook helps us encounter the triune God, Father, Son, and Spirit, not on a literal mountaintop but in daily ascents to the Holy Scriptures where each member of the Godhead glitters theological brilliance onto the pages of our embodiment: honing our biblical and theological interpretation, transfiguring our desires, and transforming our agency closer to his likeness.

—Matthew D. Kim, professor of preaching and pastoral leadership, George W. Truett Chair of Preaching and Evangelism, Truett Seminary, Baylor University

Biblical scholars treat all sorts of theological themes. Why then is historical-critical biblical scholarship not enough by itself? In this major study, the eminent theologian Kevin Vanhoozer answers this question. With the erudite rigor and gentlemanly patience for which he is known, he sifts through a vast array of approaches and arguments. I love his emphasis on Christ's transfiguration, an event that literally reveals the theophanic and eschatological power of God's Word in history, requiring the eyes of faith and calling forth divine-human communion.

—Matthew Levering, James N. Jr. and Mary D. Perry Chair of Theology, Mundelein Seminary

Vanhoozer ranges widely and thought-provokingly in this lucid and challenging book. It will surely become a landmark in discussions of what it means to read the Bible theologically.

—R. W. L. Moberly, professor of theology and biblical interpretation, Durham University

An ambitious book from a trustworthy yet always-refreshing voice, *Mere Christian Hermeneutics* is Vanhoozer's clarion call to embrace the daring possibility of faithful biblical interpretation. Given his life's work, Vanhoozer is able to ascend through the complexity and dissolution of hermeneutics to the light of clarity. Rigorous enough to serve as a formative textbook for beginning exegetical theologians and capacious enough to invigorate mature practitioners of the craft, all readers will be revived to kneel at the feet of God's voice in Scripture and become faithful respondents, "canonically aware and redemptively responsible." This is a beautiful book that will become, I wager, a giant in the field because it so faithfully points to the light of Christ.

—Amy Peeler, Kenneth T. Wessner Professor of
New Testament, Wheaton College

From a giant in systematic thinking about the Bible comes a monumental and generous volume that promises to lead biblical and theological scholars from different traditions together in a task they share with all believers: to hear God speak in the Scriptures and thereby to be changed into the likeness of his Son. The title's *mere* has little to do with modesty or limits, but trades on the word's original sense of "pure" and "gleaming." For Vanhoozer explores how reading Scripture is properly done in the service of entering into God's glory. This goal orders his presentation around the reality of Christ's transfiguration, with Scripture as the divine avenue for participating in this transformative truth. Creatively conceived, richly articulated, and faithfully penetrating, Vanhoozer's book marks—for Protestants, Catholics, and evangelicals alike—a converting invitation as much as a scholarly landmark.

—Ephraim Radner, professor emeritus of historical theology,
Wycliffe College at the University of Toronto

What a gift this book is to our age. It is not just an expansive survey of a vast field, nor just an invitation to cooperate and come to terms, nor just a curated ensemble of helpful techniques and methods. Beyond all that, Vanhoozer has set forth here a coherent and comprehensive vision for the interdisciplinary work of interpreting Scripture. *Mere Christian Hermeneutics* reaches the heights of clarity and throws light in all directions.

—Fred Sanders, professor, Torrey Honors College, Biola University

This book is what we need now. Before the turn of the century many of us struggled with the meaning of meaning, and Kevin Vanhoozer's *Is There a Meaning in This Text?* helped us find a way through everything that was going on. *Mere Christian Hermeneutics* by Vanhoozer goes further and emphasizes the outcomes of Scripture study in terms of righteousness and loving and serving the Lord. The idea that there is such a thing as mere Christian hermeneutics—a shared interpretive perspective of all Christians everywhere from the resurrection to the second coming—needs attention. Vanhoozer helps readers grapple with the dynamics of and variations within this shared perspective by showing how frames of reference and reading cultures shift interpretation. Every student and every pastor needs to read *Mere Christian Hermeneutics*. I know how much it already has helped me.

—Gary Edward Schnittjer, distinguished professor of Old Testament
at Cairn University, coauthor of *How to Study the Bible's Use of the Bible*,
author of the award-winning *Old Testament Use of Old Testament*

Vanhoozer is my favorite modern writer on hermeneutics, and this is my favorite book of his on the topic. Not only does he tackle the toughest questions, but he does so in a way that is both grounded in the literal sense and extends this literality to a transfigural theological reading. Employing the transfiguration, he shows us why we must interpret not only grammatically and historically but theologically and eschatologically. While theological interpretation has suffered from lack of clarity, this book shows why we must read theologically and how we ought to do so. My hope is that evangelical hermeneutics will be transfigured by this important and timely work.

—Patrick Schreiner, associate professor of New Testament and biblical theology, Midwestern Baptist Theological Seminary

Faithful interpretation of the beauty and depth of Scripture requires sensitivity to its literary, theological, and transformative elements; however, modern-day discipline-entrenched academics have fashioned these elements into tools of division, obscuring Scripture's beauty with man-made towers of scholarly achievement. In *Mere Christian Hermeneutics*, Kevin Vanhoozer reminds us that interpretation is not a siloed endeavor for competing craftsmen but rather an exercise in knowing and seeing God in the face of Christ as God's people read and are transformed by his Word. Building on biblical themes such as ascent and transfiguration, Vanhoozer masterfully constructs a proposal for a fully formed "literal sense" that takes seriously Scripture in all its beauty and depth as God's address to us. If taken seriously, *Mere Christian Hermeneutics* can overcome the various divides that affect not only the academy but also the global church, drawing God's people together under the light of Christ.

—Brandon D. Smith, chair of the Hobbs School of Theology and Ministry, associate professor of theology and early Christianity, Oklahoma Baptist University; cofounder, the Center for Baptist Renewal

Mere Christian Hermeneutics explores a way for all Christians—biblical scholars, theologians, clergy, and laity alike—to read Scripture theologically, the way it is meant to be read, on its own terms. This way combines both letter and spirit on a Christ-bound journey to the mountaintop. Vanhoozer is a reliable guide as readers ascend the slopes of Mount Tabor to behold the human flesh and divine glory of the Word of God (written and incarnate) and then seek to reflect that light of Christ to the world. In this excellent and insightful volume, he exhorts the church to build, once again, something so desperately needed: a Christian reading culture that unites rather than divides.

—Keith Stanglin, professor of historical theology, Harding School of Theology, executive director, Center for Christian Studies

According to Thomas Aquinas, it is better to illuminate than merely to shine, to deliver to others contemplated truths than merely to contemplate. Over the past several decades, Kevin Vanhoozer has distinguished himself as one of the brightest of lights in the constellation of Christian theology and has devoted himself to enlightening others through his teaching and writing. In the present volume, Vanhoozer delivers truths long contemplated to the reading public for its greater illumination. With the help of a clear distinction (between Scripture's literal sense and its providential frame of reference) and a lucid analogy (Christ's divine light is to his body as Scripture's "transfigural" sense is to its letter), Vanhoozer illumines a pathway to reading Holy Scripture within the providential economy of divine light that shines most fully in the face of Jesus Christ and that summons us to hear his voice (Matt 17:5). *Mere Christian Hermeneutics* is a clarion call to faithful and fruitful biblical interpretation.

—Scott R. Swain, president, James Woodrow Hassell Professor of Systematic Theology, Reformed Theological Seminary, Orlando

Kevin Vanhoozer has a gift for revitalizing evangelical theology with imaginative paradigms. This hermeneutical magnum opus does it again! The transfiguration paradigm coherently extends his earlier thinking—on textual meaning, the drama of doctrine, and thus theological exegesis—yet sheds new light on an enduring challenge and a glorious reality: the canonical, Christological extension of Scripture's literal sense.

—Daniel Treier, Gunther H. Knoedler Professor of Theology, Wheaton College and Graduate School

Kevin Vanhoozer is someone who I am glad has shaped the reading cultures in which I participate. This present volume exemplifies all of the reasons for my gratitude: a meticulous attention to the theological nature of interpretation, a clear emphasis on the need for moral and spiritual transformation of the reader, and a resolute priority on the ontology of Scripture as guide for hermeneutics. Not only that, but here he both shows and tells: through an insightful engagement with Christ's transfiguration and other figurally related biblical texts, Vanhoozer proves to us the rich promise of his theological vision. I am thankful for his intuitive influence on my work, and this book clearly illustrates why.

—Fellipe do Vale, assistant professor of biblical and systematic theology, Trinity Evangelical Divinity School

MERE CHRISTIAN HERMENEUTICS

MERE CHRISTIAN HERMENEUTICS

Transfiguring What It Means to Read the Bible Theologically

KEVIN J. VANHOOZER

ZONDERVAN ACADEMIC

ZONDERVAN ACADEMIC

Mere Christian Hermeneutics

Published in Grand Rapids, Michigan, by Zondervan. Zondervan is a registered trademark of The Zondervan Corporation, L.L.C., a wholly owned subsidiary of HarperCollins Christian Publishing, Inc.

Requests for information should be addressed to customercare@harpercollins.com.

Zondervan titles may be purchased in bulk for educational, business, fundraising, or sales promotional use. For information, please email SpecialMarkets@Zondervan.com.

ISBN 978-0-310-16023-6 (audio)

Library of Congress Cataloging-in-Publication Data

Names: Vanhoozer, Kevin J., author.
Title: Mere Christian Hermeneutics : Transfiguring What It Means to Read the Bible Theologically / Kevin J. Vanhoozer.
Description: Grand Rapids : Zondervan, [2024] | Includes bibliographical references and index.
Identifiers: LCCN 2023057923 (print) | LCCN 2023057924 (ebook) | ISBN 9780310234388 (hardcover) | ISBN 9780310114512 (ebook)
Subjects: LCSH: Jesus Christ--Transfiguration. | Hermeneutics.
Classification: LCC BT410 .V36 2024 (print) | LCC BT410 (ebook) | DDC 232.9/56—dc23/eng/20240329
LC record available at https://lccn.loc.gov/2023057923
LC ebook record available at https://lccn.loc.gov/2023057924

Cover design: Brian Bobel Design
Cover image: © Universal History Archive / GettyImages
Interior design: Sara Colley

Printed in the United States of America

24 25 26 27 28 LBC 7 6 5 4 3

For Dan Treier

Contents

Part 2: Figuring Out Literal Interpretation

Part 3: Transfiguring Literal Interpretation

Preface

The philosophers have only interpreted the world, in various ways. The point, however, is to change it.
—Karl Marx

Can biblical interpretation change the world? It may be a moot point in light of widespread biblical illiteracy, a consequence of the decline of biblical civilization in America, and in the West in general.[1] There was a time, however, when biblical interpretation shaped civilization. The patristic period created a culture of reading that inhabited a Christian symbolic universe, a universe that is no more, thanks to the "Big Crunch" of secular modernity that flattened it.[2] There is today an urgent need to recover Christian practices of reading the Bible theologically, for the sake of the well-being of the church, academy, and world alike.

The 2010 Cape Town Commitment, the product of the Third Lausanne Congress, issued a call to action, urging theological educators to recenter the study of the Bible "as the core discipline in Christian theology."[3] This is not a plea for a return to Christendom, much less for the supremacy of a single denomination, system of theology, or exegetical method. It is a call for a return to biblical Christianity, for a theological approach to reading Scripture with and for the people of God, past and present, from east, west, north, and south. It is a call to respect the heritage of literal and spiritual interpretation. It is a call to see exegesis, systematics, and church history alike as properly theological disciplines. It is, I submit, a call for a "mere Christian" hermeneutics: a

1. See Grant Wacker, "The Demise of Biblical Civilization," in *The Bible in America: Essays in Cultural History*, ed. Nathan O. Hatch and Mark A. Noll (Oxford: Oxford University Press, 1982), 121–38; and Mark A. Noll, *America's Book: The Rise and Decline of a Bible Civilization, 1794–1911* (Oxford: Oxford University Press, 2022).

2. On the contribution of the church fathers to these developments, see Lewis Ayres, "Seven Theses on Dogmatics and Patristics in Catholic Theology," *Modern Theology* 38, no. 1 (2022): 45.

3. "A Confession of Faith and a Call to Action," Part IIF, 4(D), https://lausanne.org/content/ctc/ctcommitment#p2-1.

principled approach to biblical interpretation that (1) asks what we are doing in reading the Bible, particularly for its literal sense, and (2) emerges from both the historic consensus on the essentials of the faith and a church-based understanding of what the Bible is primarily for.

We live on the far side of the "demise of biblical civilization," that momentous revolutionary change when modern people no longer read the Bible as telling the true story of the world. Of the many factors behind the collapse of the Bible's de facto authority, perhaps the most devastating was interpretive disagreement not only over what it says but, more radically, over how to read it.

Biblical Christianity matters. It therefore behooves us to ask what it means to be "biblical," and "literal." The suffix provides a clue. *Logical* means "relating to or being in accord with logic." *Comical* means "relating to comedy." *Ethical* means "relating or conforming to certain standards of behavior." Similarly, being *biblical* means speaking, thinking, and acting in accordance with the Scriptures, and *literal* means reading in accordance with the letter. Sadly, many people, including confessing Christians, have lost the ability to discern (or even discuss) whether a particular idea or practice is warranted by Scripture—or to define what *literal* means.

It was James Barr who first alerted me to the importance of being able to say what it means to be biblical, as well as to the challenge of defining what it means to be literal. Simply holding a "high" view of Scripture is no guarantee that one's interpretation will be sound. Nor does citing verses here and there make for a biblical theology; heretics do this too. Barr castigated so-called fundamentalists for their supposed "literal" interpretations, showing in example after example how poor their readings actually were, at times not even getting the genre right (is it I, Lord?).[4] How, then, can we get the Bible right? There are so many ways to read, so many schools of biblical interpretation, so many "methods for Matthew," to cite one title in the "Methods in Biblical Interpretation" series.[5] That there is a conflict of interpretations is well known. The more intense conflict, however, is between approaches to interpretation and competing visions of what biblical interpretation is for.

The present book is about what it means to read the Bible *theologically*. In 2010 Miroslav Volf declared the renewed interest in theological interpretation of the Bible to be "the most significant theological development in the last two decades," comparable to the rediscovery of the Trinitarian nature of God in the early twentieth century.[6] Most significant, perhaps, but surely one of the most

4. See, e.g., James Barr *Fundamentalism* (Philadelphia: Westminster, 1978); and Barr, *Escaping from Fundamentalism* (London: SCM, 1984).

5. *Methods for Matthew*, ed. Mark Allan Powell (Cambridge: Cambridge University Press, 2009).

6. Miroslav Volf, *Captive to the Word of God: Engaging the Scriptures for Contemporary Theological Reflection* (Grand Rapids: Eerdmans, 2010), 14.

controversial and misunderstood developments. I served as general editor of the award-winning *Dictionary for Theological Interpretation of the Bible*, yet despite its being a *dictionary*, a definition of "theological interpretation of Scripture" (henceforth TIS) proved elusive. In the introduction, I confidently said what theological interpretation *is not*, gestured toward what it is (e.g., it pertains to God), yet concluded by acknowledging a smorgasbord of approaches operating under the general rubric.[7] Minimally, we could say that TIS is "interpretation that keeps theological concerns primary."[8]

Much to my chagrin, TIS fell less like a bombshell than a lead balloon into the playground of the exegetes. Historical and systematic theologians were generally enthused, but many (not all) biblical scholars came to regard theological interpretation with a hermeneutic of suspicion. What was new about TIS was worrisome; what was good about it was old news, something biblical scholars had already been doing. The following evaluation is representative: "Theological Interpretation of Scripture is partly disparate movement, partly a call to reformation in biblical interpretation, partly a disorganized array of methodological commitments in hermeneutics, partly a serious enterprise and partly (I suspect) a fad."[9]

There is some truth to every part of this verdict. For example, many parties were scaling the mountain that is TIS by different routes. Having observed (and tried) several of these attempts, however, I have concluded there is a better way. Like the Sherpas who serve as both guides and bearers of camping equipment, ropes, food, and even oxygen canisters, I here plot a new course, although it remains to be seen whether I am climbing Sinai or Tabor (or both). In any case, it is a mountain with light on top.

Twenty years ago, I wrote another book about biblical interpretation.[10] Its primary aim was to respond to the postmodern challenge that drained the Bible (and preaching) of authority by claiming that texts, including biblical texts, have no stable, authoritative, or objective meaning.[11] My argument was theological but pursued two related projects simultaneously, flip-flopping between general and special hermeneutics, so that it was not always clear on which track the

---

7. Kevin J. Vanhoozer, introduction to *Dictionary for Theological Interpretation of the Bible* (Grand Rapids: Baker Academic, 2005), 19–25.

8. Stephen Fowl, "Christian Theological Interpretation," in *The New Cambridge Companion to Biblical Interpretation*, ed. Ian Boxall and Bradley C. Gregory (Cambridge: Cambridge University Press, 2023), 189.

9. D. A. Carson, "Theological Interpretation of Scripture: Yes, But . . ." in *Theological Commentary: Evangelical Perspectives*, ed. R. Michael Allen (London: T&T Clark, 2011), 187.

10. Kevin J. Vanhoozer, *Is There a Meaning in This Text? The Bible, the Reader, and the Morality of Literary Knowledge* (Grand Rapids: Zondervan, 1998). A tenth anniversary edition, with a new preface, was published in 2009.

11. The meaning of *meaning* continues to be controversial. For a recent discussion, see Steven Cassedy, *What Do We Mean When We Talk About Meaning?* (Oxford: Oxford University Press, 2022).

engine was running. Was I arguing that *all* books should be read "theologically," or only the Bible? Answer: I was arguing that all books should be read like the Bible, namely, by trying to do justice to the "real presence" of authorial meaning by inferring their communicative intent from what authors actually did with their words. I inadvertently led some readers to think that I was saying the Bible should be read like every other book, such that biblical hermeneutics was a subset of general hermeneutics, when in fact I was trying to argue the opposite. So much for authorial intent!

While reading Scripture is in many respects similar to reading books in general, reading the Bible is ultimately marked by an even greater dissimilarity. What primarily makes reading the Bible *like* reading other books is that both have human creatures as their authors; what makes reading the Bible *unlike* reading other books is that its primary author is God. To say that is to make a confession of faith. The question is, for people of faith, what difference should this make? Minimally, it means that biblical interpretation is not simply a matter of textual mechanics or scholarly expertise. The Bible is more—but not less!—than a piece of history and literature. Archaeology, philology, and literary criticism all have a place, but finally they are but stations on the way to the cross.

The goal of the present book is to think about biblical interpretation in the Bible's own theological terms. This leads me to privilege what I call the economy of light, namely, the way the God who in himself is the Father of lights (Jas 1:17) communicates his light to the world in Christ (John 8:12) into our hearts (2 Cor 4:6), by the illumination of the Spirit. This in turn leads me to privilege Jesus' transfiguration as a climactic moment in the history of God's luminous self-communication. In looking back to the Old Testament and forward to Christ's crucifixion and exaltation, the transfiguration provides a capsule summary of the economy of light and, in so doing, gives us a distinctly theological purchase on the nature of the biblical text, the process of reading, and its effect on the reader. I was encouraged along the way by my discovery that Jerome, centuries before me, had also seen hermeneutical significance in the transfiguration (see chapter 7 below).

Two other things led me to the foot of this holy hermeneutical, sacred story mountain. The first was a 2011 conference co-organized by Hans Boersma and Matthew Levering and sponsored by Regent College in Vancouver: "Heaven on Earth? The Future of Spiritual Interpretation?" The conference brought Roman Catholic and Protestant biblical scholars and systematic theologians together to discuss the relationship between grammatical-historical and spiritual-theological exegesis. Brian Daley led off as the Roman Catholic keynote speaker, and I brought up the rear with the evangelical keynote address,

"Ascending the Mountain, Singing the Rock: Biblical Interpretation Earthed, Typed, and Transfigured," the seed of the present book.[12]

The second contributing factor was not a onetime but recurring event. For years I have taught a doctoral seminar titled "Advanced Theological Prolegomena." (It's more exciting than it sounds.) Each class includes PhD students from four different disciplines: Old Testament, New Testament, church history, and systematic theology. The aim is to promote interdisciplinary, integrative reflection by asking: (1) In what sense are all four properly *theological* disciplines? (2) What does each discipline contribute to the common task of reading the Bible as Christian Scripture in and with the church, yesterday and today? That the course usually includes international students, including some from the Majority World, only makes it more exciting: given all this diversity, in what does our unity consist?

Both the conference and the course suggested to me the need for a "mere Christian" hermeneutics: a way of thinking about hermeneutics that could overcome historical, ethnic, denominational, and especially disciplinary divides. Would it be possible, I wondered, to do for biblical hermeneutics what C. S. Lewis did for Christian belief in his book *Mere Christianity*? Lewis responded to the plurality of Christian traditions by documenting the widescale agreement about the essentials of the faith. Lewis likened this "mere Christianity" (as Richard Baxter called it) to a hall that connected the various "rooms" in God's "household."[13] In the present work, the various "rooms" represent different approaches to biblical interpretation and, as Lewis observed about hell, they are locked from the inside. I argue that interpreters need to leave their interpretive silos and mingle in the hall to converse with those who read the Bible differently. The notion of a "mere" hermeneutics alternately made me laugh, then gasp, at the sheer folly and magnitude of the task: achieving interpretive peace after centuries of interpretive conflict.[14]

The book you are about to read does provide principles for theological interpretation, but not a detailed step-by-step method. Nor does it provide an exhaustive survey of the kinds of criticism and interpretive approaches that lay claim to the TIS rubric. While I engage different approaches to biblical

12. The conference papers were published in two places, first, in *Modern Theology* 28, no. 4 (2012), then as a book coedited by Hans Boersma and Matthew Levering, *Heaven on Earth? Theological Interpretation in Ecumenical Dialogue* (Oxford: Blackwell, 2013).

13. See further C. S. Lewis, *Mere Christianity* (1952; repr., San Francisco: HarperSanFrancisco, 2001), xv–xvi.

14. *Mere Hermeneutics* is the third of what I like to think of as my "Mere Trilogy," which began with a book coauthored with Dan Treier on "Mere Evangelicalism" (*Theology and the Mirror of Scripture: A Mere Evangelical Account* [Downers Grove, IL: IVP Academic, 2015]) and continued with a book on "Mere Protestantism" (*Biblical Authority after Babel: Retrieving the Solas in the Spirit of Mere Protestant Christianity* [Grand Rapids: Brazos, 2016]).

interpretation from a variety of times and traditions, I do so not to draw up a list of hermeneutical heroes and villains, but for the sake of formulating a positive, integrative proposal. My fundamental claim is that we need all the theological disciplines, and several kinds of biblical criticism, to read the Bible rightly, in ways that do justice to both its human and divine authorship.

Can biblical interpretation change the world? Yes, and the particular change I have in view is a transfiguration. "Transfiguring biblical interpretation" refers both to the process of rethinking biblical hermeneutics in light of the transfiguration of Jesus, "the radiance of the glory of God" (Heb 1:3), and to the change interpreting the Bible this way makes, not least in the reader. Transfiguring biblical interpretation attends both to the Bible's literal sense and to the light in the letter.

I dedicate this book to Dan Treier on the occasion of his fiftieth birthday. He has been, if not all things to all people, then at least many things to me: student, colleague, coeditor, coauthor, colaborer on the bridge, counselor, critic (of this book too), and, most importantly, friend. Unfortunately, Dan, unlike Christmas gifts, this one is not returnable because, as you well know, a text is authorial discourse, fixed by writing—and by (as you also know) extensive revisions.

Transfiguration Sunday, 2023

Acknowledgments

The idea for the present book stemmed from Katya Covrett's invitation to write a textbook on theological interpretation of Scripture: its nature, purpose, and practice. Katya organized a brainstorming session with a number of biblical scholars and theologians, including Dick Averbeck, Mark Gignilliat, Tim Gombis, Michael Graves, Nijay Gupta, Charles Halton, Jon Laansma, Jonathan Lunde, and Klyne Snodgrass. I am grateful to Katya for the original invitation and for her ongoing, indeed longsuffering, editorial help.

Mickey Klink and Nathan Chambers offered helpful feedback on particular chapters. I am thankful for their charitable but honest comments. Doug Sweeney remains my go-to source for all things Luther and Edwards: I'm grateful for his steering me toward the right primary sources and, in general, for his friendship and encouragement. The same goes to those faculty colleagues who participate in our interdepartmental Deerfield Dialogue Group and offered comments on chapter 6 and the conclusion: Fellipe do Vale, Steve Greggo, Donald Guthrie, Dana Harris, Josh Jipp, Michelle Knight, Mimi Larson, Te-Li Lau, David Luy, Craig Ott, Madison Pierce, and Lawson Younger.

I'm grateful as well to Richard Muller for supplying me from his virtual stacks with several choice essays and books on the literal sense, and to Erik Lundeen, who was kind enough to let me see his dissertation on Johannes Oecolampadius's sixteenth-century search for the literal sense, just days after successfully defending it. Finally, I'm happy to acknowledge and thank Arnold Huijgen and Hans Burger for sharing drafts of their essays on Hans Boersma's sacramental exegesis, and to Mike Kibbe and Patrick Schreiner for their willingness to share prepublication versions of their respective forthcoming books on Jesus' transfiguration.

The manuscript benefited from discussions with my PhD students who devoted several Wednesday evening sessions, in person and then later via Zoom, to a chapter-by-chapter analysis. To Will Bankston, YK Hwang, Wilson Jeremiah, TaeJung Kim, Caleb Lindgren, Roy McDaniel, Kenny Silva, and Matt

Wiley: thank you for your many helpful stylistic and substantive suggestions. I owe Matt a double portion because, as my TA, he read everything twice. Finally, I want to thank David McNutt and Matt Estel, my editors at Zondervan, for their helpful queries, comments, and suggestions for improving the manuscript before tucking it into bed.

Introduction

An Experiment in Biblical-Theological Criticism

The knowledge of God is a mountain steep indeed and difficult to climb—the majority of people scarcely reach its base.

—Gregory of Nyssa, *The Life of Moses*

If, as Gerhard Ebeling maintained, the history of the church and the history of biblical interpretation are the same thing, then all who care about the present and future church should care about the present and future of biblical interpretation.[1] Sound doctrine and true worship alike depend on reading the Bible rightly and on responding rightly to what we read. Christian faith and life are inextricably tied to Holy Scripture—to the human words that, by God's wise determination, communicate God's own word. But what is right reading, and where do we learn it: in the academy or church? Is it a matter of biblical scholarship, "spiritual" interpretation, some combination of the two, or something else altogether? If the Bible is God's word—a divine address, a use of language to establish personal relationship—then biblical interpretation is our listening and answering speech.[2]

Perhaps we can at least agree on this: if being biblical is implicit in being a Christian, then so is hermeneutics—the study of the nature, principles, methods, and purposes of interpretation—and theology, in particular, assumptions about God's relationship to Scripture (inspired authorship) and its right reading (illumined interpretation). After all, we answer to God by answering Jesus'

---

1. Gerhard Ebeling, "Church History as the History of the Exposition of Holy Scripture," in *The Word of God as Tradition: Historical Studies Interpreting the Divisions of Christianity* (Philadelphia: Fortress, 1968), 11–31.

2. Eugene Peterson describes prayer as "answering speech." *Answering God: The Psalms as Tools for Prayer* (San Francisco: Harper & Row, 1989), 6. Reading the Bible rightly, to hear the Word of God, is in many ways like prayer. See further Daniel J. Brendsel, *Answering Speech: The Life of Prayer as Response to God* (Wheaton, IL: Crossway, 2023), esp. ch. 4, "Praying in Response to Scripture."

question, "But who do you say that I am?" only by reference to the canonical Scriptures and the broader story of God's relation to the history of Israel recounted therein.[3] This gives rise to an urgent follow-up question: Are seminaries and churches teaching hermeneutics and helping Christians read the Bible profitably in ways that rightly identify Christ, effectively train disciples in the way of Christ, and in general build up the body of Christ?[4] If Scripture is the lifeblood of the church, biblical interpretation is its circulation system: translation, preaching, commentary, lived tradition—all are forms of biblical interpretation. This book describes local churches and seminaries alike as "reading cultures," and calls for a distinctly theological reading of the Bible as a way of being answerable to its literal meaning.[5]

Some may take offense at the idea that there is a right way to read the Bible, that it pertains to the literal sense, and has something to do with theology. After all, *right reading* implies there must be a *wrong reading*, and this sets off alarm bells in an age that has had its fill of totalitarian colonial oppression.[6] Moreover, *right reading* requires a standard that one can use to judge whether a particular reading is conforming or nonconforming. Who am I—who is *anybody*—to play judge and jury, laying down the hermeneutical law and deciding whether an interpreter is guilty of first-degree man(uscript) slaughter (i.e., bearing false witness) or the lesser offense of exegetical jaywalking (i.e., ignoring authorial intention)?

For centuries there was widespread agreement that the basis for right reading, theological interpretation, and doctrinal development was the Bible's literal sense. Yet there was no consensus as to the definition of the literal sense. Indeed, *literality* has proven to be one of the more elusive concepts in the history of ideas. "Literal" interpretation is today associated with understanding statements and texts in a straightforward, simplistic manner, without consideration of figurative meanings that may be intended. When journalists and others describe present-day evangelicals as those who believe "in the literal truth of the Bible," it is thus easy to dismiss them as biblical literalists, as one does those who hold to other far-fetched beliefs, such as the earth being flat.

Modern relativism and postmodern indeterminism have convinced many

3. See further *Christology and Scripture: Interdisciplinary Perspectives*, ed. Andrew T. Lincoln and Angus Paddison (London: T&T Clark, 2008).

4. See further Ched Spellman and Jason K. Lee, *The Seminary as a Textual Community: Exploring John Sailhamer's Vision for Theological Education* (Dallas: Fontes, 2021). Fun fact: Sailhamer took the idea of a "textual community" from a lecture I gave in 1990 at Trinity Evangelical Divinity School when John and I were on the faculty.

5. I discuss the nature and function of reading cultures more fully in chapter 1. See also the entry in the glossary.

6. See Iain Provan, *The Reformation and the Right Reading of Scripture* (Waco, TX: Baylor University Press, 2017).

that *reading rightly* is in the eye of the beholder. The concept of *reading rightly* implies a bounded set, in which a particular reading is either right or wrong. By way of contrast, *reading well* suggests a centered-set picture of interpretation, in which a particular reading may be closer or further from whatever makes reading right. Everyone makes some kind of judgment between better or worse interpretations. My aim in this book is to "save" the literal, in part by providing a richer and more theologically adequate definition. To define the literal sense, however, we must begin by describing what a text *is, is doing,* and *is for,* and to do so with categories informed by theology, not just philosophy.[7]

The Experiment: From Methods of Criticism to Criticism of Methods

The Evangelists wrote their gospels to identify Jesus as the Christ. The author of the fourth gospel admits to being selective in his material: "Now there are also many other things that Jesus did. Were every one of them to be written, I suppose that the world itself could not contain the books that would be written" (John 21:25). One might say the same about books on biblical interpretation. The bay of biblical studies is filled with fishing boats, each one trawling for meaning.[8] What each catches depends on several factors: where to fish, how deep, what bait to use, whether to use line, spear, or net, and so forth. Success or failure may also depend on the degree of one's patience.

An exegetical method is essentially a disciplined way of reading, the formalization of an interpretive insight, intuition, or interest—a way of answering a particular question. Consider, for example, the different ways of reading the Gospels. Some exegetes have a special interest in comparing the similarities and differences between Matthew, Mark, and Luke. As in the famous Abbott and Costello routine, they want to know who's on first (or who came first). That interest fuels redaction criticism. Those with a literary interest may practice narrative criticism, with an eye to the different ways each gospel tells the story of Jesus. Feminists have a special interest in the Evangelists' depiction of women and the way Jesus related to them. Still others have a historical bent and investigate the social customs and common conceptual worldview of first-century Palestinian Jews, which is what the Evangelists were. Each of these interpretive

7. In the nineteenth and twentieth centuries, philosophers took the lead in making hermeneutics into a theory of understanding all expressions of human life, not simply written texts. See Hans-Georg Gadamer, "The Universality of the Hermeneutical Problem," in *Philosophical Hermeneutics* (Berkeley: University of California Press, 1976), 3–17.

8. I am borrowing George Guthrie's apt analogy from "Boats in the Bay: Reflections on the Use of Linguistics and Literary Studies in Biblical Studies," in *Linguistics and the New Testament: Critical Junctures,* ed. Stanley E. Porter and D. A. Carson (Sheffield: Sheffield Academic, 1999), 23–35.

interests gives rise to a particular form and practice of biblical criticism and, at the limit, an interpretive community that shares that interest and practice.

There are many interpretive interests. A legitimate interpretive interest generates a method of reading that contributes in some way to genuine understanding of some aspect or dimension of the text. One perennial interest has been the meaning of the text, though what people mean by *meaning* varies. Consequently, it is best to ask people not to use the term, and instead say what they m***. As we will see, the fate of the literal sense is tied up with this confusion about what people mean by *meaning*.[9]

Texts are complex, stratified realities, involving words, sentences, structure, and genre. Accordingly, interpreters require multiple methodological approaches, working on different levels (e.g., lexical, semantic, historical, literary) to do them and their meanings justice. Each method yields certain insights, but no one method catches everything relevant to textual understanding. Gadamer's *Truth and Method* makes this point compellingly: one's choice of method predetermines the kind of truth one then discovers.[10] To prefer one method to the neglect of others is to risk methodological reductionism, a myopic mistake: to use one method exclusively is to limit what sort of truth about the text to which one will have access. Interpreters who insist that the text means only what their method discovers are like scientists who reduce reality only to what can be perceived by their theories and instruments. They are like explorers who insist the world extends only as far as what their flashlights illumine. It is presumptuous to think that any one academic discipline, theory, or critical tool will catch the sacred fish. There are more things in discourse and text than are dreamed of in critical theory.

"'All things are lawful,' but not all things are beneficial" (1 Cor 10:23 NRSV). The apostle Paul was probably not thinking of interpretive approaches when he cited this Corinthian slogan, but it is nevertheless apt. Not every permissible exegetical method is expedient—or edifying. Certain ways of reading the Bible may not hurt the church, but neither do they help it respond to the apostle Peter's exhortation to "grow in the grace and knowledge of our Lord and Savior Jesus Christ" (2 Pet 3:18). Consequently, we need not only to "test the spirits" (1 John 4:1) but also to test the hermeneutics. We need to conduct an experiment in criticism.

An experiment is a procedure for testing a hypothesis. C. S. Lewis proposed an experiment to evaluate ways of reading. His experiment reverses the normal

9. See further George B. Caird, "The Meaning of Meaning," in *The Language and Imagery of the Bible* (London: Duckworth, 1980), 37–61; and Christopher D. Spinks, *The Bible and the Crisis of Meaning: Debates on the Theological Interpretation of Scripture* (London: T&T Clark, 2007).

10. Hans-Georg Gadamer, *Truth and Method*, trans. Joel Weinsheimer and Donald G. Marshall (London: Sheed and Ward, 1989).

procedure of judging a person's taste by the things they read. Instead, he proposed to judge literature "by the way men read it."[11] If one or more readers love a book, even after repeated readings, then it cannot be too bad. Lewis's hypothesis is that "good literature [is] that which permits, invites, or even compels good reading."[12] Lewis acknowledged a complication, a fly in the ointment: "The most obvious objection to judging books by the way they are read is the fact that the same book may be read in different ways."[13] If this is true of literature in general (and it is), how much more is it the case with the Bible?

Consider what I call my "three laws of hermeneutical motion": (1) Every type of criticism developed in the academy eventually gets applied by someone to biblical interpretation; (2) every cultural trend or social development eventually moves people to read the Bible from that particular perspective or with that special interest (e.g., feminism, postcolonialism, liberation, etc.); and (3) there is no more telling intellectual and cultural barometer than biblical interpretation. Given this plurality, how can we discern which approaches to biblical interpretation are legitimate? Many exegetes draw on the resources of general hermeneutics (i.e., principles for valid interpretation of books *in general*) when trying to distinguish right from wrong reading.[14] The general assumption is that right reading follows from having the right method (for reading books in general), and that reading the Bible is no different from reading Plato, Dickens, or Updike.

My experiment in biblical-theological criticism works a variation on Lewis's. Instead of judging "right readers" or "right readings" on the basis of the critical methods they use, I propose *judging the rightness of critical methods by the kind of theological readings, readers, and reading cultures they beget.*[15] I define a *bad* exegetical method as one that forbids, forestalls, or frustrates any theological reading of the Bible, and a *good* exegetical method as one that is open to, facilitates, or necessitates some kind of theological reading.[16] If an interpretive approach engenders faithful theological reading, and a reading culture that produces answerable readers, then it qualifies as a good interpretation regardless of its general hermeneutical merits or demerits. Why the emphasis on "theological"? First, because the Bible is the word from God to the people of God that teaches about God and is useful for training in godliness. Second, because reflection on

---

11. C. S. Lewis, *An Experiment in Criticism* (Cambridge: Cambridge University Press, 1961), 104.

12. Lewis, *Experiment in Criticism*, 104. He also said, "The ideally bad book is the one of which a good reading is impossible" (113).

13. Lewis, *Experiment in Criticism*, 113.

14. See, e.g., E. D. Hirsch's *Validity in Interpretation* (New Haven, CT: Yale University Press, 1967).

15. And, as I shall argue in part 3, by the kind of transfigurations certain kinds of reading enable.

16. See the related proposal of John Frederick and Ryan A. Brandt, "*Regula Catholica, Regula Interpretatio*: A Summary and Way Forward for Theological Interpretation of Scripture," in *Theological Interpretation of Scripture as Spiritual Formation*, ed. Ryan A. Brandy and John Frederick (Leiden: Brill, 2022), 305–30.

reading the Bible should be informed by what Christians believe, "one cannot be committed to orthodoxy and read Scripture as if God did not exist."[17]

According to my experiment—a theological criticism of interpretive methods—the criteria for interpretive *goodness* are a function not of general hermeneutics, literary criticism, or philosophy, but of doing justice to what the Bible ultimately is and is for: a divine address, mediated by and fixed in human writing, for the sake of human transformation. This is the final justification for giving hermeneutical pride and place to Christian theology, and to what we might call *theological criticism*.[18] Again, my experiment tests the hypothesis that a reading is good if it enables the reader to understand and do justice to what she is reading: human discourse, to be sure, but also the word of God. A reading is good if it begets not just any reader response, but a responsible response, or, stated differently, if it begets not a sovereign but an *answerable* subject (answerable to God).

An observation by Lewis sheds further light on why theology is necessary for reading Scripture rightly. He opened his study of Milton's epic poem *Paradise Lost* with an important thesis: "The first qualification for judging any piece of workmanship from a corkscrew to a cathedral is to know *what* it is—what it was intended to do and how it is meant to be used."[19] To conduct our experiment, then, we must know what the text *is*, *is doing*, and *is for*. We cannot know any of these things about the Bible, however, without drawing on explicitly theological realities. We must accept the Bible for what it really is: not merely "the word of men but . . . the word of God" (1 Thess 2:13).

Divine Address: "Today, If You Hear His Voice . . ."

The first step in interpretation is determining *what* one is reading. Right reading is never less than reading along the textual grain—reading prose as prose, poetry as poetry, history as history, and so forth. Questions pertaining to literary genre—identifying *what kind* of text—therefore loom large. Our inquiry begins even further back, however, with the question, what is a *text*? Or, more specifically, what are *biblical texts*? The answer to that—"the word of God in the words of men"—requires deploying not only *God* but three additional theological categories: divine voice, divine discourse, and divine promise.

17. Seth Heringer, "Preparing to Read: Theological Presuppositions and Biblical Interpretation," *Journal of Theological Interpretation* 17, no. 1 (2023): 130–31.

18. Cf. Joseph Ratzinger's similar call for a "criticism of criticism" in his "Biblical Interpretation in Crisis: On the Question of the Foundations and Approaches of Exegesis Today," in *Biblical Interpretation in Crisis: The Ratzinger Conference on Bible and Church*, ed. Richard John Neuhaus (Grand Rapids: Eerdmans, 1989), 6.

19. C. S. Lewis, *A Preface to Paradise Lost* (London: Oxford University Press, 1942), 1.

Divine Voice: What the Bible *Is*

The people of Israel were the original recipients of what they now call the Hebrew Bible and what Christians call the Old Testament. They had heard the voice of God, a fearsome thing: "Behold, the LORD our God has shown us his glory and greatness, and we have heard his voice out of the midst of the fire" (Deut 5:24). The law God first laid down in speech was then preserved in writing, as were later prophecies. As Paul said, Israel was entrusted with "the oracles of God" (*ta logia tou theou*; Rom 3:2).

According to Scripture, Israel was the elect recipient of a divine address, a speech directed to a particular person or group. An addressee is in an "I-Thou" relation.[20] Modern liberal theologians agreed but emphasized the personal encounter, not what was said. They also tended to view Scripture as the human authors' attempt to express the significance of their religious experience.[21] James Barr's view is representative: "We do not have any idea of ways in which God might straight-forwardly articulate thoughts or sentences to men; it just doesn't happen."[22] The Bible is on this view less a divine address than, at best, a humanly authored record of revelation or, at worst, a projection of human religious ideals onto a celestial blank slate.

The biblical authors beg to differ: "Long ago God spoke to our ancestors in many and various ways" (Heb 1:1 NRSV). "The word of the LORD came to . . ." is one of the most frequent phrases in the Old Testament (see Gen 15:1; 1 Sam 15:10; 1 Kgs 18:1; Isa 38:4; et al.). Indeed, it is striking how many acts ascribed to God by the biblical authors are *speech acts*. Nevertheless, even conservative evangelicals sometimes stop short of viewing the Bible as divine address. It has become commonplace to hear that the Bible "is written *for* us, but not *to* us."[23] The apostle Paul, like every other biblical author, is too historically and culturally distant—not to mention *dead*—to address me personally: "Reading Paul's letters today is quite literally reading someone else's two-thousand-year-old mail: we do *not* share with Paul and his readers their moment in time."[24] Jane Austen's letters to her sister Cassandra afford fascinating glimpses into the personality of one of my favorite authors, yet they are not directed to me. To read someone else's mail is to eavesdrop on a private conversation. However, this

---

20. Martin Buber, *I and Thou* (New York: Scribner, 1970), 53.

21. George A. Lindbeck calls this tendency, typical of modernity's "turn to the subject," the "expressive-experiential" approach to biblical religion and doctrinal theology. *The Nature of Doctrine: Religion and Theology in a Postliberal Age* (Philadelphia: Westminster, 1984), 31–32.

22. James Barr, *The Bible in the Modern World* (London: SCM, 1973), 17.

23. This idea occurs frequently in John Walton's writings. See, e.g., *The Lost World of Genesis One: Ancient Cosmology and the Origins Debate* (Downers Grove, IL: IVP Academic, 2009), 9. Walton does not intend to call into question the Bible's status as God's Word, only to remind us that its original audience comes from an ancient culture that inhabited a different conceptual world.

24. Peter Enns, *How the Bible Actually Works* (New York: HarperOne, 2019), 258 (emphasis original).

is *not* the way the church reads the Bible. Christians who read say, Ephesians, are not eavesdroppers on someone else's conversation because Paul was God's "chosen instrument" (Acts 9:15) for communicating God's word—and not to his original recipients only.

The voice Israel heard out of the midst of the fire was "the voice of the living God" (Deut 5:26). Moses repeats what God said on Mount Sinai to the first generation to a second generation in the book of Deuteronomy, and there is a clear expectation that God will speak his covenant word to future generations as well (Deut 4:9–24; 30:1–10). Centuries later, King Darius wrote, "He is the living God, enduring forever" (Dan 6:26). Centuries after that, Peter identified Jesus as "the Christ, the Son of the living God" (Matt 16:16). The risen Christ is "Lord both of the dead and of the living" (Rom 14:9), including biblical interpreters today, which is why John Webster said both the Bible and its readers belong to "the domain of the revelatory presence of Christ."[25] The Bible is part of the pattern of divine communication and communion over which the risen Lord presides and in which he presents himself. The Bible is not only "the manger in which Christ lies"[26] but a bed the Lord has made for himself. Unlike the human authors of Scripture who are dead and buried, then, the risen Christ is alive—communicatively present and active.

Søren Kierkegaard was keenly aware that readers of the Bible stand before the living God: "*It is I to whom it is speaking; it is I about whom it is speaking.*"[27] To read the Bible as if it were addressed to someone else, therefore, is to succumb to third-person Christianity, in which the words and actions of God concern *them*, not *us*. By way of contrast, biblical interpretation for Kierkegaard, like discourse itself, "is *irreducibly second-personal.*"[28] That Bible reading is a *second-person* affair is also a guiding conviction of the present work. I therefore agree with Scott Swain: "In dealing with the Bible interpretively, we are not rational subjects dealing with an inert object; we are instead rational subjects addressed by the divine Subject and called to loving attention and fellowship."[29]

The doctrine of inspiration preserves this emphasis on the Bible as divine

---

25. John Webster, *The Domain of the Word: Scripture and Theological Reason* (London: T&T Clark, 2012), 38.

26. Martin Luther, "Preface to the Old Testament," in *Martin Luther's Basic Theological Writings*, ed. Timothy F. Lull (Minneapolis: Fortress, 1989), 119.

27. Søren Kierkegaard, *For Self-Examination* and *Judge for Yourself!*, ed. and trans. Howard V. Hong and Edna H. Hong (Princeton, NJ: Princeton University Press, 1990), 35 (emphasis original).

28. Ross Inman, "Theology in the Second Person: Christian Dogmatics as a Mode of Prayer," in *Analyzing Prayer: Theological and Philosophical Studies*, ed. Oliver D. Crisp, James M. Arcadi, and Jordan Wessling (Oxford: Oxford University Press, 2022), 122 (emphasis original). See also Joshua Cockayne, *Contemporary with Christ: Kierkegaard and Second-Personal Spirituality* (Waco, TX: Baylor University Press, 2020), esp. chs. 3, 7.

29. Scott R. Swain, *Trinity, Revelation, and Reading: A Theological Introduction to the Bible and Its Interpretation* (London: T&T Clark, 2011), 7.

address, as expressed by the Nicene Creed's description of the Holy Spirit as one "who spoke [Lat. *est locutus*] by the prophets."[30] To locate the Spirit's speaking exclusively in the past, however, is to subscribe to a deistic picture of God's relation to his word, according to which God orated, and then let his word get on with it, without further action or assistance.[31] According to the author of Hebrews, however, the Holy Spirit *speaks* the words of Psalm 95:7–11, even though they originally proceeded from the mouth of David centuries earlier: "Therefore, as the Holy Spirit says, 'Today, if you hear his voice . . .'" (Heb 3:7). Verb tenses always matter, but especially so here. The author of Hebrews is writing to Christians centuries later but insists that the promise of entering God's rest still stands (Heb 4:1), even if the original recipients to whom it was directed do not (because they have since died). God therefore appoints another day as *today*, namely, the day to hearken and respond to his voice (Heb 4:7). The "today" of the author of Hebrews and his original audience is, of course, long past. Yet God continues to address the church through this passage, such that the original reader's *today* (our yesterday) becomes *today* anew, for contemporary readers too: "The writer believes that through his discourse (a sermon comprised of a series of scriptural expositions), he himself communicates that divine word and effects an encounter between his hearers and the God who speaks."[32] If the author of Hebrews could view the Spirit who spoke through David as speaking *today* (i.e., to his audience), then we should too.

The Bible is the medium of divine address.[33] To read the Bible as God's word is therefore to encounter something living and active (Heb 4:12): the voice of God, God personally speaking, the triune God in communicative action, doing things with, in, and through human words. We are not the first recipients of Scripture, its immediate addressees. But when, in corporate worship, the lector proclaims, "The word of the Lord," after the Scripture reading, the congregation thanks God for something present, not simply a relic from the past. "God is the author of Scripture and still speaks in it, and there is no sense that authoring Scripture and speaking through it are heterogeneous activities only remotely connected to one another."[34] What God is *not* doing in speaking

30. One such prophet is Jeremiah: "The ontology of the book of Jeremiah as simultaneously the words of Jeremiah and the words of God sets the text itself as a location of God's activity." Andrew H. Shead, *A Mouth Full of Fire: The Word of God in the Words of Jeremiah* (Downers Grove, IL: InterVarsity, 2012), 284.

31. Deism is the idea that God created the world and then withdrew, leaving it to its own devices, and thus ceasing to act in relation to it.

32. Jonathan I. Griffiths, *Hebrews and Divine Speech* (London: Bloomsbury T&T Clark, 2014), 2.

33. For more on the doctrine of Scripture, see my two essays: "Holy Scripture," in *Christian Dogmatics: Reformed Theology for the Church Catholic*, ed. Scott Swain and Michael Allen (Grand Rapids: Zondervan, 2016), 30–56; and "Holy Scripture," in Michael Allen, ed. *The New Cambridge Companion to Christian Doctrine* (Cambridge: Cambridge University Press, 2023), 119–38.

34. Francis Watson, "Hermeneutics and the Doctrine of Scripture: Why They Need Each Other," *International Journal of Systematic Theology* 12, no. 2 (2010): 127.

"today" is adding to or distorting what the prophets and apostles said. As we shall see, the Spirit does not *change* the meaning of the words but *revoices*, *reactivates*, and *resituates* the discourse in and for a new redemptive-historical context.[35]

Divine (and Human) Discourse: What the Bible *Is Doing*

The Bible *is* a human medium, a sanctified or set-apart creaturely means by which the Creator "throws his voice," as it were, into creation.[36] Scripture is not an inert object to be studied, as if reading the Bible were an "I-It" relation. It is rather a means for encountering the living God, "the primary means by which God presents himself to us."[37] Reading the Bible is thus an "I-Thou" affair—but this is not how many biblical interpreters see it.

Robert Morgan and John Barton compare the Bible to a corpse: "Texts, like dead men and women, have no rights, no aims, no interests. They can be used in whatever way readers or interpreters choose."[38] They make an important point: approaches to biblical hermeneutics typically reflect the interpretive interests of the readers, which may or may not correspond to the communicative interests of the authors. It is also true that texts are neither persons nor agents. Strictly speaking, a piece of writing cannot *do* anything; it just is, a sleeping message awaiting the reader's princely kiss of life. Talk of what the biblical text is doing is more accurately described as what *someone* is doing in, with, or through the text: "texts are best viewed as actions performed on a variety of levels."[39] The author is the person who uses the text to say something, and *persons*, as agents, have rights, aims, and interests.[40] The pertinent question is: Which person, or persons—human and divine, including the third divine person, the Holy Spirit—may legitimately claim authorial rights over a given text?

Every biblical interpreter assumes something or other about whose use counts, and about how God relates (or does not relate) to that use. Signs have

35. See further Gregory W. Lee: "The locutions that mediate God's speech remain canonically constant, but the illocutions adopt new force according to the contours of redemptive history. God is faithful to his unchanging Word, but this Word is living, not static." *Today When You Hear His Voice: Scripture, the Covenants, and the People of God* (Grand Rapids: Eerdmans, 2016), 216–17.

36. Of course Jesus Christ is the definitive human medium of God's communicative presence and activity. I intend here simply to show the standard Protestant doctrine of Scripture, reflected in multiple Reformation-era confessions. See also "John Owen on Communication from God," in J. I. Packer, *The Quest for Godliness: The Puritan Vision of the Christian Life* (Wheaton, IL: Crossway, 1990), 81–96.

37. Timothy Ward, *Words of Life: Scripture as the Living and Active Word of God* (Downers Grove, IL: IVP Academic, 2009), 177.

38. Robert Morgan and John Barton, *Biblical Interpretation* (Oxford: Oxford University Press, 1988), 7.

39. Charles Altieri, *Act and Quality: A Theory of Literary Meaning and Humanistic Understanding* (Amherst: University of Massachusetts Press, 1981), 10.

40. It is common for publishers to add, under the copyright, something like the following formula: "The right of [author's name] to be identified as the Author of the Work has been asserted by him/her."

no agency of their own, hence a theological account of what the Bible is, is doing, and is for must not be content with defining the Bible in semiotic terms. Letters and words have meaning potential, but it takes a personal agent using language to actualize it.[41] Dictionaries do not define abstract signs but describe word *usage*. To confess the Bible as God's word is to acknowledge *God's use* of human words and sentences as constituting their ultimate meaning and communicative intent. There may be no more important theological presupposition affecting one's reading than this: deciding whose use of biblical words determines their meaning.[42]

To read the Bible is to grapple with language, not a language system (that way structuralism lies) but with the actual use of language in context: *discourse*. The Bible is discourse: something (the sense) someone (the author) says (the predication) to someone (the addressee) about something (the referent) in some way (the genre) at some time (the occasion) for some purpose (the telos).[43] Furthermore, the Bible is human *and divine* authorial discourse. Everything in biblical interpretation depends not only on semantics—signs and referents (i.e., *what is said; about what*)—but also on the pragmatics or context of use (*who* is speaking, *when, to whom, in what way*, and *for what purpose*).

Discourse is a core concept in the present work. Viewing the text as discourse, fixed in writing, enables interpreters to do justice to what the text *is*: something God personally says and does. What is divine about the Bible is not the words, which are fully human—there is nothing heavenly about Hebrew and Greek—but the discourse. God speaks—and in speaking performs communicative acts—in and through the human discourse, without suppressing or manipulating the cognitive and communicative capacities of the human authors. The great advantage of discourse analysis is that it incorporates and integrates other types of criticism that, left to their own devices, focus on one aspect only of the total discourse phenomenon.[44]

Discourse analysis truly comes into its own when it describes the many things speakers do with words and the ways they do them. Recognizing that

41. Darren Sarisky's otherwise very helpful treatment of reading the Bible theologically fails sufficiently to take divine authorship into account, ascribing speech agency to the text instead. *Reading the Bible Theologically* (Cambridge: Cambridge University Press, 2009), 282.

42. A key premise in the present work is that our assumptions about the nature of Scripture shape our methods for interpreting it. Stated as a formula: ontology (what we think the text is) precedes epistemology (our methods for coming to knowledge of what it means).

43. See further my essay "The Apostolic Discourse and Its Developments," in *Scripture's Doctrine and Theology's Bible: Studies in the New Testament's Normativity for Christian Dogmatics*, ed. Markus Bockmuehl and Alan Torrance (Grand Rapids: Baker, 2008), 191–207.

44. George Lindbeck made this point in his important, though underappreciated essay, in which he compares and contrasts Brevard Childs's canonical approach, Richard Hays's narrative approach, and Nicholas Wolterstorff's authorial discourse approach. "Postcritical Canonical Interpretation: Three Modes of Retrieval," in *Theological Exegesis: Essays in Honor of Brevard S. Childs*, ed Christopher Seitz and Kathryn Greene-McCreight (Grand Rapids: Eerdmans, 1999), 26–51.

authors do more with words than inform casts new light on the notion that the word of God is "living and active" (Heb 4:12).[45] The Bible is God's word not merely because it contains supernaturally revealed information, but because its human words are the vehicle for a variety of divine speech acts. The nature of the Bible thus calls for theological interpretation inasmuch as "God speaking and God acting are often one and the same thing."[46] What Scripture is, the voice of God, enables what it does: "I the LORD have spoken; I will accomplish it" (Ezek 17:24 NRSV).[47]

Divine Purpose: What the Bible *Is For*

The Bible is "holy" Scripture because God has set it apart for a divine purpose. God's "ten words" or commandments (Exod 20:1–17) are set-apart words that regulate the life of a set-apart people (Exod 19:6). Indeed, at many times and in many ways, God gave all the books of the Bible to establish and preserve his covenant people as his treasured possession (Exod 19:5; Deut 7:6). God's promise, even more than God's law, creates the covenant: "And I will walk among you and will be your God, and you shall be my people" (Lev 26:12).[48] This was a reiteration of God's earlier promise to Abraham to make of him a great nation (Gen 12:2–3; 17:4–8). We can generalize the point: the ultimate purpose of the Bible is to generate and govern a covenant people.[49] There is arguably no more personal, or intimate, speech act than the exchange of vows in a marriage ceremony, where the words uttered bind the speaker to the addressee: "I do"; "I will." This is precisely what the Lord God promises Israel: to be her faithful husband, come what may. The promise is the paradigmatic speech act. Unlike statements, a promise does not describe something but commits the speaker to doing something: "When God promises something happens, and the covenant gives substance to this."[50] The point is worth pondering: without an original anchoring promise, there would be no covenant between God and Abraham.[51] The only way to make a covenant is to utter an oath with self-involving obligations (Gen 26:3; cf. Heb 6:17). As God's verbal *fiats* created light and everything

---

45. See further my *Is There a Meaning in This Text? The Bible, the Reader, and the Morality of Literary Knowledge* (Grand Rapids: Zondervan, 1998).

46. Ward, *Words of Life*, 26 (emphasis original).

47. For more on divine discourse, see my "Triune Discourse: Theological Reflections on the Claim That God Speaks," in *Trinitarian Theology for the Church: Scripture, Community, Worship*, ed. David Lauber and Daniel Treier (Downers Grove, IL: InterVarsity, 2009), 25–78.

48. According to Anthony Thiselton, it was William Tyndale who "pioneered the instinct to regard God's speaking as his act, especially in promise." Anthony C. Thiselton, *Promise and Prayer: The Biblical Writings in the Light of Speech-Act Theory* (Eugene, OR: Cascade, 2020), 3.

49. For more on covenant discourse, see Swain, *Trinity, Revelation, and Reading*, 40–52.

50. Thiselton, *Promise and Prayer*, 10.

51. Paul speaks of "the covenants of promise" in Ephesians 2:12.

else in nature (Gen 1:3), so God's promise to be Israel's God created an eternal covenant (Heb 9:15; 13:20).

One of the first divine promises comes early in the biblical story (Gen 3:15 NIV: "he [which a mere Christian hermeneutic will eventually identify as Christ] will crush your [Satan's] head")—the first intimation of the gospel, also known as the *proto-evangelium*. The last promise comes at the very end of the story: "Surely I [Jesus] am coming soon" (Rev 22:20). Everything God does between the beginning and the end of the biblical story confirms that he is as good as his word. It is precisely because God fulfills his promises that his words are *true*. This is also the criterion for discerning a true prophet (Deut 18:22) and, by extension, for discerning that *God* is true (2 Sam 22:31; Ps 18:30; Rom 3:4).

God's promise to create a people for himself is a central biblical theme. According to Luther, "The chief topic of all of Holy Scripture is to know and comprehend God as the one who promises."[52] How God makes good on his promise to Abraham is arguably the arc of the whole biblical story: Jesus Christ is the unexpected fulfillment of the promise that lies at the heart of the Old Testament; the coming of the Holy Spirit to unite believers to Christ is the startling fulfillment of the divine promise at the heart of the New Testament. The Father makes good on his promise by sending the Son; the Son makes good on his promise (to never leave or forsake his disciples) by sending his Spirit: "Behold, I am sending the promise of my Father upon you" (Luke 24:49; cf. John 14:26; Acts 1:4; 2:33). The last surprise, so big that it took time for the apostles to wrap their minds around it, was that the promise was not for Jews only but also for the Gentiles—hence the reference to "better promises" (Heb 8:6).

The Bible is divinely inspired human testimony to a divine testament—to God's covenant promise to be with and for his people. The triune God who spoke to the prophets in many and various ways now uses Scripture in many and various ways to publish and administer his covenant for the sake of building up his new covenant community, the church. What Scripture is ultimately for is enabling communion—covenant fellowship with the triune God who bespoke it and about whom it bespeaks.

Human Answerability: ". . . Do Not Harden Your Hearts"

The present experiment in biblical criticism evaluates interpretive methods by the kind of readers and readings they beget. Our experiment now requires us to

52. Martin Luther, *Luther's Works*, vol. 8, *Lectures on Genesis Chapters 45–50* (St. Louis: Concordia, 1968), 201.

extend Lewis's point, about the importance of first knowing what things are, to readers and the process of reading. We must therefore return to the question of the identity of its addressees: the "to whom" of biblical discourse. Is the divine address directed to contemporary biblical interpreters too, or are they simply listening in on someone else's covenantal discourse? Taking God's purpose for writing into account allows us to identify the "to whom" of the divine address: any person willing to take these words to heart. Let me therefore say a few words about who right-minded Bible readers are, how they should read, and what their reading is for.

Who Readers Are: Answerable Persons

Many approaches to biblical hermeneutics depict the reader as a sovereign knowing subject, free to choose which interpretive method to deploy. The assumption is that the text is a passive body on which the reader operates, a corpse into which the reader breathes life. Our experiment subverts this assumption: it is the biblical text that awakens slumbering readers to the reality of God, and to themselves before God.

The celebrated opening statement of Calvin's *Institutes*—that self-knowledge and knowledge of God are interrelated—has hermeneutical significance.[53] Humans know themselves as creatures to whom their Creator directs certain speech acts: questions, commands, warnings, assertions, and, yes, promises. "Hermeneutics is significant if and only if we are to view ourselves as most fundamentally objects of another's address, and not subjects in and through whom reason communes with itself."[54] According to Calvin, biblical statements do more than describe states of affairs; they often place the reader in situations that demand a response.[55] In informing us, the Bible also questions us—*places us* before God, renders us accountable to God. To read Scripture for its divine address is to approach a holy place; it is to climb with Moses to meet God.

To read the Bible theologically is to adopt a certain posture before the text. Those whom God addresses are in no position to lord it over the text, methodologically or otherwise. The first thought of the biblical interpreter must not be "I read, therefore I am (a sovereign subject)," but rather, "I read, therefore I am answerable (to God)." Reading the Bible involves "a readiness to be addressed and confronted."[56] The biblical interpreter is one who stands under the text,

---

53. The precise line is "Nearly all the wisdom we possess . . . consists of two parts: the knowledge of God and of ourselves." John Calvin, *Institutes of the Christian Religion*, ed. John T. McNeill, 2 vols. (Philadelphia: Westminster, 1960), I.1.1.

54. Watson, "Hermeneutics and the Doctrine of Scripture," 141.

55. See further Gilbert Vincent, *Exigence éthique et interprétation dans l'oeuvre de Calvin* (Geneva: Labor et Fides, 1984).

56. John Webster, *Word and Church: Essays in Christian Dogmatics* (Edinburgh: T&T Clark, 2001), 80.

not over it (cf. Neh 8:4–5): "Understanding is receptivity to the communication of another. Without being addressed by another, there can be no understanding. . . . To be addressed is to be perceived as one who *lacks* a knowledge of whatever is to be communicated, and as one who is *in need of* this knowledge."[57] We best read the Bible theologically, before God, by adopting the posture of prayer: on our knees.

Scripture requires more than parsing verbs, more than intellectual assent to its propositions, more even than application of its moral principles. There is nothing personal, or demanding, about data processing. Every divine speech act—indicative, interrogative, and imperative alike—poses a tacit question to the reader, namely, "How will you respond to what has been said, and to the person who has said it?" Such *answerability* is more radical than the literary critical "reader-response"; the latter involves interpretation, the former the whole of life.[58] If we keep in mind what the Bible is for, our most important answer must be deeply personal, even existential: "Let it be to me according to your word" (Luke 1:38). There is no alibi for being or reading. In reading Scripture, a biblical interpreter locates herself *coram Deo* ("in the presence of God").

The Bible's opening chapters depict God addressing his human creatures who quickly go out of their way to avoid being answerable: "But the Lord God called to the man and said to him, 'Where are you?'" And he said, 'I heard the sound of you in the garden, and I was afraid, because I was naked, and I hid myself'" (Gen 3:9–10). The divine address continues to strip readers naked. Responding to God's word has been, and always will be, an existentially fraught affair. Biblical interpreters are answerable not only for the "correctness" of their reading but for the way they respond to what they read, and to the one *who is saying it*. Abraham's "Here I am" (Gen 22:1), Isaiah's "Here I am" (Isa 6:8), and Mary's "Let it be to me according to your word" (Luke 1:38) all signal a readiness to hear and obey, the paradigmatic posture before the divine address.

To read the Bible rightly, one must do more than leverage the Bible for the sake of one's own interpretive community, a strategy that fails to go beyond identity politics. To read the Bible theologically is to have one's politics, agenda, and identity—one's very sense of self—stripped bare before the text: "Naked I came from my mother's womb" (Job 1:21). At the other extreme, Kierkegaard worried that too many Christians interpret the Bible "objectively" to defend themselves against the transformative potential of the text: "To be alone with Holy Scripture! I dare not! If I open it—any passage—it traps me at once; it

57. Watson, "Hermeneutics and the Doctrine of Scripture," 140.

58. On reader-response criticism, see my "The Reader in New Testament Study," in *Hearing the New Testament: Strategies for Interpretation*, ed. Joel B. Green, 2nd ed. (Grand Rapids: Eerdmans, 2010), 301–28.

asks me. . . . Have you done what you read there? . . . But one can also defend oneself against God's Word. . . . Take Holy Scripture, lock your door—but then take ten dictionaries, twenty-five commentaries, then you can read it, just as calmly and coolly as you read newspaper advertising."[59]

Kierkegaard knew from experience how easily spiritual procrastination can hide under the guise of scholarly busyness. If even the scholars disagree about how to read the Bible, who am I to prefer my own opinion? A passage can have no claim on us if we are unable to determine what exactly it is saying: "If the bugle gives an indistinct sound, who will get ready for battle?" (1 Cor 14:8). The conflict of scholarly interpretations provides, for some, the perfect excuse for not rallying to God's cause, to defer ever having to answer the divine address.

True understanding, of the biblical text and of oneself, takes place only in God's presence, signified by his face or voice. God's Word "embraces and contains me always, already, and forever, far from being subject to my embracing or containing it."[60] The biblical text is a mirror (Jas 1:22–25) in which we see our true faces, as fallen and potential recipients of saving grace. We also see God's face gazing at us from the mirror of the text.[61] In Calvin's words, "It is certain that man never achieves a clear knowledge of himself unless he has first looked upon God's face."[62] Kierkegaard agreed with Calvin about the reciprocity of self-knowledge and knowledge of God, but insisted that such knowledge comes in and through reading Scripture: "[There is] no true self-knowledge without knowledge of God or without being before God. To be in front of the mirror is to be before God."[63] True understanding also means *acting* on the basis of what one sees: "My acts become the best commentary, the best gloss, the most rigorous explication of these luminous words that God has given me the grace to be able to gather into my soul and my voice."[64]

Adam knew himself to be an answerable subject because of the Creator's address: "Where are you?" (Gen 3:9). It remains a penetrating question. To read the Bible is to enter into its world, at least momentarily, a world dominated by the word of God that addresses us, and by the God who awaits our response. New Testament exegete Ulrich Luz may have been right to worry, however, that "modern exegesis of our text leads us into a different world. It asks not how hearers and readers participate in the story; it primarily asks historical

---

59. Kierkegaard, *For Self-Examination*, 31–32.

60. Jean-Louis Chrétien, *Under the Gaze of the Bible* (New York: Fordham University Press, 2015), 9.

61. For an extended development of the mirror image, see Kevin J. Vanhoozer and Daniel J. Treier, *Theology and the Mirror of Scripture: A Mere Evangelical Account* (Downers Grove, IL: IVP Academic, 2015).

62. Calvin, *Institutes* I.1.2.

63. Kierkegaard, *For Self-Examination*, 234.

64. Chrétien, *Under the Gaze of the Bible*, 30.

questions about the origin of our story."[65] Where are we? What world—what story, what text—do we readers inhabit? To think theologically about the process of reading the Bible is to see reading itself as taking place on holy ground, an event of divine address and human answerability.

What Readers Do: Bear Faithful (or Unfaithful) Witness

A "mere Christian" hermeneutic focuses on the things for which all Bible readers are accountable, regardless of their particular interests, contexts, methods, traditions, interpretive communities, or scholarly degrees. Mere Christian hermeneutics refers to essential things readers need to know (e.g., that the Old Testament and New Testament belong together) and do (e.g., pray) to follow "the way the words go" and understand biblical discourse.[66] The way readers follow or do not follow the biblical words is an index to their understanding (including their self-understanding), and to their discipleship. In brief, *mere hermeneutics refers to those basic principles espoused by all Christians, everywhere, and at all times for reading the Bible as the church's Scripture.*[67]

Brevard Childs did not explicitly speak of "mere Christian hermeneutics," but he expressed a similar idea: "I strongly feel that there is a family resemblance in the responses of the Church [to biblical interpretation], in spite of the enormous diversity with the Christian exegetical tradition."[68] Indeed. In speaking of "mere Christian hermeneutics" I have in mind *what all Spirit-illumined readers have in common regardless of the differences in their particular exegetical methodologies.*[69] "Method" (from Gk. *meta* + *hodos* ["way"]) names a particular way of interpreting, of pursuing an interpretive interest. By way of contrast, mere hermeneutics is less a formal procedure than a meta-methodological guide, a rule of interpretive way. Answerability involves more than being able to give an account of one's exegetical methodology. It is more like the barometer of our existence, an indicator of our relationship to God. There is nothing "mere" (in the sense of inconsequential) about that.

---

65. Ulrich Luz, *Matthew 8–20* (Minneapolis: Fortress, 2001), 403.

66. "The way the words go" is Bruce D. Marshall's description of the literal sense. See his "Absorbing the World: Christianity and the Universe of Truths," in *Theology and Dialogue: Essays in Conversation with George Lindbeck*, ed. Bruce D. Marshall (Notre Dame, IN: University of Notre Dame Press, 1990), 94.

67. Brandon D. Smith makes a similar point, insisting that three premodern "sensibilities"—to the way the words go (literal sense); to the overall coherence of the Bible (christological referent); to the transformative purpose (sanctifying aim)—"inform a basic *Christian* reading of Scripture." *Taught by God: Ancient Hermeneutics for the Modern Church* (Brentwood, TN: B&H Academic, 2024), 182.

68. Childs, "Allegory and Typology within Biblical Interpretation," in *The Bible as Christian Scripture*, ed. Christopher R. Seitz and Kent Harold Richards (Atlanta: Society of Biblical Literature, 2013), 310.

69. Cf. Richard Briggs: "Hermeneutics consists not least in the negotiation of agendas—typically, competing agendas—held by different stakeholders in the text." "The Hermeneutics of Reading Genesis," in *Reading Genesis after Darwin*, ed. Stephen C. Barton and David Wilkinson (Oxford: Oxford University Press, 2009), 58.

The author of Hebrews exhorts his readers not to harden their hearts when they hear God's voice (or read his word). What is of hermeneutical significance to him has less to do with producing technically precise readings than it does with approaching the text in the right posture. Interpreters are prone to misread in one of two ways, each equally deadly. The one partakes of pride, the other sloth.[70] Prideful readers use biblical texts to promote their own views and voices rather than those of the text. Pride also shows up in the inordinate esteem in which interpreters may hold their own methods while looking down on others. Pride need not listen; it already knows. Interpretive pride thus leads to bearing false witness and, at the limit, idolatry. The second form of misreading, at the other end of the spectrum of deadly interpretive sin, is sloth. Sloth, too, is a form of unfaithful witness, in which the interpreter fails either to attend or to respond to the Bible's summons. Both pride and sloth are species of hard-heartedness, for which the Bible provides troubling examples. Consider, for example, the Lord's imperative to Israel: "Render true judgments, show kindness and mercy to one another, do not oppress the widow, the fatherless, the sojourner, or the poor" (Zech 7:9–10). What the Lord says here lays the foundation for a flourishing community characterized by justice and peace, which is why what comes next, a description of the people's lack of response, is so shocking: "But they refused to pay attention and turned a stubborn shoulder and stopped their ears that they might not hear. They made their hearts diamond-hard lest they should hear the law and the words that the Lord of hosts had sent by his Spirit through the former prophets" (Zech 7:11–12). This is the very portrait of the kind of close-minded and hard-hearted reading that stops understanding dead in its tracks.

The New Testament uses two related Greek terms for hard-heartedness. The first is derived from the word for stone (*poros*), and in four of its five occurrences it is associated with a lack of understanding (Mark 6:52; 8:17; John 12:40; 2 Cor 3:14), the last in connection with reading Moses. The other term for hardness or stubbornness of heart is *skleros* as in *arteriosclerosis*: the hardening of the arteries. This is a serious disease: the buildup of fats and cholesterol on the walls of the arteries can impede the flow of oxygen and other nutrients to the heart. The buildup of resistance to God's word in one's heart is equally dangerous. False gods and sinful habits can restrict the flow of truth and grace in the reading of the Bible. Call it hermeneutical arteriosclerosis.

Right reading of the Bible, the kind that attends to, and answers, the divine address, requires more of readers than using the right methods or following the right procedures. Right reading is a "process that requires a particular attention, vigilance, and availability."[71] These are not steps in a method but interpretive

70. I refer to these as the "two deadly interpretive sins" in *Is There a Meaning in This Text?*, 462–63.
71. Chrétien, *Under the Gaze of the Bible*, 2.

virtues: dispositions of the mind and heart that arise from a deep desire for understanding and for doing justice to the voice of another—an author. No single method can guarantee right reading; right reading requires right-hearted readers. Elsewhere I have argued for the importance of the interpretive virtues—personal characteristics like honesty, openness, attentiveness, and humility—dispositions that are conducive to textual understanding.[72] These virtues are necessary if readers are to bear true rather than false witness to authorial discourse and textual meaning, where bearing true witness is a matter of saying what one has heard in the text rather than what one might have preferred it to say.[73] Forming interpretive virtues—particular dispositions and habits of reading—is very much part of our experiment in biblical-theological criticism. For we are examining approaches to biblical interpretation by looking at, among other things, the kind of readers they form: "the tree is known by its fruit" (Matt 12:33).

Emphasizing right reading rather than right methodology makes for strange bedfellows. Richard Longenecker affirmed the inspiration and authority of the New Testament but did not think that readers today can or should imitate the way the apostles read, preferring the more academically respectable grammatical-historical method. Yet he also affirmed Paul's encouraging us to read Scripture *"as participants in the eschatological drama of redemption."*[74] This is almost the same language Peter Martens uses to describe how, for Origen, biblical interpretation was a way of life: "Origen contextualized the interpreter of Scripture—scholarly commitments included—within the Christian drama of salvation . . . that culminated in the vision of God."[75] As we shall see, Longenecker and Origen belonged to two very different reading cultures. For earlier Christians, the ideal reader is one who answers the divine address by bearing faithful witness, not least by actively participating in the eschatological dramatic subject matter of the text.

What Reading Is For: Communion with God; Training in Godliness

In the epilogue to *An Experiment in Criticism,* Lewis opined that reading good literature enlarges our being: "In reading great literature I become a thousand men and yet remain myself."[76] Reading Scripture rightly yields an even greater

72. Vanhoozer, *Is There a Meaning in This Text?*, 376–77, 466–67.

73. For more on interpretive virtue, see chapter 9 below.

74. Richard Longenecker, *Biblical Exegesis in the Apostolic Period*, 2nd ed. (Grand Rapids: Eerdmans, 1999), xxxv (emphasis original).

75. Peter Martens, *Origen and Scripture: The Contours of the Exegetical Life* (Oxford: Oxford University Press, 2012), 6; cf. 246.

76. Lewis, *Experiment in Criticism*, 141.

good, becoming like *one* man, Jesus Christ, through a *transformation* of the self. Theologically speaking, a reader's ontology or deepest identity—what defines a person at the core of one's being—is a function not of ethnicity or culture or social location, but of creaturehood and *covenantal* location: in Christ (or not).

In his High Priestly Prayer, Jesus tells the Father that he has given to his disciples "the words that you gave me, and they have received them." This reception was not a passive recording of information, for Jesus goes on to say that they "have come to know in truth that I came from you; and they have believed that you sent me" (John 17:8). Nothing transforms our being more than coming to know God and oneself before God. This is precisely what reading the Bible theologically is ultimately for. The divine address demands an answer and graciously gives what it demands. Some parts of the Bible were written to solicit belief—for example, that Jesus is the Christ (John 20:31)—others, obedience (Deut 8:1). Together the diverse modes of divine address communicate the supreme good of knowing God: communion.

Perhaps the most visible and tangible way the biblical interpreter enters into right relationship with God is through prayer—talking to God. The right reader response to the divine address is dialogical: "Here I am" (Gen 22:1). As Robert Alter notes, "Dialogue is the vital center of biblical narrative."[77] Many of the most important events are conveyed through dialogue: "For the biblical writers, then, it was clearly of paramount importance to show people relating to each other through speech."[78] This is especially so when one of the dialogue partners is God. I want to extend the point, going beyond Alter, to biblical interpretation itself. Reading the Bible to hear God's word is itself intrinsically dialogic. Even the reaction of hard-hearted readers is a kind of response ("No thanks"). According to Charles Taylor, dialogue enables a mode of being together that makes possible a shared take on the world, which he calls "joint attention."[79]

When readers of the Bible read rightly, their attention is focused on the same subject matter as the author's. The concept of authorial intention here comes into its own. I have argued elsewhere that it refers primarily not to what an author *planned* to do (i.e., the motive one has for writing), but to that to which authorial discourse is attending. To *intend* something is to direct one's *attention* to it.[80] Attention is "the concentration of the whole self in a moment of time."[81] Understanding is a form of joint attention, a veritable meeting of

77. Robert Alter, *The Art of Bible Translation* (Princeton, NJ: Princeton University Press, 2019), 103.

78. Alter, 103.

79. Charles Taylor, *The Language Animal: The Full Shape of the Human Linguistic Capacity* (Cambridge, MA: Belknap, 2016), 65, 90.

80. See further my *Is There a Meaning in This Text?*, 246–67.

81. Craig Dykstra, *Vision and Character: A Christian Educator's Alternative to Kohlberg* (New York: Paulist, 1981), 51.

the minds, author's and reader's. It is a key factor in interpersonal communion: "Come now, let us reason together, says the LORD" (Isa 1:18).[82] Reading the Bible theologically enables us to attend to the world and ourselves the way God sees the world and us. According to John Owen, the principal end of Scripture is "to beget in the minds of men faith, fear, obedience, and reverence of God, to make them holy and righteous. . . . It is given to make us *humble, holy, wise* in spiritual things . . . to make us to love God and to live unto him."[83]

Mere Christian hermeneutics views reading as much more than information processing. Those who aspire to right reading would do well to heed what Augustine says about the Psalter being a handbook of right reader responses, a tutor for right-hearted reading: "If the psalm is praying, pray yourselves; if it is groaning, you groan too; if it is happy, rejoice. . . . Everything written here is like a mirror held up to us."[84] Right readers must pray and practice biblical truth: "What Scripture is *for* is the conversion of human affection."[85] Serious and sincere reading, the kind of prayerful reading that results in saying yes to God, thus involves not merely intellectual assent but wholehearted consent to God's communicative intentions. The Psalms, together with the rest of the Bible, teach us both what God is like and how humans ought to respond to him in every type of situation imaginable. This is what we see David doing in writing the Psalms and what readers do when they pray the Psalms: "Submitting to the authority of God entails making God's will our own and living our lives in accordance with it."[86] Praying the Psalms and the rest of Scripture helps us attend and conform to what is real: the will of God expressed in the word of God.[87]

Ascending the Mountain: The Plan of the Book

"Life with God in the house of God—this was the original goal of the creation of the cosmos."[88] How an unholy people can come into the presence of a holy God is the chief complication in the biblical narrative to which the gospel is the solution. In Christ, YHWH has opened a way for humanity to dwell in the

82. See further Kelly M. Kapic, *Communion with God: The Divine and the Human in the Theology of John Owen* (Grand Rapids: Baker Academic, 2007).

83. John Owen, "The Causes, Ways, and Means of Understanding the Mind of God, as Revealed in His Word," in *The Reason of Faith* (Glasgow: Falconer, 1801), 261–62.

84. Augustine, *Expositions of the Psalms: 1–32*, trans. Maria Boulding (New York: New City, 2000), 347.

85. Jason Byassee, *Praise Seeking Understanding: Reading the Psalms with Augustine* (Grand Rapids: Eerdmans, 2007), 110 (emphasis original).

86. Vincent Brümmer, *What Are We Doing When We Pray?* (Aldershot, UK: Ashgate, 2008), 61.

87. See further Bruce Waltke and Fred Zaspel, *How to Read and Understand the Psalms* (Wheaton, IL: Crossway, 2023).

88. L. Michael Morales, *Who Shall Ascend the Mountain of the Lord? A Biblical Theology of the Book of Leviticus* (Downers Grove, IL: InterVarsity, 2015), 17.

divine presence.[89] Moses' encounter with the divine presence on Mount Sinai is a key point in the story. It is on the mountain that the Lord God speaks to Moses. The tabernacle perpetuates Moses' mountaintop experience by serving as the "tent of meeting" (Exod 29:44), "an architectural embodiment of the mountain of God . . . whereby the holy of holies corresponds to the summit," with the tables of law, originally given on Sinai, now kept in the ark of the covenant within the holy of holies, the summit's typological counterpart.[90]

Israel's story traces "the movement from Sinai, where Israel was consecrated to God in the wilderness, to Zion, as Israel inherited the land of Canaan."[91] The urgent question, for Israel and for us, is "Who shall ascend the mountain of the Lord, and how?" We know that the blood of sheep and goats ultimately failed to make Israel right before the Lord: "What to me is the multitude of your sacrifices? says the Lord; I have had enough of burnt offerings of rams and the fat of well-fed beasts" (Isa 1:11). The people of God remain answerable for their covenant unfaithfulness, and so the rest of the Bible's storyline describes the new Passover God provides, enabling people to dwell in his presence.

Ascending the mountain to meet God is a biblical trope. Jesus, too, goes up the mountain at certain key points in his ministry (Matt 5:1; 14:23; 15:29). The Psalms of Ascent (Pss 120–134) were probably sung by pilgrims on their way up to the temple on Mount Zion, and the Hebrew term for "ascent" suggests both "steps" and "going up."[92] This is a compelling image for reading the Bible as well. The psalmist asks, "Who shall ascend the hill of the Lord? And who shall stand in his holy place?" (Ps 24:3). The answer—"He who has clean hands and a pure heart, who does not lift of his soul to what is false and does not swear deceitfully" (v. 4)—also stands as a description of the right-minded and right-hearted reader of Scripture. This and other passages encouraged early Christian theologians to compare the process of biblical interpretation to ascending the mountain. Gregory of Nyssa's classic *The Life of Moses* relates Moses' pilgrim's progress up the mountain of God, a lifelong journey of the soul toward the vision of God. Reading the Bible to hear the word of God requires a similar ascent.

Centuries later the apostle Peter had a similar mountaintop experience. He was one of the three disciples who, along with James and John, accompanied Jesus up a high mountain, where Jesus heard the voice of God and was transfigured. The Gospels depict Peter's response to this event as both awkward and

89. This is also the primary theme and theology of the book of Leviticus according to Morales, *Who Shall Ascend*, 23.

90. Morales, 96.

91. Morales, 224.

92. See David C. Mitchell, *The Songs of Ascents: Psalms 120 to 134 in the Worship of Jerusalem's Temples* (Newton Mears, Scotland: Campbell, 2015), ch. 3.

inappropriate—a definite cringe moment.[93] Although commentators differ over the nature of Peter's error, the text makes clear that neither Peter nor the other two disciples had rightly interpreted the event. Luke comments that Peter "did not know what he was saying" (Luke 9:33 NIV); Mark said, "He knew not what to answer" (Mark 9:6 ASV). If answerability is a measure of understanding, we have to conclude that, at least at this point, Peter had no answer for what he had just seen.[94]

I invite readers to join me in ascending the mountain. There is perhaps no better picture of what is involved in reading the Bible theologically, particularly when my primary case studies—Moses on Mount Sinai and Jesus on Mount Tabor—feature accounts of humans having mountaintop experiences of God's glorious presence. To ascend the mountain is to chart a pathway into the Holy Scriptures, up to the place where God speaks and humans listen. The ultimate objective is to ascend, with Moses, Peter, and the rest of the people of God, the mount of Jesus' transfiguration, there to see Jesus in all his glory. We do not climb this mountain just "because it's there," but because there is nowhere else, and no one else, to whom we can go to hear about salvation in Christ. As Peter says to Jesus, "You have the words of eternal life" (John 6:68).

I have structured the argument in the form of two ascents, both having to do with transfiguration, in different ways. However, before we begin our ascent, part 1 surveys the terrain and the ways in which earlier mountain climbers have attempted the ascent. Chapters 1–3 explore the way in which habits of reading the Bible have generated disparate "reading cultures" and the way these reading cultures were dichotomized both in the medieval period (e.g., scholastic versus monastic) and in modernity (e.g., exegesis versus theology). These more diagnostic chapters help us to understand how we got to where we are, Bible readers formed by disordered reading cultures, caught between the cross-cultural currents of church and academy. I argue that reading at such cultural cross-purposes has not served the cross of Christ.

Parts 2 and 3 make different ascents up the mountain of biblical interpretation, though they intersect at several key points. The focus of part 2 is the letter of the biblical text ("what someone says"). The aim is to define and then follow the literal sense, something of great interest to both exegetes and theologians. Biblical interpretation is challenging, not only because of the myriad conflicting interpretations, many of which have divided the church, but also because of the conflict of interpretive methods, interests, and communities (viz., historical, ethnic, denominational, and disciplinary). Accordingly, the secondary aim is to

93. See further in chapter 7.

94. Peter later recalls Jesus' transfiguration with greater understanding (see 2 Pet 1:16–18).

reconcile these alienated interpretive communities, for their segregation has not served well the cause of literal interpretation—or the church.

Chapters 4 and 5 set forth a constructive proposal concerning the literal sense and literal interpretation. I clarify the precritical distinction between "literal" and "figural" interpretation, distinguish literal from literalistic interpretation, and retrieve the practice, common to Medieval and Reformation-era interpreters, of giving thick, theologically rich descriptions of the literal sense. I identify divergent frames of reference as one of the root causes of confusion about the literal sense and insist that a mere Christian hermeneutic do justice to the theological subject matter of Scripture: what the letter is *about*. The goal is to do honor to both the philological principle, championed by exegetes who follow the way the words go in their grammatical-historical context, and the christological principle, favored by theologians who follow the way words go in canonical context toward their eschatological referent. To this end, I argue that theological descriptions of the literal sense require interpreters to adopt both grammatical-historical and what I call grammatical-eschatological frames of reference. This leads to the first way in which the proposal is *trans-figural*, namely, by following the way certain trajectories cut *across* ("trans") times and testaments, linking biblical persons, places, and events ("figures").

Part 2 reads the letter of the text with a "trans-figural" frame of reference that attends to the letter in its multiple contexts: grammatical, literary, canonical, redemptive-historical, and eschatological. The aim throughout is to reconcile various reading cultures or interpretive communities that are either opposed or indifferent to one another: West versus East, ecclesial (monastic) versus academic (scholastic), systematic theology versus biblical scholarship, premodern versus modern. What we find at the summit of part 1 is the *formal principle* of mere Christian hermeneutics: a trans-figured literal sense.

Part 3 repeats our ascent, but this time by a different path and in company with the disciples on Mount Tabor. The focus now is the light of Christ, the subject matter of Scripture ("what something is said *about*") and the *material principle* of mere Christian hermeneutics, namely, the knowledge of God concentrated and communicated in the shining face of Jesus Christ. Accordingly, chapters 6 through 9 trace the economy of light—the ordered way in which God communicates the saving knowledge of himself from creation through Christ to consummation.

Jesus' transfiguration is an underappreciated hermeneutical resource, which Western theology has for the most part neglected (the one prominent exception being Jerome). The chapters in part 3 situate Jesus' transfiguration in the broader economy of light, namely, the ordered way God communicates his self-knowledge through redemptive history, thereby transferring sinners from the domain of darkness to the kingdom of the true light of the world (John 1:9; 9:5; Col 1:13). Jesus' transfiguration features as a crucial episode in this economy of light. The transfiguration takes place at a key moment, situated between the creation of light that God spoke into being (Gen 1:3) and the glory of God that will provide light in the new Jerusalem (Rev 21:23), and is perhaps the most important revelatory event in the economy of light between creation and consummation. It is also an event that exposes the limits of what a modern critical mindset can (or cannot) see: the glory of God in the face of Christ.

The transfiguration is an excellent case study for our experiment in biblical-theological criticism.[95] First and foremost, *it provides a unique vantage point from which to think about the ends and means of Christian hermeneutics in distinctly christological terms.* Far from being a weird footnote to Jesus' person and work of marginal importance, the transfiguration yields a key insight into what the whole Bible is about, shows us how to connect the letter of the text to the light of Christ, and graphically depicts what the effect of reading Scripture rightly should be on the reader: seeing Jesus, "the focal point that gathers all the rays of light that issue from Scripture."[96] Second, the transfiguration locates readers between a critical mindset that tends to overlook the supernatural and a precritical mindset that some may feel sees meaning that is not there. Whereas part 1 follows the letter of the text to what it is about, part 2 explores how the light of Christ transfigures both the letter and the reader by directing both to their proper end: the glory of God.

"Transfiguring interpretation" is shorthand for the attempt to combine scholarly exegesis, with its philological attention to the letter, and spiritual interpretation, with its concern for reading in such a way that readers understand in ways that conform them to the image of Christ. It is an attempt to read the Bible theologically, in, with, and for the church, while nevertheless profiting from the modern insights gleaned in the academy. To anticipate: transfigural interpretation attends to the letter of the text in order to discern in it the light of Christ. What earlier generations called the spiritual sense is, according to the view set forth here, the "transfigural" sense, namely, the glory of the literal sense. To see Christ in the letter is not to see something "other" in the text, as in "allegorical" interpretation; rather, it is to see "how much more" there is to the literal referent. Transfigural interpretation stands for the whole hermeneutical process of glorifying the biblical letter for the sake of the reader's glorification.

Parts 2 and 3 are both about ascending the mount of "transfiguration," then,

---

95. The question is whether modern biblical scholarship is able to perceive what Thomas Schreiner argues is the center of Paul's theology, namely, the glory of God in Christ. *Paul, Apostle of God's Glory in Christ: A Pauline Theology*, 2nd ed. (Downers Grove, IL: IVP Academic, 2020).

96. Dane C. Ortlund, "Christocentrism: An Asymmetrical Trinitarianism?," *Themelios* 34, no. 3 (November 2009): 318.

but by two different paths. In each case, the goal is to hear the word of God (divine address) with understanding (answerability). The result is the transfiguration of biblical hermeneutics, made something more glorious than other kinds of textual interpretation. For part of the peculiar glory of biblical interpretation is the reconciliation of the hitherto alienated disciplines of biblical studies and theology, originally partners, not competitors. Exegetes and theologians must recognize the importance of collaboration in order to hold together the philological and christological principles necessary for right reading of the Bible. The final goal is to form readers who are not simply "finely aware and richly responsible"[97] persons on whom nothing is lost but, rather, persons who are *canonically aware and redemptively responsible*—attentive and answerable to the divine address in the words of the prophets and apostles, the divine flame in the midst of a burning book, the light of Christ in the letter of the text.

Come, let us go up to the mountain of the Lord. (Isa 2:3; Mic 4:2)

97. The phrase is from a novel by Henry James (*The Princess Casamassima*), as cited repeatedly by Martha Nussbaum in her *Love's Knowledge: Essays on Philosophy and Literature* (Oxford: Oxford University Press, 1990), 37, 84, 136, 148.

PART 1

Reading the Bible in and out of Church

The Divided Domain of the Word

No style or form or pattern of biblical interpretation necessarily deserves the designation theological. Perhaps the most we can say is that theological interpretation is any form of human readerly activity that seeks to discern Christ in and through Scripture.... An ecclesial hermeneutic, therefore, is necessarily a hermeneutic of discipleship, a form of reading that takes shape in the wake of Christ's address and hopes for it ever anew.

—Derek W. Taylor, *Reading Scripture as the Church*

Learning to read is the first and most important step in a child's education, the principal doorway to learning about everything else. Reading both informs and forms, which is why children of God down through the ages have sought to figure out what the Bible means, why it matters, and how they should respond to or participate in the Bible's story.[1] Serious and sustained Bible reading, at once reflective and practical, is the soul of theology and the beating heart of the body of Christ, the church.

Hermeneutics is the art and science of interpretation—the study of the principles and practices necessary for textual understanding. It is a second order discipline that asks, *"What exactly are we doing when we read, understand, or*

1. Lewis Ayres argues that early Christianity and the development of doctrine is largely the story of how Christians adopted a set of reading practices found in ancient Greek and Latin traditions of literary commentary. Lewis Ayres, "'There's Fire in That Rain': On Reading the Letter and Reading Allegorically," *Modern Theology* 28, no. 4 (2012): 618–19.

apply texts?"[2] If biblical hermeneutics is scientific, however, it is not because it uses the same principles and procedures as philosophical, literary, or legal hermeneutics. The Bible is not simply one member of a larger set. If biblical hermeneutics is scientific, it is only because its procedures are in accordance with the nature of what it is trying to interpret.[3] To read the Bible as the word of God therefore involves the science of God (i.e., theology) and the life or culture to which this science, this project of seeking to know God, gives rise. Biblical hermeneutics is not rocket but theological science; the Bible is not a manual for going to the heavens but a story about heaven coming down to earth.[4]

Christian theology begins by acknowledging both the difference and the relation between God and the world, namely, the Creator-creature distinction, sometimes referred to simply as "the Christian distinction."[5] It is expressed in the first commandment: "You shall have no other gods before me" (Exod 20:3). This includes Hermes, the fabled messenger god, from whom the term *hermeneutics* derives. To avoid methodological idolatry, "God" must qualify "hermeneutics," not vice versa. To subordinate the task of faith seeking understanding (theology) to an independent science of textual understanding (hermeneutics) is to elevate Hermes above his station. Christian interpreters must not worship other gods in the high places of interpretation theory.

This is a book about reading the Bible theologically—and thinking theologically about Bible reading. The latter task involves thinking about authors, texts, subject matter, and readers in relation to God and God's word. Because we learn how to read in community, we must also think theologically about *culture*, the breeding ground of habits of reading.[6] Perhaps more than other hermeneutics textbooks, we will also think theologically about the "social imaginary" that has taken captive modern Western scholarship. By social imaginary I mean the story that frames our everyday beliefs and practices, the "ways people imagine their social existence"[7]—and their reading cultures. By "reading culture," I have something more specific in mind than a community that values

2. Anthony C. Thiselton, *Hermeneutics: An Introduction* (Grand Rapids: Eerdmans, 2009), 4 (emphasis original).

3. To put it in terms of a formula: ontology (what something is) determines epistemology (how it is known). For this understanding of science, see my "T. F. Torrance: Christ the Key to Creation and Theological Science," in *Science and the Doctrine of Creation*, ed. Geoffrey H. Fulkerson and Joel Thomas Chopp (Downers Grove, IL: IVP Academic, 2021), 121–47.

4. John Wesley, expressing his desire to be "a man of one book," said, "I want to know one thing, the way to heaven," but he was speaking in a soteriological, not astronomical, register. See *The Works of John Wesley*, vol. 1 (Nashville: Abingdon, 1984), 104–5.

5. See Robert Sokolowski, *The God of Faith and Reason: Foundations of Christian Theology* (Washington, DC: Catholic University of America Press), 23–26.

6. One early call for reading Scripture in community was Stephen E. Fowl, *Engaging Scripture: A Model for Theological Interpretation* (Oxford: Blackwell, 1998).

7. Charles Taylor, *A Secular Age* (Cambridge, MA: Belknap, 2007), 171.

and enjoys reading. Think of a reading culture as the social space where reading happens, together with the values, practices, and aims that characterize that space. A reading culture forms readers. It thus involves *people* (e.g., scholars; pastors; laypeople) and *places* (e.g., home, academy, church).

Not every reading culture acknowledges the Bible as the word of God. Students at secular universities who enroll in "The Bible as Literature" classes belong to one kind of reading culture, participants in Bible Study Fellowship to quite another. What is ultimately at stake is whether and to what extent we acknowledge the Bible, rather than some other texts, as the final arbiter of truth, not least about God. What is at stake, in sum, is nothing less than biblical civilization. My ultimate concern, then, is with reforming churches and seminaries so that they become the kind of reading cultures that can form readers to inhabit the strange new world that has been brought into being by the gospel of Jesus Christ.[8]

This book is for those who, like me, care about biblical literacy and are concerned about the conflict of biblical interpretations. It is for those who, like me, are puzzled about the nature and method of literal interpretation. It is for those who, like me, want to live under the lordship of Christ in every area of their lives, including their study of the Bible. The present book takes a distinctly Christian, and theological, approach to the theory and practice of biblical interpretation. To read the Bible Christianly and theologically is to enter onto holy ground, the domain of the living and active word of God. Unlike reading other texts, reading God's word involves a faithful and obedient standing *under* and following *after*.

Though biblical hermeneutics is not rocket science, it does involve political science, insofar as reading the Bible as Scripture in the church, the *polis* or city of God, has everything to do with forming readers into "fellow citizens with the saints and members of the household of God" (Eph 2:19), men and women who are able, always and everywhere, to inhabit the city of God, practicing the presence of God in Christ through the Spirit to the glory of God. No project is more theological than that.

The chapters in part 1 set the stage by introducing several key issues pertaining to reading the Bible theologically. In particular, I examine the longstanding tension between two types of reading cultures, the one oriented more to the letter (and literal sense), the other to Spirit (and spiritual sense). But we begin with reading cultures, biblical literacy, and the aim of reading.

---

8. Reading John Webster's *The Culture of Theology* (Grand Rapids: Baker Academic, 2019) has proved formative of my own thinking.

CHAPTER 1

Forming Reading Cultures

From Biblical Literacy to Gospel Citizenship

Theological interpretation is reading the Bible with a concern for the enduring truth of its witness to the nature of God and humanity, with a view to enabling the transformation of humanity into the likeness of God.

—R. W. L. Moberly[1]

The notion of a reading culture—a set of interpretive practices shared by a community and formative of its members—calls attention to the way literacy is constitutive of good citizenship. Since ancient Athens, one of the purposes of education has been to prepare citizens to participate in democracy. There are things people need to know in order to exercise the privileges and responsibilities commensurate with being a French, Nigerian, or Korean citizen. Call this need-to-know information *cultural literacy*.[2] Whereas literacy means knowing how to read and write, cultural literacy pertains to the ability to say and do things commensurate with good citizenship. For example, every American needs to know what "all men are created equal" means and how "endowed by their Creator with certain unalienable Rights" is to be lived out with others in just institutions.

1. R. W. L. Moberly, "What Is Theological Interpretation of Scripture?," *Journal of Theological Interpretation* 3, no. 2 (2009): 162 (emphasis original).

2. See E. D. Hirsch Jr., *Cultural Literacy: What Every American Needs to Know* (New York: Vintage Books, 1988).

Interpretive Communities, Constitutions, and Covenants

The most important document for American cultural literacy is, of course, the Constitution. To become United States citizens, immigrants must read, write, and speak English, pass a civics test, and, most intimidating of all, "understand and agree with the U.S. Constitution."[3] It's a tall order, particularly when even the finest legal minds, the Supreme Court justices, do not always agree on what it means, or even on how to read "America's Scripture."[4]

Jaroslav Pelikan's *Interpreting the Bible and the Constitution* is a fascinating comparative study of normative Scripture: Christian and American. As a historian of doctrine, Pelikan's primary interest was "the fundamental problem of the relation between the authority of the original text and the authority of the developing doctrine in the ongoing life and history of the community."[5] The parallels are indeed remarkable. There are weighty tomes on constitutional interpretation that pit "originalists" (those who insist on interpreting the Constitution to discover the original authorial intent) against those who affirm a "living Constitution," insisting that meaning develops over time, and thus requires taking historical precedents into account, which is to say, tradition.[6] What interests me in this debate is the interpretive community's role in fostering literacy.

The Bible, like the Constitution, is the founding document of a historic community—the people of God—whose members are citizens of a "holy nation" (1 Pet 2:9). Pelikan saw four interpretive communities vying for bragging rights as to who is reading the Constitution rightly, and in each case, they have counterparts in the church: (1) "We the people" (citizens, the congregation), (2) academic scholars (professors of law, biblical exegetes), (3) professional practitioners (lawyers, pastors), (4) an authoritative hierarchy (Supreme Court justices; sessions, synods, and bishops). The Protestant Reformers insisted that the responsibility for reading the Bible to determine what God is saying should not be reserved for an elite. Martin Luther's notion of the priesthood of all believers was a call not for interpretive anarchy but for widespread biblical literacy. Each Christian, as a citizen of heaven (Phil 3:20), has the privilege *and*

---

3. *The USCIS Policy Manual*, vol. 12, chap. 7, "Attachment to the Constitution," https://www.uscis.gov/policy-manual/volume-12-part-d-chapter-7.

4. See Thomas C. Grey, "The Constitution as Scripture," *Stanford Law Review* 37, no. 1 (1984): 1–25.

5. Jaroslav Pelikan, *Interpreting the Bible and the Constitution* (New Haven, CT: Yale University Press, 2004), 75.

6. For a general survey of approaches, see Lackland H. Bloom, *Methods of Interpretation: How the Supreme Court Reads the Constitution* (Oxford: Oxford University Press, 2009). For an examination of the idea that what is authoritative is the authors' or founding fathers' original intention, see the Pulitzer Prize–winning book by Jack N. Rakove, *Original Meanings: Politics and Ideas in the Making of the Constitution* (New York: Vintage Books, 1996).

responsibility to read the Bible, not as isolated but as gathered individuals, in community.[7] Still, every citizen needs to have a certain core knowledge: it is what enables Americans to be American, the French to be French, and Christians to be Christian. Of course, the Bible is wholly unlike the Constitution because its authority comes not from "We the people" but from "I . . . the Lord your God" (Exod 6:7).[8] The church is not a democracy, but a Christocracy, for Christ is head of its body politic (Eph 5:23; Col 1:18).

The Bible does not use the term *cultural literacy*, but the idea features prominently when Israel was first constituted a "holy nation" (Exod 19:6). There were certain things every Israelite had to know. For example, Passover was the fledgling nation's Fourth of July, a celebration of independence from Egypt: "And when your children say to you, 'What do you *mean* by this service?' you shall say, 'It is the sacrifice of the Lord's Passover, for he passed over the houses of the people of Israel in Egypt, when he struck the Egyptians but spared our houses'" (Exod 12:26–27, emphasis added). After receiving the Law on Mount Sinai, Moses calls for Israel's obedience to the statutes and rules by which they are to live as a holy nation: "For what great nation is there that has a god so near to it as the Lord our God is to us. . . ? And what great nation is there, that has statutes and rules so righteous as all this law that I set before you today?" (Deut 4:7–8). Moses then instructs Israel to teach the divine decrees to their children: "When your son asks you in time to come, 'What is the *meaning* of the testimonies and the statutes and the rules that the Lord our God has commanded you?' then you shall say to your son, 'We were Pharaoh's slaves in Egypt. And the Lord brought us out of Egypt with a mighty hand. . . . And the Lord commanded us to do all these statutes, to fear the Lord our God, for our good always, that he might preserve us alive, as we are this day" (Deut 6:20–24, emphasis added).

The question of meaning, and the core knowledge of what it means to be part of the people of God, arises again as Israel is about to enter the promised land, when the Lord miraculously parts the Jordan as he had earlier parted the Red Sea. Joshua orders twelve men, one from each tribe, each to take a stone from the middle of the riverbed and place it at Gilgal, where the people set up camp: "When your children ask their fathers in times to come, 'What do these stones *mean*?' then you shall let your children know, 'Israel passed over this Jordan on dry ground.' For the Lord your God dried up the waters of the Jordan for you until you passed over . . . that you may fear the Lord your God forever'" (Josh 4:21–24, emphasis added).

7. See further my *Biblical Authority after Babel: Retrieving the Solas in the Spirit of Mere Protestant Christianity* (Grand Rapids: Brazos, 2016), 155–60.

8. For a treatment of the two different meanings of "We the people" that has bedeviled constitutional interpretation, see Randy E. Barnett, *Our Republican Constitution: Securing the Liberty and Sovereignty of We the People* (New York: HarperCollins, 2016).

All three questions about meaning—about the Passover, the Ten Commandments, the memorial at Gilgal, respectively—concern what Israelites need to know as competent citizens of their holy nation. Each pertains to foundational events in Israel's history. Interestingly, the answers to these three questions ("What does *x* mean?") require knowing a larger story. The meaning of the Law is inseparable from its place in the narrative about God's mighty acts of deliverance. To be a culturally literate member of ancient Israel, then, was to understand oneself to be part of a covenant people constituted—called into being—by the grace of God: "And the Lord has declared today that you are a people for his treasured possession" (Deut 26:18).

The church, like Israel, is an elect people—"a chosen race, a royal priesthood, a holy nation" (1 Pet 2:9)—beholden to a new covenant, based not on law but gospel (Luke 22:20; 2 Cor 3:6). Members of the church can say, "Our citizenship is in heaven" (Phil 3:20), because their deepest identity is not the earthly place they inhabit but their being in Christ. Paul asks his readers to live as citizens of the gospel: "Only let your manner of life be worthy of the gospel of Christ" (Phil 1:27).[9] No matter their place of origin, Christians are now "fellow citizens with the saints and members of the household of God" (Eph 2:19), with all the privileges and responsibilities appertaining thereunto. The Bible is the covenant document, the church's constitution, because in the power of the Spirit, it is the founding text that *constitutes* the gathered assembly as a holy nation: one people under God—and God's word. To be a citizen of the gospel who knows what constitutes her holy nation is thus to be a person of the book. Biblical literacy and Christian cultural literacy stand or fall together.

Biblical Interpretation and the Formation of Christian Culture

Fast-forward through Israel's history, past the entrance into the promised land, subsequent exile and return, to first-century Palestinian Judaism. The question of the law's meaning was still paramount and, according to Josephus, "The Pharisees . . . [were] considered the most accurate interpreters of the laws."[10] They were experts in the *letter* of the law, both because they often interpreted it fastidiously and because they were proficient in devising legal loopholes to get around it. It was one of these lawyers—an expert in the Mosaic law, perhaps a Pharisee (cf. Luke 7:30)—who put Jesus' biblical literacy to the test, asking,

9. The verb Paul used here (*politeuesthe*) could be literally translated "live as a citizen" or "let your citizenship be."

10. Josephus, *Jewish War II*, viii.14.165, Loeb Classical Library (Cambridge, MA: Harvard University Press, 1927).

"Teacher, what shall I do to inherit eternal life?" Jesus responds with a question of his own, turning the question of biblical literacy back upon the lawyer: "What is written in the Law? How do you read it?" (Luke 10:26). Interestingly, the Greek omits the direct object. Jesus is therefore asking, "How do you read?" or, as one version has it, "How readest thou?" (Luke 10:26 ASV). That way of putting the question may indicate that Jesus is concerned not simply with a technical detail, but with the lawyer's fundamental approach to biblical interpretation. So, "How do you read?" along with Jesus' earlier query to his disciples, "Who do you say that I am?" (Luke 9:20), may be the two most important questions for which every professing Christian is answerable.

Legalistic interpretations of first-century Jewish culture failed to capture the true meaning of the Mosaic law. God's treasured possession had become not a holy but a hypocritical nation whose corporate life testified to their misunderstanding of their constitutional text, as Jesus made clear: "You search the Scriptures because you think that in them you have eternal life; and it is they that bear witness about me" (John 5:39). It was such hermeneutical differences that led the Jewish authorities to seek to kill Jesus, for his way of reading the Scriptures challenged and subverted religious conventions, in particular, Jewish interpretive authority.

The God-breathed Scriptures have a God-given purpose: they are profitable "for teaching, for reproof, for correction, and for training in righteousness, that the man of God may be complete, equipped for every good work" (2 Tim 3:16–17). All Scripture is profitable for training competent citizens of heaven. The biblical interpreter's proper vocation is to read Scripture so as to become wise unto salvation, as well as fit for living in and representing the kingdom of heaven. This was the signature emphasis of patristic hermeneutics.[11] To read the Bible theologically, then, is to remember what the Bible is and what it is for: it is the word of God that forms the people of God. "Once you were not a people, but now you are God's people" (1 Pet 2:10). The Bible provides a reminder of who God is, what God has done, who we are before God, and what we are to do for God.

What does being the people of God involve and require? The most important ingredients include a shared history (memory), a common life (identity), and ways of reading normative Scripture (understanding). Reading the Bible theologically is both a characteristic practice of Christian culture and a means of forming and reforming Christian culture, the way the people of God seek "to inhabit the world which is brought into being by the staggering good news

11. See Richard S. Briggs, "Premodern Interpretation and Contemporary Exegesis," in *The New Cambridge Companion to Biblical Interpretation*, ed. Ian Boxall and Bradley C. Gregory (Cambridge: Cambridge University Press, 2023), 301–17.

of Jesus Christ, the world of the new creation."[12] Among the central practices that need to be cultivated in and for a Christian culture "are textual practices, habits of reading."[13] Culture involves people in a particular place engaging in particular practices that reflect their beliefs and values. What distinguishes a properly Christian culture is its concern to indwell a space formed by God's word. Moreover, the practices that comprise a Christian culture are not merely natural but result from a triune work of grace.

A Christian culture, viewed theologically, is more than a this-worldly phenomenon. It is not a merely human project but a work of the Son and Spirit, God's "two hands." It is a human response to a divine address that interrupts the old way of doing things, as did the voice of the risen Jesus when he stopped a young man in his tracks, saying, "Saul, Saul, why are you persecuting me?" (Acts 9:4). Christians similarly read their constitutional texts, the Old Testament and New Testament, in the presence of their risen Lord, whose words they are. Christian habits of reading the Bible are thus part of an "eschatological" culture. Mere Christian hermeneutics is about reading the Bible in that peculiar eschatological space that defines and generates Christian culture: *the presence of Christ in the power of his Spirit*. Reading the Bible rightly—as what it is, the word of God—thus involves a reading culture created and sustained by the word of God. The implications are staggering. For, if merely human reading cultures—whether academic, leisure, literary, or religious—are able to form readers, how much more could a mere Christian hermeneutic, in an eschatologically charged space, be transformative?

Such ideas were familiar to early Christians who read the Bible to be built up into Christ. The text was for them "the verbal form of divine pedagogy,"[14] profitable for training in righteousness, and gospel citizenship. Keeping in mind this pedagogical function of biblical interpretation is the necessary backdrop for understanding the early church as a reading culture and the earliest chapters of the history of biblical interpretation. We will never be able to sympathize with patristic or medieval interpreters, or even read them correctly, unless and until we appreciate their concern to read Scripture in ways that edify the church. Even if we decide we cannot read the Bible exactly as they did, we can still learn from the Fathers what should be our reading's *aim*.

Patristic and medieval interpretation reminds us that the Bible has formative potential. Frances Young's valuable work *Biblical Exegesis and the Formation of Christian Culture* demonstrates that, in many respects, "the early Church was

12. Webster, *Culture of Theology*, 43.

13. Webster, 45.

14. John J. O'Keefe and R. R. Reno, *Sanctified Vision: An Introduction to Early Christian Interpretation of the Bible* (Baltimore: Johns Hopkins University Press, 2005), 22.

more like a school than a religion in the social world of antiquity."[15] Christians continued to use tools of classical culture but directed them not to classical but biblical literature. "The Bible replaced Homer as the authoritative religious or philosophical text."[16] Stories about Abraham and David replaced those of Achilles and Ulysses as the core curriculum on which moral learning was based—Christian *paideia*, training of children in the Christian way. Here, in the patterns of reading Scripture in the early church, lay the basis of biblical civilization.

According to Young, it was Origen who first "professionalized" biblical interpretation and turned Scripture into "the basis for a complete educational system with primary, secondary and tertiary levels."[17] This same Origen is, ironically, the whipping boy of modern biblical scholarship, the abusive father who does violence to the biblical text with his flights of fancy. What most people know about Origen is that he associated the literal sense with the "body" of the text, in other words, with the lowest rank, then went on to suggest that this level of meaning is appropriate only for babes in Christ—interpretive K–12, as it were (cf. Heb 5:12–13). Origen associated the text's "soul" with the moral or spiritual meaning, appropriate for the more mature—those in interpretive college. The highest degree of hermeneutical education, the grad school of interpretation as it were, is the level of the "spirit" and involves discerning spiritual truths. Origen's use of Paul's benediction—"May your whole spirit and soul and body be kept blameless at the coming of our Lord Jesus Christ" (1 Thess 5:23)—as a proof text for his three-tiered allegorizing has not won him any friends either.

We shall return to Origen, and the various levels of meaning, in due course. It would be a shame, however, if those inclined to dismiss Origen were to throw out his pedagogical baby with the allegorical bathwater. Because reading the Bible is formative, and not merely informative, the twin questions, "Why am I reading the Bible?" and "What sort of person must I be in order to read it for the purpose it was written?" are not only relevant but essential to mere Christian hermeneutics. As Webster said, "It is more important to lay out an anthropology of the reader than to establish a set of methodological directives for reading."[18] I intend to pursue both ends, for my experiment in biblical-theological criticism is also an experiment in Christian culture, specifically, Christian *reading* culture. It asks: What kind of readings, *and readers*, do certain ways of exegeting and interpreting produce?

---

15. Frances Young, *Biblical Exegesis and the Formation of Christian Culture* (Cambridge: Cambridge University Press, 1997), 244.

16. Young, 75.

17. Young, 292.

18. Webster, *Culture of Theology*, 73.

We learn to read in community. The values and practices of that community constitute its reading culture. To explore the history of biblical interpretation is therefore a cross-cultural experience. Not all Christians read the Bible in the same way or value the same reading practices. For many biblical scholars, it is primarily an academic practice. By way of contrast, for the church fathers, it was primarily a purpose-driven pedagogy: "The purpose of biblical exegesis, implicit and explicit, was to form the practice and belief of Christian people, individually and collectively."[19] One of the reasons that reading the church fathers can often be disorienting, then, is that earlier Christians "*embraced* the concerns we tend to separate out into scholarship, theology, *praxis*, and spirituality."[20]

One of the most significant, yet least appreciated features, of this patristic synthesis was "that it provided a literature which shaped Christian discourse *and fed the Christian imagination*."[21] In the words of patristic scholar Lewis Ayres, "the Scriptures are a providentially ordered resource for the shaping and reformation of the Christian's imagination and desire."[22] The point must not be missed: the prevailing social imaginary in the early church was scriptural, not secular. And this, I hope to show, is where the conflict between premodern, modern, and postmodern reading cultures really lies, *in the differences of their respective social imaginaries*. The very way modern Christians think about reading the Bible is conditioned by the prevailing social imaginary that in turn informs the dominant reading practices in society, the academy, and even the church. For this reason, the early church presents a challenge to contemporary Christians: to think theologically about reading the Bible; to specify what role God plays in biblical interpretation. Again, the challenge is to see the reading culture that has shaped us for what it is and to acknowledge the influence of the prevailing social imaginary on that culture. For reading Scripture theologically requires an active and alert, canonically formed imagination, an apprenticeship as it were in the society of biblical literature—not the professional society (SBL) that goes by that name but, rather, the unity in diversity of the literature that comprises the Christian canon and the cloud of witnesses who have read them as cohering in Christ.[23]

---

19. Young, *Biblical Exegesis and the Formation of Christian Culture*, 299.

20. Young, 299 (emphasis original). With some significant exceptions (e.g., the Puritans), those who speak of spiritual formation in connection with biblical interpretation tend to be Roman Catholics and Eastern Orthodox. Angela Harvey describes her own approach to spiritual reading as "Wesleyan Orthodox." See her *Spiritual Reading: A Study of the Christian Practice of Reading Scripture* (Eugene, OR: Cascade, 2015). Conspicuous by its absence is a Reformed Protestant account. Filling this lacuna is one of the burdens of the present work.

21. Young, 299 (emphasis added).

22. Lewis Ayres, "The Soul and the Reading of Scripture: a Note on Henri de Lubac," *Scottish Journal of Theology* 61, no. 2 (2008): 189.

23. See further the helpful book by David I. Starling, *Hermeneutics as Apprenticeship: How the Bible Shapes Our Habits and Practices* (Grand Rapids: Baker Academic, 2016).

On the Making of Reading Cultures: Three Historical Examples

Consider three brief examples from different eras of biblical interpretation. Each illustrates the importance of biblical interpretation in the formation of Christian culture.[24]

Augustine (Fifth Century)

In the ancient world, "to be educated . . . was to be a reader."[25] Brian Stock's *Augustine the Reader* is all about Augustine's attempt "to lay the theoretical foundation for a reading culture."[26] For Augustine, the consummate pastor-theologian, the purpose of Christian teaching (doctrine) is discipleship, and the proper end of biblical interpretation is community formation. Augustine's *On Christian Doctrine* (*De doctrina christiana*) influenced the way Christians read their Bibles for well over a thousand years.[27] Good exegesis required the reader's moral and spiritual formation, not simply choosing the right method. Indeed, the aim of interpretation—to read in ways that foster the love of God and neighbor—was more important than the particular method: "So anyone who thinks that he has understood the divine scriptures or any part of them, but cannot by his understanding build up this fourfold love of God and neighbor, has not yet succeeded in understanding them."[28] No amount of technical precision can make up for biblical interpretations that pursue technical knowledge but not love: "The reader, then, has his or her own telos: the proper relationship with God and with his or her neighbor."[29]

Can biblical interpretation change the world? At the very least, it can form a culture. This was Augustine's purpose in writing his manual for biblical

---

24. Space prevents me from doing full justice to any one of them. Each has been the subject of extensive scholarly scrutiny and multiple monographs, and I do not pretend to have discovered something original. I have tried here and throughout this work to do due diligence to both primary and secondary sources. The fact that the argument of the present book is normative rather than descriptive is no excuse to ride roughshod over history or to treat classic texts in a slipshod way. However, the nature of my topic—reading the Bible theologically in and for the church catholic—requires a certain ambitious synthetic reach.

25. William Harmless, ed. *Augustine in His Own Words* (Washington, DC: Catholic University of America Press, 2010), 156.

26. Brian Stock, *Augustine the Reader: Meditation, Self-Knowledge, and the Ethics of Interpretation* (Cambridge, MA: Belknap, 1996), 1.

27. See Grover Zinn, "The Augustinian Tradition of Sacred and Secular Reading Revised," in *Reading and Wisdom: The De doctrina christiana of Augustine in the Middle Ages*, ed. Edward English (Notre Dame, IN: University of Notre Dame Press, 1995), 61–83.

28. Augustine, *On Christian Teaching* 1.36.40, trans. R. P. H. Green (Oxford: Oxford University Press, 1999), 27.

29. James A. Andrews, *Hermeneutics and the Church: In Dialogue with Augustine* (Notre Dame, IN: Notre Dame University Press, 2012), 291. On the importance of authorial intention for Augustine, see *On Christian Doctrine* 1.36.40–41.

interpretation: to instill certain habits of reading in his congregation—a rule for reading that would blossom into a rule for community life.

Hugh of St. Victor (Twelfth Century)

Hugh of St. Victor's treatise *Didascalicon, or, On the Study of Reading* is to the twelfth-century what Augustine's *On Christian Doctrine* was to the fifth: an epoch-making, culture-forming handbook to biblical interpretation and Christian learning. For Hugh, all learning in other areas was preparatory for the Christian's primary vocation: reading the Bible. The fruit of reading Scripture is twofold "because it either instructs the mind with knowledge or equips it with morals."[30] What Hugh ultimately wants readers to learn is Christ himself (cf. Eph 4:20): "Learning and, specifically, reading, are both simply forms of a search for Christ the Remedy, Christ the Example and Form which fallen humanity, which has lost it, hopes to recover."[31]

Hugh likened learning Scripture to building a cathedral. Biblical literacy is therefore a kind of "construction project, a process of building up the whole person."[32] The comparison is fitting, for Hugh believed that "the subject matter of all the Divine Scriptures is the work of man's restoration."[33] One scholar therefore dubs Hugh a "second Augustine" and "reformer": "Hugh conceives of Christian existence in this life as aiming at the construction of a dwelling place, an *aedificatio* for the presence of God within human persons, through their reformation (*reformatio*) in the image of God."[34] To be "re-formed," in this context, means being rebuilt in the image of Christ, conformed to his form, largely by repairing the soul through an apprenticeship to Scripture. For Hugh, "biblical interpretation is not merely *about* God's restorative work, it is itself that work of restoration."[35] Hugh was representative of the twelfth century monastic culture that pursued spiritual formation largely through reading and meditating on Scripture, reading cultures that gave equal attention to grammar (the knowledge of letters) and spirituality (the search for God).[36]

---

30. *The Didascalicon of Hugh of Saint Victor: A Medieval Guide to the Arts*, trans. Jerome Taylor (New York: Columbia University Press, 1991), 127.

31. Ivan Illich, *In the Vineyard of the Text: A Commentary on Hugh's Didascalicon* (Chicago: University of Chicago Press, 1993), 10.

32. Ian Christopher Levy, *Introducing Medieval Biblical Interpretation: The Senses of Scripture in Premodern Exegesis* (Grand Rapids: Baker Academic, 2018), 148.

33. From *De sacramentis christianae fidei*. Cited in Boyd Taylor Coolman, *The Theology of Hugh of St. Victor: An Interpretation* (Cambridge: Cambridge University Press, 2010), 13.

34. Coolman, *Theology of Hugh of St. Victor*, 3.

35. Paul Rorem, *Hugh of Saint Victor* (Oxford: Oxford University Press, 2009), 121.

36. The two cultural values came together in their cultural practice of *lectio divina* ("divine reading"), a way of reading prayerfully and contemplatively. I will say more about monastic culture and its contrast with "scholastic" culture in subsequent chapters.

The Reformers (Sixteenth Century)

Can biblical interpretation change the world? Yes, because it already has. The Reformation is an obvious exhibit of the way in which a reading culture (the Protestant Reformation) can effect social, intellectual, and political changes. Luther and Calvin were keen to translate the Bible into the vernacular languages of their respective nations so that the formative power of the gospel would be accessible to all: "The study of the Bible was meant to be transformative at the most basic level of the human person, *coram deo*. It was meant to lead to communion with God."[37] At the time of Luther's death mid-sixteenth century, there were some half a million copies of his German translation in print, a combustive cultural force that eventually changed the face of Europe: "It was through textual production that Luther hoped to reform religious life, by reaching beyond the structures of the church to a popular religious movement."[38]

The Reformers continued to value the liberal arts inasmuch as they contributed to biblical literacy. In his 1520 treatise *To the Christian Nobility*, Luther called for reform in the church but also in the academy: "Above all, the most important and most usual teaching, in both the universities and the lower schools, ought to be concerned with the Holy Scriptures."[39] Calvin, too, believed in education for everyone, encouraging—nay, mandating!—parents in Geneva to teach their children the catechism.[40] The Geneva Academy, founded in 1559, was the first Protestant university, and Calvin's teaching in the academy was part of his duty as a pastor. Moreover, the academy's curricular structure "sent the message that scriptural exegesis as taught in the theology lectures was not an academic discipline separate from the clergy's day-to-day work, but was rather an integral part of it."[41] Teachers (the "doctors" of the church) were to train pastors in the reading of the Bible, and pastors were to teach their congregations.

In Geneva Calvin had the title "Reader," and he more than lived up to it, writing commentaries on almost every book in the Christian canon. He compared reading to seeing (through the "spectacles" of Scripture), hearing, and

---

37. Timothy George, *Reading Scripture with the Reformers* (Downers Grove, IL: IVP Academic, 2011), 21.

38. Brian Cummings, *The Literary Culture of the Reformation: Grammar and Grace* (Oxford: Oxford University Press, 2002), 16.

39. Cited in *Martin Luther: Selections*, ed. John Dillenberger (Garden City, NY: Anchor Books, 1961), 475. See also Luther, "To the Councilmen of All Cities in Germany That They Establish and Maintain Christian Schools," in *Martin Luther's Basic Theological Writings*, ed. Timothy E. Lull (Minneapolis: Fortress, 1989), 704–35.

40. See further Randall C. Zachmann, *John Calvin as Teacher, Pastor, and Theologian: The Shape of His Writings and Thought* (Grand Rapids: Baker Academic, 2006).

41. Karin Maag, "Calvin and Students," in *The Calvin Handbook*, ed. Herman J. Selderhuis (Grand Rapids: Eerdmans, 2009), 167.

even eating (cf. Jer 15:16), such is its power to penetrate the heart.[42] In his 1559 preface to the *Institutes*, "To the Reader," Calvin explained that the purpose of his doctrinal instruction was to make smooth the path of reading the Bible so that readers "may be able both to have easy access to it and to advance in it without stumbling."[43] Knowledge of sound doctrine was central to the task of reading the Bible: "There was a symbiotic relationship between the *Institutes* and the commentaries in that both served the purpose of elucidating scripture, but from different perspectives."[44] Calvin himself described doctrinal theology as "a key to open a way for all children of God into a good and right understanding of Holy Scripture."[45]

Finally, although Calvin was part of the humanistic movement that sought to do justice to literary texts, including the Bible, in their original languages, he believed reading Scripture makes unique demands upon the reader. Readers must approach the Scriptures as Moses did the burning bush, "as if there the living words of God were heard."[46] Gilbert Vincent argues that, for Calvin, there was an ethical dimension to biblical interpretation; readers must respond not simply to bits of information but to the world-shattering event of being addressed by God.[47] In addition to making sense of textual content (the letter), readers have to contend with the voice of God and the claim of lordship that voice makes on their lives: "In this text we are arrested and addressed by God."[48] The event of being addressed by God created an eschatological culture of reading, a reading by those "on whom the end of the ages has come" (1 Cor 10:11)—and those to whom the King of the ages has spoken.[49] The salient point is that, for Calvin, the reader's context includes "being addressed by God."

---

42. John Calvin, *Institutes of the Christian Religion*, ed. John T. McNeill, 2 vols. (Philadelphia: Westminster, 1960), 1.6.1.

43. Calvin, *Institutes*, 4. His approach to reading may have been influenced by the monastic tradition of *lectio divina*. See Wesley A. Kort, "Calvin's Theory of Reading," *Christianity & Literature* 62, no. 2 (2013): 190. Kort adds, "As Luther took 'vocation' out of the monastery and applied it to the lives of all Christians, so Calvin took the discipline of *lectio divina* . . . and made it a central and defining act of Christian life and identity" (191).

44. Bruce Gordon, *Calvin* (New Haven, CT: Yale University Press, 2009), 108. Cf. Kort: "The principal purpose of theology and doctrine for Calvin is to clarify and to protect the act of reading Scripture." "Calvin's Theory of Reading," 198.

45. Calvin, "Subject Matter of the Present Work," *Institutes*, 7.

46. Calvin, I.7.1. In saying, "as if," Calvin was not saying that we must simply *imagine* the Bible to be the word of God. Rather, as Kort explains, Calvin uses the Latin *sicut* to express "a hesitancy before the actuality of the living word of God in reading Scripture." "Calvin's Theory of Reading," 195.

47. See Gilbert Vincent, *Exigence éthique et interprétation dans l'oeuvre de Calvin* (Geneva: Labor et Fides, 1984).

48. Webster, *Culture of Theology*, 71.

49. Webster defined an eschatological culture as a culture "which is generated, sustained, and perfected, and also exposed to radical questioning, by the utterly gratuitous presence of God in the risen Jesus through the Holy Spirit's working." *Culture of Theology*, 53.

Toward What Kind of Reading Culture?

Since the time of ancient Israel, the people of God have read and responded to the word of God written in ways that are formative of culture—that complex whole of beliefs, values, and practices. Patristic, medieval, and Reformation readers alike valued the liberal arts and especially grammar. Indeed, the twin foci of Bible reading were *God* and *grammar*.

The first challenge of early Christians was to speak rightly of God in relation to biblical testimony about Jesus Christ. God is one, yet Scripture ascribes divine qualities to the Son and the Spirit and ascribes actions to them of which only God is capable (e.g., creation). Under canonical pressure, the fourth-century council of Nicaea formulated a Trinitarian grammar of biblical discourse: the God the Bible depicts is one in nature and three in person (Father, Son, and Spirit).[50] A later council formulated a grammatical rule for speaking about Jesus Christ according to the logic implicit in the biblical testimony about him: the Son of God is one (divine) person with two natures (divine and human).[51] These grammatical rules for talking (and thinking) rightly about God also function as rules for right reading. To these two rules we could add what is arguably the first rule of the grammar of God: never confuse the Creator with anything creaturely. We might group these three rules pertaining to the Trinity, Christology, and the Creator-creature distinction under the rubric of the "mere Christian" doctrine of God.

In the context of early Christianity, "grammar" means more than the study of parts of speech. It is the first of the liberal arts and stands at the intersection of literacy, biblical interpretation, education, and culture. *Grammata* is the Greek word for "letters," a catch-all term for "arts and letters," or simply the humanities: "Rather than one discipline among many, *grammatica* had an essentially constitutive function, making a certain kind of literacy and literary culture possible."[52] Grammar was "the foundation of literacy,"[53] and to study *grammatica* was to study the arts of speech and reading. Historians can therefore speak of the patristic, medieval, and even the Reformation eras of the church as

50. C. Kavin Rowe rightly notes, "This [canonical] pressure moves us to the conclusion that YHWH is not the Father alone. . . . Read canonically, then, the full unity of God as expressed through the name *kyrios* is that of Father, Son, and Spirit." "Biblical Pressure and Trinitarian Hermeneutics," *Pro Ecclesia* 11, no. 3 (2002): 303–4.

51. R. B. Jamieson and Tyler R. Wittman, *Biblical Reasoning: Christological and Trinitarian Rules for Exegesis* (Grand Rapids: Baker Academic, 2022).

52. Martin Irvine, *The Making of Textual Culture: "Grammatica" and Literary Theory 350–1100* (Cambridge: Cambridge University Press, 2006), xiv. Jean Leclercq agreed: "Thus grammar is the first stage and the foundation of general culture." *Love of Learning and Desire for God: A Study of Monastic Culture* (New York: Fordham University Press, 1982), 17.

53. Cummings, *Literary Culture of the Reformation*, 20.

"grammatical" cultures: the set of reading practices, including the *goods* of those reading practices, that were part and parcel of their respective ways of life.[54]

The premodern term *grammatica* is thus far more capacious than its modern counterpart: "grammar." *Grammatica* covers everything to do with literacy, including the principles for textual interpretation: "*grammaticus* . . . designate[s] a man 'who knows how to read'—that is, not only how to decipher the letters, but how to understand the texts."[55] In sharp contrast, modern grammar refers exclusively to the study of the elements, structure, and syntactical rules of a given language. Students who study the grammar of New Testament Greek in exegesis classes typically have in mind the latter. For them, grammar is the linguistic equivalent of organic chemistry inasmuch as both study the basic constituents of their respective disciplines: syntax in the one case, molecules in the other.

Here is a universal truth: every Christian reader belongs to some reading culture. Reading cultures differ from one another, at least in part, by the way they understand and relate *God* and *grammar*. In the Middle Ages, for example, people read texts aloud; they heard the "voices of the pages" which, in the case of the biblical text, were voices that conveyed the voice of God.[56] In monastic reading cultures, some monks searched for God so fervently that, in their one-track devotion, they sometimes bypassed the letter: "*Mea grammatica Christus est*" ("My grammar is Christ"), declared Peter Damian.[57] The Reformers were equally devoted to Christ, though they were unwilling to cut ties to the biblical letters, the anchors that held them fast to the prophetic and apostolic testimony.

In modern times, the pendulum has swung to the other side. Pride of place in biblical studies today goes to getting the grammar right. This is partly because many people learn to read the Bible in an academic culture where linguistics is next to godliness. Modern linguistics provides new tools for analyzing sentence meaning. Some biblical interpreters do not simply read but *diagram*, producing visual illustrations, often with the aid of increasingly powerful software, that clarify the flow of the argument and the meaning of the thoughts conveyed.[58] When applied beyond the level of the sentence, however, diagramming may be less helpful. It is difficult to capture the way in which various literary genres may affect sentence meaning and relationships (try diagramming the book of Proverbs or *Huckleberry Finn*). Outside biblical studies, we normally do not

54. The term "grammatical culture" comes from Irvine, *Making of Textual Culture*, 1.

55. Leclercq, *Love of Learning and Desire for God*, 17. See also the chart of the divisions of *grammatica* in Irvine, *Making of Textual Culture*, 6.

56. Leclercq, *Love of Learning and Desire for God*, 15.

57. Cited in Leclercq, 260.

58. See, e.g., the Propositional Outline feature of Logos Bible Software, https://www.logos.com/grow/how-to-quickly-diagram-a-biblical-passage/ (accessed March 9, 2023).

speak of "exegeting" short stories or novels written in our native tongue, nor do we diagram sentences when reading C. S. Lewis's *Narnia Chronicles*, much less *Moby-Dick*. Still, all readers today inhabit some kind of reading culture whose values and aims generate and govern particular ways of reading.

To paint with a broad brush: modern readers objectify grammar, viewing language at a critical distance as something that can be studied neutrally, even impersonally. What do conjunctions, verb tenses, and dependent clauses have to do with Jerusalem? In his study of Greek grammar, Daniel Wallace speaks of "unaffected meaning," namely, "the meaning of the construction in a vacuum—apart from contextual, lexical, or other grammatical intrusions."[59] Wallace goes on to note, rightly, that we cannot leave the matter there: "The nature of language is such that *grammar cannot be isolated from other elements* such as context, lexeme, or other grammatical features."[60] A reductionist approach that pays attention to morphology and syntax only, abstracting bits of language from the lived context in which people use them, may technically count as grammatical, but it is not conducive to textual understanding. There is a certain kind of exegesis that murders to dissect. It is important, then, not to give the impression that knowledge of grammar, narrowly conceived, is the be-all and end-all of reading. A reading culture that is grammatical in this reductionist sense forms readers to be mere technicians of textuality, not answerable subjects.[61] How, then, shall we integrate our dual interests in *God* and *grammar*? What *other* kinds of attention to the letter of the text are necessary to do justice to the Bible as the word of God in human words? The present book is an extended answer to this important question.

The first step toward forming a reading culture that accords with Holy Scripture is to acknowledge the existence, and influence, of reading cultures. For some readers may resist the idea that they belong to any culture that might affect their reading, other than the "scientific" culture of biblical scholarship. The cure for this naivete is a good dose of church history. Travel is equally educational. Those who have eyes to see and ears to hear quickly come to understand that culture pertains not only to *those* people over *there*, but to all of us. Every person's biblical interpretation is culturally conditioned, minimally, by the reading culture to which he or she belongs.

Let me now set forth my working assumption: *the kind of exegesis we do depends on the nature of the reading culture into which we have been socialized.*

59. Daniel B. Wallace, *Greek Grammar beyond the Basics: An Exegetical Syntax of the New Testament* (Grand Rapids: Zondervan, 1996), 2.

60. Wallace, xiii (emphasis original).

61. I am reminded of my college piano teacher John Nordquist's distinction between those who play notes and those who love them. This comment performed a baptism of my imagination as I began to see reading musical scores as a form of textual interpretation.

Remember, a reading culture is a community that values and practices a certain way of reading. Reading cultures generate interpretations and, more importantly, form readers to conform to their community's standards and practices. It may help to distinguish literacy as linguistic competence (i.e., the ability to speak and understand a particular language) from literacy as literary competence (i.e., the result of successful socialization into the habits and practices of a particular reading community). *Readers are deemed "literate" if they achieve competence in a particular community's reading practices.*

Rudolf Bultmann famously asked, "Is exegesis without presuppositions possible?"[62] My question is slightly different: *Is exegesis without reading cultures possible?* Biblical interpreters do well to examine not only the presuppositions they bring to the text, but also the ways their presuppositions and interpretive practices have been formed by the particular reading culture they inhabit. It matters because the ways Christians read the Bible eventually shape Christian culture. A disordered reading culture will form a disordered Christian culture (and vice versa). It is a kind of hermeneutic circle: *reading cultures form readers, and readers form (or hand on) reading cultures.*

Not all reading cultures are created equal, as Jesus' sobering comment reminds us, when he told his listeners they could not understand him "because you cannot bear to hear my word" (John 8:43). The aim of mere Christian hermeneutics is to ensure that reading cultures form readers who can attend to, and bear, Jesus' words. A rightly ordered Bible-reading culture is one that rightly orders the paired interpretive interests in *grammar* and *God*. Doing justice to each does not necessarily entail giving each equal time, but rather, giving each its proper *due*. Clarifying how to handle the letter of the text (grammar) and how it relates to the light of Christ (God) will occupy the lion's share of our attention.

In his widely used textbook, Michael Gorman attempts to balance grammar and God by defining biblical exegesis as scholarly reading: "the careful historical, literary, and theological analysis of a text."[63] He also mentions "close reading," the "deliberate, word-by-word and phrase-by-phrase consideration of all the parts of a text in order to understand it as a whole."[64] Such reading honors the letter and forms a kind of reading culture that ought not be despised. The urgent question, however, concerns the role of theology. Different reading cultures attune readers to attend to different things. How are seminaries and

---

62. Rudolf Bultmann, "Is Exegesis without Presuppositions Possible?," in *Existence and Faith* (London: Hodder and Stoughton, 1961), 289–96.

63. Michael Gorman, *Elements of Biblical Exegesis: A Basic Guide for Students and Ministers*, 3rd ed. (Grand Rapids: Baker Academic, 2020), 4.

64. Gorman, 4. Matthew Malcolm views exegesis similarly, "as intentional, attentive, respectful interpretation of a particular written text." *From Hermeneutics to Exegesis: The Trajectory of Biblical Interpretation* (Nashville: B&H Academic, 2018), 6.

churches forming Bible readers to attend not only to grammar but to God? What, if anything, is distinctly theological about biblical interpretation?

To read the Bible "like every other text" is to do it an injustice, because in important respects, it is *not* like any other text, for God is involved in the production (writing) and reception (reading) of the Bible in a way that is qualitatively different from his involvement with other texts. While the reading of the Bible is in some respects similar to the reading of other books, overall it is marked by an even greater dissimilarity: "What makes the Bible *like* other books is the fact that it has authors; what makes the Bible *unlike* other books is that its primary author is God."[65]

Literate readers—those who achieve understanding—attend to what is said and make themselves answerable to it. God is spirit, and those who read his word must read in spirit and truth (cf. John 4:24). The kind of biblical literacy that builds up citizens of a holy nation ultimately attends to the *grammar* of the word *of God*. Moreover, doing justice to *of God* means attending to the letter in canonical as well as historical context.[66] This gives rise to a different kind of reading culture, one that values attending to the whole of Scripture as well as its individual parts. A Christian reading culture will therefore foster a habit that may at first glance strike some to be paradoxical: *close canonical reading*.[67]

Reading the Bible theologically requires more than close canonical reading, however. To read the Bible theologically is to be attentive not simply to its original historical context or even theological content, but also to the way in which the text effects a breaking in of God's word into the reader's own context, making the reader one of those "on whom the end of the ages has come" (1 Cor 10:11). The question that remains is how readers should respond to, and be formed by, what Webster called the "eschatological culture" brought into being by the living and active word of God that invades and interrupts our worldly places.[68] To read the Bible theologically is to inhabit a context into which God breaks in.

My purpose in this first chapter has been to call attention to the importance of reading cultures and to the fact that Christians belong to a peculiar, *eschatological* reading culture. We must therefore come to understand authors, texts, readers, and the process of reading itself in relation to God and the gospel of God. This is our proper theological context. It is therefore important not

---

65. Kevin J. Vanhoozer, *Is There a Meaning in This Text? The Bible, the Reader, and the Morality of Literary Knowledge* (Grand Rapids: Zondervan, 1998), 4.

66. As English grammar studies the parts of speech and rules implicit in rightly formed English sentences, a *canonical* grammar studies prophetic and apostolic speech, the rules implicit in their speech of God, as well as the rules for relating the subject matter of the Old Testament and New Testament.

67. I will say more about this in chapters 4–6.

68. Webster, *Culture of Theology*, 53.

to confuse the eschatological culture that all Christians share with particular ethnic, national, disciplinary, or denominational cultures. The goal is a *mere* Christian hermeneutic that accords with our eschatological Christian culture, a hermeneutic that will form readers to read canonically, in spirit and truth—readers who know they are answerable to God for their interpretations and their lives.

CHAPTER 2

Exegesis in a Toolshed

A Conflict of Reading Cultures

Oh, of course, there is another meaning, another interpretation of the word "father," which insists that my father, though a monster, though a villain to his children, is still my father simply because he begot me. But this meaning is, so to speak, a mystical one.

—Fyodor Dostoyevsky, *The Brothers Karamazov*

Chapter 1 called attention to some factors that are often kept behind the scenes of (and out of textbooks on) biblical interpretation: (1) that the final purpose of biblical interpretation is the formation of a Christian culture, the education and edification of a biblically literate community able to demonstrate its understanding by adopting a manner of life commensurate with their gospel citizenship; (2) that there are several ways of being biblical, different kinds of "reading cultures," each of which forms readers to attend to the letter of the text in different ways; and (3) that to think theologically about what it is to read the Bible as the living and active word of God brings into view the unique eschatological context of the reader, as well as the possibility of a distinct, eschatologically charged reading culture. The net result is a striking, and perhaps controversial, new spin on the *context of the reader*, which typically is thought to be a function of race/ethnicity, gender, class—a sociopolitical rather than theological matter.

This chapter sets out two more things every reader ought to know about biblical interpretation. First, that throughout church history, there has been a recurring tension between two kinds of reading cultures, a recurrence easy to overlook because the terms describing the tension vary. Second, that when this tension becomes too pronounced, the result is a pathological polarization in which each culture devalues or perhaps dismisses the contribution of the other. Such exclusion serves the cause neither of biblical literacy nor of Christ.

I here provide a sketch of this pathological development, with the intent of setting forth a more hopeful course. However, sometimes, to move forward, it helps to know how we arrived where we are, at our current impasse, hence the brief excursus below on the history of biblical interpretation. I will argue in subsequent chapters that the tension this chapter identifies can be restorative rather than debilitating. My hope is that currently divided reading cultures will beat their interpretive swords into plowshares and their methodological spears into pruning hooks, that discipline will no longer take up arms against discipline, nor train their students to continue turf wars. My hope, in brief, is that biblical scholars and theologians will embrace rather than exclude one another's approaches. Before they can do that, however, we have to take both parties to the toolshed.

C. S. Lewis: Taking Biblical Interpreters to the Toolshed

The toolshed in question is the one Lewis featured in his short but insightful four-page essay, "Meditation in a Toolshed."[1] Imagine entering a dark toolshed. There is a crack at the top that lets in a ray of light. When one looks *at* the sunbeam, all one can see are specks of dust floating in it. Lewis contrasted *looking at* the beam with *looking along* it, which happens when one steps into the light and sees, not specks of dust, but green leaves outside the toolshed and, beyond them, the sun itself. Lewis drew an important moral from this simple metaphor: "Looking along the beam, and looking at the beam are very different experiences."[2]

Once one grasps the distinction between looking *at/along*, said Lewis, one finds it everywhere. A young man in love sees his beloved, and suddenly everything is right with the world. A neuroscientist looking *at* the young man's love from the outside sees something else. The "grammar" of neuroscience frames the young man's love in terms of visual stimuli and biochemical reaction. Lewis observed, "You get one experience of a thing when you look along it and another when you look at it."[3] Interestingly, Lewis did not apply his little parable to reading, but we can. Some readers look *at* the text; others look *along* it.

1. In C. S. Lewis, *God in the Dock: Essays on Theology and Ethics* (Grand Rapids: Eerdmans, 1970), 212–15.

2. Lewis, "Meditation in a Toolshed," in *God in the Dock*, 212.

3. Lewis, "Meditation in a Toolshed," 213.

To look *at* the text is to maintain a critical distance. It means reading with a certain detachment. "Looking at" is a kind of close reading, but one that favors analysis. Those who adopt a critical or analytic posture stand outside the world of the text, looking in. Lewis thought this critical mindset to be one of the hallmarks of modernity, with its valuation of scientific objectivity. Looking *at* privileges an *external* frame of reference, the better to bring certain textual features into focus. Readers who look *at* the text from their critical vantage point often assume that their frame of reference is superior to "insider" views: "The people who look *at* things have had it all their own way; the people who look *along* things have simply been brow-beaten. It has even come to be taken for granted that the external account of a thing somehow refutes or 'debunks' the account given from inside."[4]

Lewis may not have been thinking about hermeneutics while meditating in his toolshed, yet his *at/along* distinction recalls Søren Kierkegaard's similar worry about reading Scripture in modernity.[5] The relevant text is *For Self-Examination*, a reflection on the requirements for being a true Christian, including what every Christian ought to know about reading the Bible as Scripture. Kierkegaard pondered the comparison in James 1:22–27 between a person who sees and remembers his image in a mirror and a person who hears and does God's word. According to Kierkegaard, James's parable "warns against the error of observing the mirror only instead of seeing oneself in the mirror."[6] To miss seeing yourself in the mirror of Scripture—learning the truth about your nature, identity, and fate—is to miss out on half of Christian wisdom, whose sum, according to Calvin, is "the knowledge of God and of ourselves."[7] Readers who look *at* the text only will not see themselves in it.

To be sure, looking *at* the mirror of Scripture can be informative. Yet, no matter how closely we examine the mirror itself—its shape, its surface, its size—the very purpose of the mirror is short-circuited unless and until we see faces. Lewis's and Kierkegaard's parables serve as prophetic warnings against prioritizing a certain kind of critical *looking at*. Kierkegaard viewed his own "unscientific" manner of reading the Bible as a corrective to the reading habits of modern biblical scholarship. No doubt both Lewis and Kierkegaard would

4. Lewis, "Meditation in a Toolshed," 213.

5. See further Timothy Houston Polk, *The Biblical Kierkegaard: Reading by the Rule of Faith* (Macon, GA: Mercer University Press, 1997); Hugh S. Pyper, *The Joy of Kierkegaard: Essays on Kierkegaard as a Biblical Reader* (New York: Routledge, 2014); Joel D. S. Rasmussen, "Kierkegaard the Reader of Scripture," in *T&T Clark Companion to the Theology of Kierkegaard*, ed. Aaron P. Edwards and David J. Gouwens (London: T&T Clark, 2020), 111–38.

6. Søren Kierkegaard, *For Self-Examination* and *Judge for Yourself!*, ed. and trans. Howard V. Hong and Edna H. Hong (Princeton, NJ: Princeton University Press, 1990), 25.

7. John Calvin, *Institutes of the Christian Religion*, ed. John T. McNeill, 2 vols. (Philadelphia: Westminster, 1960), I.1.1.

resonate with Paul Ricoeur's *cri de coeur*: "Beyond the desert of criticism, we wish to be called again."[8] This is a poignant expression from a leading twentieth-century hermeneutic philosopher of a desire to encounter something in the text beyond what can be critically examined, classified, or explained by critical theories. To modify Ricoeur's adage: "Beyond the desert of criticism, we wish to *look along*."

Man cannot live by looking *at* bread only. Ricoeur's desire to get beyond critical *looking at* is part and parcel of his longing for a "second naivete," a post-critical faith that does not renounce the critical moment—the suspicion that appearances may be deceiving rather than reflective of reality—but nevertheless moves beyond it. In a poignant passage, Ricoeur invoked the example of Moses, who before dying was able to get at least a glimpse of this promised land, a meaning that survives the "desert of criticism." Ricoeur believed that modern learning made the first naivete, a trust in the Bible's literal sense and historical narratives, impossible. His second naivete discovers meaning in the text read as a symbolic or metaphorical narrative rather than one that is literal and historical. I think Ricoeur was right in what he affirmed (the desire to be called again), but wrong in what he denied (the truth of the Bible's literal sense).[9] I believe the story of the Bible to be true not because I have looked *at* it (critically) and found its history to be reliable, but rather, because by looking *along* it, I am able to see everything else, myself included.[10]

As to the dilemma—to look *at* or *along*, to be critical or naive—story is for Lewis the partial solution.[11] It is thanks to the narrative imagination—a kind of thinking that puts together what analytic reason takes apart—that readers are able to *look along* the text and enter into its beam of light: its storied world. The imagination is a cognitive faculty that excels in making and discovering meaningful connections between things.[12] Thinking biblically invites and includes both a critical, analytic moment that excels at looking *at*, and an imaginative, synthetic moment that enables us to look *along*. Both kinds of thinking are ingredients in interpretive wisdom.

Lewis himself was an exemplary reader, more concerned to "receive" a literary work on its own terms than to foist upon it his own critical theory

8. Paul Ricoeur, *The Symbolism of Evil* (Boston: Beacon, 1969), 349.

9. See further my *Biblical Narrative in the Philosophy of Paul Ricoeur: An Essay in Hermeneutics and Theology* (Cambridge: Cambridge University Press, 1990).

10. From C. S. Lewis, "Is Theology Poetry?," in *Weight of Glory: And Other Addresses* (New York: HarperCollins, 2001), 116–40.

11. What I call the literary imagination or story, Lewis in his essay called *myth*.

12. For a fuller account of the imagination and its role in theology, see my "The Discarded Imagination: Metaphors by Which a Holy Nation Lives," in Kevin J. Vanhoozer, *Pictures at a Theological Exhibition: Scenes of the Church's Worship, Witness, and Wisdom* (Downers Grove, IL: IVP Academic, 2016), 17–46.

and practice.[13] This is precisely what it means to be *called* beyond the desert of criticism. The first plea the Bible, or any literary work, makes to the reader is respectful attention: "Look. Listen. Receive."[14] We "receive" a work when "we exert our senses and imagination and various other powers according to a pattern invented by the artist."[15] This "according to" is another way of saying "looking along," or *looking in the direction indicated by the author's text.* To understand what is written, readers must follow the way the author's words go. To receive a work is to enter into its way of seeing. The first commandment of biblical interpretation is therefore "Look along the textual beam of light."

It is important not to confuse the second naivete—the faithful imagination—with gullibility or *uncritical* thinking. The lesson of the toolshed is not that one way of looking is right and the other wrong: "One must look both *along* and *at* everything."[16] The Christian view of the world is set forth in Scripture as a unified story. And yet in the story the incarnation happens. The Word was made flesh at a particular time and place in history—*without ceasing to be myth,* that is, presented in story form; hence we cannot understand Jesus' incarnation apart from its setting in a much longer narrative (the Old Testament). To be truly Christian (or biblical), "we must both assent to the historical fact and also receive the myth (fact though it has become) with the same imaginative embrace which we accord to all myths."[17] What does this distinction between looking *at*/*along* have to do with reading cultures?

C. P. Snow: The Two Cultures

The reason why we can find examples of looking *at* and *along* "all day long," as Lewis observed, is that they have developed into two different cultures of reading. Take, for example, C. P. Snow's famous 1959 Rede Lecture, "The Two Cultures," which distinguishes between the arts and science, two different ways of thinking about and experiencing the world. Snow spoke from personal experience of each: "By training I was a scientist: by vocation I was a writer."[18] Although he had a foot in both camps, he felt as though he were moving among two groups, "comparable in intelligence, identical in race, not grossly different in social origin, earning about the same incomes, who had almost ceased to

13. For a sustained appeal to C. S. Lewis as an expert guide to reading the Bible, see John C. Collins, *Reading Genesis Well: Navigating History, Poetry, Science, and Truth in Genesis 1–11* (Grand Rapids: Zondervan, 2018), esp. 25–29 and 62–67.

14. C. S. Lewis, *An Experiment in Criticism* (Cambridge: Cambridge University Press, 1961), 19.

15. Lewis, *Experiment in Criticism*, 88.

16. Lewis, "Meditation in a Toolshed," 215.

17. Lewis, "Myth Became Fact," in *God in the Dock*, 67.

18. C. P. Snow, *The Two Cultures* (Cambridge: Cambridge University Press, 1993), 1. Snow studied infrared spectroscopy at Cambridge's Cavendish Laboratory but later became a novelist.

communicate at all, who in intellectual, moral, and psychological climate had so little in common that . . . one might have crossed an ocean."[19]

The concept of the "two cultures" was Snow's way of making sense of his mid-twentieth-century intellectual context: "This is a problem of the entire West. . . . I believe the intellectual life of the whole of western society is increasingly being split into two polar groups."[20] Snow called the first group "literary intellectuals" and the second "physical scientists."[21] Each had its own values, ways, jargon, and methodology. The problem was that the two groups were unable to communicate with one another. Even though Snow did not use the term, it is fair to describe these two groups as reading cultures. The sciences and the humanities read the world differently, according to different rules and conventions—different grammars.

Taken together, Lewis's two ways of looking and Snow's two cultures pose a crucial question: Is biblical interpretation an instance of looking *at* or *along*? Should biblical hermeneutics give rise to a reading culture more like the sciences or the arts (or neither)? Whereas premodern Bible readers were more concerned with becoming the right kind of person than they were about methodology, the seventeenth-century turn to empirical science and the eighteenth-century Enlightenment turn to rationality set new standards for responsible knowers.[22] By the nineteenth century, the *Oxford English Dictionary* was defining science as the use of physical and experimental processes for coming to know the material world. Every intellectual enterprise, including the study of the Bible, was now obligated to show that it employed critical methods that could yield genuine knowledge, if it wanted to be counted a science.

Biblical and theological scholars were not immune to these developments. Many nineteenth-century exegetes and theologians were keen to don the mantle of science, in part to give a certain prestige to their readings. Many modern biblical critics accepted the new science, turning their attention to historical, literary, and cultural analysis, procedures for looking *at*.[23] Not to be outdone, certain theologians claimed that they, too, employed a scientific method. The

19. Snow, 2.

20. Snow, 3.

21. More recently, Iain McGilchrist has argued that the two cultures are symptoms of a more fundamental duality, the divided brain, composed of left and right hemispheres, with very different ways of processing information and experiencing the world. See his *The Master and His Emissary: The Divided Brain and the Making of the Western World*, exp. ed. (New Haven, CT: Yale University Press, 2019). Thanks to Matt Wiley for calling my attention to this book, and the parallel with Snow's "two cultures."

22. See further Lawrence M. Principe, *Scientific Revolution: A Very Short Introduction* (Oxford: Oxford University Press, 2011); and John Robertson, *The Enlightenment: A Very Short Introduction* (Oxford: Oxford University Press, 2015).

23. For a survey of different forms of biblical criticism and of the impact of other disciplines on biblical scholarship, see *The Oxford Handbook of Biblical Studies*, ed. J. W. Rogerson and Judith M. Lieu (Oxford: Oxford University Press, 2008).

nineteenth-century Princeton theologian Charles Hodge maintained that the Bible "is to the theologian what nature is to the man of science. It is his storehouse of facts."[24] Modern exegetes and theologians could therefore claim, with some warrant, that their respective disciplines constituted a "science of the Bible." As the next chapter will show, the two disciplines have since gone their separate ways, similar to the divergence of Snow's two cultures, and with the same disheartening result: "Between the two a gulf of mutual incomprehension—sometimes . . . hostility and dislike, but most of all lack of understanding. They have a curious distorted image of each other."[25]

In retrospect, Snow's two cultures contrast, though of some pedagogical value, is ultimately too simplistic and outdated. To begin with, there are so many specialized subdisciplines in the academy today that we should perhaps speak of not two but of one hundred and two cultures. Still, a good case could be made that there is in modern universities a rough and ready distinction between two kinds of reading cultures: the humanities focus on reading books that treat the human condition (literature); the natural sciences read the physical world (the "book of nature"). If anything, however, the plurality of disciplines and approaches to reading merely exacerbates the problem: To what kind of reading culture should Christian readers belong?

Members of the theological disciplines do well to heed intellectual historian Stefan Collini's advice to academics: "The rigid divisions between disciplines, the lack of mutual comprehension, the misplaced feelings of superiority or disdain in various professional groups—these should be seen as *problems,* not fatalistically accepted as part of the immutable order of things."[26]

I agree. The rest of this chapter therefore aims to put contemporary disputes over how to interpret the Bible into a broader historical perspective. This is the first step in resolving the reading culture wars that have divided, and continue to divide, biblical interpreters—and the church, past and present.

Crosscurrents of Biblical Interpretation: A Brief History of a Recurring Tension

Thus far this chapter has established that there is a distinction between looking *at* texts and looking *along* them, and that these two ways of looking have some affinities with the two "cultures" of the sciences and humanities. The origins

24. Charles Hodge, *Systematic Theology* vol. 1 (Grand Rapids: Eerdmans, 1979), 10.

25. Snow, *Two Cultures,* 4. I will return to exegesis and theology as two contrasting reading cultures in chapter 3.

26. Snow, lx–lxi.

of this duality are far more ancient, however. Indeed, there is good reason to believe that these two reading cultures are as old as biblical interpretation itself.

Hermeneutics has to do with the what, how, and wherefore of textual interpretation: What kind of text are we reading? How is it to be read? Why are we reading? The *what* question is easily answered: biblical interpreters are reading the books of the Bible. Though there is some question as to the outer limits of the canon, there is a widespread consensus that the sixty-six books in the Protestant Bible make up the common core. Where Christian communities diverge is over how to read and the purpose(s) reading serves. The diverse reading cultures we are considering, then, differ chiefly over the *how* and *why* of reading, and over which question is most important. Prioritizing the *how* question generates a different kind of reading culture than does prioritizing the *why*. The former focuses on *process*, the latter on *purpose*. I have been at pains to bring this dynamic to light because, as with so many other aspects of culture, we are likely not to be aware of it until we meet those from another culture, or become travelers ourselves, from one place, or time, to another. It is worth calling out various reading cultures, for many people simply assume that their way of reading the Bible is normal, if not normative.

Let me suggest, provisionally, that there is a family resemblance between looking *at*, the sciences, and the *how* question, on the one hand, and looking *along*, the humanities, and the *why* question on the other. My aim is to provide an account of what it means to read the Bible theologically that does justice to both questions. In the previous chapter, I suggested that premodern readers like Augustine, Hugh of St. Victor, and Calvin shared this aim. Before we can rush to formulate a "mere hermeneutic" (an approach to reading Scripture on which all Christians should agree), however, we have to identify and deal with the conflicts that have characterized the history of biblical interpretation. These conflicts pertain not simply to different readings of the same biblical text, but to different ways of reading biblical texts. It is the practices associated with these disparate ways that have given rise to reading cultures that, despite their common interest in the same sacred page (the *what*), are not on the same page as concerns the process (the *how*) and purpose (the *why*). Again, nothing is more effective at disabusing people of the notion that their way of reading the Bible is normal or normative (or that they have no reading culture) than making them familiar with the history of biblical interpretation.

This is not the place to mount an exhaustive survey, nor am I the person to do it. Many excellent reference books are available for that purpose.[27] My purpose is

27. I recommend in particular Keith D. Stanglin, *The Letter and Spirit of Biblical Interpretation: From the Early Church to Modern Practice* (Grand Rapids: Baker Academic, 2018). See also *A History of Biblical Interpretation*, vol. 1, *The Ancient Period*, ed. Alan J. Hauser and Duane F. Watson (Grand Rapids:

more modest and focused: to trace a recurring tension between two cross-cultural reading currents—what the New Testament describes as the contrast between "letter" and "spirit"—through the major periods of premodern church history (viz., patristic, medieval, Reformation).[28] As the next chapter will show, this tension eventually reached a breaking point when, in modernity, biblical studies and systematic theology part company and go their separate disciplinary ways.

Antioch and Alexandria

In surveying the history of biblical interpretation, it is important not to lump all approaches in the early church under the same "premodern" rubric. Whether one describes them as "schools," "trajectories," or "traditions," Antioch and Alexandria have come to represent contrasting reading cultures within early Christianity.[29] Bernard Ramm divided his own survey of the historical schools of interpretation into "allegorical" and "literal," and this is where we find Alexandria and Antioch respectively.[30] Yet it is also important not to reduce everything in early Christian biblical interpretation to a tale of two cities. Each was interested in doing justice to both the literal and the spiritual senses of Scripture, the difference being one of emphasis, with Antioch putting more emphasis on the "letter," and Alexandria stressing the "spirit" of the letter.[31] John Cavadini's generalization is helpful: "For the fathers, the literal sense of Scripture was *ordered towards* the spiritual sense(s)."[32] Be that as it may, the

---

Eerdmans, 2003); Karlfried Froelich, *Biblical Interpretation in the Early Church* (Philadelphia: Fortress, 1984); Christopher A. Hall, *Reading Scripture with the Church Fathers* (Downers Grove, IL: InterVarsity, 1988); Brandon D. Smith, *Taught by God: Ancient Hermeneutics for the Modern Church* (Brentwood, TN: B&H Academic, 2024); John L. Thompson, *Reading the Bible with the Dead: What You Can Learn from the History of Exegesis that You Can't Learn from Exegesis Alone* (Grand Rapids: Eerdmans, 2007); *Dictionary of Major Biblical Interpreters*, ed. Donald K. McKim (Downers Grove, IL: IVP Academic, 2007); *The Oxford Handbook of Early Christian Biblical Interpretation*, ed. Paul M. Blowers and Peter W. Martens (Oxford: Oxford University Press, 2019); and *Biblical Interpretation in the Era of the Reformation: Essays Presented to David C. Steinmetz in Honor of His Sixtieth Birthday*, ed. Richard A. Muller and John L. Thompson (Grand Rapids: Eerdmans, 1996).

28. By "premodern" (or "precritical"), I am referring to the period before the late seventeenth-century European Enlightenment, a complex intellectual and social movement characterized by the premium it put on autonomous reason, unchained from tradition and religious authority, and critical thinking. It is important at the outset not to make this contrast too neat or too simplistic. Many interpreters sought to do justice to both aspects. For an examination of how Paul's statement, "The letter kills, but the Spirit gives life" (2 Cor 3:6), has been interpreted down through the centuries, see *The Spirit and the Letter: A Tradition and a Reversal*, ed. Paul S. Fiddes with Günter Bader (London: Bloomsbury T&T Clark, 2013).

29. Peter W. Martens describes Antioch and Alexandria as two "exegetical cultures" in *Adrian's "Introduction to the Divine Scriptures": An Antiochene Handbook for Scriptural Interpretation* (Oxford: Oxford University Press, 2017), 15–16.

30. Bernard Ramm, *Protestant Biblical Interpretation*, 3rd ed. (Grand Rapids: Baker, 1970), 24–50.

31. See further, Brian E. Daley, *God Visible: Patristic Christology Reconsidered* (Oxford: Oxford University Press, 2020).

32. John C. Cavadini, "From Letter to Spirit: The Multiple Senses of Scripture," in *The Oxford Handbook of Early Christian Biblical Interpretation*, ed. Paul M. Blowers and Peter W. Martens (Oxford: Oxford University Press, 2019), 127.

respective emphases associated with Antioch and Alexandria respectively lie at the headwaters of what eventually become opposing reading cultures.

The Origen of Allegorical Interpretation

If we can still speak of a "school" of Alexandria, Origen may well lay claim to being its principal. Modern biblical scholars are often more inclined to identify him as an abusive church father because of his "crimes against textuality" (i.e., allegorical flights of fancy). What is incontrovertible is his influence in early Christianity. He wrote what were arguably the first comprehensive treatments of text criticism, hermeneutics, and theology.[33] Frances Young describes Origen as "the first scholarly exegete of Scripture,"[34] adding, "he created Christian scholarship."[35] Origen's work therefore makes an apt opening case study for our experiment in biblical-theological criticism.[36]

Origen's "school" was a center for Christian learning that served catechumens (new Christians preparing to be baptized) and students preparing to become teachers. There was only one primary textbook, Scripture, and Origen studied it with the same tools and principles used with the Greco-Roman classics of antiquity. Many of these "grammatical" techniques—establishing a reliable text, clarifying difficult terms, determining allusions to other texts—are standard issue even today. Less familiar is the Neoplatonic interpretive framework for reading the Bible that Origen inherited from Philo of Alexandria.[37] The one word that best describes Origen's reading, as controversial as it is biblical (Paul uses it in Gal 4:24), is *allegorical*. We must therefore take care in defining it.

The etymology is Greek: *allos* ("other") and *agoreuein* ("to speak in public"; cf. *agora*). To allegorize is to speak of one thing (a hidden or symbolic meaning) in terms of another (the surface meaning). Strictly speaking, an allegory means something *other* than what a person *says*. This disconnect or "otherness" is typical of allegorical writing and interpretation. John Bunyan's *Pilgrim's Progress* is an allegory of the Christian life. On one level (the earthly), it is the story of

33. Origen's *Hexapla* apparently put six different versions of the Old Testament text side by side for critical comparison. Most of his extant works are homilies, parts of commentaries, and the entirety of his masterpiece *On First Principles* (in Latin translation).

34. Frances Young, "Divine Discourse: Scripture in the Economy of Revelation," in *The Oxford Handbook of Early Christian Biblical Interpretation*, ed. Paul M. Blowers and Peter W. Martens (Oxford: Oxford University Press, 2019), 80.

35. Frances Young, "The Interpretation of Scripture," in *The First Theologians: An Introduction to Theology in the Early Church*, ed. G. R. Evans (Oxford: Blackwell, 2004), 27.

36. Origen's work is, as we shall see, a hermeneutical lightning rod for modern biblical exegetes, and the church has rejected certain of his doctrinal teachings, such as his notion of the preexistence of souls. It would be a mistake, however, to disregard too quickly everything he has to say about exegesis, for no interpretive approach is foolproof.

37. See further Joseph Wilson Trigg, *Origen: The Bible and Philosophy in the Third-Century Church* (Atlanta: John Knox, 1983), esp. ch. 3, "Platonism."

an individual's journey from one place to another, but on the *other* level (the spiritual), it is a story about the Christian life. In similar fashion, "allegorical interpretation (*allegoresis*) is understood as explaining a work . . . as if there were another sense to which it referred."[38]

Allegorical interpretation predates Christian theology, for it was a part and parcel of Hellenistic literacy, and hence of "general" hermeneutics.[39] It was commonplace to read Homer's stories of the gods to find a meaning deeper than the surface letter, especially when that surface meaning appeared to be either untrue or unedifying. Read allegorically, however, as having symbolic meaning on another level, these stories were repositories of philosophical truths. Origen was aware both of this Hellenistic reading practice and of the fact that Philo had appropriated it for the purpose of making the Jewish Scriptures more compelling to educated Greek readers. The key (Platonic) insight: as the visible realm of earthly things is but a shadow of the invisible realm of essential things, so the letter of the text has a corresponding hidden truth.

Origen baptized allegorical reading practices, claiming Pauline precedent. Paul uses the term *allegoreo* and interprets the story of Hagar and Sarah allegorically as representing the slavery and freedom that characterize the old and new covenants respectively (Gal 4:22–31): "The habit of reading the Old Testament on this principle [allegorically] was, for Origen, one of the distinguishing marks of the Christian way of reading Scripture as opposed to that of the Jews."[40] The Jews, said Origen, could not get beyond the "letter" that kills to the "spirit" that gives life (2 Cor 3:6). However, the apostles never set down rules for allegorical interpretation, explaining *how* to get from letter to spirit (the "other" meaning). This was the lacuna that Origen sought to rectify in book 4, chapter 2, of *On First Principles*.

Origen stated that the Bible has three sorts of meaning, corresponding to the threefold division of body, soul, and spirit (1 Thess 5:23).[41] Consider, for example, how Origen allegorized the instructions in Exodus 12:9 concerning the Passover lamb: "Do not eat any of it raw or boiled in water, but roasted." Christ is the true Passover lamb, slain before the foundation of the earth (Rev

---

38. Rita Copeland and Peter T. Struck, "Introduction," in *The Cambridge Companion to Allegory* (Cambridge: Cambridge University Press, 2010), 2.

39. General hermeneutics pertains to principles of textual interpretation that may be applied to any and every text; special hermeneutics pertains to the unique challenges of interpreting particular kinds of texts (e.g., legal, religious). A perennial question for biblical interpreters is whether reading the Bible requires special in addition to general hermeneutics.

40. G. R. Evans, *The Language and Logic of the Bible: The Earlier Middle Ages* (Cambridge: Cambridge University Press, 1984), 115.

41. Origen, *On First Principles* 4.2.4, trans. G. W. Butterworth (Notre Dame, IN: Ave Maria, 2013). Origen also appealed to the Septuagint (mis)translation of Proverbs 22:20–21, which speaks of portraying the meaning of Scripture "in a threefold way" (4.2.4).

13:8). Christ is also the Logos, hence, "What is the flesh of the divine words if not the divine Scriptures?"[42] To read literally is to eat the text raw; to read morally is to boil it in water. Neither reading eats the Paschal text as it ought to be eaten, namely, cooked in fire (i.e., read spiritually).[43] Some scholars think Origen distinguished three tiers of readers (beginners, experienced, experts). It is more likely that he was thinking about the same readers progressing from one level of meaning to the other.[44] Origen largely abandoned the tripartite division in his actual reading and concentrated on the twofold distinction between literal and spiritual interpretation: "In practice, there are two levels of meaning."[45] The first pertains to history; the latter to the mystery of salvation. In Origen's words, "These mysteries which were made known and revealed to them by the Spirit, the prophets portrayed figuratively through the narration of what seemed to be human deeds and the handing down of certain legal ordinances and precepts."[46]

The aim of spiritual interpretation is to read for the spiritual sense, which Origen identified as the intention of the Holy Spirit, the ultimate author of Scripture. Origen believed the Holy Spirit inserted certain "stumbling blocks" into the literal sense to force readers "to a higher and loftier road."[47] In his commentary on Psalm 1, Origen compared the letter of the text to a "locked door" that only "the key of David" (i.e., fulfilled prophecy) can open.[48] The spiritual sense is thus the pearl of great price hidden in the shell of the letter, "a kind of outer covering and veil for spiritual meanings."[49] To plumb the letter's depths, one must have the Spirit of Christ, for "the Spirit searches all things, even the deep things of God" (1 Cor 2:10 NIV).

Origen held letter and spirit together by means of an incarnational analogy. Whereas Plato's Forms remain in heaven, the Son of God took human form. Jesus came in the flesh, but hidden in that flesh was his divinity, the spiritual sense as it were: "The Incarnation . . . provides for Origen the guarantee of

---

42. Origen, *Treatise on the Passover and Dialogue with Heraclides and His Fellow Bishops on the Father, the Son and the Soul*, trans. Robert J. Daly (Mahwah, NJ: Paulist, 1992), 26.5.

43. See the discussion in Daniel Boyarin, "Origen as Theorist of Allegory: Alexandrian Contexts," in *The Cambridge Companion to Allegory*, ed. Rita Copeland and Peter T. Struck (Cambridge: Cambridge University Press, 2010), 52–53. We shall return to Origen's understanding of the literal sense in the next chapter.

44. See Karen J. Torjesen, *Hermeneutical Procedure and Theological Method in Origen's Exegesis* (Berlin: de Gruyter, 1985).

45. Young, "Interpretation of Scripture," 855.

46. Origen, *On First Principles* 4.2.7.

47. Origen, *On First Principles* 4.2.9.

48. Origen, *Philocalia*, frag. 2.1.1–10. Cited in Brian E. Daley, "Finding the Right Key: The Aims and Strategies of Early Christian Interpretation of the Psalms," in *The Harp of Prophecy: Early Christian Interpretation of the Psalms*, ed. Brian E. Daley and Paul R. Kolbet (Notre Dame, IN: University of Notre Dame Press, 2015), 14–15.

49. Origen, *On First Principles* 4.2.8.

Christian allegorical access to truth."[50] Jesus himself refers to the "sign of the prophet Jonah" (Matt 12:39)—his coming out of the belly of the whale after three days—which Origen interpreted as indicating Jesus' resurrection. The spiritual sense of the story of Jonah thus *means* something *other* than Jonah's personal history: "The truth of the events recorded to have happened . . . cannot be fully seen in the mere text and historical narrative; for each event . . . is clearly a symbol of something as well."[51] The patristic scholar Jean Daniélou noted that, for Origen, "The Bible is one vast allegory, a tremendous sacrament in which every detail is symbolic."[52]

Such claims can trigger in biblical scholars an acute allegoriphobia, to coin a term: the fear that allegorical interpretation foists meanings onto texts, that it *invents* rather than *discovers*, and that the *other* meaning is only loosely or perhaps arbitrarily tethered to the letter of the text. Iain Provan is one such biblical scholar who stands aghast at Origen's handling of the Old Testament. In his magisterial work *The Reformation and the Right Reading of Scripture*, Provan distinguishes between four kinds of hermeneutics before setting out a fifth way of his own. Origen is the ancestor of the fourth way, whose signature move is a retrieval of the "Platonist-Christian synthesis" of the early church.[53] Provan raises two principal objections to this way of reading: (1) It demeans the letter of the text, and the human author's communicative intent: "To a very great extent, for Origen the literal sense of Scripture is not of great value," to the point where he might as well speak of the *insufficiency* of Scripture's literal sense.[54] (2) It downplays communicative intent and canonical context in favor of "philosophical and ethical ideas that derive from elsewhere," specifically, a version of Platonism circulating in the environing culture.[55]

As Provan makes clear, the challenge for those who adopt Origen's way of reading is how to keep allegory from running amok, becoming "unbridled allegory."[56] Consider, for example, Pope Innocent III's claim that the true meaning of the "greater" and "lesser" lights God made on the first day (Gen 1:14–19) were, respectively, not the sun and the moon but, rather, the pope and the king. It is hard not to see such allegorical readings as a reflex of the interpretive will

50. Boyarin, "Origen as theorist of allegory," 51.

51. Origen, *Contra Celsum* 2.69, rev. ed., trans. Henry Chadwick (Cambridge: Cambridge University Press, 1980), 118.

52. Jean Daniélou, *Origen* (London: Sheed and Ward, 1955), 184.

53. Provan dubs this fourth way "Counter-Reformational Protestantism," a clever way of referring to certain Protestants (Provan has in mind Hans Boersma, among others) who appear to be on the verge of selling their Reformation birthright (e.g., *sola scriptura*; literal interpretation) for a mess of medieval pottage.

54. Iain Provan, *The Reformation and the Right Reading of Scripture* (Waco, TX: Baylor University Press, 2017), 176.

55. Provan, 178.

56. Stanglin, *Letter and Spirit of Biblical Interpretation*, 194.

to power, that is, reading the Bible in ways that promote one's self-interest. As Bernard Ramm observed, "The Bible treated allegorically becomes putty in the hand of the exegete."[57] And *silly* putty at that, given the apparently fanciful interpretive flights to which allegorists are sometimes prone.

In stark contrast to biblical scholar Provan, theologian Hans Boersma praises Origen, "the brilliant third-century biblical interpreter," for taking his metaphysical cue from Plato and Paul, insisting "that the invisible things of God are understood by means of things that are visible."[58] Origen's notion that we ascend from earthly shadows to heavenly realities assumes not an unbiblical Platonic dualism, says Boersma, but a "soft" Platonism that acknowledges the real participation of created things in the reality of God. Origen knew what Boersma would like contemporary biblical scholars to know: *"that the Bible cannot be interpreted without prior metaphysical commitments and that we need Christian Platonism as an interpretive lens in order to uphold Scripture's teaching."*[59]

We have not heard the last of Origen. He figures prominently in subsequent chapters, both as a philologist and as one concerned with the formation of ideal interpreters. But he has already helped us identify two issues with which all approaches to reading the Bible theologically must eventually deal: (1) the nature and function of the letter of the text and (2) the necessity of going beyond letter to Spirit in nonarbitrary fashion.

The Antiochene Alternative

Another reading culture, with different emphases, developed among a group of Christians in a place distant from Alexandria, both geographically and intellectually. Origen's willingness to identify the meaning of biblical texts with something other than its literal sense alarmed a group of fourth- and fifth-century Syrian theologians in the city of Antioch. The "school" of Antioch took a more conservative approach to biblical interpretation: "Fundamentally the Antiochenes approached texts philologically, reacting against the identification of allegory where there was nothing in the text to suggest that that was intended."[60]

Diodore of Tarsus stressed the importance of understanding the historical context and the plain word-for-word meaning of the text, declaring, "We

---

57. Ramm, *Protestant Biblical Interpretation*, 30.

58. Origen, *Commentary on the Canticle of Canticles*, 3.12. Cited in Hans Boersma, *Scripture as Real Presence: Sacramental Exegesis in the Early Church* (Grand Rapids: Baker Academic, 2017), 5. For a similar approach, see Craig Carter, *Interpreting Scripture with the Great Tradition: Recovering the Genius of Premodern Exegesis* (Grand Rapids: Baker Academic, 2018).

59. Hans Boersma, *Five Things Theologians Wish Biblical Scholars Knew* (Downers Grove, IL: IVP Academic, 2021), 40 (emphasis original).

60. Young, "Interpretation of Scripture," 853.

far prefer *to historikon* [history, factuality] to *allegorikon* [allegory]."[61] John Chrysostom was typically Antiochene in his sober, restrained, grammatical, "matter-of-fact exposition of the text."[62] Diodore understood allegorical interpretation to imply a complete divorce from the historical sense, however, and recent scholars fault him for reading Origen uncharitably. Be that as it may, the Antiochenes voiced a legitimate concern about the locus of Scripture's truth, and the extent to which it must be found on the ground, as it were, rooted in the text and historical events, rather than somewhere else (i.e., allegorically).

Three concepts figure prominently in the Antiochene approach: *historia*, *theoria*, and typology. Each is shorthand for the particular way Antiochenes sought to distinguish their approach from allegorizing while preserving the relationship between letter and spirit. The Antiochenes saw Origen's allegorical readings as undermining biblical *historia*, the plain meaning of the historical narrative: "Antioch cannot tolerate arbitrary interpretation of prophetic and other texts that have been disconnected from their historical roots. The text should be a window, not a warped mirror."[63] One of the sharpest Antiochene diatribes against the allegorists is found, interestingly enough, in Theodore of Mopsuestia's comment on Paul's reading in Galatians 4 of the story of Hagar and Sarah (Gen 16–21).[64] Theodore began by alluding to "people" who overturn the meaning of Scripture: "By breaking up everything placed there they fabricate from themselves certain foolish fictions and give their folly the name of allegory." He conceded that Paul uses the term *allegoreo*, but insisted that Paul means something different than Origen: "For the apostle does not do away with the narrative, nor does he get rid of what happened long ago."[65] Both parts of Theodore's reasoning deserve our attention.

First, Paul "does not get rid of what happened long ago." Theodore insisted on the historical basis of the story of Sarah and Hagar (although he may have exaggerated the extent to which Origen denied it): "For they say that not even Adam actually existed as Adam, since it strikes them they should interpret scripture as much as possible 'spiritually'—they want their folly to be called spiritual interpretation. So they say that paradise did not exist as paradise nor

61. From his *Quaestiones* on the Octateuch. Cited in R. C. Hill, "Diodore of Tarsus," in *Dictionary of Major Biblical Interpreters*, ed. Donald K. McKim (Downers Grove, IL: IVP Academic, 2007), 375.

62. Jaroslav Pelikan, *The Preaching of Chrysostom: Homilies on the Sermon on the Mount* (Philadelphia: Fortress, 1967), 19.

63. Robert C. Hill, *Reading the Old Testament in Antioch* (Atlanta: Society of Biblical Literature, 2005), 144.

64. See also the summary of John Chrysostom's reading of Galatians 4 in Smith, *Taught by God*, 48–53.

65. Theodore of Mopsuestia, *Commentary on the Minor Pauline Epistles*, trans. Rowan A. Greer (Atlanta: Society of Biblical Literature, 2010), 113.

the serpent as the serpent. I should like to say to them that by breaking up the *historiam* they no longer have a *historiam*."[66]

Theodore is not, of course, a modern historical critic: the primary emphasis of *historia* is less on what can be empirically shown to be the case, on the basis of evidence, than it is on the subject matter that the narrative is about.

Second, Paul "does not do away with the narrative." At least this is how the translator, Rowan Greer, rendered *historiam*: narrative. Greer cautioned against reading modern ideas of "historical" or "literal" into our understanding of patristic exegesis. Translating *historia* as narrative or story puts a different spin on the Antiochene objection to allegorical interpretation. It is not simply that the allegorists deny factuality. Rather, in Greer's words, "Their mistake is to break up the narrative and to interpret its component parts without reference to the narrative as a whole."[67] The Antiochenes insisting that the *historia* or narrative was "true" does not quite mean what a modern historian means.[68]

This brings us to the second technical term that characterizes Antiochene reading culture, *theoria* (from the Greek verb *theoreo* = "to behold or contemplate"). *Theoria* describes the Antiochene way of engaging in spiritual interpretation. It is hard to pinpoint exactly what *theoria* is or involves. The key claim is that *theoria* is not a flight *from* the literal sense but a deeper insight *into* it. Theodoret assured his readers that he and his fellow Antiochenes did not "rely on the letter that killeth; instead, by getting within it, we search for the Spirit's meaning, and enlightened by him we take spiritually the Spirit's sayings."[69] Consider how Diodore deployed the term to describe what Paul is doing in Galatians 4:

> We shall treat of [the text] historically and literally and not stand in the way of a spiritual and more elevated insight [*theoria*]. The historical sense, in fact, is not in opposition to the more elevated sense [*theoria*]; on the contrary, it proves to be the basis and foundation of the more elevated meanings. One thing alone is to be guarded against, however, never to let the discernment process [*theoria*] be seen as an overthrow of the underlying sense, since this would no longer be discernment [*theoria*] but allegory: what is arrived at in defiance of the content is not discernment [*theoria*] but allegory. The apostle

66. Theodore of Mopsuestia, 115.
67. Theodore of Mopsuestia, xiv.
68. So James L. Kugel and Rowan A. Greer: "The *historia* was the obvious narrative meaning of the text and must not be confused with the modern use of 'history' as a way of talking about the reconstruction of what really happened by using the texts as historical evidence." *Early Biblical Interpretation* (Philadelphia: Westminster, 1986), 195.
69. Theodoret, *Praef.* in *Patrologia graeca* 81.37. Cited in Hill, *Reading the Old Testament in Antioch*, 152.

> [Paul] . . . never overturned the historical sense by introducing discernment despite calling discernment [*theoria*] allegory.[70]

Theoria attempts to hold together the underlying literal sense and the more elevated spiritual sense. But how? There is no scholarly consensus.[71] One of the disputed issues is whether the prophets intended their words to have a second, christological referent, or whether this reference to Christ, and *theoria* itself, is a hermeneutical maneuver of the reader, perhaps the result of the Spirit's illumination. According to Richard Perhai, *theoria* most closely resembles typological interpretation: "Typologizing does not deny that the original events occurred. It does not demand that the type be (fully) realized initially in the Scripture, though it lies there latently as a 'prefigure.'"[72] On this view, then, the spiritual sense does not float above but inheres in and adheres to the literal sense or *historia* (the narrative sequence of events). Scholars at least agree that the Antiochenes offer a corrective to allegorical exegesis "by establishing the biblical author's original intent within the historical circumstances of his day while also seeking, where relevant, the fuller soteriological relevance (*theoria*) of each text by relating it to the whole of salvation history with Christ as its origin and goal."[73]

Reconsidering the Distinction

To this point, we have been assuming that Antioch and Alexandria represent opposing reading cultures, a typological versus an allegorical approach to biblical interpretation.[74] But do they? The Antiochenes were just as concerned to interpret spiritually, like the Alexandrians, as they were to avoid allegorizing, unlike the Alexandrians. This makes the attempt to distinguish the two reading cultures more challenging.

Church fathers in Antioch and Alexandria began with the plain or literal sense: "the way the words run." Moreover, both reading cultures tried to relate

---

70. Diodore of Tarsus, *Commentary on Psalms 1–51*, trans. Robert C. Hill (Atlanta: Society of Biblical Literature, 2005), 4.

71. Bradley Nassif surveys scholarship on Antiochene exegesis from 1880 to 1993 in "The 'Spiritual Exegesis' of Scripture: The School of Antioch Revisited," *Anglican Theological Review* 75, no. 4 (1993): 437–70. Richard J. Perhai reviews scholarship on Antiochene *theoria* since 1991 in *Antiochene Theoria in the Writings of Theodore of Mopsuestia and Theodoret of Cyrus* (Minneapolis: Fortress, 2015), 113–204.

72. Perhai, *Antiochene Theoria*, 71. Bradley Nassif agrees that *theoria* often resembles typology but at other times bears a greater resemblance to a literal method of messianic exegesis.

73. Bradley Nassif, "Antiochene *Theoria* in John Chrysostom's Exegesis," in *Exegesis and Hermeneutics in the Churches of the East*, ed. Vahan S. Hovhanessian (New York: Peter Lang, 2009), 54.

74. We will return to the question of typology in chapter 4, where we will examine it in greater depth. For the moment it is salutary to recall Andrew Louth's comment that the typology/allegory distinction is better characterized by Henri de Lubac's distinction between *allegori facti* (an association of events) and *allegori verbi* (a purely verbal association). See Andrew Louth, *Discerning the Mystery: An Essay on the Nature of Theology* (Oxford: Clarendon, 1983), 119.

the literal and spiritual aspects of the biblical text. This is where we begin to see a divergence: each took "the way the words ran" and then ran further with it—albeit in different directions. Lewis Ayres, a leading patristic scholar, distinguishes these two ways of reading as the "grammatical" and "figural."[75] The key insight, however, is this: both Antiochene *theoria* and Alexandrian *allegoria* count as "figural" strategies. Therefore, instead of hastily dismissing certain spiritual interpretations as "allegorical," Ayres prefers to speak in terms of "figural and bad figural exegesis."[76] This is a helpful terminological proposal. It invites us to think harder about what the difference between good and bad figural exegesis is, rather than simply dismissing interpretations we do not like by labeling them allegorical.

In addition to respecting the letter and practicing figural interpretation, Antiochenes and Alexandrians each read the Bible to foster Christian culture. These three commonalities lead one historian of exegesis to conclude that "the Antiochene school of interpretation has more in common with Origen than it does with modern, historical-critical exegesis."[77] While examples of Origen seemingly disparaging the letter can be found, his deepest intent was to honor it: "Origen argues that allegorical readers should look for the spiritual (which is to say the *real*) import *of* the letter, rather than a meaning *in place of* the letter."[78] As to his alleged use of Neoplatonism to discover higher truths, some scholars see Christology playing that role, not philosophy: "Origen's allegorical interpretation of the OT simply is christological interpretation."[79]

For the above reasons, recent scholars caution against drawing too sharp a distinction between the two reading cultures. Everyone still agrees that the Antiochenes denounced Origen's allegorical interpretations of Scripture. As to the exact nature and degree of the disagreement, and the Antiochene alternative, however, scholarly opinion varies. The extreme positions—that there is basically no difference between the two; that Antiochenes are precursors of grammatical-historical exegesis as we know it today—are best avoided.

Is the contrast between *theoria* and *allegoria* a distinction without a difference? Frances Young makes a compelling case that the typical Alexandria/Antioch contrast is too rigid and simplistic. For Young, the real distinction pertains to how we perceive the relation between what the text says ("letter") and what the text is about ("spirit"). Accordingly, the real question is this:

75. Lewis Ayres, *Nicaea and Its Legacy: An Approach to Fourth-Century Trinitarian Theology* (Oxford: Oxford University Press, 2004), 34.

76. Ayres, 38.

77. Stanglin, *Letter and Spirit of Biblical Interpretation*, 68.

78. David Dawson, *Christian Figural Reading and the Fashioning of Identity* (Berkeley: University of California Press, 2001), 54.

79. Stanglin, *Letter and Spirit of Biblical Interpretation*, 63.

How do these two ancient reading cultures differ in forming readers to move from letter to spirit? Alexandrians view words as symbols referring to higher truths—but one needs to have the key to the code: "For Origen the Platonist, both the created order and the text of Scripture were symbolic of the eternal world of spiritual realities. Symbols and types he understood in terms of something standing for something else, so that the words of Scripture became a kind of code to be cracked by allegorical reading."[80] On this view, the way the words run to their higher spiritual meaning is a function not of the words themselves but of a symbolic code external to the biblical text.

By way of contrast, Antiochene readers follow the way the words go by attending to the text itself, taken as a coherent narrative whole. There is a spiritual meaning, but it reflects the deeper meaning of the text itself and not something outside it: "The 'ikon' will resemble the person or event which it represents, but symbols are not representations in that sense; symbols are 'tokens' or 'signs' whose analogous relationship with what is symbolized is less clear."[81] If we merge Young's categories with Ayres's, we can describe the two reading cultures in these terms: symbolic-figural (Alexandria) versus ikonic-figural (Antioch). Only the former, symbolic-figural, is true allegory, because the text refers to something *other* than what it says: "The objection to Alexandrian allegory is that it treats texts as a collection of arbitrary tokens, not as 'mirroring' in its narrative coherence the truths which may be discerned within it."[82] This is indeed a real difference, but it is not as simplistic as "letter versus spirit," nor does "typology versus allegory" expose what lies at its root.

Young's crucial insight is that "the key interpretative question concerns the proper *identification* of that referent."[83] The idea of a frame of reference—the interpretive assumptions that enable readers to identify *what authors are speaking about*—will loom large in later chapters. For now, it suffices to point out that premodern interpreters employed frames of reference that differed from one another in some respects, yet in other respects overlapped with one another in important ways, distinguishing them from modern frames of reference. Stated differently: unlike modern readers, all the church fathers read spiritually, but not in the same way. A mere Christian hermeneutic eventually has to justify the move from (literal) sense to (spiritual) referent: "The differences lie in the kind of reference found convincing, and the range of cross-reference permitted."[84]

80. Young, "Alexandrian and Antiochene Exegesis," in Hauser and Watson, *A History of Biblical Interpretation*, 351.

81. Frances Young, *Biblical Exegesis and the Formation of Christian Culture* (Cambridge: Cambridge University Press, 1997), 210.

82. Young, *Biblical Exegesis and the Formation of Christian Culture*, 175.

83. David Dawson, *Christian Figural Reading and the Fashioning of Identity* (Berkeley, CA: University of California Press, 2002), 5.

84. Young, *Biblical Exegesis and the Formation of Christian Culture*, 136.

The Antiochenes insisted that any spiritual interpretation had to be warranted by the narrative itself. This, then, was the force and function of Antiochene *theoria*: it was a spiritual discernment into the patterns and types that make up the unified biblical narrative.[85]

I have been using Antioch and Alexandria figuratively to represent two ways of moving from letter to spirit, from what the text says to what it is about. What differentiates the two reading cultures is the way each "frames" the text in order to determine its referent. Like *reading culture*, the notion of a *frame of reference* may be new to many readers, including students of hermeneutics. Both are essential to my argument and to mere Christian hermeneutics. To read with a frame of reference is to examine the text from a particular angle, put a certain set of questions to it, and filter the readers' perceptions of what the text is about. To cite Walter Moberly, an Old Testament scholar who makes frequent use of the idea, "The questions one asks and the answers that appear plausible are inseparable from the wider frame of reference and assumptions within which one works."[86] I propose that we accept Young's distinction and define allegorical interpretation as that which uses some code *other than* (*allos*) the biblical text itself as the frame of reference by which to move from the letter to what the text is "really" about, the "spiritual" meaning. In symbolic-figural interpretation, then, something other than the textual narrative serves as the frame of reference—as what we look through to discern what the text is speaking about (i.e., its referent).

Antioch and Alexandria represent not a facile contrast between letter and spirit, but different reading cultures, each with its own distinct frame of reference. Culture remains the operative term because it involves a set of beliefs, values, and practices, particularly about frames of reference (i.e., ways of seeing the world). As we will see throughout the present work, we can distinguish one reading culture from another in large part by identifying the frame(s) of reference to which they give priority. The most important frame of reference for the Antiochenes, for example, is the *historia*, or narrative of the text itself, considered as a unified whole.

The next stop at this point is Augustine, the key bridge figure linking the patristic and medieval ages. His hermeneutical handbook, *De Doctrina Christiana*, combines the best of Antioch and Alexandria and sums up what he wanted Christian leaders to know about reading and teaching the Bible to the

85. The transfigural approach I adopt in the present work could be seen as an evangelical Protestant gloss on an essentially Antiochene hermeneutic.

86. R. W. L. Moberly, "Pentateuch," in *The New Interpreter's Dictionary of the Bible*, vol. 4, Me–R, ed. Katherine Doob Sakenfeld (Nashville: Abingdon, 2009), 434.

faithful.[87] It also set the stage, and the parameters, for biblical interpretation throughout the medieval era in the West.[88]

For present purposes, however, we need only sketch Augustine's strategy for moving from letter to spirit, that is, from the wording of the text to the text's subject matter or, in Augustine's own terms, from "sign" to "thing."[89] To simplify what could be a very long story, Augustine's main concern was to provide guidance for pastors who had to prepare and deliver sermons, the primary means for building up the church in the faith: "The sermon, on Augustine's model, is paradigmatic for theological interpretation, 'paradigmatic' because . . . directed toward the ecclesial community to engender the double love of God and neighbor."[90] Having received a classical education, Augustine knew that one of the priorities in interpretation is determining what the text is fundamentally about. His hermeneutical classic *De Doctrina Christiana* ("On Christian Teaching," or "Teaching Christianity") sets forth what Augustine understood this to be: Scripture is fundamentally about the love of God poured out in Christ. Coming to know what Scripture is about also provides a criterion for distinguishing legitimate and illegitimate interpretations. When confronted by a plurality of possibilities, prefer the reading that best fosters love of God and neighbor.[91] Against such reading there is no law; indeed, such interpretations fulfill why the law was given in the first place (Matt 22:37–40): "So anyone who thinks that he has understood the divine scriptures or any part of them, but cannot by his understanding build up this double love of God and neighbor, has not yet succeeded in understanding them."[92]

Augustine's approach combines the Antiochene attention to the literal sense with the Alexandrian concern for spiritual substance. If the literal meaning is not edifying, Augustine believed he had license to provide a spiritual interpretation. Augustine interpreted Paul's observation that "the letter kills, but the Spirit gives life" (2 Cor 3:6) as saying "that we should not take in the literal sense any figurative phrase which in the proper meaning of its

---

87. R. P. H. Green's translation is a good place to start. See Augustine, *On Christian Teaching* (Oxford: Oxford University Press, 1997).

88. According to Stanglin, "The history of biblical interpretation in the medieval West begins and ends with Augustine." *Letter and Spirit of Biblical Interpretation*, 78. Levy agrees: "It was [Augustine's] *De doctrina christiana* that stood as the principal interpretative paradigm throughout the Middle Ages." Levy, *Introducing Medieval Biblical Interpretation*, 19.

89. See Richard A. Norris, "Augustine and the Close of the Ancient Period of Interpretation," in *History of Biblical Interpretation*, Hauser and Watson, 380–408.

90. James A. Andrews, *Hermeneutics and the Church: In Dialogue with Augustine* (Notre Dame, IN: Notre Dame University Press, 2012), 11. Andrews defines "sermon" as "the rhetorical delivery of what one understands from scripture in order to evoke the proper response" (225).

91. Augustine credited Ambrose, bishop of Milan, with helping him to overcome unworthy literal pictures of God (e.g., as having arms) by introducing him to the deeper allegorical meaning.

92. Augustine, *On Christian Teaching* 1.36.40, trans. Green, 27.

words would produce only nonsense, but should consider what else it signifies, nourishing the inner man by our spiritual intelligence."[93] Although Augustine admitted that interpreters have an obligation to recover the author's communicative intent,[94] when this is not possible, or when the author's intention is unclear, the thing to do is read in such a way as to build up Christian faith, hope, and love.

Monastic and Scholastic

In this chapter I have been tracing the roots of two reading cultures that persist even today. We learned that patristic interpreters had different ideas about the *how* of biblical interpretation but not about the *why*. Augustine expressed this well in concluding that the *purpose* of biblical interpretation—building up the church in various ways—outweighs disagreements about the process. Differences over both the process and the purpose became more pronounced in the study of the Bible in the Middle Ages. Location once again was the key factor, though the focus now was not cities but institutions, specifically the monastery and the university: two reading cultures that began to grow further and further apart.

The Rise of Monasteries: Lectio Divina

One point of contention between reading cultures concerns frames of reference: the way one moves from grammar (letter) to God (spirit). A second point of contention concerns the reasons why Christians read the Bible. I agree with Moberly: "The crucial question, which is prior to questions of method and sets the context for them, is that of purpose and goal. To put it simply, *how we use the Bible depends on why we use the Bible*."[95]

Consider, for example, the difference between reading the Bible as an exercise in daily devotions versus appealing to the Bible in the context of doctrinal disputes. The difference is worth keeping in mind and may explain some of the distance modern readers experience when they encounter patristic and medieval interpretations. It is telling that, for centuries after Augustine, the main context for reading the Bible was the monastery; the university came later.

In the monastery, monks combined their study of grammar with their devotion to God. The medieval monastery was perhaps the quintessential reading

---

93. Augustine, "On the Spirit and the Letter," in *Nicene and Post-Nicene Fathers Series* 1, vol. 5, ed. Philip Schaff (Edinburgh: T&T Clark, 1995), 6 (IV).

94. Augustine, *De doctrina christiana* 3.27.38, trans. Edmund Hill (New York: New City, 2014).

95. R. W. L. Moberly, *The Old Testament of the Old Testament: Patriarchal Narratives and Mosaic Yahwism* (Minneapolis: Fortress, 1992), 2. Young agrees: "The use to which a work of literature is put surely influences the way it is understood." *Biblical Exegesis and the Formation of Christian Culture*, 215.

culture, aided and abetted by prayer.[96] A well-known saying attributed to Cyprian of Carthage commends prayer and reading as representative of the monk's daily routine: "At times you speak with God, at times he speaks with you."[97] The goal of this monastic reading culture was spiritual maturity, not the discovery of a single meaning: "Theorists and teachers of *lectio divina* concern themselves more with the process of reading than with its result."[98] *Lectio* involved reading aloud, with a running commentary that allowed the master to explain difficult words and provide other comments, including references to the *Glossa ordinaria* or collection of helpful observations (glosses) by previous authors. "*Lectio* divides into prayer and study."[99] Guigo II's *Ladder of Monks* outlines this practice of reading for the sake of sanctification in four stages, four steps on a ladder by which monks get closer to God: *lectio divina* (divine reading), *meditatio* (repetition of and reflection on the reading), *oratio* (prayer), and *contemplatio* (communion with God).[100] Biblical interpretation in this monastic reading culture was largely an exercise in piety for the sake of wisdom rather than knowledge.

In a 2009 address contrasting monastic and scholastic theology, Pope Benedict XVI characterized the former's practice as "love of words and the desire for God."[101] The wording is almost identical to Jean Leclercq's classic *The Love of Learning and the Desire for God: A Study of Monastic Culture*. St. Benedict represented for Leclercq the epitome of the monastic reading culture: "We find in germ the two components of monastic culture: studies undertaken, and then, not precisely scorned, but renounced and transcended, for the sake of the kingdom of God."[102]

The Rise of Universities: Sacra Doctrina

The early monastic schools fostered another type of reading culture as well. In the tenth and eleventh centuries, some of the large cathedrals attracted students who came to learn to read Scripture with a master. These cathedral schools were the forerunners of the great European universities. Though it was all in the family (of God), monks in monasteries often criticized the monks at

96. "The activity of reading is found at the very heart of monastic culture." Duncan Robertson, *Lectio Divina: The Medieval Experience of Reading* (Collegeville, MN: Liturgical, 2011), 6.

97. Cited in Robertson, xi.

98. Robertson, xv.

99. Ivan Illich, *In the Vineyard of the Text: A Commentary on Hugh's Didascalicon* (Chicago: University of Chicago Press, 1993), 65.

100. For a contemporary apology for *lectio divina*, see Angela Harvey, *Spiritual Reading: A Study of the Christian Practice of Reading Scripture* (Eugene, OR: Cascade, 2015). Interestingly, she makes a distinction "between interpretation and reading here to consider reading as primarily . . . an interior activity, whereas interpretation is directed more towards communication" (4–5).

101. Benedict XVI, "Monastic Theology and Scholastic Theology," October 28, 2009, https://www.vatican.va/content/benedict-xvi/en/audiences/2009/documents/hf_ben-xvi_aud_20091028.html.

102. Leclercq, *Love of Learning and Desire for God*, 12.

these schools ("schoolmen" or "scholastics") for losing sight of the larger pedagogical aim of Bible reading: the formation of mature souls.

It is difficult to define the essence of "scholasticism." As with the "schools" of Alexandria and Antioch, we must not insist on rigid definitions or identify scholasticism with a single method. What we can say with confidence is that scholasticism formed a different kind of reading culture, which formed readers to have different sensibilities than they would have developed in a monastic reading culture.[103] Whereas *lectio divina* promoted a reading culture of the Bible in a liturgical context aimed at developing spirituality, readers in the schools attended to Scripture as *sacra pagina* in the context of the schoolroom, for the sake of developing doctrine, using the recognized scholarly standards and scientific methods of the day.

One of the fixtures in scholastic reading culture was the practice of *quaestio* and *disputatio*. As a master read and commented on a biblical text, questions arose that pertained less to the grammar than to the logic of the argument, particularly when what one biblical author said seemed to contradict another. For example, Genesis 2:3 states that on the seventh day "God rested from all his work," yet Jesus says in John 5:17, "My Father is working until now." (The "answer" to this *quaestio* distinguishes the work of creating and the work of sustaining/directing creation). Other places that raised questions had to do with the implications of what was said. For example, what did Jesus mean in Matthew 26:26 when, at the Last Supper, he declared, "This is my body"? (The answer to that *quaestio* remains a matter of Protestant dispute.) At any rate, the most persistent and penetrating questions were set aside for separate treatment, perhaps in a *disputatio* (public debate) over a doctrinal topic. These attempts, perhaps the ancestor to current analytic theology, sought to resolve contradictions in the text, or between church fathers, by drawing linguistic or logical distinctions, as Aristotle had suggested in his treatise *De interpretatione*.[104] The scholastic approach was after its own fashion interested in the literal sense too, particularly as concerned the clarification and implications of its meaning.

Over time, as the questions became more complex and organized, the disputations took on a life of their own. *The Book of Sentences*, Peter Lombard's twelfth-century compilation of important answers to the perennial questions arising from reading the Bible, were culled from centuries of church tradition

103. See further Ulrich G. Leinsle, *Introduction to Scholastic Theology* (Washington, DC: Catholic University of America Press, 2010).

104. Aristotle noted that often an apparent contradiction in fact amounts only to an equivocation. Eliminate the ambiguity, and the problem goes away. For his analysis of the ills of equivocation, see his *On Interpretation* 6. For more on analytic theology, see Thomas H. McCall, *An Invitation to Analytic Christian Theology* (Downers Grove, IL: InterVarsity, 2015); Oliver D. Crisp and Michael C. Rea, ed., *Analytic Theology: New Essays in the Philosophy of Theology* (Oxford: Oxford University Press, 2009).

and eventually became, alongside the Bible, the standard textbook of theology in the medieval university.[105] It consisted of thousands of quotations stating the opinions of varied religious authorities (e.g., Gregory, Hilary, Augustine). Unlike Scripture, however, the *Sentences* followed not a chronological but a topical order. For hundreds of years, every aspiring theologian (even Martin Luther) had to write a commentary on Lombard's *Book of Sentences*. This practice gave rise to a new genre of theology with its own aim and logic: "Reading the Bible and dealing with theological questions had always gone hand in hand, but in the university there was now emerging a distinction between the sacred page (*sacra pagina*) of Scripture and the church's sacred teaching (*sacra doctrina*) as discrete fields of inquiry and fields of study."[106]

Peter Abelard compiled a similar textbook, *Sic et Non* ("Yes and No"), of 158 questions (e.g., "Must human faith be completed by reason, or not?"; "Is God a single unitary being, or not?"), but with a view to showcasing the divergent opinions of the church fathers.[107] Having exposed these contradictory opinions, he then provided rules for resolving them, such as acknowledging that the same term can have several meanings. By the thirteenth century, this practice of focusing on conceptual rather than lexical questions had become its own academic discipline. University theology embraced the language arts but went beyond them, developing a new interest in dialectic (the science of argument) rather than rhetoric and, in the process, introducing a *reasoned* reading whose aim was to resolve logical problems—call it analytic theology.[108] In this academic reading culture, conceptual cleanliness is next to godliness.

Thomas Aquinas's work represents the thirteenth-century medieval university at its best. Although Thomas also wrote commentaries, he is primarily known for his *Summa Theologica*, a cathedral of the intellect, a comprehensive catalog of questions and answers concerning God and the works of God, ordered topically, which is to say, according to reason and logic. It is an impressive synthesis of the Christian faith, drawing upon Scripture and its interpretation by the church fathers, all wrapped up in Aristotelian categories. It made for a coherent theological package but altogether different from what his contemporaries were producing in the monasteries. Here is the point: the medieval university was forming readers to ask different kinds of questions, with different frames of reference, than those typically asked in the monastery.

---

105. See further Philipp W. Rosemann, *The Story of a Great Medieval Book: Peter Lombard's Sentences* (University of Toronto Press, 2013).

106. Stanglin, *Letter and Spirit of Biblical Interpretation*, 102.

107. See Peter Abelard, *Sic et Non: A Critical Edition*, ed. Blanche Beatrice Boyer and Richer Peter McKeon (Chicago: University of Chicago Press, 1978).

108. See further, G. R. Evans, *Old Arts and New Theology: The Beginnings of Theology as an Academic Discipline* (Oxford: Oxford University Press, 1980).

Reconsidering the Distinction

G. R. Evans, contemplating the parting of the monastic and scholastic ways, concludes that there must be a place for both *lectio* and *disputatio*, for both a subjective and an objective aspect to biblical interpretation. Evans associates the monks with the former in view of their "cultivating the capacity for response in themselves and others," whereas "the academics concentrate upon the objective and technical side of biblical criticism."[109] Pope Benedict similarly refused to take sides, calling instead for faith and reason to enter into reciprocal dialogue: "Faith is open to the effort of understanding by reason; reason, in turn, recognizes that faith does not mortify her but on the contrary impels her towards vaster and loftier horizons."[110] Not everyone views the marriage of faith and reason in such rosy terms, however: "Scholastic reading then becomes a professional task for scholars—and scholars who, by their definition as clerical professionals, are not an edifying example for the man in the street."[111]

In light of these long-standing cross-cultural reading currents, the urgent questions for biblical interpreters today are these: Into what kind of reading culture have we been, or are we being socialized? Should we be trying to preserve, dismantle, or rethink the distinction that distinguishes Antioch from Alexandria and monasteries from universities? What kind of reading cultures should local churches and seminaries be, and what kind of readers should they be trying to cultivate? With these questions in mind, we now turn to our story's sequel: Whatever happened to those two ancient reading cultures and the tension between them?

---

109. G. R. Evans, *The Language and Logic of the Bible: The Earlier Middle Ages* (Cambridge: Cambridge University Press, 1984), 165.

110. Benedict XVI, "Monastic and Scholastic Theology."

111. Illich, *In the Vineyard of the Text*, 81.

CHAPTER 3

Biblical Studies and Theology as Polarized Reading Cultures

The State of the Question

Theology is thus most properly an invitation to read and reread Scripture, to hear and be caught up by Scripture's challenge to a repentant, non-manipulative heeding of God's Word.

—John Webster, *Holy Scripture*

The preceding overview of the history of biblical interpretation is incomplete: it failed to mention the Reformation and what happened next. Providing an exhaustive survey of the history of exegesis is not possible, nor is it my intent. Instead, I have chosen to sketch, in rather broad brushstrokes, the trajectory of two reading cultures, each interested in grammar and God, and hence literal and spiritual interpretation. These two streams flow through Protestant church history too: "post-Reformation Protestant scholasticism" is a real thing.[1] And as many recent studies have shown, there is significant continuity between the interpretive principles of early modern (i.e., sixteenth- and seventeenth-century) Protestant exegetes and their premodern forebears. Together with patristic and medieval interpreters, the Reformers and their immediate successors confessed the unity of Scripture, agreed that clearer passages explain those that are more obscure (the *analogia scripturae*), looked to the consensus tradition for additional

1. The best single source is Richard A. Muller, *Post-Reformation Reformed Dogmatics: The Rise and Development of Reformed Orthodoxy, ca. 1520 to ca. 1725*, 4 vols., 2nd ed. (Grand Rapids: Baker Academic, 2003).

help (*analogia fidei*), and agreed that Christ is the ultimate subject matter (*scopus*) of the Scriptures. "Because of the continued and assumed importance of these features to the exegetical task, it is proper to regard early Protestant exegesis as closer in spirit to the medieval period than to the later, modern period."[2]

Experts tend to be protective about their particular eras; a good church historian is, after all, an advocate of the past. Accordingly, when it comes to comparing the medieval and modern periods of biblical interpretation, G. R. Evans, a medievalist, can perhaps be forgiven for commending monks and theologians in the Middle Ages who, despite their differences, enjoyed a consensus about the God-given nature of the Bible, in sharp contrast to moderns, about whom Evans says, "No consensus has yet been reached on the way in which the Bible should be approached and the questions which should be asked about it."[3] Indeed. This contemporary lack of consensus about how best to approach biblical interpretation is the subject of the present chapter.

What does it mean to be biblical? As the preceding survey has shown, this is a polarizing question, one that has led to contrasting reading cultures. Three types of polarization are of particular interest insofar as each contributes to the formation of a reading culture. Interestingly enough, the division between Protestants and Roman Catholics is not a major part of the story. While it looms large in church history, it is not one of the three sources of polarization I consider here. Why not? Because the same three forms of polarization—epochal (premodern/modern), institutional (church/academy), and disciplinary (biblical studies/theology)—have created stress fractures in Roman Catholicism as they have elsewhere.[4]

The most significant result of the tension we have been examining is not denominational but epochal: premodern versus modern. Getting clear on what makes biblical interpretation modern will therefore be our first order of business. For it is in modernity that the tension between scholastic and monastic reading cultures metastasizes into a second polarization, between academy and church, and between what Michael Legaspi calls "the Academic Bible" and the

2. See Keith D. Stanglin, *The Letter and Spirit of Biblical Interpretation: From the Early Church to Modern Practice* (Grand Rapids: Baker Academic, 2018), 147. Stanglin also acknowledges certain discontinuities, such as the diminishing authority of tradition and the greater emphasis on the literal sense and human authorial intent among Protestants (147–50).

3. G. R. Evans, *The Language and Logic of the Bible: The Earlier Middle Ages* (Cambridge: Cambridge University Press, 1984), 168.

4. See, e.g., Joseph Ratzinger, "Biblical Interpretation in Crisis: On the Question of the Foundations and Approaches of Exegesis Today," in *Biblical Interpretation in Crisis: The Ratzinger Conference on Bible and Church*, ed. Richard John Neuhaus (Grand Rapids: Eerdmans, 1989); and my "Expounding the Word of the Lord: Joseph Ratzinger on Revelation, Tradition, and Biblical Interpretation," in *The Theology of Benedict XVI: A Protestant Appreciation*, ed. Tim Perry (Bellingham, WA: Lexham, 2019), 66–86.

church's "Christian Scripture."[5] The third, and perhaps most painful polarization, between biblical studies and theology, is a product of the first two. Care must be taken, however, lest we simply project the church/academy distinction onto that between biblical studies and theology. There is no one-to-one correspondence. Many biblical scholars and theologians have a foot in both camps. There are people of faith working in the academy. Nevertheless, the center of gravity for "serious" biblical interpretation has taken a sharp scholastic tack. The location of this third polarization, then, between biblical studies and theology, is *within* the church and academy alike. It is this latter disciplinary polarization—the contrasting reading cultures of biblical studies and systematic theology—that is the primary focus of the present chapter. Most churchgoing Christians have no inkling that biblical scholars and theologians speak different languages, have different interpretive interests, or inhabit different reading cultures, yet it is true. Their fields have become distinct specializations, each with its own journals, jargon, degree programs, and professional societies.[6]

We begin by examining the consequences for biblical interpretation of the "epochal" shift to modernity. Next, we examine the way in which modernity exacerbates the tension between the two reading cultures we surveyed in chapter 2. The chapter concludes with a clarion call to all biblical interpreters to return to church, becoming active participants in an ecclesial reading culture where the purpose of reading Scripture is clear, even if the process is not.

Epochal Polarization: When Modern Biblical Interpreters Lost Interest in Theology

I cannot hope to explain satisfactorily the origins of the modern world, but I will try to describe the principal changes that have most affected the disciplinary reading cultures we know today as biblical studies and theology. Earlier I mentioned the "demise of biblical civilization." Think of it as a revolution in hermeneutic paradigms, what Hans Frei called the "great reversal" in hermeneutics that took place in the eighteenth century.[7] Before then the biblical narrative was the interpretive framework with which almost everyone in the West made sense of the world. After modernity, however, many Westerners view the Bible as merely another worldly object to be explained by the various sciences (e.g., archaeology, ancient history, cultural anthropology, sociology, religious studies).

5. Michael Legaspi, *The Death of Scripture and the Rise of Biblical Studies* (Oxford: Oxford University Press, 2011), viii.

6. In fact, the fragmentation is actually more radical. Today it is not enough to say that one is either a biblical scholar or theologian: there are multiple subspecializations under each of these headings.

7. Hans Frei, *The Eclipse of Biblical Narrative: A Study in Eighteenth and Nineteenth Century Hermeneutics* (New Haven, CT: Yale University Press, 1974), 130.

The ultimate result: theologians lost interest in biblical exegesis, and biblical exegetes lost interest in theology.

Scot McKnight, in his *Five Things Biblical Scholars Wish Theologians Knew*, rightly identifies one source of the paradigm shift: "Frames matter."[8] The person who "frames" a discussion sets the ground rules for how a topic will be discussed. To frame an issue is to influence how people view and may respond to it. Let us call what frames a discussion about texts and their meaning a *frame of reference*. It is essentially the set of assumptions and values that informs the reader's perspective—the way a reader looks at the text. I cannot overstate the importance of reading with the right frame of reference, for it shapes both the questions a reader brings to the text and what she sees there. Perhaps we can now appreciate the formative impact of reading cultures: *reading cultures instill certain interpretive intuitions and practices, training readers to use certain frames of reference rather than others*. Frames matter.

Adieu to Allegorizing?

Modern scholars are quick to anathematize ancient allegories as self-serving and arbitrary flights of exegetical fancy. After citing Augustine's interpretation of Jesus' parable of the good Samaritan—in which the wayfarer is Adam; the robbers, the devil and his minions; the priest who passed by, the ministry of the Old Testament; the Samaritan himself, Jesus; and the innkeeper, the apostle Paul—C. H. Dodd made a withering comment: "To the ordinary person of intelligence . . . this mystification must appear quite perverse."[9]

Origen gave a similar reading of the parable—and receives a similar slap down from modern biblical scholarship. According to Origen, "The man who was going down is Adam. Jerusalem is paradise, and Jericho is the world. The robbers are hostile powers. The priest is the Law, the Levite is the prophets, and the Samaritan is Christ."[10] Origen went on to make even more surprising identifications, suggesting that the inn to which the Samaritan took the man is the church, the innkeeper the apostle Paul, and the Samaritan's promise to return a reference to Jesus' second coming. Modern exegetes are typically scornful of such detailed allegorical readings. New Testament scholar Craig Blomberg is clearly exasperated with what he takes to be an arbitrary and anachronistic reading: "No one in [Jesus'] original audience . . . could ever have been expected to associate the Samaritan's innkeeper with the apostle Paul!"[11]

---

8. Scot McKnight, *Five Things Biblical Scholars Wish Theologians Knew* (Downers Grove, IL: IVP Academic, 2021), 149.
9. C. H. Dodd, *The Parables of the Kingdom* (London: Nisbet, 1935), 13.
10. Origen, *Homilies on Luke*, trans. Joseph T. Lienhard (Washington, DC: Catholic University of America Press, 1996), 34.3–4.
11. Craig Blomberg, *Interpreting the Parables* (Downers Grove, IL: InterVarsity, 1990), 32.

For many modern biblical scholars, premodern biblical interpretation is a *foreign* reading culture, so strange that one wonders whether premoderns and moderns actually share "one Lord, one faith, one baptism" (Eph 4:5). The ancient logic that made sense of the aforementioned allegorical associations escapes most moderns. The differences run deep, to one's basic intuitions about the nature and value of biblical interpretation. Jonathan Haidt's observation as to why "good people" are increasingly polarized over politics and religion may apply here too. According to Haidt, "*Intuitions come first, strategic reasoning second.*"[12] The context of his remarks is moral intuitions and reasoning, but the same may be true of hermeneutical intuitions and exegetical reasoning. For example, moderns have their own ideas about what counts as sound exegetical intuitions: not moral but *interpretive righteousness*. Modern incomprehension of premodern reading cultures ("What were they thinking?") has less to do with reasoning than with contrasting interpretive intuitions. Where do interpretive intuitions come from? They come from being socialized into a particular reading culture. The conclusion should be obvious: the foreignness moderns often feel when they encounter premodern biblical interpretation should not lead to their summary dismissal of such readings as primitive, much less perverse. Rather, interpretive humility should lead them to inquire further into the differing hermeneutical intuitions and conceptions of the interpretive good that gave rise to premodern ways of reading the Bible in the first place.

John O'Keefe and R. R. Reno are modern readers who sympathize with biblical scholars' concerns with allegorizing—up to a point. For they do not think that the church fathers were out of their right interpretive minds. Instead, they feel the need to go the second mile to understand the logic behind, say, allegorical interpretation: "For us . . . the first step toward understanding patristic exegesis was a moment of self-criticism. . . . Slowly, we began to realize that the key issue rested in our preconceptions about what is significant about texts."[13] A moment of self-criticism is precisely what Haidt recommends as well: for, without it, we are but what C. S. Lewis terms *chronological snobs*, who assume the superiority of modernity simply because it is newer than the past.[14] It is difficult, however, to step outside one's habitual frame of reference to look, not at the text, but at the way we typically approach it.

The ancients inhabited a "saturated" frame of reference in which earthly, natural things are transitory signs of an eternal, supernatural realm of higher

12. Jonathan Haidt, *The Righteous Mind: Why Good People Are Divided by Politics and Religion* (New York: Vintage Books, 2013), xx (emphasis original).

13. John J. O'Keefe and R. R. Reno, *Sanctified Vision: An Introduction to Early Christian Interpretation of the Bible* (Baltimore: Johns Hopkins University Press, 2005), 7.

14. C. S. Lewis, *Surprised by Joy: The Shape of My Early Life* (New York: Harcourt, Brace, Jovanovich, 1966), 207–8.

realities. Advocates contend that early and medieval theologians used an "Ur-Platonism" as a metaphysical framework for interpreting Scripture: "The Platonist-Christian synthesis made it possible to regard creation, history, and Old Testament as sacramental carriers of a greater reality."[15] Hans Boersma, in his *Five Things Theologians Wish Biblical Scholars Knew* (the companion volume to McKnight), makes two points germane to the present discussion in a chapter titled "No Plato, No Scripture." He claims, first, that Christian Platonism is the necessary metaphysical scaffolding for making sense of the key teachings of Scripture, not simply one of many possibilities.[16] Second, he points out that the alternative to Christian Platonism is not no metaphysics but an *alien* metaphysic, less hospitable to the biblical message.

The concern about bidding adieu to allegorical interpretation, then, is that moderns may have inadvertently invited something even more sinister into the interpreter's house. At least the premodern frame of reference enabled biblical interpreters to read supernaturally, for the mystery beyond the history, whereas modern frames of reference tend to filter out that supernatural mystery. What frame of reference do we moderns inhabit that leads us to think of allegorical interpretations as so strange, if not perverse?

Installing an Immanent Frame of Reference: The Modern Social Imaginary (Part 1)

Charles Taylor's *A Secular Age* is well known and rightly admired for its incisive insight into the roots of modernity. The question that motivates his inquiry has everything to do with frames of reference: "Why is it so hard to believe in God in . . . the modern West, while in 1500 it was virtually impossible not to?"[17] My question is similar: Why is it so hard to interpret the Bible spiritually in the modern West while from 330 to, say, 1830 it was virtually impossible not to?[18] The answer has less to do with the rise of science or arguments against God's existence than with something more radical: an epochal "disenchantment," in which the taken-for-granted picture of a supernaturally saturated, meaningful creation was replaced by that of an impersonal order of matter in meaningless motion. Taylor describes modernity as a revolution in our social imaginary, "the way that we collectively imagine, even

15. Hans Boersma, *Heavenly Participation: The Weaving of a Sacramental Tapestry* (Grand Rapids: Eerdmans, 2011), 38. See also Craig A. Carter, *Interpreting Scripture with the Great Tradition: Recovering the Genius of Premodern Exegesis* (Grand Rapids: Baker Academic, 2018), 66–84.

16. Hans Boersma, *Five Things Theologians Wish Biblical Scholars Knew* (Downers Grove, IL: IVP Academic, 2021), 62.

17. Charles Taylor, *A Secular Age* (Cambridge, MA: Belknap, 2007), 539.

18. My *terminus ad quem*, 1830, is only an approximation. It is difficult to provide an exact date, for the loss of a supernatural frame of reference for interpreting the Bible, and everything else, was a gradual process.

pretheoretically, our social life in the contemporary Western world."[19] The social imaginary is profoundly implicated in our earlier discussions of reading cultures, interpretive intuitions, and frames of reference. Indeed, it is more fundamental than those three, for it is what integrates them. Taylor defines the social imaginary as the set of storied assumptions that underlies our shared understanding of reality and undergirds our everyday practices. It is that taken-for-granted picture of the way the world goes. This picture is not something explicitly taught, but caught, not a theory one learns in the classroom, but on the street: "it is carried in images, stories."[20]

Like a scientific paradigm, a social imaginary is not easily dislodged. This is because it is not usually something we look *at*, to evaluate critically, but what we look *through*: it is the window that frames our view of the world. A change of social imaginary is an epochal change, a change in worldview. Such a change requires a shaking of the imaginary's foundations.[21] In a real sense, a social imaginary is the taken-for-granted story in which individuals live and move and think their communal being. Think of the social imaginary as the operating system, as it were, of human existence. We live in a secular age, says Taylor, because we inhabit a secular (from Lat. *saeculum* = world) social imaginary—because a this-worldly picture holds our imaginations captive.

In describing secularity, Taylor introduces another idea that bears on what we have said about reading cultures and frames of reference, the windows through which readers view the biblical text. The "immanent frame" is Taylor's term for the picture of a self-enclosed world of nature that moderns inhabit: the world *incurvatus in se*, a space-time cosmos curved in upon itself and thus sealed off from the sacred or other-worldly.[22] In the house of the secular interpreter, the immanent frame is a window frame of reference that, instead of letting light in, keeps most of it out. There is no room for the supernatural or spiritual in the immanent inn. To inhabit the immanent frame is to be conscious only of what appears or occurs in the closed causal nexus of space-time. In an immanent frame, no one moment is more important than another, and life is just "one damn thing after another."[23] Time on this view is *shut off* from eternity, less ecclesial than Ecclesiastes time: "What has been is what will be, and what has been done is what will be done, and there is nothing new under the sun" (Eccl 1:9). Qohelet here gives voice to something like the immanent frame, a worldview by which we come "to understand our

19. Taylor, *A Secular Age*, 146.

20. Taylor, 172.

21. Jesus' world-subverting parables are an example of such "shaking."

22. Martin Luther used *incurvatus in se* ("turned in upon oneself") to describe the sinner's self-centered preoccupation with self, in contrast with the outward orientation of one who loves God and others.

23. An early twentieth-century proverb of uncertain attribution.

lives as taking place within a self-sufficient immanent order."[24] It is, in a word, existence without transcendence.

It is hard to exaggerate the impact of the immanent frame on modern biblical interpretation. First and foremost, it did away with the traditional picture of the God/world relationship, thus spawning a new, "critical" reading culture (see below). Benedict de Spinoza was one of the first biblical interpreters to appreciate the revolutionary nature of the new frame of reference. He rejected the divine authorship of the Bible and instead examined it as only a human product, composed in an immanent frame, and thus subject to the same historical and cultural forces as any other book. Furthermore, given the immanent frame, there can be no final purpose in reading, no transcendent good such as the knowledge of God, or godliness, to be aimed at.[25]

Matthew Levering worries that even believing modern biblical scholars may inadvertently reduce biblical history to what can fit into an immanent frame of reference: "Once the 'historical' is understood as a solely linear temporal continuum, then a separation of historical exegesis from patristic-medieval exegesis becomes inevitable."[26] Flat-earthers, meet flat-texters—interpreters who force biblical history into immanent frames of reference, thereby limiting themselves to this-worldly explanations of what actually happened in Israel's and Jesus' history. Levering agrees with modern scholars that we should study the Bible in its original contexts, yet he protests when those immanent contexts are all that interpreters consider.[27]

The great merit of Taylor's account of secularity is its highlighting the all-important role of the social imaginary in determining the frames of reference interpreters use to make sense of reality—and the Bible. The great merit of Levering's account is its reminder that exegesis always presupposes some understanding of what history *is*. For his own part, Levering insists that "the historical includes a participation in realities known by faith."[28] Given the Bible's own claims about divine action in the world, there is no reason to reduce the vertical, open-to-transcendent dimension of history to a closed horizontal structure of this-worldly cause and effect: "The loss of a participatory framework cuts off the literal/historical sense from the spiritual sense and makes it increasingly difficult to see in the literal/historical sense anything but a set of immanently enclosed concepts."[29] We need not follow Levering in seeing history's relation to

24. Taylor, *A Secular Age*, 543.

25. By way of contrast, chapter 9 makes a case that the end or telos of biblical interpretation is the transfiguration of the reader into greater Christlikeness.

26. Matthew Levering, *Participatory Biblical Exegesis: A Theology of Biblical Interpretation* (Notre Dame, IN: University of Notre Dame Press, 2008), 4.

27. Levering, 1.

28. Levering, 7.

29. Levering, 145.

the transcendent as "participatory" (this way Plato lies), but we must follow him in insisting that multiple frames of reference are needed to get biblical history right, including frames of reference that are open to transcendence. We must agree, in other words, that God's mighty acts in history burst the immanent frame wide open.

Criticism and the Great Hermeneutical Reversal: The Modern Social Imaginary (Part 2)

In addition to enclosing history in an immanent frame, the new secular social imaginary also provided a new frame of reference for conceiving knowledge. Immanuel Kant's famous "Copernican revolution" worked a thought experiment on thought itself: the "naive" view pictures knowledge as the mind registering sensations, passively conforming to objects. Kant compared this naive (precritical) epistemology to the naive (prescientific) view that the sun and stars revolve around their spectators on earth. As Copernicus demonstrated, this hypothesis fails to explain the motion of these heavenly bodies. The Copernican view reverses the picture: it is the earth that moves around the sun (not vice versa); the sun and stars remain at rest. Kant's equally epoch-making proposal was a "Copernican revolution" in epistemology: knowledge occurs not when the mind passively conforms to its object, but when the object conforms to the structure of our minds. Kant argued that the mind's categories order and make sense of our experience.[30] He also insisted that we can only know what we experience. Because experience is limited to the immanent frame (the space-time causal nexus), and because God is not an item in the world, Kant concluded that there can be no knowledge of God. Religion is useful as a prop to morality but, like everything else, it is a human phenomenon subject to critical scrutiny and so remains "within the limits of reason alone."[31]

Kant's Copernican revolution matters because it is the epitome of critical thinking, the impetus of the secular social imaginary, and the foundation of biblical criticism. To be "critical" is to be aware of the limits of human knowledge, and to be suspicious of surface appearances and naive opinion that masquerade as knowledge and truth. Kant was not the first critical thinker, of course, yet there is good cause to regard him as the Father of Criticism inasmuch as he criticizes reason itself, which is to say, he determines its rightful limits. Kant's manifesto "What Is Enlightenment?" urged modern thinkers to "dare to reason" for themselves rather than hiding behind the skirts of church

30. Immanuel Kant, *Critique of Pure Reason*, 2nd ed., trans. Norman Kemp Smith (London: Macmillan, 1933), 22.

31. See Immanuel Kant, "*Religion within the Boundaries of Mere Reason* (1783)," in *Religion and Rational Theology*, The Cambridge Edition of the Works of Immanuel Kant, trans. and ed. Allen W. Wood and George Di Giovanni (Cambridge: Cambridge University Press, 1996).

dogma and tradition.[32] Other scholars, like Spinoza, had been critical of the Bible.[33] It was patently obvious to him that Moses could not have written the Pentateuch, for the simple reason that Deuteronomy records his death. But it was Kant who grounded this signature move of criticism in a critical philosophy. For modern criticism is first and foremost a *style of thought* that cuts across the academic disciplines, "a style of interpretation driven by a spirit of disenchantment."[34] Less than a century after Kant, this critical mindset was alive and well, having created a reading culture that dominated the field of biblical studies, best expressed by W. K. Clifford's critical credo: "It is wrong always, everywhere, and for anyone to believe anything upon insufficient evidence."[35] Similarly, Van Harvey, a twentieth-century historian, contended that it is *immoral* for a historian to believe something unless there is sufficient evidence. Can one believe the patriarchal narratives, or the story of Israel's journey to and from Egypt? The modern, critical answer is *no*—at least not without sufficient evidence. For, as Spinoza archly observed, it is one thing to establish the "sense of Scripture," quite another to determine "the truth of things."[36] We come to know the former by reading the Bible, but we come to know the latter only when we examine what we have read in the light of critical reason.

Modern criticism—the suspicious work of reason—is the perfect style of thought given the authority of modernity's immanent frame. There was a time when Augustine's interpretation of the parable of the good Samaritan seemed right and proper, and when biblical accounts of God's action in the world were unproblematic. Those times are gone. The modern secular imaginary now inclines us to look for natural explanations, both for the miracle stories the Bible recounts and the Bible itself. The mandate of modern biblical criticism is to provide an exhaustive account of the text as a historically and culturally conditioned human document. Again, the reflex of the critical mind is to be suspicious of appearances in order to penetrate to reality. Many biblical critics have spent their careers trying to reconstruct what *actually* happened rather than accept what the texts report to have happened.[37] They do so with an immanent (i.e., historicist) frame of reference, which insists on explaining events in relation to

---

32. See Immanuel Kant, *Foundations of the Metaphysics of Morals, and What Is Enlightenment?*, trans. Lewis White Beck (New York: Liberal Arts, 1959), 85–91.

33. One of the earliest works to employ a more secular frame of reference for reading the Bible was Baruch Spinoza's 1670 *Theological-Political Treatise* (Cambridge: Cambridge University Press, 2007).

34. Rita Felski, *The Limits of Critique* (Chicago: University of Chicago Press, 2015), 2.

35. W. K. Clifford, "The Ethics of Belief," in *Lectures and Essays* (London: Macmillan, 1886), 346.

36. Spinoza, *Theological-Political Treatise*, 100.

37. See, e.g., Thomas L. Thompson, *The Historicity of the Patriarchal Narratives: The Quest for the Historical Adam* (Harrisburg, PA: Trinity Press International, 2002); John van Seters, *In Search of History: Historiography in the Ancient World and the Origins of Biblical History* (New Haven, CT: Yale University Press 1983); Israel Finkelstein and Amihai Mazar, *The Quest for the Historical Israel: Debating Archaeology and the History of Early Israel*, ed. Brian B. Schmidt (Atlanta: Society of Biblical Literature, 2007); William

their immediate historical contexts only.[38] In the modern social imaginary, the Bible is like Samson shorn of his locks, as weak (and historically conditioned) as any other book (cf. Judg 16:7).

Meanwhile, modern theologians were losing interest in theology. Those who accepted Kant's critique of reason, like Friedrich Schleiermacher, made religious experience rather than revelation the focus of their study.[39] Alongside the eclipse of biblical narrative, then, we have also to mention the "eclipse of God's agency."[40] Modern theologians thus "changed the subject": the object of their study was no longer God (theology proper), but human religious experience (anthropology). Passengers on this railway are greeted at the terminal by the open arms of Ludwig Feuerbach.[41]

Theologians lost interest in theology, then, by paying more attention to religious experience in general and less to the testimony of the prophets and apostles.[42] Sometime in the seventeenth century, the conversation drifted away from the specifics of doctrinal Christianity toward philosophical arguments for (and against) the existence of God. At the origin of modern atheism, Michael Buckley argued, is philosophical apologetics.[43] How can defending theism count as evidence that modern thinkers were losing interest in theology? Because it shows (1) that they were substituting the generic God of the philosophers for the triune God of the gospel, and (2) that they thought rational arguments and objective evidences (e.g., design in nature) could settle the matter. In sum, the struggle between atheism and theism was no longer a matter of biblically informed faith, but philosophically adjudicated reason.

One last feature of Taylor's account of secularization is worth mentioning. The alleged superiority of the modern historicist imaginary is, he claims,

---

G. Dever, *What Did the Biblical Writers Know and When Did They Know It? What Archaeology Can Tell Us about the Reality of Ancient Israel* (Grand Rapids: Eerdmans, 2001).

38. A good example of historicism is the work of Ernst Troeltsch, who insisted on explaining the life of Jesus and the rise of early Christianity in terms of their immediate historical contexts. See his *The Social Teaching of the Christian Churches*, 2 vols. (New York: Harper Row, 1960).

39. For Schleiermacher, doctrines are not descriptions of the divine nature but "accounts of the Christian religious affections set forth in speech." *The Christian Faith* (Edinburgh: T&T Clark, 1928), 76.

40. Mark Allan Bowald, *Rendering the Word in Theological Hermeneutics: Mapping Divine and Human Agency* (Aldershot, UK: Ashgate, 2007), 13–23.

41. Feuerbach is the grandmaster of the masters of hermeneutical suspicion, for he interprets statements about God as code for what humans ultimately venerate. The essence of religion, and its secret, is that theological statements are actually anthropological statements, expressions of qualities we deem divine. See further Ludwig Feuerbach, *The Essence of Christianity*, trans. George Eliot (Buffalo, NY: Prometheus Books, 1989); and Van Harvey, *Feuerbach and the Interpretation of Religion* (Cambridge: Cambridge University Press, 1995).

42. I am indebted to Nicholas Lash, "When Did the Theologians Lose Interest in Theology?," in his *The Beginning and End of "Religion"* (Cambridge: Cambridge University Press, 1996), 132–49, for the material in this paragraph.

43. "Theology alienated its own nature by generating a philosophy that functioned as apologetics." Michael J. Buckley, *At the Origins of Modern Atheism* (New Haven, CT: Yale University Press, 1987), 358.

misplaced. What made the secular picture more believable was not scientific proof, as if physics could disprove God. On the contrary, what makes the modern secular imaginary compelling is its claim to be *ethically* superior—hence Clifford's and Harvey's claim that it is *morally* wrong to believe things without sufficient evidence. In other words, in the secular imaginary, suspicion—a distrust of appearances—is a *virtue*: "It is seen as the stance of maturity, of course, of manliness, over against childish fears and sentimentality."[44] To describe faith in such terms is *already* to inhabit the secular imaginary, however. Those who know the real thing know better (cf. 2 Thess 1:4; Jas 1:3).[45]

Disciplinary Polarization: The Divided Domain of Biblical Interpretation

Chapter 2 described how the ancient tension between ways of reading the Bible grew in intensity during the medieval era and eventually reached a breaking point, with biblical scholars and theologians going their separate disciplinary ways in the modern academy. These two ways (call them, for lack of better terms, the "historical" and the "theological") drifted even further apart in the twentieth century, though recently there have been encouraging signs of a rapprochement.[46] Still, alongside the great reversal in hermeneutics, we must also mention the great divorce between biblical and theological studies, the two principal disciplines in the domain of the word.[47]

Biblical scholars and systematic theologians have pursued their respective interpretive interests for the past two centuries and, for much of that period, have not been on talking terms. There is a disciplinary dividing wall of indifference, if not of outright hostility. Even when the topic is theology, biblical scholars and theologians take different approaches and speak their own languages, following paths first charted by J. P. Gabler in the eighteenth century, when he distinguished the descriptive historical task of "biblical theology" (i.e., saying what the biblical authors thought about God) from the normative task of "dogmatic theology" (i.e., saying what people today should think about

44. Taylor, *Secular Age*, 365.

45. Nicholas Hardy argues that biblical criticism never did attain the neutrality to which it aspired, but rather served the interests of various ecclesiastical and political institutions. See his *Criticism and Confession: The Bible in the Seventeenth Century Republic of Letters* (Oxford: Oxford University Press, 2017).

46. In addition to the St. Andrews conferences on Scripture and theology (see below), I would point to the 2007 founding of the *Journal of Theological Interpretation*, whose purpose is to allow biblical interpreters to employ theological frames of reference.

47. Myk Habets contends that biblical studies and systematic theology represent different approaches to theological interpretation of Scripture. General hermeneutical concerns (i.e., those that pertain to the author-text-reader triad) dominate the biblical approach, in contrast to what Habets calls the *theological* theological interpretation of Scripture typical of systematic theologians ("*Theological* Theological Interpretation of Scripture," *International Journal of Systematic Theology* 23, no. 2 [2021], 235–58).

God).[48] Gabler's aim was praiseworthy: he wanted to make sure that dogmatic theologians were not simply cherry-picking biblical texts that would support their preferred positions. Gabler assigned to the "biblical" theologian the task of describing the religious ideas of the biblical authors on their own terms and in their own historical contexts. Biblical theologians were not to use the Bible to prove this or that confessional statement. The unintended consequence of this disciplinary division of labor, however, is that at present "exegetes cooperate more naturally with philologists, sociologists, and historians than with systematic theologians."[49]

Churches and seminaries must grapple with the fact that both biblical studies and systematic theology have been affected by modernity such that they have become separate reading cultures. There is pressure in the academy, not least from the sciences and other fields of study, for biblical scholars and theologians to accept the parameters of the immanent frame: historicism for exegetes; rationalism for theologians. Even within that common immanent frame, however, exegetes and theologians continue to work with different frames of reference that lead them to put different kinds of questions to the biblical text. To generalize (and live dangerously): from early modern times until around the 1970s, biblical exegetes tended to employ an array of critical methods that focused on some aspect of the world "behind" the text. For their part, theologians tended to direct their attention to some aspect of the world "in front of" the text. A few examples will have to suffice, but a bit of background concerning these prepositional "worlds" may help to show what is at stake.

The distinction between the worlds "behind," "of/within" and "in front of" the text are now commonplace in biblical hermeneutics. They represent interpretive approaches, typical of general hermeneutics, that are author-centered, text-centered, or reader-centered, respectively.[50] The world *of* the text is made up of words and has a coherence of its own, thanks to its literary structure and plot.

48. See the translation and commentary by John Sandys-Wunsch and Laurence Eldredge, "J. P. Gabler and the Distinction between Biblical and Dogmatic Theology: Translation, Commentary, and Discussion of His Originality," *Scottish Journal of Theology* 33 (1980): 133–58. See also Krister Stendahl's related distinction between "what it meant" and "what it means" in his "Biblical Theology, Contemporary," in *Interpreter's Dictionary of the Bible* (Nashville: Abingdon, 1962), 1:418–32. I discuss both definitions of biblical theology, along with that of Geerhardus Vos, in my "Staurology, Ontology, and the Travail of Biblical Narrative: Once More unto the Biblical Theological Breach," *Southern Baptist Journal of Theology* 23, no. 2 (2019): 7–33.

49. Arnold Huijgen, Koert van Bekkum, and Hans Burger, "Biblical Exegesis and Systematic Theology: Toward Mutual Benefit," *Journal of Reformed Theology* 16 (2022): 174–75.

50. W. Randolph Tate, *Biblical Interpretation: An Integrated Approach*, rev. ed. (Peabody, MA: Hendrickson, 1997), xx. Jonathan Pennington describes the three worlds as "three avenues." *Reading the Gospels Wisely: A Narrative and Theological Introduction* (Grand Rapids: Baker Academic, 2012), ch. 6. Paul Ricoeur referred to "the world of/within the text" to indicate a way of being-in-the-world that has the potential to reconfigure the reader's existence. See further my *Biblical Narrative in the Philosophy of Paul Ricoeur: A Study in Hermeneutics and Theology* (Cambridge: Cambridge University Press, 1990), 87–90.

Exegetes distinguish this storied world *within* the text from the historical world *behind* the text. The latter includes the sociocultural context of the authors and editors who produced it. Finally, the world *in front of* the text is that of its readers, who bring the world of the text into their lives, if only for a moment. This plurality of textual worlds raises an interesting question to be taken up in the next chapter: In which "world" do we find the text's literal meaning?

The World *behind* the Biblical Text: Reading with Historical Frames of Reference

One characteristic of the modern secular imaginary is historical consciousness: that ever-present awareness that what humans think and do is conditioned by their social context. When modern biblical scholars read biblical texts, they want to learn as much as possible about the various forces—social structures, cultural practices, political powers, and so on—that may have contributed to their composition and content. Historical consciousness and critical thinking are the twin sources of the "historical-critical" approach. The core presupposition is that to arrive at textual meaning readers must go *behind* the text (and its surface appearance) in order to understand its historical occasion, cultural context, sources, authors, and original audience. The interpretive intuition behind historical criticism seems sound: to understand any stranger, it helps to know something about that person's background and context.

Context looms large in hermeneutic textbooks. It has been said that "the three most important rules in interpretation are context, context, and context."[51] But what *is* a context, how *large* is a context, and how many *kinds* of context are there? Modern exegetes tend to read the Bible with a historical frame of reference, hence pride of place goes to the original context, including the material culture, artifacts, and cognate languages and literatures that together make up the world *behind* the text.[52] The lack of precritical interest in, or knowledge of, the original context is one of the primary reasons modern biblical critics tend to dismiss them.

Much depends on which context(s) an interpreter decides to privilege, and why. John Monson says the study of the original context "offers a vantage point from which to evaluate the disparate readings of the biblical text and to identify those that are grounded within the physical and cultural soil of the biblical authors. It represents a potentially more objective ('constrained') view from the world of the text, but outside the confines of the text—a view that has only become available during the past century."[53]

51. Often attributed to J. Vernon McGee.

52. See further W. W. Hallo and K. L. Younger, eds., *The Context of Scripture*, 3 vols. (Leiden: Brill, 1997–2002).

53. John Monson, "Contextual Criticism as a Framework for Biblical Interpretation," in *Israel: Ancient Kingdom or Late Invention?*, ed. Daniel Block (Nashville: Broadman & Holman, 2008), 54.

Does the context that determines meaning belong exclusively to the world *behind* the text? Monson is willing to acknowledge a canonical context that stretches the notion of original context "to include the occasion when original texts were compiled into book form and then ultimately canonical form in order to address later audiences with the divine witness."[54] Other biblical scholars are not so hospitable. They see no good reason why other books in the canon should be treated differently than any other contemporaneous sources.[55] For, within the immanent frame, one cannot appeal to God's agency, and the only other explanation as to why some books are "in" and others "out" is that the people responsible for compiling the canon had more political power than their opponents.[56]

Some historians make very modest claims about the world behind the text; others construct metanarratives of their own. N. T. Wright identifies himself as a historian with a mandate to understand the New Testament authors in light of their own historical context (Second Temple Judaism); the alternative to reading them on their own terms in their own world is to misinterpret them.[57] In Wright's opinion, this is precisely what patristic and Reformation theologians have done with doctrines like justification by faith: "If you want to understand how ideas and phrases are used in the first century it helps to look at the first century, not the fourth century [i.e., Nicaea] . . . (still less the sixteenth century AD [i.e., the Reformation]!)."[58] Wright speaks for modern biblical scholarship when he observes that it is "the theologians' flight from history . . . that has done the real damage."[59] To understand the world *behind* the New Testament text, Wright reconstructs the story that informs its authors' worldview. This story—about Jesus' death fulfilling Israel's hope for a new exodus, seen as a final return from exile—is less important than the fact that Wright thinks it is necessary to reconstruct it and his choice to privilege the context of Second Temple Judaism in doing so. In Wright's view, right reading

54. John Monson, "Original Context and Canon," in *Interpreting the Old Testament Theologically: Essays in Honor of Willem A. VanGemeren*, ed. Andrew T. Abernethy (Grand Rapids: Zondervan, 2018), 32.

55. James Barr, *Holy Scripture: Canon, Authority, Criticism* (Louisville: Westminster John Knox, 1983), 67.

56. For examples of arguments to this effect, see Bart Ehrman, *Lost Christianities: The Battles for Scripture and the Faiths We Never Knew* (Oxford: Oxford University Press, 2003); Bart Ehrman, *Lost Scriptures: Books That Did Not Make It into the New Testament* (Oxford: Oxford University Press, 2003); Elaine Pagels, *The Gnostic Gospels* (New York: Random House, 1979).

57. John H. Walton takes a similar approach to the Old Testament and focuses on interpreting it in light of the cognitive environment, its ancient Near Eastern context. See his *Ancient Near Eastern Thought and the Old Testament: Introducing the Conceptual World of the Hebrew Bible*, 2nd ed. (Grand Rapids: Baker Academic, 2018).

58. N. T. Wright, "Historical Paul and 'Systematic Theology': To Start a Discussion," in *Biblical Theology: Past, Present, and Future*, ed. Carey Walsh and Mark W. Elliott (Eugene, OR: Cascade, 2016), 153.

59. N. T. Wright, "Responding to Exile," in *Exile: A Conversation with N. T. Wright*, ed. James M. Scott (Downers Grove, IL: IVP Academic, 2017), 324.

depends on reconstructing the original frame of reference that makes sense of Jesus as the climax of Israel's story.

Richard Hays, a fellow New Testament scholar, wonders whether interpretive privilege belongs to a historical frame of reference that works independently of its creedal counterpart.[60] Hays says that Wright assembles his historical evidence only to make "a highly intuitive, synthetic leap of induction that generates a master hypothesis."[61] That master hypothesis is his reconstructed metanarrative allegedly operating behind the text—the story of Israel's covenant, exile, and return—distinct from the particular narratives of the individual Gospels. It is, says Hays, "a critically abstracted construct."[62] Hays worries that the voices of the individual Evangelists disappear, swallowed up by the "real" story Wright claims to have discovered in the world behind the text. Hays also wonders whether the story Wright historically reconstructs from the world behind the text "obsessively forces all the evidence into the single mold of the exile and return pattern."[63] Hays notes that Wright is able to read even the parable of the prodigal son "as a story about Israel's exile and restoration."[64] Hays confesses, "No matter how many times I read Tom's elegant treatment of the parable, I simply can't persuade myself that this is what Jesus meant."[65] What shall we say then? Having begun *behind* the text in order to clarify it, are we now perfected by something *other* than the text?

Wright believes he can correct church tradition by going behind the text, but Hays counters, asking, "Why not acknowledge that the church's tradition might provide aid rather than hindrance in seeking to understand the New Testament's witness about the identity of Jesus?"[66] For his own part, Hays thinks that a historical frame of reference alone is inadequate; readers of the New Testament will not get even their historical investigation right if they neglect the canonical form of the story.[67] It is an important disagreement. Hays also cites the late Robert Jenson, a theologian, throwing gas on what is already a burning fire: "But what if the church's dogma were a necessary hermeneutical principle of historical reading, because it describes the true ontology of historical being?"[68] What if? The salient point is simply this: when attempting

60. Richard B. Hays, "Knowing Jesus: Story, History and the Question of Truth," in *Jesus, Paul and the People of God: A Theological Dialogue with N. T. Wright*, ed. Nicholas Perrin and Richard B. Hays (Downers Grove, IL: IVP Academic, 2011), 44. I will say more about creedal frames of reference below.

61. Hays, 46.

62. Hays, 49.

63. Hays, 55.

64. Hays, 55.

65. Hays, 55.

66. Hays, 57.

67. Hays, 61.

68. Robert W. Jenson, "Identity, Jesus, and Exegesis," in *Seeking the Identity of Jesus: A Pilgrimage*, ed. Richard B. Hays and Beverly Roberts Gaventa (Grand Rapids: Eerdmans, 2008), 50.

to reconstruct the world behind the text, historians, too, may be tempted to speculate and offer a narrative account of what really happened that is at odds with the biblical narrative. Such historical/speculative reconstructions may turn out to be a distinctly modern form of allegorizing, that is, of saying the text really *means* (or is about) something *other* than what it plainly says. As we will see in the next section, systematic theologians speculate too; I am therefore in no position to cast the first stone. But this debate is not about disciplinary one-upmanship. Mere Christian hermeneutics must not pit theology against history or doctrine against grammatical-historical interpretation. The cause of reading the Bible theologically is not served by simplistic contrasts.

Interpreting the Bible with a historical frame of reference, alert to the original contexts of the authors, has produced undeniable exegetical dividends. At a bare minimum, we need to know something about the original contexts to understand the semantic range of the Hebrew and Greek terms that make up the text: "There is worth in historical analysis of biblical language because the semantic value of terms changes over time, and historical work highlights precisely this: meaning is use, and such use varies across different historical contexts."[69] One of the five things exegete Scot McKnight wants theologians to know is that "theology needs historically shaped biblical studies."[70] Divine revelation takes place not in a vacuum but in concrete historical and cultural contexts. McKnight challenges the individualistic way the New Testament term *gospel* has been understood in the context of modern evangelicalism. He criticizes the popular "soterian" frame of reference, according to which the gospel is about the possibility of an individual's salvation from sin and guilt through faith in Christ's atoning death. A close reading of the Gospels in their original context discovers instead what McKnight calls a "King Jesus gospel," namely, the proclamation that God's project is to establish his kingdom on earth, which is less about the salvation of individuals than the establishment of a social order marked by justice and *shalom*.[71] Biblical studies thus help provide the proper frame of reference for the gospel itself.

Again, everything depends on one's frame of reference. The problem in modern biblical studies is not with the historical frame as such, but with its *immanence*—the closed-in-upon-itself worldview that shuts out God and divine action. This has disastrous material and methodological implications.[72] To read the Bible in the immanent frame changes the subject: biblical scholars no longer

69. Darren Sarisky, *Reading the Bible Theologically* (Cambridge: Cambridge University Press, 2019), 185.

70. This is the title of chapter 3 in McKnight, *Five Things Biblical Scholars Wish Theologians Knew*.

71. See Scot McKnight, *The King Jesus Gospel: The Original Good News Revisited* (Grand Rapids: Zondervan 2011).

72. See Brad East, "The Hermeneutics of Theological Interpretation: Holy Scripture, Biblical Scholarship and Historical Criticism," *International Journal of Systematic Theology* 19, no. 1 (2017), 30–52.

read the Bible to come to know God but, rather, to understand the biblical authors' thoughts about God. When modern theology becomes a kind of religious anthropology, the disciplinary divide only deepens: "Where the subject matter of biblical exegesis and of dogmatic theology is not taken to be the same, there exists no real ground for mutual interaction between the two disciplines."[73]

In an immanent frame of reference, the Bible has a natural history only. C. S. Lewis was well acquainted with naturalism, which he describes as a "hangover" from our night out with modernity: "We all have Naturalism in our bones and even conversion does not at once work the infection out of our system."[74] Metaphysical naturalism is the belief that only the physical world—matter in motion—is real. Its first cousin, methodological naturalism, insists that Christian doctrine has no bearing on one's views on either the nature of the biblical text or how it should be read. It is simply illegitimate to read the Bible as anything else than the words of culturally and historically conditioned human authors. The immanent historical frame, so understood, is exclusionary because it shuts out any consideration of the transcendent, including divine authorship. The problem with naturalism lies not in what it affirms, but in what it denies: "theological reading does not deny the reality of the immanent features of the world or the gains that have been made by historical consciousness. What it does do, however, is to deny the ultimacy and finality of the immanent frame."[75] If only immanent frames of reference are hermeneutically acceptable, then the only thing biblical studies has to say to theology is, "Keep out!"

The World "in Front of" the Biblical Text: Reading with Conceptual, Confessional, and Contextual Frames

Despite my intent to promote a theological reading culture, it would be a mistake to assume that theologians are automatically the book's heroes. Modern theologians have "changed the subject" and are also complicit in the demise of the Bible's literal interpretation. Theologians, too, approach the Bible with frames of reference taken from somewhere other than the biblical text (usually philosophy). Many have eagerly plundered the Egyptians—and the Greeks, Germans, French, and others—for various conceptual schemes in order to make the Bible, and the Christian faith, more intelligible to their contemporaries. Augustine did something similar with Plato, as did Thomas Aquinas with Aristotle. In every case, theologians have interpreted the Bible aware of their contemporary context, and of the world of their readers, *in front of* the text.

73. C. Kavin Rowe and Richard Hays, "Biblical Studies," in *Oxford Handbook of Systematic Theology*, ed. John Webster, Kathryn Tanner, and Iain Torrance (Oxford: Oxford University Press, 2007), 452.

74. C. S. Lewis, *Miracles: A Preliminary Study* (New York: Macmillan, 1947), 197.

75. Sarisky, *Reading the Bible Theologically*, 364.

Paul Tillich's *Systematic Theology* is a case in point. Tillich was remarkably attuned to the world in front of the text. His "method of correlation" begins by determining which questions modern men and women are asking, then shows how the Bible answers them.[76] He listened to mid-twentieth-century culture and detected an underlying anxiety, a sense that people are threatened by the end of their finite existence (death) and meaninglessness, the two forms of "non-being" to which he thought the Bible provides a solution. To this problem, the Bible provides an answer—when read with an existentialist frame of reference. Tillich believed that modern people no longer seriously believed in a God "out there." God, for Tillich, is not an object of knowledge but the "ground of our being."[77] Tillich read the Gospels not as factual records or evidence for reconstructing the past, but as symbolic expressions of the disciples' understanding of existence in light of their religious experience of Jesus' cross and resurrection, which symbolize the "power of new being."[78]

Tillich's systematic theology is a cautionary tale. Though he gets high marks for contemporary intelligibility, he fails the test of biblical fidelity. The most glaring theological problem is that it is not clear whether Jesus needs to have actually risen from the dead in order to serve as the symbol of the power of new being.[79] Because he read the Bible as symbolic myth, reconstructing what is behind the text (and what actually happened) is secondary. What counts most is bringing the Bible into the world of the twentieth-century, where it is read not as an account of God's building project (to form a people for himself) but of the human quest for ultimate reality.[80] Although the Gospels appear to recount the history of Jesus, in Tillich's frame of reference they become ontological parables: symbolic stories about the relation of finite human being to being-itself. Tillich's theology turns out to be yet another allegorical interpretation, in which what the Bible is really about (existentialism) is *other* than what its authors appear to be saying.[81]

---

76. Paul Tillich, *Systematic Theology*, vol. 1 (Chicago: University of Chicago Press, 1951), 59–65.

77. In line with his method of correlation, "God" is the answer to the question of the precariousness of our being.

78. For a more complete evaluation of Tillich's Christology as overly beholden to the mid-twentieth-century world in front of the text, see Colin J. D. Greene, *Christology in Cultural Perspective: Marking Out the Horizons* (Grand Rapids: Eerdmans, 2003), 128–32.

79. See David Kelsey, *The Fabric of Paul Tillich's Theology* (New Haven, CT: Yale University Press, 1967).

80. See Paul Tillich, *Biblical Religion and the Search for Ultimate Reality* (Chicago: University of Chicago Press, 1955).

81. David Bentley Hart turns conventional wisdom on its head, suggesting that modern theologians like Tillich are the true allegorists: "Historians or hermeneuticians frequently assert that what most alienates modern readers from the methods of premodern exegetes is the latter's passion for allegory. But this is false. If anything, we today are much more culturally predisposed than our forebears to an unremitting allegorization of the tales we tell or books we read, no matter how elaborate or tedious the results. . . . The same critic who might prissily recoil at the extravagances of a patristic figural reading of the Book of

David Tracy argues that what makes theology "modern" is its willingness to employ a variety of philosophical frames of reference in order to make sense of the Bible in the contemporary situation: "What modernity provides for the naming of God . . . is a series of seemingly endless debates on the correct ism, that is, the correct set of abstract propositions which name and think God."[82] This accords well with Tracy's own conception of theology as the correlation of *theos* (God) with *logos* (concept), speaking of God within a particular philosophical frame of reference and intelligibility. This is precisely what biblical scholars worry about—theology being "systematic" insofar as it uses conceptual schemes drawn from elsewhere than the biblical text to render the Bible intelligible for readers in front of the text. There are myriad such schemes or systems of ideas (*-isms*): their name is Legion, not least because they have imperial ambitions. Some of the leading conceptual schemes that modern theologians have appropriated most often include Marxism, feminism, and panentheism.[83] Critics of systematic theology may feel like asking, "What else is new? Have not theologians *always* imposed frames of reference drawn from in front of the text?" Think, for example, of Thomas Aquinas's wholesale appropriation of Aristotle (adjusted for revelation).

Others worry about theologians imposing not philosophical but confessional frames of reference. One reason Calvinists and Arminians find biblical support for their respective traditions is because both parties read the Bible with theological grids already in place. When biblical exegetes look askance at "theological interpretation of Scripture," this is often why. Their worry is exacerbated when they read claims like this: "Proper interpretation proves itself to be such when our reading of Scripture accords with what the church teaches."[84] Such statements appear to resolve the tension between biblical studies and theology by demanding an unconditional surrender on the part of biblical scholarship. To many Protestant ears, this seems to get things the wrong way around: church doctrine must accord with the Scriptures, not vice versa. Be that as it may, biblical scholars worry that both Protestant and Roman Catholic

---

Numbers might feel not the slightest dismay at the transformation of Prospero into an ironic indictment of colonialism, or of Horatio Hornblower into an inflexibly erect emblem of the 'phallic signifier.' What makes the spiritual allegories of ancient pagan, Jewish, and Christian exegetes so alarming to modern sensibilities is not that they were allegories but that they were so disconcertingly spiritual." "Ad Litteram," in *A Splendid Wickedness and Other Essays* (Grand Rapids: Eerdmans, 2016), 274–77.

82. David Tracy, "Literary Theory and the Return of the Forms for Naming and Thinking God in Theology," *Journal of Religion* 74 (1994): 307.

83. Tracy describes panentheism—the view that everything is in the God who is greater than the world—as "the one permanent achievement of modern theologies of God." "The Return of God in Contemporary Theology," in *On Naming the Present: God, Hermeneutics, and Church* (Maryknoll, NY: Orbis, 1994), 41.

84. R. R. Reno, *The End of Interpretation: Reclaiming the Priority of Ecclesial Exegesis* (Grand Rapids: Baker Academic, 2022), xv.

theologians tend to interpret the Bible with creedal and confessional rather than textual frames of reference.

The concern is valid. However, it is no more problematic to employ confessional or creedal frames of reference than it is historical frames of reference, provided they enable rather than disable understanding of what the Bible says. Arguably, this is precisely what the Nicene creedal frame of reference does in specifying the deity of the Son and the Trinitarian nature of God. Reno says, "I defy anyone to identify a way of thinking about God, history, and human destiny that is at once more metaphysically self-conscious than the Nicene tradition and more thoroughly and constantly invested with exegetical substance."[85] For Protestants, at least, ecclesial frames of reference, including Nicaea, have only ministerial, not magisterial authority. All are ultimately answerable to the way the biblical words go. Frames of reference are unavoidable in biblical interpretation and, as we have seen, the danger of speculation, even allegorizing, lurks in historical and conceptual/confessional frames alike.

One more set of interpretive frames that privilege the world in front of the text deserves mention: those that defer to the present context. In the modern and postmodern academy, ancient and contemporary contexts vie for the attention of biblical critics. To the extent that we are in the "age of the reader," the advantage has shifted to present contextual frameworks.[86] Historical-critical approaches continue to have ample representation in academic biblical scholarship. However, the trend in recent decades has been toward what, for lack of a better term, we might call *identity frames of reference*. These interpretive frameworks privilege the multiple worlds in front of the text represented by contemporary interpreters themselves. For example, the interpretive interest that governed Latin American liberationist theological readings of the Bible in the 1960s was not "going to heaven" but "justice on earth," a frame of reference that privileged the perspective of the poor. The concern to read the Bible in ways that advocate for various people groups (e.g., ethnic; gender-based; the disabled) and foster social justice in the world in front of the text has generated multiple contextual frames of reference. Each in its own way represents a "postcolonial" frame of reference aimed at correcting a perceived injustice against a marginalized or oppressed people group.[87]

---

85. Reno, 23.

86. For further analysis of this turn to the reader in contemporary hermeneutics, see my *Is There a Meaning in This Text? The Bible, the Reader, and the Morality of Literary Knowledge* (Grand Rapids: Zondervan, 1998), ch. 4, and my "The Reader in New Testament Interpretation," in *Hearing the New Testament: Strategies for Interpretation*, ed. Joel Green, 2nd ed. (Grand Rapids: Eerdmans, 2010), 259–88.

87. For more on postcolonial biblical interpretation, see R. S. Sugirtharajah, *Postcolonial Criticism and Biblical Interpretation* (Oxford: Oxford University Press, 2002). For a balanced critique of contextual approaches to biblical interpretation, see Taimaya Ragui, *Confessing Community: An Entryway to Theological Interpretation in North East India* (Minneapolis: Fortress, 2023).

Whereas modernity freed interpreters from the shackles of authoritative tradition, postmodernity seeks to free interpreters from the illusion of the "view from nowhere,"[88] namely, the idea that scientific methodology affords interpreters the kind of objectivity about textual meaning that the natural sciences have in their own domains. In the wake of postmodern pushback, however, the new trend is to elevate the "view from *here*"—the in-front-of-the-text world of a particular people group. The significance of this development cannot be overstated. By and large, the context that many contemporary biblical interpreters privilege today is not that of the original author, but their own. What matters to many contemporary readers is the world in front of the text: reading the Bible in one's own context in ways that advance the interests of one's personal and/or communal identity.[89] This desire to make ancient texts address contemporary issues can easily lead to the cynical assumption that interpretation always says more about the reader than it does the text.

The War of the Worlds: Polarized Reading Priorities

Biblical interpreters today are caught in a "war of the worlds" scenario. On the one hand are the multiple worlds *in front of* the text, as we have just seen. These are in altogether different orbits than the worlds *behind* the text. Nor have we yet mentioned the world *of* or *within* the text, namely, the narrative world constructed by authors, projected by the text, and encountered by readers.[90]

The tension we have been tracing has led theology and biblical studies to go their separate ways. The fragmentation of the theological disciplines has become even more pronounced in modernity.[91] The divisions between reading cultures that exist today are both between the theological disciplines and within them. When Markus Bockmuehl was appointed professor of New Testament at Oxford University, his inaugural lecture struck a disconsolate note, asking whether there was any consensus still to be had about the object of New Testament studies.[92] What should New Testament scholars be look-

88. I take this phrase from the book by Thomas Nagel, *The View from Nowhere* (Oxford: Oxford University Press, 1986), which explores the tension between viewing the world objectively ("from nowhere in particular") on one hand and being honest about one's particular location on the other. This same tension characterizes biblical interpretation, though as I'm suggesting here, the pendulum has of late swung toward the side of particularity and locatedness: "the view from here, right here."

89. Each of the aforementioned various identities and many others not mentioned here have their own working groups at the annual meetings of the Society of Biblical Literature and the American Academy of Religion.

90. One seminal example of a literary approach to biblical interpretation is Robert Alter, *The Art of Biblical Narrative* (New York: Basic, 1981). See also Meir Sternberg, *The Poetics of Biblical Narrative: Ideological Literature and the Drama of Reading* (Bloomington: Indiana University Press, 1985).

91. See further Edward Farley, *Theologia: The Fragmentation and Unity of Theological Education* (Minneapolis: Augsburg Fortress, 1994).

92. Markus Bockmuehl, "The Troubled Fortunes of New Testament Scholarship," in *Seeing the Word: Refocusing New Testament Study* (Grand Rapids: Baker, 2006), 27–74.

ing at in their study of the New Testament, how should they be looking at the New Testament, and what are they reading the New Testament for? Similar questions could be asked about Old Testament studies or systematic theology. Contrary answers abound. Some readers will find this apocalyptic tone—my setting the disciplinary doomsday clock at 11:59 p.m.—to be exaggerated. By some standards, the biblical-theological disciplines are flourishing, particularly if the number of academic journal articles and doctoral dissertation publications are any indication. On this reckoning, the modern academic-commentary-industrial complex has never been healthier or more productive.

And yet what motivates this prodigal academic production does not necessarily serve the church or the seminary. Theological education is but a noisy gong or clanging cymbal if it is not helping students to read the Bible well in order to understand God truly. As we have seen, however, biblical studies and systematic theology have generated two opposing reading cultures with different aims, interests, and procedures. To complicate matters further, each reading culture is writing biblical commentaries.[93] Pastors now face the challenge of deciding what kind of commentaries to read as aids to sermon preparation and to their understanding of biblical Christianity. Should they privilege the world "behind" the text and look at it with a historical frame of reference, or should they accord interpretive privilege to some world "in front of" the biblical text derived from their ecclesial tradition or from the prevailing philosophies and cultural currents of the day?[94]

As we have seen, the present polarized situation did not happen overnight but was the result of a centuries-long development. Complementary medieval reading cultures have hardened into separate intellectual cultures, which Oliver Crisp defines as a discipline "that identifies itself as having a distinctive approach to its subject matter and a particular methodological approach to its subject."[95] The main casualty of this cross-cultural conflict may not be pastors needing help but the very subject matter of the biblical text, which the disciplines frame in disparate, often polarizing, ways. In their zeal for their own respective frames of reference, biblical studies and systematic theology have perhaps lost sight of the Bible's own frame of reference, which, as we will see, is a function of the literal sense. The ultimate victim in this hermeneutical cold war, this disciplinary war of the textual worlds, may prove to be the world *of* the

93. The commentary series arising from biblical studies are too numerous to mention. What is noteworthy, however, is the rise of commentary series authored primarily by theologians. See, e.g., the (now defunct) Brazos Theological Commentary on the Bible series (Baker Academic) and the International Theological Commentary series (T&T Clark).

94. As we have discussed, there are also conflicts between the *various* worlds in front of the text.

95. Oliver Crisp, *Analyzing Doctrine: Toward a Systematic Theology* (Waco, TX: Baylor University Press, 2019), 28.

text. And now I am referring not only to the narrative world *within* the text, but to the text as divine address, which belongs to an eschatological culture—the domain of the living and active word of God—requiring a theological frame of reference. Again, a theological frame of reference does not do away with the historical but, rather, views the historical as a field of divine action, including divine communicative action.[96]

My concern going forward is how to overcome the debilitating disciplinary polarization that may have begun as a constructive tension but, in modernity, has resulted in a pathological division of exegetical labor. The authors of a 2022 essay only slightly exaggerate: "It is remarkable that no elaborate methodology for cooperation between biblical studies and systematic theology exists to date."[97] Walter Brueggemann thinks the tension is here to stay: "There can, in my judgment, be no final resolution of the tension between the systematizing task of theology and the disruptive work of biblical interpretation."[98] Constructive tension turns into an unhealthy polarization, however, when biblical interpreters slip into thinking in terms of a disciplinary "them versus us." It will take more than individual goodwill to heal the breach, for as I have been arguing, the problem is one of conflicting reading cultures. Insofar as "biblical studies" and "theology" have institutional dimensions (e.g., academic departments; professional societies; journals), those who have been trained in the academy have been socialized into what amounts to rival political identities that jostle for institutional power (e.g., to set curricula). The way forward will require reform of the institutions that foster the reading cultures that form readers of the Bible.[99]

The identity politics I have in view here pertains not simply to historically marginalized or special interest groups, but to the powers that shape exegetes' and theologians' interpretive intuitions, and thus their respective self-conceptions as biblical interpreters. Of course, many streams—familial, ethnic, geographic, denominational, and professional, for example—feed into a person's identity, though they may not always be operative in one's reading of the Bible. One of the unfortunate effects of modern specialization, however, is that exegetes and theologians now define their approaches to biblical interpretation in contrast to one another, to the point that they often seem to represent polar opposites. Biblical scholars trained to look at the biblical text through

96. I relate this to typology and typological interpretation at greater length in a later chapter.

97. Huijgen, Van Bekkum, and Burger, "Biblical Exegesis and Systematic Theology," 187. The authors go on to offer seven theses as "a groundwork for developing such a fruitful cooperation." I try to do the same in parts 2 and 3 of the present work.

98. Walter Brueggemann, *Theology of the Old Testament: Testimony, Dispute, Advocacy* (Minneapolis: Augsburg, 1997), 107.

99. Bible colleges, seminaries, and divinity schools: this means you!

a historical frame of reference may consider it as a personal affront when a theologian praises Augustine's allegorical reading of the Psalms. Conversely, a theologian may resent the suggestion that reading the Bible with Trinitarian presuppositions is "eisegesis."[100]

Ezra Klein's *Why We're Polarized* is not about biblical interpretation (the title refers to America's political fissures), but many of his insights nevertheless apply. For example, "The most important psychological imperative most of us have in a given day is protecting our idea of who we are."[101] Nothing makes us identify with our interpretive tribe so passionately as the perception that we are being attacked, or the prospect that our tribe is losing power and influence. I firmly believe that the primary self-conception of biblical scholars and theologians should be their common identity "in Christ," not their tribal identities, whether disciplinary or denominational. Klein's advice to Republicans and Democrats is worth quoting: "The path of wisdom on identity politics is to be mindful of which of our identities are being activated, so that we can become intentional about which identities we work to activate."[102]

We do not have to allegorize Miroslav Volf's *Exclusion and Embrace* to appreciate how his reflections on identity, otherness, and reconciliation apply to today's polarized Bible reading cultures. The history of biblical interpretation includes more than its fair share of exclusions: mutual anathemas. Modern biblical critics once found it easy to dismiss medieval allegorizing—until David Steinmetz took up the latter's case, arguing for the superiority of precritical exegesis: "The medieval theory of levels of meaning in the biblical text, with all its undoubted defects, flourished because it is true, while the modern theory of a single meaning, with all its demonstrable virtues, is false."[103] In light of such polarizing claims (superiority implies inferiority), it is tempting for both biblical scholars and theologians to think in terms of "them versus us." Yet, as Volf helpfully points out, there is a distinction between healthy differentiation and unhealthy exclusion: "We are who we are not because we are separate from the others who are next to us but because we are *both* separate *and* connected, *both* distinct *and* related; the boundaries that mark our identities are both barriers and bridges."[104] It may be more comfortable to stay within one's own interpretive culture, but this serves the cause of neither truth nor Christ: "A certain kind of distance from one's primary social group—refusal to identify fully with it or any

---

100. I draw both examples from personal experience.

101. Ezra Klein, *Why We're Polarized* (New York: Avid Reader, 2020), 96.

102. Klein, 262.

103. David Steinmetz, "The Superiority of Pre-critical Exegesis," *Theology Today* 37 (1980): 38.

104. Miroslav Volf *Exclusion and Embrace: A Theological Exploration of Identity, Otherness, and Reconciliation* rev. ed. (Nashville: Abingdon, 2019), 59.

of its political [read: *exegetical*] projects—is essential if the Christian faith is not to be given an exclusionary form."[105]

Our present polarized situation raises serious questions about the reading cultures within which pastors and their congregations are formed. Locating pastors in the church and theologians in the academy has resulted in a theological anemia in the pastorate and an ecclesial anemia among academic theologians. At stake is the pastor's self-conception and sense of vocation: "We don't expect pastors to be *theologians*, certainly not scholars, at least not of a professional variety."[106] In modernity, the social location of the academy is not only distant from that of the local congregation, but worlds apart, thus prompting several urgent questions: Into what kind of reading culture does the academy socialize prospective pastors? What does literal interpretation mean in the context of the modern academy? How can readers do justice to both grammar and God? Is spiritual interpretation desirable and, if so, is it still possible?

Fortunately, there are positive signs that the tide is beginning to turn. Dialogue and cooperation between biblical scholars and theologians is not as rare today as it was fifty years ago. The University of St. Andrews has hosted several conferences that brought together biblical scholars and systematic theologians to think about a particular biblical book. In his introduction to the volume on the Gospel of John, Richard Bauckham writes, "The two disciplines are natural partners who have lost the means of effective communication with each other, so absorbed have they become in their own issues."[107] The time is therefore ripe for building hermeneutical bridges. What the church needs now is disciplinary integration, not segregation. Interpreters of the word, unite!

Beyond Polarization: Taking Biblical Studies and Theology Back to Church

Our brief survey of the state of the question—the relationship between the two reading cultures of biblical studies and systematic theology—is nearing its end. The question, in brief, is: "Whither biblical interpretation?" Volf's title, *Exclusion and Embrace*, provides the answer and a positive way forward: not exclusion, but embrace—but not so hard as to suffocate. It is not a question of one side losing, much less disappearing. It is, rather, a matter of "making space

105. Volf, 319 (emphasis original).

106. Gerald Hiestand and Todd Wilson, *The Pastor Theologian: Resurrecting an Ancient Vision* (Grand Rapids: Zondervan, 2015), 11. See also Kevin J. Vanhoozer and Owen Strachan, *The Pastor as Public Theologian: Recovering a Lost Vision* (Grand Rapids: Baker Academic, 2015).

107. Richard Bauckham, "Introduction," *The Gospel of John and Christian Theology*, ed. Richard Bauckham and Carl Mosser (Grand Rapids: Eerdmans, 2008), x. Subsequent St. Andrews Conferences on Scripture and Theology have produced three other volumes, on Genesis, Galatians, and Hebrews.

in oneself for the other."[108] What Volf says about alienated individuals trying to reconcile also applies to the two cultures we have been describing: "I do not want to be myself only: I want the other to be part of who I am and I want to be part of the other."[109] This may require both exegetes and theologians to readjust their self-conceptions. It also involves reforming their respective cultures so that each fosters the kind of readers who are open to one another's disciplinary contributions.

Can we talk—and listen—to one another? It's a real question. Even Christians who share the same confessional framework may find themselves thinking about exegesis very differently, depending on the disciplinary reading culture into which they have been socialized. Good fences may make good neighbors, but to love our neighbors we have to do more than stay in our own yards. To have a genuine conversation, we must learn the dialogical virtues—patience, openness, charity, and humility—particularly when our interlocutors have different interpretive intuitions. Pope Francis identifies the lack of dialogue as the root of much exclusion, and this applies to polarized Bible reading cultures: "The attitude of listening . . . spurs us to pull down walls of misunderstandings, and to create bridges of communication, overcoming isolation and closure in one's small world."[110]

Yuval Levin's *A Time to Build* is not about biblical interpretation, but its lessons nevertheless apply. Levin, like Klein (see above), is troubled by the toxic polarization in American politics, though his diagnosis differs from Klein's. According to Levin, the fundamental problem is that both rival parties view social institutions "not as molds that ought to shape their behavior and character but as platforms that allow them greater individual exposure and enable them to hone their personal brands."[111] Whereas Levin is concerned with the American nation, my concern is with polarization in the church, a holy nation (1 Pet 2:9).

Exegetes and theologians need to go back to church. What does this mean? The issue is not whether individual biblical scholars and theologians have a personal faith (for the sake of the present discussion, let us assume they do). The issue, rather, has to do with the kind of reading practice into which exegetes and theologians have been socialized. Church is not simply a safe space where biblical scholars and theologians can become friends, though it should be that

108. Volf, *Exclusion and Embrace*, 98.

109. Volf, 143.

110. "Audience with volunteers of 'Telefono Amico Italia,'" *Summary of Bulletin: Holy See Press Office*, March 13, 2017, https://press.vatican.va/content/salastampa/en/bollettino/pubblico/2017/03/11/171011a.html.

111. Yuval Levin, *A Time to Build: From Family and Community to Congress and the Campus, How Recommitting to our Institutions Can Revive the American Dream* (New York: Basic Books, 2020), 6.

too. *The church should be the community that generates and governs the interpretive aims and interests of biblical scholars and theologians alike.* Not every ecclesial reading culture will use the same confessional framework, yet whatever their particular denominational (or nondenominational) slant, every church should, minimally, be forming readers to read with a distinctly theological interest: to know and love God. Reading the Bible in the church should affect the kinds of questions and frames of reference that biblical scholars and theologians prioritize and bring to the text.

Levin's description of institutions is instructive: "When I speak of institutions . . . I mean the durable forms of our common life. They are the frameworks and structures of what we do together."[112] The church is an institution in this organic sense. It forms mature disciples and citizens of the gospel through preaching, administering the sacraments, and works of mercy, all of which proceed from faith in Christ. Tragically, however, the church is one of the institutions, along with governments, big business, and the media, in which people today have lost confidence. Levin suggests, somewhat counterintuitively, that the present polarization in American politics stems not from these institutions being too powerful but too weak: they lack the ability to form people into citizens who know how to work together to accomplish important social tasks. Levin proposes that instead of abandoning we need to strengthen these historic institutions, precisely for the sake of better personal formation: "Enduring progress happens soul by soul, but that is actually why it can only happen through the institutions of society, which touch and form each of us."[113]

The church is one such formative institution; the academy is another. The question today for academies and churches (and their seminaries) alike is not simply "What are they teaching?" but rather, "What kind of students (and readers) are they forming?" According to Levin, in the academy "a progressivism that leans toward identity politics is the reigning orthodoxy."[114] As we have seen, identity politics generates a self/other mentality that can have a polarizing tendency. Levin rightly sees that the purpose of social institutions is to form persons with the virtues necessary for their particular vocations: "To be such a professional is not only to have a certain job but almost to become a certain type of human being."[115] If this is true of professionals in general, how much more is it true of biblical scholars and theologians. Biblical scholars and theologians must go to church in order to understand that they ultimately serve not a special interest group (i.e., their own guild) but the church—the whole people of God.

112. Levin, 19.
113. Levin, 41.
114. Levin, 105.
115. Levin, 69.

Going back to church means remembering what the Bible, and the church, is and is for: "But you are a chosen race, a royal priesthood, a holy nation, a people for his own possession, that you may proclaim the excellencies of him who called you out of darkness into his marvelous light" (1 Pet 2:9). Biblical scholars and systematic theologians need to go back to church to be reminded that, in the final analysis, they are on the same side because they serve the same Lord and his cause, namely, God's plan to make all things new in Christ, through the Spirit: "Where the subject matter of biblical exegesis and dogmatic theology is thought to be the same, the two disciplines are of necessity inseparable."[116] The distinction between biblical scholars and theologians is not redundant, for exegetes focus on understanding the biblical authors on their own terms, while theologians restate what the prophets and apostles say to make it intelligible and applicable in the present: "Yet, in continuity with the ancient church, there is no final division between biblical interpretation and theological reflection, for they are united in the common task of attending to the subject matter of scripture."[117]

The polarization of exegesis and theology has not served the church, but there is no need to vilify either side. If we must have villains, I can think of two only: "flat-texters" (biblical scholars who deny any depth dimension to historical reference, thus ruling out the possibility of divine action) and "free-texters" (theologians whose interpretive frames float free of the text altogether, thus ruling out the possibility of biblical authority). Fortunately, most of these belong to small scholarly sects in the academy, socially isolated from the general population. Mere Christians, regardless of their disciplinary or confessional location, must "*commit ourselves to act otherwise* in the future."[118]

The mere Christian hermeneutics set out in the present work calls for reform in both reading cultures insofar as in the one, biblical studies, theology comes too late, while in the other, systematic theology, Scripture figures too little. The way forward asks exegetes and theologians to go back to church—and to do so without forgetting what they learned at school.[119] To that end, we now turn to exploring what it means to read for the Bible's literal sense with a distinctly theological frame of reference. Does traditional grammatical-historical interpretation have a place in mere Christian hermeneutics? Absolutely! Does it have the place to itself? Not quite. Does it have pride of place, with power to veto other forms of interpretation? Read on.

116. Rowe and Hays, "Biblical Studies," 452.
117. Rowe and Hays, 452.
118. Volf, *Exclusion and Embrace*, 341 (emphasis original).
119. See further Daniel J. Treier, *Introducing Theological Interpretation of Scripture: Recovering a Christian Practice* (Grand Rapids: Baker Academic, 2008).

PART 2

Figuring Out Literal Interpretation

The Letter of the Text

My God, my God, thou art a direct God, may I not say a literal God, a God that wouldst be understood literally and according to the plain sense of all thou sayest, but thou art also . . . a figurative, a metaphorical God too, a God in whose words there is such a height of figures.

—John Donne, *Devotions upon Emergent Occasions* (1624), Expostulation XIX

To this point, we have flagged the problem of conflicting reading cultures. The loser has been the biblical text, which has too often been caught in cross-cultural crossfire, a conflict over which frame(s) of reference are legitimate, and why. Negotiating these tensions—biblical studies versus systematic theology; premodern versus modern versus postmodern; the West versus the rest—requires, first, determining what the biblical text is, second, clarifying what we mean by "literal" sense and "literal" interpretation, and third, specifying a frame of reference that would allow for an enriched literal interpretation that, without distorting the letter of the text, enables "spiritual" reading as well. Both the church and the seminaries that train her pastors should be reading cultures that form readers to do justice to the letter of the text in the presence of Christ, the one whose voice is speaking in the Scriptures, the one who is the subject matter of the Scriptures, and the one to whom the Scriptures ultimately belong.

Having established in part 1 the significance of reading cultures, the chapters in part 2 examine criteria for right reading. The focus here is on the norm of theological interpretation of Scripture, namely, the literal sense, and on specifying what it means to read "according to the letter." The burden of these two chapters is to specify what the literal sense is and to distinguish it from populist literalism and other misconceptions. Frames of reference once again play an important role. To do justice to the letter of the text as human-divine discourse, its subject matter, and its canonical context, those who read the Bible theologically must ultimately adopt an eschatological frame of reference and a style of grammatical-eschatological exegesis. Doing so opens up new possibilities for a reading that is at once literal and figural/spiritual, thus retrieving a "christoscopic" way of reading the Bible for its plain canonical sense that the Reformers have in common with the church fathers and with Christian readers everywhere and at all times.

CHAPTER 4

Defining *Sensus Literalis* (Part 1)

From Grammatical Sense to Eschatological Reference

The problem of the literal may be the most fundamental problem in the theory of interpretation.

—Brian Cummings[1]

This chapter explores what is arguably of greatest interest to biblical scholars and systematic theologians alike, though perhaps for different reasons: the literal sense. Many exegetes understand their vocations in terms of doing justice to the letter of the text—the way the words run. Many theologians agree with Thomas Aquinas that the proper basis for Christian doctrine is Scripture's literal sense: "All the senses are founded on one—the literal—from which alone can any argument be drawn."[2] Both exegetes and theologians often assume we know what "literal" means. We do not. In the history of ideas, literality is an "essentially contested concept."[3]

There is an urgent need to clarify the meaning of the literal sense, and to distinguish literal interpretation from both nonliteral and literalistic alternatives. Determining the meaning of *sensus literalis* is, says Brevard Childs, "one

1. Brian Cummings, "Literally Speaking, or, the Literal Sense from Augustine to Lacan," *Paragraph* 21, no. 2 (1998): 200.

2. Thomas Aquinas, *Summa Theologica* I.1.10.

3. See further W. B. Gallie, "Essentially Contested Concepts," *Proceedings of the Aristotelian Society* 54 (1956): 167–98. An essentially contested concept is one that "inevitably involves endless disputes about their proper uses on the part of their users" (169).

of the burning issues of theology."[4] The reason why a consensus has not been reached, I submit, has to do with prior decisions to privilege certain frames of reference rather than others, decisions often made by default, a function of the particular reading culture to which one belongs, and by the social imaginary that sustains it.

We begin our inquiry into the meaning of the literal with what is arguably the exegete's primary interest: philology, the practice of giving loving attention to words and the way words go. I then offer a fivefold typology of approaches to literality and commend a synthetic model that befits a mere Christian hermeneutic. The next section analyzes further that important yet often insufficiently acknowledged factor in literal interpretation that I introduced in chapter 3: *frame of reference*. My fundamental claim is that disagreements regarding literal interpretation have to do with the different frames of reference readers employ. Such decisions proceed as much from one's social imaginary as from philology proper, a claim I demonstrate by contrasting the *immanent* frame (and the modern secular imaginary that begat it) with a recent attempt to retrieve a *transcendent* frame of reference (associated with a premodern sacramental imaginary). This leads to an examination of the difference frames of reference make for reading the Old Testament and to the question, ought Christians to have a frame of reference that enables them to see the Old Testament as literally about Jesus Christ? The chapter concludes by observing the way the book of Hebrews reads the literal sense of Scripture christologically, thanks to a frame of reference that is as eschatological as it is historical.

Philology: Reading the Letter with Loving Attention

Philology—"the love of words" (*philia* + *logos*)—refers to the entire enterprise of attending to and understanding a work of written discourse.[5] What does it mean to love words and to give loving attention to the way the words go in biblical texts? The reading culture wars we examined in part 1 amount to differences in opinion on precisely this point. *Ad fontes*: to the original sources, yes! But with which frame(s) of reference?

4. Brevard Childs, "The *Sensus Literalis* of Scripture: An Ancient and Modern Problem," in *Beiträge zur alttestamentlichen Theologie: Festschrift für Walther Zimmerli Zum 70. Geburtstag*, ed. Herbert Donner, Robert Hanhart, and Rudolf Smend (Göttingen: Vandenhoeck & Ruprecht, 1977), 92. Surprisingly, there is no single monograph that provides a comprehensive historical survey and conceptual analysis of what "literal" means.

5. "The love of words" is the definition and last line of James Turner's *Philology: The Forgotten Origins of the Modern Humanities* (Princeton and Oxford: Princeton University Press, 2014), 386.

General and Special Philology

Erasmus was a Renaissance philologist who cared about getting the biblical text right. He devoted his knowledge of Hebrew, Greek, and Latin to the publication of the first critical edition of the Greek New Testament. Although he did not use the term *discourse*, his understanding of how words work agrees with what we said earlier about the Bible as divine/human: "It happens that not a little light is thrown on the understanding of the sense of Scripture if we weigh up not only what is said, but also by whom it is said, to whom it is said, in what words it is said, at what time, and on what occasion; what proceeds, and what follows."[6]

It is a crucial philological point: the interpreter's topic is not words in isolation, but discourse—*what someone says to someone about something at some time in some way for some purpose*. We have already discussed the divine author and purpose of biblical discourse. The present chapter focuses on two other elements: *what* someone says (the "sense" of discourse) and what something is said *about* (the "referent" of discourse).

Before we examine sense and reference, though, it may be worth noting that the disciplinary debates in divinity, about how to read the Bible, have their counterpart in the humanities. The historian of ideas James Turner bemoans the way that philology, which (like theology) used to be a unified enterprise, has devolved into a number of disparate studies that have gone their own disciplinary ways. Turner wants these estranged academic specializations to reunite into a "philological family."[7] Only such a reunion can effectively ground the human sciences and resist the encroachment of the natural sciences, which in the late nineteenth-century supplanted philology as the paradigm of knowledge. Ah, humanities! Ah, textual understanding! He mourns the loss of an agreed-upon set of principles for loving words and understanding texts largely because he views philology as central to many fields of knowledge, the "king of the sciences."[8] The parallel with the way biblical scholars and theologians have grown apart is striking. Turner acknowledges that both stories—the dissolution of biblical interpretation and of textual interpretation in general—are intertwined, joined at the hip by philology.[9]

Three tendencies have deposed the king. First, modern science, with its empirical testing and instrumental success, has displaced the humanities as the paradigm of knowledge in the university. Second, analytic philosophers began to understand their study as contrary to philology. "Philosophy was logical,

---

6. Desiderius Erasmus, *Ratio seu Methodus compendio perveniendi ad veram theologiam*, cited in John Barton, *The Nature of Biblical Criticism* (Louisville: Westminster John Knox, 2007), 128.

7. Turner, *Philology*, 383.

8. Turner, x.

9. Bernard Ramm highlighted the "philological principle" in his account of the Protestant system of hermeneutics (*Protestant Biblical Interpretation*, 113–15).

deductive, precise in conclusions. . . . Philology was interpreting, empirical, treating in probabilities."[10] The third factor was the dissolution of philology into divergent disciplinary fiefdoms, each with its own methods, jargon, and professional societies. "Scholars in the modern humanities . . . seek legitimacy by demonstrating expert control of separated territories."[11] What Turner sees as undermining the humanities, the loss of philology as an integrative discipline, was in my opinion a contributing factor to the undermining of *divinity*, the British academic term for the study of theology, and the task of understanding the word of God. To read the Bible theologically involves more than philology but not less.

Turner thinks that all would be well in the humanities if only they could get their philological groove back. Michael Legaspi is not so confident. The humanities require more than studying texts in their historical contexts: "Scholarship inevitably serves some larger vision of life. Scholarship is . . . the fruit of the culture to which scholars belong."[12] This is why we began our experiment in biblical-theological criticism by looking at competing reading cultures. For what lies at the core of a reading culture is also what is at the center of Augustine's two cities: an object of love that orients and motivates that city's work. At the center of humanities is the love of words. The philologist asks, "What do I love when I love these words?" Augustine asked, "What do I love when I love my God?" Christians who want to read the Bible theologically ask, "What do I love when I love the biblical words as the word of God?"

Rightly Ordering One's Love of Words and the Word

Biblical scholars think themselves more philologically inclined than theologians because biblical studies pays more attention to the particulars of the text than dogmatics.[13] To love words is to love everything about them: their etymologies, cognates, grammatical forms, historical *Sitz im Leben*, and so forth. Only a biblical scholar like James Barr could write an entire book on biblical words for time.[14] In our increasingly specialized times, however, many academic fields are devoted to the study of language: comparative, structuralist, evolutionary, and cognitive linguistics, to name but a few.[15] Our question—what do we love

10. Turner, *Philology*, 381.

11. Michael L. Legaspi, "The Consolation of Philology," *First Things*, October 2015, 66.

12. Legaspi, 67.

13. On love as involving attention, see Iris Murdoch, who defined attention as the "loving gaze directed upon an individual reality." Iris Murdoch, *Sovereignty of Good* (London: Routledge & Kegan Paul, 1970), 30. See also Martha Nussbaum, who calls for reading that is "finely aware and richly responsible." Martha C. Nussbaum, *Love's Knowledge: Essays on Philosophy and Literature* (Oxford: Oxford University Press, 1990), 84.

14. James Barr, *Biblical Words for Time* (London: SCM, 1962).

15. For the breadth of topics under "language sciences," see Patrick Colm Hogan, ed., *The Cambridge Encyclopedia of Language Sciences* (Cambridge: Cambridge University Press, 2010).

when we love the biblical words as the word of God?—becomes more urgent given this plethora of approaches.

For serious students of the Bible, the first step in giving loving attention to biblical words is to learn to read them in the original Hebrew and Greek. It is one thing to know a foreign language, however, quite another to know what speakers and writers are doing with it. We need a diversity of exegetical methods to do justice to the various dimensions of biblical discourse. For example, the insight that Matthew used the Gospel of Mark in composing his own gospel led to redaction criticism: the study of how editorial changes communicate their own intentionality and theological slant. By way of contrast, tradition criticism arises from the insight that certain biblical texts took shape over time, and that many "tradents" had a hand in the final product, leaving the reader the challenge of discerning and sorting the various layers of this handing on and the various circumstances that led to these developments.[16] Such critical approaches may be forms of loving attention. "To attend to something is to approach it with a just and loving eye, and therewith to perceive it in its unbounded particularity and complexity and so as it truly is."[17] It is important to keep in mind, however, that written discourse is multifaceted. Several critical methods may be valid, but they may be pursuing different agendas, different interpretive interests, different loves. What we need is an integrative approach that pursues all relevant lines of inquiry. Call it *philological* criticism.

C. S. Lewis was a philologist *par excellence*. His loving attention to all things lexical is on display in his *Studies in Words*, in which he offered sundry field reports from his lifelong observations of words in their "native habitat."[18] According to Lewis, "Language exists to communicate what it can communicate,"[19] though readers must be alert to the myriad ways authors have used words at different times and for different purposes. Context is all important: "When someone speaks about the Stations of the Cross we do not think about railway stations nor about our station in life."[20] If we are not alert and attentive to an author's particular communicative intent, we are liable to read the words as if we had written them, and in that case, "What we get may still be . . . a poem; but it will be our poem and not his."[21] This may be a forgivable lapse in a high school English essay, but it is a serious offense when, in reading Scripture, one substitutes one's own word for God's. For Lewis, the philologist's vocation was

16. For redaction, tradition, and other forms of criticism, see further Richard N. Soulen and R. Kendall Soulen, *Handbook of Biblical Criticism*, 4th ed. (Louisville: Westminster John Knox, 2011).

17. Bridget Clarke, "Iris Murdoch and the Prospects for Critical Moral Perception," in *Iris Murdoch, Philosopher*, ed. Justin Broackes (Oxford: Oxford University Press, 2012), 236.

18. C. S. Lewis, *Studies in Words*, 2nd ed. (Cambridge: Cambridge University Press, 1967), 2.

19. Lewis, *Studies in Words*, 313.

20. Lewis, *Studies in Words*, 11.

21. Lewis, *Studies in Words*, 11.

modest and straightforward: "Find out what the author actually wrote and what the hard words meant and what the allusions were to, and you have done far more for me than a hundred new interpretations . . . could ever do."[22]

Fittingly, Lewis pointed out that "sense" derives from the Latin *sentire* ("to perceive, feel, know") and suggested that when it pertains to meaning and interpretation, it is probably a figurative use of literally finding one's way. Biblical scholars are keen for theologians to respect the philological principle: to love and do justice to the biblical texts by attending to their literal sense, following the way the words go. From the biblical scholar's standpoint, theological interpretation goes wrong, or gets lost, whenever it imports doctrinal concerns that are foreign to the historical author's communicative intent. Such incursions risk violating Lewis's afore-mentioned philological principle.

The etymology of philology (the *philo* or love of *logos*) suggests another possible meaning of the term. The prologue to John's gospel introduces Jesus as the *logos* who was with God in the beginning, was God, and who became flesh (John 1:1–18). Moreover, the Logos who became flesh uses human *logoi* (words) to speak about himself. "In John, Jesus is what *is* spoken even as he *does* the speaking."[23] How one responds to the words of the Word is, for John, a matter of eternal life or death. Moreover, love for the Word entails keeping or obeying his words (John 14:21, 24). According to John Webster, Holy Scripture is set-apart human discourse appointed by the Son himself as a means of his self-attestation: "Here, too, in the matter of his coming to be known, he is 'before all things' (Col 1:17)." If language exists to communicate what it can communicate, then Christian theologians contend that biblical language exists to communicate Christ.[24] What philologists of Scripture ultimately love about biblical words is that *they are the words the Word speaks.*

It is not my intent to prolong the reading culture wars that have alienated biblical studies and systematic theology. On the contrary, my aim is to resolve the interpretive conflict (blessed are the hermeneutical peacemakers). The way forward is to show that the two principles, philological and christological, stand in complementary rather than competitive relation to one another. There need be no contradiction between loving biblical words and the living Word, nor between loving the textual letter and the light of Christ that shines through it.[25]

We need not assume that biblical scholars are the only ones who attend to biblical words with loving attention. Both biblical scholars and theologians can

22. Lewis, *Experiment in Criticism*, 121.

23. Robert H. Gundry, *Jesus the Word according to John the Sectarian* (Grand Rapids: Eerdmans, 2002), 49.

24. John Webster, *The Domain of the Word: Scripture and Theological Reason* (London: T&T Clark, 2012), 35.

25. Part 3 will give a more systematic account of reading the Bible in the economy of light.

give loving attention to the letter, then, but they may do so in different ways and at different levels. The point is worth repeating: both biblical scholars and theologians can be biblical. There is a difference between the way the words go (sense) and the destination at which they eventually arrive (referent). As Peter Leithart notes, "We get at the riches of Scripture precisely by luxuriating in the letter."[26] If there is a conflict between their respective reading cultures, then, it concerns how best to attend to the letter of the text, or how to order one's philological and christological loves. More pointedly, does loving the letter mean attending to what is said (sense) or to what it is said about (referent)?

Literality (Part 1): Construing the Sense of the Letter

Theologians throughout church history have acknowledged the literal sense as the authoritative touchstone in doctrinal disputes. The key questions have always been "Where stands it written?" and "What does it say?" Pius XII, in his important 1943 papal encyclical on biblical scholarship, *Divino Afflante Spiritu*, agreed with Aquinas when it described discovering and expounding the literal sense as the exegete's "foremost and greatest endeavor."[27] Roman Catholics and Protestants agree: theological truth must be in accordance with "the way the words run."[28] To identify Scripture as divine discourse fixed by writing is to agree with Warfield: "What Scripture says, God says."[29] Even twentieth-century theologians like Dietrich Bonhoeffer insisted, "The exact wording must be taken seriously."[30] Authority bereft of meaningful content is all bark, no bite. What Christians believe—sound doctrine—depends on what the Bible says. It is one thing to have a high view of Scripture but quite another to read it rightly; alas, the one does not necessarily lead to the other.

The Challenge of Reading "according to the Letter"

Despite widespread agreement that literality matters for exegesis and theology, we lack consensus on what it means to read "according to the letter." Our

---

26. Peter Leithart, *Deep Exegesis: The Mystery of Reading Scripture* (Waco, TX: Baylor University Press, 2009), vii.

27. *Divino Afflante Spiritu*, §23, https://www.vatican.va/content/pius-xii/en/encyclicals/documents/hf_p-xii_enc_30091943_divino-afflante-spiritu.html.

28. Lewis Ayres, *Nicaea and Its Legacy: An Approach to Fourth-Century Trinitarian Theology* (Oxford: Oxford University Press, 2004), 32, who takes the phrase from Eugene Rogers's translation of Thomas Aquinas's *circumstantia litterae* (*De Potentia*, q. 4, a.1, c). William Tyndale earlier referred to "the way the words go" in the prologue to his translation of the Pentateuch.

29. B. B. Warfield, "Inspiration," in *The International Standard Bible Encyclopedia*, vol. 3, ed. James Orr (Chicago: Howard-Severance, 1915), 1473–83.

30. Dietrich Bonhoeffer, *Theological Education at Finkenwalde: 1935–1937*, ed. Mark Brocker and H. Gaylon Barker (Minneapolis: Fortress, 2013), 541.

first task is to say what literal interpretation is *not*. This involves distinguishing *literal* from *literalistic*. Much depends on distinguishing the kind of literal interpretation associated with philology from more popular forms of literalism that yield overly literalistic interpretations that are tone-deaf to the way words actually work.

To read *ad litteram* means reading "according to the letter" (from Lat. *littera*).[31] A. J. Jacobs illustrates one extreme version of what this might mean in his best-selling satire, *The Year of Living Biblically: One Man's Humble Quest to Follow the Bible as Literally as Possible*.[32] Most of the book recounts the absurd situations he gets into by strictly applying rules meant for ancient Israel in modern-day Manhattan, for example, "stoning" blasphemers—with pebbles. The book reinforces the popular prejudice against biblical literalism: it is irrelevant, out of touch, and, ironically enough, *unlettered*—a crude, uncultured way of reading according to the letter so strictly that it ends up becoming a kind of illiteracy.[33] A "literalistic" interpretation tries to follow the way the words go *without attending to the context of their use*. As such, it is a superficial form of reading, hence its negative connotation. Problems emerge when we fail to distinguish literalistic from literal readings.

Early Christians sometimes associated literalistic interpretations with Jewish readers who were unable to see past the letter to that to which it pointed: Jesus Christ. On the other hand, Luther championed the literal sense in contrast to allegorical readings, which he worried made Scripture into a nose of wax, easily twisted. However, simply contrasting literal with either literalistic or allegorical falls short of saying what the literal sense *is*. Interestingly, the Reformers' invective against allegorizing did not prevent them from reading the Old Testament christologically, a paradox that led one Reformation historian to conclude, "Protestant literalism is nowhere near so literal as it wants us to be."[34] Today people often use *literal* for emphasis, often in a nonliteral way, as in "Vanhoozer's lecture was literally electrifying" (no, it wasn't) or "Vanhoozer's lecture was so convoluted, I literally died of boredom" (no, you didn't). Everyone uses the term, then, but few are able to say exactly

31. According to David Bentley Hart, ancient and medieval exegetes read Scripture "with an exactingly scrupulous attention to what was written on the page, in every detail, and with every discernible shade of significance." "*Ad Litteram*," in *A Splendid Wickedness and Other Essays* (Grand Rapids: Eerdmans, 2016), 275.

32. A. J. Jacobs, *The Year of Living Biblically: One Man's Humble Quest to Follow the Bible as Literally as Possible* (New York: Simon & Schuster, 2007). The book also spawned "Living Biblically," a short-lived CBS television sitcom that aired in 2018.

33. Adrian Thatcher goes further, arguing that literal interpretation produces not simply comic but tragic effects, including corporal punishment, racism, and colonialism. "The Literal Sense of Scripture: A Hermeneutical Disaster," *Modern Believing* 53, no. 1 (2012): 5–12.

34. Brian Cummings, "Protestant Allegory," in *The Cambridge Companion to Allegory*, ed. Rita Copeland and Peter T. Struck (Cambridge: Cambridge University Press, 2010), 185.

what *literal* means. Like Augustine with time: we know what it (literality) is—until someone asks us.[35]

Frances Young dismisses *literal* as a "thoroughly ambiguous" term, of no help in enabling us to understand how biblical interpreters read in accordance with the letter: "The inadequacy of the term 'literal' for making meaningful distinctions in the history of exegesis is equaled by its inadequacy for understanding what is going on in modern discussions, especially at the popular level."[36] This leads us to ask, does literal interpretation actually exist? It is conspicuous by its absence from the two-volume *Oxford Encyclopedia of Biblical Interpretation*, which examines over fifty types of interpretation, including ethnic (e.g., African American, Latina/o, Korean), confessional (e.g., Wesleyan, Lutheran, Pentecostal), liberative (e.g., feminist, transgender, womanist), critical (e.g., historical, narrative, disability), and thematic (e.g., economics, orality, pop culture), but not "literal."[37] It would appear that Brevard Childs's statement remains as true today as when he first made it five decades ago: "There are few more perplexing and yet important problems in the history of biblical interpretation than the issue of defining what is meant by the *sensus literalis* of a text."[38]

Models of Literality: A Fivefold Typology

In popular usage, "literal" expresses the straightforward meaning of an utterance. In scholarly treatments, literal interpretation typically focuses on the verbal, authorial, or historical dimension of an utterance.[39] The contrast in both cases is with "figural" speech, which has another meaning in addition to the literal. The reality is more complex. The best way to understand the various uses of "literal" is to set out a fivefold typology, according to which the literal is the (1) verbal, (2) authorial, (3) historical, (4) literary, or (5) "ruled" sense.

Verbal Sense

The *Catechism of the Catholic Church* defines the literal sense as "the meaning conveyed by the words of Scripture and discovered by exegesis."[40] Groups of letters acquire conventional meanings when they become recognizable words in a particular language: *pain* means one thing in English but something else in French ("bread"). The literal meaning is the dictionary meaning, a description of how speakers ordinarily use a word in a particular language.

---

35. See Augustine, *Confessions*, bk. 11.

36. Frances Young, "Literal Meaning," in *Dictionary for Theological Interpretation of the Bible*, 401.

37. See *The Oxford Encyclopedia of Biblical Interpretation*, ed. Steven L. McKenzie, 2 vols. (Oxford: Oxford University Press, 2013).

38. Childs, "The *Sensus Literalis* of Scripture," 80.

39. See, e.g., Kathryn Greene-McCreight, "Literal Sense," in *Dictionary for Theological Interpretation of the Bible*, 455–56.

40. *Catechism of the Catholic Church* (New York and London: Doubleday, 1995), art. 116.

While it is tempting to define the literal sense in terms of verbal meaning, it rests on a mistaken assumption, namely, that every word has a basic, context-independent meaning—its "proper" meaning. In reality, most words have a range of possible uses: the "semantic range" of a term is the sum total of potential meanings a given word has at a given time. Time is a relevant factor because verbal usage is not fixed in stone. Words have histories, with varied contexts and multiple uses; you can no more control the way words go than you can direct the wind (as we are seeing with *literal* itself).

Authorial Sense

It is important not to confuse sentence meaning with speaker meaning. "He's hot" may seem to be a straightforward predication, but what it actually means depends on the context of its utterance, which might be a hospital, tennis tournament, casino, or college mixer. The verbally encoded information (the sentence) underdetermines the literal sense (what a speaker is doing with it). Sentences alone are often not sufficient for understanding how the words go.

Reading according to the letter on this second view is a function of language use by persons in particular contexts.[41] The central claim is that meaning is purposive communicative action: authors *actualize* the semantic potential of words by using them in particular ways. Meaning is thus a species of intentional action by personal agents. "All actions have intentions . . . and all intentions envision some action."[42] However, psychological intention alone (*intending to*) is not enough. Meaning is an affair not of consciousness but of intentional communicative action: what authors *do* with words. Whether the literal sense includes not only what an author explicitly says but also implies (the technical term is "implicature") is a topic of ongoing discussion.[43] Still, those inclined to identify the literal sense with authorial intention agree that interpretation is a matter of inferring the author's communicative intent from the way an author has put the words in motion, directing them to "run" in a particular direction.

Some would describe as literal only those speech acts where the words run in the conventional way; others insist that the literal sense just is the author's intended sense, or senses, conventional or not.[44] In any case, this combination

---

41. See further Dan Sperber and Deirdre Wilson, "Pragmatics," in *The Oxford Handbook of Contemporary Philosophy*, ed. Frank Jackson and Michael Smith (Oxford: Oxford University Press, 2007), 468–95.

42. John Farrell, *The Varieties of Authorial Intention: Literary Theory beyond the Intentional Fallacy* (London: Palgrave Macmillan, 2017), 21.

43. H. P. Grice coined the term *implicature* in his essay "Logic and Conversation," in *Studies in the Ways of Words* (Cambridge, MA: Harvard University Press, 1989), 22–40.

44. John Lennox uses the term *literalistic* to designate a word's ordinary (i.e., verbal) sense and *literal* for the sense intended by the author. *Seven Days That Divide the World: The Beginning according to Genesis and Science* (Grand Rapids: Zondervan, 2011), 25.

of the verbal (words) and occasional (the particular context of their use), the semantic and the pragmatic, gives rise to what has become a standard definition of the literal sense: "The sense which the human author directly intended and which the written words conveyed."[45] This approaches what Luther had in mind when, in debate with Erasmus, he rejected allegorizing: "Instead, we must everywhere stick to the simple, pure, and natural sense of the words that accords with rules of grammar and the normal use of language."[46]

Many biblical interpreters—including Roman Catholics, evangelicals, and mainline Protestants—agree that the literal sense of Scripture "is that which has been expressed directly by the inspired human authors."[47] To affirm biblical inspiration is to affirm that "this sense is also intended by God, as principal author."[48] The question of whether God accommodates his intention so that it corresponds without remainder to that of the human author, or whether the divine authorial intent makes words *run further* than their human authors could have intended, is an important point to which we shall return below. Be that as it may, if literal meaning is a function of authorial intent, it is fixed for all time, for "actions taken in the past, including artistic utterances, cannot change, however much our understanding of them [may]."[49]

Historical Sense

A third view identifies the literal sense with the historical referent, the physical thing or event in the world to which the words run (i.e., point, signify). Vincent Crapanzano, an anthropologist, says that a culture of literalism pervades modern America's religious and secular life, particularly in two places: conservative evangelicalism and the Supreme Court. He describes literalism as a style of interpretation, characterized by a focus on the referential function of language, an unambiguous correlation of word and thing, a single commonsense meaning of words, and an emphasis on "originalism."[50]

James Barr defined the literal in terms of physicality: "Physicality affords a simple, commonsense, one-to-one correspondence between the entities referred to and the words of the text."[51] This fits well into the modern social imaginary, in which the real is the empirical. Interestingly, Barr thought fundamentalists and

---

45. Raymond E. Brown, "Hermeneutics," in Brown, ed., *New Jerome Biblical Commentary* (Englewood Cliffs, NJ: Prentice Hall, 1990), 1148.

46. Martin Luther, "On the Bondage of the Will," in *Luther and Erasmus: Free Will and Salvation*, trans. E. Gordon Rupp and Philip S. Watson (Philadelphia: Westminster, 1959), 221.

47. J. L Houlden, ed., *The Interpretation of the Bible in the Church* (London: SCM, 1995), 52.

48. Houlden, 52.

49. Farrell, *Varieties of Authorial Intention*, 241.

50. Vincent Crapanzano, *Serving the Word: Literalism in America from the Pulpit to the Bench* (New York: New Press, 2000), 2–3.

51. James Barr, "Literality," *Faith and Philosophy* 6 (1989): 415.

modernists agree that literal meaning equals historical correspondence, though fundamentalists believe the Bible is literally true while modernists either reserve judgment or take a more skeptical view. For his part, Rowan Williams, former archbishop of Canterbury, objects to this "disastrous shrinkage" of the literal sense to a one-to-one correspondence with historical fact.[52]

"Taking the Bible literally" meant something different to premodern Christian readers for whom history meant the true story of what God had said and done in history. Although they acknowledged that the people, things, and events that make up the biblical story may mean *more* than history, they do not mean *less*. Premodern readers did not even think of distinguishing a historical reality *behind* the textual account. For example, Augustine saw the literal sense of Genesis as *historia*, a true account of what happened, the basis for further transhistorical truths (i.e., spiritual senses). Similarly, in the *City of God*, Augustine argued that the Genesis account of Eden can be understood in a spiritual sense as Paradise without sacrificing the historical truth of what happened in a real place on earth. While Augustine was open to interpreting the river that flowed out of Eden to become four rivers as referring to the four classic virtues or the four gospels, he nevertheless insisted on their literal meaning too: "No one, then, forbids us to understand Paradise according to these, and perhaps other, more appropriate, allegorical interpretations, while also believing in the truth of that story as presented to us in a most faithful narrative of events."[53]

Literary Sense

More recently, Hans Frei emphasized the literary or narrative nature of biblical history, largely as a reaction to modern biblical criticism's tendency to identify the literal sense with its historical referent.[54] Frei thought the modern interest in "what *actually* happened" inclines readers to treat biblical narrative as a source, not a story with its own literary integrity. Paul Noble explains, "For the Reformers, the literal sense was a *literary* sense; but for critical scholars it became 'literalistic.'"[55] Frei insisted that the literal sense of biblical narrative is the story itself, not some truth or moral to which the story may refer or represent.[56] His point is subtle yet important. For Frei, the literal sense is bound to the literary form. The literal meaning of biblical narrative is the story itself, a

52. Rowan Williams, "The Literal Sense of Scripture," *Modern Theology* 7 (1990): 124.

53. Augustine, *The City of God against the Pagans*, bk. XIII, 21, trans. R. W. Dyson (Cambridge: Cambridge University Press, 1998), 568–69.

54. Interestingly, the French term *histoire* can mean either "story" or "history."

55. Paul R. Noble, "The *Sensus Literalis*: Jowett, Childs, and Barr," *Journal of Theological Studies* 54 (1993), 15.

56. See Hans Frei, *The Eclipse of Biblical Narrative: A Study in Eighteenth and Nineteenth Century Hermeneutics* (New Haven, CT: Yale University Press, 1974).

function of the world *within* rather than *behind*, the text.[57] As such, it is history-like (not history-lite).

Brevard Childs identified the literal with the literary as well, though the form he had in mind was not narrative but the Christian canon in its entirety, the "final form" of the biblical texts: "I am convinced that when the Reformers spoke of the literal sense of the Biblical text as normative (*sensus literalis*) they had in mind the canonical sense and not a hypothetical projection of what scholars thought originally happened."[58] Childs, like Frei, insisted that the literal sense is that to which the biblical texts bear witness in their literary form. According to Frei, "Calvin, like Luther, saw Christ as the subject matter of the whole Bible."[59] Childs agreed: "For Calvin, the *sensus literalis* IS Jesus Christ."[60] To interpret literally, according to this fourth view, is to grasp the content of the text in, under, and through its literary form.

Plain or "Ruled" Sense

Strictly speaking, *canon* correlates with a particular community for whom its texts are considered authoritative: the church. Our final model for understanding literality therefore puts the accent on the community of faith, the social location of the biblical canon, not its literary form. This model ties literal sense to the common usage not of its author but of its recipients: "The plain sense is 'the way the words run' *for a community in the light of that community's techniques for following the argument of texts.*"[61] The literal sense becomes the "plain" sense, the sense taken as obvious by a particular interpretive community that reads the Bible as its canonical Scripture. Literality is thus a combination of the verbal sense and *ruled* reading, Katherine Greene-McCreight's term for reading in accordance with a community's rule of faith.[62]

What counts as literal on this model is a function of *ruled reading practices*. Disagreement over how best to describe the nature and authority of these rules complicates the picture, however. On the one side are those who privilege the interpretive community's ingrained instincts: "The plain sense is a consensus reading."[63] For example, Lewis Ayres defines the literal sense as "that which results

57. We shall return to Frei's account of biblical narrative in the following section.

58. Brevard Childs, "The Old Testament as Scripture of the Church," *Concordia Theological Monthly* 43 (1972): 721.

59. Frei, *Eclipse of Biblical Narrative*, 20.

60. Cited in Daniel R. Driver, *Brevard Childs, Biblical Theologian: For the Church's One Bible* (Grand Rapids: Baker Academic, 2010), 92 (emphasis original).

61. Ayres, *Nicaea and Its Legacy*, 32 (emphasis added).

62. Kathryn Greene-McCreight, *Ad Litteram: How Augustine, Calvin, and Barth Read the "Plain Sense" of Genesis 1–3* (New York: Peter Lang, 1999), ix.

63. Kathryn Tanner, "Theology and the Plain Sense," in *Scriptural Authority and Narrative Interpretation*, ed. Garrett Green (Philadelphia: Fortress, 1987), 63.

from ascribing to the words, phrases, and other textual units the meaning that is commonly given them by reasonably well-educated readers in a reading community."[64] Community consensus becomes the stabilizing factor—the rule—for determining the literal sense. Ayres maintains that the early church canonized not simply a particular set of texts but "a particular set of reading methods."[65] We could say of this first option that the literal sense is the plain *ecclesial* sense. The weakness of this position is twofold, however: (1) It is difficult to determine *which* reading community's practices should rule. (2) There is a risk that the community's readings are simply self-fulfilling prophecies, deaf to the possibility that they may have misconstrued the text: "the plain sense of a text is not considered here as if it were anything 'in itself,' apart from an interpretive practice of using texts. . . . The plain sense is itself a product of an interpretive tradition."[66]

Perhaps to avoid these potential weaknesses, Brevard Childs proposed an alternative way of relating the rule of faith to Scripture's literal sense. The canon (Gk. *kanon* = "rule") is not simply a list of authoritative books but also "the rule that delineates the area in which the church hears the word of God."[67] The canon provides the rule for its own reading by providing the necessary context for discerning *what it is about*: "Exegesis does not confine itself to registering only the verbal sense of the text, but presses forward through the text to the subject matter (*res*) to which it points."[68] The two-testament Bible thus lives up to its own standards concerning lawful testimony (cf. Deut 19:15). When read canonically, the Old Testament and New Testament together witness to the Father's plan to create a holy nation in the Son through the Spirit.

Augustine made a similar point centuries before: "We find scattered through the scriptures, and marked out by learned Catholic expositors of them, a kind of canonical rule, which we hold on to most firmly, about how our Lord Jesus Christ is to be understood to be God's Son."[69] Childs and Augustine thus envisaged a kind of ruled reading that is text based rather than community based. What "rules"—guides and governs—our reading of the Bible on this view is the canon itself. The rule of faith is not an invention but a discovery of the community, and what the rule discovers is what the canon is essentially about.[70]

64. Lewis Ayres, "The Word Answering the Word: Opening the Space of Catholic Biblical Interpretation," in *Theological Theology: Essays in Honour of John Webster*, ed. R. David Nelson, Darren Sarisky, and Justin Stratis (London: Bloomsbury T&T Clark, 2015), 41n7.

65. Ayres, "Word Answering the Word, 40.

66. Tanner, "Theology and the Plain Sense," 64. For more on the problems associated with adopting an extracanonical or "communitarian" rule of faith, see John C. Peckham, *Canonical Theology: The Biblical Canon, Sola Scriptura, and Theological Method* (Grand Rapids: Eerdmans, 2016), 124–30.

67. Brevard Childs, *Biblical Theology in Crisis* (Philadelphia: Westminster, 1970), 99.

68. Brevard Childs, "Toward Recovering Theological Exegesis," *Ex Auditu* 16 (2000): 123.

69. Augustine, *The Trinity*, 2nd ed. (Hyde Park, NY: New City, 2015), II.1.2 (98).

70. See further Ched Spellman, *Toward a Canon-Conscious Reading of the Bible: Exploring the History and Hermeneutics of the Canon* (Sheffield: Sheffield Phoenix, 2014).

Though the idea of letting doctrine "rule" one's reading of Scripture may sound unbiblical, the intent is precisely the reverse: "To be guided under the authority of sound doctrine, then, means practically the same thing as *canonical* literal reading, using Scripture to interpret Scripture. Put simply, to be ruled is to be scriptural and vice versa."[71] There is therefore a sense in which "ruled reading" is simply another way of describing biblical reasoning.[72]

Ruled reading in this second sense is a way of reading Scripture *biblically* and of giving pride of place to the *canonical* usage of words in determining their literal sense. This comes close to what John Peckham calls "intrinsic canonicity," where Scripture is understood "as the corpus of writings commissioned by God to be the 'rule' or 'standard' of Christian faith and practice."[73] What ultimately rules reading—and thus what constitutes the "plain sense"—turns out to be a function of *sola Scriptura*.[74] Greene-McCreight comes to a similar conclusion in her book-length study of how Augustine, Calvin, and Barth understood the plain sense: "Ruled reading is an 'intra-biblical' and not an extra-textual explanatory device. That is, the prior understanding of what the biblical texts are 'about' is taken from scripture and not from a set of external philosophical or scientific commitments and reapplied to scripture. . . . Ruled reading thus allows scripture to interpret itself."[75]

The two types of ruled reading we have just surveyed—call them the *communal* and the *canonical*—stand in tension with each another. Olivier-Thomas Venard compares them to two asymptotes, two lines that approach the same curve but never quite meet.[76] Greene-McCreight speaks of countervailing forces: "The concern to honor verbal sense pulls the reader toward 'static exegesis' . . . while Ruled reading pulls the reader toward (limited) 'dynamic' exegesis."[77] Hans Frei's question about the literal sense remains as apt and urgent as ever: Does it stretch or will it break?[78]

---

71. David Graham, "Defending Biblical Literalism: Augustine on the Literal Sense," *Pro Ecclesia* 25, no. 2 (2016): 179.

72. For a book-length argument along these lines, see R. B. Jamieson and Tyler R. Wittman, *Biblical Reasoning: Christological and Trinitarian Rules for Exegesis* (Grand Rapids: Baker Academic, 2022).

73. Peckham, *Canonical Theology*, 19.

74. Peckham: "The practitioner of canonical *sola Scriptura* posits the canon itself as rule not because she naively thinks the canon requires no interpretation but because she does not believe *any* rule or normative interpreter (other than God) could actually eliminate hermeneutical diversity" (*Canonical Theology*, 134).

75. Greene-McCreight, *Ad Litteram*, 248.

76. See his essay "Les deux asymptotes," in *Le sens littéral des Écritures*, ed. Olivier-Thomas Venard (Paris: Cerf, 2009).

77. Greene-McCreight, *Ad Litteram*, 246.

78. Hans Frei, "The 'Literal Reading' of Biblical Narrative in the Christian Tradition: Does It Stretch or Will It Break?," in *The Bible and the Narrative Tradition*, ed. Frank McConnell (Oxford: Oxford University Press, 1986), 36–77.

Literality (Part 2): Toward Which Frame of Reference?

The preceding survey began by examining the literal sense and ended with a consideration of literal reference. What ultimately rules reading, and literal interpretation, is the particular frame of reference that filters the words' sense, allowing what is being talked about to come into focus. The reason we lack a consensus as concerns literality "is that interpreters over the centuries see this same 'literal sense' through a different set of spectacles."[79] Consider, for example, the contrast between confessional and scientific exegesis (or as Don Collett calls them, Nicene and scientific reason), respectively: "It is helpful to think of these two frames of reference as contrasting rules of faith for relating Scripture's literal sense to the theological reality of which it speaks."[80] The present section builds on this crucial insight that literal interpretation is beholden to frames of reference.

What readers take as the "plain" or literal sense depends on which particular frame of reference they employ. It follows that reading "according to the letter" always involves something in addition to the letter. Exegesis without presuppositions is not possible, for literal interpretation always involves a frame of reference, whether we acknowledge it or not. Different frames of reference—whether critical, confessional, or contextual—function as ersatz rules of faith.[81] In thesis form: What "ruled reading" rules is one's choice of frame of reference, and one's frame of reference affects how we read "according to the letter." In this chapter and the next, I make the case that we need all five models of literality discussed above in order to do justice to the Bible as human-divine discourse.[82]

On the Very Idea of a Frame of Reference

The idea of a "frame of reference" is conspicuous by its absence from most hermeneutic textbooks, yet its influence is enormous and undeniable. It is the lens through which the plain sense comes into view, enabling readers to say what the words they are reading are *about* (i.e., the referential dimension of discourse). The conflict over literal interpretation boils down to choices about divergent frames of reference. Some analysis of this important concept is therefore in order.

---

79. G. T. Sheppard and Anthony Thiselton, "Biblical Interpretation in the Eighteenth and Nineteenth Centuries," in *Dictionary of Major Biblical Interpreters*, ed. Donald K. McKim, 2nd ed. (Downers Grove, IL: InterVarsity, 2007), 45.

80. Don C. Collett, *Figural Reading and the Old Testament: Theology and Practice* (Grand Rapids: Baker Academic, 2020), 161.

81. In the following two chapters, I argue for the superiority of a properly theological frame of reference, generated and governed by a scriptural imaginary and canonical rule of faith.

82. My overarching claim will be that literal meaning is equivalent to discourse meaning. Each of the five models calls attention to various aspects of discourse.

Sense and Reference

We owe the conceptual distinction between sense and reference to an 1892 essay by Gottlob Frege, the father of analytic philosophy.[83] The *sense* of a word or text pertains to one's mental concept of an object; the *referent* is the real-world object to which that sense or concept corresponds. "The morning star" and the "the evening star" both refer to the planet Venus, but under very different descriptions.

My definition of discourse—what someone says to someone about something at some time in some way for some purpose—involves more but not less than sense and reference.[84] Frege's German term for reference, *Bedeutung*, derives from the verb *deuten* ("to point towards"). It reminds us that discourse is always *about* something. As Augustine knew, signs indicate things. While the *sense* is "what someone says," the *reference* is that about which that something is said. Literal meaning and interpretation involve both sense (what is said) and reference (that about which something is said). The literal *sense* is the *way* words run; the literal *referent* is that *to which* the words run.

Frames of Reference in General

Frances Young contends that the real source of the confusion over "literal" interpretation is, and always has been, disagreement over how to answer the question, "What does the text refer to?"[85] This was what patristic debates over literal and allegorical interpretation were really about: the question of reference.[86] It is a crucially important insight. The sense of discourse is relatively easy to pinpoint using the tools of philology (*hapax legomena*—terms that occur only once—are the exception to the rule because it is harder to get a sense of their semantic range). Discerning what a discourse is *about* requires more than dictionary skills, however.

In the context of physics, a frame of reference is a coordinate system that allows observers to determine where an object is, which direction it is going, and how fast.[87] In the context of everyday experience, the earth is our frame of reference, which is why we speak of the sun rising and setting (i.e., in relation to the earth's horizon). A frame of reference is that set of ideas and assumptions that inform and influence the way we make sense of things. In the context of literary

---

83. Gottlob Frege, "On Sense and Reference," in *Translations from the Philosophical Writings of Gottlob Frege*, ed. Peter Geach and Max Black, 3rd ed. (Oxford: Blackwell, 1980), 56–78.

84. Note that this definition includes the various dimensions of discourse, including its content, author, addressee, referent, manner, occasion, and aim.

85. Young, "Literal Meaning," 401.

86. Frances M. Young, *Biblical Exegesis and the Formation of Christian Culture* (Cambridge: Cambridge University Press, 1997), 119–38.

87. The laws of physics are invariant, but our observations are relative to our own frame of reference. As Einstein pointed out, if we were traveling at the speed of light, time would appear to stop.

interpretation, a frame of reference refers to all the things that influence how a reader attends to the letter of the text, and thus to what the reader sees there.

Think of a frame of reference as what structures the interpreter's house. It is the set of assumptions with which an interpreter is most "at home." A frame of reference is something we inhabit and look through, a window that opens out onto the text. Windows both limit what can be seen and frame the way we see the world outside. This is precisely what a frame of reference does: it predisposes readers to attend to the letter in certain ways rather than others and gives them an initial sense of what to look and listen for.

Different frames of reference privilege certain contexts and not others. I have been speaking of "the way the words go," a paraphrase of Thomas Aquinas's *circumstantia litterae* ("the circumstances of the letters").[88] To see something in context is to identify the relevant circumstances that make that thing intelligible. If the literal sense pertains to the way words go or run, then *context* specifies the kind of ground under their feet—the circumstances of a particular discourse. For example, if readers inhabit a frame of reference that privileges authorial discourse, they will privilege the author's original historical context.

To get a better handle on the role of frames of reference in textual interpretation, consider Jane Austen's 1816 novel *Emma*. Literary critics agree on the basic plot: girl wants girl to meet boy; girl attempts to make the ideal match; girl meets her match. The basic story—what is said, the *sense*—is straightforward. Not so its reference. Literary critics debate what *Emma* is really about: masculinity, social status, women's liberation? Something else? One collection of critical essays devotes half the book to helping readers place *Emma* in its original cultural milieu. The frame of reference here for these essays is decidedly sociohistorical. One author attends to Austen's cultural background: the essay includes photographs of various objects Austen refers to in the story, such as "a large-sized square pianoforté." Other essays adopt very different frames of reference, reflecting the varied interests (and contexts) of twenty-first-century readers. Several critics read *Emma* in light of current debates over gender, with a particular interest in the novel's representation of masculinity (through the characterization of Emma's father and Mr. Knightley). One critic adopts a Marxist frame of reference and focuses on the social realities of class and status. Another reads the novel with an overriding interest in the question, "Is Jane Austen a feminist?"[89]

Critical dispute over the meaning of *Emma* continues. Note well: Austen's English is not the problem; her prose is a model of grammatical correctness. The

88. Thomas Aquinas, *De Potentia* 4.1, https://isidore.co/aquinas/QDdePotentia4.htm.
89. See further the essays in *Emma: A Case Study in Contemporary Criticism*, ed. Alistair M. Duckworth (Boston: Bedford and New York: St. Martin's, 2002).

real issue pertains to what *Emma* is really about: masculinity, femininity, social class, courtship and marriage, something else? The conflict of interpretations over *Emma* boils down to contrasting frames of reference. Modern critics reflect modern values and interests, and probably the various literary theories prevalent in the schools that socialized them into academic reading cultures. And this is the key point: frames of reference are functions of reading cultures, and reading cultures, as we have seen, are cultivated by the prevailing social imaginaries. All three—frame of reference, reading culture, and social imaginary—shape the expectations readers bring to texts, both as to "what there *is*" (in the world), and "what is *there*" (in the text).

Framing the Problem: "We Wish to See Jesus" (John 12:21)

Walter Moberly, an Old Testament scholar, mentions frames of reference so often in his *Old Testament Theology* that "frame of reference" has an entry in his subject index.[90] This is understandable, for everything in Old Testament exegesis depends on what one thinks it is about. As Heiko Oberman explained, "Since early in the history of the Christian Church, the Old Testament has posed the chief exegetical problem to the biblical interpreters."[91] To see why this is so, we have only to ask whether Christian readers are right to see Christ in the Old Testament.

What ought to rule a Christian reading of the Old Testament? Which frame(s) of reference may we legitimately use, and whence comes their legitimacy? The question has proved controversial since the early church: Can Christians read the Hebrew Scriptures as testimony to Jesus Christ without doing violence to the letter of the text? To put it bluntly, is the Old Testament *literally* about Jesus Christ?

We are transitioning from *Emma* to Esther, and all the other books in the Old Testament, but the issue is the same: Which frame of reference allows us to see what these texts are really about? A good case can be made for reading the Old Testament within a Jewish frame of reference: insofar as the Old Testament is Hebrew Scripture, it belongs first and foremost in the Jewish synagogue, to be interpreted according to Judaism's rule of faith. However, patristic and medieval Christians often dismissed Jewish readings as "all letter, no spirit." This slight makes many contemporary biblical scholars and theologians uncomfortable; some are no longer inclined to appropriate the Hebrew Scriptures for Christian

90. See the various entries under "frame of reference" in Walter Moberly, *Old Testament Theology: Reading the Hebrew Bible as Christian Scripture* (Grand Rapids: Baker Academic, 2013), 316.

91. Heiko Oberman, *Forerunners of the Reformation: The Shape of Late Medieval Thought Illustrated by Key Documents* (Philadelphia: Fortress, 1981), 281.

purposes in the wake of the Holocaust. Moberly himself acknowledges that the Old Testament was originally Israel's Scripture (viz., the Hebrew Bible), yet he takes with equal seriousness the reality that these documents are also part of Christian Scripture.

Does the Old Testament text provide its own frame of reference, or are Christians free to use their own faith-based frames of reference? Do Christian readings impose something alien on a hapless Old Testament text, supplanting ancient Near Eastern frames of reference with others? Moberly wonders whether reading the Old Testament in a Christian frame of reference stifles the Old Testament's own voice: "Will not Christian faith only hear what it wants to hear?"[92] Many biblical scholars have precisely this worry, namely, that Christian theological readings of the Old Testament run roughshod over the literal sense, refusing to let the texts have their own say. Hays rightly describes the concern: "Modern historical criticism characteristically judges . . . that the New Testament's christological readings of Israel's Scripture are simply a big mistake: they twist and misrepresent the original sense of the texts."[93] The modern critical climate requires readers to discard faith's frame of reference in order to interpret the text according to the letter in its original historical context.[94] If the Bible is like every other ancient text, then this critical approach, and its frame of reference, makes perfect sense.

On the other hand, if being scientific means that one's method accords with the nature of the object being examined, then it behooves us to clarify what the Bible is (ontology), to whom it is directed (audience), and what it is for (teleology). If the Bible is indeed divine address, then any frame of reference that mutes the voice of God risks being less than fully scientific. The mere Christian hermeneutical assumption I have adopted in the present work views the Old Testament and New Testament as unified divine discourse. The theologically salient point is this: *God* is the someone speaking, by means of the prophets; the *people of God* the someone spoken to; *covenantal communion* between divine Lord and human servants the ultimate purpose. What is currently at issue is what this discourse, and in particular the Old Testament, is about.

Irenaeus's rule of faith serves as a frame of reference that helps readers connect the Old Testament and New Testament to understand precisely what

92. Moberly, *Old Testament Theology*, 30.

93. Richard B. Hays, *Reading Backwards: Figural Christology and the Fourfold Gospel Witness* (Waco, TX: Baylor University Press, 2014), 3.

94. See further Stanglin's helpful summary of the principles of historical-critical exegesis in Keith D. Stanglin, *The Letter and Spirit of Biblical Interpretation: From the Early Church to Modern Practice* (Grand Rapids: Baker Academic, 2018), 178–85.

the Scriptures are about (their *hypothesis*).[95] Some biblical scholars complain that the rule is an extratextual tradition that stifles the discrete witness of the Old Testament authors.[96] I prefer a more charitable interpretation, namely, that the rule serves as an "*executive summary* of scriptural teaching."[97] It is not a supplement to, but a function of the biblical text, construed as a canonical whole. Specifically, the rule reminds readers that the two testaments belong together, twin witnesses to the one God's plan of salvation summed up in Jesus Christ.

May Christian readers today legitimately approach the Old Testament, rule in hand, and, like the Greeks who approached Philip, say, "We wish to see Jesus" (John 12:21)? Or does christological reading run afoul of the letter of the Old Testament text and its literal interpretation? It is a stark alternative, not least because choosing a frame of reference is something for which readers are answerable, ultimately to Jesus himself: "For if you believed Moses, you would believe me; for he wrote of me" (John 5:46). Does following Jesus include following the way Jesus read the Old Testament, a *hermeneutical discipleship*, as it were? What is at stake is a decision less about exegetical methods than a decision as to what the Bible is fundamentally about: "The quest for a framework of interpretation is a quest not as much for method as for a way of finding coherence between the Hebrew Scriptures and the Christian story."[98]

I resonate with Moberly's desire to employ more than one frame of reference and to retain the enduring philological and historical insights of modern biblical scholarship. The way forward, I believe, is to make the latter penultimate, placing legitimate concerns "within a frame of reference that puts different questions to the texts."[99] The goal is a thick description of biblical discourse that is able to do justice to everything the authors, human and divine, are saying and doing in the text. We therefore need as many forms of criticism and frames of reference as are required to do justice to and understand what the Bible is, is doing, and is for. What Scripture *is*, is a many-splendored, multilayered thing; what it therefore calls for is a multilayered interpretive response.

---

95. I'm attributing the rule of faith to Irenaeus, but in fact there is no one authorized version. There were several versions of the rule of faith circulating in the early church, yet they all agreed on the doctrinal essentials (i.e., orthodoxy) and, as such, could be seen as an early expression of mere Christian theology. See further Everett Ferguson, *The Rule of Faith: A Guide* (Eugene, OR: Cascade, 2015).

96. For one example of such nervousness, see J. R. Daniel Kirk, "Colonizing Biblical Interpretation," Storied Theology, April 22, 2016, http://www.patheos.com/blogs/storiedtheology/2016/04/22/colonizing-biblical-interpretation/.

97. V. Philips Long, "Irenaeus, Scripture, and the 'Rule of Truth': Of Kings, Foxes, and Mosaics," *Crux* 54, no. 2 (2018): 20.

98. Rowan Greer, in James L. Kugel and Rowan A. Greer, *Early Biblical Interpretation* (Philadelphia: Westminster, 1986), 151.

99. Moberly, *Old Testament Theology*, 4.

Framing Literal Interpretation: Of Secular and Sacred Imaginaries

To learn to read is to be socialized into a system of beliefs, values, and conventions—a reading culture—that makes sense of texts thanks to particular frames of reference. Frames of reference are first cousins to fiduciary frameworks (Polanyi), paradigms (Kuhn), and plausibility structures (Berger).[100] To exchange one frame of reference for another requires people to adopt, if only temporarily, new cognitive spectacles, a new way of seeing the world. It requires, in short, a conversion of the imagination. To a great extent, the story of literal interpretation is the story of shifting social imaginaries, epochal moments when what changes is not the picture (i.e., what the Bible says), but what frames and gives that picture meaning.

The Immanent Frame and the Secular Social Imaginary

The previous chapter introduced the first of these changes: the early modern shift to the immanent frame. We need not repeat that story here. What is of immediate interest, however, is the way the immanent frame shapes what readers take as literal. According to Hans Frei, early modernity experienced something like a Copernican revolution in biblical interpretation: "It is no exaggeration to say that all across the theological spectrum the great reversal had taken place; interpretation was a matter of fitting the biblical story into another world with another story rather than incorporating that world into the biblical story."[101]

Frei did not use Charles Taylor's terminology to describe this hermeneutical reversal, but he could have, for he identified the moment when the West exchanged one social imaginary (biblical, supernatural) for another (secular, naturalistic). Frei's "eclipse of biblical narrative" was essentially the moment when the biblical frame of reference for interpreting reality went dark. Henceforth, the stories determining the plausibility structures of Western culture come from the natural and social sciences, not the Old Testament and New Testament.

Frei's rubric—the eclipse of biblical narrative—was well chosen. The word of God is no longer a lamp for secular feet nor a light for our modern path. With few exceptions, biblical images and stories no longer inform, much less rule, the modern secular imaginary. What caused the eclipse? Just this: a secular picture

100. See Michael Polanyi, *Personal Knowledge: Towards a Post-Critical Philosophy* (Chicago: University of Chicago Press, 1962); Thomas Kuhn, *The Structure of Scientific Revolutions* (Chicago: University of Chicago Press, 1962); Peter Berger and Thomas Luckmann, *The Social Construction of Reality: A Treatise in the Sociology of Knowledge* (New York: Anchor, 1967).

101. Frei, *Eclipse of Biblical Narrative*, 130.

took us captive. Frei's analysis corroborates what I have been saying about the centrality of frames of reference. What Frei objected to in modern theology is the way it tears apart the literal sense from its reference. To read with an immanent frame of reference is to assume that the text is about either what is *behind* it (the historically reconstructed facts) or *above* it (the mythological or philosophical truth): "In either case, history or else allegory or myth, the *meaning* of the stories was finally something different from the stories or depictions themselves."[102]

Frei rightly understood that the immanent frame of reference has implications for literal interpretation and Christology alike. The gospel narratives are not about historically reconstructed figures *behind* the text or some moral/religious quality symbolized by Jesus as the immanent frame would have it. Rather, when literally interpreted—that is, according to their own *narrative* frame of reference—the Gospels are about Jesus, whose story they tell. Frei's insight and special contribution was his insistence that biblical narrative provides its own *intratextual* frame of reference. It follows that there is no access to the subject matter of the text apart from the narrative itself.[103] The literal sense and Christology thus stand or fall together: "It was largely by reason of this centrality of the story of Jesus that the Christian interpretive tradition in the West gradually assigned clear primacy to the literal sense in the reading of Scripture."[104]

The Transcendent Frame and the Sacramental Social Imaginary

Frei was not the only theologian to chafe under the constraints of reading the Bible with modernity's immanent frame of reference. One particularly robust reaction reinstalls what we might term a *transcendent* frame, largely because of the Platonic presuppositions with which it is associated. While it strives to be theological, it remains to be seen whether it, too, fails to do justice to the literal sense. At the very least, it provides more evidence of the impact of frames of reference on literal interpretation of the Bible.

---

102. Frei, *Eclipse of Biblical Narrative*, 11 (emphasis original).

103. For Frei, "intratextual" readings make the narrative into its own frame of reference, whereas "extratextuality" takes something outside the text (e.g., ancient Near Eastern history or existentialism) as the frame of reference for interpreting the text.

104. Frei, "'Literal Reading' of Biblical Narrative," 39. Frei's own account of Jesus' referential status is somewhat obscure. Frei is reticent to say much more about his reality or his resurrection other than to insist that *in the storied world of the Gospels*, Jesus Christ is alive. His critics worry that Frei freed literal interpretation from its thrall to one kind of immanent frame (the historical) only to imprison it in another (the literary). See, e.g., Jason A. Springs, *Toward a Generous Orthodoxy: Prospects for Hans Frei's Postliberal Theology* (Eugene, OR: Wipf & Stock, 2016), esp. ch. 4, "But Did It *Really* Happen? Frei and the Challenges of Critical Realism and Historical Reference," 85–104.

Sacramental Exegesis: Beyond Literal Interpretation?

Among proponents of theological interpretation of Scripture are certain Protestants who wish to recover a premodern frame of reference, a metaphysical framework they describe as "sacramental ontology" (Hans Boersma) or "Christian Platonism" (Craig Carter). They are allied with Roman Catholic *nouvelle théologie*, a mid-twentieth-century movement spearheaded by Jean Daniélou and Henri de Lubac, that sought to recover patristic reading practices to offset the disenchantment of modern biblical criticism.

Some scholars lay the blame for the loss of the sense of the sacred at the doorstep of the Reformation's call for literal interpretation.[105] Boersma laments the Reformers' "abandonment of a premodern sacramental mindset in which the realities of this-worldly existence pointed to greater, eternal reality in which they sacramentally shared."[106] What moderns call secular—the self-enclosed realm of space-time—is for Boersma something that "participates" in "the higher time of God's eternity."[107] Earthly reality in its parts and as a whole is, for Boersma, a kind of sacrament that partakes of heavenly reality: "My Christian Platonist convictions persuade me that everything around us is sacramental, in the sense that everything God has created both points to him and makes him present."[108] In a Christian Platonist frame of reference, the created order "sacramentally represented the supernatural reality of the mystery of God."[109] Boersma is right to see that the best way to counter the modern secular imaginary is to propose an alternative, in his case, a *sacramental* social imaginary. It is a bold attempt to reenchant our secular age by substituting a supernaturally saturated, *transcendent* frame of reference. Boersma's Christian instincts are spot on, though we need to proceed with caution, for it is not self-evident that his Platonist-sacramental frame of reference is generated and governed by the biblical text itself.

The problem with grammatical-historical methods, according to Boersma, is their complicity with the disenchanted world of secular modernity, namely, their tendency to acknowledge only the flat, linear, temporal aspect of history. In

---

105. See Brad S. Gregory, *The Unintended Reformation: How a Religious Revolution Secularized Society* (Cambridge, MA: Belknap, 2012), and my attempt to rebut the charge in Kevin J. Vanhoozer, *Biblical Authority after Babel: Retrieving the Solas in the Spirit of Mere Protestant Christianity* (Grand Rapids: Brazos, 2016), 10–13.

106. Hans Boersma, *Heavenly Participation: The Weaving of a Sacramental Tapestry* (Grand Rapids: Eerdmans, 2011), 2.

107. Hans Boersma and Matthew Levering, "Spiritual Interpretation and Realigned Temporality," *Modern Theology* 28, no. 4 (2012): 589. See also Levering, *Participatory Biblical Exegesis: A Theology of Biblical Interpretation* (Notre Dame: Notre Dame University Press, 2011).

108. Hans Boersma, *Scripture as Real Presence: Sacramental Exegesis in the Early Church* (Grand Rapids: Baker, 2017), 1.

109. Hans Boersma, *Nouvelle Théologie and Sacramental Ontology: A Return to Mystery* (Oxford: Oxford University Press, 2009), 7.

a series of books, Boersma speaks of "sacramental hermeneutics," "sacramental exegesis," and "sacramental reading." What makes biblical interpretation sacramental is its insistence on an ontological relation between the natural and the supernatural. The Bible, too, is sacramental, a temporal reality that mediates the eternal Word of God. Boersma notes the interchangeability of the Latin terms *mysterium* and *sacramentum*, citing de Lubac's notion that the New Testament is the mystery hidden within the "sacrament" of the Old Testament.[110]

How, then, does Boersma relate philology to Christology and explain the relation between the biblical letter and the Lord of whom it speaks? His sacramental approach lends itself to allegorizing, "a sacramental kind of interpretation that looks for the deeper, hidden meaning beneath the literal, or historical, meaning of the text."[111] What legitimates allegorical interpretation for Boersma, however, is not philosophy but Christology. Though both Platonic and sacramental ontology have an interest in "heavenly participation," Christianity insists that the transcendence in which we participate is not Being in general but the eternal Logos of God, the second person of the Trinity. Is the Old Testament literally about Jesus Christ? Boersma's short answer is a qualified "yes." The literal sense is "the starting point (*sacramentum*) of a search for the greater, more christological reality (*res*) of the gospel."[112]

The Seriously Literal Exegete Strikes Back

In yet another iteration of the tension between biblical studies and theology that we have been tracing, two Old Testament scholars distinguish their own frames of reference from Boersma's sacramentalism. Christopher Seitz takes his bearings from Irenaeus's focus on the history of salvation. In the Old Testament, God was "demonstrating in advance, by types, things to come."[113] Seitz believes Irenaeus stayed closer to the text with his emphasis on God promising things he would later fulfill than Boersma's notion of God's sacramental presence. The salient contrast is between God *acting in advance* and *being from above*. Another point of tension concerns the relationship of philology and Christology. Boersma objects to Seitz's "christological literalism," the belief "that it is by means of a literal reading of the Old Testament that we arrive at the ontological reality

110. Boersma, *Nouvelle Théologie*, 155.

111. Boersma, *Heavenly Participation*, 140. It is worth noting that Boersma believes one's theology of the Lord's Supper is intimately tied to one's view of biblical interpretation. Somewhat surprisingly, however, he associates (and criticizes) the notion that Christ is "really present" in the Eucharist with a "realist" understanding of Scripture that exaggerates the literal or historical meaning, to the detriment of the deeper, spiritual meaning.

112. Boersma, *Heavenly Participation*, 152.

113. Irenaeus, *On the Apostolic Preaching*, trans. John Behr (Crestwood, NY: St. Vladimir's Seminary Press, 1997), 70.

(that is, the christological and trinitarian faith of the church)."[114] On the contrary, it is "only *because the believer already knows the ontological reality* . . . that he is now able to discern Christ's presence also within the Old Testament as its deepest allegorical truth."[115] The difference is telling. Whereas Seitz views the canon's literal sense pressuring and propelling the reader forward to Christ, the climax of the covenant, Boersma insists that readers can find Christ in the Old Testament only because they have already met him in the New Testament: "Christ is first, Scripture second. . . . Though historical types may *chronologically* foreshadow Christ, *ontologically* they follow him and are patterned on him."[116] Discerning Christ in the Old Testament is, for Boersma, a matter not of christological literalism but of christological allegorizing.[117]

Another Old Testament scholar, Iain Provan, distinguishes his "seriously literal" way of reading the Bible from Boersma's "counter-Reformational Protestantism." What particularly bothers Provan is the way Boersma elevates the church's great tradition into "the context in which all the Scriptures . . . must be read."[118] Provan resents the way in which Boersma uses the literal sense as a mere stepping stone to a spiritual interpretive pilgrimage rather than "the single, fixed textual meaning" that was the touchstone of the Reformers and their heirs. Provan speaks for many biblical scholars when he expresses his concern that "spiritual readers" too often fail to think well about the "literal."[119]

Provan also objects to the way in which Boersma privileges the Christian Platonist frame of reference, on the grounds that doing so calls the authority and clarity of Scripture into question: "The 'spiritual depths' of biblical texts are not 'hidden' in them."[120] He also worries that "sacramental ontology" may be another term for "analogy of being."[121] While Boersma's intent is to retrieve a Christ-centered picture of created reality as existing through, for, and in Christ (Col 1:16), not everything in creation is part of the economy of saving grace the way baptism and the Lord's Supper are. Daniel Treier rightly formulates the problem: "If everything becomes 'sacramental,' then nothing is sacred."[122] I have argued elsewhere that the apostle Paul distinguished between being "in

---

114. Hans Boersma, *Five Things Theologians Wish Biblical Scholars Knew* (Downers Grove, IL: InterVarsity, 2021), 26.

115. Boersma, *Five Things Theologians Wish Biblical Scholars Knew*, 28.

116. Boersma, *Five Things Theologians Wish Biblical Scholars Knew*, 13, 33.

117. Boersma uses this contrast to describe de Lubac's position (christological allegorizing), which is also his own view (*Five Things Theologians Wish Biblical Scholars Knew*, 28).

118. Iain Provan, *The Reformation and the Right Reading of Scripture* (Waco, TX: Baylor University Press, 2017), 17.

119. Provan, 93.

120. Provan, 638.

121. A point suggested to me by Philip Cary in personal correspondence (August 20, 2019).

122. Daniel J. Treier, "*Heavenly Participation*: The Weaving of a Sacramental Tapestry—A Review Essay," *Christian Scholar's Review* 41 (2011): 71.

general" (ontology) and being "in Christ" (soteriology).[123] All creatures stand in some kind of relation to their Creator, but only the elect are included in the life and fellowship of the triune God. I agree with Jeremy Mann: "Sacramental ontologies generally fail to capture the created world's dynamic history [i.e., creation, fall, redemption, consummation] in the arc of Scripture."[124]

Biblical narrative raises questions that only theological ontology can answer.[125] I therefore sympathize with Boersma's and Carter's attempt to retrieve a frame of reference that brings theological realities into focus. Yet I also sympathize with seriously literal exegetes who push back against exaggerated claims about needing to read the Bible in a Platonist frame of reference in order to be Christian, particularly when "the Bible does not use the language of 'being' in frequent, sustained, theoretical ways."[126] The urgent question is "*Which* frame of reference best accords with the biblical testimony to God's reality, relation to the world, and presence in Scripture?"

Several theologians, responding to Boersma, highlight the contrast between the vertical dynamic of Christian Platonism with its upward pull (i.e., participation in God) and the more horizontal dynamic of salvation history with its eschatological pull.[127] My own sympathies are with the latter. So, too, I believe, are those of the author of Hebrews (see below). By "eschatological," I mean what pertains to the end of history, the doctrine of "last things," *and* whatever happens when the God who is outside creation breaks into it. Eschatology pertains not simply to the end of history, but to God's presence and activity in the midst of history. Biblical narrative relates what the eternal God is doing in our time to bring about a new time. The concept of inaugurated eschatology—the characteristic New Testament theme that the kingdom of God is "already/not yet"—reminds us that God is not simply above the world, in a heavenly realm of Platonic Forms, but enters into our world to make it heavenly (i.e., filled with his presence).

---

123. Kevin J. Vanhoozer, "The Origin of Paul's Soteriology: Election, Incarnation, and Union with Christ in Ephesians 1:4 (with special reference to Evangelical Calvinism)," in *Reconsidering the Relationship between Biblical and Systematic Theology in the New Testament*, ed. Benjamin E. Reynolds, Brian Lugioyo, and Kevin J. Vanhoozer (Tübingen: Mohr Siebeck, 2014), 177–212.

124. Jeremy R. Mann, "Sacramental Ontology and Calvin: Toward a Re-enchanted World," *Bulletin of Ecclesial Theology* 4, no. 2 (2017): 31. For further analysis and evaluation of sacramental ontology, see Jeremy Mann, "Is the World Sacramental? Ontology, Language, and Scripture," in *Creation and Doxology: The Beginning and End of God's Good World*, ed. Gerald Hiestand and Todd Wilson (Downers Grove, IL: IVP Academic, 2018), 79–98.

125. See my "Staurology, Ontology, and the Travail of Biblical Narrative: Once More unto the Biblical Theological Breach," *Southern Baptist Journal of Theology* 23, no 2 (2019): 7–33.

126. Daniel J. Treier, "'Christian Platonism' and Christological Interpretation," *Reformed Faith & Practice* 5 no. 3 (2020): 43.

127. See the essays by Hans Burger and Arnold Huijgen in *Scripture and Theology: Historical and Systematic Perspectives*, ed. Tomas Bokedal, Ludger Jansen, and Michael Borowski (Berlin: de Gruyter, 2023).

What the Bible *is* and what the Bible *is about* are equally eschatological, divine realities that no immanent frame of reference can bring into focus. A mere Christian hermeneutic therefore reads the Bible keeping in mind the eschatological nature of both its *form* (divine address) and *content* (divine subject matter). We turn now to consider how the Old Testament and New Testament do the same. Both Isaiah and the book of Hebrews would have us see Jesus by attending to the letter of the text with an eschatological frame of reference, in an eschatological reading culture, and for an eschatological purpose.

Framing Isaiah; Framing Hebrews: Is the Literal Always Earth-Bound?

Framing Isaiah: Do Old Testament Prophets Say More Than They Can Know?

At the beginning of his public ministry, Jesus entered into a Jewish reading culture (a synagogue) and read from Isaiah 61 ("The Spirit of the Lord God is upon me, because the Lord has anointed me to bring good news to the poor"; v. 1). The Gospel of Luke recounts what happened next: "And he rolled up the scroll. . . . And the eyes of all in the synagogue were fixed on him. And he began to say to them, 'Today this Scripture has been fulfilled in your hearing'" (4:20–21). What an astounding comment! Was Jesus interpreting Isaiah or using the text for his own purposes? What frame of reference could Jesus have been using to come to his conclusion?

Childs and Moberly read Isaiah as scholars indebted to modern biblical studies and as saints who read with a Christian conviction that Isaiah is referring to Jesus Christ: "The Christian community has consistently affirmed throughout its history . . . that what the Bible, taken as a whole, is *literally about* is *Jesus Christ*."[128] But (to echo Nicodemus), "How can these things be?" (John 3:9).

In 2001 Childs published "a technical, modern commentary" on the book of Isaiah that left him painfully aware of how many hermeneutical and theological questions he had failed to address.[129] In particular: Could twenty-first-century readers read in continuity with those church fathers and other earlier Christians? Is there a "family resemblance" between Christian readings of Isaiah down through the centuries? Such questions led Childs to write *The Struggle to Understand Isaiah as Christian Scripture*.[130] The bulk of the book surveys how Christians have read Isaiah from New Testament times, through

128. Richard Burnett, "John Calvin and the *Sensus Literalis*," *Scottish Journal of Theology* 57, no. 1 (2004): 2.

129. Brevard S. Childs, *Isaiah* (Louisville: Westminster John Knox, 2001).

130. Brevard S. Childs, *The Struggle to Understand Isaiah as Christian Scripture* (Grand Rapids: Eerdmans, 2004).

the patristic, medieval, and Reformation periods, to the present. He noted that modern biblical critics fail to wrestle with Isaiah as Christian Scripture, preferring to adopt a purely historical frame of reference. For example, in his 1821 commentary, Wilhelm Gesenius lodged numerous critical complaints against traditional Christian interpretations, such as the identification of the servant in Isaiah 42–53 with Jesus. Even conservative commentators like A. B. Davidson struggled with this, insisting that Jesus is the *fulfillment* of the servant of the Lord (Isa 53) but not the *referent* of the prophet's discourse: "It can hardly be doubted that the prophet's thought is national . . . the servant is a creation of the prophet's mind, the ideal Israel itself."[131]

Walter Brueggemann, Childs's token postmodern reader, "flatly repudiates any claim that the book of Isaiah predicts or anticipates Jesus Christ."[132] According to Brueggemann, says Childs, there is "no ontological connection" between the two testaments. The New Testament's use of the Old Testament is a leap of creative imagination, for it "does not rest on any textual basis derived from the Old Testament itself. Rather, the New Testament writers have consistently read back into the Old Testament a Christian interpretation."[133] Childs rebutted the charge, noting that Irenaeus's rule of faith provides a frame of reference that enables readers to see how Christ is what makes the two testaments one Scripture.[134] Each testament retains its own integrity, yet together they form an integral unity, held together by the reality that undergirds their joint witness: the person and work of Jesus Christ.[135] For Childs, the rule of faith is first and foremost *intrinsic* to the canon, not a coercive imposition: "The canonical shape provides the larger framework of Scripture—a rule of faith—within which the interpretive function of exegesis is guided."[136] One may of course read the Old Testament as the Hebrew Bible, in distinction from the New Testament, with a Jewish frame of reference, but to do so is to adopt a history of religion rather than theological framework: "Both tasks are legitimate, but they are different in goal and procedure."[137]

Which task should those who value literal interpretation pursue? Can they follow Jerome's example and view Isaiah the man as an evangelist and his text as a "fifth gospel," on the grounds that "he describes all the mysteries of Christ and the Church so clearly that you would not think he is prophesying about what is to come, but rather composing a history of what

131. A. B. Davidson, "The Book of Isaiah Ch. XLff," *The Expositor*, ser. 2, vol. 8 (London: Hodder and Stoughton, 1884), 358–59.

132. Childs, *Struggle to Understand Isaiah*, 294.

133. Childs, *Struggle to Understand Isaiah*, 294.

134. Childs, *Struggle to Understand Isaiah*, 304.

135. Childs, *Struggle to Understand Isaiah*, 313.

136. Childs, *Struggle to Understand Isaiah*, 317.

137. Childs, *Struggle to Understand Isaiah*, 321.

has already happened"?[138] Interestingly, it is Jon Levenson, a modern Jewish biblical scholar, who sheds light on what is at stake in one's choice of frame of reference: "The problem is that by making *historical* context sovereign and regulative, historical criticism destroys the *literary* context that is the Bible (either Jewish or Christian) as a whole and often even the smaller literary context that is the book, the chapter, or whatever."[139] Levenson here points out that, in a real sense, Jews and Christians are reading different texts. For Jewish readers, the canonical context of Isaiah does not include the Gospels; for Christians, it must.

The implications for literal interpretation are enormous. Levenson rightly perceives the organic connection between frame of reference and context, that what counts as "literal" is context dependent, and that there are other relevant contexts in addition to that of the original historical situation. Literal interpretation—doing justice to the letter of the text—therefore requires *thick description*: a reading that takes account of all *relevant* contexts that have a bearing on what authors mean by their words (i.e., the who, what, where, when, how, and why of discourse): "If one wants to answer the question of what person *S* is doing, one must select a level or mode of description from a number of available alternatives."[140] Moberly rightly concludes that such multicontext, multilayered readings are preferable to speaking of a *sensus plenior* ("fuller meaning").[141]

How might we give thick descriptions of the vexing Isaianic passages concerning the servant of the Lord (Isa 52:13–53:12)? It is difficult to identify someone who fits this description *within* Isaiah's own historical frame of reference. On the other hand, modern biblical critics scoff at the suggestion that Isaiah could speak of things *beyond* his own frame of reference. So, is Isaiah referring to Christ? Yes and no, says Moberly. Yes if we read Isaiah in the context of the Christian canon, but no if we read in terms of his own historical frame of reference. Does Moberly think Isaiah is "literally" about Christ or not? It is hard to say. As a trained biblical scholar, he is keen not to introduce into the Old Testament texts ideas that are not there. As a Christian, he is keen

---

138. Jerome, prologue to his Latin translation of Isaiah, in *Biblia Sacra Vulgata*, 5th ed. (Stuttgart: German Bible Society, 2007), cited in Moberly, *Old Testament Theology*, 146–47.

139. Jon Levenson, *The Hebrew Bible, the Old Testament, and Historical Criticism: Jews and Christians in Biblical Studies* (Louisville: Westminster John Knox, 1993), 100.

140. René van Woudenberg, *The Epistemology of Reading and Interpretation* (Cambridge: Cambridge University Press, 2021), 209.

141. Moberly, *Old Testament Theology*, 158. Elsewhere he says that "the canonical status of the biblical documents requires that Christian interpreters be able to read the text in more than one context." Moberly, "Biblical Hermeneutics and *Ecclesial* Responsibility," in *The Future of Biblical Interpretation: Responsible Plurality in Biblical Hermeneutics*, ed. Stanley E. Porter and Matthew R. Malcolm (Downers Grove, IL: IVP Academic, 2013), 150.

to read the Old Testament texts as testimony to the same God that the New Testament calls the Father of Jesus Christ. He hopes thereby to do justice both to the "letter" of the text through the use of scholarly methods and to the "spirit" of the text by reading Old Testament and New Testament together within the Christian frame of reference, namely, the rule of faith. Yet the question remains: Is Isaiah *literally* about Jesus Christ?[142]

Like Moberly, I do not wish to discount Isaiah's frame of reference. The original author's voice must be heard. Neither the sense nor the semantic range of Hebrew words changes when they become part of Christian Scripture. At the same time, Christians believe that the prophets *said* more than they could consciously *know* about "what person or time the Spirit of Christ in them was indicating when he predicted the sufferings of Christ" (1 Pet 1:11). Better: the prophets knew *what they were saying*, but they did not know exactly what, or whom, they were speaking *about*. They understood the sense of their discourse but not its ultimate referent. This way of viewing the matter explains why we still need the hard work of philology to clarify the sense of the words, and other frames of reference than Isaiah's to understand the *referent* of his discourse that his words ultimately indicate. Strictly speaking, then, what is "fuller" is not the sense, but the reference, of their discourse—not *sensus* but *referens plenior*.[143] Any frame of reference that mutes the divine discourse is, in the final analysis, less than fully critical.

A final analogy may help to bring my own discourse, what I am talking about, into sharper focus. In the 1990s a series of *Magic Eye* books zoomed to the top of bestseller lists, spurred on by the subtitle: "A New Way of Looking at the World." The technical term for these illustrations is "stereogram": an apparently random image that, when viewed the right way, with both eyes, reveals a 3D image. The *literalistic* way of looking at the image sees only the surface made up of repeated patterns, signifying nothing. Those who look at the image in this way see the letter, as it were, but *not what it is about*. To see what it is about, viewers need the right (stereoscopic) frame of reference. The essential point, not to be missed, is that the 3D image—the referent—is really there and, when it comes into focus, there is no doubt whatsoever about what one is looking at. Something similar takes place, I submit, when we read

142. Elsewhere, in a study of Abraham and Jesus, Moberly again deals with christological interpretation. Walter Moberly, *The Bible, Theology, and Faith: A Study of Abraham and Jesus* (Cambridge: Cambridge University Press, 2000). Strangely, there is no discussion of Jesus' statement in John 8:56: "Your father Abraham rejoiced that he would see my day. He saw it and was glad." One wonders what frame of reference Jesus had in mind.

143. Cf. Elliot Johnson's related notion of *references plenior* in his "Author's Intention and Biblical Interpretation," in *Hermeneutics, Inerrancy, and the Bible*, ed. Earl Radmacher and Robert D. Preus (Grand Rapids: Zondervan, 1984), 428.

the Old Testament with a Christian frame of reference (the rule of faith).[144] The image of Christ, the final referent of Scripture, is really there, and clearly visible—but only when we look along the letter of the text with the right frame of reference.

Framing Hebrews: Toward What Kind of Heavenly Participation?

The book of Hebrews serves as an apt case study for thinking about historical/theological frames of reference, and for the dialogue between biblical studies and systematic theology.[145] It presents the reader with an exegetical dive with a high degree of difficulty, challenging interpreters to explain how its author relates the literal and spiritual senses of Scripture, and to specify what frame of reference he uses to read the Old Testament.

No biblical text sounds more Platonic than Hebrews. Consider the way the author compares and contrasts Israel's earthly priest and tabernacle with their celestial counterparts, asserting that the one is "a copy and shadow of the heavenly things . . . according to the pattern [*typos*]" shown to Moses (Heb 8:5). Luke Timothy Johnson associates *typos* ("type") with Plato's eternal forms, the spiritual template of a (less real) material representation, a contrast that illustrates "the Platonic worldview of Hebrews."[146] James W. Thompson agrees, arguing that the author of Hebrews works with "a Platonic metaphysic."[147] Christian-Platonists believe they have strong warrant from Hebrews for viewing Old Testament persons and events as "sacraments that participate in the New Testament reality."[148] Still to be determined, however, is the nature of earth's participation in heaven: is it sacramental and/or Platonic and, if not, is the only alternative a merely earth-bound literal sense?

On a strictly lexical level, it is noteworthy that *upodeigma* ("copy" in Heb 8:5) "is *never* used by *any* ancient author, let alone by Philo or Plato, in reference to a Platonic copy."[149] If a Platonic scheme of participation were in view, the author of Hebrews could have described the earthly tabernacle as a *mimesis* of the heavenly. As Robert Gundry points out, the Old Testament law, priests,

144. In the following chapter, I describe this right frame of reference as not stereoscopic but "christoscopic." For instructions on how to view 3D Magic Eye images, see https://www.magiceye.com/faq/.

145. See *The Epistle to the Hebrews and Christian Theology*, ed. Richard Bauckham, Daniel R. Driver, Trevor A. Hart, and Nathan MacDonald (Grand Rapids: Eerdmans, 2009); and *Christology, Hermeneutics, and Hebrews: Profiles from the History of Interpretation*, ed. Jon C. Laansma and Daniel J. Treier (London: Bloomsbury T&T Clark, 2012).

146. Luke Timothy Johnson, *Hebrews: A Commentary* (Louisville: Westminster John Knox, 2006), 202.

147. J. W. Thompson, *The Beginnings of Christian Philosophy: The Epistle to the Hebrews* (Washington, DC: Catholic Biblical Association of America, 1982), 52.

148. Benjamin J. Ribbens, "Hebrews as Participatory Exegesis," *Journal of Theological Interpretation* 15, no. 1 (2021): 102.

149. Kenneth Schenck, *A Brief Guide to Philo* (Louisville: Westminster John Knox, 2005), 84.

and sacrifices were shadows not of some timeless reality, but of "the world to come" (Heb 2:5; cf. 10:1). It is therefore more accurate to view these earthly shadows as *fore*shadows.[150] C. K. Barrett agreed with viewing the relationship between earthly and heavenly in temporal rather than spatial terms: "Jesus is primarily . . . an actor in the eschatological drama of redemption rather than a mediator standing between the real and phenomenal worlds."[151]

The dualism in question is not Plato's distinction between the earthly realm of shadows/appearances and the heavenly realm of ideas / real things but the Pauline distinction between two ages, this age and the age to come.[152] This is an apocalyptic and eschatological dualism whose roots lie in the Old Testament but come to full fruition only in the redemptive history of Jesus Christ.[153] In this framework, heaven and earth are not antithetically polarized, for Christ will appear on earth again (Heb 9:28). In an apocalyptic frame of reference, the destruction of the present world is followed by a new creation.[154] Hebrews does not explicitly mention a new heaven and new earth, but it does depict the Son as "heir of all things" (Heb 1:2) and does mention "the world to come" (Heb 2:5).[155] Jesus is the one who brings God's kingdom—heaven, the sphere of God's reign—to earth, thereby fulfilling Old Testament messianic prophecy.[156] In this frame of reference, simultaneously messianic and eschatological, participation in the kingdom of heaven is less Platonic than covenantal, a matter of confessing, celebrating, and conforming to God's reign *on earth*, the dominion of the messianic King.

---

150. Robert H. Gundry, "To Plato or Not to Plato?," *Books & Culture* 17 (March/April 2011): 25–26.

151. C. K. Barrett, "The Eschatology of the Epistle to the Hebrews," in *The Background of the New Testament and Its Eschatology*, ed. W. D. Davies and D. Daube (Cambridge: Cambridge University Press, 1956), 389.

152. For an early statement of the distinction, see Geerhardus Vos, *The Pauline Eschatology* (Grand Rapids: Baker, 1979). Jewish apocalyptic is arguably a better frame of reference for reading Hebrews than Christian Platonism. See Jihye Lee, *A Jewish Apocalyptic Framework of Eschatology in the Epistle to the Hebrews* (London: Bloomsbury T&T Clark, 2021). On Jewish apocalyptic more generally, see John J. Collins, *The Apocalyptic Imagination: An Introduction to Jewish Apocalyptic Literature*, 3rd ed. (Grand Rapids: Eerdmans, 2016); *The Jewish Apocalyptic Tradition and the Shape of New Testament Thought*, ed. Benjamin E. Reynolds and Loren T. Stuckenbruck (Minneapolis: Fortress, 2017); and Christopher Rowland, *The Open Heaven: A Study of Apocalyptic in Judaism and Early Christianity* (New York: Crossroad, 1982).

153. See further Brian D. Ingraffia, *Postmodern Theology and Biblical Theology: Vanquishing God's Shadow* (Cambridge: Cambridge University Press, 1996).

154. There is currently a lively debate over the "apocalyptic Paul," which in part concerns the frame of reference Paul uses in theologizing. See Jamie Davies, *The Apocalyptic Paul: Retrospect and Prospect* (Eugene, OR: Cascade, 2022). I take no position on that debate here, though I would say that apocalyptic as a literary genre is narrower than an eschatological frame of reference, though compatible with it.

155. See further Edward Adams, "The Cosmology of Hebrews," in *The Epistle to the Hebrews and Christian Theology*, 122–39.

156. See further Joshua W. Jipp, who claims that "Jesus' messianic kingship functions as a root metaphor or basic assumption for reading the New Testament." Joshua W. Jipp, *The Messianic Theology of the New Testament* (Grand Rapids: Eerdmans, 2020), 313.

Earth- or Christ-Bound? The Eschatological Orientation of the Bible's Literal Sense

This chapter has confirmed that at the root of different understandings of the literal are decisions about what it means to lovingly attend to the letter of the text and about which frames of reference ought to have priority. I claimed that what influences our choice of frames is often the reading culture into which one has been socialized and the prevailing social imaginary that shapes the values, beliefs, and practices of that reading culture. Biblical interpretation is thus considerably more complex than learning the steps of a particular exegetical method. For behind critical approaches and interpretive methods lurk subterranean Copernican revolutions that affect the social imaginary. For modern scholars socialized to read with immanent frame of reference, the way the words run is this-worldly, a matter of natural history only, making it difficult, if not impossible, to see Christ in the Old Testament. The author of Hebrews, together with the rest of the prophets and apostles, sees things with a different frame of reference that includes both a horizontal and vertical axis. Platonism lacks the all-important eschatological dimension: the notion that God, who transcends time, has nevertheless entered into it, vocally and bodily, to redeem and renew it. This christological truth—that the Word through whom all things were created has entered into it and spoken—has philological consequences.

God has commissioned and inspired the words of the prophets and apostles, words that ultimately run to Jesus Christ. Doing justice of the letter of the text therefore means situating it in an eschatological frame of reference, ruled by a scriptural imaginary: the story of God forming a holy nation (Exod 19:6; 1 Pet 2:9), making all things subject to Christ (1 Cor 15:28) and the earth his footstool (Isa 66:1; cf. Matt 5:35; Heb 10:13). Biblical discourse is messianic kingdom discourse. Christ is the realization of the eternal purpose of God "to unite all things in him, things in heaven and things on earth" (Eph 1:10). All this to say: the eschatological subject matter of the text calls for an eschatological frame of reference. Otherwise it will not come into focus but remain so many squiggly lines that form no coherent pattern.

There is another reason to read with an eschatological frame of reference. Hebrews is God's address to God's people, hence to interpret it on its own terms requires more than focusing on the world behind, within, or in front of the text. None of those worlds captures the context of "being addressed by God." God's presence in Scripture is communicative, a speaking presence that, like the kingdom it proclaims, breaks into the world of author and reader alike. It is eschatological because it is a breaking (and speaking) into time and space from one who is beyond them. The world *of* Hebrews is not the historical reality behind it, nor the narrative world within it, nor the contemporary context of the reader. Rather, the world *of* Hebrews is the world entered into by reading it, the real world, in which God is eschatologically present, actively addressing the reader via the letter of the text: "Today, if you hear his voice" (Heb 3:7, 15; 5:7).[157] *The Word of God is not simply the content of the Bible, but the voice of God speaking to us in and through it.* Let it therefore not be said of Hebrews' Christian readers that Christ "came to his own, and his own people did not receive him" (John 1:11).

The discourse of Hebrews is Christ-bound, not merely earth-bound. Christ is both the ultimate speaker and referent of the text, and it requires theological interpretation to articulate how this is so. At the same time, although Christ is the subject matter of the text, he is not strictly speaking a part of the text: "His nature is not textual, but personal. . . . Christ is the center of the Scriptures, not in semantic or thematic terms, but in a distinctly theological sense."[158] Christ is the *external* center of Scripture, by which I mean (1) that Christ is not simply a character in the text but also its commissioning editor; and (2) that Christ is not simply a figure in history but the eternal Son of God who comes into our world in his own manner and time.[159]

It may be helpful to draw a distinction between an eschatological *context* and an eschatological *frame of reference*. We read the Bible today in an eschatological context because it exposes us to the divine address; we read the Bible with an eschatological frame of reference because it is about events pertaining to the end of the ages. As to eschatological context, Paul tells his own readers that events in Israel's history "happened to them as an example, but they were written down for our instruction, on whom the end of the ages has come" (1 Cor 10:11). If eschatology has to do with the breaking in of the age to come into this age, then Paul's identification of his readership as those "on whom the end of the ages has come" situates them, and us, squarely in an eschatological context.

As to reading with an eschatological frame of reference, this derives from Jesus' own reading of the Old Testament: "*Today* this Scripture has been

---

157. "The Letter to the Hebrews exists in this sphere, the sphere of the apostles who partake in the history of revelation as its witnesses and ministers, and the sphere of the interpreters who participate in the history of revelation as its addressees and hearers" (John Webster, "One Who Is Son: Theological Reflections on the Exordium to the Epistle to the Hebrews," in *Epistle to the Hebrews and Christian Theology*, 70).

158. Arnold Huijgen, "Reinventing the Quadriga: Connecting Biblical Exegesis and Systematic Theology through the Anagogical-Eschatological Sense of Scripture," in *Scripture and Theology: Historical and Systematic Perspectives*, ed. Tomas Bokedal, Ludger Jansen, and Michael Borowski (Berlin: de Gruyter, 2023), 406.

159. For Christ as "external center" of Scripture, see Ingolf Dalferth, "Die Mitte ist außen: Anmerkungen zum Wirklichkeitsbezug evangelischer Schriftauslegung," in *Jesus Christus als die Mitte der Schrift: Studien zur Hermeneutik des Evangeliums*, ed. Christof Landmesser (Berlin: de Gruyter, 1997), 173–98.

fulfilled in your hearing" (Luke 4:21, emphasis added). This accords with Jesus' broader hermeneutical claims: "[The Scriptures] bear witness about me" (John 5:39); "Moses . . . wrote of me" (John 5:46). The Old Testament Scriptures bear witness to Jesus because *all* biblical discourse is oriented toward fulfillment in Christ. Jesus is eschatologically present in all the Scriptures. Everyone agrees that the literal sense has to do with the *historia* of the Bible. The surprise is coming to understand how this *historia*, whether story or history, has an eschatological orientation. Eschatology is the true north of biblical history and the literal sense.

Everything we have said up to this point is but an appetizer for the main course, to be served up in the following chapter, a retrieval of an expansive approach to literal interpretation that reconciles what has been put asunder: verbal sense and christological referent. To take the literal sense with all seriousness means using all those frames of reference that are needed to understand the Bible as human and divine discourse: not only *what* is said, but *by whom, about what,* and *to whom* it is said. The goal is to set forth the contours of a "mere Christian hermeneutic" shared by patristic, medieval, and Reformation readers alike, a way of attending to the literal sense that brings into focus the already/not-yet referent of redemptive history. Only such an eschatological frame of reference allows both philology and Christology to come into their own. The Christ-bound literal sense that comes into focus in this frame of reference is the supreme norm of Christian doctrine and the goal of theological interpretation of Scripture. Both biblical scholars and systematic theologians make vital contributions to clarifying *what is said* (sense) and *that about which* something is said (reference), respectively. Each is necessary for a seriously literal interpretation that follows the way the biblical words go, through history and all the way to their eschatological fulfillment, a way of reading that in the next chapter I call grammatical-eschatological exegesis.

CHAPTER 5

Defining *Sensus Literalis* (Part 2)

From the Figural to the Trans-figural

Figural interpretation is not a method, but a way of reading the Bible that recognizes the unity of Scripture and the presence of Christ throughout.
—Peter Leithart[1]

The literal sense of Scripture is the foundation and the source of all interpretation, but the Christological sense is the summit and the crown of all interpretation.
—Martin Luther, *Lectures on Galatians* 4:4–5

This chapter continues my attempt to define the literal sense in a way that enables biblical scholars and theologians to overcome their disciplinary differences and get on the same sacred page. My fundamental thesis is that the Bible's literal meaning calls for a theological reading that is a faithful and obedient response to the summons of its divine author, not an alien imposition. I agree with Childs: "The biblical text itself exerts theological pressure on the reader, demanding that the reality which undergirds the two witnesses [Old Testament and New Testament] not be held apart and left fragmented, but rather critically united."[2]

The previous chapter argued that loving attention to the letter of the biblical text means doing justice to what it is and is about—the inbreaking of

1. Peter Leithart, *Deep Exegesis: The Mystery of Reading Scripture* (Waco, TX: Baylor University Press, 2009), 18.

2. Brevard Childs, "Towards Recovering Theological Exegesis," *Ex Auditu* 16 (2000): 127.

God's Word into history—and that this entails reading in (the reader's) eschatological context. The literal sense is the "plain sense"—yes, but plain *to whom?* It is a good question, for it reminds us that *to someone* is part of discourse. What is plain to a particular reader will depend on the frame of reference they bring to the text, which is why the idea of a "mere Christian hermeneutics" will strike many readers as naive. We therefore begin with an account of where the root of the conflict of biblical interpretation really lies, which is considerably deeper than disputes over the relative merits of this or that method. Nor is it a conflict that can be resolved simply by an interpreter deciding "to be a neutral observer, prescinding from any kind of faith-commitment in order to get at the truth."[3] Previous chapters have shown that behind professions of alleged neutrality lie deeper commitments to an often-unacknowledged frame of reference and social imaginary.

By way of preview, here is my mere Christian hermeneutical credo. I believe (1) that there is indeed a distinctly Christian way of reading Scripture as a unified canon; (2) that it appears in every period of church history, even if it is not always the dominant scholarly approach; (3) that it appears in exemplary manner in the Protestant Reformers, who were as much heirs of patristic and medieval ways of reading as they are precursors to ours;[4] (4) that this "reformed catholic" way of reading for the plain sense traces the movement of typological figures across the canon, yielding a *plain canonical, trans-figural* literal sense.[5]

This chapter sets forth a catholic (i.e., mere Christian) reading practice inflected by the Reformation, a literal *cum* figural mode of interpretation ruled by a social imaginary generated and governed by Scripture itself. The domain of this scriptural imaginary is the church, the creature of the Word, to which it is the corporate response.[6] It follows that literal interpretation will mean something different in the church than the academy thanks to the respective frames of reference each privileges. It is in the church, that reading culture that acknowledges the need to read the Bible in canonical context to hear the divine address, that Christ comes to be seen as the Bible's literal referent.

---

3. John Barton, *The Old Testament: Canon, Literature, and Theology; Collected Essays of John Barton* (New York: Routledge, 2016), 204.

4. See also Hans Moscicke, who speaks of an "ecumenical hermeneutic." "The Theological Presuppositions of Ancient Christian Exegesis: G. K. Beale and Henri de Lubac in Conversation," *Journal of Theological Interpretation* 10, no. 1 (2016): 125–43. Christopher Seitz speaks of "canonical catholicity," by which he means an approach to biblical interpretation that focuses on typology and characterizes both Roman Catholic (e.g., Paul Beauchamp) and Protestant (e.g., Brevard Childs) readers. Christopher Seitz, *Convergences: Canon and Catholicity* (Waco, TX: Baylor University Press, 2020).

5. I am attempting a retrieval of an old reading practice in a new theological key: a *trans-figural* interpretation that follows the way biblical words (and figures) go, across the canon, to their ultimate christological referent.

6. John Webster views the domain of the Word as constituted by the communicative presence and activity of the triune God. Webster, *Domain of the Word*, 3.

Tactics vs. Strategy: Where the Conflict Really Lies

Why do the interpreters rage?[7] A large part of the present work—too large!—has dealt with the conflict of interpreters, interpretations, and interpretive approaches. Paul Ricoeur described reading in general as "a struggle with the text,"[8] and with other readers who approach the text with different questions or interests. Ricoeur devoted a whole book to the latter: *The Conflict of Interpretations.*[9] Alas, church history is replete with examples of the conflict—disciplinary, theoretical, ideological, and denominational—of biblical interpretations.

What is the real source of this conflict? Where do Bible readers disagree, and why? According to Sandra Schneiders, "Everyone can agree that the objective of New Testament interpretation is to arrive at an understanding of the meaning of the text. But there the agreement ends, because the meaning of meaning itself . . . is disputable."[10] It may be helpful to tease out the idea of interpretive conflict further, using a distinction between "tactics" and "strategy" that originated, appropriately enough, with Carl von Clausewitz's famous 1832 treatise *On War.*[11] It is fitting, inasmuch as the conflict of interpretations has made the literal sense a casualty of war.

Exegetical Tactics: Interpretive Means

A war is a series of "engagements." Clausewitz observed that it is one thing to execute these engagements or battles, another to coordinate them in order to win the war: "One has been called *tactics,* and the other *strategy.* . . . Tactics teaches *the use of armed forces in the engagement;* strategy, *the use of engagements for the object of the war.*"[12] Tactics require science (e.g., the use of engineering in siege warfare), whereas strategy requires more holistic and long-term thinking. Tactics concern what to do "on the ground" to achieve immediate goals (means); strategy is a matter of the overarching aims and objectives (ends).

The distinction is important if we are to determine where the conflict of interpretations really lies. Let us grant that reading Scripture involves a struggle

---

7. Cf. Psalm 2:1.

8. *A Ricoeur Reader: Reflection and Imagination,* ed. Mario J. Valdés (New York: Harvester Wheatsheaf, 1991), 494. I will return to this idea in chapter 9.

9. Paul Ricoeur, *The Conflict of Interpretations: Essays in Hermeneutics,* ed. D. Ihde (Evanston, IL: Northwestern University Press, 1974).

10. Sandra Schneiders, *The Revelatory Text: Interpreting the New Testament as Sacred Scripture,* 2nd ed. (Collegeville, MN: Liturgical, 1999), 13.

11. Carl von Clausewitz, *On War,* ed. and trans. Michael Howard and Peter Paret (Princeton, NJ: Princeton University Press, 1984).

12. Clausewitz, 128.

to understand. To read the Bible is to enter into an interpretive engagement. Modern biblical studies focused largely on exegetical tactics rather than strategy—at least until the advent of liberation and advocacy approaches. Mainstream biblical scholarship "has been guided by its espousal of . . . a method, namely, historical criticism, rather than by a developed hermeneutical theory."[13] Whether a biblical scholar uses, say, source, form, or redaction criticism is a tactical, not strategic matter; in all three cases, the aim is to understand some aspect of the world behind the text.

Tactics and strategy are equally important in achieving victory in war, yet tactics must serve strategic goals. Strategy is magisterial, tactics ministerial.[14] The moral should be clear. Seriously literal interpreters will not prevail in the conflict of interpretations until they begin thinking in terms of strategy and not tactics alone. The strategist keeps in mind the aim of the struggle, and this determines everything else: where to pour one's resources, which battles to fight. Mere Christian hermeneutics is primarily about strategy. This is where the conflict of interpretations really lies.

Hermeneutical Strategies: Interpretive Ends

What is probably Clausewitz's best-known quote identifies what is at stake in the conflict of interpretations: "War is a mere continuation of politics by other means."[15] Politics pertains to ways power and authority are used to achieve certain ends for a certain group of people who inhabit a certain place (e.g., city [Gk. *polis*], region, or country). If the deepest source of the conflict of interpretations is less about tactics (i.e., exegetical procedures) than strategy, then a mere Christian hermeneutic must attend to the ends of biblical interpretation. In particular, we must ensure that interpretive tactics serve interpretive ends—and take care that our interpretive ends are not self-serving.

People read the Bible with a wide range of interpretive interests: to learn more about the ancient Near East; to reconstruct a text's composition history; to learn how people in ancient cultures treated women, children, and the disabled. None of these scholarly interests is explicitly political, theological, or conducive to conflict. However, it is possible to read the Bible strategically, in ways that support one's own community's *power* interests, which is to say, for political ends. The conflict of interpretations today is largely over identity politics—what kind of people we wish to become or wish others to become—and how this relates to what God is doing in Christ. We therefore need to update Frei's

13. Schneiders, *Revelatory Text*, 23.

14. Michel de Certeau deployed the tactics/strategy distinction differently in *The Practice of Everyday Life*, 3rd ed. (Berkeley: University of California Press, 1984). He viewed "tactics" as subversive ways ordinary people cope with or subvert the "strategies" put in place by social institutions.

15. Clausewitz, *On War*, 87.

analysis of the eclipse of literal interpretation: whereas early moderns privileged an immanent frame of reference that shrunk the literal sense to the empirical referent in the world behind the text, late moderns are more inclined to privilege an immanent frame of reference and read for the sake of transforming the world in front of the text. Both strategies unfortunately eclipse the literal sense.

"Let My People Go": Liberative Aim, Emancipatory Interpretation

Identity politics dominates large swathes of biblical interpretation. The updated fourth edition of one of the standard hermeneutic textbooks now features a section on "Exegesis: Identity and Advocacy." Reading the Bible in a way that furthers the interests of one's gender, ethnicity, and social class have, for many, become their exclusive interpretive strategy: "Interpretive approaches closely related to the identity of the reader quite naturally give way to advocacy."[16] Various liberationist, postcolonial, and feminist approaches to biblical interpretation focus on promoting shapes of human freedom and flourishing, not on reconstructing "what actually happened."[17] For example, Elizabeth Schüssler Fiorenza denies revelatory status to any biblical text that is not emancipatory for women, deeming any interpretation that is not emancipatory for women to be unethical.[18]

Both the title and the argument of David Janzen's book *The Liberation of Method* sums up the strategic aim of interpretive identity politics.[19] Instead of asking whether a reading conforms to this or that critical method, Janzen thinks we should ask whether a reading contributes to the emancipation of oppressed minorities and to greater justice for all. The best way to ensure justice, he argues, is to privilege readings that come from the two-thirds world and from the various colors in the Rainbow Coalition or the LGBTQIA+ community whose voices have been suppressed or excluded from the discussion. The strategic goal is liberation, and the ethical reading is the one that contributes to greater emancipation of the oppressed, whether or not it conforms to standardized exegetical methods.

The idea that we need "liberating" from Western methods is somewhat

16. See John H. Hayes and Carl R. Holladay, *Biblical Exegesis: A Beginner's Handbook*, 4th ed. (Louisville: Westminster John Knox, 2022), ch. 11, "Exegesis: Identity and Advocacy," 185.

17. See further R. S. Sugirtharajah, ed., *Exploring Postcolonial Biblical Criticism: History, Method, Practice* (Oxford: Wiley-Blackwell, 2011); and Alejandro F. Botta and Pablo R. Andinach, eds., *The Bible and the Hermeneutics of Liberation* (Atlanta: Society of Biblical Literature, 2009); Elisabeth Schüssler Fiorenza, *Bread Not Stone: The Challenge of Feminist Biblical Interpretation*, rev. ed. (Boston: Beacon, 1995).

18. Elisabeth Schüssler Fiorenza, "The Ethics of Interpretation: Decentering Biblical Scholarship," *Journal of Biblical Literature* 107 (1988): 101–15.

19. David Janzen, *The Liberation of Method—The Ethics of Emancipatory Biblical Interpretation* (Minneapolis: Fortress, 2021).

ironic, for the Enlightenment was itself a call for liberation: "Throughout the modern period, the appeal to the literal sense has frequently embodied an emancipatory impulse that seeks to free the Bible from the overlay of ecclesial interpretation and control."[20] Cardinal Ratzinger (later Pope Benedict XVI) issued a similar call for a liberation from the illusion that biblical scholarship (i.e., "method") is neutral and scientific. We need, he said, a "criticism of criticism."[21] Scott Hahn's *Politicizing the Bible* argues that "modern" interpreters were not disinterested scholars but reformers of a sort who wished to remake society by liberalizing it, which is to say, by liberating it from the domain of the church and received theological opinion.[22] If this is right, then what is "modern" about biblical interpretation is not simply its scientific probing of the text but its subordination of biblical interpretation to political ends and ultimately a "secular magisterium."[23] As with cultures, so with eras: each has its own insights and blind spots. Ratzinger did not intend his "criticism of criticism" to be a scorched-earth policy that leaves nothing of modernity standing. He simply wanted to point out the sociopolitical interests behind "free" critical thinking.

If, per my experiment in biblical-theological criticism, we are to judge forms of criticism by the kind of readers they beget, it may be that neither the historical-critical method nor its ideological successors get passing marks. Modern democratic politics (like modern critical exegesis) is largely procedural rather than teleological, more intent on preserving the smooth operation of freedom (i.e., lack of restraint) than on acknowledging its proper end or purpose (i.e., what freedom is *for*). D. C. Schindler, a critic of modernity, describes this liberative aim as a flight from reality, by which he means the created order, the only objective criterion for assessing what is truly good for human beings.[24] When democracy (freedom *from* an authoritative state) does not correspond to created nature (freedom *for*), it becomes diabolical (Gk. *dia-ballo* = "to divide"),

20. Richard N. Soulen and R. Kendall Soulen, "Literal Sense," in *Handbook of Biblical Criticism*, 4th ed. (Louisville: Westminster John Knox, 2011), 118.

21. Joseph Cardinal Ratzinger, "Biblical Interpretation in Crisis: On the Question of the Foundations and Approaches of Exegesis Today," in *Biblical Interpretation in Crisis: The Ratzinger Conference on Bible and Church*, ed. Richard John Neuhaus (Grand Rapids: Eerdmans, 1989), 6. See also Jeffrey L. Morrow, "The Politics of Biblical Interpretation: A 'Criticism of Criticism,'" *New Blackfriars* 91 (2010): 528–45.

22. See Scott W. Hahn and Benjamin Wiker, *Politicizing the Bible: The Roots of Historical Criticism and the Secularization of Scripture, 1300–1700* (New York: Crossroad, 2013); and Scott W. Hahn and Jeffery L. Morrow, *Modern Biblical Criticism as a Tool of Statecraft (1700–1900)* (Steubenville, OH: Emmaus Academic, 2020).

23. Hahn and Morrow, *Modern Biblical Criticism*, 229. The authors credit this point to Jon Levenson, who claimed that "historical criticism is the form of biblical studies that corresponds to the classical liberal political ideal . . . the realization of the Enlightenment project in the realm of biblical scholarship." Jon Levenson, *The Hebrew Bible, the Old Testament, and Historical Criticism: Jews and Christians in Biblical Studies* (Louisville: Westminster John Knox, 1993), 118.

24. D. C. Schindler, *Freedom from Reality: The Diabolical Character of Modern Liberty* (Notre Dame, IN: University of Notre Dame Press, 2017).

tearing apart the fabric of society as individuals go their own way, in interpretation and everywhere else. This is Augustine's City of Man, a place marked by love of oneself (and others like oneself), pride in oneself (and one's identity group), and advocacy for oneself. It is a strategy that leads to war—and to an eclipse of the literal sense in favor of a liberative frame of reference.

"One in Christ": Incorporative Aim, Conciliatory Interpretation

Mere Christian readers have a different interpretive strategy, a new frame of reference, and a new goal for human flourishing: "For freedom Christ has set us free" (Gal 5:1). Identity politics is presently divisive because the prevailing secular assumption is that freedom is autonomous, a will-to-power to do what is right in one's own eyes. By way of contrast, the Bible depicts freedom as acting in accordance with one's created nature and God's word. Disputes over interpretive methods are but the surface ripples of crosscurrents aswirl in the deeper waters of disputes over human nature and destiny. The real conflict of biblical interpretation lies here: in differences over what the Bible is really about and over the frames of reference that give us access to this reality.

We can still speak of the end of biblical interpretation in terms of identity politics, but in the Christian community, the *polis* of God, identity is not socially constructed but divinely bestowed, a matter of the image of God and formation unto Christlikeness. The church exists to conform individuals in its gathered assemblies to their new identity "in Christ" (2 Cor 5:17), citizens of a holy nation (1 Pet 2:9), people who know how to represent the kingdom of God everywhere to everyone at all times. The primary strategic aim for the church as a reading culture is becoming "wise for salvation through faith in Christ Jesus" (2 Tim 3:15), being built up "to the measure of the stature of the fullness of Christ" (Eph 4:13).[25] To read Scripture theologically is to hold to an incorporative aim: building up the body of Christ (Eph 4:12). One way to do this is to surrender one's own interpretive interests to the interests of the text ("always being reformed by the word of God"). Another way is to put the interest of the whole body ahead of one's self-interest. Augustine expressed something similar when he identified love of God and neighbor as the aim of reading Scripture—and of the politics of the City of God.[26] The overall strategy is individual and corporate formation unto Christlikeness.

---

25. Rebekah Eklund makes a similar point, arguing that Christians read the Bible for the good of "transformative knowledge of God: the increase of wisdom." "The Goods of Reading: Theological Interpretation and Scripture Reasoning," *Journal of Scriptural Reasoning* 9, no. 1 (2010), https://jsr.shanti.virginia.edu/back-issues/vol-9-no-1-december-2010-the-fruits-of-scriptural-reasoning/the-goods-of-reading-theological-interpretation-and-scriptural-reasoning/.

26. Augustine, *On Christian Teaching*, trans. R. P. H. Green (Oxford: Oxford University Press, 2008), 1.86.

An incorporative aim—union first and foremost with Christ, and therefore with one another—lies at the heart of mere Christian hermeneutics. This aim gives rise to a distinct "conciliatory" interpretation, a process that aims at achieving unity through recourse to councils.[27] Gathering together to work through one's differences with others is preferable to going to war. It is also the pattern we see in the New Testament. When the early Christians disagreed about what to require of Gentile converts, they met, in council, at Jerusalem. There was debate, to be sure, but not division. The varying sides eventually came to a common mind: "For it has seemed good to the Holy Spirit and to us . . ." (Acts 15:28).

Identity politics, in the sense of working out Christian identity in Christ in our particular place and time, lies at the heart of reading the Bible as Christian Scripture. The burden of this digression into identity politics is to remind us that identity in Christ is the province of the whole church (i.e., catholic), not of any one special interest group. Interpreters and interpretive communities are not gladiators competing in an arena for power and prestige, but delegates in a round-table discussion, a council assembled to discover what the Spirit is saying to the church.[28] The conflict of interpretation easily becomes toxic, especially in the context of identity politics. Differences in the church over biblical interpretation should therefore be worked out in councils that beat the sword of toxicity into the plowshare of catholicity.[29]

Theological Vision: Toward a Reformed Catholic Scriptural Imaginary

Mere Christian hermeneutics is fundamentally a matter of strategy, not tactics. The emphasis is less on using particular methods rather than others than on ordering whatever exegetical procedures one uses to the right theological ends. Interpretive ends become disordered when we seek to read the Bible as something other than what it is: human-divine discourse. Yet deeper even than interpretive tactics and strategies lies vision, a grasp of the whole process of interpretation, which I have described as human response to divine address. The deepest conflict of interpretations lies here, in whether or not one decides to describe the whole process of biblical interpretation in theological terms.

Despite ongoing differences over tactics and strategy, there is common hermeneutical ground on which Christians, past and present, may unite, regardless

27. Both "council" and "conciliate" derive from the Latin *concilium*, meaning "assembly."

28. See David K. Strong and Cynthia A. Strong, "The Globalizing Hermeneutic of the Jerusalem Council," in Craig Ott and Harold A. Netland, eds. *Globalizing Theology: Belief and Practice in an Era of World Christianity* (Grand Rapids: Baker Academic, 2006), 127–30.

29. See further Kevin J. Vanhoozer, *Biblical Authority after Babel: Retrieving the Solas in the Spirit of Mere Protestant Christianity* (Grand Rapids: Brazos, 2016), 230–31.

of their particular contexts, countries, or confessions. It is a common theological vision characterized by "reformed catholicity,"[30] shorthand for the way Christian communities across centuries and cultures have always read Scripture, a way that Protestant Reformers retrieved and epitomized, albeit imperfectly.

The rule of faith, that quasi-creedal summary of the triune God's works of salvation in Jesus Christ,[31] expresses the theological vision behind reformed catholicity. I have already described the rule as an executive summary of Scripture. My focus here will therefore be on the scriptural imaginary that the rule presupposes, and on which a theological vision of the literal sense depends. For, as we have already seen, the secular social imaginary clouds the vision of biblical interpreters by exiling God, and the notion of divine action, from the realm of academic discourse. Recall that a social imaginary is the tacit story that frames our everyday thinking and experience. Biblical narrative goes into eclipse, and biblical interpretation into disorder, when people no longer see God, the world, and themselves by its light.

George Lindbeck, a Lutheran, provided an insightful account of how the faith of the catholic church is linked to the scriptural imaginary:

> From the beginnings until well past the Reformation, those for whom the study of Scripture was the soul of theology . . . read it as a Christ-centered and typologically-unified whole with figural applications to all reality. *Its world was for believers the truly real one within which they thought and lived.* It was primarily a means for understanding other things rather than an object for study (though it was also that).[32]

This claim has everything to do with the right theological vision and framework of reference for literal interpretation. In Lindbeck's words, "A scriptural world is thus able to absorb the universe. It supplies the interpretive framework within which believers seek to live their lives and understand reality."[33] From another location on the Protestant spectrum, James McClendon, a Baptist, said something similar:

> The baptist vision is the way the Bible is read by those who (1) accept the plain sense of Scripture as its dominant sense and recognize their continuity with

30. See Michael Allen and Scott R. Swain, *Reformed Catholicity: The Promise of Retrieval for Theology and Biblical Interpretation* (Grand Rapids: Baker Academic, 2015).

31. So Allen and Swain, 108–9.

32. George Lindbeck, "Two Kinds of Ecumenism: Unitive and Interdenominational," *Gregorianum* 70 (1989): 657–58 (emphasis added).

33. George Lindbeck, *The Nature of Doctrine: Religion and Theology in a Postliberal Age* (Philadelphia: Westminster, 1984), 117.

> the story it tells, and who (2) acknowledge that finding the point of the story leads them to its application, and who also (3) see past and present and future linked by a "this is that" and "then is now" vision, a trope of mystical identity binding the story now to the story then, and the story then and now to God's future yet to come.[34]

This is only the tip of the catholic iceberg: there is a broad Christian consensus that the biblical narrative relates the true story of God, the world, and humanity.

This scriptural imaginary was precisely what fell into eclipse when biblical scholars and theologians exchanged the Bible's own framework for extratextual frameworks of meaning and truth drawn from elsewhere, usually a temporarily fashionable philosophical *ism* (e.g., deism, existentialism). The loss of this catholic consensus in modernity prompted Lindbeck to call for a "postcritical retrieval of classic scriptural hermeneutics," a recovery of the world- and identity-shaping narrative imagination of the biblical canon.[35] Read as the true story of the world, "the Bible had consensus-and-community forming power."[36] The moral: catholicity is a function of the scriptural imaginary. Reading with a scriptural imaginary is part and parcel of a mere Christian hermeneutics and identity.

What Lindbeck said about the biblical narrative serving as the story by which we see everything else (which is what I mean in speaking of a scriptural imaginary) comes close to James Hamilton's definition of biblical theology: "The world does have a true story. The Bible tells it. . . . To do biblical theology is to think about the whole story of the Bible."[37] The story of the Bible constitutes a "symbolic universe": "the set of images, patterns, types, symbols, and signifiers that furnish the minds of the biblical authors."[38] Hamilton sees the task of biblical theology as enabling readers to inhabit the Bible's symbolic universe. This involves seeing the connections between events in its unified story, as well as the relation of the Bible's story to the stories of our own lives. This is precisely the function of a social imaginary. The conflict of interpretive approaches lies not on the level of tactics, but strategy and competing visions that animate and control the process of biblical interpretation. The root of the conflict lies at the

---

34. James W. McClendon, *Systematic Theology*, vol. 2: *Doctrine* (Nashville: Abingdon, 1994), 45.

35. George A. Lindbeck, "Postcritical Canonical Interpretation: Three Modes of Retrieval," in *Theological Exegesis: Essays in Honor of Brevard S. Childs*, ed. Christopher Seitz and Kathryn Greene-McCreight (Grand Rapids: Eerdmans, 1999), 26.

36. Lindbeck, "Two Kinds of Ecumenism," 658.

37. James M. Hamilton, *What Is Biblical Theology? A Guide to the Bible's Story, Symbolism, and Patterns* (Wheaton, IL: Crossway, 2014), 12.

38. Hamilton, 64. Interestingly, Hamilton avoids the term *figures*, though arguably it fits here.

level of the social imaginary, and whether it is secular or scriptural, which is to say, theological (i.e., God-centered).

Having located where the conflict really lies—in rival visions of Christian identity and competing social imaginaries—we turn now to examine how this conflict affects the way Christians think about literality and read for the literal sense.

Mere Christian Figuration: Beyond Typology and Allegory

The scriptural imaginary—the symbolic universe of biblical narrative that connects the Old Testament to the New Testament and constitutes them a unified story—is a prerequisite for reading the Bible theologically. It is also a hallmark of mere Christian hermeneutics, that canonical and consensual—which is to say reformed catholic—practice of reading the Bible as Christian Scripture. What is this practice, and how does it relate to literal interpretation? In chapter 4, I argued that the right frame of reference is less Platonist and sacramental (above/below) than Pauline and eschatological (already/not yet). Here I explore why this frame of reference calls for "figural" reading. My thesis is twofold: (1) figural interpretation of the Bible corresponds to, and unfolds, the scriptural imaginary itself (the story of the triune God's saving action in the world); (2) figural interpretation is less an exegetical tactic than it is a hermeneutic strategy informed by a theological vision.

Types of Figural Reading: Presuppositions and Practice

Although Hamilton sees a close connection between the Bible's symbolic universe (biblical theology) and "figural" interpretation, it is telling that he shies away from the term because, in his words, "*figural* now seems to be used to refer to connections forged by the interpreter *apart from* exegetical details in the text."[39] His hesitation is understandable and reflects the concerns modern biblical scholarship has with premodern interpretations. And yet no single term better describes the heart and soul of mere Christian biblical interpretation than *figural*. Figural interpretation is as universal (catholic) a reading practice as literal interpretation. And therein lies the paradox: *Can a mere Christian hermeneutic be both literal and figural?* Before we can answer, we must define our terms, and this entails clarifying the distinction between allegory and typology, the two main species of figural interpretation. The burden of this section is to show why figural reading is integral to seriously literal interpretation.

39. Hamilton, 62 (emphasis original).

All readers regularly encounter figures of speech whereby we speak of one thing in terms of something else. The Bible is filled with similes, symbols, and metaphors that speak of God as a shepherd (Ps 80:1), shield (Ps 84:11), fortress (2 Sam 22:2), and so forth. The kind of figures with which we are presently concerned pertain less to speech than to persons, things, and events. A figure, in the sense I am using the term here, is the result of a divine intention to establish a relationship between two or more things, such that the former represents or betokens the latter: "One event or utterance figures another when, while remaining unalterably what it is, it announces or communicates something other than itself."[40] Human speech agents do things with words, but God communicates by doing things with *things*. *Figuration*—the making of figures—is a way of viewing and experiencing things as part of a unified pattern of divine activity in history. These figures are the glue that unify biblical narrative and give it coherence. For example, Paul in Romans 9 and 11 uses "Israel" to refer not only to the historical ethnic community whose story the Old Testament tells, but also to the new community defined by faith in Christ. Israel *figures* the church. Such figuration is more than rhetorical: Paul is saying that "God has expanded Israel by including gentiles in a way that preserves the continuity of that community's identity with the Israel made up of Jews."[41]

God is the primary figurative agent. It is God who expands the meaning of "Israel" even as he remains faithful to the original community.[42] Here, then, is the mere Christian principle of figural interpretation: *Human readers figure God's figurations after him.* The figural reading I examine here is thus a distinctly Christian practice arising from distinctly Christian theological convictions, in particular, an affirmation of divine authorship of history.

The Fundamental Presupposition: A Providential Ordering of Time, Word, and Thing

The first principle of figural reading, divine providence, is as theological as it gets—and as historical. To repeat, the biblical figures are more than forms of speech; rather, they are elements in the divine grammar of history. Figural interpretation presupposes that the meaningful patterns connecting persons, things, and events in the biblical story are grounded in the divinely intended patterns that make up historical reality. Call it "figural realism." Figural realism stakes theological claims about real world history. And this,

40. Paul Griffiths, *Song of Songs*, Brazos Theological Commentary on the Bible (Grand Rapids: Brazos, 2011), lvii.

41. John David Dawson, *Christian Figural Reading and the Fashioning of Identity* (Berkeley: University of California Press, 2002), 21.

42. This is a key point in Gregory W. Lee, *Today When You Hear His Voice: Scripture, the Covenants, and the People of God* (Grand Rapids: Eerdmans, 2016), 192–217.

finally, is why the social imaginary is so important: to read figurally is to hold to a particular worldview in which divine action looms large. God, by speaking, forms both things *and the connections between things*, even things centuries removed. Moreover, these things (figures) are story-shaped, in the sense that their existence has a beginning, middle, and ending, all of which are divinely authored. Figural realism affirms an intelligible order to created reality because God speaks intelligibly and is faithful to his word. Figural interpretation is the mere Christian way of discerning this order, set forth in speech—"figured"—in the biblical texts.

Scripture consistently depicts God as acting in history to reveal his will, realize his plans, and fulfill his promises. The doctrine of divine providence is a kind of grammatical rule for following the way the biblical words go when they speak of the God/world relationship. To inhabit the scriptural imaginary is to look along the biblical text and believe, with the biblical authors, that God is working out the purpose of his will in his own time and way, prefigured in the history of Israel but definitively revealed only in the person, history, and work of Jesus Christ.

Figural realism illumines not only the connection between Old Testament and New Testament but also the connection between biblical text and the reader's lived reality. For example, the "exodus" refers not simply to a past event (God's delivery of Israel from bondage in Egypt) but to a characteristic pattern of divine saving action that culminates in what God is doing in Christ, which is why Luke described Jesus' impending death as a "departure" or *exodos* (Luke 9:31), the ultimate realization of the deliverance that Israel's exodus from Egypt foreshadowed and prefigured. The biblical figures make up not only a symbolic universe but a coherent narrative, connected not only chronologically but by "providential affiliation through time, as later and earlier witnesses are canonically associated."[43] Israel's exodus and Jesus' exodus become figures through which Paul reads his own life, leading him to declare, "I have been crucified with Christ" (Gal 2:20). Other biblical figures, like Israel's wilderness wanderings, feature prominently in hymns such as William Williams's "Guide Me, O Thou Great Jehovah," in which the contemporary singer *is* Israel wandering in the wilderness.[44] God's word written continues to have figurative power insofar as it constitutes an always-relevant frame of reference that makes sense of who and where we are as readers of Scripture.

---

43. Christopher Seitz, *Prophecy and Hermeneutics: Toward a New Introduction to the Prophets* (Grand Rapids: Baker, 2007), 122.

44. See the discussion in Bruce Hindmarsh, "*Lectio Evangelica*: Figural Interpretation and Early Evangelical Bible Reading," in *Every Leaf, Line, and Letter: Evangelicals and the Bible from the 1730s to the Present*, ed. Timothy Larsen (Downers Grove, IL: IVP Academic, 2021), 43–45.

A Reformed Catholic Practice: Figural Interpretation Today

In a secular age that reads the world and the Bible within an immanent frame of reference, figural interpretation appears thoroughly fictive: an imaginative human construction. It is no wonder, then, that what I have described as a catholic (universal) Christian reading practice has fallen on hard times. It is a fateful fall, for readers ultimately fail to understand the Bible's true literal meaning unless and until they can read figurally. I realize this is a controversial claim. Many evangelical Protestants put allegorical, spiritual, and figurative interpretations into the same "nontextual" basket. In the next section, I therefore propose a criterion with which to distinguish "good" from "bad" figuration. The immediate task, however, is to explain why figural reading matters.

The twentieth-century rediscovery of figural reading owes much to Erich Auerbach, a literary critic who detected in the Old Testament a distinct style from what he saw in other ancient histories like Homer's: "Figural interpretation establishes a connection between two events or persons in such a way that the first signifies not only itself but also the second, while the second involves or fulfills the first."[45] Auerbach cited the way in which the sacrifice of Isaac prefigured the sacrifice of Christ, noting how such figuration cannot be contained by an immanent frame: "a connection is established between two events which are linked neither temporally nor causally—a connection which it is impossible to establish by reason in the horizontal dimension."[46]

Credit for discovering Auerbach, and for teasing out the significance of figuration for Christology, goes to Hans Frei. His struggle to understand the eclipse of biblical narrative in modern biblical criticism resulted in his bringing into sharper focus the nature of precritical reading. It was precisely the sense that the biblical texts made up one unified story, thanks to figuration, that was lost when critics read Scripture as man-made rather than God-given: "The interpretive means for joining them [the several biblical stories] was to make earlier biblical stories figures or types of later stories and of their events and patterns of meaning."[47] Significantly, Frei saw figuration as an extension of literal interpretation: "It was literalism at the level of the whole biblical study and thus of the depiction of the whole of historical reality."[48] The col-

45. Erich Auerbach, *Mimesis: The Representation of Reality in Western Literature* (Princeton, NJ: Princeton University Press, 1968), 73. See also his seminal essay, "Figura," in *Scenes from the Drama of European Literature* (Gloucester, MA: Peter Smith, 1973), 11–76; and James W. Skillen, "Reengaging Figural Interpretation: The Impact of Erich Auerbach," *Calvin Theological Journal* 52, no. 2 (2017): 181–203.

46. Auerbach, *Mimesis*, 73.

47. Hans Frei, *The Eclipse of Biblical Narrative: A Study in Eighteenth and Nineteenth Century Hermeneutics* (New Haven, CT: Yale University Press, 1974), 2.

48. Frei, 2.

lapse of figural interpretation compromised the Bible's ability to function as Christian Scripture.[49]

The canon is the literary space that generates and governs the figural extensions of the literal sense: "*As the Son and the Father are one, so, too, is the witness to them from the Old and New Testaments*."[50] Christopher Seitz insists that Old Testament figures are not confined to a distant past but are forward-looking, having "an extensional dimension arising from the historical and literal sense."[51] The discrete witness of the Old Testament has everything to do with reading it forward, not as predictions but as prefigurations of Christ, "disclosures of Christ . . . in the scripture's own literal sense."[52] From the beginning, Seitz seems to suggest, God was acting and authoring in figural ways, orienting Old Testament persons, places, and things to their eschatological fulfilment in Jesus Christ. It therefore follows that "the first witness [that is, the Old Testament] is not being retrofitted. . . . The first witness has been so formed by God in its literal sense in advance; it is pre-formed."[53]

Yes and no, says Richard Hays, a New Testament scholar, who agrees that the New Testament authors read the Old Testament figurally, but disagrees that they were extending the literal reading forward. On the contrary, the New Testament authors were reading *backward*: the figural correspondence "is necessarily retrospective rather than prospective."[54] Hays thinks the Gospels teach us to read the Old Testament "for latent figural meanings unsuspected by the original author and readers."[55] Most of what earlier generations identified as messianic prophecies are, in Hays's view, examples of retrospective figural reading, for the way Jesus fulfills them typically "comes as a poetic surprise, a surprise that *reconfigures* our understanding of the precursor texts and transforms any conscious intention of the Old Testament authors."[56] Hays ultimately locates figural associations "not in human intentionality [whether of author or

49. See also Dawson's *Christian Figural Reading and the Fashioning of Identity*, an important book that engages Auerbach, Frei, and Daniel Boyarin and argues against a supersessionist understanding of figural reading, according to which Christian readings "replace" Jewish meanings and identity by allegorizing them away. Dawson defends Origen's figural reading as a counterexample.

50. Christopher R. Seitz, *Figured Out: Typology and Providence in Christian Scripture* (Louisville: Westminster John Knox, 2001), 6 (emphasis original).

51. Christopher R. Seitz, *The Elder Testament: Canon, Theology, Trinity* (Waco, TX: Baylor University Press), 6.

52. Seitz, *Elder Testament*, 27.

53. Seitz, *Elder Testament*, 46.

54. Richard B. Hays, *Reading Backwards: Figural Christology and the Fourfold Gospel Witness* (Waco, TX: Baylor University Press, 2014), 2. To be precise: the act of grasping the figural connection must be retrospective. See Richard B. Hays, *Echoes of Scripture in the Gospels* (Waco, TX: Baylor University Press, 2016), 347–48.

55. Hays, *Reading Backwards*, 15.

56. Hays, "Figural Exegesis and the Retrospective Recognition of Israel's Story," *Bulletin for Biblical Research* 29 (2019): 43.

reader] but in the mysterious providence of God, who is ultimately the author of the correspondences woven into these texts and events, correspondences that could be *perceived* only in retrospect."[57] As to ontology, then, Hays is a figural realist, though as to epistemology, he is a figural relativist.[58]

The most thorough recent account of figural interpretation is Don Collett's *Figural Reading and the Old Testament: Theology and Practice*. Collett insists that reading the Old Testament as Christian Scripture does not require Hays's notion of reading backward, which "effectively erases the Old Testament's figural sense as a canonical medium for brokering its christological sense."[59] There is nothing deficient about the Old Testament's witness to Jesus Christ if the Old Testament is "literally" about Jesus. However, to make good on this claim, Collett has to rescue the literal sense from its bondage to modern historicity—and, he believes, from the notion of the historical author's original intention. His thesis is that figural interpretation is "a species of historical reading rooted in the Scripture's literal sense."[60] However, Collett's literal sense is not merely the historical or authorially intended sense. It is rather "embedded within a creational and providential 'rule' for reading Scripture's canonical, final, or 'full' form."[61] It is worth spelling out this "rule" in further detail.

Collett's frame of reference is decidedly theological, reflecting the Genesis account of time as created and providentially ordered by God: "Scripture's theological sense is mediated through inspired words in a given historical context *and* through the relation of those words to a larger, providentially constructed network of figurally related things."[62] The figural meaning of a person, thing, or event is a function of its final place in God's purposive order. For example, when Joseph's brothers sold him into slavery, they intended evil, "but God meant it for good" (Gen 50:20). Tellingly, Collett defines *historia* as "the reality of a life lived under God's providence."[63] This is worlds apart from the way secularists (and some modern biblical scholars and theologians) would define history within the immanent frame. Collett summarizes his view in a nice turn of phrase: "Meaning . . . is not an affair of human consciousness but an affair of providence."[64] Of course, if everything is potentially connected to everything

57. Richard B. Hays, *Echoes of Scripture in the Gospels* (Waco, TX: Baylor University Press, 2016), 359 (emphasis added).

58. By "relativist," I mean only that Hays thinks humans can come to know figural associations retrospectively, that is, *relative* to their post-resurrection position.

59. Don C. Collett, *Figural Reading and the Old Testament: Theology and Practice* (Grand Rapids: Baker Academic, 2020), 145.

60. Collett, 2.

61. Collett, 3.

62. Collett, 107.

63. Collett, 15.

64. Collett, 109.

else, thanks to God's creative omnipotence, then the frame of reference grows exponentially, making it harder to stick the landing on determinate meaning: "What the text means can never be delimited by those [historical] contexts alone because of the eternal nature and voice of the triune Lord who speaks in and through them."[65]

God speaks through "the royal *person* of David, the redemptive *event* of the Exodus, the sacred *institutions* of the tabernacle and the temple."[66] These are all historical realities; Collett clearly wants to root figural reading in the literal sense. But what does he mean by *literal*? Although a figure's meaning is related to its original historical context, the operative term is not provenance but providence: "The literal sense speaks of itself (that is, the historical and original context native to its own day) but at the same time also speaks of something 'other'—namely, the theological reality that gave birth to the literal-historical sense in the first place."[67] The "home" of literal meaning is, for Collett, partly verbal but mainly external (God's providential purpose) and thus only partially mental or intentional (i.e., residing in authorial consciousness). Jesus says, "He [Moses] wrote of me" (John 5:46), but did the Old Testament authors have Jesus "in mind"? Collett shifts the center of semantic gravity away from Moses' conscious awareness to his words: "The Old Testament's christological sense is not grounded in the conscious intentions of biblical authors but in the inspired words they penned."[68] Collett wants to make meaning a function of divine providence, not human subjectivity. I only regret that he does not forge a stronger tie between divine providence and divine authorship: God does things with things *and words*.

Contemporary biblical scholars and theologians alike sense the need to return to figural reading in order to recover the unity of Scripture and explain the way the Old Testament prefigures Christ. Two disputed issues stand out: (1) Who is the agent of figuration (Old Testament authors, New Testament authors, the divine author); and (2) how do figures relate to the literal sense? I have already answered the first: figuration is a function of divine authorship, first of history, then of biblical texts. Collett rightly emphasizes God's providence over history, but he needs to say more about God's providence over philology in order to do justice to the literal sense. We turn now to address the

65. Collett, 55. Collett relies on Ephraim Radner's complex work *Time and the Word: Figural Reading of the Christian Scriptures* (Grand Rapids: Eerdmans, 2016). Radner argues that figural reading "is not really a 'method'" (7) but, rather, a way of identifying what the Bible is talking about (i.e., a theory of reference): "this is that." For a summary and evaluation, see Daniel J. Treier, "Keeping Time: Human Finitude and Figural Interpretation," *Pro Ecclesia* 27 no. 3 (2018): 289–99.

66. Collett, 46.

67. Collett, 29.

68. Collett, 130.

second issue: whether, and how, the Old Testament may be read figurally *and* in a responsible, *text-based* manner.

Figuring Out Allegory and Typology: A Distinction without a Difference?

We are trying to set forth a mere Christian mode of reading that is as literal as it is figural, but definitions continue to elude us. From the early church until post-Reformation times, there was a consensus that the Old Testament speaks of Christ in terms of figures that mean something other than what they straightforwardly say. We must not minimize the danger of arbitrary figuration, the bogeyman of modern biblical scholars. Figural interpretation must not be a stratagem for letting untethered allegorizing in through the hermeneutical back door. The way forward is to revisit an older distinction between typology and allegory as modes of figural interpretation.

Both terms have biblical *bona fides*. "Type" (Gk. *tupos*; Lat. *figura*) occurs several times (Rom 5:14; 1 Cor 10:6; Heb 8:5), and Paul famously uses the term allegory (Gk. *allegoria*) once (Gal 4:24).[69] Early Christian readers were quick to justify their own allegorizing by appealing to Paul's example. We must be cautious, however, not to identify ancient words with modern concepts too quickly. It is difficult to determine whether early Christians, eager to discover Christ in the Old Testament, distinguished in their own minds typological from allegorical readings. Here we may recall our conclusion in chapter 2 that what distinguishes typology from allegory is the latter's use of something other than the biblical narrative (*historia*), like Christian Platonism, as a framework for establishing connections between things. Everyone knows that the Reformers had a pronounced allergy to allegory. If figural reading is equivalent to allegorizing, it is difficult in the extreme to imagine that figural reading could be an ingredient in mere Christian hermeneutics. And yet these same Protestant Reformers, champions of the literal sense, also read figurally. Go figure!

Quarrels about Words? A Distinction Unfolds

In the mid-twentieth century, several scholars made a concerted effort to "save" figural interpretation by distinguishing between typology and allegory. Gerhard von Rad claimed that the notion that Old Testament types prefigure Christ is neither arbitrary nor mystical, but "simply corresponds to the belief that the same God who revealed himself in Christ has also left his footprints in

69. Paul's allegorical interpretation of Hagar and Sarah as representing two mountains and two covenants (Hagar = Sinai = old covenant = flesh vs. Sarah = heavenly Jerusalem = new covenant = Spirit) is well known for the difficulties it presents. The chief difficulty may be terminological. Though Paul uses the term ἀλληγορούμενα ("allegorically") in Galatians 4:24, what he does is more accurately described as typological.

the history of the Old Testament covenant people."[70] Leonhard Goppelt defined types as persons, institutions, or events that are "divinely ordained representations . . . of future realities that will be even greater or more complete,"[71] adding that typology was how New Testament authors interpreted the Old Testament. For example, John the Baptist identified Jesus typologically when he says, "Behold, the Lamb of God, who takes away the sin of the world!" (John 1:29).

Hays views typology not as a method of exegesis but as a way of thinking. "Typists" think in narrative patterns, with a scriptural imaginary in which God's saving acts in history are promissory notes, anticipating future acts about which one can say, "How much more!" A number of biblical scholars jumped on the typological bandwagon. Not only was typology *not* allegory, but its promise/fulfillment schema opened up a way for the spiritual sense (the fulfillment) to be compatible with historical-criticism.[72] Typology provided a way of relating past, present, and future "in terms of a historical correspondence and escalation in which the divinely ordered prefigurement finds a complement in the subsequent and greater event."[73]

Meanwhile, in the French-speaking world, church historians were disputing how best to describe Scripture's patristic interpretation. Jean Daniélou suggested that the fathers' exegetical practice contained resources for coping with the "increasing rupture between exegesis and theology" that was characteristic of mid-twentieth-century Roman Catholic and Protestant scholarship alike.[74] Daniélou distinguished typology, a distinctly Christian form of figural reading, from allegory, a tradition of figural reading with roots in Hellenistic and rabbinic sources. His stated purpose was to distinguish "what in the Fathers belongs to ecclesiastical tradition and is strictly speaking typology, and what has its origin in extraneous sources, especially in the allegory of Philo."[75] What distinguishes the two kinds of figuration is the way in which each relates, or fails to relate, to salvation history. Types are "a figure of events to come."[76] Typology

---

70. Gerhard von Rad, "Typological Interpretation of the Old Testament," *Interpretation* 15 (1961): 36.

71. Leonhard Goppelt, *Typos: The Typological Interpretation of the Old Testament in the New Testament* (Grand Rapids: Eerdmans, 1982), 18.

72. For a survey of developments in biblical scholarship, see David L. Baker, *Two Testaments, One Bible: The Theological Relationship between the Old and New Testaments*, 3rd ed. (Downers Grove, IL: IVP Academic, 2010), 169–89; Mitchell L. Chase, *40 Questions about Typology and Allegory* (Grand Rapids: Kregel, 2020), 107–16; and Tibor Fabiny, "Typology: Pros and Cons in Biblical Hermeneutics and Literary Criticism," in *Figura and Fulfillment: Typology in the Bible, Art, and Literature* (Eugene, OR: Wipf & Stock, 2016), 138–55.

73. E. Earle Ellis, *The Old Testament in Early Christianity: Canon and Interpretation in the Light of Modern Research* (Grand Rapids: Baker, 1992), 106.

74. Jean Daniélou, "Les orientations présentes de la pensée religieuse," *Études* 249 (1946): 8.

75. Jean Daniélou, *From Shadows to Reality: Studies in the Biblical Typology of the Fathers* (London: Burns & Oates, 1960), viii.

76. Daniélou, *From Shadows to Reality*, 12.

denotes a relationship between two persons, things, or events, each of which belongs to the same sacred history; allegory does not.

Henri de Lubac, a medievalist, objected to Daniélou's distinction, claiming that it was neither scriptural nor an accurate description of patristic interpretation. When the church fathers used the term *allegory* or interpreted allegorically, they were following the apostle Paul, not Philo. Besides, the term *typology* is of recent vintage, dating only from 1840 or so, and so was not available to the church fathers.[77] In response, Daniélou acknowledged the relative youth of the term but insisted that the conceptual distinction it helps identify is indeed ancient: "The main thing, after all, is to make the distinction between the two things quite clear—which Fr. de Lubac does not, perhaps, altogether succeed in doing."[78] The "two things" to which Daniélou refers are two kinds of figural reading: the good ("typology") and the not so good ("allegory"). Daniélou provides a helpful illustration of "good" figural interpretation: "In the Exodus, in the death and resurrection of Christ, and in Baptism, it is the same redeeming action which is accomplished on different levels of history—that of the figure, of the reality, and of the sacrament."[79]

It did not help calm down their disagreement when both Daniélou and de Lubac wrote books on Origen, the one claiming him as an exemplar of typology, the other as a champion of allegory. As we have seen, Origen is indeed a lightning-rod figure in the history of biblical interpretation.[80] R. P. C. Hanson distinguished between two kinds of allegory, Hellenistic and "Palestinian," identifying Origen with the bad (Hellenistic) kind whose link between the original event and its nonliteral referent was arbitrary.[81] Daniélou maintained that, in addition to its loose connection with the framework of salvation history, allegory leads to interpretations with too many fanciful details, whereas typology limits its power of figural invention by staying rooted to its center of gravity, the continuous narrative that culminates in the gospel of Jesus Christ. Ironically, what is ultimately at issue in this dispute between the two species of figural interpretation is the literality of the divine action recounted in the Bible.

The quarrel over figural interpretation continues. Frances Young acknowledges that the term *typology* is a modern construct but thinks it is still useful.[82]

77. Andrew Louth, *Discerning the Mystery: An Essay on the Nature of Theology* (Oxford: Clarendon, 1983), 118.

78. Jean Daniélou, *Origen* (New York: Sheed and Ward, 1955), 327n2.

79. Jean Daniélou, *The Bible and the Liturgy* (Notre Dame, IN: University of Notre Dame Press, 1956), 87.

80. See Dawson, *Christian Figural Reading and the Fashioning of Identity*, chs. 5, 6.

81. R. P. C. Hanson, *Allegory and Event: A Study of the Sources and Significance of Origen's Interpretation of Scripture* (Richmond: John Knox, 1959).

82. Frances M. Young, *Biblical Exegesis and the Formation of Christian Culture* (Cambridge: Cambridge University Press, 1997), 152.

We find typology, she suggests, in the context of overall narrative coherence. Allegorical references, in contrast, are untethered; they refer to something other than or external to the story of which they are a part. According to Young, typology "requires a mirroring of the supposed deeper meaning in the text taken as a coherent whole, whereas allegory involves using words as symbols or tokens, arbitrarily referring to other realities by application of a code, and so destroying the narrative, or surface, coherence of the text. . . . Typology remains true to the narrative, allegory translates narrative into propositions."[83]

To restate Young's formulation of the distinction in terms of the present work: typology employs a text-based frame of reference for reading biblical narrative, whereas allegory employs a frame of reference taken from elsewhere than the text.[84] The emerging consensus is that "typology and allegory are *competing* forms of nonliteral exegesis, the former the successful variety, the latter its unsuccessful, nonliteral twin."[85] Two points are worth noting: first, there is an unfortunate tendency among modern scholars to conflate literal with literalistic; second, even those who affirm the consensus view do not always agree on how to draw the distinction.

Typology Lost? The Distinction Grows Strangely Dim

The alliance between mid-twentieth-century biblical and patristic scholars seeking to defend the distinction between typology and allegory began to unravel at century's end as the distinction came under fire from both sides, largely because of further research into early Christian allegory: "'Typology' is a modern construct. Ancient exegetes did not distinguish between typology and allegory, and it is often difficult to make the distinction, the one shading into the other all too easily."[86] This is particularly true of Origen, who meant something different by "typology" and "allegory" than what those terms have come to mean in the twentieth century.

Thomas Luxon blames the Reformers for muddying the waters by making what he thinks is nothing more than a rhetorical distinction: "Typology . . . is allegory that denies it is allegory."[87] What drives this denial, says Luxon, is Christianity's dualistic distinction between this age and the age to come, the flesh and the spirit. Dualistic thinking requires allegorical discourse: if

83. Young, 162.

84. This formulation of the typology/allegory distinction recalls George Lindbeck's distinction between intratextual and extratextual theology in his *The Nature of Christian Doctrine* (Louisville: Westminster John Knox, 1984).

85. Peter Martens, "Revisiting the Allegory/Typology Distinction: The Case of Origen," *Journal of Early Christian Studies* 16, no. 3 (2008): 295.

86. Young, *Biblical Exegesis*, 152.

87. Thomas Luxon, *Literal Figures: Puritan Allegory and the Reformation Crisis in Representation* (Chicago: University of Chicago Press, 1995), 22.

the heaven to come is the true reality, then earthly realities are only shadowy allegories—dim figures of the eternal world to come. Typology is simply a Protestant dodge, "a euphemism for allegory designed to mark Protestantism's continued commitment to allegorical structures of thought," namely, a dualistic, two-world frame of reference.[88] As I suggested earlier in connection to Christian Platonism, however, it is an open question as to whether earth/heaven should be conceived vertically, in terms of above and below, rather than redemptive-historically, in terms of already/not yet.[89]

Surprisingly enough, Brevard Childs once proposed dropping the distinction altogether and reclaiming allegory as the best catchall term for Christian figural interpretation, which he described as "the struggle to discern the mystery of Christ."[90] Childs credited his own change of heart and mind as concerns allegory to Andrew Louth's chapter "Return to Allegory," part of his book *Discerning the Mystery*.[91] The key question for any form of exegesis, says Louth, is whether it enables us to hear the voice of God in Scripture. Allegory is "a means of ensuring that we do not evade the fundamental 'ontological difficulty' which opens us to the ultimate mystery of Christ contained in the Scriptures."[92] Allegorical interpretation is thus the quest for the "other," "higher," "deeper," or "spiritual" reference—the truth of the theological subject matter. Hence, "the heart of the problem of allegory turns on the nature of the referentiality of the biblical text."[93] The importance of frames of reference has been a recurring theme of the present work. Here, too, I believe we best explain the difference between the two modes of figural reading by specifying their respective frames of reference.

It may be useful to pause and recall where we are and why we are here. We are attempting to set forth a mere Christian hermeneutic, a figural way of reading the Bible that (so I am claiming) enjoys catholic continuity across the many centuries, cultures, and confessional statements that appear to divide us. Those who deny the typology/allegory distinction tend to view Christian figural reading as allegorical. We can describe this situation as "typology lost." The new champions of describing figural reading as allegorical insist that they are not

88. Luxon, 40.

89. Cf. Collett: "The movement to distinguish typology from allegory in the mid-twentieth century was an attempt to translate the vertical nature of *theological* other-speaking in allegory and figure into a horizontal form of *historical* other-speaking, thereby rendering biblical figures safe for public consumption by modern biblical interpreters" (*Figural Reading and the Old Testament*, 48n72). Luxon seems to be making a similar point about the Protestant Reformers.

90. Brevard S. Childs, "Allegory and Typology in Biblical Interpretation," in *The Bible as Christian Scripture*, ed. Christopher R. Seitz and Kent Harold Richards (Atlanta: Society of Biblical Literature, 2013), 304.

91. Childs refers to "Louth's brilliant chapter" in "Allegory and Typology in Biblical Interpretation," 304.

92. Andrew Louth, *Discerning the Mystery*, 112.

93. Childs, "Allegory and Typology in Biblical Interpretation," 304.

flying *from* history but, rather, further *into* the depths of history: "The allegorical sense represents our attempt to understand the mystery we discern here."[94] The new allegorists worry that without some kind of spiritual interpretation, "the biblical text can only be an object of archaeological interest."[95]

As we have seen, nothing bothers seriously literal interpreters more than the arbitrary lists of correspondences that allegorical interpretation apparently licenses ("This means *whaaat?*"). Biblical scholars want to know whether allegorizers have anything like air traffic control to rein in flights of exegetical fancy. Christian allegorizers are not free to "figure out" indefinitely, for Scripture presents them with a magnetic field of figures, with Christ as the "magnetic pole" and the rule of faith as the "field of force."[96] As Jason Byassee puts it in his study of Augustine's allegorical interpretation of the Psalms, "*Christ* is the guarantor against allegorical flights of fancy, the 'control' that fixes our readings on the ground."[97]

Recent scholarship on Origen, our arch-allegorizer, has focused on the role of the reader's edification.[98] It is almost as if Origen was conducting his own experiment in biblical-theological criticism, judging the validity of allegorical interpretations on the basis of how well they equipped the reader to progress toward the soul's perfection: "By examining this drama as it was inscribed on Scripture's pages, ideal interpreters also participated in it."[99] Martens is keen to present Origen's figural interpretation as "a way of life."[100] To Origen's credit, he intended his allegorizing to foster a reading culture governed by the scriptural imaginary, a reading culture that would foster readers who see themselves as the people of God on a journey back to God culminating in the vision of God.[101] The question remains: Is *allegory* the best way to construe the figural reading that I think characterizes a mere Christian hermeneutic?

---

94. Louth, *Discerning the Mystery*, 117. Louth adds, "What Daniélou calls 'typology' they [the Fathers and medieval theologians] call 'allegory'" (118). Louth says the distinction is better characterized by de Lubac, who distinguished between *allegoria facti* and *allegoria verbi*, stipulating that the latter becomes only empty wordplay unless it is based in the former.

95. Young, *Biblical Exegesis*, 3.

96. Louth, *Discerning the Mystery*, 121.

97. Jason Byassee, *Praise Seeking Understanding: Reading the Psalms with Augustine* (Grand Rapids: Eerdmans, 2007), 40.

98. See, in particular, Karen J. Torjesen, *Hermeneutical Procedure and Theological Method in Origen's Exegesis* (Berlin: W. de Gruyter, 1983); and Peter W. Martens, *Origen and Scripture: The Contours of the Exegetical Life* (Oxford: Oxford University Press, 2012).

99. Martens, *Origen and Scripture*, 6.

100. Martens, *Origen and Scripture*, 1.

101. Treier notes a similar concern in biblical typology. Referring to Paul's statement that what happened to Israel are examples, "types," for us (Paul's readers), Treier says, "For an event to be written is to enable its encouragement of our proper response to God." "Typology," in *Dictionary for Theological Interpretation of the Bible*, ed. Kevin J. Vanhoozer (Grand Rapids: Baker, 2005), 826.

Guarding the Good Conceptual Deposit: A Distinction Regained

Although Young thinks the allegory/typology distinction does not precisely map onto different ways of figural reading in the early church (e.g., Alexandrian versus Antiochene), she continues to think that the term *typology*, though anachronistic, is a useful "heuristic tool" for differentiating patristic modes of reading.[102] The crucial differences between forms of figural reading "lie in the way in which the correspondence and divergencies are conceived."[103] Young herself distinguishes between two ways texts refer to things. In "symbolic" *mimesis*, the reader needs an extratextual code to discover the reference. The figural correspondence here depends on something *outside* the text itself. However, in "ikonic" *mimesis* the correspondence relation is intratextual insofar as the other meaning (the "spiritual" referent) is organically related to the narrative coherence or world of the text (*historia*).[104] In Young's reconstituted concept of typology (ikonic *mimesis*), the frame of reference is integrally related to the text itself, whereas in allegory (symbolic *mimesis*), it is not.

There is no end to quarreling over words. Those who deny any distinction between modes of figuration—between legitimate and illegitimate figural interpretation—risk losing the possibility of rightly tethering the figural/spiritual to the literal sense. What is ultimately at stake in deciding whether to label the reformed catholic tradition of reading typological or allegorical is thus the fate of the literal sense. For the sake of biblical faithfulness and Christian orthodoxy, we must be able to distinguish a warranted or "good" figural reading from its unwarranted or "bad" counterpart. And to do this, we need to have more than descriptions of how so-and-so reads the Bible. Evaluative criteria are necessary if we are to provide a normative rather than descriptive account of figural interpretation. Even Origen distinguished between proper and improper figural exegesis, and some such distinction is also what Daniélou and others have tried to articulate by differentiating typology from allegory.[105] It is one thing to insist that we preserve the *terms* of the distinction, however, quite another to preserve the *distinction* itself.[106] My claim is that mere Christian readers have always worked with some such distinction, even if it has not always been formulated in the same way.

---

102. Young, *Biblical Exegesis*, 193.

103. Young, 191.

104. Benjamin Ribbens likens ikonic *mimesis* to looking "*along* the text." "Typology of Types: Typology in Dialogue," *Journal of Theological Interpretation* 5, no. 1 (2011): 86. Ribbens goes on to identify three further subtypes of ikonic *mimesis*.

105. Martens lists five tacit guidelines in Origen's work with which to distinguish proper from improper figural reading. See Martens, "Revisiting Allegory and Typology," 310–12.

106. Cf. David Yeago's insight that we can express the same judgment with different concepts. "The New Testament and the Nicene Dogma: A Contribution to the Recovery of Theological Exegesis," *Pro Ecclesia* 3 (1994): 152–64. Similarly, I suggest that we can preserve the same distinction with different terms.

For the sake of good historical description, the Origen scholar Martens proposes that we discontinue using "allegory" and "typology" as labels, largely because they are anachronistic.[107] He nevertheless acknowledges that patristic theologians like Origen made a conceptual distinction between better and worse modes of figural reading. Martens therefore urges contemporary interpreters to find alternative labels for these modes and, furthermore, to "develop a conversation around the criteria for successful nonliteral [that is, "figural"] scriptural interpretation."[108] I second the motion, with a couple amendments. First, we need to expand the discussion beyond patristic theologians, because biblical interpreters in every age have had to distinguish between appropriate and inappropriate figural reading. Some such distinction has always been an ingredient in a mere Christian hermeneutic, for figural reading is not a license for interpretive relativism. Second, I am not convinced that all figural reading is a form of nonliteral interpretation, though I readily grant that it is non*literalistic*. The kind of figural reading I advocate, my mere Christian alternative to typological and allegorical interpretation, is *trans-figural*. It only remains to show its compatibility with literal interpretation, a task to which we now turn.

Grammatical-Eschatological Exegesis and the "Trans-figural" Literal Sense

The figural interpretation characteristic of the catholic tradition does not negate the literal sense but is rather its prolongation and culmination. After all, both medieval interpreters and the Reformers searched for ways to acknowledge the full "spirituality of the letter."[109] The reformed catholic practice of reading I set forth here attempts to do justice to both the figural/spiritual and literal aspects of the biblical text. The "reformed" qualifier of catholicity calls attention to a set of emphases shared by the Reformers—loving and obedient attention to the letter of the biblical text (grammar), the importance of divine authorship (figuration), canonical context (Scripture interprets Scripture), and Christ-centered redemptive history—not to a particular Protestant confession.

To do justice to the Bible's literal sense, we must interpret the biblical figures that make up the world of the text with an eschatological frame of reference, remembering that we are dealing with divine authorial discourse about the course of redemptive history. To anticipate: "good" figural reading thickens,

---

107. For a counterargument, see Brent Parker's "Typology and Allegory: Is There a Distinction? A Brief Examination of Figural Reading," *Southern Baptist Journal of Theology* 21, no. 1 (2017): 57–83, in which he provides four reasons for keeping the terminology as well as the distinction.

108. Martens, "Revisiting Allegory and Typology," 316.

109. Christopher Ocker, *Biblical Poetics before Humanism and Reformation* (New York: Cambridge University Press, 2002), 219.

extends, or deepens the literal sense; "bad" figural reading thins, stymies, or subverts the literal sense. What I shall call *trans-figural* interpretation derives not from general or philosophical hermeneutics but from a uniquely scriptural phenomenon, namely, the way in which biblical figures connect "across" (Lat. *trans*) times and testaments so as to make up a coherent unified narrative centered on Jesus Christ. To follow the way the biblical words go is to be caught up in their divine trans-figuration: "This moving *across* the text of the Bible, not past it, is what makes early commentary feel so different and foreign to modern readers."[110] To anticipate: my claim is that what people often refer to as the spiritual sense (i.e., "good" figuration) is actually the *eschatological fullness* of the literal-historical sense. It is not the bare historical but the historical-eschatological frame of reference that enables the literal sense to come into its own—or rather, into all its glory.

The Literal Sense and Trans-figural Realism

A mere Christian hermeneutic promotes literal reading that is both literary and literate, alert both to the way an author refers to reality and to the nature of the reality referred to.[111] I have argued that figural readers *discover* a divinely intended meaning already present in the Old Testament, albeit tacitly. When Paul says that Israel's wilderness wanderings "took place as examples [*tupoi*] for us" (1 Cor 10:6), he is not simply drawing a moral from a story, as if he were an apostolic Aesop. On the contrary, he is speaking of *typification*, "a pattern or archetype that prefigures a later fulfillment in which both cast light on the other."[112] C. H. Dodd famously suggested that the New Testament authors likely learned how to read the Old Testament from Jesus.[113] Was Jesus respecting the Old Testament's literal sense, or was he using it to say something its authors were not saying when, on the road to Emmaus, he interpreted to the disciples "in all the Scriptures the things concerning himself" (Luke 24:27)?

The Bible's typological associations, first observed by Jesus himself, are not invented, haphazard, nor artificial. Again, they are the result of prior divine figural intention. Jesus was no creative anti-realist when it comes to the semantics of

---

110. Mark Gignilliat and Jonathan T. Pennington, "Theological Commentary," in *A Manifesto for Theological Interpretation*, ed. Craig G. Bartholomew and Heath A. Thomas (Grand Rapids: Baker Academic, 2016), 241.

111. Cf. the similar distinction between literal-factual and literal-literary in Richard S. Briggs, *Theological Hermeneutics and the Book of Numbers as Christian Scripture* (Notre Dame, IN: University of Notre Dame Press, 2018), 58. Elsewhere I have defined the literal sense as "the sense of a literary act." Kevin J. Vanhoozer, *Is There a Meaning in This Text? The Bible, the Reader, and the Morality of Literary Knowledge* (Grand Rapids: Zondervan, 1998), 312.

112. Kimlyn J. Bender, *1 Corinthians* (Grand Rapids: Brazos, 2022), 167.

113. C. H. Dodd, *According to the Scriptures: The Substructure of New Testament Theology* (London: Nisbet, 1952), 126–27.

biblical language and literature. He was not conjuring up associations between Israel's history and his own that had no basis in something real. Rather, Jesus makes known the plan of salvation, and the correspondences that constituted it, that had been set in place "before the foundation of the world" (Eph 1:4).

Jesus' hearers did not always understand: "This figure of speech Jesus used with them, but they did not understand what he was saying to them" (John 10:6). The problem had nothing to do with his vocabulary or his pronunciation, yet his meaning still eluded his listeners. On one occasion, Jesus cites Zechariah 9:9: "Fear not, daughter of Zion; behold, your king is coming, sitting on a donkey's colt" (John 12:15). John observes, "His disciples did not understand these things at first, but when Jesus was glorified, then they remembered that these things had been written about him and had been done to him" (v. 16). That the disciples came to understand the figure only later has nothing to do with its verbal meaning, which did not change; rather, it had everything to do with the disciples' inability to follow Jesus' words to their proper referent. It is a point worth emphasizing: what changed was not Jesus' meaning but the disciples' understanding.

As we have seen, figural interpretation allows readers to explore the rich network of meaningful connections between biblical persons, things, and events that are the narrative infrastructure of the scriptural imaginary. Similar to typology, it is a way of thinking biblically and theologically—thinking God's thoughts after him, tracking the way his eternal purpose has been realized in Jesus Christ (Eph 3:11).[114] To look *along* the biblical text is to read figurally, tracing the correspondences between Old Testament prefigurations and their fulfillment in Christ. How we label this "good" figural reading matters less than being able to say what makes it good. My mere Christian alternative to both allegory and typology is to describe the right kind of figural reading as *trans-figural*. It remains only to show how the way the *figures* go connects to the "way the words run"—the literal sense.

Textual understanding is the ability to follow what has been said to what it has been said *about*. To follow the way biblical words run across history, through the centuries, from shadowy anticipations to bright revelations, from figure to figured, is to read *trans-figurally* (= "across-figures"). Hence my thesis: *Trans-figural interpretation follows the way the biblical words run across or beyond figures to the realities those figures foreshadow and anticipate.*

It should be obvious that reading trans-figurally requires a biblically informed scriptural imaginary. How else can one follow God's figurations after

114. "Typology is not a method of biblical interpretation, but a way of thinking" (David L. Baker, describing Goppelt's position, in Baker, *Two Testaments, One Bible: The Theological Relationship between the Old and New Testaments*, 3rd ed. (Downers Grove, IL: IVP Academic, 2010), 173.

him? The crucial point as regards the literal sense is that trans-figural interpretation follows figural trajectories that are really there, in history, in the world opened up by the letter of the biblical text, which is also the real world.[115] To paraphrase the poet Gerard Manley Hopkins: the world of the Bible is charged with the grandeur of God—and his figurations.[116] The reality of this world, divine figurations and all, cannot be grasped by immanent-only frames of reference, or by historical-critical methods of reading. This trans-figural reality only comes into view thanks to a scriptural imaginary. My interim conclusion: the literal sense of the text, what the Bible's divine author is really talking about, demands figural—or as I am now calling it, *trans-figural*—interpretation. For unless we can follow the way the words go, from figure to figured, we will neither understand nor ascertain the literal sense.[117] My claim, then, is that *trans-figural interpretation thickens, extends, and deepens the literal sense, precisely by following the way the words go, from figure to what is figured.*

The Literal Sense: Divine Authorial Discourse and Canonical Intentionality

All the elements necessary for defining the literal sense—the letter of the text, discourse, context, frame of reference, hermeneutical strategy, interpretive vision—are now on the table, though we have yet to see how they fit together. To see how they do, we must return to the notion of divine authorial discourse and the question of its context(s).

The matter to clear up is whether reading divine discourse trans-figurally entails a change in meaning. I intend to show that it does not. Following the way the divine author's words and figures run, from their original sense to their final destination, neither adds to nor distorts the verbal sense (i.e., the *something* of something said). The semantic range of biblical words is fixed, determined by their original use at a certain time. What *does* change (because it gets trans-figured) is the referent (the something *about which* something is said)—and the reader's understanding.[118] The decisive point, not to be missed, is this: the verbal content of a sentence will always underdetermine its reference until we know *whose discourse* it is. What is finally at issue in trans-figural interpretation

115. We could call these figural trajectories either typologies or allegories provided we acknowledge them as verbal, historical, and divinely intended.

116. An allusion to the famous opening line from Gerard Manley Hopkins's poem "God's Grandeur": "The world is charged with the grandeur of God" (in Gerard Manley Hopkins, *Poems and Prose* [London: Penguin Classics, 1985], 27).

117. My claim is that trans-figural reading is commonplace in the patristic, medieval, and Reformation periods, as well as in their evangelical descendants (for an example of the latter, see Hindmarsh, "*Lectio Evangelica*," 32–54).

118. Note, too, that the particular change in question does not alter but, rather, adds to or "thickens" the original referent.

and its relation to the literal sense is the Bible's nature as discourse. The literal meaning is a function not simply of the words used but of the way the author uses words. It follows, then, that literal interpretation must attend not to verbal sense only but to all aspects of biblical discourse, in particular *who* is speaking (the author), *about what* (the referent), and *to whom* (the audience).

Literality pertains to *the way the words run*. To define a text as "discourse fixed by writing"[119] reminds us to specify *how* and *why* the words are running in just this way, *where* they are heading, and *who* is running them in that direction. The Antiochenes, of course, knew the literal sense "covered the whole meaning of the writer, including his metaphors and figures."[120] When Paul refers to Israel's miraculous drinking water from a rock at the beginning and end of their wilderness wanderings (Exod 17:6; Num 20:11), and then says, "the Rock was Christ" (1 Cor 10:4), he does not change the verbal sense of either Old Testament passage. Instead, he identifies their ultimate referent. This final referent (Christ) makes clear what the semantic content (a water-giving rock) was always ultimately about, even if the original hearers (like Jesus' disciples) could not appreciate it at the time.[121] We know that Jesus viewed himself as the source of life-giving water (John 4:10; cf. John 7:38–39, 19:34; Rev 22:1). If literality is a function of the way the words go, then trans-figural interpretation enables the letter of the text to complete its course.[122]

Everything depends on *who* is doing what with biblical words. Who, in the final analysis, is the author of the Bible? There is a spectrum of positions. At one end are those who, even if they affirm biblical inspiration, bind the literal sense to the communicative intent of the original human author. These readers "seek the mind of God in the mind of the human authors of Scripture, and not somewhere else."[123] One critic dubs this way of thinking the "instrumentalization of the literal sense," for on this view the letter is a means for recovering the human author's inspired consciousness.[124] At the other end of the spectrum are those who want to locate meaning not in the inspired authors' consciousness (i.e., what they were aware of at the time of composition) but in the inspired words themselves, in their providentially arranged canonical context. I want to

---

119. Paul Ricoeur, *Hermeneutics and the Human Sciences: Essays on Language, Action, and Interpretation* (Cambridge: Cambridge University Press, 1981), 145.

120. Beryl Smalley, *The Study of the Bible in the Middle Ages* (Oxford: Basil Blackwell, 1952), 14.

121. See further Darrell L. Bock, "Single Meaning, Multiple Contexts and Referents," in *Three Views on the New Testament Use of the Old Testament*, ed. Kenneth Berding and Jonathan Lunde (Grand Rapids: Zondervan, 2007), 125.

122. For an extended analysis of this passage, see my "Ascending the Mountain, Singing the Rock: Biblical Interpretation Earthed, Typed, and Transfigured," *Modern Theology* 20, no. 4 (2012): 781–803.

123. Iain Provan, *The Reformation and the Right Reading of Scripture* (Waco, TX: Baylor University Press, 2017), 91.

124. Collett, *Figural Reading and the Old Testament*, 128.

examine both ends of the spectrum, though my aim is to propose an alternative closer to the middle.

Two recent works, both by Old Testament scholars, spell out what it means to read the Old Testament theologically as Christian Scripture. Each wants to marry literal and spiritual interpretation in responsible fashion, via reference to the Bible as a canonical whole, yet each is apparently unaware of the other's work. Also of interest is how each aspires to the mantle of Reformation hermeneutics yet struggles to give an adequate account of *whose* communicative intent comes through at the canonical level, and how.

Iain Provan's "fifth way" of reading the Bible, "seriously literal interpretation," claims to stand in fundamental continuity with the Reformers. He also allows for figural reading, which, following Frei, he describes as "literalism at the level of the whole biblical story."[125] This is a significant claim, one that does not neatly fit the typology for literality we examined in the previous chapter. Provan rightly contends for a literality beyond the sentence level. For example, Psalm 2 probably functioned as a royal coronation psalm, to be sung when a new king was crowned in ancient Israel. However, when read in the context of the whole book of Psalms, probably dating from the postexilic period, Psalm 2 speaks about a king who is yet to come. In the larger context of the whole Psalter, that is, the literal meaning of Psalm 2 has to do with messianic hope.[126] It would therefore appear that even a seriously literal interpreter like Provan is willing to accept "a double literal sense."[127] Here is his key claim: "To read literally is to read biblical texts not only as they were first uttered or written by their originators, but also as they have been placed in larger literary entities and in conversation with other texts that are also part of the whole canonical collection of Scripture."[128]

It is a crucial point, one that is as catholic as it is reformed: to read the Old Testament Christianly is to read it as canonical Scripture, a unified and integral whole.

The mention of canon raises several questions. First, why should we read the disparate texts that comprise the Old Testament, written by different people at different times, as a meaningful whole? We could appeal to the intentions of the anonymous canonizers responsible for Scripture's final form, as Childs did, but this prompts a second query: What makes *their* intentions so special? Why should the intentions of an unknown group of canonizers create the context that determines the literal sense, the norm of Christian doctrine?

125. Frei, *Eclipse of Biblical Narrative*, 2, cited in Provan, *Reformation and the Right Reading of Scripture*, 100.

126. See Provan, *Reformation and the Right Reading of Scripture*, 95.

127. Provan, 96.

128. Provan, 102.

The unknown identity of the canonizers prompts a third question: *Whose* communicative intention are we seeking when we read biblical words in canonical context? After all, texts on their own lack communicative intent; they are not persons or communicative agents.[129] It is therefore not entirely clear who Provan thinks is the author of the Old Testament texts' canonically intended christological sense.[130] The question remains: Whose communicative intent informs the canonical Scriptures and oversees their final form?

Don Collett arrives at a similar inconclusive conclusion as Provan, albeit by a different route. Like Provan, Collett wants both to preserve the Bible's literal sense and extend it by tying it not to human authorial consciousness but "to the canonical profile and figural shape of its words."[131] This enables Old Testament authors to speak more than they know: the link between their words and Christ is real, but it is a link forged not mentally (i.e., in the minds of the human authors) but figurally, that is, in a divinely ordered (providential) history. Locating literality in human authorial consciousness (the fateful misstep of modern biblical scholarship, in Collett's opinion) limits the referent to what the human authors were aware of at the time of writing, thus effectively short-circuiting figural interpretation.[132]

Neither Provan nor Collett makes explicit appeal to divine authorial intentionality in their respective explanations as to how the words of the Bible run past the limits of what their human authors could have known at the time of writing. Provan appeals to canonical intentionality, Collett to the providentially ordered figural relation between inspired words and things. In addition, Collett worries that *sensus plenior* (the idea that God intends a "fuller" meaning not intended by the human author) works to the detriment of the literal sense inasmuch as literality gets "kicked upstairs, as it were, into the hidden realm of divine authorship and intention."[133] How, he wonders, can we access divine authorial intention? This is the right question. To make sense of canonical

129. This is a disputed point. Some contemporary literary theorists speak of the *intentio operis* ("the intention of the work"). See Umberto Eco, *The Limits of Interpretation* (Bloomington: Indiana University Press, 1990).

130. This explains why Provan concludes that the Reformers do not practice what they preach when it comes to literal interpretation. Provan complains that Luther "frequently cuts across the communicative intent of the text" (*Reformation and the Right Reading of Scripture*, 219), and even Calvin "sometimes failed to follow [his stated hermeneutical method] through in practice" (220). As to Provan's defense of the idea of canonical communicative intentions (see 618), I am not as persuaded as he seems to be by the argument in Charles J. Scalise, *Hermeneutics as Theological Prolegomenon: A Canonical Approach* (Macon, GA: Mercer University Press, 1994), which draws mainly on philosophical (e.g., Ricoeur; Gadamer) rather than properly theological sources.

131. Collett, *Figural Reading and the Old Testament*, 129.

132. "The construction of the authorial self that underwrites the hermeneutics of Descartes, Locke, and Schleiermacher substitutes a particular version of authorial intentionality for the providential intentionality at work in Scripture's formation history" (Collett, *Figural Reading and the Old Testament*, 128).

133. Collett, 140.

intentionality (Provan) and of the way inspired Old Testament words witness to Christ (Collett), we need a coherent and robust account of divine authorial communicative intent and of the proper context for discerning it.[134]

Like Provan, Mark Gignilliat espouses a notion of canonical intentionality. Unlike both Provan and Collett, however, Gignilliat acknowledges the whole canon as God's word and "identifies the authorial voice of the text with its final form."[135] It is because God is the primary author of the canonical Scriptures that we can "go beyond the epistemic horizons of the authors and editors" and discern divinely intended figural associations.[136] Acknowledging the Bible as divine discourse supplies the missing link between canonical intention and literality.

Bruce Waltke's "canonical process" approach to interpreting the Psalms moves in a similar direction. The Psalms, especially but not exclusively the messianic psalms, are about a son of David who is also David's Lord (Matt 22:41–45), a "puzzle that finds resolution only in Jesus Christ himself."[137] Waltke thinks the Davidic king who features so prominently throughout the Psalms is a figure of Christ. His is neither an undisciplined allegorical or a strict historical reading but, rather, a "canonical process" approach, which recognizes "that the text's intention became deeper and clearer as the parameters of the canon were expounded."[138] Significantly, Waltke maintains "that the original authorial intention was not changed in the progressive development of the canon but deepened and clarified."[139] He distinguishes his approach from *sensus plenior* because he believes the canonical process *deepens* rather than deviates from the original meaning. As the canon developed, "lesser and earlier representations were combined to form greater units that are more meaningful than their component parts."[140] Waltke, like Gignilliat, acknowledges that reading in canonical context ultimately makes sense only on the assumption of divine authorship.

Recall Thomas Aquinas's identification of the literal sense with the

134. My proposal resembles Jean Gerson's fifteenth-century criterion for discerning what he called the "theological literal sense," a function not of surface grammar alone but of the communicative intent of the Holy Spirit. See further Karl Froehlich, "'Always to Keep the Literal Sense in Holy Scripture Means to Kill One's Soul': The State of Biblical Hermeneutics at the Beginning of the Fifteenth Century," in *Literary Uses of Typology from the Late Middle Ages to the Present*, ed. Earl Miner (Princeton, NJ: Princeton University Press, 1977), 20–48.

135. Mark S. Gignilliat, *Reading Scripture Canonically: Theological Instincts for Old Testament Interpretation* (Grand Rapids: Baker Academic, 2019), 44.

136. Gignilliat, *Reading Scripture Canonically*, 92. Gignilliat also calls attention to the way in which the canon puts pressure on the reader to identify YHWH as the triune God, the subject matter and speaker of the Old Testament (93).

137. Bruce K. Waltke and Fred G. Zaspel, *How to Read and Understand the Psalms* (Wheaton, IL: Crossway, 2023), 30.

138. Waltke and Zaspel, 525.

139. Waltke and Zaspel, 526.

140. Waltke and Zaspel, 529.

circumstantia litterae ("the way the words run"). When God, the divine author of the canon, "makes the words run a certain way," he does not change their sense (i.e., the direction they run); rather, he makes them run *further.*[141] God's trans-figurative intent makes words go the second semantic mile, enabling them to signify not simply lambs and tabernacles, but the sacrificial death of Jesus Christ. Yet this intent comes into focus only in canonical context.[142] God's trans-figurative intent does not violate verbal meaning (i.e., the letter) but directs and orchestrates it. There is therefore no need to distinguish canonical intentionality and authorial intent (contra Provan) or providential ordering and authorial intent (contra Collett) when God is the authorial agent of the canon. What God ultimately intends his discourse to mean becomes clear only in canonical context:

> For the Christian figural reader of the biblical text, God is both enactor and interpreter of the events depicted by the text. They have meaning and significance because they are the idiom in which God acts and speaks. Although one may refer to a figure "announcing" its fulfillment, it is ultimately God who does the announcing, for a person or an event is a *figura* precisely because it begins an extended divine utterance that embraces subsequent persons and events.[143]

My claim, then, is twofold: (1) divine authorial intent comes into focus in canonical context, and (2) this canonical intentionality is synonymous with God's trans-figural intent. Trans-figural interpretation follows the way God makes the biblical words run and figures fly: beyond the human authorial intent, through history, across the canon, and from their original to their ultimate referents. It is akin to Jacques Lefèvre d'Étaples's "literal prophetic sense," namely, "the intention of the prophet and of the Holy Spirit speaking in him."[144] When prophets say more than they can know, they are not talking nonsense, even if they cannot identify the future referent. When read in canonical context,

141. Interestingly, the French word for meaning, *sens*, also means "direction," which perhaps explains why we can think of the literal sense in terms of "the way the words run." Both meaning and authorial intention have to do with directedness—the direction to which consciousness tends in attending to something.

142. John Piper makes an interesting point about human authors meaning more than they could be aware of: "You do this every time you use the little abbreviation *etc.*" John Piper, *Reading the Bible Supernaturally: Seeing and Savoring the Glory of God in Scripture* (Wheaton, IL: Crossway, 2017), 318. Piper also acknowledges that God, the divine author, sometimes refers to more than the human authors were aware of. And, though Piper does not use the term, he says something that comes close to what I mean by divine trans-figural intent: "God always has more in mind to communicate than the human authors do" (321).

143. Dawson, *Christian Figural Reading and the Fashioning of Identity*, 85.

144. James Samuel Preus, *From Shadow to Promise: Old Testament Interpretation from Augustine to the Young Luther* (Cambridge, MA: Belknap, 1969), 137.

what they were really talking about all along comes into focus. We can describe this divinely intended literal sense as the *totus sensus*: the whole meaning of the divine author, including the figural and trans-figural intent.[145]

To read canonically is to interpret each part of Scripture in light of the whole, tracing figural trajectories from figure to figured, which is to say, reading trans-figurally. We read theologically "by pursuing the literal sense by way of dialogue with God."[146] The divine author creates figural connections, thereby progressively revealing his mind. God's plan of salvation to bring all things under one head, even Christ (Eph 1:10), devised "before the foundation of the world," is revealed trans-figurally, in canonical context. We could also describe this as "close canonical reading."[147] It is a matter of attending to the particulars and the big picture simultaneously. Close canonical reading entails reading the biblical text, the whole text, and nothing but the text. This is the best way to ascertain the divinely intended, literal meaning. Indeed, we might even describe the literal sense as the "plain canonical sense." At least one church council made this explicit. The 2008 Jerusalem Declaration affirms that the Bible is to be "read, preached, taught and obeyed *in its plain and canonical sense*, respectful of the church's historic and consensual reading."[148] It is "plain" because it reveals the mystery of redemptive history with human words and simple figures; it is "canonical" because the divine communicative intent comes into view only in the context of the whole of redemptive history as set forth in the canonical Scriptures. The literal sense is canonically plain to those who, in the spirit of reformed catholicity, read the letter of the text trans-figurally and understand that the whole Bible is ultimately about Jesus Christ.

The Literal Sense as Grammatical-Eschatological

If trans-figuring interpretation is reading for the divine authorial intent in canonical context, with one exegetical eye fixed on what the words meant in their original context, while the other follows the divine authorial intent across the canonical figures until it is finally figured out in Christ, then what exactly is the literal sense? There are several things to keep in mind in providing a

145. Vern S. Poythress offers a suggestive model for relating human and divine authorship: "Isaiah's intention was that we should understand whatever God intended by his words" ("Divine Meaning of Scripture," *Westminster Theological Journal* 48 (1986): 259.

146. Richard S. Briggs, "Premodern Interpretation and Contemporary Exegesis," in *The New Cambridge Companion to Biblical Interpretation*, ed. Ian Boxall and Bradley C. Gregory (Cambridge: Cambridge University Press, 2023), 312.

147. See further *Close Reading: The Reader*, ed. Frank Lentricchia and Andrew Dubois (Durham, NC: Duke University Press, 2003). Part 3 of the present work is partly intended as an extended example of close canonical reading, attending particularly to the economy of light that spans the Old Testament and New Testament and climaxes in Christ.

148. Art. 2 of the Jerusalem Declaration, a product of the first meeting of the Global Anglican Future Conference (GAFCON).

definition. First, we should avoid drawing a hard and fast contrast between literal and spiritual, for some kind of spiritual interpretation is part and parcel of a mere Christian hermeneutics that reads the Old Testament as Christ-bound discourse.[149] Second, and relatedly, we should avoid defining literal in contrast to the grammatical. Words, and the relationships between words, matter. Third, we should avoid defining the literal sense apart from authorial action, for sense (something said) is an integral component of discourse. Fourth, we should avoid defining the literal sense apart from divine authorship or limit divine authorship to the semantic constraints and historical contingencies of the Bible's human authors. Fifth, we should not define the literal sense apart from the canonical context, for it is one of the relevant contexts by which we determine what the divine author was doing with his divinely inspired human discourse. Sixth, and finally, we must avoid defining the literal sense apart from the eschatological frame of reference that allows the final subject matter of biblical discourse to come into focus.

This last point is worth exploring further, for it pertains to reference, which, as Young rightly reminds us, is what the debate between typology and allegory was really about: how to move from word (what is said) to thing (that about which something is said) to determine what the author's discourse is ultimately about. Not every frame of reference does justice to the through line of redemptive history, which is about God making good on his covenant promises or to their eschatological fulfillment in Christ. Trans-figural interpretation specifies the kind of figural reading that respects the literal sense by following the direction of the letter from its original sense and historical referent to its final eschatological referent. The trans-figural dynamic is horizontal, not vertical: there is an important difference between the salvation-historical eschatological movement and the Platonic upward movement.[150] In that respect, at least, trans-figural and typological interpretation have something in common.[151] Both are figural readings that take "into account correspondences . . . between events or people in an eschatological framework,"[152] what Provan calls "the now and not yet of biblical hermeneutics."[153] Eschatology broadens, but does not negate,

149. Figural interpretation is "spiritual" for at least two reasons: first, because it reads for a higher meaning and truth than the historical; second, because the Holy Spirit is necessary to see that the Old Testament is a witness to the reality of Jesus Christ.

150. See Hans Burger, "Quadriga without Platonism: In Search for the Usefulness of the Fourfold Sense of Scripture in Dialogue with Hans Boersma," in *Scripture and Theology: Historical and Systematic Perspectives*, ed. Tomas Bokedal, Ludger Jansen, and Michael Borowski (Berlin: de Gruyter, 2023).

151. Recall that "trans-figural" is my suggested alternative to both "typological" and "allegorical" types of figural interpretation.

152. Mark S. Gignilliat, "Paul, Allegory, and the Plain Sense of Scripture: Galatians 4:21–31," *Journal of Theological Interpretation* 2, no. 1 (2008): 140.

153. From Provan's lecture "Seriously Literal Interpretation" at the London School of Theology (February 13, 2017) as reported in Joseph Hartropp, "How to Read the Bible: Take It Literally but Take

the historical frame of reference typically associated with literal interpretation: "'Eschatological framework' refers to the canonical reality of biblical texts as they speak beyond their historical particularity to ultimate eschatological realities in God's redemptive economy."[154] Trans-figural interpretation takes its bearing from the letter of the text, following the divine authorial intent in its canonical context, on its redemptive-historical trajectory to its christological destination. Trans-figural interpretation therefore reads for the literal sense, construed as the sense of divine authorial discourse.

How does trans-figural interpretation, and the approach to mere Christian hermeneutics that it represents, stand in relation to previous attempts to relate literal and spiritual modes of reading, such as the medieval *quadriga*? The medieval *quadriga* was also a Christian frame of reference, one that saw every biblical text as a meaningful part of a christological whole: what God has done, is doing, and will do in Christ.[155] According to Peter Leithart, "The quadriga incarnates the New Testament's already–not yet eschatology in hermeneutical practice."[156] Indeed, of the three traditional spiritual senses, the one with which my trans-figural proposal has the closest affinity is the anagogic or eschatological, broadly conceived. The "already" sense of the biblical letter indicates a "not yet" fully realized reality. I therefore agree with Arnold Huijgen: "When the eschatological sense of Scripture is taken as the first of the spiritual senses . . . the historical dynamic of the drama between God and his people under the Old Testament and the eschatological tension between the present and the not-yet in the New Testament can tie Biblical studies and systematic theology together."[157]

What, then, is the literal sense that, according to Aquinas, alone deserves to establish Christian doctrine? Whatever definition we offer must take care not to neglect the various aspects of biblical discourse: the spiritual/christological, grammatical, human authorial/historical, divine authorial/supernatural, canonical, and eschatological. It must also make efforts to distinguish "literal"

It Seriously," *Christianity Today*, February 14, 2017, https://www.christiantoday.com/article/how.to.read.the.bible.take.it.literally.but.take.it.seriously/104700.htm. See also his claim that the literal and the typological (my "trans-figural") are "two aspects of the same way of reading." Iain Provan, *The Reformation and the Right Reading of Scripture* (Waco, TX: Baylor University Press, 2017), 100.

154. Gignilliat, "Paul, Allegory, and the Plain Sense of Scripture," 140n22.

155. Peter Leithart makes a similar point in calling readers of Scripture to pay attention to four things: who does what to whom; what the passage says about Jesus; what the passage says about *you* in Jesus; what the passage says about your *future* in Jesus. Peter Leithart, *Theopolitan Reading* (West Monroe, LA: Athanasius, 2020): 112–13.

156. Peter Leithart, "The Quadriga or Something Like It: A Biblical and Pastoral Defense," in *Ancient Faith for the Church's Future*, ed. Mark Husbands and Jeffrey P. Greenman (Downers Grove, IL: IVP Academic, 2012), 121.

157. Arnold Huijgen, "Reinventing the Quadriga: Connecting Biblical Exegesis and Systematic Theology through the Anagogical-Eschatological Sense of Scripture," in *Scripture and Theology: Historical and Systematic Perspectives*, ed. Tomas Bokedal, Ludger Jansen, and Michael Borowski (Berlin: de Gruyter, 2023), 404.

from "literalistic." My proposed definition flies in the face of what most modern readers mean when they speak of reading the Bible "literally." My definition seeks to do justice to all that the Bible is and does: *the literal meaning of Scripture is the meaning of the letter, viewed as human-divine authorial discourse, when read in canonical context with an eschatological frame of reference.*[158] Two items in this definition merit further scrutiny.

Note, first, how everything begins with the letter of the text. The "spiritual" sense does not hover over and apart from the letter (this way "bad" figuration lies); rather, the spiritual sense pertains to the eschatological, itself a function of the end of history. The divine trans-figural intent directs the grammatical sense of the letter from its immediate historical referent to its eschatological referent. Accordingly, literal or trans-figural interpretation (they are equivalent notions) follows the grammatical sense of the letter from its immediate historical referent along the through line of its redemptive-historical frame of reference to the fullness of its ultimate eschatological referent. This is a reading that is as literal (i.e., letter-bound) as it is spiritual (i.e., Christ-bound). *The spiritual sense on this account is the eschatological fullness of the literal sense.*

Although "trans-figural" captures the complexity of literal interpretation, we could also call the kind of literal reading I am advocating *grammatical-eschatological* exegesis. This term has several advantages. First, it reminds us that everything starts with the letter of the text and with the way the authors, human and divine, make the words run. Second, it reminds us that we will understand what the Bible is ultimately about only when we read it with an eschatological frame of reference. The problem with grammatical-historical exegesis is that it can be done with an immanent frame of reference.[159] This is not the case with grammatical-eschatological exegesis, which refuses to be constricted by the immanent frame. Grammatical-eschatological exegesis is therefore better able to give a *thick* description of the Bible's literal sense.[160]

A second noteworthy feature of my proposed definition is its canonical built-in. What canonizes biblical discourse is the divine "superintention"

---

158. It is worth noting that Christians do not read the literal sense of Scripture the way they do any other book. This chapter provides a *theological* account of the Bible's literal sense, not a general hermeneutical account. I make no apologies for that, as general hermeneutics takes us only so far in interpreting Scripture. To return to our metaphor of fishing boats: general hermeneutics can cast into the sea of the Old Testament, but it will never catch the sacred fish.

159. This is also the weakness of Carl Henry's "literal-grammatical sense." Carl F. H. Henry, *God, Revelation, and Authority*, vol. 2, *God Who Speaks and Shows, Fifteen Theses, Part One* (Waco, TX: Word, 1976), 15.

160. I would not object to labeling it "grammatical-Christological," but I prefer grammatical-eschatological both because it contrasts with (but does not contradict) grammatical-historical and because it calls attention to reading with an eschatological rather than immanent frame of reference. An eschatological frame of reference is one that views history as open to and receptive of divine action and divine in-breaking.

that makes of human words God's words.[161] However, the divinely intended meaning—what God's word is ultimately about—becomes apparent only when the biblical texts are read together in canonical context. To be sure, God himself is not context-bound the way human authors are; his authorial word is "living and active" (Heb 4:12) but not free-floating. Nevertheless, without context, God's word could not settle down as it were and so acquire its "plain canonical" determinate meaning. The literal meaning (as opposed to the literalistic) is the trans-figural meaning.

To read literally, then, according to the divine author's intent, is to read trans-figurally, attending to the way the letters run across the canon from their original historical situation and referent to their eschatological fulfillment. Trans-figural reading thus serves the cause of *theologically thick* literal meaning (as opposed to one that is theologically thin and *literalistic*). We can now provide a summary account of the Bible's literal sense, and of the grammatical-eschatological exegesis that accords with reading the Bible theologically. The literal sense is grammatical, in accordance with the letter, when read in an eschatological (redemptive-historical) frame of reference, in canonical context, for the divine author's trans-figural intention or plain canonical sense. The key takeaway: Scripture's literal sense necessitates a properly *theological* interpretation and a hermeneutical strategy that aims to follow the divine figuration where it leads.

We turn now to consider some representative examples of "mere Christian" literal interpretation. While they do not explicitly mention grammatical-eschatological exegesis or the trans-figural sense, something very much like these notions nevertheless characterizes their interpretive practice.

A Reformed Catholic Paradigm: Christoscopic Interpretive Vision

To speak of mere Christian hermeneutics is to claim that, despite appearances, all sides in the disputes over biblical interpretation, that is, all *orthodox* participants, share a significant amount of common ground—or rather *holy* ground: theological assumptions pertaining to the divinely inspired nature of biblical discourse and its Christ-centered subject matter. Mere Christian hermeneutics is a proposal for how to read the Bible in a particular reading culture: the one, holy, catholic, and apostolic church. Of course, not every biblical interpretation is created equal. Though catholic means "universal," we should not infer that

161. A *superintention* is the divine author's communicative intention to say or do something with the human discourse of Scripture that does not go against the original meaning but takes it further, extending it from figures to what is figured.

anything goes, or that every interpretation is as good as another. We must qualify catholicity by *reformed*, by which I mean that set of emphases shared by the Protestant Reformers, including loving and obedient attention to the letter of the biblical text (grammar), the importance of divine authorship (figuration), canonical context (Scripture interprets Scripture), Christ-centered redemptive history, and a willingness to have one's interpretation challenged and, if need be, corrected by the text (*semper reformanda*).

The Protestant Reformers are representative, even exemplary, literal interpreters of the Bible. They are not, of course, the only such Christian interpreters; indeed, such a claim for exclusivity would fly in the face of my argument and the concept of mere Christianity itself. Indeed, one of the things that commends the Reformers as role models is their concern to read in continuity with the church fathers, who, as we have seen, also valued what I have here described as literal interpretation. The Reformers represent the catholic reading tradition of the church in a Protestant key.

Let me here raise a potential objection. In naming dead white European males as exemplary interpreters, am I not betraying my own Western, racist, and sexist biases, thus confirming postmodern suspicions that biblical interpretation amounts to nothing more than a will to political power, a desire to form communities that will serve my own interests? Am I creating a catholicity after my own image? It is an important question.[162]

In reply, let me say, first, that I believe no one culture, denomination, or group of people has a monopoly on the gospel or its interpretation. I believe in "Pentecostal plurality," the idea that it takes many exegetical methods, and many interpretive communities from different times and different places to achieve a plenary understanding of Scripture.[163] Second, the Reformers lived in a "kairos" moment in the history of biblical interpretation, betwixt and between the premodern and the modern, and I believe they often represent the best of both eras. Third, though they professed the supreme authority of the Bible, the Reformers also cherished tradition, so much so that they claimed to be more truly catholic, more in line with their patristic and medieval forebears, than their Roman counterparts.[164] Finally, the Reformers preserve a healthy tension

162. The objection recalls C. S. Lewis's comments on "Bulverism," the attempt to falsify an argument, not by addressing the argument itself, but by pointing out where it came from: "You say that because you're a [fill in the ethnicity, sex, class, or confessional tradition of your choice]." In Lewis's words, "Bulverism tries to show that the other man has causes and not reasons." "'Bulverism' or, the Foundation of 20th Century Thought," in C. S. Lewis, *God in the Dock: Essays on Theology and Ethics* (Grand Rapids: Eerdmans, 1970), 275.

163. See my *Is There a Meaning in This Text?* 419–20.

164. Like Provan, I am using "reformed" to indicate an approach "that is consistent with magisterial Reformation principles and practices, rather than being exclusively (or merely) Protestant, or indeed more narrowly Calvinist (Reformed)." Provan, *Reformation and the Right Reading of Scripture*, 21.

between valuing the letter (philology) and the spirit of the text (Christology). The claim, in brief, is that the Protestant Reformers read the Bible in ways that their patristic and medieval forebears could recognize, even if the rhetoric the Reformers employed (e.g., Luther's "I hate allegories") suggests radical discontinuity. The Reformers cast off the external finery of medieval allegorizing, not its beating heart. The vision that animated their reading of Scripture was that of hearing and meeting the God of their salvation, of coming to know God as it were face-to-face, in the face of Jesus Christ reflected in the mirror of the text. I therefore disagree with those who say the Reformers fell into "the Protestant error" of eliminating the figural in favor of the literal sense.[165] The Reformers had more in common with the late-medieval church than with the modern academy. Put differently, it was not the Protestant Reformers who made the literal sense modern by reading the Bible within an immanent frame of reference. Again, in speaking of "reformed" catholicity, I am referring to a way of reading the Bible that puts the accent on discerning the divine trans-figural intention, in canonical context, with an eschatological frame of reference.

A mere Christian hermeneutic strives not for the lowest but the *richest* common denominator. "Mere" contrasts with "parochial." The emphasis is on what is essential, not eccentric. Like Provan, I am seeking a "way for *all* Christian readers of Scripture to approach it."[166] Unlike Provan, however, I give more credence to how the Reformers actually read. Whereas Provan thinks the Reformers' practice of literal interpretation did not always live up to their principles,[167] I tend to think the reverse: the Reformers' readings display more unanimity than their hermeneutical principles. They show more than they can tell: their exegetical practice displays more agreement about what literal interpretation is than they could articulate.[168]

This chapter, in speaking of transfigural interpretation, has set out what I take to be a reformed catholic practice. To read transfigurally, I argued, is to read for the grammatical-eschatological sense of the letter, *a theologically extended literality*. It is theological because it attends to the divine authorial communicative intent as discerned in canonical context. It is extended because it incorporates the more remote eschatological reference as well as the more immediate and historical original. The Reformers are representative of

165. Collett raises this question, too, but answers with a qualified *no* (*Figural Reading and the Old Testament*, 113).

166. Provan, *Reformation and the Right Reading of Scripture*, 21 (emphasis original).

167. Provan, 216–20.

168. I would say something similar about Provan. We agree on how to read the Bible, but we give slightly different accounts of what we're doing. Specifically, he posits an equivalence between the human and divine authorial intent, which is why he has to speak of the "text's" (rather than the divine author's) canonical intent. By way of contrast, I maintain that canonical intent just is the intent of the divine author, which is not identical with, or circumscribed by, that of the human author.

the mere Christian theological vision that sees the whole process of biblical interpretation as answering the Word with which God addresses us in Scripture. That "Word," of course, is Jesus Christ. When the Reformers read for the *theological literal* sense of the Scriptures, they, like their forebears, read christologically.

We turn now to some brief examples of reformed catholic practice in reading theologically for this thick, trans-figural literal sense. My aim in so doing, in addition to giving examples of best interpretive practice, is to show that I have not invented something new. Trans-figural biblical interpretation is not a novelty but a revival of a practice that is as Protestant as it is catholic.[169]

Martin Luther

Luther is well known for his abhorrence of allegories, yet he nevertheless insisted that the Old Testament is about Christ. He had affinities with the late medieval tendency to "fold" the spiritual meanings into the literal, "toward an increasingly 'fat' literal sense; meaning that was traditionally ascribed to one of the three spiritual senses was now being attributed to the *sensus literalis*."[170] Richard Muller's summation is apt: "The doctrinal, moral and eschatological dimensions of the *quadriga* were not lost but rather were found more precisely lodged in the literal sense."[171]

Whereas Nicholas of Lyra saw a "double literal sense" (*duplex sensus literalis*) in Old Testament prophecy—an immediate historical referent and a deferred spiritual/eschatological/christological referent—Luther posited a single literal sense whereby the Old Testament text refers directly to Jesus Christ, albeit in the mode of promise.[172] Where Nicholas saw references to both Solomon and Christ in 1 Chronicles 17:13 and 22:10 ("He shall be my son, and I will be his father"), Luther insisted that these passages refer literally to Christ only: "This historical sense was basically future-oriented."[173] There is no need of figures or types: "For Luther, Christ himself was truly present, even if not yet incarnate, in

169. See further Allen and Swain, *Reformed Catholicity*; and Matthew Barrett, *The Reformation as Renewal: Retrieving the One, Holy, Catholic, and Apostolic Church* (Grand Rapids: Zondervan, 2023).

170. Erik Herrmann, "Luther's Absorption of Medieval Biblical Interpretation," in *The Oxford Handbook of Martin Luther's Theology*, ed. Robert Kolb, Irene Dingel, L'Ubomir Batka (Oxford: Oxford University Press, 2014), 82.

171. Richard Muller, "Biblical Interpretation in the Sixteenth and Seventeenth Centuries," in *Dictionary of Major Biblical Interpreters*, ed. Donald K. McKim (Downers Grove, IL: IVP Academic, 2007), 26.

172. Jacques Lefèvre d'Etaples also held to a "double literal sense," in his case, a literal historical and literal prophetic sense. The latter had a "spiritual" fulfillment, but it remains literal because it was "the intention of the prophet and of the Holy Spirit speaking in him" (Preus, *From Shadow to Promise*, 137).

173. Lee-Chen A. Tsai, "The Development of Luther's Hermeneutics in His Commentaries on the Psalms" (unpub. PhD diss., University of Aberdeen, 1989), 186. See also Brian T. German, *Psalms of the Faithful: Luther's Early Reading of the Psalter in Canonical Context* (Bellingham, WA: Lexham, 2017).

the Old Testament era."[174] For this reason, Luther was hesitant to acknowledge figural meaning in the Old Testament: "While allegory eradicates the historicity of the Old Testament events, typology annuls the historical presence of Christ in the Old Testament."[175]

Luther saw no contradiction between the philological and christological principles. Indeed, he "believe[d] Christ to be the *sensus literalis* of Scripture on the basis of the Bible's messianic promise."[176] We might say Luther practiced grammatical-eschatological exegesis under a different name: "It is Luther's conviction that Scripture's fixation upon Jesus Christ as its central subject matter is a reality about the literal sense referent of the biblical text in its 'letter.'"[177] Accordingly, Luther serves as a paradigmatic trans-figural interpreter of the Bible's literal sense *avant la lettre*: "Luther's major contribution to hermeneutics lies in the fusion of literal and spiritual in a new and dynamic relationship."[178]

Johannes Oecolampadius

The Basel Reformer Johannes Oecolampadius's commentary on Isaiah (1525) "gives us an example of a major Reformer who did not let the interest in *sensus literalis* undermine a sensitivity to biblical depth."[179] Although Oecolampadius himself described his reading as "allegorical," it "shows fascinating hermeneutical affinities to twentieth-century developments in Vosian biblical theology and in typological interpretation."[180] This confusion over the nature of Oecolampadius's figural reading makes him an excellent case study of trans-figural literal interpretation.

For Oecolampadius, the immediate historical referent of the Old Testament gives rise not to three spiritual senses, but to a triadic eschatological fulfillment: "In the New Testament, redemptive history has three fundamental stages: (1) the work of Christ on earth, (2) the application of redemption to the church, and (3) the consummation when Christ returns."[181] Oecolampadius's "allegories" are in fact tightly regulated, divinely intended trans-figural correspondences,

174. Erik Lundeen, "In Search of the Literal Sense: Johannes Oecolampadius (1482–1531) and the Exegetical Tradition on Isaiah" (unpub. PhD diss., Baylor University, 2022), 270.

175. Heinrich Bornkamm, *Luther and the Old Testament* (Minneapolis: Fortress, 1969), 250.

176. William M. Marsh, *Martin Luther on Reading the Bible as Christian Scripture: The Messiah in Luther's Biblical Hermeneutic and Theology* (Eugene, OR: Pickwick, 2017), xi.

177. Marsh, 193.

178. Arthur S. Wood, *Luther's Principles of Biblical Interpretation* (London: Tyndale, 1960), 34. See also the helpful discussion in Todd R. Hains, *Martin Luther and the Rule of Faith: Reading God's Word for God's People* (Downers Grove, IL: IVP Academic, 2022), 8-20.

179. Vern Poythress, "Typology and Christocentricity in the Hermeneutics of Johannes Oecolampadius," *Westminster Theological Journal* 81 (2019): 295.

180. Poythress, 295. "Vosian" here means in the manner of Geerhardus Vos (1862–1949), the father of a distinctly Reformed approach to biblical theology.

181. Poythress, 302.

discovered as he attended to the redemptive-historical through line in canonical context. Unlike Luther, Oecolampadius did not view Christ as the sole literal referent of Old Testament prophecy. Isaiah's references to Cyrus (Isa 44:28; 45:1) refer literally to Cyrus and figurally to Christ. Similarly, Isaiah 40–48 is about the return of the Jews from their exile in Babylon under Cyrus *and* Christ's delivery of his people from sin and death.

Oecolampadius's reformed catholic credentials are impeccable. In addition to his extensive working knowledge of several church fathers and his knowledge of both Hebrew and Greek, he was an assistant to Erasmus, a friend of Melanchthon, an acquaintance of the Hebraist Johannes Reuchlin, a colleague of Zwingli, and author of numerous biblical commentaries appreciated by Calvin and Bucer. However, more than anything else, it is Oecolampadius's insistence that Christ is the *scopus* or goal of Scripture, which he takes from the Greek patristic theologians (and Erasmus), that makes him my mere Christian hermeneutical patron saint.[182]

Athanasius used the Greek term *skopos* "to describe the general perspective or frame of reference with which the Scriptures are rightly to be interpreted . . . the basic pattern of meaning that is perceived when the interpreter not only looks at the written words but looks through them at the objective center of reference."[183] For Athanasius, "the meaning of the words written is not found in the letters as such but in the divine actions they express."[184] To identify the *scopus* of biblical discourse is to grasp what the divine discourse in Scripture is finally about. Oecolampadius found the spiritual (that is, christological) content within an "expanded literal sense [that] contained the truths about what Christians ought to believe, do, and hope."[185] To call Christ the goal or *scopus* of the divine address is to understand that "everything written in Scripture was about him and for the benefit of his church."[186] Oecolampadius's formula—"*Scriptura scopus Christus*" ("The scope of Scripture is Christ")[187]—is a theological vision statement. It provides a framework for understanding what the whole process of biblical interpretation is ultimately about and why it matters. We read the word of God to come face-to-face with the Word of God.

182. Erik Lundeen devotes chapter 2 of his dissertation to the influence of Erasmus. Lundeen "In Search of the Literal Sense." Jeff Fisher says that the primary source was the Eastern church fathers. *A Christoscopic Reading of Scripture: Johannes Oecolampadius on Hebrews* (Göttingen: Vandenhoeck & Ruprecht, 2016), 59–66.

183. Thomas F. Torrance, as cited in Kathryn Greene-McCreight, "He Spoke through the Prophets," in *Nicene Christianity: The Future for a New Ecumenism*, ed. Christopher R. Seitz (Grand Rapids: Brazos, 2001), 171.

184. Thomas F. Torrance, *Divine Meaning: Studies in Patristic Hermeneutics* (Edinburgh: T&T Clark, 1995), 232.

185. Fisher, *Christoscopic Reading of Scripture*, 37.

186. Fisher, 53.

187. From his commentary on Hebrews, cited in Fisher, 53n3.

In his study of Oecolampadius's commentary on Hebrews, Jeff Fisher labels his approach "christoscopic."[188] As the term suggests, it has to do with seeing (*scopic*) Christ (*christo-*) as the ultimate referent of the textual letter. It is a particular way of being christocentric, one that views Christ as the reference, subject matter, or "about what" of biblical discourse. Christoscopic interpretation is neither myopic nor reductionist, for Oecolampadius had in mind the person and work of Jesus Christ in relation to the reign and glory of God. Christoscopic reading is another way of describing what I have termed grammatic-eschatological exegesis: "Oecolampadius integrated the traditional 'anagogic,' 'ecclesiologic-eschatological' and tropological senses into the 'spiritual' sense which is directed to Christ and his kingdom."[189] In sum, Oecolampadius uses *skopos* to describe a "theologically literal" meaning that corresponds to the divine authorial intention in canonical context.[190]

John Calvin

Arguably no biblical interpreter straddles the premodern and modern eras more than John Calvin. It was Calvin, for instance, who expressed misgivings about identifying the literal sense of certain psalms with their christological reading. This led Philip Schaff to declare Calvin the founder of modern exegesis.[191] Indeed, some of Calvin's contemporaries accused him of so historicizing these interpretations as to de-Christianize them—hence the Lutheran Aegidius Hunnius's treatise castigating the "Judaizing Calvin."[192] When commenting on Psalm 22:1 ("My God, my God, why have you forsaken me?"), Calvin spent considerably more time relating the verse to David than to Christ, largely from a desire to honor the natural (i.e., literal) sense, and to offer interpretations that he could defend to the Jews of his day.[193]

On the other hand, it would be inaccurate, or at least incomplete, to place Calvin on the side of historical rather than theological interpretation. Calvin admitted that the Hebrew Scriptures "should be read with the aim of finding

188. Fisher, 30.

189. Peter Opitz, "Exegetical and Hermeneutical Work of Oecolampadius, Zwingli and Calvin," in *Hebrew Bible, Old Testament: The History of Its Interpretation*, vol. 2, ed. Magne Saebø (Göttingen: Vandenhoeck & Ruprecht, 2008), 411.

190. So Paul Blowers: "*Skopos* raises the issue of 'intended' meaning, which . . . properly belongs not to the original scriptural authors . . . but to God, the true author of Scripture, who is guiding the audience of his Word *teleologically* toward the grand fulfillment of all scriptural 'prophecy' in the mystery of Jesus Christ." "Eastern Orthodox Biblical Interpretation," in *A History of Biblical Interpretation*, vol. 2, ed. Alan J. Hauser and Duane F. Watson (Grand Rapids: Eerdmans, 2003), 178.

191. See Philip Schaff, "Calvin as a Commentator," *Presbyterian and Reformed Review* 3 (1892): 462–69.

192. See further G. Sujin Pak, *The Judaizing Calvin: Sixteenth-Century Debates over the Messianic Psalms* (Oxford: Oxford University Press, 2010), ch. 5.

193. See further Barbara Pitkin, *Calvin, the Bible, and History: Exegesis and Historical Reflection in the Era of Reform* (Oxford: Oxford University Press, 2020).

Christ in them."[194] He also had a healthy, though not uncritical, respect for patristic exegesis. Calvin affirmed with church tradition the unity of the Old Testament and New Testament: "The context of any single book is the rest of the Holy Scripture. No book can be interpreted as if it stood outside the Bible."[195] I am hard pressed to think of a clearer endorsement of reading in canonical context than that. For such reasons, Sujin Pak classifies Calvin as a precritical exegete yet cautions that he "cannot be so easily distanced from modern principles of exegesis either."[196]

Everything depends on what we identify as Calvin's preferred frame of reference. His respect for philology and his reverence for Christ urged him to forge an exegetical *via media*. As David Puckett observes, "The Jewish approach robs Jesus Christ of his honor; the Christian approach robs the Old Testament of significance for its original audience. A mediating position is necessary."[197] Calvin mediated philology and Christology by reading with an eschatological frame of reference in which, thanks to divine trans-figural intent, historical figures like David serve as figures of Christ. Furthermore, Calvin viewed the substance of the Old Testament and New Testament—the covenant of grace summed up in Christ—as essentially the same,[198] enabling him to assume a "natural coherence between literal and figural reading, and . . . the need of each for supplementation by the other."[199] For Calvin, the salvation history of the Old Testament is as christoscopic as the New Testament.[200]

As we have seen, trans-figural interpretation does not distort but *extends* the literal sense. According to Erik Lundeen, Calvin held to a similar notion—an "extensive single literal sense" that admitted multiple referents.[201] For example, in his commentary on Galatians 4:24 (Paul's "allegorical" interpretation of Sarah and Hagar), Calvin said that what Paul was really doing with the Genesis text was not allegory but an "anagoge." Scott Manetsch clarifies Calvin's thought: "Paul has not distorted the genuine meaning of the Old Testament narrative, for Abraham's household (through Sarah and Isaac) was *literally* God's church. . . . Paul was, technically speaking . . . drawing a figure

194. John Calvin, *Gospel according to John 1–10*, Calvin's New Testament Commentaries, vol. 4 (Grand Rapids: Eerdmans, 1995), 139.

195. T. H. L. Parker, *Calvin's Old Testament Commentaries* (Louisville: Westminster John Knox, 1993), 81.

196. Pak, *Judaizing Calvin*, 8.

197. David L. Puckett, *John Calvin's Exegesis of the Old Testament* (Louisville: Westminster John Knox, 1995), 120.

198. See Calvin, *Institutes* I.10.23.

199. Frei, *Eclipse of Biblical Narrative*, 27.

200. So Pitkin, *Calvin, the Bible, and History*, 26.

201. See table 7.1, summarizing four different views of literal reference held by the Reformers, in Lundeen, "In Search of the Literal Sense," 267.

that accorded with the literal sense."[202] Calvin's own comment on Galatians 4:22 is telling: "A mystical interpretation of this sort (*anagoge*) was not inconsistent with the true and literal meaning."[203]

There is a fascinating kinship between Calvin's anagoge, the anagogic spiritual sense of the medieval *quadriga* (traditionally the one that corresponds to some future or heavenly referent) and what in the present book I am calling the eschatological frame of reference: "The anagogical sense, properly speaking, dealt with heavenly or eschatological realities. Calvin's anagoge, in contrast, usually pointed to Christ and New Testament realities, which was the traditional role of the allegorical sense."[204] In his commentary on Zechariah, Calvin described how Israel defeated her enemies, adding, "This is an anagoge—that is, once we have held to the literal sense of the prophet, we can then easily pass over to the spiritual kingdom of Christ."[205] This is but another example of reading trans-figurally for the literal sense. What I have been calling grammatical-eschatological exegesis has Protestant precedent.

Consider, finally, Calvin's comment on Genesis 3:15: "And now we have to cross over from the serpent to the author of evil himself; and this is not only a comparison but a true literal anagoge."[206] This transference from figure to figured makes sense because Christians today participate in the same redemptive history as the biblical characters. What legitimates this transference—or *trans-figuration*—is Calvin's Christian conviction that the Old Testament and New Testament share a common subject matter, namely, salvation in Christ. That Calvin's understanding of the literal sense could include such anagogical correspondences is evidence of the elasticity of the concept *literal*.[207] The Reformers, said David Steinmetz, advocated "a letter pregnant with spiritual significance, a letter big-bellied with meanings formerly related by the *quadriga* to allegory or tropology."[208] Barbara Pitkin agrees, grouping Calvin with other reformed catholic interpreters who tend "to overstuff this single, literal sense with spiritual meanings."[209]

---

202. Scott Manetsch, "John Calvin and the Theological Interpretation of Scripture," in *Hearing and Doing the Word: The Drama of Evangelical Hermeneutics* (London: T&T Clark, 2021), 167.

203. John Calvin, *Commentary on the Epistles of Paul to the Galatians and Ephesians* , trans. William Pringle (Edinburgh: Thomas Clark, 1854), 136.

204. Lundeen, "In Search of the Literal Sense," 292n82. Cf. Randall C. Zachmann: "Anagoge stresses the elevation from the temporal sign to the spiritual reality it represents." "Calvin as Analogical Theologian," *Scottish Journal of Theology* 51, no. 2 (1998): 162.

205. Calvin, *Ioannis Calvini opera quae supersunt omnia*, vol. 44, ed. G. Baum, E. Cunitz, and E. Reuss (Brunswick: Schwetschke, 1890), 283, cited and trans. Lundeen, "In Search of the Literal Sense," 294.

206. Cited in Parker, *Calvin's Old Testament Commentaries*, 72.

207. See Richard Burnett, "John Calvin and the *Sensus Literalis*," *Scottish Journal of Theology* 57, no. 1 (2004): 1–13.

208. David C. Steinmetz, "Divided by a Common Past: The Reshaping of the Christian Exegetical Tradition in the Sixteenth Century," *Journal of Medieval and Early Modern Studies* 27 (Spring 1997): 249.

209. Pitkin, *Calvin, the Bible and History*, 8.

Martin Bucer

It is fitting that we conclude our sampling of reformed catholic interpreters with Martin Bucer, not because he is the best known or most prolific but, rather, because he is an excellent representative of mere Christian hermeneutics. Bucer was both a bridge figure and a bridge builder.[210] He straddled academic disciplines (viz., biblical studies and theology) and eras (late medieval/early modern).[211] He worked hard to forge doctrinal agreements between Protestant factions that were drifting farther apart. He has been called "an apt hermeneutical mentor for our age," both because he exemplifies the way biblical studies and theology ought to work hand in hand and because he reminds us that both ultimately exist to serve the church.[212]

Bucer's aim as an interpreter was "to determine with the greatest possible clarity what the respective biblical author had intended to say."[213] To this end, he read Hebrew and interpreted messianic psalms in dialogue with Jewish exegesis to learn more about the historical context and plain sense (*peshat*) of the Old Testament text. Knowing the grammar and historical context is essential, but so is recognizing the aim or *scopus* of a passage: because Bucer held to a unity of the two peoples of the Old Testament and New Testament, "the church is just as central a player in his interpretations of these [messianic] Psalms as is Christ."[214] Bucer's christological readings of the messianic psalms therefore discovered the church, the *body* of Christ, as part of the extended literal sense. The blessings God conferred on the saints of old apply by "transference" to the church and may therefore be read figurally.[215] Indeed, Pak argues that for Bucer, "the central meaning of all of Scripture [was] the restoration of God's people through the saving act of Christ."[216]

Thomas Cromwell's Cambridge Injunctions of 1535, a turning point in the English Reformation, mandated that all theology lectures were to be based on the Bible alone—"according to the letter"—rather than on what had hitherto

210. Pak notes that Bucer was "a significant mediating figure between the exegeses of Luther and Calvin" (*Judaizing Calvin*, 7).

211. Martin Greschat observes that Bucer's biblical interpretations are "remarkably modern and progressive." *Martin Bucer: A Reformer and His Times* (Louisville and London: Westminster John Knox, 2004), 82. Wesley Hill, assessing Bucer's lectures on Ephesians, concludes that he "remains a pioneer and model." "The Text of Ephesians and the Theology of Bucer," in *Reformation Readings of Paul: Explorations in History and Exegesis*, ed. Michael Allen and Jonathan A. Linebaugh (Downers Grove, IL: IVP Academic, 2015), 161.

212. Brian Lugioyo, "Martin Bucer's Reading of Ephesians," in *Reformation Readings of Paul: Explorations in History and Exegesis*, ed. Michael Allen and Jonathan A. Linebaugh (Downers Grove, IL: IVP Academic, 2015), 124.

213. Greschat, *Martin Bucer*, 82.

214. Pak, *Judaizing Calvin*, 57.

215. So David F. Wright, "Bucer, Martin," in *Dictionary of Major Biblical Interpreters*, ed. Donald K. McKim, 2nd ed. (Downers Grove, IL: InterVarsity, 2007), 252.

216. Pak, *Judaizing Calvin*, 62.

been the standard textbooks (e.g., Peter Lombard's *Sentences*). Bucer therefore had to display all his reformed catholic interpretive powers in his 1550–51 lectures on Ephesians at Cambridge University, in which he moved seamlessly from philology to Christology, demonstrating his humanist and his catholic credentials by giving equal attention to exegesis and theology.

Bucer believed that Ephesians addresses not only first-century Christians but his own sixteenth-century English audience and, indeed, all future generations of believers. He insisted that to read Scripture rightly we must pray to and listen for the Spirit "as conscientiously as possible."[217] Technical knowledge of the grammar on its own cannot yield right understanding of what the Spirit is saying to the church.

Bucer read Ephesians as providing a compendium of Christian doctrine—everything believers need to know about the principal topics (*loci*) of the mystery of salvation in Christ and the Christian life that is its result. Paul's aim (*scopus*) "is the increase of piety, not only in knowledge, but also in practice, both among the Ephesians and ourselves."[218] Bucer discovered particular doctrinal *loci* (e.g., election, ecclesiology) in every chapter, yet the one essential doctrine that pervades the whole epistle is "the mystery of Christ" (Eph 3:4). In commenting on this phrase, Bucer clarified the grammar and other philological matters and then unpacked the meaning of Paul's argument. The humanist *loci* method served the needs of exegesis and theology alike: "The interpreter would identify the chief points (*loci*) that an author made in his work, and then gather them together to come to an understanding of the author's argument."[219]

Bucer's lectures on Ephesians serve as a poignant reminder and encouragement: it is possible to do theology in partnership, not competition, with exegesis; it is possible to do theology in the university in a way that serves the church. As Bucer stated, "True theology is not theoretical or speculative but active and practical. Indeed, the end of it is to act, that is, to live a godly life."[220] For all these reasons, Bucer's Cambridge lectures on Ephesians represented, for a brief moment, what it might look like to combine in one person what I have here described as two contrasting reading cultures: the scholastic and monastic. These lectures also provide a sterling example of the trans-figural reading I have been advocating: a literal interpretation in a reformed catholic key that follows the way the letters go, from history to unfolded mystery. In Bucer, as in

---

217. Bucer, cited in N. Scott Amos, *Bucer, Ephesians and Biblical Humanism: The Exegete as Theologian* (Cham, Switzerland: Springer, 2015), 99.

218. Bucer, cited in Amos, 125.

219. Amos, 133–34. Amos contrasts Bucer's method with Calvin's. Whereas Bucer incorporated a discussion of the *loci* into his exposition, Calvin kept his discussions separate, reserving extended theological reflection for his *Institutes* (Amos, 134–38).

220. Bucer, commentary on John 14, trans. by and cited in Amos, 7.

other reformed catholic interpreters, we see the exegete as true theologian, the theologian as true exegete.[221]

Summary

In the conclusion to her classic *The Study of the Bible in the Middle Ages*, Beryl Smalley likened Hugh and Andrew of St. Victor to "men building on the site of a buried city, unaware of the civilization lying beneath their feet."[222] She was alluding to the centuries-long loss of literal (Antiochene) interpretation they rediscovered. The literal sense has been lost and found on more than one occasion, although even when it was found, it has not always led to Christ.

The Reformers themselves disputed the nature of the literal sense and interpretation. I have here tried to provide an account that makes sense of their common practice, even if they described it in different terms. Though the concepts I have introduced may be new and unfamiliar, the underlying position for which I have argued—a mere Christian hermeneutic—is in line with the reformed catholic tradition. Even as Protestant a post-Reformation theologian as Francis Turretin could agree with Thomas Aquinas, up to a point: "The literal sense is not so much that which is derived from proper words and not figurative . . . but that which is intended by the Holy Spirit and is expressed in words either proper or figurative."[223] There is also widespread agreement that though the literal sense is one, it has dual aspects, for the divine author's letter (discourse) encompasses the mystery of Christ. Again, what counts is not the surface grammatical meaning only but what an author has said/done.[224] We must neither confuse nor conflate the *sensus literalis* (literal sense) with the *littera* (literalistic sense), the way the words run under authorial direction with the surface grammatical meaning.

We come now to the end of part 2, and our first ascent up the mount of interpretation. We have moved from the literal to the figural and trans-figural in an argument directed "towards giving the literal sense a fuller content, *sensus literalis plenior*."[225] I have provided a definition of the literal sense and an apology for literal interpretation, but there has been more theory than practice—the typical soft spot in many accounts of what it means to read theologically. Accordingly, the chapters in part 3 focus on one figure in particular, light, and

221. This is also the thesis of Amos, 5.

222. Smalley, *Study of the Bible*, 357.

223. Francis Turretin, *Institutes of Elenctic Theology*, vol. 1, trans. George Musgrave Giger, ed. James T. Denison Jr. (Phillipsburg, NJ: P&R, 1992), 150.

224. This was certainly true for Luther: "The true meaning of the text could never be reduced to defining the text but always had to include how the text worked on its hearers and readers." Timothy J. Wengert, *Word of Life: Introducing Lutheran Hermeneutics* (Minneapolis: Fortress, 2019), xii.

225. Clifton Bruno, "Discerning the Literal Sense: Bringing Together Biblical Scholarship and Dogmatic Theology," *Nova et vetera* 19, no. 1 (2021): 256.

trace its trans-figuration across the canon, from creation to consummation. Thus begins our second ascent up the mount of biblical interpretation. It, too, will be trans-figural, but for a different reason. For the destination of our second ascent, following the figure of light, leads us to the one who is light incarnate, to his transfiguration, and to ours in him.

PART 3

Transfiguring Literal Interpretation

The Light of Christ

The Incarnation is the first stage of a process that is to reach fulfillment in the Transfiguration, that is, in the penetration of the world by the light of Christ.

—Jean Daniélou[1]

It is not just that we read the transfiguration, but also that, in some important sense, the transfiguration "reads" us.

—Stephen Barton[2]

Treat the Scripture of God as the face of God.

—Augustine[3]

Mere Christian hermeneutics calls churches and seminaries to foster reading cultures that can overcome the modern division of biblical scholarship and theology in order to form literate citizens of the gospel. My primary aim in part 1 was to change the way interpreters think about themselves as readers and about understanding the Bible as Christian Scripture. Readers are not autonomous subjects who use critical tools or methods on an inert text. Rather, readers are answerable subjects, responsible for hearing, doing justice,

1. Jean Daniélou, *Salvation of the Nations* (London: Sheed and Ward, 1950), 50.

2. Stephen Barton, "The Transfiguration of Christ according to Mark and Matthew: Christology and Anthropology," in *Auferstehung–Resurrection*, ed. Friedrich Avemarie and Hermann Lichtenberger (Tübingen: Mohr Siebeck, 2001), 232.

3. Augustine, *Sermon* 22.7 in *The Works of Saint Augustine*, vol. 2, trans. Edmund Hill (Hyde Park, NY: New City, 2009), 46.

and responding to the divine address that accompanies the human discourse of the Bible. Part 1 was more concerned with fostering certain exegetical sensibilities than with providing a specific exegetical method.

Part 2 set out a mere Christian account and definition of the literal sense. Theologians across the Catholic-Protestant spectrum agree *that* the literal sense is authoritative. The challenge is to say *what* the literal sense is. As we saw, a thick understanding of the literal sense requires grammar, an eschatological frame of reference, a trans-figural hermeneutical strategy, a canonical context, and a christoscopic vision. Our first climb up the mountain of biblical interpretation was trans-figural, employing a scriptural imaginary, eschatological frame of reference, and hermeneutical strategy that followed the way the biblical figures run—to Jesus Christ. My proposed definition of the literal sense—*the meaning of the human-divine authorial discourse when read in canonical context and viewed through an eschatological frame of reference*—constitutes the authoritative norm of Christian theology, the *formal principle* of mere Christian hermeneutics.

We now turn our attention in part 3 to the *material principle* of mere Christian hermeneutics: the light of Christ or, more expansively, the knowledge of God in the face of Christ. This second ascent up the mount of interpretation is "transfigural" too, though it is Jesus' transfiguration, a climactic event in an all-encompassing triune "economy of light," that is the center of attention. The Bible, and biblical interpretation, now appear as ingredients in a broader work of God, a work of enlightening, in which the Father communicates the light of his self-knowledge in the radiance of the Son through the shining of the Spirit: *light from light for light*.[4] How the triune God communicates the light that he is to those who walk in darkness is not one more frame of reference but, rather, an overarching framework for understanding the Bible's composition and interpretation alike. Interpreters who read Scripture rightly participate in this triune mission and ministry of illumination, demonstrating their understanding of the light of Christ gleaned from the letter of the text by walking as children of light (Eph 5:8). The word is a lamp unto our path, yes, but "The Lord is my light and my salvation" (Ps 27:1). But we begin at the beginning, with light from Genesis and the genesis of light.

4. As we will see, the economy of light is another way of thinking about the economy of revelation, though because of the close connection between light and life (John 1:4), it pertains to the economy of redemption as well.

CHAPTER 6

Shedding Light on Literality

Light Wrought

Now when God said, "Let there be light," and light was made, did He say this on a certain day or before the beginning of days? If He said it by the Word, who is coeternal with Himself, He certainly did not speak in time. On the other hand, if He spoke in time, He did not speak by His eternal Word but by a creature subject to time; and so light could not be the first creature.

—Augustine, *The Literal Meaning of Genesis*, bk. 1, ch. 9

The opening verses of Genesis immediately put to the interpretive test everything we have been saying about the literal sense, literal interpretation, and frames of reference. Since the early church, the creation narratives have defied the finest theological minds to do them justice. More recently, Genesis 1–3 has figured prominently in the dialogue between science and theology. Whole books have been written on reading Genesis "after Darwin."[1] Our particular concern, however, is Genesis 1:3, "And God said, 'Let there be light,' and there was light," and what this might have to do with the light of Christ that is our particular focus in part 3. The story of light—how it came to be, what it is, what it does, how it relates to Jesus Christ—provides both a fitting exegetical case study for our approach to literal interpretation and a theological framework for understanding what it means to read the Bible theologically. My hope is that

1. *Reading Genesis after Darwin*, ed. Stephen C. Baron and David Wilkinson (Oxford: Oxford University Press, 2009).

interpreting Genesis 1:3 and the nature of the light of which it speaks will shed some light on literality itself.

My immediate aim is twofold: to give a literal interpretation of "Let there be light" and, in so doing, to illuminate literality. Accordingly, we begin with some observations about the frames of reference contemporary interpreters commonly employ to read Genesis and what they often miss: the significance of God's *literal* acts of speaking. I then give a brief overview of the history of interpretation of Genesis 1:3 before offering my own interpretation of "Let there be light," the initial moment in an ensuing economy of light of which biblical interpreters are significant, if only momentary, flashes.

Framing Creation: On Reading Genesis 1:3 Literally

To ponder the meaning of God's creation of light raises at least three questions: (1) What does it mean to take the creation account "literally," and how might a literal reading relate to modern science? (2) Does God literally *speak* light into being, and if so, what can we learn about the nature of divine action? (3) To what does this bespoken light literally refer, and how might it relate to the claim that "God is light" (1 John 1:5)? The present section examines the first two questions. The answer to the third question comes in the final section, aided and abetted by the history of exegesis that we examine in the second.

What Is Genesis 1 Literally About?

If, as Thomas Aquinas stated, the literal sense alone is the proper basis of Christian doctrine, then the crucial question as concerns the doctrine of creation is simply this: What does Genesis 1 literally mean? What is the creation narrative ultimately about? The way interpreters answer depends on the frame of reference they adopt, which in turn determines the kinds of questions they ask. One need only peruse the vast array of interpretations to see that this is so.[2] The questions modern interpreters typically ask have to do with whether Genesis contradicts or is in accord with modern science. The default assumption is that Genesis 1–2 is about cosmological origins. This then leads to debates over the length of the six days or whether Genesis 1 gives an accurate chronological and scientific account of the beginnings of the heavens and the earth.

This material is well trod, and I do not want to get bogged down with questions concerning, say, the length of the six days.[3] My focus is rather on

2. For a survey of interpretive approaches, see *Since the Beginning: Interpreting Genesis 1 and 2 through the Ages*, ed. Kyle R. Greenwood (Grand Rapids: Baker Academic, 2018).

3. I agree with Henri Blocher that it is "essential to get rid of the deep-seated feeling once and for

the creation of light as (1) a clue as to what Genesis is really about and (2) the opening act in the larger story of light that spans the Scriptures. What is truly at stake, theologically speaking, has less to do with the length of the days of creation and more to do with God the Creator. What matters theologically is that God (literally) created by speaking, and that by (literally) speaking God acts. *These two theological truths are essential for reading the rest of Scripture rightly.*

To take the measure of the interpretive challenge, however, let us briefly consider three approaches and their respective frames of reference, which have figured prominently in recent interpretations of Genesis 1. Doing so also serves as a kind of summary review of the way frames of reference influence what readers take to be the literal sense.

1. "Young-earth creationists" read Genesis 1 as a factually true historical narrative that, as such, makes scientific claims about the timing and mechanism of the origins of the cosmos.[4] The assumption that Genesis narrates the literal truth about how the world was made leads creationists to conclude that Genesis 1 conflicts rather than harmonizes with modern science. In their way of thinking, the only alternative to a straightforward literalistic (i.e., grammatical) reading is the slippery slope of figural interpretation, on which literality begins to slide and is impossible to stop. If God did not create the universe in six twenty-four-hour days, why not dismiss the literal truth of everything else in Genesis and in the Gospels, as well? The concern over the historicity of the resurrection is understandable. However, to consider all biblical narrative as unadorned history is too simple and risks sliding into not allegorizing but overly literalistic misreading. There are other ways of referring to the real and making historical truth claims than straightforward chronology. The identification of literary genre is the beginning of interpretive wisdom.[5]

2. At the other end of the spectrum are modern biblical critics who read Genesis 1–2 as ancient literature—myth, not modern science. On this view, the biblical authors' frame of reference reflects the ancient Near Eastern cosmological assumptions of their day. The Bible should thus be read like any other prescientific text that deals with the world's origins. "Whatever the first chapters of Genesis offer, there is one thing that they certainly do not offer, namely,

---

all that figurative language would be inferior to literal language, somewhat less worthy of God." Henri Blocher, *In the Beginning: The Opening Chapters of Genesis* (Downers Grove, IL: IVP Books, 1984), 49.

4. So Todd Beall: "Genesis 1 should be read . . . as historical narrative that is meant to be taken literally." "Reading Genesis 1–2: A Literal Approach," in *Reading Genesis 1–2: An Evangelical Conversation*, ed. J. Daryl Charles (Peabody, MA: Hendrickson, 2013), 45.

5. See also Kenneth L. Gentry's literalist critique of the literary framework view: *As It Is Written. The Genesis Account: Literal or Literary? Dismantling the Framework Hypothesis* (Green Forest, AR: Master Books, 2016), as well as James B. Jordan, *Creation in Six Days: A Defense of the Traditional Reading of Genesis One* (Moscow, ID: Canon, 1999).

a literal account of events that actually happened prior to and during the early history of humanity."[6]

3. "Concordists" take a middle position, intentionally reading Genesis in ways that avoid conflicting with modern science. For example, proponents of the day-age theory take the six days figuratively, as referring to vast periods of time, long enough to explain the old age of the universe and to allow for the evolution of species (e.g., "old-earth creationism").[7] Concordists accept the scientific consensus as to the age of the earth and the physicalist frame of reference that goes with it.

Each of the above approaches reads Genesis 1 with one eye on modern science. One wonders, however, whether their frames of reference enable readers to penetrate to the theological joints and marrow of the opening verses, which are as much, if not more, about God the Creator than the cosmos God creates. I agree with Derek Kidner, who said, "It is no accident that *God* is the subject of the first sentence of the Bible. . . . The passage, indeed the Book, is about Him first of all; to read it with any other primary interest . . . is to misread it."[8] We require a frame of reference that does justice to all aspects of Genesis 1: its historical claims, its literary way of making those claims, *and* its theological subject matter.[9] To read Genesis 1 well, we must "negotiate between historical, literary-canonical, and theological frames of reference."[10]

Did God "Literally" Speak?

Genesis 1 is historical insofar as it makes truth claims about something that happened, even if it cannot be independently verified. Genesis 1 is literary "because it communicates doctrine in an artful way."[11] For example, Genesis 1 is exalted prose that narrates God's speech acts "in the beginning." Genesis 1 is also theological, because what exalts its prose is not simply its poetic form but

6. Kenton Sparks, "Genesis 1–11 as Ancient Historiography," in *Genesis: History, Fiction, or Neither? Three Views on the Bible's Earliest Chapters*, ed. Charles Halton (Grand Rapids: Zondervan, 2015), 111. See also John Walton, "Reading Genesis 1 as Ancient Cosmology," in *Reading Genesis 1–2*, 141; and Nathan J. Chambers, "Interpretive Categories and the Ancient Near Eastern Context," in *Reconsidering Creation Ex Nihilo in Genesis 1* (Winona Lake, IN: Eisenbrauns, 2020), ch. 1.

7. See, e.g., Hugh Ross, *Navigating Genesis: A Scientist's Journey through Genesis 1–11* (Covina, CA: RTB, 2014). See also the articles, for and against, young-earth and old-earth creationism respectively in *Dictionary of Christianity and Science*, ed. Paul Copan, Tremper Longman III, et. al. (Grand Rapids: Zondervan, 2017), 131–47.

8. Derek Kidner, *Genesis* (Downers Grove, IL: InterVarsity, 1979), 43.

9. For a book-length attempt to do just this, see Peter J. Leithart, *Creator: A Theological Interpretation of Genesis 1* (Downers Grove, IL: IVP Academic, 2023). See also C. John Collins, *Reading Genesis Well: Navigating History, Poetry, Science, and Truth in Genesis 1–11* (Grand Rapids: Zondervan, 2018).

10. Chambers, *Reconsidering Creation Ex Nihilo in Genesis 1*, 235.

11. Bruce K. Waltke, *Genesis: A Commentary* (Grand Rapids: Zondervan, 2001), 31.

its exalted content. "God speaks and acts in majesty to create the world and everything in it."[12]

Questions prompted by reading Genesis 1 in relation to a scientific frame of reference have misdirected our attention. The crucial point in the creation narrative is not the length of the days or whether Scripture conflicts with modern science. The essential claim is that God spoke all things, visible and invisible, into being. Genesis 1 is *literally* about creation. It is the story of God freely acting out. To read Genesis 1:1–3 well, and literally, we must therefore employ a theological frame of reference. When we do so, two truths come into focus. The first is that God is the Creator, a personal agent; creation is his free act. The second truth is implied by the first: God creates by speaking; creation is his speech act. These two truths are, in turn, essential for reading the rest of Scripture rightly (i.e., theologically): God acts; God speaks. These are the twin bases of a mere Christian hermeneutic.

Framing Creation

Before commenting on the creation of light, a word about the opening words of Genesis is in order. There are three major interpretations of the phrase "In the beginning, God created the heavens and the earth." Genesis 1:1 may describe (1) an absolute beginning (i.e., a claim about cosmological origins); (2) a relative beginning (proponents of this view often translate it "In the beginning, *when* God created . . ."; or (3) a thematic beginning that serves as a title or summary of what is to come in the rest of the chapter. This is a notoriously difficult interpretive crux, and this is not the place for an exhaustive discussion. What follows are a few reasons for preferring a combination of the first and third views, according to which what God does in the beginning sets the stage for everything else that follows.[13]

The verb *bara'* ("created") is used exclusively with God as subject, and its perfect tense form suggests a completed act.[14] A comparison with other ancient Near Eastern creation accounts makes it clear that, in addition to whatever else it may be doing, Genesis is demythologizing as it were myths like *Enuma Elish* that depict the gods struggling with recalcitrant matter in order to create. Reading within a canonical context provides further corroboration. The psalmist declared,

12. Vern S. Poythress, *Interpreting Eden: A Guide to Faithfully Reading and Understanding Genesis1–3* (Wheaton, IL: Crossway 2019), 127.

13. The following provide more thorough-going defenses of the first (traditional) view: Chambers, *Reconsidering Creation Ex Nihilo in Genesis 1*, ch. 4; C. John Collins, *Genesis 1–4: A Linguistic, Literary, and Theological Commentary* (Phillipsburg, NJ: P&R, 2006), 50–55; Poythress, *Interpreting Eden*, 291–321; Victor P. Hamilton, *The Book of Genesis, Chapters 1–17*, NICOT (Grand Rapids: Eerdmans, 1990), 103–7.

14. See Collins, *Reading Genesis Well*, 160–61.

"By the word of the Lord the heavens were made. . . . For he spoke, and it came to be" (Ps 33:6, 9). The New Testament says, "Every good gift and every perfect gift is from above, coming down from the Father of lights" (Jas 1:17); Genesis 1 indicates that "the first mode of creaturely existence is receptivity—the receipt of being and life."[15] Finally, reading in canonical context with an eschatological frame of reference reminds us that Genesis 1 is the beginning of a long story that ends with Revelation, confirming God's sovereignty over the royal priesthood that is the centerpiece of the created realm (Exod 19:6; 1 Pet 2:9; Rev 5:10).[16]

What is primarily at stake in Genesis 1:1–3 is the identity and nature of God, his absolute transcendence and authority over all things. Did God create the world out of nothing (*ex nihilo*), or did God have to struggle with a preexistent medium? Philology alone cannot provide a definitive answer. Biblical exegetes who insist on reading with an ancient Near Eastern frame of reference alone contend that the concept of creation *ex nihilo* "was not yet a significant theological idea."[17] However, Janet Soskice rightly encourages us to widen our frame of reference as concerns what counts as biblical: "*Creatio ex nihilo*, if not 'in the Bible,' is certainly biblical. It is a scripturally driven piece of Christian metaphysics."[18] Christians are right to read Genesis 1:1–3 in canonical context and to feel the canonical pressure of passages like Romans 4:17 ("the God . . . who calls into existence the things that do not exist") and Hebrews 11:3 ("By faith we understand that the universe was created by the word of God"). The doctrine of creation *ex nihilo* matters because it is fundamentally a theological rather than a cosmological claim. It affirms "that God, from no compulsion or necessity, created the world out of nothing—really nothing—no preexistent matter, space, or time."[19] *Ex nihilo* creation matters because the main concern of Genesis 1 is to establish a categorical distinction between the creator God and the created world.

To read Genesis 1 without acknowledging an implicit *ex nihilo* creation is to risk going wrong everywhere else in one's biblical interpretation.[20] For to misconstrue the relationship of God and the world is to misidentify the divine

15. Simon Oliver, "Every Good and Perfect Gift Is from Above: Creation *Ex Nihilo* before Nature and Culture," in *Knowing Creation: Perspectives from Theology, Philosophy, and Science*, vol. 1, ed. Andrew B. Torrance and Thomas H. McCall (Grand Rapids; Zondervan, 2018), 44.

16. See further Mark Smith, *The Priestly Vision of Genesis 1* (Minneapolis: Fortress, 2010).

17. James E. Atwell, *The Sources of the Old Testament: A Guide to the Religious Thought of the Hebrew Bible* (London: T&T Clark, 2004), 4.

18. Janet Soskice, "Why *Creatio ex nihilo* for Theology Today?," in *Creation ex nihilo: Origins, Development, Contemporary Challenges*, ed. Gary A. Anderson and Markus Bockmuehl (Notre Dame, IN: Notre Dame University Press, 2018), 40.

19. Soskice, 38.

20. On whether *ex nihilo* creation is explicit versus implicit in Genesis 1, see the helpful discussion about implicature in relevance theory and Genesis 1 in John W. Hilber, *Old Testament Cosmology and Divine Accommodation: A Relevance Theory Approach* (Eugene, OR: Cascade, 2020), 175–81.

protagonist of the story. Unlike Marduk, the god of Babylonian creation myth, YHWH does not have to engage in an arm-wrestling contest with Leviathan or with anything else in the heavens and the earth. "Creation *ex nihilo* means that God does not need to establish His identity over-against any external reality."[21] The doctrine of creation *ex nihilo* therefore provides a helpful theological frame of reference—and rule for reading the rest of the Bible.

The six days describe God's *works* of distinction (i.e., the separations of light/dark, sky/water, water/land). Genesis 1:1 announces a more radical distinction, that between God's uncreated being and the created beings he speaks into existence. "God alone gives form and gives being. . . . This is the passage's great doctrine."[22] Genesis 1:3 ("And God said, 'Let there be light,' and there was light") supports creation *ex nihilo*. "The idea of creation by the word preserves first of all the most radical essential distinction between Creator and creature. Creation . . . is rather a product of his personal will."[23] In sum, Genesis 1:1 identifies God as all-sufficient, "such that the world depends on him and not he on it."[24] So much for the nature of God the Creator. We turn now to examine the moment and means of creation itself.

Does God Literally Speak?

As many commentators note, the focus of Genesis 1:3 and, indeed, of the whole first chapter, is on *God saying*, as indicated by the refrain that marks all six days: "And God said." *God saying* is arguably the main thing that happens in Genesis 1; the entire created order is a by-product of *God saying*. It is therefore imperative that readers of Genesis 1 use a frame of reference that highlights and makes sense of God's speech acts.[25] Are we as readers meant to take *literally* the description of God speaking? Augustine asked a whole passel of questions about this: Did God say this in time or eternity? On his own or by means of a creature? Audibly or inaudibly? In what language? And to whom was it directed? Immediately after this barrage, he commented, "But perhaps this is an absurdly material way of thinking and speculating on the matter."[26] After all, Augustine

---

21. Chambers, *Reconsidering Creation Ex Nihilo in Genesis 1*, 229.

22. Blocher, *In the Beginning*, 66–67. The six days are divine accommodations to human ways of thinking, figures of speech that the divine author intended to be seen as periods of indeterminate length, perhaps twenty-four-hour days, perhaps not.

23. Gerhard von Rad, *Genesis: A Commentary* (Louisville: Westminster John Knox, 1973), 49–50.

24. Collins, *Reading Genesis Well*, 209.

25. Older source critics posit two sources behind Genesis 1:1–2:4, which Herbert May dubs "Acts" and "Words." On his view, the "Acts" source is preexilic; it was later exilic and postexilic editors, reacting against Babylonian dualism, who saw God himself as the cause of light and thus insisted on his speaking it into being. See Herbert Gordon May, "The Creation of Light in Genesis 1:3–5," *Journal of Biblical Literature* 58, no. 3 (1939): 203–11.

26. Augustine, *The Literal Meaning of Genesis*, trans. John Hammond Taylor, vol. 1 (New York: Paulist, 1982), 1.2.5.

knew, from John 1:1, that the Son is the Word who was with God in the beginning, and this led him to suggest that God's saying was less a material sound and more "an immaterial utterance of God in His eternal Word."[27]

The real point of theological interest in my view lies in the question, does God *literally do* anything? After all, *saying* is a verb, a doing word indicating some form of action. Readers must therefore deal with the logically prior question: What does it mean for God to literally act, to do anything? This is as crucial a theological issue as the Creator/creation distinction itself. If God does not act, then there is nothing to narrate, and we would have to read the Genesis story as myth, a symbolic expression of a universal truth, not a historical event. Read on its own terms, however, whether prosaic or poetic, the creation narrative is an account of something that actually happened. "The cosmos begins with a great sound, not a Big Bang but a Big 'Be!'"[28]

These sounds, moreover, continue. There would be no covenant history if the eternal God had not communicated, in words spoken and written, as Scripture represents him as doing. If God did not literally speak, there is no way to explain how God could make his purposes known. We can go further. For, unless God literally speaks, he cannot have done most of the actions the Bible depicts him as performing: giving the procreation mandate to Adam and Eve, promising to make Abraham a great nation, laying down the law by which Israel was to keep covenant, prophesying a future Messiah, declaring sinners innocent, and so forth. There could be no covenant without an initial covenanting speech act, a promise or oath (cf. Gen 26:3; Heb 6:17). It is no coincidence, then, that "the word of the Lord" which made the heavens (Ps 33:6), ruled Israel (Deut 5:22), guided kings (1 Sam 15:1), came to the prophets (Jer 1:4), and multiplied disciples (Acts 6:7) is a key biblical theme with its own causal force: "[My word] shall not return to me empty, but it shall accomplish that which I purpose" (Isa 55:11). Speaking is a form of action, a way of doing certain things, so much so that "God speaking and God acting are often one and the same thing."[29]

God's saying "Let there be light" is nevertheless a speech act of a different order. While humans can, under the right conditions, do things with words (e.g., "I now pronounce you husband and wife"), only God can create and give form to things that previously did not exist simply by speaking (Rom 4:17). Unlike human declaratives, God's declaratives are also generative. In Luther's words, "He created the world and all things with the greatest ease, namely, by

27. Augustine, *Literal Meaning of Genesis* 1.4.9.

28. Peter J. Leithart, *Creator: A Theological Interpretation of Genesis 1* (Downers Grove, IL: IVP Academic, 2023), 196.

29. Timothy Ward, *Words of Life: Scripture as the Living and Active Word of God* (Downers Grove, IL: InterVarsity, 2009), 26. See also my "The Bible—Word of God?," in *Reading the Bible Today*, ed. Lydia Jaeger (Grand Rapids: Zondervan, 2024).

speaking. Accordingly, there is no more effort for God in His creation than there is for us in the mention of it."[30] God, then, is a speech agent, but we must be careful to acknowledge the asymmetry between divine and human speech agency.

This brings us back to our opening question: *Does* God literally speak or do anything? Stated differently, what is the right interpretation of Genesis 1:3: "And God said, 'Let there be light,' and there was light"? Saying is an action, and actions take time, but God says *fiat lux* before time existed. Thanks to grammatical "aspect," biblical Hebrew comes as close as is linguistically possible to expressing an atemporal "pure action."[31] Various English translations have been proposed to capture this atemporality, including "God saith, 'Let light be;' and light is" or "And God said—Light, be, And light was."[32]

James Barr represented a generation of modern biblical scholars and theologians for whom the whole idea of divine action has become problematic in a scientific age where the God of the gaps has less and less room to maneuver: "We do not have any idea of ways in which God might straightforwardly communicate articulate thoughts or sentences to men; it just doesn't happen."[33] Others, noting the problems the notion of divine causality raises for modern science, ask, "Does the 'God who acts' really act?"[34] Still others, reflecting on "God is spirit" (John 4:24), similarly insist, "Language . . . cannot be literally predicated of pure spirit."[35] How can we take *God saying* literally if God has no body parts, such as a tongue and a mouth? And how can we take divine action in general literally, given the prevailing naturalistic frame of reference of our scientific age?

Once again, much depends on how we conceive of literality and on our continuing to distinguish literal from literalistic interpretations. The urgent question for literal interpreters is simply this: Which set of assumptions should readers bring to Genesis 1 to understand rightly the authors' (human and divine) communicative intentions? One does not need to be modern to avoid overly literalistic readings. Luther is a case in point: "Not that God actually spoke,

30. Martin Luther, cited in *Luther's Works*, vol. 1 *Lectures on Genesis Chapters 1–5*, ed. Jaroslav Pelikan (St. Louis: Concordia, 1958), 22. See also Christoph Schwöbel, "'We Are All God's Vocabulary': The Idea of Creation as a Speech-Act of the Trinitarian God and Its Significance for the Dialogue between Theology and Sciences," in *Knowing Creation: Perspectives from Theology, Philosophy, and Science*, vol. 1, ed. Andrew B. Torrance and Thomas H. McCall (Grand Rapids; Zondervan, 2018), 47–68.

31. For a fuller explanation, see Jonathan Yovel, "The Creation of Language and Language without Time: Metaphysics and Metapragmatics in Genesis 1," *Biblical Interpretation* 20 (2012): 205–25.

32. Yovel, 219.

33. James Barr, *The Bible in the Modern World* (London: SCM, 1973), 17.

34. Frank B. Dilley, "Does the 'God Who Acts' Really Act?," in *God's Activity in the World: The Contemporary Problem*, ed. Owen C. Thomas (Chico, CA: Scholars, 1983), 45–60.

35. Sandra Schneiders, *The Revelatory Text: Interpreting the New Testament as Sacred Scripture* (Collegeville, MN: Liturgical, 1999), 28.

for he has no mouth, tongue, teeth, or lips as we do. But he who created and formed the mouth of all men can also make speech and the voice."[36] William Alston elucidated Luther's insight, helpfully distinguishing literal from literalistic thanks to a distinction between analogy and univocity. Alston began by defining action, human or divine, as "a change that is brought about by a volition or intention."[37] He then showed that employing vocal cords is not necessary to speaking. God *literally*—really and truly—speaks, but not *univocally*, the way we men and women do, with tongues, teeth, and vocal cords. God can do what humans do, but in his own Godlike way. "'God speaks' is a literal but analogical claim. It is analogical because divine discourse is both like and unlike human discourse; but this is not metaphor, because the performance of illocutionary acts belongs properly and primarily to God and only derivatively . . . to human creatures."[38]

God therefore *says* (but not as humans might), "Let there be light," and as a result, there was light. God produced real-world effects by "speaking his mind." That God forms and enacts intentions, thereby making a difference outside himself, is the epitome of personal agency. God's "speak-acting" is less an anthropomorphic description of God's agency than a theomorphic description of ours. Creaturely images of God can only bring about *some* effects through speaking, but God's speaking is universally effectual. Human speech acts fail—warnings go unheeded; promises are left unfilled; truth claims prove false—not so God's word. God's speech acts confer being and, as Genesis 1 goes on to show, order creation. God's speech generates and governs. This distinctive divine speak-acting follows from the singular Creator-creature distinction. That God *speaks* light into being, along with everything else, attests to his sovereign lordship: creation is an intentional and intelligible divine work, not an overflow (emanation) of God's own being. God's *fiat lux* is *ex nihilo* creation in action and at work.

That God literally speaks is foundational for the present project in two ways. First, on a formal level, God's speech acts serve as the criterion and norm for the plain canonical sense of Scripture (i.e., what God is doing with biblical words in canonical context). Second, on the material level, what God does by speaking—the various types of divine discourse, including the Word becoming flesh (John 1:14)—is what the Bible is *literally* about. We fail to interpret Scripture literally unless we read biblical narrative as an account of God's

36. Luther, "How Christians Should Regard Moses," in *Martin Luther's Basic Theological Writings*, ed. Timothy F. Lull (Minneapolis: Fortress 1989), 136–37.

37. William Alston, *Divine Nature and Human Language: Essays in Philosophical Theology* (Ithaca, NY: Cornell University Press, 1989), 96.

38. Merold Westphal, "On Reading God the Author," *Religious Studies* 37 (2001): 273. For a fuller discussion of these matters, see my *Remythologizing Theology: Divine Action, Passion, and Authorship*, Cambridge Studies in Christian Doctrine, ser. 18, repr. ed. (Cambridge: Cambridge University Press, 2012), 207–11.

communicative acts in the spatiotemporal world he spoke into being in the first place.[39] It is surely significant that both creation and redemption involve divine speech acts. "Paul uses creation as a metaphor for what happens to a person at conversion [and] the metaphor denotes something real at a deeper level than the merely physical."[40] God justifies by *declaring* someone righteous: "When the judge in the law-court justifies someone . . . he *creates* the status the vindicated defendant now possesses, by an act of *declaration*."[41] Creation and redemption are things God does with words, mighty speech acts and divine interjections that create being from nonbeing. We turn now to consider precisely what God brings into being in saying, "Let there be light."

"What Light through Yonder Cosmos Breaks?" Genesis 1:3 in the History of Exegesis

Light is the only entity mentioned in the Genesis account that is created strictly by fiat, rather than out of something else (e.g., "Let the earth sprout vegetation"; Gen 1:11). What, then, is this light?[42] There is no better way into the conflict of interpretations than to experience it, and the best way to experience it is to survey the history of biblical interpretations.[43] What follows is a snippet of this history, a much-abridged survey of various commentaries on Genesis 1:3, ranging from the fourth to the twenty-first centuries. I have two purposes: first, to explore further the centrality of interpretive assumptions and frames of reference; second, to advance our understanding of both light and literality. Dipping into the history of exegesis of "Let there be light" will, I trust, shed light on the nature of light and on literal interpretation itself.[44]

39. The real conflict in interpreting Genesis 1 is not between theology and science, but between different understandings of divine action. See Collins, *Reading Genesis Well*, 282–83.

40. John C. Lennox, *Seven Days That Divide the World: The Beginning according to Genesis and Science* (Grand Rapids: Zondervan, 2011), 102.

41. N. T. Wright. *Justification: God's Plan and Paul's Vision* (Downers Grove, IL: InterVarsity, 2009), 69.

42. For a "history of ideas" approach to light, see Bruce Watson, *Light: A Radiant History from Creation to the Quantum Age* (New York: Bloomsbury, 2016). See also the chapters in part 1 of *Light from Light: Scientists and Theologians in Dialogue*, ed. Gerald O'Collins and Mary Ann Meyers (Grand Rapids: Eerdmans, 2012).

43. A good general survey is Keith D. Stanglin, *The Letter and Spirit of Biblical Interpretation: From the Early Church to Modern Practice* (Grand Rapids: Baker Academic, 2018). For a comprehensive survey of interpretations of Genesis 1 and, in particular, the length of the six days, see Andrew J. Brown, *The Days of Creation: A History of Christian Interpretation of Genesis 1:1–2:3* (Dorset, UK: Deo, 2014).

44. Fun fact: In his *Lectures on Genesis*, Luther mentioned Jerome's claim that Jewish rabbis forbade anyone under age thirty to read or expound Genesis 1 for others (Luther, *Lectures on Genesis*, 3). Fortunately, I satisfy this condition. Those who want a more complete history of interpretation are advised to start with Philo's "On the Creation," in *The Works of Philo: Complete and Unabridged*, trans. C. D. Yonge (Peabody, MA: Hendrickson, 1993). An Alexandrian Jew steeped in Hellenistic philosophy, Philo brought a Neoplatonic frame of reference to bear on his reading of Genesis.

Basil of Caesarea

Basil of Caesarea's (330–379) *Hexameron* was the first Christian treatise (originally a Lenten series of homilies) on the six days of creation (from Gk. *hexa-*, meaning "six"). It is often cited as an example of a more literal approach to Genesis than one finds in, say, Origen. Indeed, Basil gives an anti-allegorical diatribe that culminates with a kind of "I do *not* have a dream" speech. Basil said, "When I hear 'grass,' I think of grass."[45] His literalism stands in stark contrast to "dream interpreters" (allegorists) who "bestow on the Scriptures a dignity of their own imagining."[46] Nevertheless, Basil rightly insisted that Genesis 1 is less concerned with the world of nature than with the majesty of the Father Almighty, maker of heaven and earth. What thus comes to the fore in his literal interpretation is ultimately a theological frame of reference.

Grass is grass, but what did Basil think of when he heard, "Let there be light"? According to Andrew Louth, Basil used the science of his day to fill out the bare outline he found in Genesis, something he could do "because he is quite clear that the scriptural account is not a scientific account."[47] The creation of light is the moment when God "illuminated" the world, "made the light circulate . . . distributing its splendor rapidly in every direction."[48] God did not create the sun and moon until the fourth day, said Basil, so that the ignorant would "not consider the sun as the origin and the father of light."[49] Knowing the human propensity to sun worship, God created it on the fourth day and set it in the heavens to put it in its place (literally!). The sun is not the primordial light, only "a vehicle for that original light."[50]

Basil mentioned other lights that are vehicles for the "true light of the world," namely, Jesus Christ (John 8:12). For example, the apostle Paul speaks of saints as "luminaries of the souls which they instructed," probably an allusion to his related notion that believers "shine as lights in the world" (Phil 2:15).[51]

---

45. Basil of Caesarea, *Hexaëmeron* 1–9, in *St Basil: Exegetic Homilies*, Fathers of the Church 46, trans. Agnes Clare Way (Washington, DC: Catholic University of America Press, 1963), 9.1, 135.

46. Basil, 136. It bears mentioning that Basil waxes more allegorical in his interpretation of the Psalms. See further Stephen M. Hildebrand, *Basil of Caesarea* (Grand Rapids: Baker Academic, 2014), 44–52. See also John A. McGuckin's claim that Basil is not castigating spiritual interpretation in general, only "excessive allegorization of details such that the moral import of the text's overarching *skopos* loses itself in a welter of secondary details." "Patterns of Biblical Exegesis in the Cappadocian Fathers: Basil the Great, Gregory the Theologian, and Gregory of Nyssa," in *Orthodox and Wesleyan Scriptural Understanding and Practice*, ed. S. T. Kimbrough (New York: St. Vladimir's Seminary Press, 2005), 45. For a vigorous rebuttal of the claim that Basil is a literalist, see Craig D. Allert, *Early Christian Readings of Genesis One: Patristic Exegesis and Literal Interpretation* (Downers Grove, IL: IVP Academic, 2018), 161–202.

47. Andrew Louth, "The Six Days of Creation according to the Greek Fathers," in *Reading Genesis after Darwin*, ed. Stephen C. Baron and David Wilkinson (Oxford: Oxford University Press, 2009), 48.

48. Basil, *Hexaëmeron* 2.7.

49. Basil, 6.2.

50. Basil, 6.2.

51. Basil, 6.2.

Basil thus grasped the importance of distinguishing God's primordial light from various created lights, parsing light in an array of conceptual hues: "May the Father of the true light, Who has adorned day with celestial light, Who has made the fire to shine which illumines us during the night, Who reserves for us in the peace of a future age a spiritual and everlasting light, enlighten your hearts in the knowledge of truth."[52] Augustine picked up the latter link, between light and intellectual illumination, and ran with it.

Augustine

No one strove more mightily, or more often, to clarify the literal sense of Genesis 1 than Augustine.[53] His first two swings were misses, by his own admission: "I wanted to test my capabilities in this truly most taxing and difficult work [of literal interpretation]. But in explaining the Scriptures, my inexperience collapsed under the weight of so heavy a load and, before I had finished one book, I rested from this labor which I could not endure."[54] Augustine's third try, *The Literal Meaning of Genesis*, on which he labored for some fourteen years, is widely acknowledged as one of his most significant exegetical works, even though it covers only the first three chapters (i.e., the six days and the first sin). In addition to his three official commentaries on Genesis, he also expounded on the days of creation in *Confessions* (books 11–13) and *City of God* (book 11).[55]

As his title indicates, Augustine's principal aim was to offer a literal interpretation of the creation narrative—"a faithful record of what happened."[56] In general, Augustine sought the meaning intended by the author (Moses), though he admitted it was often difficult to determine, in which case he relied on the analogy of Scripture and catholic tradition: "Let us choose the one [interpretation] which appears as certainly the meaning intended by the author. But if this is not clear, then at least we should choose an interpretation in keeping with the context of Scripture and in harmony with our faith."[57]

What most strikes modern readers are the varied questions Augustine asked: Is light something material or spiritual? Was light the first thing created, or was it "the heavens and the earth" (Gen 1:1)? What is the connection

52. Basil, 2.8.

53. For an account of these efforts, see Yoon Kyung Kim, *Augustine's Changing Interpretations of Genesis 1–3: From De Genesi Contra Manichaeos to De Genesi Ad Litteram* (Lewiston, NY: Mellen, 2006). See also Gavin Ortlund, *Retrieving Augustine's Doctrine of Creation: Ancient Wisdom for Current Controversy* (Downers Grove, IL: IVP Academic, 2020).

54. Augustine, *The Retractions*, trans. M. Inez Bogan, Fathers of the Church, vol. 60 (Washington, DC: Catholic University of America Press, 1968), 1.17, 76.

55. See Roland J. Teske, "Genesis Accounts of Creation," in *Augustine through the Ages: An Encyclopedia*, ed. Allan D. Fitzgerald (Grand Rapids: Eerdmans, 1999), 379–81.

56. Augustine, *Literal Meaning of Genesis* 1.1.19.

57. Augustine, *Literal Meaning of Genesis* 1.21.41.

between the light created on day one and the lights created on day four (Gen 1:14)? Clearly, the nature and role of light is an important interpretive crux. Augustine struggled to understand how there could be light before the creation of the luminaries (sun, moon, stars) on day four, what kind of pre-solar light it was, and where that light went during the evening of the first three days. He knew, of course, that the sun does not really go away at night: "There is always day in one place and night in another."[58]

What, then, is the nature of this light that precedes sunlight? If the "earth" mentioned in Genesis 1:1 refers to the whole material universe, which God then separated into the waters below and the heaven above (Gen 1:6–8), then "the heavens" mentioned in verse 1 cannot refer to the sky "up there." Augustine concluded that "the heavens" refer to the immaterial or spiritual created order, allowing him to fill in an otherwise puzzling gap in the Genesis narrative, which nowhere explicitly treats the creation of angels.[59] If angels are not eternal, then there must have been a time when they were not and hence a time when they began to be. Augustine appealed to Job 38:7: "When the stars were made, all my angels praised me with a great voice."[60] Augustine thought the angels were created on the first day to be inhabitants of the "heavenly city" above.[61] Pursuing this line of reasoning further, he inferred that the light created with the angels in the heavens is not physical but immaterial or spiritual. So the light created on the first day is not physical, nor can it be equated with "the true Light which is coeternal with the Father," namely, the Word that was with God in the beginning.[62]

Augustine's reading was complex and at times convoluted, yet to his credit he eventually specified the literal meaning of the spiritual light God spoke into being on day one: God's illumination of the angels' intellects. Augustine contrasted this literal interpretation (where light *figures* knowledge) as preferable to the literalist interpretation of light as something physical. "Let there be light" refers to God enabling the angels to know his plan for creation. "The angels first saw the creature in the Word of God, and thus the creature was originally produced in the knowledge of the angels."[63] Augustine's interpretation, while it will strike some as implausible, may appear more compelling when read in conjunction with John 1:3: "Through him [the Logos] all things were made" (NIV). The notion seems to be that Christ is the template of every created thing, the sum total of the divine ideas expressed in creation. There was light on the first

58. Augustine, *Literal Meaning of Genesis* 1.10.21.

59. Augustine, *Literal Meaning of Genesis* 1.17.32. Augustine had first come to this position in his *Confessions*, bk. 12.

60. At least this is what Augustine read in the Latin translation of the LXX rendering of Job 38:7.

61. Augustine, *Literal Meaning of Genesis* 5.19.37. See also Augustine, *City of God* 11.9.

62. Augustine, *Literal Meaning of Genesis* 1, 17, 12.

63. Augustine, *Literal Meaning of Genesis* 4.31.48.

day when the angels "first saw in the Word of God those works to be made before they were actually made."[64] In brief, the light God created before the sun is what the angels come to know in contemplating the Word through whom all things were made, the Word who is also "the light of the world" (John 8:12).

Identifying the light God spoke into being with angelic knowledge also helped Augustine explain how there could be evening and morning before the sun was created on day four. The six days are days of angelic learning—celestial "school days," as it were. Evening and morning refer to the two modes of this angelic knowledge, respectively. In the morning (i.e., "daytime"), angels see the essence of things in the Word of God, then, in the evening, God creates these things and the angels know them as they exist. "The knowledge the angels have of the spiritual, eternal ideas is like the day, while the knowledge they have of time-bound creation is like the evening."[65] The six days of creation are a divine accommodation, God's manner of speaking about the angels' progressive comprehension of what was actually an instantaneous work of creation.[66]

We may wonder how equating the creation of light with the illumination of angelic intelligence could count as literal rather than allegorical interpretation. Augustine anticipated the objection: "These interpretations, of course, are different from our ordinary understanding of light in the material sense. But it is not true that material light is literally 'light,' and light referred to in Genesis is metaphorical 'light.'"[67] Augustine here raised the intriguing possibility that the truest and most literal light is the light of the mind, not the eyes. After all, even today we speak of seeing as something either physical (ocular) or spiritual (intellectual). In the words of one of Augustine's contemporary defenders, "Because the divine Word is uncontainable in human words, one concludes paradoxically that even the literal sense of the text transcends its letter. . . . Christian readers of Scripture, therefore, cannot help but ascend from the literal to the figural."[68]

Augustine's reading of Genesis 1:3 suggests that the truer and more literal light is spiritual (i.e., intellectual illumination). Physical light is, paradoxically, but a type or shadow compared to the real thing. And the truest light is, of course, Christ himself. "He is literally the Light but metaphorically a stone."[69]

---

64. Augustine, *Literal Meaning of Genesis*,4.32.49.

65. Allert, *Early Christian Readings of Genesis One*, 284.

66. See further Augustine's similar treatment of angelic knowledge in *City of God* 11.7.

67. Augustine, *Literal Meaning of Genesis* 4.28.45. See also Elizabeth Klein, *Augustine's Theology of Angels* (Cambridge: Cambridge University Press, 2018), 5.

68. David Graham, "Defending Biblical Literalism: Augustine on the Literal Sense," *Pro Ecclesia* 25, no. 2 (2016): 174, 193. For an argument that what Augustine took to be the literal sense includes several levels, including a spiritual sense, see Kim, *Augustine's Changing Interpretations of Genesis 1–3*, 163–67.

69. Augustine, *Literal Meaning of Genesis* 4.28.45. Augustine was referring to John 8:12 ("I am the light of the world") and Mark 12:10 ("The stone that the builders rejected has become the cornerstone"), respectively.

Augustine thus rejected the literalist interpretation of Genesis 1:3, preferred the figural reading, and was open to the trans-figural possibility that the creation of light prefigured the incarnation of the "light of the world."

Thomas Aquinas

By the twelfth century, there were two competing views on Genesis 1: Augustine's instantaneous creation theory and the alternative propagated by Gregory, Jerome, Bede, and others, which recognized an original creation ("in the beginning"), a work of "distinction" (days one through three), and a work of "adorning" (days four through six).[70] Thomas Aquinas's discussion of the six days, which he patterned after the latter scheme, merits examination given his comments on both the nature of the literal sense and the nature of light.

It was Thomas Aquinas, we may recall, who insisted that theologians appeal to the literal sense to establish doctrine.[71] However, because God is the ultimate author of Scripture, who "by one act comprehends all things by His intellect," Thomas was unwilling to limit legitimate interpretive options to what was in the mind of the human author only.[72] Significantly, Thomas never used this notion of the plurality of the literal sense in his actual exegesis to invoke an "anything goes" relativism. Instead, he deployed it to explain more modestly "that a legitimate diversity in theological understanding could well be the intention of the Holy Spirit and even of the Spirit's instrument, the human author of Scripture."[73] Interpretations may therefore be viable if they accord with the context ("the circumstance of the letter") and the creed (the catholic faith). The interpretation of Genesis 1 is a case in point. Augustine and the Greek fathers disagreed over whether unformed matter in general was created prior to particular formed things. Thomas thought that Genesis 1 and the creed allowed for both interpretations. He was therefore open to the possibility that the Spirit granted Moses the knowledge of both truths "under one letter such that whichever of these meanings is the meaning of the author [*sensus auctor*]."[74]

Thomas treated the first day of creation in four articles in his *Summa*

70. See further Brown, *Days of Creation*, 66–79. See also the thirteenth-century work of Robert Grosseteste, *On the Six Days of Creation*, trans. C. F. J. Martin (Oxford: Oxford University Press, 1996), who tried to synthesize the various views.

71. Thomas Aquinas, *Summa Theologica* 1, 1, art. 10.

72. Thomas Aquinas, *Summa Theologica* 1, 1, art. 10. Note, too, that when Thomas spoke of authorial intention, he often meant the act of willing a certain end, as in, "John the Evangelist principally intends to show the divinity of the incarnate Word." This fits with what I said in part 1 about tying literal meaning to the whole discourse—what authors say about something to someone in some way—and not simply the words themselves.

73. Mark F. Johnson, "Another Look at the Plurality of the Literal Sense," *Medieval Philosophy and Theology* 2 (1992): 141.

74. Thomas Aquinas, *De potentia* 4.1.

Theologica, asking whether light is a "body" or a "quality."[75] The first thing he wanted to know was whether the term *light* was used literally when referring to spiritual things, such as the knowledge of angels. His response fits with what we described as the *extended* literal sense: "In its primary meaning [light] signifies that which makes manifest to the sense of sight; afterwards it was extended to that which makes manifest to cognition of any kind."[76] Both kinds of light, physical and spiritual, involve illuminative power.[77] It is fitting, Thomas thought, that God created light first. For light "is common to terrestrial and celestial bodies," and "all other things are made manifest by light."[78] However, whereas for Augustine the light created in Genesis 1:3 pertained to the knowledge of angels, Thomas associated light with human intelligence: what is "seen" in the mind's eye.[79] Thomas thus viewed the sensible light that illumines our eyes as an image of the intelligible light that illumines our mind's eye. Physically, light enables physical sight, but we also know things "by participating in an inner intelligible light, which God gives."[80]

Like other Christian commentators, Thomas Aquinas read Genesis 1:3 in tandem with 1 John 1:5: "God is light, and in him is no darkness at all." If God's essence is light, Thomas reasoned, then no created entity could have light as an essential property, for that would make it equal with God. If God's being is light, and if to be is to be in act, then God is that singular source that actively illumines the minds of angels and humans alike. Thomas was aware, of course, that John 1:9 ("The true light, which gives light to everyone, was coming into the world") also has an important bearing on the literal interpretation of Genesis 1. The creation of light anticipates the incarnation of Christ. "Aquinas thus understands the primary mission of the Son to be the illumination of our intellects."[81] Christ is the essential source of light for every intelligent creature

---

75. Thomas Aquinas, *Summa Theologica* 1, 67.

76. Thomas Aquinas, *Summa Theologica* 1, 67. Note, however, that Thomas took physical light as the baseline and spiritual light as the figural extension, whereas Augustine moved in the other direction, taking spiritual light as the (literal) baseline meaning. For more on how Thomas adapted Aristotle's views, see ch. 2, "The Physics of Light," in David L. Whidden III, *Christ the Light: The Theology of Light and Illumination in Thomas Aquinas* (Minneapolis: Fortress, 2014), 47–68.

77. Cf. Thomas Aquinas's comment on Job 37:3: "Among all the sensible effects light is the most spiritual." Thomas Aquinas, *The Literal Exposition on Job*, trans. Anthony Damico (Atlanta: Scholars, 1989), 405.

78. Thomas Aquinas, *Summa Theologica* 1, 67, art. 4.

79. So Marie-Dominique Chenu, *Toward Understanding Saint Thomas* (Chicago: G. Regency, 1953), 171. There is debate over Thomas Aquinas's appropriation of Augustine's notion of divine illumination. The issue is whether divine light creates an intrinsic cognitive capacity (Aristotle's "active intellect," the power to abstract forms from things) or functions as an extrinsic influence that bestows actual cognitive content. For a rehearsal of this debate and a compelling case for Thomas's Augustinian credentials, see Lydia Schumacher, *Divine Illumination: The History and Future of Augustine's Theory of Knowledge* (Oxford: Wiley-Blackwell, 2011).

80. Whidden, *Christ the Light*, 143. Unlike humans, who have to abstract forms from things seen, the angels, being immaterial, know things more immediately.

81. Whidden, *Christ the Light*, 113.

who comes into the world, the Word who illumines darkened intellects through his Spirit. "The acts of Christian theological intelligence are a natural work of the human mind, and they are 'spiritual' in that as such they are moved by God the Holy Spirit, who is the light of the mind."[82] In sum, *light is knowledge that originates in and is ordered to the triune God*. What is striking is that Thomas intended this as a literal interpretation of Genesis 1:3, in contrast with the allegorical reading he gave elsewhere, according to which "Let there be light" means "Let Christ be born in the church."[83]

Martin Luther

Like Augustine before him, Martin Luther displayed a Captain Ahab–like obsession in pursuing the textual equivalent of the great white whale, the literal meaning of Genesis: "I will devote the remaining years of my life to an exposition of the Books of Moses."[84] Luther preached, taught, and commented on Genesis longer than any other biblical text, including an eighteen-month series of sermons and eight volumes worth of lectures delivered over a span of ten years.[85] In contrast to Augustine, however, Luther's primary interest was the later chapters, which by reading literally enabled him "to interpret the believer's own life as a struggle for faith and faithfulness."[86]

Luther read literally while fully committed to discovering the "spirituality of the letter," by which he meant its real subject matter or *scopus*: Jesus Christ.[87] In his 1523 "Preface to the Old Testament," he expressed his conviction that the Old Testament is Christian Scripture: "Here you will find the swaddling cloths and the manger in which Christ lies."[88] Christ appears as a *literal promise* from God as early as Genesis 3:15, the *protoevangelium* or first indication of the gospel: "He shall bruise your head, and you shall bruise his heel." Such statements, alongside other messianic promises, render Genesis "an entirely evangelical book."[89] Luther read Genesis as a prophetic witness to

82. John Webster, "Editorial," *International Journal of Systematic Theology* 14 no. 4 (2012): 379. We shall return to the triune nature of divine illumination at the end of the chapter.

83. See the discussion of Thomas Aquinas's commentary on Galatians 4:7 in Whidden, *Christ the Light*, 214.

84. Luther, *Lectures on Genesis Chapters 1–5*, ix.

85. The first eight volumes of *Luther's Works* published by Concordia are all devoted to his lectures on Genesis.

86. Mickey L. Mattox, "Faith in Creation: Martin Luther's Sermons on Genesis 1," *Trinity Journal* 39 (2018): 208. Mattox observes, "If for Luther there is a how-to book for the Christian life, Genesis is it" (209).

87. The phrase "spirituality of the letter" is Ocker's way of describing the goal of the later medieval exegesis with which he associated Luther. Christopher Ocker, *Biblical Poetics before Humanism and Reformation* (Cambridge: Cambridge University Press, 2002), 219.

88. Luther, "Preface to the Old Testament," in *Luther's Works*, vol. 35, *Word and Sacrament I*, ed. E. Theodore Bachmann (Minneapolis: Fortress, 1960), 236.

89. Luther, "Preface to the Old Testament," 237. Cf. Adina Miriam Yoffie: "To the orthodox

Christ, and without this christological subject matter, "even the knowledge of the language is nothing."[90]

As concerns Genesis 1, Luther believed Moses spoke literally about what God does in time, and what God did took time. Luther concluded, "The world, with all its creatures, was created within six days, as the words read."[91] Luther had harsh words for Augustine's idea that God created everything instantaneously: "Augustine resorts to extraordinary trifling in his treatment of the six days, which he makes out to be mystical days of knowledge among the angels, not natural ones."[92] Concerning Genesis 1:3 in particular, what most impressed Luther was God's speaking.[93] Light comes into being only through the Word that was with God and was God. "Therefore in the beginning and before every creature there is the Word, and it is such a powerful Word that it makes all things out of nothing."[94] As to the nature of the created light, Luther acknowledged that it was difficult to say, though he thought it must be "true and physical," for one should not "without reason depart from the rules of language or . . . by force read meanings into words."[95] Light is light. Well, not quite. For in connection with the fourth day of creation, he said the "crude light of the first day was perfected by the addition of new creatures: the sun, the moon, the stars, etc."[96] He refused to say more about the nature of this "crude light" except that "the astronomers are the experts from whom it is most convenient to get what may be discussed about these subjects."[97] Luther's literal interpretation is thus a mixed bag: the literal meaning of "Let there be light" refers to "natural" light, whereas the literal meaning of "And God said" pertains to the Word through whom all things were made.

Lutherans . . . the Christological sense of Genesis 3:15 was its *sensus literalis*." "Biblical Literalism and Scholarship in Protestant Northern Europe, 1630–1700" (PhD diss., Harvard University, 2009), 183.

90. Luther, "Preface to the Old Testament," 249. For more on Luther's various prefaces to the Bible, see William M. Marsh, *Martin Luther on Reading the Bible as Christian Scripture: The Messiah in Luther's Biblical Hermeneutic and Theology* (Eugene, OR: Wipf & Stock, 2017), 28–161.

91. Luther, *Lectures on Genesis*, 5. Robert Letham claims that Luther is "the first of the major exegetes" to view the days as twenty-four hours each. Robert Letham, "'In the Space of Six Days': The Days of Creation from Origen to the Westminster Assembly," *Westminster Theological Journal* 61 (1999): 164. Note should be taken, however, of the influence on Luther of Nicholas of Lyra's 1322 *Postilla litteralis* (the first running commentary on the Bible to be printed). Lyra rejected Augustine's interpretation of the six "days" of angelic knowledge as "far from the literal sense," preferring to view each as indicating a span of twenty-four hours, even before the creation of the sun. See C. Patton, "Creation, Fall and Salvation: Lyra's Commentary on Genesis 1–3," in *Nicholas of Lyra: The Senses of Scripture*, ed. Philip D. W. Krey and Lesley Smith (Leiden: Brill, 2000), 23.

92. Luther, *Lectures on Genesis*, 4.

93. For Luther on creation as a speech act, see Oswald Bayer, *Martin Luther's Theology: A Contemporary Interpretation* (Grand Rapids: Eerdmans, 2008), 101–4.

94. Luther, *Lectures on Genesis*, 17.

95. Luther, *Lectures on Genesis*, 19.

96. Luther, *Lectures on Genesis*, 40.

97. Luther, *Lectures on Genesis*, 41.

John Calvin

While it is an exaggeration to dub John Calvin the founder of modern historical-grammatical exegesis, Calvin's humanist training did lead him to assign priority to verbal meaning and authorial intent in describing literal interpretation: "The true meaning of Scripture is the natural and simple one."[98] This accords with Calvin's tendency to see Genesis as a "popular" work, written so that ordinary people can understand it. Genesis contains need-to-know information about the origins of the cosmos and the covenant. Moses wrote "to render [the invisible] God, as it were, visible to us in his works."[99] In general, Calvin is keen to avoid two errors: a preoccupation with nature that is forgetful of God; on the other, a speculation over the divine essence that is forgetful of God's works. The literal sense serves a pedagogical purpose, instructing the faithful in the substance of the faith. God's purpose in creating was ultimately covenantal: to form a people for himself in, with, and under Christ. "We are companions of the Patriarchs: for since they possessed Christ as the pledge of their salvation when he had not yet appeared, so we retain the God who formerly manifested himself to them."[100]

Calvin tied his theology to the text, to the way the words go. This reflects his training as a humanist. He was equally committed to reading the Bible as Christian Scripture.[101] One example of his devotion to the letter of the text is his refusal to interpret the mention of God in Genesis 1:1 as referring to the Trinity. Yes, the divine name ("Elohim") is in the plural form, but Calvin cautioned readers "to beware of violent glosses."[102] It is "frivolous" to see a reference to Christ—at least not until two verses later, when Calvin associated "and God said" (Gen 1:3) with "all things were made through him" (John 1:3)! Apparently, Calvin first caught a glimpse of the Trinity only when the Word acted out in Genesis 1:3–5, speaking order into being by separating light from darkness: "The act of distinguishing his wisdom begins to be conspicuous" only with the creation of light.[103] In human experience, plants and trees need sunlight to grow.

98. John Calvin, *The Epistles of the Apostle Paul to the Galatians, Ephesians, Philippians, and Colossians*, trans. T. H. L. Parker (Grand Rapids: Eerdmans, 1965), 84–85.

99. John Calvin, *Genesis*, trans. John King (Edinburgh: Banner of Truth Trust, 1975), 58.

100. Calvin, *Genesis*, 66. Greene-McCreight notes that Calvin's literal interpretations include figural reading because persons and events in Israel's history are types of Christ and the story of the church. Kathryn Greene-McCreight, *Ad Litteram: How Augustine, Calvin, and Barth Read the "Plain Sense" of Genesis 1–3* (New York: Peter Lang, 1999), 98.

101. Stephen Edmondson identifies a convergence between Renaissance historiography and theological interpretation in Calvin's interest in the Bible's depiction of history as the history of the covenant Mediator, Jesus Christ. Stephen Edmondson, "Christ and History: Hermeneutical Convergence in Calvin and Its Challenge to Biblical Theology," *Modern Theology* 21, no. 1 (2005): 3–35. Rebekah Earnshaw unpacks the various ways Calvin could be considered to be a "biblical theologian." Rebekah Earnshaw, *Creator and Creation according to Calvin on Genesis* (Göttingen: Vandenhoeck & Ruprecht, 2020), 31–38.

102. Calvin, *Genesis*, 71.

103. Calvin, *Genesis*, 75. Cf. Karl Barth, who after reading Genesis 1:3 and John 1:3 together said the

"The existence of light is the sine qua non for the existence of anything else."[104] However, the biblical narrative is so ordered that the creation of the sun takes place on day four, after the earth had already sprouted plants and vegetation. Calvin thought this intentional. Humans are prone to idolatry, particularly sun worship (and astrology), hence the creation of the sun is delayed so that we understand that the life-giving property of light belongs to God alone.[105] We are meant, said Calvin, "to refer all things to him."[106]

At one point in his commentary, Calvin alluded to Ptolemaic astronomy, saying that "the earth, like a little globe, is placed in the center [of the circuit of heavens]."[107] Yet he was quick to add that Moses was not speaking as a philosopher or astronomer about these matters. Moses was not making scientific claims about the relative size of the sun, moon, and stars; rather, he was speaking phenomenologically, in terms of how things appear in everyday human experience: "Moses here addresses himself to our senses."[108] Calvin acknowledged Genesis 1 to be a nonscientific account of creation and interpreted it literally as such. The purpose of the creation narrative is to provide guidance to ordinary readers, not astronomers. "For as it became a theologian, he [Moses] had respect to *us* rather than to the *stars*."[109] The frame of reference that guided Calvin's reading was the biblical narrative itself, nothing else, and it is precisely this commitment that saved his literal interpretations from being tied to any one scientific theory.[110]

Gordon J. Wenham

Gordon Wenham's commentary, several centuries downstream from Calvin, is representative of many twentieth-century evangelical approaches that have sought to continue and improve on the Reformers' manner of literal interpretation. Wenham examines the opening chapters of Genesis in relation to various forms of biblical criticism, ancient Near Eastern parallels, the rest of the Bible, and modern thought. He agrees with those who see Genesis 1 as "a polemic against the mythic-religious concepts of the ancient Orient."[111] God

---

Fathers "were right when they saw glimpses of the whole mystery of the Trinity" in "Let there be light." Barth, *Church Dogmatics* III.1 (Edinburgh: T&T Clark, 1958), 116.

104. Hamilton, *Book of Genesis*, 119.

105. Calvin's objection to astrology is parallel to his objection to allegory: in both cases, the temptation is to read these signs "according to our fancy." *Genesis*, 84; cf. the discussion in Greene-McCreight, *Ad Litteram*, 129.

106. Calvin, *Genesis*, 82.

107. Calvin, *Genesis*, 61.

108. Calvin, *Genesis*, 85.

109. Calvin, *Genesis*, 85–86.

110. Cf. Greene-McCreight: "Calvin seems to want to guard the literal reading from the necessity of committing itself to any one worldview." *Ad Litteram*, 125.

111. Gordon J. Wenham, *Genesis 1–15*. Word Biblical Commentary, vol. 1 (Nashville: Thomas Nelson, 1987), 37.

does not have to struggle with recalcitrant matter but lays down the law, as it were, ordering creation by his authoritative, wise, and powerful word.

The "comment" section of Wenham's commentary exposits the text's verbal meaning; the "explanation" relates Genesis to wider theological discussions. There is a nod to source criticism, though Wenham devotes the bulk of his discussion to what is more certain (the final form) before tackling what is less certain (the various underlying sources and their development). His overriding goal is the discovery of the original meaning of Genesis, namely, what it meant to its final editor and first readers.[112]

Wenham describes Genesis 1 as "the majestic opening chapter" that introduces the two main subjects of the whole of Scripture: God the Creator and humanity his creature (and their relation). Genesis 1 sets the stage for all the stories to follow, identifying the God of Abraham, Isaac, and Jacob as the Creator of the heavens and the earth. As to the creation of light, Wenham notes that Genesis 1:3–5 contains, in simple sequence, the same sevenfold formula found in all six days of creation: (1) announcement ("God said"); (2) command ("let there be"); (3) fulfillment ("and there was"); (4) execution ("light"); (5) approval ("was good"); (6) a subsequent explanatory word ("God called"); and (7) an enumeration of the days ("the first day"). Wenham sees in the separation of light from darkness an anticipation of God's election of Israel to be a holy (i.e., set-apart) nation: "God is, as it were, prejudiced in favor of light."[113] He further notes that light, though not itself divine, stands metaphorically for life, salvation, the commandments, and the presence of God. Wenham does not say what light literally is. However, he does bemoan the overly literalistic way in which the six days have been interpreted, citing the difficulty of accounting for light before the creation of the sun.[114] He sees the schema of the six days as a narrative device that expresses the coherence and purposiveness of the Creator's work, not a chronological or scientific account of the actual process. As with all language we use to speak of God, the six days are analogical.[115] Finally, Wenham argues that the text itself discourages readers from interpreting Genesis 1 with a scientific frame of reference: "When allowed to speak for itself, Genesis 1 looks beyond such minutiae."[116]

Genesis 1 is chiefly about God: his speech, his action, and in particular his speech action, all of which are to be taken literally, though not literalistically. Light came to be as a result of a distinctly divine speech act (call it a "generative")

---

112. Wenham, xlv.

113. Wenham, 18.

114. Wenham, 39; cf. 18.

115. See further Collins's discussion of analogical days as "God's workdays." Collins, *Genesis 1–4*, 124–25.

116. Wenham, *Genesis 1–15*, 40.

that brings into being what it says. As to what the light so created literally is, we have sampled representative commentators. What remains to be thought is whether created light is physical or spiritual and, if the latter, what that is and involves. Our survey may have raised more questions than it answers, though it also provided the hint of a promising way forward, some crumbs pertaining to the relationship between physical light, knowledge, and the Word through whom all things were made, "the true light, which gives light to everyone" (John 1:9).

Making Known: A God-Bespoke Economy of Light

Part 3 presents Scripture and its readers as constituents in the all-encompassing biblical story of light, from creation to consummation. We have dipped our toe into the history of exegesis of Genesis 1:3 to get help knowing what light is. We now turn to consider what light does and what God was doing in creating light. The first order of business, however, is to clarify the relation between created light and God's own uncreated light. Only then may we, secondly, explain the literal meaning of God creating light, an act that marks the beginning of the shining forth of the triune God. Clarifying the way God administers and communicates light provides a comprehensive and compelling framework for viewing biblical interpretation itself as a participation in the light that God is: "In your light do we see light" (Ps 36:9).

Is God Literally Light? God's Being *Ad Intra*

"God is light" (1 John 1:5) and God creates light (Gen 1:3), yet God does not create himself. Jesus said, "I am the light of the world" (John 8:12), yet it is an egregious error to say with Arius that when God created light he also spoke the Son into being as his first and greatest creature. God is light, and there is light in the universe, but it does not follow that created light is an overflow or emanation of God's being. Literal interpreters of Genesis 1 must take care, then, both to relate and distinguish the light God is from the light God creates. In the words of Irenaeus, "He may most properly be termed light, but he is nothing like that light with which we are acquainted."[117] A more recent theologian puts it like this: "Created light is not divine; what it is may be hard enough to fathom, but whatever it is, God is not an exponential expansion of it—'that than which a brighter cannot be conceived.' God's being is strictly non-commensurable."[118] God is the one "who dwells in unapproachable light" (1 Tim 6:16).

117. Irenaeus, *Adversus Haereses* 2.13.14.

118. Ivor Davidson, "Divine Light: Some Reflections after Barth," in *Trinitarian Theology after Barth*, ed. Myk Habets and Phillip Tolliday (Eugene, OR: Pickwick, 2011), 62.

To affirm that God *is* light is to understand that God is the source of his own being. God lights everything, but nothing lights God. Aseity applies to his luminosity as it does to all his other perfections. God *is* light, holy and wholly light. As Creator, God is set apart, morally and metaphysically, from all things, visible and invisible. "God is light" is a statement about God's essential nature and character, the majestic resplendence he is in himself. There was no time when God was not light, for the light of God's being is an *ad intra* divine perfection. "God's light is his triune glory in himself, in the plenitude of the relations in which his perfect life eternally subsists."[119] That God is light means that God's life in himself—the immanent Trinity—is itself glorious. As white light contains all the colors of the rainbow, so God's glory encompasses all his perfections. God's light is his glory and his glory is his light. That there is no darkness in God means that he has need of nothing else to be fully himself; God is eternally free to be all that he is in himself.

Athanasius picked up on the concept of light to explain how the Son relates to the Father in eternity as the radiance of light relates to the source of light: "He is the expression of the Father's Person, and Light from Light."[120] The mutual glorification that characterizes the relation of Father and Son in eternity is the inner radiance of God's life as light (John 17:5). Each of the three persons of the Trinity knows and makes known the glory of the other two. To confess that God dwells in unapproachable light is to acknowledge the perfect plenitude of God's life in himself: one source (Father), radiance (Son), and illumination (Spirit).[121] Yet, in his sovereign freedom, God is also free to go out of himself as it were to shine on or share his light with what is not God. This God does in creating through his Son (John 1:3), the same Son who is "the radiance of the glory of God" (Heb 1:3)—or as the Nicene Creed has it, "light from light."

That God's uncreated light differs from created lights receives corroboration from Isaiah: "The sun shall be no more your light by day . . . but the Lord will be your everlasting light" (Isa 60:19). The book of Revelation's description of the new Jerusalem seconds the motion: "And the city has no need of sun or moon to shine on it, for the glory of God gives it light, and its lamp is the Lamb" (Rev 21:23; cf. 22:5). This verse explains the nature of God's own light as the radiance of his glory.[122] The Son is not only the light of the world but "the radiance of the glory of God," and the Son radiates the light that God is

---

119. Ivor Davidson, "Foreword" to Andrew R. Hay, *God's Shining Forth: A Trinitarian Theology of Divine Light* (Eugene, OR: Pickwick, 2017), x.

120. Athanasius, *Apologia contra Arianos* 1.9. Jaroslav Pelikan explored light imagery in Athanasius in his *The Light of the World* (New York: Harper & Brothers, 1962).

121. For a further treatment of this theme, see Hay, *God's Shining Forth*, 29–54.

122. See Ioan Chirila, "*Let There Be Light!* Gen. 1:3 in the Interpretation of the Primordial Light," *Studia Universitatis Babes-Bolyai. Theologia Orthodoxa* 65, no. 1 (2020): 9.

because the Son is "the exact imprint of his [God's] nature" (Heb 1:3). A light without radiance is no light at all, only darkness, but "God is light, *and in him is no darkness at all*" (1 John 1:5, emphasis added). Those who walk in darkness, by way of contrast, do not know God, for they have no fellowship with him (1 John 1:6). Elsewhere in Scripture light appears as a source of life (John 1:3), symbol of truth (Ps 43:3), and means of knowledge (Ps 119:130). Indeed, there is a special connection between light and knowledge: "To say God is light is to confess the effective, illuminating presence of God the revealer."[123] The God who is light thus enlivens and illumines all things by his sheer luminosity and brightness—in other words, by creating light.[124]

"Let There Be Light": God's Work *Ad Extra*

God's generative speech act "Let there be light" is the point of connection "between the *opus ad extra* and the *opus ad intra* that precedes it; i.e., that God remains in Himself at the very time when in His utterance He proceeds out of Himself."[125] That God creates light by speaking it into being is an external publication of the internal perfection God is. This too is God's glory, namely, his right "to prove and declare, to denote and almost as it were to make Himself conspicuous and everywhere apparent as the One He is."[126] The glory of God includes the freedom and the act by which God makes himself and the sum of his perfections known. "They are the coming into being of light outside Him on the basis of the light inside Him, which is Himself."[127] In brief, God's glory includes both the "inshining" and the outshining of his light. God is uncreated, "archetypal" light; what God speaks into being is created, "ectypal" light.

In creating, the triune God begins to act *out*: not "Gentlemen, start your engines" but, rather, "Let us (Father, Son, and Spirit) begin our operations, our work *ad extra*." This is an example not of reading the Trinity *into* Genesis 1:3 but, rather, of reading the Trinity *out* of it. We are not forcing the Trinity into Genesis; on the contrary, we are sensitive to the canonical pressure on Genesis 1.[128] For to read Genesis 1:3 in canonical context is to understand that the one who is light (God the Father) freely and graciously decides to provide illumination for something other than himself. Natural light is a prototype of revelation and a promissory note, for the "Father of lights" from whom every good and

123. John Webster, *Confessing God: Essays in Christian Dogmatics II* (London: T&T Clark, 2005), 40.

124. See "Light," in *Dictionary of Biblical Imagery*, ed. Leland Ryken, James C. Wilhoit, Tremper Longman III (Downers Grove, IL: InterVarsity, 1998), 509–12; and the discussion in Daniel L. Akin, *1, 2, 3 John*, New American Commentary (Nashville: B&H, 2001), 62–73.

125. Barth, *Church Dogmatics* III.1, 110.

126. Barth, *Church Dogmatics* II.1, *Doctrine of God* (Edinburgh: T&T Clark, 1957), 641.

127. Barth, 647.

128. On the notion of "canonical pressure" and its relevance to the Trinity, see C. Kavin Rowe, "Biblical Pressure and Trinitarian Hermeneutics," *Pro Ecclesia* 11 no. 3 (2002): 295–312.

perfect give from above comes (James 1:17) eventually sends his Son, "light from light," into the world, later to be further illumined by the Spirit. In the words of Gregory of Nazianzus, "We receive the Son's light from the Father's light in the light of the Spirit. . . . It is the plain and simple explanation of the Trinity."[129]

We are finally in a position to offer a literal interpretation of "Let there be light." At the very beginning of his wondrous works, God makes known *ad extra* the glory of his own *ad intra* being. The God who is light eternal begins in the beginning to shine forth light. Why light? To enlighten is to make known. In Augustine's words, "Light bears testimony of itself. . . . It is its own witness to itself in order to make itself known."[130] Light, physical and mental, is a transcendental condition of visibility and intelligibility. Light is the necessary condition for the very possibility not merely of angelic (so Augustine) but also of human perception and conception, the basis for understanding anything whatsoever. Without light, the world would be unintelligible, the book of nature unreadable, its divine author unknown.

Genesis 1:3 narrates God's first outward act of self-communication, the moment he established an intelligible universe, an ordered means of making known something of his own divine life to creatures that are not divine.[131] Physical light illumines—makes itself and other things known—in a way that imitates the self-revelation of the God who is light. That the very first step in the process of creating the world was the creation of light is fitting, for light, physical and mental (i.e., intelligence), is the condition for knowing everything else. The creation of physical light is the means by which God shows his work. This is also the purpose of the visual aids—the two great lights—created on day four. Another purpose of having days and nights "is to establish the alternating patterns of darkness and light to allow for historical progression and the drama of creation."[132] This, too, is crucial for the process of making known God's glory: "For light is the revelation of the will of God, and the heavenly bodies, above all the sun, are His servants in the sense that they indicate to man *the seasons given him for the recognition of this revelation.*"[133] God structures human being-in-time, lighting (and darkening) the stage on which the drama of creation, fall, and redemption is played out.

Scripture narrates world history in terms of God giving light to a people

---

129. Gregory of Nazianzus, *Fifth Theological Oration: On the Holy Spirit*, 31.3, in *On God and Christ* (Crestwood, NY: St. Vladimir's University Press, 2002), 118.

130. Augustine, *Homilies on the Gospel of John* 35, 4, as cited in Jean-Louis Chrétien, *Under the Gaze of the Bible* (New York: Fordham University Press, 2015), 87.

131. Jonathan Yovel argues that in saying, "Let there be light," God also creates language as a performative medium, another instrument of intelligibility, in addition to light itself. "Creation of Language," 214–16.

132. Chambers, *Reconsidering Creation Ex Nihilo in Genesis 1*, 222.

133. Barth, *Church Dogmatics* III.1, 165 (emphasis added).

who walk in darkness, the willful ignorance of sin. God's giving light is arguably the driving force behind creation and redemption alike. The technical term describing these works of the triune God *ad extra* is "economy" (Gk. *oikonomia* = "household management"; "plan" in Eph 1:10; 3:9). By "economy of light," then, I mean *the way in which God effects his eternal purpose to make himself known to creatures in space and time.* The economy of light is the external means by which God executes his plan conceived "before the foundation of the world" (Eph 1:4) to reveal himself, to "show the immeasurable riches of his grace in kindness toward us in Christ Jesus" (Eph 2:7). Genesis 1:3 recounts the opening phase of this plan in describing the creation of light. We might paraphrase Genesis 1:3 as "Let there be an economy of making known," a place and time to show forth God's glory. Or, more plainly, "*Let us reveal.*" The creation of light is a divine statement of intent, a declaration of iridescence: to be and act in time in ways that correspond to his eternal being.[134]

Creation is a theater for the glory of God.[135] In creating light, the triune God begins to publish (make public) his perfections. God saw that the light was good (Gen 1:4) because its creaturely goodness—its ability to reveal or make known—reflected, though to a lesser degree, God's own revelatory goodness: "For his invisible attributes . . . have been clearly perceived, ever since the creation of the world, in the things that have been made" (Rom 1:20). Oecolampadius said something similar, describing light as "a thing which enlightens minds, which teaches the truth. God created light, so that his works might be made clear."[136] According to Paul Blowers, "Genesis 1 was already, for patristic exegetes, a 'tableau' or montage of the whole divine economy and pointed ahead to the mystery of salvation and the appearance of the 'new creation.'"[137]

God's speaking light into being marks the first chapter in a story of revelation that spans the Scriptures and involves the first publication of the collected works of the triune God. God literally speaks light into being, and created light illumines—speaks back, as it were: "Creation is a rhetorical act, the outward

---

134. On "economy of light," see Kevin J. Vanhoozer and Daniel J. Treier, *Theology and the Mirror of Scripture: A Mere Evangelical Account* (Downers Grove: IL: IVP Academic, 2015), 58–59, 85–90; and Ike Miller, *Seeing by the Light: Illumination in Augustine's and Barth's Readings of John* (Downers Grove, IL: IVP Academic, 2020), 181–87. New Testament scholar Franz Overbeck was the first to use the term "economy of light," and he did so in connection with his study of how the various "lights" (e.g., John the Baptist, Jesus, John the Evangelist, et al.) in the Gospel of John worked and related to one another. Franz Overbeck, *Das Johannesevangelium: Studien zur Kritik seiner Erforschung* (Tübingen: J. C. B. Mohr, 1911), 416–17.

135. Calvin frequently refers to the heavens and earth as a *theatrum* in which we perceive God's glory. See, for example, *Institutes* 1.5.8, 1.6.2, and 1.14.20.

136. Iojannes Oecolampadius, *An Exposition of Genesis*, trans. Mickey L. Mattox (Milwaukee: Marquette University Press, 2013), 63.

137. Paul M. Blowers, *Drama of the Divine Economy: Creator and Creation in Early Christian Theology and Piety* (Oxford: Oxford University Press, 2012), 8.

address of the eternally speaking God."[138] In creating light, God makes known and creates the means for further making known. "What else is the entire creation," Luther asked, "than the Word of God uttered by God, or extended to the outside?"[139] Barth similarly saw creation as "the temporal analogue, taking place outside God, of that event in God Himself by which God is the Father of the Son."[140] The creation of light literally refers, then, to the first work of the economic Trinity, the setting in temporal motion of God's eternal plan to make himself and his glory known to creatures who could reflect his glory back to him. "For the light we now see is *literally*, and not merely analogically, 'a glance at the glory of God.'"[141]

The suggestion that Genesis 1:3 marks the beginning of God's work *ad extra* is hardly a fanciful exercise in allegorical exegesis. When read rightly, with a theological frame of reference, the creation of light in Genesis 1:3 is literally about divine action, namely, the creation of conditions of intelligibility, actualizing the possibility of *creaturely knowing and God's making known.*

The Economy of Light as Framework for Biblical Interpretation

In this chapter, I have discussed the literal meaning of "Let there be light" and attempted to shed light on literality in doing so. Divine authorial action—God's doing things with words—lies behind both notions. God literally speaks light into being, and both light and speech are means of illumination that enable creaturely knowledge. "By faith we understand that the worlds have been framed by the word of God" (Heb 11:3 ASV). Commentators continue to dispute whether the six days of Genesis 1 are metaphorical; on this point, there is room for diverse interpretations. However, as concerns God speaking, we must read literally (though not literalistically). To do justice to the creation narrative, one need not insist that God created in six twenty-four-hour days, but one should affirm creation *ex nihilo*, and one must affirm creation *ex locutione* (out of [literal] speech), namely, effectual commands by which God "calls into existence the things that do not exist" (Rom 4:17).[142]

In pursuing these connections between light and literality, have we strayed from mere Christian hermeneutics? By no means. The Bible, *and its interpretation*, are themselves ingredients in the economy of light: "Your word is a lamp

138. Leithart, *Creator*, 237.

139. Luther, *Lectures on Genesis*, 22.

140. Barth, *Dogmatics in Outline* (London: SCM, 1949), 52.

141. Catherine Pickstock, "What Shines Between: The *Metaxu* of Light," in *Between System and Poetics: William Desmond and Philosophy after Dialectic*, ed. Thomas A. F. Kelley (New York: Routledge, 2016), 118–19 (emphasis added).

142. The Genesis formula "let there be" is a peculiar speech act, unique to God—what I am here calling a "generative"—that brings about the reality it describes.

to my feet and a light to my path" (Ps 119:105). What I have called the material principle of mere Christian hermeneutics (the light/knowledge of God that shines forth in Christ through the Spirit) undergirds the formal principle (the Bible's literal meaning), and this for two reasons. First, because the Bible is an ingredient in the economy of light, a divinely commissioned, set-apart creaturely auxiliary, a minister of light, as it were. Second, the interpretation of the Bible is part of the economy of light. Multiple frames of reference are allowed and encouraged, but only insofar as they contribute to the illumination of Scripture's subject matter: the knowledge of the glory of God or, in a word, the light of Christ. Readers, too, play a significant role in the economy of light.[143] Barth noted the connection between the way light makes God known and the way apostles make the gospel known: "The light created by God is implicitly what the apostolic office is explicitly. . . . When He creates light, God erects this sign and ordains this witness."[144] When later Scriptures speak of Christians as "children of light" (Eph 5:8; 1 Thess 5:5), these are not simply figures of speech "but highly exact representations of the meaning already given to the creation, existence, and function of light in Gen. 1:3."[145]

To read the Bible well is to put any number of exegetical frames of reference at the service of the economy of light. The economy itself provides a hermeneutical framework for understanding the story of God's communicating light in creation, revelation, and redemption alike: (1) It reminds us that the enlightening of our minds is a joint triune work that originates with the Father (light's *source*), proceeds through the Son (light's *radiance*), and is completed by the Holy Spirit (light's *illumination*). (2) It provides theological categories for coordinating the various frames of references and exegetical methods, enabling interpreters to give thick descriptions of the extended literal sense. (3) It orients us to the aim for which God gave us Scripture in the first place, which has everything to do with forming readers to reflect the light of Christ, able to walk as "children of light" (Eph 5:8). To read the Bible theologically is to participate in this economy of light, following the words and the light where they lead. "The end of reading Holy Scripture is to know the mind of God who is its primary author and interpreter."[146] Understanding the Bible as God's word takes place in the economy of light or not at all.

Jesus' transfiguration is a frequently overlooked topic in Western theology. This is unfortunate because it is a linchpin in the economy of light. Accordingly, the transfiguration serves in the chapters to come not simply as one more case

143. See ch. 9 below.
144. Barth, *Church Dogmatics* III.1, 120.
145. Barth, III.1, 120.
146. John Webster, "Illumination," in *The Domain of the Word: Scripture and Theological Reason* (London: T&T Clark, 2012), 61.

study in the history of exegesis but, rather, and more importantly, as a lens through which to think about what it means to read the Bible literally and theologically, which is to say, for understanding the letter of the text—and the light of the knowledge of the glory of God (2 Cor 4:6) that illuminates it.

CHAPTER 7

The Transfiguration of Christ

Light Revealed

There was joy for the Prophets and the Apostles by this ascent of the mountain. The Prophets rejoiced when they saw his humanity, which they had not known. The Apostles also rejoiced when they saw the glory of his divinity, which they had not known . . . and they looked to one another: the Prophets to the Apostles and the Apostles to the Prophets.

—Ephrem the Syrian, Sermon on the Transfiguration[1]

What, if anything, does Jesus' transfiguration have to do with biblical interpretation? Obviously, it is a narrative account that, like other biblical texts, calls for interpretation, and I will indeed provide an interpretation in due course. But there is more, much more. The transfiguration offers something altogether more wonderful than an exercise in biblical hermeneutics. To ascend Mount Tabor with the disciples is to gain a precious vantage point on both the identity of Jesus and the whole process of reading the Bible literally and theologically. This is hardly a self-evident claim. Readers will therefore be forgiven if they ask, in the words of Nicodemus, "How can these things be?" (John 3:9).

By way of response, I will develop an idea I take from Jerome's commentary on Mark 9:1–7. I have already said that biblical interpretation is like ascending a mountain, but Jerome likened it to ascending Mount Tabor in

1. "Of Our Venerable Father Ephrem the Syrian: Sermon on the Transfiguration of Our Lord and God and Saviour, Jesus Christ," Wayback Machine, last updated November 3, 2008, https://web.archive.org/web/20140225061435/http://anastasis.org.uk/on_the_transfiguration.htm.

particular. Those who cannot make the climb, he said, "have Jesus down below," according to the bare letter only. They cannot see his shining clothes or face. Nor can philosophers make Jesus' face or clothes shine either, because "their treatises are all of earth."[2] The way to Jesus is via theological interpretation of the Bible. "We are standing on the mountain with [Moses and Elijah] when we understand the Scriptures spiritually."[3] In an intriguing move, Jerome likened spiritual interpretation to Jesus' transfiguration: "Take any prophetical witness, any evangelical parable, if you consider merely the letter, there is nothing shining in it."[4] Monks at the medieval abbey of St. Victor similarly saw the literal sense as *pulchre lucens*, "transparent to the divine light."[5] In the spirit of Jerome, and with the Victorines and other reformed catholic interpreters, I therefore propose to climb the hermeneutical mountain once more to search for the light of Christ shining, not apart from the text, but rather in and through its letters.

The burden of this chapter, then, is to situate Jesus' transfiguration in the economy of light for the sake of clarifying the task of biblical interpretation. We begin by exploring the "analogy of bodiliness" (*analogia corporis*), namely, the similarity between the body of Jesus and the "body" of the biblical text. At the heart of the analogy is what transfiguration—"the most dramatic instance of change [*metamorphosis*] in the New Testament"[6]—does to each body, respectively. To clarify the nature of Jesus' bodily change, we examine the transfiguration in the Synoptic Gospels, the history of exegesis, and, in a surprising twist, the Gospel of John. The chapter concludes by setting forth five theses on the transfiguration of Jesus as a guide to reading the Bible literally and theologically. To anticipate, the transfiguration—a change in Jesus' *figure*—is emblematic of the changes required in our reading, and in us as readers, when we read the Bible theologically.

The Meaning of Transfiguration and the Transfiguration of Meaning

Western theology has largely neglected Jesus' transfiguration. The omission is unfortunate because this mountaintop event is a linchpin in the economy of light, a capsule summary and climax of the story of God's self-communication

---

2. Jerome, *The Homilies of St. Jerome*, vol. 2, trans. Marie Liguori Ewald (Washington, DC: Catholic University Press of America, 1966), 164.
3. Jerome, 165.
4. Jerome, 163.
5. Beryl Smalley, *The Study of the Bible in the Middle Ages* (Oxford: Basil Blackwell, 1952), 370.
6. Ian Curran, "Transformed," *Christian Century*, July 15, 2008, 26.

ad extra that began with the creation of light.[7] By way of contrast, the transfiguration features prominently in Eastern theology, which associates it with the divinization of Jesus' humanity and with salvation as "deification" or *theosis*. Eastern Orthodoxy reminds us that "certain sorts of attention to the material are the best way into understanding 'spirit.'"[8] Western exegetes and theologians do well to look east in the winter of our hermeneutical discontent, to be warmed by the light of the Son, even as they continue to feel the critical chill at their backs.[9]

The Transfiguration in the Economy of Light: What Kind of Change?

Descriptions matter. There are many nontheological ways of describing biblical interpretation, ways that rely more on theories drawn from, say, psychology, sociology, or literary theory rather than Christian doctrine. Who gets to describe the process of biblical interpretation, and what makes some descriptions better than others? Critical theories abound, but if we want to avoid reading the Bible like any other book, we need to give a biblical and theological account of what it is to read the Bible as Christian Scripture. Two orienting convictions lie behind my proposal. (1) The subject matter of theology—the economy of light, God's mighty luminary acts by which he makes himself known—must dictate our approach and the way we describe it. (2) The transfiguration, far from being a marginal (and somewhat weird) footnote to Jesus' person and work, yields a particularly fecund insight into this subject matter.

Why transfiguration? In the first place, Jesus' transfiguration is arguably the most important event between creation and consummation in the biblical story of light. The transfiguration may not belong to the core of the gospel, but it "stands as a gateway to the saving events of the gospel and is a mirror in which the Christian mystery is seen in its unity. . . . Here the diverse elements in the theology of the New Testament meet."[10] Indeed, according to one commentator, the transfiguration "presents the Gospel in microcosm."[11] Jesus' transfiguration is a kind of *précis*, a "light motif" of the whole drama of redemption.

7. Patrick Schreiner, noting the transfiguration's links to Jesus' death and future glory, says it "is a microcosm of the gospel. It reveals the great mystery of Christianity." *The Transfiguration of Christ: An Exegetical and Theological Reading* (Grand Rapids: Baker Academic, 2024), 3.

8. Rowan Williams, *Looking East in Winter: Contemporary Thought and the Eastern Christian Tradition* (London: Bloomsbury Continuum, 2021), 6.

9. I am riffing off of Rowan Williams's *Looking East in Winter*, itself an allusion to an image used by the fifth-century author Diadochos of Photike.

10. Arthur Michael Ramsey, *The Glory of God and the Transfiguration of Christ* (London: Longmans, Green and Co.,1949), 144.

11. Allison Trites, "The Transfiguration of Jesus: the Gospel in Microcosm," *Evangelical Quarterly* 51, no. 2 (1979), 67–79. See also Allison A. Trites, *The Transfiguration of Christ: A Hinge of Holy History* (Hantsport, Nova Scotia: Lancelot, 1994).

Second, the placement of the transfiguration in the gospel narratives, between Peter's confession and Jesus' crucifixion, is significant. As Augustine saw, the transfiguration is "a lens through which to survey the whole sweep of divine condescension from incarnation to crucifixion."[12] The transfiguration also invites reflection on the relationship of Jesus' saving work (soteriology) and future glory (eschatology), the earthly and the heavenly. In particular, it highlights the *eschatological* nature of the light of Christ inasmuch as it represents a moment "where finite and infinite, present and eschatological future overlap in . . . an epiphany."[13] The transfiguration is a space-time preview of end-time consummation, a glimpse of "what happens when the divine reality is fully manifest in human existence."[14]

Third, the transfiguration provides another fascinating case study in the history of exegesis and opportunity to think further about the relationship of exegesis and theology. Studying the transfiguration casts light (the operative term) on the ways in which exegesis, historical theology, and systematic theology interrelate, as well as serving as a promising promontory on which readers from East and West can meet, perchance for mutual edification. For all these reasons, the transfiguration proves to be the keystone of mere Christian hermeneutics.

The transfiguration also presents certain challenges, both as concerns the event itself and its bearing on biblical interpretation. The exegetical challenge is to say what the transfiguration is about: what *literally* happens to Jesus on Mount Tabor? My proposal hinges on how we describe the change in question. If it were to involve a substantial change in Jesus, for example, it would prove a fateful paradigm for biblical interpretation: to change the meaning of the letter into something else altogether would wreak havoc on literal interpretation. This was precisely the Reformers' worry about allegorical exegesis, that it reads the text as meaning something *other* than what it says. However, this is arguably not the function of light, which exists not to obscure but rather to clarify.

From Body of Jesus to Letter of the Text

If it is right to inquire about the light of Christ (reference) in the letter of the text (sense), then the transfiguration of Jesus is of more than passing interest. There is a certain analogy, an *analogia corporis*, between what happens to Jesus' body in the transfiguration and what happens to the letter of the biblical text in theological interpretation. By body of the text, I mean both the letters that comprise it and its basic content. The analogy implies that readers experience

12. Michael Cameron, "Transfiguration: Christology and the Roots of Figurative Exegesis in St. Augustine," *Studia Patristica* 33, ed. E. A. Livingstone (Leuven: Peeters, 1997), 44.

13. Williams, *Looking East in Winter*, 7.

14. Ian Curran, "Transformed," *Christian Century*, July 15, 2008, 27.

something similar in biblical interpretation to what the disciples experienced at Jesus' transfiguration. In a nutshell: *the light shining from Christ's face is to his body as the transfigural sense is to the letter of the biblical text.*

Hans Frei was right to discern "a strong interconnection" between Christology and the literal sense.[15] After all, it was the gospel story, with its climax of God raising Jesus from the dead, that led theologians to acknowledge the priority and authority of the literal sense. That Christ assumed flesh—really lived, really died, really rose from the dead—is a necessary presupposition for right understanding (1 John 4:2–3; 2 John 7). Note the order: first theology, then hermeneutics. Frei's work brilliantly documents the ripple effect of modernity on both Christology and the literal sense when biblical scholars began to read the Gospels with immanent frames of reference.[16] Who/what do we say Jesus *literally* is? To prioritize extratextual frames of reference is to revise the literal sense, and to revise the literal sense is to lose the agreed-upon subject matter of Christianity: the story of what God was doing in and through the body of Jesus Christ (Rom 8:3).

Frei understood Jesus' identity as a function of the story the Gospels tell about him. For example, the story of the resurrection identifies Jesus as *the one who is now living.* Curiously, Frei made next to nothing of the transfiguration as an element in Jesus' identity description. This is regrettable, for as a matter of canonical record, the transfiguration occupies a pivotal place in all three narratives of the Synoptic Gospels, offering a powerful, if not decisive, clue to his identity, as we will see below. Moreover, if the fate of Christology and the literal sense are indeed bound together, as Frei rightly believed, then it is worth exploring whether and to what extent what happens to Jesus' body in the transfiguration has a counterpart effect on the letter of the biblical text.[17]

As to who Jesus literally is, the orthodox creeds formalized the biblical testimony that the eternal Word who was with God assumed a truly human nature, including a physical, fleshly body. The Nicene and Chalcedonian formulas, in affirming Jesus Christ as one person with two natures, provided both a frame of reference and rules for rightly reading the gospel narratives.[18] Interestingly, Patrick Schreiner thinks the transfiguration "might be the clearest narrative

---

15. Hans Frei, *Types of Christian Theology* (New Haven, CT: Yale University Press, 1992), 5.

16. See esp. Hans Frei, *The Eclipse of Biblical Narrative: A Study in Eighteenth and Nineteenth Century Hermeneutics* (New Haven, CT: Yale University Press, 1974). Cf. my earlier discussion of Frei and literality in ch. 4 above.

17. The correlation is even closer once one factors in the observers/readers: in both cases, believing interpretation may be a condition for seeing the light. We shall return to this point below in discussing the role of the disciples in the transfiguration story.

18. See Jamieson and Wittman's principle 6 and rules 7–9 in R. B. Jamieson and Tyler R. Wittman, *Biblical Reasoning: Christological and Trinitarian Rules for Exegesis* (Grand Rapids: Baker Academic, 2022), 126–78.

picture we have of the two natures of Christ in one person."[19] It reveals Jesus' "double Sonship": he is both the eternal Son of God ("light from light") and the messianic son of David.[20] The transfiguration marks the moment where both the preexistent glory of the eternal Son and the future glory of the messianic Son are revealed together. I believe the letter of the biblical text has an analogous dual-aspect character in its capacity as human-divine discourse.

The transfiguration narrative centers its attention on Jesus' face, which according to Matthew, "shone like the sun" (Matt 17:2). According to Emmanuel Levinas, even pale, nonshining faces elude our conceptual grasp: "The face speaks."[21] This is the fundamental insight of his ethics: other persons must be recognized as having infinite worth; they must not be theorized, thematized, or totalized—all ways of demeaning unique persons, reducing them to faceless members of a set. If even ordinary human faces are beyond rational categorization, how much more the shining face of the God-man. Maximus the Confessor deemed the face of Jesus ineffable because it is the locus through which God's light shines. "For Maximus, revelation . . . in the transfiguration, is the saturating gift of the divine Logos."[22] A saturated phenomenon, like Jesus' shining face, is "so overwhelmingly 'given' . . . that it defies any 'intentional' human subjectivity and so also, by its excess, subverts conceptualization."[23] Faces speak, and Jesus' face exceptionally so—but can we speak about his face?

The French term for face is *la figure*. In this light, "transfigural" could now connote either that which runs across (*trans-*) the face or a face-to-face encounter. The latter recalls my introductory suggestion that reading the Bible theologically is ultimately a matter of divine address and human answerability, itself a kind of face-to-face encounter—especially when we remember that the "face" (Heb. *panim*) of God signals God's presence.[24] Combining the two senses produces a suggestive new meaning, with "transfigural" indicating the way the light of Christ shines from his face, through the letter of the text, into our faces. To read transfigurally is thus to transfer the light from Christ's face into ours. Of course, biblical interpreters do not literally see the face of the divine author,

19. Schreiner, *Transfiguration of Christ*, 4.

20. Schreiner is convinced that "one cannot understand the depth of the transfiguration without dogmatic categories" (*Transfiguration of Christ*, xii).

21. Emmanuel Levinas, *Totality and Infinity: An Essay on Exteriority* (Dordrecht: Kluwer Academic, 1991), 66.

22. Paul Blowers, "The Transfiguration of Jesus Christ as 'Saturated Phenomenon' and as a Key to the Dynamics of Biblical Revelation in Saint Maximus the Confessor," in *What Is the Bible? The Patristic Doctrine of Scripture*, ed. Matthew Baker and Mark Mourachian (Minneapolis: Fortress, 2016), 91.

23. Blowers, 92–93. See also Merold Westphal, "Transfiguration as Saturated Phenomenon," *Journal of Philosophy & Scripture* 1, no. 1 (Fall 2003): 26–35.

24. God's face is often linked with God's favor. We will examine Jacob's "face-to-face" encounter with God (Gen 32) in chapter 9 below.

but they do hear his voice. If the face speaks, might we say that the voice—and the letter that conveys it—shines?

To posit an analogy between the transfigured body of Jesus and the transfigured letter of the biblical text, we must be as able to say what literally happens to Jesus' face as we are to say what it means for the biblical letter to serve as a conduit of (spiritual) light.[25] What exactly happens, then, to the transfigured Jesus? Does something similar really happen to the letter of the biblical text? Is there a parallel between readers attending to the body of the text and the disciples seeing the glorified Christ?[26] To answer these questions is to gain a precious foothold in our interpretive ascent from the grammatical-historical to the grammatical-eschatological sense of Scripture.

From Textual Letter to Spiritual Interpretation

We are exploring a "transfigural" analogy, namely, that the light shining from the face of Christ is to his body what the spiritual sense is to the letter of the text. Recall that light, *God making known*, is the material principle of mere Christian hermeneutics. To get from light in general to the light streaming from Jesus' face, however, we must answer two questions: (1) What exactly happened to Jesus (i.e., what does transfiguration mean)? (2) To what might the transfiguration of the letter possibly refer? The burden of the remainder of this chapter is to investigate and respond to this pair of questions.

Some readers may still harbor doubts about the wisdom of assigning any hermeneutical significance to Jesus' transfiguration, or using it to justify spiritual interpretation. I will state the objection as forcefully as I can: If there is a parallel between Jesus' body and the body of the biblical text, then the transfiguration, because it involves a metamorphosis from one thing into something else, would provide a warrant not for literal but *allegorical* interpretation, for it would make the letter mean something *other* than what it says. If that were the thrust of my analogy, then, to transfigure the letter would be to *disfigure* it. Clearly, the first step is to clarify the nature of the metamorphosis that lies at the core of Jesus' transfiguration.

Jesus' face "speaks," yes, but what does it say? If we are to use the transfiguration as a framework for understanding what it means to read the Bible theologically, we must first interpret the transfiguration narrative itself. Here, too, however, we discover a conflict of interpretations. This should come as no surprise, given what we have discovered about the role of frames of reference.

25. According to de Lubac, both Scripture and the incarnation are "incorporations" (i.e., embodiments) of the Logos. See the chapter "The Incorporation of the Logos" in his *History and Spirit: The Understanding of Scripture according to Origen* (San Francisco: Ignatius, 2007), 385–426.

26. Stating it this way anticipates the debate about the transfiguration itself: Was it something that happened to Jesus or to the disciples? Was it "objective" or "subjective" (or both)?

The challenge of reading the Bible theologically is that of finding frames of reference that proceed from and accord with the economy of light—frames of reference that correspond to what the Bible is and to what it is about. The general tendency among modern New Testament scholars who read with historical-critical frames of reference is to focus on the disciples' experience rather than on Jesus himself. In modern biblical scholarship, Jesus' face has little to say.

Henri de Lubac was one of the few who thought, as I do, that the transfiguration had hermeneutical significance.[27] De Lubac, a medievalist, prized spiritual interpretation and viewed the letter as the "sacrament of the spirit."[28] For him, to read the Bible theologically was to read for the spiritual sense, which is deeper and other than the literal. Given the above analogy, I wonder whether it is right to describe the change to Jesus' face, or to the letter of the text when read theologically, as "sacramental." Such a suggestion makes transfiguration into a kind of *transubstantiation*, in which case the letter of the text—the textual meaning; the "bread" of discourse—could be viewed as undergoing a "substantial" metamorphosis, becoming something that previously it was not.[29] Biblical scholars would be right to resist this picture, for on this view, spiritual interpretation changes the original historical meaning into something else, rendering the exegete's attempt to clarify verbal meaning a chasing after the "accidents" rather than the "substance" of the text. Fortunately, this is not the kind of spiritual interpretation de Lubac had in mind. For de Lubac, spiritual interpretation referred to the process by which Christ uses the letter of the text to render himself present to the reader. "The spiritual sense *is* the very Christ rendered in the literal sense acting as subject and object of Scripture."[30] Christ is both the agent and the content of the process. What still needs to be explained, however, is what spiritual interpretation does to the literal sense. What kind of change does it involve?

To answer this question, we now turn to consider the evidence from Scripture and its interpreters in support of my claim that Jesus' transfiguration provides a valuable framework for reading the Bible theologically. Like all

27. As William Wright observes, de Lubac appealed to early Christian exegesis of the transfiguration "as a biblically authorized token for the relationship between the Old Testament and New Testament and therefore the Christian interpretation of Scripture." William M. Wright, "The Literal Sense of Scripture according to Henri de Lubac: Insights from Patristic Exegesis of the Transfiguration," *Modern Theology* 28, no. 2 (2012): 254.

28. Henri de Lubac, *Sources of Revelation* (London: Herder and Herder, 1968), 14.

29. The Roman Catholic doctrine of transubstantiation maintains that the bread and wine in the Lord's Supper undergo a change of substance while maintaining their external form (i.e., "accidents"). That is, they appear to be the same elements, but in fact they have become the substance of Christ's body and blood. See further Brett Salkeld, *Transubstantiation: Theology, History, and Christian Unity* (Grand Rapids: Baker Academic, 2019).

30. Kevin Storer, "Theological Interpretation and the Spiritual Sense of Scripture: Henri de Lubac's Retrieval of a Christological Hermeneutic of Presence," *Journal of Theological Interpretation* 7 no. 1 (2013): 95.

biblical narratives, the transfiguration, too, raises questions that demand theological answers. For example, What happened when Jesus' face and clothes became altered? What did the three disciples who were with Jesus actually see? Why is this episode so significant that all three Synoptic Gospels report it? As we turn to examine these and other issues in the history of biblical exegesis, I ask readers to keep in mind the possibility that the transfiguration narrative "presents us with a text whose literal meaning *is* its spiritual sense."[31]

The Transfiguration in the Synoptic Gospels

What is *literally* happening on that "high mountain" of transfiguration (Matt 17:1)? What kind of light is involved, and what does it tell us about Jesus? First, the basics. The transfiguration story appears in all three Synoptic Gospels (Matt 17:1–8; Mark 9:2–10; Luke 9:28–36), each time in the same narrative context, just after Jesus asks the disciples who they think he is. After the disciples reply, "the Christ," Jesus predicts his death and resurrection and says, "There are some standing here who will not taste death until they see the kingdom of God after it has come with power" (Matt 16:28; Mark 9:1; Luke 9:27). Jesus then takes Peter, James, and John and leads them up a high mountain, where he is transfigured. There is a show of light, some guest appearances, a voice from the cloud, and then it is over. What just happened?

General Interpretive Trends

Biblical scholars have made frequent forays into the transfiguration narrative, in sharp contrast to the theologians' neglect.[32] F. W. Beare observed that "there is probably no other pericope in the Gospels which has received such divergent interpretations as the story of the Transfiguration."[33]

Redaction Criticism: One Transfiguration in Three Narratives

Despite the many similarities between the three Synoptic accounts, modern commentators have noticed a number of significant differences.[34] For example, Matthew and Luke mention Jesus' radiant face (Matt 17:2; Luke 9:29); Mark does not. Matthew and Mark use the Greek term *metamorphoō* (Matt 17:2;

31. C. Clifton Black, "Transfigured Exegesis," in *Crisis, Call, and Leadership in the Abrahamic Traditions*, ed. Peter Ochs and William Stacy Johnson (New York: Palgrave Macmillan, 2009), 255.

32. For a list of works up to 1981, see Thomas F. Best, "The Transfiguration: A Select Bibliography," *Journal of the Evangelical Theological Society* 24, no. 2 (June 1981): 157–61.

33. F. W. Beare, *The Earliest Records of Jesus* (Nashville: Abingdon, 1962), 141.

34. See, e.g., Simon Lee: "The various tellings of the Transfiguration story indicate how these early Christians modified the [Jewish and Hellenistic trends of the times] in ways that were distinctive to their self-identity and that met their communal needs." *Jesus' Transfiguration and the Believers' Transformation*, WUNT 2 (Tübingen: Mohr Siebeck, 2009), 2.

Mark 9:2); Luke does not. In Mark Elijah's name comes before Moses' (Mark 9:4); Matthew has the traditional order, putting Moses' name first (Matt 17:3). Luke reveals what Moses and Elijah were talking about with Jesus (his "departure" or *exodus* from Jerusalem; Luke 9:31); Matthew and Mark do not. Matthew specifies that the cloud that overshadowed them was "bright" (Matt 17:5); Mark and Luke do not. The object of the disciples' fear in Matthew is the divine voice (Matt 17:5–6); in Luke they are afraid of entering the cloud (Luke 9:34), and in Mark what they are afraid of is left unspecified (Mark 9:6). Commentators typically account for these and other discrepancies by appealing either to the diverse frames of reference (e.g., Jewish, Hellenistic) that would have been familiar to the original readers or to the diverse theological agendas of the three Evangelists. For example, Simon Lee says Matthew's account "functions as a foundational legend for his community and legitimates that community's recent separation from mainline Judaism."[35] Little is said about the theological significance of the event itself.

Historicity: A Happening to Jesus or the Disciples?

Doubts about the historicity of the transfiguration have led to disagreements about its literal meaning. Several commentators, including Karl Barth, note that "the miracle happens to Jesus Himself and is not something performed by Him."[36] Was the transfiguration a miraculous event that happened to Jesus (e.g., a physical occurrence), or was it something that happened to the disciples (e.g., a psychological occurrence)? Was it an objective event or a subjective vision? Jesus instructs the disciples, "Tell no one the vision, until the Son of Man is raised from the dead" (Matt 17:9). The mention of vision complicates any hard and fast objective/subjective distinction. A subjective vision may be no better than a hallucination. On the other hand, "A vision is an historical event and can be perfectly objective . . . in the sense that in it we see exactly what we are meant (by God) to see."[37] Some commentators wonder what, if anything, a bystander would have seen. Was the transfiguration, and the light that shone from Jesus' face and clothes, visible to anyone or just to the disciples?[38] Here, too, one's interpretation will depend on one's chosen frame(s) of reference. For example, J. W. C. Wand called the transfiguration "a veridical vision," yet he failed to specify what made it true.[39] He was open to the possibility that it

35. Lee, 7.

36. Karl Barth, *Church Dogmatics* III.2 (Edinburgh: T&T Clark, 1960), 478.

37. Stephen Williams, "The Transfiguration of Jesus Christ (Part 1)," *Themelios* 28, no. 1 (Autumn 2002): 17.

38. Note the possible parallel with the "light of heaven" that shone upon Paul on the road to Damascus, a light that Paul said others saw (Acts 22:9).

39. J. W. C. Wand, *Transfiguration* (London: Faith, 1967), 62.

was a "mystical phenomenon," adding that such experiences "are almost always capable of a naturalistic explanation."[40] By way of contrast, when we read these narratives literally (as defined in part 2), in canonical context with an eschatological frame of reference, it is clear that the disciples were witnesses to a literal act of God: the Father audibly confirming Jesus' identity as the eternal Son in the bright cloud of the Spirit (Matt 17:5).[41]

Relation to the Resurrection: Anticipatory or after the Fact?

Julius Wellhausen (of documentary hypothesis fame) appealed to source criticism to suggest that the transfiguration was originally an oral tradition describing the risen Christ, which later got misplaced, making it appear to be an event in Jesus' life.[42] Gerd Theissen, somewhat similarly, thinks the transfiguration, with its scene of heavenly glory, is a misplaced ascension story.[43] However, such theories conveniently overlook the fact that the transfiguration narratives include details (e.g., the presence of Moses and Elijah; the voice from heaven) absent from the resurrection and ascension accounts.

There may nevertheless be a legitimate textual connection between the transfiguration and these events. Some commentators see an explicit link between Mark's transfiguration account and his abbreviated account of Easter morning. As is well known, the shorter, more authentic ending of the Gospel of Mark lacks a proper resurrection narrative, concluding instead on a note of the disciples' fear (Mark 16:8). The disciples' fear also receives mention in the transfiguration story (Mark 9:6). Furthermore, both stories feature white clothes: at the transfiguration, Jesus' clothes become "intensely white" (Mark 9:3), and at the tomb the disciples meet a young man "dressed in a white robe" (Mark 16:5). This echo may indicate that the two accounts are mutually explanatory: "Mark emphasizes the centrality of the resurrection of Jesus by placing his vision of the risen Christ not at the end of his Gospel, *but right in the middle*. Quite literally, the heart of Mark's Gospel, its center, is the Transfiguration account."[44]

---

40. Wand, 51. Cf. Donald Evans's discussion of Wand's position in "Academic Skepticism, Spiritual Reality and Transfiguration," in *The Glory of Christ in the New Testament: Studies in Christology*, ed. L. D. Hurst and N. T. Wright (Oxford: Oxford University Press, 1987), 181–83.

41. Schreiner comments, "Divine unity *ad intra* entails inseparable actions *ad extra*. The transfiguration reveals God as this threefold light – a light that is christologically centered but trinitarily understood" (*Transfiguration of Christ*, 58). As to identifying the Spirit with the cloud, he notes that the Evangelists all say "overshadowed" (*episkazo*), the same verb used to describe the Spirit's coming upon Mary (Luke 1:35).

42. Julius Wellhausen, *Das Evangelium Marci: Übersetzt und erklärt*, 2nd ed. (Berlin: Reimer, 1909), 69. See also Rudolf Bultmann, *History of the Synoptic Tradition* (New York: Harper and Row, 1976), 259–61.

43. Gerd Theissen, *The Miracle Stories of the Early Christian Tradition* (Edinburgh: T&T Clark, 1983), 97.

44. Chris Knights, "Metamorphosis and Obedience: An Interpretation of Mark's Account of the Transfiguration of Jesus," *Expository Times* 121, no. 5 (2010): 221 (emphasis original).

There is some irony in identifying the transfiguration as a misplaced resurrection account. As Patrick Schreiner notes, the Gospel narratives do not describe the resurrection, but the Gospel writers do describe the glory of Christ in the transfiguration.[45] Modern biblical scholars are at something of a loss knowing how to account for, or what to do with, Jesus' transfiguration glory.

The Nature of Transfiguration: What Kind of Change?

Each of the Synoptic Gospels depicts the transfiguration as a dramatic change in Jesus' external appearance. The Greek verb in Mark 9:2 is *metamorphoō*, raising the questions: What did metamorphosis mean to the original readers, and how should contemporary readers understand the nature of the change that English translations render as *transfigured*? Many modern biblical commentators insist that we must use Jewish and Hellenistic frames of reference only to identify the literary genre, but these cannot do justice to the broader canonical context or the whole economy of light.[46] Let us recall what is at stake: if there is an analogy between what happens to Jesus and what happens to the letter of the text when read theologically, then we must be absolutely clear about what kind of change transfiguration brings about. The options include the following:

1. A Change of Nature (Transfiguration as Myth)

Some interpreters contend that the transfiguration marks the point where Jesus became something he previously was not, namely, the Son of God.[47] Metamorphosis here means substantial change. Such readings might have some plausibility if the story is read as an independent tradition, but in canonical context it is unlikely, because Jesus is already identified as God's Son earlier in the Gospels, by the voice from heaven at Jesus' baptism (Mark 1:11).

2. A Preview of Future Status (Transfiguration as Apocalypse)

Most modern biblical scholars tend toward using one of two frames of reference: the apocalyptic or epiphanic. According to the first, the transfiguration is a little apocalypse, as it were: a vision of Christ's future reign. On this reading, the transfiguration is what Jesus was referring to when he said that some of his disciples would not die until they "see the kingdom of God" (Mark 9:1). The transfiguration is thus a preview of Jesus' future exaltation, be it his resurrection, ascension, heavenly session, or parousia—in any case, some glorious future

45. Schreiner, *Transfiguration of Christ*, 25.

46. Cf. John Paul Heil: "We must first determine the literary genre if we are to understand what the story is communicating to its implied audience." *The Transfiguration of Jesus: Narrative Meaning and Function of Mark 9:2–8, Matt 17:1–8 and Luke 9:28–36* (Rome: Pontifical Biblical Institute, 2000), 35.

47. See W. P. Bradley, "The Transfiguration—Credential or Answer?," *CrozQ* 12 (1935): 57–76.

that involves a change, not of Jesus' substance but *status*, from humiliation to exaltation.[48] The focus is "on Jesus' acquisition of . . . glory following his ascent to heaven, not on the manifestation of that glory at his descent from heaven."[49] Jesus' transfiguration "reflects both Hellenistic and Jewish ideas about what happened to people who ascended into the heavenly world."[50] According to this apocalyptic interpretation, the transfiguration is not a revelation of Jesus' deity but a preview of his deification. As to transfiguration light, in the Greco-Roman frame of reference, those like Hercules and Julius Caesar, when they became gods, also became shining stars, symbolized by their white, shining raiment.[51]

The light and whiteness of Jesus' face and clothing are therefore not incidental details but clues as to the *heavenly* nature of the event. Scripture typically depicts angelic beings as wearing white (Dan 7:9; Matt 28:3; Rev 15:6; 19:14), and nothing on *earth* could produce such intense whiteness. Moreover, in Jewish apocalyptic tradition, Elijah was thought to have bypassed death and attained angelic status. Finally, mountains figure in Jewish apocalyptic texts as "the place where eschatological and messianic events occur, where special divine knowledge is communicated with human mediators, and where things hidden are revealed in end times."[52] The transfiguration is thus a preview of good things to come: resurrection, ascension, even parousia. It is, in the words of one commentator, "rather like looking into a crystal ball."[53]

3. A Revelation of Present Status (Transfiguration as Epiphany)

The other main interpretation sees the transfiguration not as an apocalypse but as an epiphany, a tangible manifestation of Jesus' present identity as the divine Son of God.[54] In the words of one commentator, "Jesus does not become different from what he was before, but for a moment his appearance becomes a divine sign to humanity, the sign of his true identity."[55] Proponents of this view

---

48. For example, Howard Clark Kee describes the transfiguration as "a proleptic vision of the exaltation of Jesus" in "'The Transfiguration in Mark': Epiphany or Apocalyptic Vision?," in *Understanding the Sacred Text: Essays in Honor of Morton S. Enslin on the Hebrew Bible and Christian Beginnings*, ed. John Reumann (Valley Forge, PA: Judson, 1972), 149; and Ben Witherington III as "a parousia preview" in "Transfigured Understanding: A Critical Note on Mark 9:2–13 as a Parousia Preview," *Anglican Theological Journal* (1992): 88–91.

49. Delbert Burkett, "The Transfiguration of Jesus (Mark 9:2–8): Epiphany or Apotheosis?," *Journal of Biblical Literature* 138, no. 2 (2019): 424.

50. Burkett, 425.

51. See Ovid, *Metamorphoses*, trans. Charles Martin (New York: Norton, 2004), IX.401 (315) and XV.922 (548).

52. Lee, *Jesus' Transfiguration*, 20.

53. Dorothy Lee, *Transfiguration* (New York: Continuum, 2004), 123.

54. An early statement of this interpretation is J. B. Bernadin, "The Transfiguration," *Journal of Biblical Literature* 52 (1933): 181–89. It should be noted that, although Heil uses the term *epiphany*, his view closely resembles the apocalyptic view we have just considered (see Heil, *Transfiguration of Jesus*, 78).

55. François Bovon, *A Commentary on the Gospel of Luke 1:1–9:50* (Minneapolis: Fortress, 2002), 375.

note that Jesus does not ascend into heaven; rather, Moses and Elijah (and eventually God's glory cloud) descend on him. Jesus' radiant face and garments are not previews of his future exaltation, but a symbolic revelation of who he already is.[56] One detail is particularly important: Jesus' face does not reflect light, as did Moses' when he spoke with God (Exod 34:34–35); rather, the light radiates from within Jesus himself. Unlike Old Testament theophanies, the transfiguration centers on the appearance of Jesus' glory, not God's. On this interpretation, the transfiguration does not confer a new status on Jesus but makes known the status Jesus already has. In an epiphanic frame of reference, light is neither material nor celestial, but revelatory, "as if the air on the mountain were clearer for the onlooker and the perception keener."[57] The disciples saw not physical but uncreated light, that same light that began to make itself known on the first day of creation—light from light.

I believe that we need both frames of reference, apocalyptic and epiphanic, to do justice to the letter of the text, particularly in view of its dual authorship.[58] Yet we need not assume that human authors themselves always wrote with only one frame of reference in mind. "The author [Mark] presents his ideas on two wavelengths, one for those more familiar with Jewish traditions and another for those more familiar with Greek religious thought."[59] It follows that Jesus can appear in a single gospel as both the eschatological prophet hoped for by Israel and the Son of God. "In the Markan scheme, Jesus is not only a human or human messiah from below, but also a divine being from above."[60] Schreiner concurs, noting that Jesus is both the eternal Son who, as God, possesses uncreated light in himself and, as man, is the messianic light who receives glory from God.[61]

There is therefore no contradiction in reading the transfiguration as referring both to the future enthronement of the Son of Man and the present revelation of the Son of God.[62] Indeed, New Testament eschatology requires both the already and the not-yet, a tension Ramsey admirably captured: "On the mount of Transfiguration a veil is withdrawn, and the glory which the disciples are allowed to see is not only the glory of a future event, but the glory of Him who *is* the Son of God."[63] The transfiguration employs both present

56. So Lee, *Jesus' Transfiguration*, 23.

57. Lee, *Transfiguration*, 126.

58. However, although I included it for the sake of discussion, I do not think the first option, that the transfiguration refers to Jesus' becoming something he was not, has sufficient canonical warrant to be considered a live interpretive option.

59. Candida R. Moss, "The Transfiguration: An Exercise in Markan Accommodation," *Biblical Interpretation* 12 (2004): 76.

60. Lee, *Jesus' Transfiguration*, 45.

61. Schreiner, *Transfiguration of Christ*, 62.

62. Williams, "The Transfiguration of Jesus Christ (Part 2): Approaching Sonship," *Themelios* 28, no. 2 (Spring 2003): 19.

63. Ramsey, *Glory of God and the Transfiguration of Christ*, 119.

and future frames of reference: "Jesus *now* on earth is the very heavenly Son of Man who will come at the Parousia in the *future*."[64] The transfiguration is thus a sophisticated theological event that overcomes both the spatial divide of heaven/earth and the temporal divide of present/future by employing dual frames of reference—the eschatological "already/not-yet" and the cosmological earthly/heavenly. Both frames are necessary to bring to speech the reality of transfiguration: what happened and what it means.

Particular Interpretive Details

Any account of the meaning of the transfiguration must deal with the details of the text. Each of the five following elements appears in all three Synoptic accounts, with some variation.

The Mountain

In both ancient Jewish cosmology and throughout Scripture, mountains are the places where earth comes closest to God's own realm. They symbolize God's presence and dominion (cf. Exod 24:12–13; Ps 99:9; Isa 56:7; Matt 28:16–17). The height of the mountain makes it a "suburb of heaven"[65] and an appropriate setting for human encounters with God.[66] Second Peter 1:18 refers to the site of transfiguration as "the holy mountain."

The Three Disciples

Peter, James, and John are more than "extras" in a scene featuring Jesus, for the whole episode is arguably for their benefit. Their presence serves at least two purposes. First, it shows the fulfillment of Jesus' prediction that some of his disciples would "see the kingdom of God" (Mark 9:1) before they died. Second, the presence of two or three witnesses emphasizes the authenticity of the testimony.[67] And, as we shall see, the disciples represent us, the viewers/readers of the story.

The Light/Whiteness of Jesus' Face and Garments

"And he was transfigured" (Matt 17:2; Mark 9:2) is a divine passive, a clear case where the context suggests that the action in question was done by God. The action in question involved making Jesus' face and clothes shine like light

64. Lee, *Jesus' Transfiguration*, 46 (emphasis original).

65. Robert H. Gundry, *Mark: A Commentary on His Apology for the Cross* (Grand Rapids: Eerdmans, 1993), 457.

66. According to Terence Donaldson, Matthew's gospel gives the mountain apocalyptic, Mosaic, and enthronement connotations. *Jesus on the Mountain: A Study in Matthean Theology* (Sheffield: JSOT, 1985), 150–52.

67. I discuss the significance of the disciples' eyewitness testimony to the transfiguration (2 Pet 1:16) in the next chapter.

or become dazzling white (Matt 17:2 has "became white as light"). Matthew says Jesus' face "shone like the sun" (Matt 17:2); Luke says it "was altered" (Luke 9:29). The Evangelists use a variety of terms—"shone," "sun," "white as light" (Matt 17:2); "radiant," "intensely white" (Mark 9:3); "dazzling" (Luke 9:29)—to express what I take to be a key moment in the economy of light.[68] These special effects are hardly gratuitous; rather, they direct our attention to an event of great theological consequence. The transfiguration afforded the disciples a glimpse behind the veil of Jesus' flesh, revealing his true identity, an outward manifestation of his inner being.[69] That his face shone like the sun implies that the light was not *on* his face but emanating *from* it. "To behold the luminous human face of Jesus is, literally, to behold the human face of the Father's Son and so too the face of the Father."[70] One commentator describes the transfiguration as an "inside out" revelation: "What Jesus *was within* was once made visible without."[71] It was a revelation of the reality that Nicaea would articulate centuries later: "light from light."

Moses and Elijah

The presence of Moses and Elijah, like the other details, are for the disciples' (and readers') benefit. Their presence adds further texture to what is already a rich event. They are conversing with Jesus, and Luke notes that the topic was Jesus' "departure" (Gk. *exodos*)—a reference to his death, resurrection, and ascension (and to God's deliverance of Israel from Egypt)—that he was about to accomplish in Jerusalem (Luke 9:31). Moses represents the law, while Elijah represents the prophets and is the harbinger of a new eschatological order (Mal 4:5). Both previously had mountaintop experiences of God (theophanies), which may explain why Luke says they "appeared in glory" (Luke 9:31).[72] Nevertheless, the disciples saw only Jesus' glory (Luke 9:32). Moses and Elijah are not competitors with Jesus but "foils to highlight that he alone is God's beloved Son to be heard."[73] This may also explain the inaptness (and ineptness) of Peter's

---

68. Luke does not say "was transfigured" (μετεμορφώθη), but "the appearance of his face was altered" (Luke 9:29), perhaps to avoid giving his Greek audience a misleading impression of the kind of change involved: "According to Luke, Jesus does not become different from what he was before, but for a moment his appearance becomes a divine sign to humanity, the sign of his true identity" (Bovon, *A Commentary on the Gospel of Luke 1:1–9:50*, 375).

69. This is precisely what the economy of light is all about: the publication to others of the knowledge God has of himself.

70. Thomas G. Weinandy, *Jesus Becoming Jesus: A Theological Interpretation of the Synoptic Gospels* (Washington, DC: Catholic University of America Press, 2018), 230.

71. Frederick Dale Bruner, *Matthew: A Commentary*, vol. 2, *The Churchbook*, rev. ed. (Grand Rapids: Eerdmans, 2004), 167 (emphasis original).

72. "The correspondence between Exodus 33 and 1 Kings 19 is uncanny, suggesting that Moses and Elijah appear on the Mount of Transfiguration because they both longed to see the glory of God." Schreiner, *Transfiguration of Christ*, 86.

73. Gundry, *Mark*, 458.

suggestion to set up three tents—one each for Moses and Elijah as well as Jesus (Matt 17:4; Mark 9:5; Luke 9:33)—for Jesus was *already* "tenting" among them (cf. *eskēnōsen*, "to dwell in a tent," in John 1:14), the tabernacle of divine glory made flesh. Deliverance and glory would come through Jesus and his cross, no one or nothing else.

The Voice out of the Cloud

The divine voice declaring Jesus as the Son of God (Matt 17:5; Mark 9:7; Luke 9:35) is arguably the climax of the transfiguration, articulating what the light displays. It is also the moment that causes the disciples to be afraid (Luke 9:34). For the bright, overshadowing cloud, the shining and the speaking, all signal the mysterious, overwhelming presence of God.[74] Readers of the Old Testament are familiar with God's speaking out of thick clouds (Exod 19:9; 24:15; 33:9; 34:5). Yet the transfiguration marks only the second time that God speaks in the entirety of the Synoptic Gospels, the other instance being Jesus' baptism, where he pronounces a similar formula: "This is my beloved Son" (Matt 3:17; Mark 1:11; Luke 3:22). As Dale Bruner comments, "In the Synoptic Gospels, God the Father talks directly to earth only twice . . . and both times God says exactly the same thing . . . *the single most important fact that God wants the church and the world to know*."[75] Each Evangelist also records a second divine utterance, the imperatival "Listen to him." This brief command is, for Bruner, "what this story is finally about."[76] If Jesus is the light of God become the light of the world, it is only fitting that we listen to him, and him only. The transfiguration story ends aptly, with the disciples seeing "Jesus alone" (Matt 17:8; Mark 9:8; Luke 9:36), reminding us that Jesus is God's first and last word, the Alpha and Omega (Rev 22:13).[77]

Transfiguration by the Letter: A Grammatical-Eschatological Exegesis

Descriptions matter, particularly when the event is a key turning point in the life and ministry of Jesus Christ. The various witnesses to the transfiguration—the three disciples, the three Synoptic Evangelists, the biblical scholars we have surveyed, and earlier interpreters we have yet to hear from—employ distinct frames of reference arising from their respective context(s).[78] Some of these (viz.,

---

74. Patrick Schreiner says "the transfiguration is *the* theophany par excellence" *Transfiguration of Christ*, 88 (emphasis original).

75. Bruner, *Matthew: A Commentary*, 2:172.

76. Bruner, 2:173.

77. See further Kevin J. Vanhoozer, "Theological Commentary and the 'Voice from Heaven': Exegesis, Ontology, and the Travail of Biblical Interpretation," in *On the Writing of New Testament Commentaries*, ed. Stanley E. Porter and Eckhard J. Schnabel (Leiden: Brill, 2013), 269–98, esp. 285–95.

78. I could have said, from their "grammatical/cultural contexts"—let the reader understand!

historical-critical or literary-ideological) are unable either to see Christ as the light of God or to listen to him as God's first and last Word. They are therefore unable to do justice to the Evangelists' literal sense, a function of their apostolic frame of reference.

Jesus' transfiguration is a saturated phenomenon, an audio-visual event replete with theological significance. The grammatical-eschatological approach to literal interpretation set forth in part 2 incorporates various frames of reference, including an eschatological-doxological frame of reference without which we cannot do justice to the transfiguration as a display of the glory of God in the face of Christ. Jesus' own words immediately preceding the transfiguration, about the disciples' *seeing the kingdom of God*, or as Matthew puts it, seeing "the Son of Man coming in his kingdom" (Matt 16:28), call for such a frame of reference.

The transfiguration was a display of Jesus' already/not-yet glory. The narrative identifies Jesus as Son of God and Son of Man, the man born to be king—but only after suffering and dying. The details of the story render the transfiguration an object lesson for the benefit of the disciples and us, a resplendent making-known that Jesus' words and deeds constitute the coming kingdom of God in power and glory, though these are hidden momentarily beneath the veil of Jesus' flesh.[79] The whole episode constituted an impressive audio-visual aid to Jesus' difficult teaching that his suffering and death must precede the coming of his kingdom, a vivid preview to the gospel truth that "Jesus will truly become Jesus in accomplishing his own exodus."[80]

Luke alone uses the term glory (*doxa*) in connection with the transfiguration, and he does so twice, the first time in connection with Moses and Elijah. Luke says they "appeared in glory" (Luke 9:31), which need not mean that they were themselves glorious. For Luke adds, more precisely, that the disciples "saw his [Jesus'] glory and the two men who stood with him" (Luke 9:32). Moses and Elijah stand at some distance from the glory, indicating "that the glory present at the Transfiguration is best taken as being proper to Jesus alone."[81] The key elements of the transfiguration—the shining face, radiant clothes, the voice from out of the overshadowing cloud—all point to Jesus' present/future glorious status.[82] To see Jesus' glory in this way *is* to see the coming of God's kingdom. We will say more in due course about the nature of this glory and its relation to what

79. That the thrust of the object lesson pertains to Jesus' glory and honor receives an important corroboration from 2 Peter 1:16–17, a text we will examine further in the next chapter: "we were eyewitnesses of his majesty"; "he received honor and glory from God the Father."

80. Weinandy, *Jesus Becoming Jesus*, 234.

81. Benjamin Thomas, *An Anglican Hermeneutic of the Transfiguration* (New York: Peter Lang, 2013), 24.

82. By glorious status, I am thinking of Jesus' ascension and second coming more than the resurrection. Tellingly, those who saw the risen Christ did not see his face shining like the sun.

I am calling an eschatological-doxological frame of reference. For the present, it is enough to call attention to the relationship between glory and light. Both have to do with a resplendence that shows itself; both make known and enable something to be seen. The transfiguration shows and tells that Jesus is his Father's Son, "light from light," in human form.

What does "glory" look like? What did the disciples literally see? The Evangelists find it difficult to describe this light, as we did the uncreated light of Genesis 1:3. Whereas Genesis 1:3 concerns protological light, the disciples witnessed eschatological light, a glimpse of eternity breaking into time, giving Jesus' face and clothes an otherworldly brilliance, revealing his divine nature and anticipating his glorified humanity and lordship in the age to come. The transfiguration is a paradigmatic event that obliged its witnesses to make transfigural connections to other persons, places, and events (e.g., Moses' encounter with God on Mount Sinai) in order to communicate its meaning and significance, connections that depend upon a biblically informed imagination that enables us to see *this* as *that*.

Historical and literary frames of reference are indispensable starting points, but they do not pierce to the division of body and spirit—the textual joints and marrow—or enable us to discern the thoughts and intentions of the authors, human and divine. Mere Christian hermeneutics calls for something more, a *canonical* and *catholic* frame of reference that reflects the perspective of a cloud of witnesses: the Law and the Prophets; Christians from past and present, East and West.

The Transfiguration in the History of Exegesis

We turn now to listen to representative voices from the great cloud of interpreter-witnesses to see what further light may be shed on Jesus' transfiguration. By and large, readers from East and West, across the centuries and confessional traditions, agree that the transfiguration is a making known of Christ's already/not-yet glory, a significant episode in the economy of light in which the triune God makes known his plan of salvation. Our immediate concern, however, is to see whether readers also agree that there is an *analogia corporis*, a textually based, hermeneutically significant correspondence between the body of Jesus and the letter of the text. A mere Christian hermeneutic, if it is to live up to its name, must be more than idiosyncratic.

Patristic

The Greek and Latin fathers lacked access to what, thanks to modern biblical scholarship, we now know about the historical and cultural context of the Evangelists. Nevertheless, patristic readings of the transfiguration made three essential gains—in theology, eschatology, and hermeneutics respectively—thanks in large part to their willingness to read with a supernatural frame of reference. First, they approached the text as Christians, and with a Nicene frame of reference that helped them interpret the transfiguration as a revelation of Christ's deity. "Their existential rather than academic concern as well as their ecclesiological orientation provide the Fathers with a dual hermeneutic principle: the personal faith . . . of the exegete and . . . the participation in the total experience of the Church."[83] Second, they understood the transfiguration as testimony to a present-future reality, an event that was historical and eschatological: the coming of the future kingdom of God in the person and work of Jesus. And third, they understood the transfiguration provided a crucial key to rightly interpreting the Old Testament. This third feature is my special focus here.[84]

There is a wealth of patristic material on the transfiguration.[85] Irenaeus made a passing reference, seeing it as the fulfillment of Moses' request in Exodus 33:12–22 to see God's glory.[86] However, the first in-depth treatment is Origen's, particularly his commentary on Matthew.[87]

Origen

Origen was alert to the light of Christ shining through the letter of the text. The Lord reveals "the radiance of his thoughts in phrases of Scripture."[88] Yes, but what should modern biblical scholars make of Origen's equating Jesus' bright clothing with Scripture ("the words and letters of the Gospels") or his suggestion that the white that bleaches can achieve (cf. Mark 9:3) is the laundry equivalent of the wisdom of worldly readers?[89]

Before dismissing such claims as allegorical fiddle-faddle, those who count themselves of hermeneutically sound and righteous mind would do well to remember Origen's exegetical concerns and frame of reference. Origen consistently displayed two overarching concerns when commenting on the

---

83. Peter A. Chamberas, "The Transfiguration of Christ: A Study in the Patristic Exegesis of Scripture," *St. Vladimir's Theological Quarterly* 14, no. 1–2 (1970): 62.

84. The best study of patristic interpretations of the transfiguration is John Anthony McGuckin, *The Transfiguration of Christ in Scripture and Tradition* (Lewiston, NY: Mellen, 1986).

85. See, e.g., Brian E. Daley, trans., *Light on the Mountain: Greek Patristic and Byzantine Homilies on the Transfiguration of the Lord* (Yonkers, NY: St. Vladimir's Seminary Press, 2013).

86. Irenaeus, *Against Heresies* 4.20.9.

87. Brian Daley notes that Origen's comments on Matthew 17:1–9 are representative of patristic interpretation, and that they had a significant influence on subsequent patristic interpretation of this passage. Daley, "Introduction," *Light on the Mountain*, 24–25, 54.

88. Origen, *Commentary on Matthew* 12.39, as trans. and cited in Daley, *Light on the Mountain*, 58.

89. Origen, *Commentary on Matthew* 12.38, in Daley, *Light on the Mountain*, 57. Ramsey cites this as a conspicuous example of Origen's allegorizing (*Glory of God and the Transfiguration of Christ*, 130).

transfiguration: first, to describe the dual human-divine nature of Jesus Christ in such a way that the former uniquely reveals the latter; second, to acknowledge the importance of spiritual maturity for spiritual perception. The transfiguration brings these two themes, divine descent (incarnation) and human ascent (salvation), together. At one point, Origen referred suggestively to the transfiguration as "the *oikonomia* [= 'economy'] on the mountain."[90] He did not name it the economy of light, but he did focus on Jesus' being transfigured "before them" (Matt 17:2; Mark 9:2), and on what the transfiguration allowed "them" to see. "The difference between those who see the Transfiguration and those who do not is a question of spiritual aptitude . . . not even all followers of Jesus are capable of seeing his divine glory."[91] Something similar holds with regard to readers and the spiritual sense of Scripture: "For Origen, holiness is accomplished through Christ and is a prerequisite for uncovering the spiritual meaning of scripture."[92]

The qualifications for seeing the light of Christ took center stage again when Origen noted that the disciples saw Jesus' shining face as he was conversing with Moses and Elijah, from which Origen deduced that while it is good to understand who Jesus is, it is even better to understand who Jesus is in relation to the Law and the Prophets: "One has seen 'Moses and Elijah in glory,' when one sees them with Jesus."[93] They are with Jesus and, in a sense, they are one with him: "For Moses, who was the law, and Elijah, who was prophecy, had become only one with Jesus, who is Gospel."[94] Jesus (the Gospel-in-person) is at one with the spiritual meaning of the letter of the Law and Prophets (the Old Testament).

For Origen, the transfiguration was about the disciples seeing Jesus in the form of God (divine glory) in, under, and through his bodily form (human flesh). At the transfiguration, "Jesus became a symbol of his own glory."[95] Again, what Origen found most significant is that only the disciples Jesus led up the mountain received the vision. Those who remained at the foot of the mountain did not see the heavenly "things above," for they were dragged down by worldly "things below." Origen drew "a connective thread between scriptural exegesis and theophanic experience," claiming that biblical interpreters make a similar

90. Origen, *Commentary on Matthew* 12.43, in Daley, *Light on the Mountain*, 65.

91. Thomas, *Anglican Hermeneutic of the Transfiguration*, 55. In context the reference is to Origen's *Contra Celsum* 2.64–65, but the point holds for his *Commentary on Matthew* as well.

92. John J. Allen, "'Go up onto a High Mountain' (Is. 40:9): Theophanic Exegesis as Mystical Ascent in *On First Principles*," *Pro Ecclesia* 29, no. 1 (2020): 109.

93. Origen, *Commentary on Matthew*, 12.38. Cited in Daley, *Light on the Mountain*, 58.

94. Origen, *Commentary on Matthew*, 12.43. Cited in Daley, *Light on the Mountain*, 65.

95. Paul M. Blowers, "Mystics and Mountains: Comparing Origen's Exegesis of the Transfiguration and Gregory of Nyssa's Exposition of the Sinai Theophany," *Phronema* 30, no. 2 (2015): 3.

ascent.[96] This ascent toward seeing and understanding has as much to do with spiritual ascesis (i.e., self-denial and spiritual formation) as it does with grammatical exegesis.[97]

Origen's exegesis of the transfiguration was one of the influences on de Lubac's understanding of the relationships between Scripture's literal and spiritual sense, and between the Old Testament and New Testament. De Lubac saw Origen's interpretation of the transfiguration as an exemplary demonstration of how the Old Testament "undergoes a conversion and exaltation in the New Testament."[98] Of particular interest is the parallel between seeing the face of Jesus shining like the sun and reading Scripture communicating the voice of God. Jesus clothes himself with humanity; the divine voice clothes itself with human words. There is one Logos but different "incorporations." "The Scripture and the Incarnation are similar in that they are both forms in which the divine Logos is present in the world."[99] In de Lubac's words, "The historical meaning and the spiritual meaning are, between them, like the flesh and the divinity of the Logos."[100] This is a succinct statement of the *analogia corporis*: "The literal sense and the flesh of Jesus are alike in that they are means by which the Logos reveals himself to human beings."[101] The likeness is analogical: the correspondence between the body of Jesus and the letter of the text, far from being fanciful, has everything to do with the activity of the Logos in the economy of light.[102]

Jerome

Among the Western church fathers, Jerome treated the transfiguration and the parallel between Jesus' body and the letter of the text most thoroughly. There were precedents. For example, in his commentary on Luke, Ambrose of Milan compared Jesus' garments to the words of Scripture, adding that unless one ascends the mountain and reads in faith, the words "will appear to you like the word of man, veiled in ambiguous sayings, not shining in the power of the Spirit."[103] Indeed, the idea that the garments (and face) of

---

96. Allen, "Go up onto a High Mountain," 114.

97. Michael Allen develops the theme of the reader's mortification in his "Dogmatics as Ascetics," in *The Task of Dogmatics*, ed. Oliver D. Crisp and Fred Sanders (Grand Rapids: Zondervan, 2017), 189–209.

98. Henri de Lubac, *Medieval Exegesis*, vol. 1, *The Four Senses of Scripture*, trans. Marc Sebanc (Grand Rapids: Eerdmans, 1998), 252.

99. Wright, "Literal Sense of Scripture according to Henri de Lubac," 256. See further Henri de Lubac, "The Incorporations of the Logos," in *History and Spirit: The Understanding of Scripture according to Origen*, trans. Anne England Nash and Juvenal Merrill (San Francisco: Ignatius, 2007), 385–426.

100. De Lubac, *History and Spirit*, 105.

101. Wright, "Literal Sense of Scripture according to Henri de Lubac," 257.

102. I hope in what follows it will become clear that I am not proposing an incarnational (dual nature) analogy but one that is specifically transfigural, pertaining specifically to the function of light in "making known" and "making glorious."

103. Ambrose, *Expositio in Lucam* 7, 12. Cited in McGuckin, *Transfiguration of Christ*, 267.

Christ corresponded to the words of Scripture became something of a patristic trope, one that Jerome explored in his commentary on Matthew more than anyone else.[104]

Jerome viewed the transfiguration as anticipating Jesus' future return in glory. He was adamant that there was no essential change to Jesus' human nature, taking pains to distinguish Jesus' transfiguration from pagan metamorphoses. In contrast to Ovid's *Metamorphoses*, for example, Jesus was not transformed into some other kind of creature: "When the splendor of the face is shown, and the brilliance of the clothing described, it is not the substance is removed, but the glory is changed (*non substantia tolliter sed gloria commutatur*). . . . The transformation added splendor; it did not make his face disappear."[105] This is Jerome's decisive rebuttal to those inclined to overspiritualize the event. *Jesus' transfigured body was glorified but still physical*: "While [Christ's substance] changed in glory, the Son of God remains the same."[106]

Jerome's homily on Mark 9:1–7 has been described as "an exposition of hermeneutical principles which uses the Transfiguration to demonstrate a 'spiritual' method of reading Scripture."[107] Indeed, this homily sets forth "the deepest formulation of his idea of Christian exegesis."[108] Jerome refused to spiritualize the humanity of Christ (i.e., Jesus' body) or the literal sense (i.e., the letter of the text). To interpret spiritually is not to override the letter but to delve deeper into it, the better to determine what it is talking about and to see the light of Christ, the knowledge and glory of God.[109] This is the context in which Jerome compared Jesus' garments to the Scriptures, the shining of his clothes to Scripture's spiritual sense. Jesus *is* the Son of God and the Bible *is* the word of God, yet only those who ascend the mountain and read in faith—in my terms, with a grammatical-eschatological frame of reference—will be able to perceive the light of Christ shimmering in the words of the biblical text: "For him who follows the word of God and ascends the mountain, climbs to the top;

104. Surprisingly, Augustine had comparatively little to say about the transfiguration and was something of a loner in thinking that Jesus' shining garments referred to the church, and that their whiteness indicated the cleanliness following the forgiveness of sins. See Augustine, *Sermon* 78, in *The Works of St. Augustine*, trans. Edmund Hill, vol. 3, pt. 3 (New York: New City, 1991), 340–44. See also Andrew Louth, "St. Augustine's Interpretation of the Transfiguration of Christ," *Studia Ephemeridis Augustinianum* 68 (Rome: Institutum Patristicum Augustinianum 2000): 375–82.

105. Jerome, *Commentarium in Matthaeum* in *Hieronymus: Commentariorum in Matheum libri 4*, Corpus Christianorum Series Latina 77, ed. David Hurst and Marcus Adriaen (Turnhout: Brepols, 1969), 147.

106. Jan Dominik Bogataj, "Jerome's Interpretation of the Transfiguration in Light of Some Recent Patristic Discoveries," *Bogoslovni Vestnik / Theological Quarterly* 81 (2021): 314.

107. Thomas, *Anglican Hermeneutic of the Transfiguration*, 65.

108. Pierre Jay, "Jerome (ca. 347–419/420)," in *Handbook of Patristic Exegesis: The Bible in Ancient Christianity*, ed. Charles Kannengiesser, vol. 2 (Leiden: Brill, 2004): 1109.

109. Jerome, *Homilies of St. Jerome*, vol. 2, 162. Jerome appeals to Paul's reading of the Sarah and Hagar episode as the story of two types of covenants to justify his own "spiritual explanation."

for him, Jesus is instantly transfigured and His garments shine exceedingly."[110] In other words, what one sees depends on where one is standing and who one is. Readers who interpret the letter with a purely historical (immanent) frame of reference see "nothing shining in it."[111] It is a sobering thought: readers who refuse to expand their referential horizons, insisting on the immediate historical referent only, end up *not* following "the way the words go."

For the biblical words go *up*, and those who follow them, reading as mere Christians, understand that the light of Christ shines in the Law and the Prophets as well as the Gospels. In contrast, those who read the Bible only "from below" know Jesus only "according to the flesh" (2 Cor 5:16). Jerome explained Peter's request to build three tents as a "from below" reading of a "from above" phenomenon: Peter failed to understand that the Law (Moses) and the Prophets (Elijah) are inseparable from the Gospel (Gospel).[112] Those who read *secundum litteram* (according to the bare letter for the grammatical sense only) are unable to make sense of biblical narrative as a unified history culminating in Christ.[113] It is only when one reads the Scriptures in faith—with a grammatical-eschatological frame of reference in canonical context—that one can perceive their truest *literal* meaning: the glory of God revealed in Christ. This explains why the narrative of the transfiguration "presents us with a text whose literal meaning *is* its spiritual sense,"[114] and how the story directs reader-disciples to ascend to a vantage point where they can see the (revealed) mystery in the (veiled) history, the dazzling face of Christ in the glimmering fabric of the canonical text.

Medieval

Is there further evidence that later interpreters read the transfiguration as having hermeneutical significance? There is, yet the documentation is sketchy because, as previously mentioned, the transfiguration never became a major topic of controversy or importance in the West.

The Venerable Bede

The Venerable Bede, the Father of English Church History, commented and preached on the transfiguration, often citing Jerome. Like Jerome, he was careful not to confuse Jesus' transfiguration with a transformation into

110. Jerome, *Homilies of St. Jerome*, 163.

111. Jerome, *Homilies of St. Jerome*, 163.

112. Augustine made the same point in his *Sermon* 78.3.

113. Cf. Wright: "According to Jerome, the defining characteristic of understanding 'according to the letter' is that it does not admit or perceive the deeper relationships between the realities in the Law and Prophets and Christ" ("The Literal Sense," 261).

114. Black, "Transfigured Exegesis," 255.

something else: "The transfigured savior has not lost the substance of the true flesh" (Lat. *transfiguratus saluator non substantiam uerea carnc amisit*).[115] Minimally, we can say that early medieval theologians resisted the urge to use the transfiguration as a warrant for allegorical interpretation, making the literal sense mean something *other* than what it says.[116]

Thomas Aquinas

Thomas Aquinas was one of the few medieval writers to give sustained attention to the transfiguration. His main interest in his commentaries pertained to the significance of Jesus' transfiguration for the believer's transformation. His primary interest in his theological treatises was, by way of contrast, more scholastic, centered on questions like: What *is* transfiguration? What does it mean? And how can divine glory be manifest in human flesh? His contemporaries posed similar questions, though tinged with a degree of literalism: How did the disciples know the two men were Moses and Elijah? Did they see the transfiguration with their eyes or in their minds?[117] How does the transfiguration relate to the beatific vision?

Thomas devoted four articles in his *Summa Theologica* to the transfiguration. He clearly viewed the transfiguration as a key moment in the history of redemption. Why? Because it was "fitting" that Jesus "should show His disciples the glory of His clarity . . . to which He will configure those who are His."[118] In brief, the transfiguration shows Jesus' disciples that they, too, have a future in the economy of light. Jesus' revelation to Peter, James, and John of the glory that would follow his suffering on the cross serves as an encouragement to disciples everywhere to persevere in the cruciform way of Christ. Jesus' suffering was a step in the Father's "bringing many sons to glory" (Heb 2:10). The transfiguration thus serves as a precious promissory note.

Thomas insisted, with Jerome, that the brightness of Jesus' face and garments represent "not a change of substance, but a putting on of glory."[119] This led him to pose a *quaestio* rather than make a comment, one that makes sense once one remembers that Thomas was reading with a frame of reference colored by Aristotelian ontological categories like "substance" and "accident." Thomas

115. Bede, *Opera Exegetica 3. In Lucae Evangelism Expositio* (Turnhout: Brepols, 1960), 205.

116. Alas, Bede himself sometimes slipped into allegorizing, as when he suggested that Jesus' altered garments refer to putting on Christ at baptism (see the discussion in Thomas, *Anglican Hermeneutic of Transfiguration*, 89).

117. See further the discussion in Aaron Canty, *Light and Glory: The Transfiguration of Christ in Early Franciscan and Dominican Theology* (Washington, DC: Catholic University of America Press, 2011). See also Kenneth Stevenson, "From Hilary of Poitiers to Peter of Blois: A Transfiguration Journey of Biblical Interpretation," *Scottish Journal of Theology* 61 no. 3 (2008): 288–306.

118. Thomas Aquinas, *Summa Theologica* Q. 45, art. 1.

119. Thomas Aquinas, *Summa Theologica* Q. 45, art. 1.

wanted to know: Did Jesus during his earthly life acquire the properties of a glorified body, one of which was "clarity"?[120] His question is really about the purposes of Jesus' transfiguration, namely, "to show men His glory, and to arouse men to a desire of it."[121] Was the light the disciples witnessed a visible manifestation of the glory of God? Thomas's reply is subtle: "The clarity which Christ assumed in His transfiguration was the clarity of glory as to its essence, but not as to its mode of being."[122] Because Jesus was not yet raised from the dead, his body had not yet acquired glory permanently. Consequently, the transfiguration records a miraculous albeit only temporary illumination of Christ's body, primarily for the benefit of the disciples.[123] For present purposes, however, the main takeaway from Thomas's discussion is that Jesus' human body was the medium for divine glory, much as the letter of the text serves as a bright medium for the knowledge of Jesus Christ.

Reformation and Early Moderns

Compared to aforementioned readings of the early church, the Reformers' interpretation of Jesus' shining face is quite dull. Ramsey's verdict is as just as it is terse: "The Reformation added little to the interpretation of the Transfiguration."[124] The Reformers and their Protestant successors contributed even less to exploring the hermeneutical potential of the transfiguration. There are exceptions. For example, Isaac Ambrose described the canonical Scriptures as "the spiritual swaddling clothes" of the Christ child, for Christ is the substance of all figures and types, and the gospel "is Christ's light."[125]

John Calvin

Given Calvin's description of Christ as the "only light of truth"[126] and his penchant for reading the Bible as a unified story of the covenant of grace becoming ever brighter, it is surprising that the transfiguration does not figure

120. The *quaestio* is a typically scholastic device, deployed when, in the course of commenting on a text, a master had to pause to address a more substantial issue or problem. The problem was that medieval theologians taught, on the basis of 1 Corinthians 15:22–24, that the resurrected body would have four "gifts," including impassibility, which Thomas worried would make his passion impossible. See Jeremy Holmes, "Aquinas' *Lectura in Matthaeum*," in *Aquinas on Scripture: An Introduction to His Biblical Commentaries*, ed. Thomas G. Weinandy, Daniel A. Keating, and John P. Yocum (London: T&T Clark, 2005), 90–91.

121. Thomas Aquinas, *Summa Theologica* Q. 45, art. 3.

122. Thomas Aquinas, *Summa Theologica* Q. 45, art. 2.

123. Cf. Thomas Aquinas: "It was not the clarity of a glorified body, since Christ's body was not as yet immortal." *Summa Theologica* Q. 45, art. 2.

124. Ramsey, *Glory of God and the Transfiguration of Christ*, 140.

125. Isaac Ambrose, *Works* (1701), 201. Cited in J. I. Packer, *A Quest for Godliness: The Puritan Vision of the Christian Life* (Wheaton, IL: Crossway, 1990), 103.

126. John Calvin, *Commentary on the Book of the Prophet Isaiah*, vol. 2, trans. William Pringle (Edinburgh: Calvin Translation Society, 1851), 322.

more prominently in Calvin's work. Even more so in light of Calvin's original contribution to the notion of the "ascent of the soul."[127] We "lift up our hearts" to the Lord not by our own efforts, Calvin suggested, but by participating in Jesus' ascension, *his* glorified humanity. The goal is fellowship with the Father in the Son through the Spirit. Calvin's vision of spiritual ascent via Jesus' ascension is inspiring. All the more surprising, then, that there is no index entry for transfiguration in the standard edition of his *Institutes*, either on its own or under "Christ, acts and life." Instead, Calvin viewed the transfiguration as one of the miraculous proofs of Christ's divinity.[128]

Calvin gave a competent though rather cautious commentary on the transfiguration. He resisted entering into subtle disputations about details such as the significance of the whiteness of Jesus' garments, or debates over whether Moses and Elijah were physically present on the mountain or merely specters. At one point, however, Calvin did invoke his important idea of divine accommodation (without using the term) in describing the transfiguration: "This transformation did not absolutely reveal Christ to the sight of His disciples as He now is in heaven but gave them such a taste of His infinite glory as they were able to receive."[129] This relates to the previously mentioned idea of spiritual ascent insofar as Calvin acknowledged that we cannot perceive the glory of Christ in its resplendent fullness until we are made like him (1 John 3:2). However, there is no mention of the relevance of this insight for the task of biblical interpretation. The Reformers' contribution to the project of transfiguring biblical interpretation yields slim pickings only, even though they agree on the importance of reading the Old Testament christologically.

Jonathan Edwards

One Protestant theologian who did contribute to my attempt to appropriate the transfiguration for the sake of mere Christian hermeneutics is Jonathan Edwards. He was uniquely positioned between the ages, as it were, with one foot in the precritical Christian tradition and another on the threshold of biblical criticism and Enlightenment modernity. Douglas Sweeney notes, "Like many early Protestants . . . Edwards practiced literal and spiritual exegesis."[130]

127. Julie Canlis, *Calvin's Ladder: A Spiritual Theology of Ascent and Ascension* (Grand Rapids: Eerdmans, 2010).

128. See the brief discussion in Stephen Edmondson, *Calvin's Christology* (Cambridge: Cambridge University Press, 2004), 198–99.

129. John Calvin, *Calvin's Commentaries: A Harmony of the Gospels: Matthew, Mark, and Luke*, vol. 2, trans. T. H. L. Parker (Grand Rapids: Eerdmans, 1972), 198.

130. Douglas A. Sweeney, *Edwards the Exegete: Biblical Interpretation and Anglo-Protestant Culture on the Edge of the Enlightenment* (Oxford: Oxford University Press, 2016), 48.

Edwards was both heir to and innovator in the Reformed interpretive tradition, and some see him as a Western figure with affinities to the East.[131] He was resolutely Protestant, yet he stood apart from his eighteenth-century peers because of his "thoroughgoing commitment to spiritual exegesis" and appreciation of Scripture's "fecundity" as much as, if not more than, its perspicuity.[132] What does "America's greatest theologian" have to contribute to our project?[133]

We must admit straightaway that, as with Calvin, there is disappointingly little that deals explicitly with the transfiguration. The key primary source is a sermon not on the Gospels but on 2 Peter 1:16: "But we were eyewitnesses of his majesty." Edwards is nevertheless helpful inasmuch as he read *all* of Scripture within a framework of understanding akin to what I have termed the economy of light. And what he *does* say about the transfiguration advances our understanding of what it means to see the light of Christ in the letter of the text.

Edwards wrote often, and copiously, on light and glory and their relationship to biblical interpretation: "Of all the similitudes [used in Scripture] to describe to us this spiritual understanding, light is that which doth most fully represent it and is oftenest used."[134] Moreover, Edwards maintained that God's glorious brightness is present not only in the gospel but in all creation, leading one Edwards scholar to declare, "The universe is God's light show."[135] If Christ is the heart of creation and the true subject matter of Scripture, we ought to expect biblical interpretation to yield "true sight" of God's glory: "Christ is the luminary, he is the sun; but the spirit of Christ is as the rays, as the very light itself. The sun don't [*sic*] enlighten us immediately, but by his beams. . . .'Tis Christ's face that shines into the heart, but 'tis the spirit of Christ are the rays by which it shines into them."[136] Edwards here posited both an objective and subjective dimension to revelatory light, dimensions we can perhaps parse, with Calvin, in terms of "word and Spirit."[137]

131. The nomenclature of "heir" and "innovator" comes from Stephen R. C. Nichols's "Jonathan Edwards' Principles of Interpreting Scripture," in *Jonathan Edwards and Scripture: Biblical Exegesis in British North America*, ed. David P. Barshinger and Douglas A. Sweeney (Oxford: Oxford University Press, 2018), 34, 40.

132. Michael J. McClymond and Gerald R. McDermott, *The Theology of Jonathan Edwards* (Oxford: Oxford University Press, 2012), 175, 178.

133. George Marsden, his biographer, refers to his reputation as "the most brilliant of all American theologians." *Jonathan Edwards: A Life* (New Haven, CT: Yale University Press, 2003), 3.

134. Jonathan Edwards, "A Spiritual Understanding of Divine Things Denied to the Unregenerate," in *Works of Jonathan Edwards* 14 (New Haven, CT: Yale University Press, 1997), 77.

135. Richard B. Steele, "Transfiguring Light: The Moral Beauty of the Christian Life according to Gregory Palamas and Jonathan Edwards," *St. Vladimir's Theological Quarterly* 52 (2008): 429.

136. Jonathan Edwards, "A Sight of the Glory of Christ" (72. II Cor. 3:18 [1728]), in *Sermons, Series II, 1728–1729*, in *Works of Jonathan Edwards Online*, vol. 43, accessed July 8, 2022, http://edwards.yale.edu/archive?path=aHR0cDovL2Vkd2FyZHMueWFsZS5lZHUvY2dpLWJpbi9uZXdwaGlsby9nZXRvYmplY3QucGw/Yy40MToxNC53amVv.

137. A distinction that eventually was parsed by Karl Barth in terms of "objective" and "subjective" revelation. *Church Dogmatics* I.1.

Edwards acknowledged an analogy of glory between the light shining from Christ's face and the light shining in and through the biblical text. He explicitly likened hearing the voice of God in Scripture to Peter's seeing the glory of God in Jesus' transfiguration: "Peter, when he saw this . . . was sure that Christ was a divine and holy person without sitting down to reason about it." In similar fashion, the saints are convicted that they are hearing God's voice speaking in the Scriptures, a "lamp" of divine glory (Ps 119:105). The excellence of Scripture is as much evidence of its divine authority and truth as "Peter's seeing the outward glory of Christ at his transfiguration."[138] The blind—sinners in the darkness of denial—cannot see even the brightest truth, which is why we need to distinguish between the objective and subjective moments in the economy of light.

Christ is the light of the world, yet we need the illumination of the Holy Spirit—the right religious "affections"—in order to see the light of Christ. A similar dynamic obtains in reading the Bible, Edwards surmised: "Spiritually to understand the Scripture, is rightly to understand what *is in* the Scripture, and what *was in it* before it was understood . . . [it is] not the making a new meaning."[139] The light is objectively there, in the text. However, a person who reads the Bible without the Spirit's enlightenment beholds spiritual things faintly, "but he that sees by divine light is like a man that views the garden when the sun shines upon it."[140] Although all readers are answerable for their interpretations, only those who have the indwelling Spirit of understanding are able to respond to the divine address as they ought, with the understanding of faith: "a man might know how to interpret all the types, parables, enigmas, and allegories in the Bible, and not have one beam of spiritual light in his mind."[141] Such a reader gets the grammar but not the glory.

Edwards rightly understood why the Spirit is necessary in the economy of light. A technical grasp of grammar is not enough. Reading Scripture rightly requires certain subjective dispositions, which Edwards discussed in his *Religious Affections* and his 1734 sermon "A Divine and Supernatural Light."[142] By supernatural light, Edwards had in mind a new spiritual sensibility the Spirit confers upon believers. What the Spirit communicates is not new information but "the power necessary to appreciate the spiritual light that radiates from

---

138. Jonathan Edwards, Misc. No. 410, in "Miscellanies," in *Works of Jonathan Edwards* 13 (New Haven, CT: Yale University Press, 1994), 470–71.

139. Jonathan Edwards, *Religious Affections*, *Works of Jonathan Edwards* 2 (New Haven, CT: Yale University Press, 1959), 280.

140. Jonathan Edwards, *The Miscellanies:a–500*, *Works of Jonathan Edwards* 13 (New Haven, CT: Yale University Press, 1993), 470.

141. Edwards, *Religious Affections*, 278.

142. The text of this sermon is Peter's confession that Jesus is the Christ (Matt 16:16), which occurred just prior to the transfiguration.

God" (and his word).[143] It is an affective power that enables its recipients to sense and appreciate—to *taste*, as it were—the text's theological subject matter. Here is how Edwards described the spiritually illuminated interpreter: "He doesn't merely rationally believe that God is glorious, but he has a sense of the gloriousness of God in his heart."[144] In sum, reading the Bible with understanding requires more than philological competence. It requires "divine and supernatural light," the illumining ministry of the Holy Spirit in our minds and hearts—not new content but the ability to see and taste the divine beauty, as it were, of the literal sense itself. This "new sense of the heart"—which I am describing as a new interpretive sensibility—has been dubbed the most original idea in all of Edwards's theology.[145]

Edwards held that the content of Scripture, the things of the gospel of Jesus Christ, are indeed glorious, objectively so, yet he also believed that readers will not be able to see what is there before their eyes, in the letter of the text, without the Spirit's supernatural work. It is thanks to the illumination of the Spirit that readers, in contemplating the things of the gospel, gain "a clear view of their divine glory."[146] This is analogous to the disciples' experience of Jesus' transfiguration. In each case, the body of Jesus and the body of the text, the light that is there radiates outward, yet it can be seen only by those who have ascended the mountain, there to be illumined by the Spirit.[147] Only hearts enlightened by the Spirit can perceive the glories of God's written word: "The truth of all these [gospel] things revealed in the Scripture . . . appear to the soul, only by imparting that spiritual taste of divine beauty."[148]

To read in the economy of light, with a Christian frame of reference, is to say with Edwards (and with John the Evangelist), "we have seen his glory" (John 1:14). Those who receive the divine light of the Spirit "see divinity in the gospel . . . behold that unparalleled, ineffably excellent, and truly divine glory shining in it."[149] Readers who behold the glory of Christ in the letter of the text, like Peter, James, and John after they had seen the glory of the transfiguration, are more than simply interpreters. They are witnesses, under oath, like

---

143. Marsden, *Jonathan Edwards*, 157.

144. Edwards, "A Divine and Supernatural Light," in *Sermons and Discourses 1730–1733*, *Works of Jonathan Edwards* 17 (New Haven, CT: Yale University Press, 1999), 413.

145. See E. Smith, "Editor's Introduction" to *Works of Jonathan Edwards* 2:30. See further Ray S. Yeo, *Renewing Spiritual Perception with Jonathan Edwards: Contemporary Philosophy and the Theological Psychology of Transforming Grace* (New York: Routledge, 2016).

146. Edwards, *Religious Affections*, 298.

147. In the case of the transfiguration, Edwards said the disciples beheld Jesus' outward glory with their physical eyes, while the Spirit manifested Jesus' "spiritual" glory to their minds. Edwards, *Religious Affections*, 300. In the case of Scripture, we behold the letter with our natural minds but require the Spirit's illumination to see the light of Christ that radiates from them.

148. Edwards, *Religious Affections*, 302.

149. Edwards, *Religious Affections*, 306.

all witnesses, to bear true witness to what they have seen and heard (Acts 4:20; 2 Peter 1:18; 1 John 1:1)—and read. To read the Bible theologically is to be a communicant in the economy of light.

Eastern (Orthodox)

A "mere Christian" frame of reference for reading Scripture cannot ignore the Eastern church, for Eastern theologians have put the transfiguration front and center, doctrinally and liturgically. The Feast of the Transfiguration (August 6) is as important for the Orthodox as Christmas or Pentecost. The transfiguration resonates deeply with Orthodoxy's theological ethos, particularly its emphasis on *theosis* (divinization): "Linking the feast with the Cross, the Resurrection and the communion of saints the services [for the Feast of Transfiguration] link it also with the primeval light which shone at the creation and with the light of the new creation wherein all things are transformed."[150] According to Vladimir Lossky, the transfiguration is more than a footnote in the quest for the historical Jesus, for it deals with "the possibility of seeing God and the nature of this vision, and . . . the possibility of deification in the real and not the metaphorical sense of this word."[151] The transfiguration also informs Eastern iconography, a pictorial representation of the theological idea that God's glory shines through material things, including Jesus' face.[152] Our focus is less liturgical than hermeneutical, on the Bible as a *verbal* icon through which shines the light of Christ. Accordingly, we will look and listen East to two homilies for the Feast of Transfiguration.[153]

John of Damascus (655–750)

John of Damascus may have delivered his homily on the Feast of Transfiguration in a church on Mount Tabor itself, the traditional site of Jesus' transfiguration.[154] The homily combines doctrinal teaching with a pastoral plea to contemplate the mystery of Christ. The language is different, yet the sentiment is similar to Edwards's insistence that spiritual understanding involves the affections of the heart, not simply the cogitations of the mind.[155]

---

150. Ramsey, *Glory of God and Transfiguration of Christ*, 138. For a study that examines the transfiguration as an icon for the transformation of all things, see Paul M. Blowers, *Maximus the Confessor: Jesus Christ and the Transfiguration of the World* (Oxford: Oxford University Press, 2016).

151. Vladimir Lossky, *In the Image and Likeness of God* (New York: St. Vladimir's Seminary Press, 1974), 60.

152. See further Solrunn Nes, *The Uncreated Light: An Iconographical Study of the Transfiguration in the Eastern Church* (Grand Rapids: Eerdmans, 2007).

153. For a comprehensive collection of such homilies, see Daley, *Light on the Mountain*.

154. Daley, 203.

155. Interestingly, John anticipated Edwards's favored image of *experiencing* the sweetness of honey when he referred to the name of Jesus as "truly the sweetest . . . of names" (Daley, 206).

For John, the transfiguration stands at the intersection of theology proper (*theologia*) and the economy of salvation (*oikonomia*). Jesus told his disciples that those who see him have seen the Father (John 15:24), and the transfiguration demonstrates it: "'And his face shone like the sun'—for it was identified hypostatically with immaterial light."[156] The transfiguration is a manifestation of the divine nature Jesus had from the beginning: "Glory did not come upon this body from outside itself, but from within."[157] Yet again we see that the transfiguration involves not a change in Jesus' body, only a deeper insight into what was already there, beneath the surface: "The divine reality dominates, and shares some of its proper light and glory with the body."[158]

Jesus remains the same, yet appears different. The "whole fullness of deity dwells bodily" (Col 2:9) in Jesus before and after the transfiguration, but it became visible in a special way. Jesus was transfigured "before them" (Matt 17:2; Mark 9:2)—the disciples. As we have seen, this is the subjective aspect to the transfiguration, a *making visible to someone*. Only the disciples who ascended the mountain were able to see Christ in his glory. John Damascene exhorts his hearers, likewise, to climb "to the peak of virtue, which is love, and there let us become observers of his glory."[159] We have a convergence of East and West: both agree that Jesus himself is the source of uncreated light and on the necessity of having the spiritual sight to see it.

Gregory Palamas (1296–1357)

Gregory Palamas was one of the "hesychast" monks who sought to experience, through prayer and mystic contemplation, a beatific vision of the uncreated, divine light of the Godhead that the disciples experienced at Jesus' transfiguration. The practice elicited criticism from other Orthodox theologians, like Barlaam of Calabria, who argued that because God is unknowable in himself, humans cannot participate in God's light. In response, Gregory drew a distinction between the transcendent and unknowable *divine essence* and the immanent workings of the *divine energies*.[160] The distinction is similar but not identical to the Western distinction of God's being *ad intra* and his works *ad extra*: "The divine *essence* is God *in his being*, and the divine *energies* are God *in his actions*."[161] According to the Orthodox, however, God's actions are not, strictly speaking, *external* works, as if they took place at arm's length from God;

156. Cited in Daley, 211.
157. Daley, 207.
158. Daley, 222.
159. Daley, 222.
160. Gregory's (extended) responses to Barlaam are gathered in a collection known as *The Triads* (Mahwah, NJ: Paulist, 1983).
161. James R. Payton Jr., *Light from the Christian East: An Introduction to the Orthodox Tradition* (Downers Grove, IL: IVP Academic, 2007), 79 (emphasis original).

rather, they are God in his manifest activity (but not hidden essence).[162] The hesychast monks aim to participate, by mystical vision, in the divine energies of transfiguring light.[163]

Christians must make a spiritual ascent with "eyes transformed by the power of the Holy Spirit" before they can see the "light on the mountain."[164] The same goes for readers of Scripture, for like Jerome, Gregory identified the letter of the text with Jesus' lucent clothing. The biblical letters are glowing too, but only those "who see the things of the Spirit in their own spirit . . . can interpret the sayings of Scripture in a divine way."[165] They are able to read (i.e., "bleach") the text in ways that "no fuller [read: interpreter] on earth" can, said Gregory, citing 1 Cor 2:14 ("The natural person does not accept the things of the Spirit of God, for they are folly to him, and he is not able to understand them because they are spiritually discerned"). Those who see the light of Christ shining in the letter of the text begin to experience, and thus participate in, the kingdom of God in all its glory and transforming power.[166]

Summary of Historical Findings

We have surveyed only a small sampling of highlights from the history of exegesis, yet we have discovered considerable overlap between East and West, and between patristic, medieval, and Reformation interpretations. The church fathers agreed that the transfiguration was a theophany, a glimpse of the light God is in himself, mediated through Jesus' human flesh, "a manifestation by Jesus to the disciples of his own divine status."[167] They further agreed that the transfiguration was a preview of a future glory of Jesus, a glory, moreover, in which believers will eventually share: "The Fathers are generally more concerned with the historical events of past, present and future which are related to the Transfiguration than they are with allegorical meanings."[168] The Fathers also saw themselves in the disciples: to see the face of Christ, they, too, needed

162. Andrew Louth, himself an Orthodox theologian, thinks that "activity" is a better translation for *energiea* than "energy." Andrew Louth, *Introducing Eastern Orthodox Theology* (Downers Grove, IL: IVP Academic, 2013), 40.

163. This is one of the key differences between Western and Orthodox theology. See further Louth, *Introducing Eastern Orthodox Theology*; and Robert Letham, *Through Western Eyes. Eastern Orthodoxy: A Reformed Perspective* (Ross-shire, UK: Mentor, 2010). Gregory also underlined the necessity of the Spirit for spiritual understanding, insisting that it was the Holy Spirit who was "shining forth through the bright cloud." Gregory, "Homily 34," in Daley, *Light from the Mountain*, 357.

164. Daley, 364.

165. Gregory, "Homily 35," in Daley, *Light on the Mountain*, 371.

166. Daley comments that Gregory's two homilies are really "a single, carefully constructed treatise on divinization: the participation of graced and disciplined human followers in the brilliance that shines forth to a unique degree in the humanity of Jesus, but which is rooted in the transcendent, inconceivable being of God." Daley, *Light on the Mountain*, 353.

167. McGuckin, *Transfiguration of Christ*, 110.

168. Chamberas, "Transfiguration of Christ," 62.

to become readers who could make the ascent to perceive the spiritual referent of the literal sense: the light of Christ in the letter of the text.

As to medieval interpretation, evangelical theologians Bobby Jamieson and Tyler Wittman strike a distinctly Thomist chord when they invoke the beatific vision in their first principle of biblical exegesis: "Holy Scripture presupposes and fosters readers whose end is *the vision of Christ's glory*."[169] One therefore wonders whether Protestants should understand the "clarity" of Scripture as signifying not only perspicuity but also *luminosity*.

One significant finding in our survey is that Protestant commentators agree with their predecessors that the transfiguration was not a metamorphosis in the pagan sense (a change into something fundamentally *other*) but, rather, a revelation of who Jesus already was. Two seventeenth-century Puritan pastors highlighted this point. Alexander Wedderburn concluded his series of twenty-two sermons on the transfiguration by saying, "There was a *Real Glorious Change* without *overturning* the true properties of his Human Body."[170] Similarly, Thomas Manton, chaplain to Oliver Cromwell, said, "Only the outward form was changed, being more full of Glory and Majesty, than it used to be or appeared to be."[171] Calvin and Edwards made clear that readers need the Spirit's illumination if they are to read with a doxological frame of reference that enables them to see that the Scriptures are ultimately about the glory of the gospel of God (Mark 1:14; Rom 1:1).

With apologies to proverbial wisdom, East and West *do* sometimes meet, as they do on Mount Tabor. First, there is an impressive consensus among theologians across the centuries and confessional divides that Jesus' transfiguration did not substantially change his human nature. We need to appreciate the transfiguration "not as a negation of the Incarnation, but as its fulfillment."[172] As the transfiguration allowed the divine nature to appear through Jesus' flesh, so spiritual interpretation allows us to hear the divine voice in the human letter of the text.

Second, Christian writers from both East and West saw the Christian life, and the reading of Scripture, in terms of spiritual ascent, involving mortification, regeneration, and illumination.[173] It is for this reason that spiritual

---

169. R. B. Jamieson and Tyler R. Wittman, *Biblical Reasoning: Christological and Trinitarian Rules for Exegesis* (Grand Rapids: Baker Academic, 2022), 3 (emphasis added). Interestingly, the transfiguration is conspicuous by its absence in their otherwise excellent study.

170. Alexander Wedderburn (1620–78), *Heaven upon Earth, or, The History of the Transfiguration of Jesus Christ Opened, and Practically Improven* [*sic*] *in Several Sermons* (Edinburgh: John Reid, 1703), 77.

171. Thomas Manton (1620–77), *Christ's Temptation and Transfiguration: Practically Explained and Improved in Several Sermons* (London: 1685), 48.

172. Andreas Andreopoulos, *This is My Beloved Son: The Transfiguration of Christ* (Brewster, MA: Paraclete, 2012), 89.

173. The image of "ascent" was based on the ascent of Moses, the subject of the following chapter.

interpretation requires a different kind of reading culture, "a different way of seeing and hearing."[174] When the Spirit ministers the word so that right-minded and right-hearted readers read Scripture rightly, what changes is not the letter of the text but the reader's frame of reference. To read for the spiritual sense is thus to read along the grain of the biblical text, in canonical context, for the christological referent. To read with this mere Christian frame of reference is to step into the light, a Spirit-illumined place that enables readers to see the light of Christ that was always/already there, in the letter of the text: "In your light [word and Spirit] do we see light [Jesus Christ]" (Ps 36:9).

The third point follows from the previous two. The transfiguration is an event in the triune economy of light. Communicating divine light—God making God known—is the common work of Father, Son, and Spirit. Heinrich Bullinger described the inseparable operations of the triune God with reference to light: "It is but one fire, even though there are three things seen in it: light, brightness, and heat. . . . And though one thing is attributed to the light, another to the brightness, and a third to the heat; yet they work inseparably."[175]

Fourth, and finally: there is widespread agreement that Jesus' transfiguration relates to his future glorification. To repeat my main point: the change/alteration/metamorphosis that took place in Jesus' face and clothes was not a change from one kind of thing to another but, rather, *an increase in glory*. This is precisely why the transfiguration is a helpful lens for thinking about biblical interpretation. *To read transfigurally is to discern the glory of the letter.* However, before we travel further down this road, a brief detour into the Gospel of John may help establish a tighter connection between the light of Christ and the letter of the text.

Transfiguration Transposed: The Glory of Christ in the Fourth Gospel

Some readers may be asking, how can the transfiguration be so central for biblical interpretation if it is not even mentioned in John's gospel? In fact, I believe the fourth gospel corroborates my claim that the transfiguration provides a framework for understanding what it means to read the Bible literally and theologically. The claim is, at first blush, admittedly counterintuitive: there *is* no transfiguration narrative in John's gospel, which is ironic, for John is named as one of the three disciples with Jesus on the mountain. Still, I believe a closer

174. Andreopoulos, *This is My Beloved Son*, 109.

175. Sermon "Of the Holy Ghost," in *The Decades of Henry Bullinger*, trans. H. I. (Cambridge: Cambridge University Press, 1851): IV:7, 326. I owe this reference to Fred Sanders (personal correspondence, n.Id.).

examination will show how important the transfiguration was for John. We begin with George Caird's remark about there being no need for the fourth gospel to narrate the transfiguration, "for to John the whole ministry of Christ, and the Cross in particular, was the revelation of that glory."[176] Alfred Loisy agreed, noting that John has no place for the transfiguration because his entire gospel is "a perpetual theophany" that displays the light of Christ in all his acts and discourses.[177] Arthur Ramsey similarly said the transfiguration does not figure in the fourth gospel, "not because John did not know of it but because he understood its meaning so well."[178] Indeed, "John takes Jesus from the mountaintop and sets him in the valley where men live and here he sets up his tent."[179] Finally, Dorothy Lee, observing the frequency of light and glory symbolism, states that the *whole* of John's gospel can be viewed as a transfiguration narrative: "John did know something of the transfiguration and chose to use it, not as a single tale, but as a motif—a series of symbols—throughout his Gospel."[180] It is an intriguing view, and one I believe to be correct.

There is space only to survey the evidence. We will begin with the prologue, John's overture to all the theological themes to come. We will then examine the signs Jesus does. We will conclude by examining examples of characters in the fourth gospel who misunderstand either Jesus' own words or previous Scripture about him. In every case, this misunderstanding is a function of people failing to see the glory of Christ. Misinterpreting God's word, it turns out, stems from an inability or failure to read transfigurally, that is, with the transfiguration as one's frame of reference and discerning Christ's glory as one's aim.

Prologue: A Word of Light

An Alternative Transfiguration Account?

John 1:1–18 may not be a transfiguration narrative, but it is a near literary relative. Consider the common elements, most of which come to a head in the stunning thematic statement, "And the Word became flesh" (1:14).

"The true light . . . was coming into the world" (1:9). Like "The Word became flesh," this statement, too, refers to the incarnation. It provides the deep background for the transfiguration, the moment where Jesus' flesh reveals its true colors as white light, the Word that was God (1:1).

"And dwelt among us" (1:14). The Greek verb translated "dwelt" could also be rendered "tented" (Gk. *skene*) and thus recalls Peter's mention of three tents.

---

176. George Caird, "The Transfiguration," *Expository Times* 67, no. 10 (1956): 294.

177. Alfred Loisy, *Le Quatrième Evangile* (Paris: Alphonse Picard et Fils, 1903), 104–5.

178. Ramsey, *Glory of God and the Transfiguration of Christ*, 124.

179. Vernon H. Kooy, "The Transfiguration Motif in the Gospel of John," in *Saved by Hope: Essays in Honor of Richard C. Oudersluys*, ed. James I. Cook (Grand Rapids: Eerdmans, 1978), 67.

180. Lee, *Transfiguration*, 101.

"We have seen his glory" (1:14). The "we" recalls the three disciples on the mountain, though it no doubt has a broader reference as well. F. F. Bruce viewed this phrase as indicating John's purpose to make his whole gospel a commentary on the transfiguration. "'We beheld his glory,' says John, and endeavors to make his readers enter into the experience which was granted to the three on the mount."[181]

"For the law was given through Moses" (1:17). Moses was with Jesus on the mountain, representing the Law. Although the prologue does not mention Elijah, it does name John the Baptist, who some identified with Elijah, whom many expected to precede the Messiah's coming (Mark 9:11; John 1:21).

Précis of the Economy of Light

Light is one of the most important and frequent symbols throughout John's gospel. I suggested earlier that "Let there be light" (Gen 1:3) refers to the divine establishment of the economy of light. That John's prologue serves as a commentary on Genesis 1 is well known. Here we may recall the connection of light with coming to know the truth. Jesus is the light because he "mediates to man that knowledge of God which is eternal life."[182] One way of construing the story of the Bible is to see it as "drama of the true light coming into the world,"[183] a world that had fallen into darkness of sin. To be sure, the divine light shone before Jesus' incarnation. Yahweh led Israel through the wilderness thanks to a pillar of fire (Exod 13:21), and the psalmist declared, "Your word is a lamp to my feet and a light to my path" (Ps 119:105). However, the climax of salvation history is the sending of the Son, and Jesus is well aware of his mission: "I have come into the world as light, so that whoever believes in me may not remain in darkness" (John 12:46). As a matter of interest, it was the German Protestant theologian Franz Overbeck who first used the phrase "economy of light," and he did so in connection with his work on the Gospel of John.[184]

"I Am the Light of the World"

The transfiguration motif features prominently in each of the two parts of John's gospel: the "Book of Signs" (chs. 2–11) and the "Book of the Passion" (chs. 12–21), where "glory" and "glorify" also feature prominently.[185] Indeed, Jesus'

181. F. F. Bruce, "The Transfiguration," *Inter-Varsity* (Summer Term 1961): 21.

182. C. H. Dodd, *The Interpretation of the Fourth Gospel* (Cambridge: Cambridge University Press, 1953), 204.

183. Ike Miller, *Seeing by the Light: Illumination in Augustine's and Barth's Readings of John* (Downers Grove, IL: IVP Academic, 2020), 153.

184. Franz Overbeck, *Das Johannesevangelium: Studien zur Kritik seiner Erforschung* (Tübingen: J. C. B. Mohr, 1911), 416–17. Cited in Karl Barth, *Witness to the Word; A Commentary on John* (Eugene, OR: Wipf & Stock, 1986), 14.

185. Dodd, *Interpretation of the Fourth Gospel*, 289.

glorification is the point of the entire gospel (8:54; 12:23, 28; 16:14; 17:1–5; 21:19). Richard Bauckham defines God's glory as "the radiance of his character, of his goodness, of who he truly is."[186] Glorification is thus the external communication, publication, or making known of the divine perfections—a radiant display of the light that God is.

The Signs Jesus Does

According to George Ladd, "John differs from the Synoptics in making the entire ministry of Jesus a manifestation of glory."[187] John's gospel arranges what Jesus says and does in a series of seven narratives, each with an accompanying discourse in which Jesus' words explain his deeds: "The truths enunciated in the discourses are given dramatic expression in the actions described."[188] Both deeds and discourses are luminous, communicating the life and light that is in the Word (1:4). John describes Jesus' works as "signs" (*semeia*), actions that symbolize the reality that Jesus goes on to explain in his accompanying discourse. For example, Jesus' healing a man born blind (John 9) follows his "I am the light of the world" discourse (John 8): the act is a symbolic object lesson that illustrates Jesus' teaching that he gives light, visual (sight) and spiritual (truth).

All seven signs, like the transfiguration, reveal Jesus' glorious identity as the heaven-sent Christ.[189] John makes this explicit early on in his gospel when he rounds out his account of Jesus' changing of water into wine by saying, "This, the first of his signs, Jesus did at Cana in Galilee, and manifested his glory" (2:11). We find a similar formula in connection with the last of the seven signs, the raising of Lazarus from the dead. When Jesus hears of Lazarus's illness, he says, "This illness does not lead to death. It is for the glory of God, so that the Son of God may be glorified through it" (11:4). Everything Jesus does in the fourth gospel signifies who he truly is, leading one scholar to comment: "Jesus' miracles are a continuous transfiguration—a continuous manifestation of glory—to those who could read their deep and profound significance."[190]

The Sign Jesus Suffers

John is adamant that the Word reveals his glory *in the flesh*. It is in the flesh that the Light tabernacles or "tents" (*eskēnō*) among us (1:14). It is in the flesh,

186. Richard Bauckham, *Gospel of Glory: Major Themes in Johannine Theology* (Grand Rapids: Baker Academic, 2015), 50.

187. George Ladd, *A Theology of the New Testament* (Grand Rapids; Eerdmans, 1993), 312.

188. Dodd, *Interpretation of the Fourth Gospel*, 384.

189. See further Lee, *Transfiguration*, 104–10.

190. Peter Riga, "Signs of Glory: The Use of '*Semeion*' in St. John's Gospel," *Interpretation* 17, no. 4 (1963): 416.

John says, that "we beheld his glory."[191] This is particularly true of Jesus' passion. Recall that in the Synoptic versions, the transfiguration serves as a hinge connecting Peter's confession and Jesus' prediction of his suffering and death. The transfiguration confirms that Jesus is the Christ and anticipates the cross, for we know from Luke that the topic of Jesus' conversation with Moses and Elijah was the "exodus" he was to make at Jerusalem (Luke 9:31).

Throughout his gospel, John establishes a connection between Jesus' death (humiliation) and glorification (exaltation), often with the term "lifted up" (Gk. *hupsoō*; see 3:14; 8:28; 12:32). Jesus speaks of the "hour" for which he has come to fulfill his mission, and "to be glorified" (12:23). Jesus then prays for the Father to glorify his name. This is when he hears a voice from heaven, which also figures in the transfiguration. Here, however, the voice says, "I have glorified it [the Father's name], and I will glorify it again" (12:28). Jesus cryptically mentions being "lifted up from the earth," but John now provides a terse explanation: "He said this to show by what kind of death he was going to die" (12:33). John also makes explicit what was only implicit in the Synoptics, namely, that the hour of Jesus' crucifixion is also the hour of his glorification.[192]

Jesus' death does not put out his light but, paradoxically, lets it shine even brighter: being "lifted up" on the cross is, literally and figuratively, an exaltation from the earth. Jesus' obedience to the point of death, his voluntary self-sacrifice, is glorious in its expression of the depth, breadth, and height of God's love for the world. Dodd expressed this eloquently: "No higher exaltation, and no brighter glory, is to be conceived than that which Christ attained in his self-oblation, since it is the absolute expression of the divine *agape*."[193] His passion, even more than his action, manifests the glorious power of God for our salvation.[194]

In John's hands, then, the transfiguration is not simply another event in Jesus' life but, rather, the key to understanding his whole story, a revelation of who he is and what he came to do. This may be why John "distributes" the transfiguration throughout his narrative, letting the radiance of Christ shine forth from beginning to end, in his deeds, discourses, death, and resurrection. John's gospel has a transfigural purpose: to tell the story in such a way as to inculcate saving faith in Jesus as the life and light of men, the glory of God

191. See Luke Irwin, "Jesus' Body and Divine Glory in John's Gospel," *Presbyterian* 47, no. 2 (2021): 69–72.

192. There are also multiple references to Jesus glorifying or being glorified by the Father in the Farewell Discourses of John 13–17. See also Jörg Frey, *The Glory of the Crucified One: Christology and Theology in the Gospel of John* (Waco, TX: Baylor University Press, 2019).

193. Dodd, *Interpretation of the Fourth Gospel*, 441.

194. Dodd commented, citing John 12:23–28; 13:31; and 17:5, "If there is any one moment of 'transfiguration' [in the fourth gospel], it is that in which [Jesus] dedicates Himself to death." *Interpretation of the Fourth Gospel*, 207n2.

in human form. Jesus' trial before the high priests and Roman authorities figures prominently in the fourth gospel (18:19–38), but in a real sense it is John's readers who are on trial.[195] Will we, contemporary readers, understand, and follow, the signs so that we too can confess, with John, "We beheld his glory"?[196]

On the Importance of Not Misunderstanding Signs

In his commentary on the fourth gospel, Raymond Brown discussed several notable characteristics of John's style. Two of these are of special interest: misunderstanding and explanatory notes.[197]

The first, misunderstanding, has received considerable attention.[198] John frequently depicts Jews and disciples alike as misinterpreting the signs, unable to penetrate beneath the surface meaning. R. Alan Culpepper's study of the fourth gospel's literary design has a chapter titled "Commentary," in which he treats misunderstanding as a rhetorical device the Evangelist uses to teach readers how to read his gospel.[199] These misunderstandings typically involve a character giving an overly literal interpretation of either Jesus' acts or Jesus' words. Behind each failure lies an anemic eschatological frame of reference. As Culpepper points out, the benefit of such misunderstandings is that they give Jesus (and the author) a further opportunity to explain the meaning of Jesus' words. For example, when Jesus tells Nicodemus that one cannot see the kingdom of God unless one is born again, Nicodemus wonders how a man can enter into his mother's womb a second time, a literalistic misunderstanding that provides the occasion for Jesus to draw an important distinction between being born of the flesh and being born of the Spirit (John 3:4–8). By the end of the episode, it becomes clear that Nicodemus is captive to an overly material (i.e., immanent) frame of reference.[200]

These misunderstandings are the backdrop for a second literary device: the authorial aside. Brown noted that there are some fifty instances of John

---

195. See Andrew Lincoln, *Truth on Trial: The Lawsuit Motif in the Fourth Gospel* (Peabody, MA: Hendrickson, 2000).

196. Riga commented that "the *semeia* are judicial, prophetical, messianic, and eschatological." "Signs of Glory," 403.

197. Raymond E. Brown, *The Gospel according to John I–XII* (Garden City, NY: Doubleday, 1966), cxxxv–cxxxvi.

198. See especially D. A. Carson's aptly named "Understanding Misunderstanding in the Fourth Gospel," *Tyndale Bulletin* 33 (1982): 59–91, which identifies sixty-four instances of misunderstanding in John and offers a thorough review of scholarship up to 1980.

199. See R. Alan Culpepper, *Anatomy of the Fourth Gospel: A Study in Literary Design* (Philadelphia: Fortress, 1983), 152–64. The summary chart (161–62) of the eighteen misunderstandings in John that are the subject of his book is particularly helpful.

200. See further Martin de Jonge, "Nicodemus and Jesus: Some Observation on Misunderstanding and Understanding in the Fourth Gospel," *Bulletin of the John Rylands Library* 53 (1970/71): 337–59.

adding a parenthetical note that either provides further explanations of names (1:41) and symbols (12:33) or corrects possible misunderstandings (e.g., after Jesus said, "Destroy this temple, and in three days I will raise it up," John 2:21 adds, "But he was speaking about the temple of his body"). These authorial asides are explicit statements of authorial intent, and John's gospel makes it clear that to mistake a speaker's or author's intent is to misunderstand what is said. Reading "from below," with immanent frames of reference only (including the grammatical-historical), fall short of the understanding the Evangelist seeks: "True understanding is a matter of grace, a gift to be granted by God himself, an inward change under the impulse of the Spirit."[201]

What exactly did Jesus' listeners miss, and how can contemporary readers of Scripture avoid making similar interpretive missteps? The most serious misunderstandings consistently concern Jesus' identity and mission.[202] It is significant that Nicodemus came to Jesus "by night" (John 3:2), a broad hint that, epistemically and spiritually speaking, he was in the dark: "Nicodemus's non-perception is a product of his failure to understand even the revelation of the Old Testament."[203] Other misunderstandings are a function of the characters' place in salvation history, before the resurrection: "His disciples did not understand these things at first, but when Jesus was glorified, then they remembered that that these things had been written about him" (John 12:16).[204] Presumably, then, those who interpret on the hither side of the resurrection are in a better position to understand Jesus and his mission. Well, not quite, for as Carson notes, other factors are also necessary: "the work of the Spirit, the place of faith, the need for elective grace or an explanatory word."[205]

If Culpepper is right about the purpose of the misunderstanding passages and explanatory asides—"to teach readers how to read the gospel"[206]—then what lesson(s) should we take away? First, we learn that the signs Jesus did are indicative of his glory. "The miracles are a continuous transfiguration—a continuous manifestation of glory—to those who could read their deep and profound significance."[207] Second, we learn that correct reading discerns the spiritual meaning through the letter. Most of Jesus' Jewish observers saw only the "letter" of the sign, its physical happening; they did not attain the spiritual understanding needed to discern God's glorious presence and activity. Third,

201. De Jonge, "Nicodemus and Jesus," 359.

202. William T. Pyle, "Understanding the Misunderstanding Sequences in the Gospel of John," *Faith and Mission* 11, no. 2 (1994): 33.

203. Riga, "Signs of Glory," 408.

204. Carson, "Understanding Misunderstandings," 79–81.

205. Carson, 84.

206. Culpepper, *Anatomy of the Fourth Gospel*, 165.

207. Riga, "Signs of Glory," 416.

we learn that the deeper, spiritual meaning John wants us to see results not from allegory but from reading *transfigurally*, that is, with an eschatological-doxological frame of reference that brings into focus the brilliant light (i.e., glory) of Christ. After all, the Son is not an "allegory" of the Father but, rather, "the radiance of the glory of God and the exact imprint of his nature" (Heb 1:3), the visible form of divine content.

To follow the way the words run in the fourth gospel and the direction to which the signs point, readers need faith—a Christian frame of reference that corresponds to the eschatological subject matter of the gospel: "While Jesus' glory was there to see in his works and words, it was visible only to those who had eyes of faith."[208] Conversely, we misunderstand the words and deeds of Jesus, and the Scriptures in general, when we read them literalistically, thereby failing to see them in all their glory.

The Transfiguration as Interpretive Framework: Five Theses

We began this chapter asking about the meaning of transfiguration and its significance for biblical interpretation. We then examined the Synoptic accounts of the transfiguration and their interpretation in East and West down through the centuries. Finally, we argued that the fourth gospel is an extended transfiguration narrative that uses its characters' misunderstandings to advance the cause of right understanding. Here we draw the threads of our argument together in five summary theses. The next chapter applies these theses to a worked example: a literal and theological reading of Moses' ascent of Mount Sinai toward his own "transfiguration" (Exod 33–34).

1. *The transfiguration has hermeneutical significance, helping us understand not only the identity of Jesus but also what it means to read the Bible literally and theologically.*

The transfiguration is first and foremost a startling confirmation of Peter's confession that Jesus is the Christ (Matt 16:16). It is epiphany and apocalypse, a revelation of who Jesus always/already is and a vision of the future glory into which he enters after his passion. The transfiguration is an "aha" moment, a decisive clue to understanding Jesus' person and work. It is more than just an

208. Kooy, "Transfiguration Motif in the Gospel of John," 66. Riga saw a parallel between the *semeia* Jesus does in the fourth gospel and the parables Jesus told in the Synoptics ("Signs of Glory," 407). Both are susceptible to misunderstanding; both require an eschatological frame of reference in order to discern the coming kingdom of God to which they point.

episode in Jesus' life. In looking back to the Law and the Prophets, and forward to Jesus' exaltation, the transfiguration is an interpretive crux of the gospel narratives. If Scripture maps the way to heaven, then the transfiguration is "part of the map legend, the apparatus we need to read the map correctly."[209] In particular, the transfiguration provides not only a clear example of how to discern the theological in the historical, but a sufficient warrant for doing so. As such, it is an anchoring event that calls for grammatical-eschatological exegesis, the project of reading to discern the light of Christ in the letter of the text. "The transfiguration is the revelation to the apostles, and in them to the whole church and all of humanity, of the final truth and reality of all things. . . . The light that shines on the apostles on the mountain of transfiguration is the light that shines in the darkness when God created the world . . . the light that will shine from the new Jerusalem."[210]

The presence of Moses and Elijah on the mountaintop means that Christians need to read Old Testament and New Testament together, a point of considerable hermeneutical significance. Thanks to their conversation with Jesus, we understand that Israel's exodus from Egypt is a figure or type of the more glorious exodus Jesus makes at Jerusalem (Luke 9:31). "When the prophetic content of the transfiguration is fulfilled, it then becomes the authoritative commentary that illuminates and enhances the meaning of the salvific events it prefigured."[211] Moreover, John's way of narrating his gospel is transfigural from the start, teaching us to read the story of Jesus in its broader canonical context as the story of light overcoming the darkness. To read transfigurally with John is to employ an interpretive framework alert for signs of divine glory in the least expected places: the letter of the Old Testament text and the cross of Christ.

2. *The transfiguration suggests an analogy* (analogia corporis) *between the human body of Christ and the letter of the biblical text, a correspondence grounded in their both being divine accommodations of the one living and active Word of God.*

Jesus is truly human. So are the Scriptures. Yet there is more to Jesus' body, and to the literal meaning of the biblical text, than their humanity. Beneath the human surface—in the one case, skeleton and skin; in the other, written letters—lies something divine, rendering both Jesus' face and the literal sense

209. Andreopoulos, *This is My Beloved Son*, 17.

210. Douglas Harink, *1 & 2 Peter*, Brazos Theological Commentary on the Bible (Grand Rapids: Brazos, 2007), 156.

211. Weinandy, *Jesus Becoming Jesus*, 238.

of Scripture conduits of light.[212] *Jesus' physical body is to his glorification what the written letter is to its spiritual sense.* This is the heart of the transfigural analogy: "His physicality . . . becomes the icon of his celestiality. . . . His body does not dissolve or become unreal . . . his humanity remains tangible, even while another identity illuminates it."[213] The transfiguration depicts Jesus' human body as a medium of divine light. The transfigural analogy teaches readers to approach the Bible ready to hear the voice of God shining in the bright canonical fabric that clothes and presents Christ.

3. *Transfigural interpretation does not change but, rather, glorifies the literal meaning.*

As many commentators have rightly noted, the transfiguration does not change Jesus into something he was not but, rather, lets the disciples see what was there all along under the veil of his humanity. Recall Jerome's formulation: "When the splendor of the face is shown, and the brilliance of the clothing described, it is not that the substance is removed, but the glory is changed. . . . The transformation added splendor; it did not make his face disappear."[214] The disciples see, in anticipatory fashion, the glory of God in Christ. Paul in Philippians 3:21 speaks of Jesus' "glorious body" though, in context, he is referring to the risen Christ. The transfiguration anticipates this, and more: who Jesus already is as well as his exaltation yet to come—resurrection, yes, but also ascension, heavenly session, and parousia.

Prior to the transfiguration, Jesus predicted that some with him would not taste death before they saw the kingdom of God. The transfiguration was this taste—and sight. The disciples saw the eschatological *is*, the already/not-yet reign of Christ. "To behold the luminous transfigured humanity of Jesus is simultaneously to behold the true living and glorious Passover/covenantal lamb of sacrifice."[215] Of course, the disciples needed a biblically informed, typological imagination to see *this* as *that*, which is precisely what we get from the other sense of "trans-figural" (the christological trajectory of figures across the canon) that was the focus of part 2.

212. It would be a mistake to conflate my transfigural analogy with a full-blown incarnational analogy between Christ and Scripture. I critique the latter in my "Triune Discourse: Theological Reflections on the Claim That God Speaks," in *Trinitarian Theology for the Church: Scripture, Community, Worship*, ed. David Lauber and Daniel Treier (Downers Grove, IL: InterVarsity, 2009), 35–41. In brief, there is nothing in Scripture that corresponds to the "one person in two natures" formula of Chalcedon. The focus of my transfigural analogy is on the way in which Christ's body and the Bible's literal sense serve to make Christ's glory known.

213. Lee, *Transfiguration*, 133.

214. Jerome, *Commentarium in Matthaeum*, 147.

215. Weinandy, *Jesus Becoming Jesus*, 234.

To read transfigurally glorifies or "magnifies" literal meaning in both senses of the term: it makes brighter and extols the letter, intensifying its clarity and enlarging its esteem. To magnify literal meaning is to see that the aim of transfigural reading is not *sensus plenior* but *sensus splendidior*, namely, the "how much more" glorious referent of the letter that is the light of Christ. It is a form of grammatical exegesis with eschatological expectations, photosensitive to the light of Christ breaking through the surface—of his literal skin and the skin of the textual letter. Transfigural reading discerns the splendor of the literal sense.[216]

4. *Transfigural interpretation is a distinctly Christian approach to reading and therefore belongs to special rather than general hermeneutics.*

As its name is, so is its nature: transfigural interpretation derives from the transfiguration of Jesus, a central episode in God's self-communication in the economy of light. It is a way of reading that attends to the light that Christ *is* (the Word who was with God, is God, and reveals God the Father) and the light that Christ *gives* (the Son's knowledge of God the Father). Whereas allegorical interpretation attempts an intellectual ascent, locating meaning and truth in some higher system of ideas (e.g., Platonism), transfigural interpretation locates meaning and truth in the history of Christ, which is why it refuses to do away with the letter. Transfigural interpretation discerns the letter's spiritual sense, which is not some allegorical *other* sense (Gk. *allos*) but a distinctly christological sense. Hence my thesis: mere Christian hermeneutics reads for the spiritual sense, best understood as the *glory* of the letter. This explains the otherwise enigmatic claim that "the transfiguration narrative presents us with a text whose literal meaning *is* its spiritual sense."[217]

5. *Transfigural interpretation is from faith to faith, requiring readers to have the "eyes of their hearts" enlightened by the Spirit (Eph 1:18).*

Transfigural interpretation involves a different way of seeing, hearing, and reading than that afforded by earthly frames of reference. Many of these remain helpful, even necessary, for the Bible's words are as fully human as is Jesus' body, and transfiguring interpretation leaves neither behind. Nevertheless, to read the Bible transfigurally is to be attuned to the eschatological realities that unify the

216. J. Gresham Machen agreed: "The writers of the Bible . . . did not know the full meaning of what they wrote, but they did know part of the meaning, and the full meaning was in no contradiction with the partial meaning but was its glorious unfolding." "Do We Believe in Verbal Inspiration?," in *The Christian Faith in the Modern World* (1936; repr., Grand Rapids: Eerdmans, 1947), 55.

217. Black, "Transfigured Exegesis," 255.

histories of Israel and Jesus and help us grasp what the Bible is really about: the glory of God in Christ. Hence to read transfigurally is to read with a doxological aim and interest: to *magnify* the literal sense and name of its divine author (1 Chr 17:24; Ps 34:3). This works a variation on Augustine's rule for reading: to choose the interpretation that best fosters love of God and neighbor.[218] The doxological rule that is part and parcel of the transfigural framework of interpretation is similar: *Choose the reading that most glorifies God and that most promotes the light of Christ in the life of the reader.*[219] This is also the aim of John's gospel, to tell Jesus' story in a way that glorifies Christ and elicits faith: light from light for light.

Transfigural interpretation is ultimately a spiritual exercise—an aspect of the obedience of faith and the eagerness of hope. Like the three disciples who accompanied Jesus to Mount Tabor, biblical interpreters need to climb to reach the mountaintop, not least by praying for the Spirit's illumination. Those who make the ascent will find the atmosphere charged with expectation, the light bedazzling, and the view astonishing.

218. Augustine, *On Christian Doctrine* 1.86.
219. I discuss the transfiguration of the reader in chapter 9.

CHAPTER 8

Transfiguring the Literal

Light Refracted

And perhaps the garments of the Word are the discourses of the Scriptures, dressing, so to speak, the divine thought: for just as he appeared to Peter, John and James in another aspect, and his garment shone with whiteness, in the same way, in the eyes of your mind, the meaning of the divine Scriptures is already being clarified.

—Ambrose, *Commentary on Luke* (9:28–36)

It is one thing to interpret the accounts of Jesus' transfiguration, quite another to use them as a lens through which to read the rest of Scripture. In chapter 7, I claimed the transfiguration has hermeneutical significance because it analogically depicts what it means to read the Bible literally and theologically. I now need to say more about the hermeneutical help it offers. May readers adopt a "take it or leave it" attitude as concerns the transfiguration? Should readers consciously employ the transfigural analogy to read the Bible well? Or must readers interpret transfigurally to comply with an implicit demand of the biblical text itself?[1] In brief, am I claiming that readers *may, should,* or *must* read the Bible transfigurally?[2]

The purpose of this chapter is to respond to this query, not least by appealing to two more apostolic witnesses: Peter and Paul. In particular, Paul's interpretation in 2 Corinthians 3 of the story of Moses' own transfiguration (Exod 34) provides an instructive case in point in both Pauline and mere

1. Attentive readers may have noted that I use *trans-figural* when I'm referring to connecting figures to what is figured, and *transfigural* when I'm thinking explicitly about the hermeneutical implications of Jesus' transfiguration. Obviously, Jesus is central to both uses, though the former stresses the letter of the text, while the latter evokes the light of Christ.

2. I am grateful to Dan Treier for phrasing the question in these three terms.

Christian hermeneutics. First, it forms part of Paul's gloss on "the letter kills, but the Spirit gives life" (2 Cor 3:6), a text at the epicenter of discussions concerning the relative merits of literal versus spiritual interpretation, and one that New Testament scholar Margaret Mitchell describes as "the Magna Carta of allegorical interpretation."[3] Second, it invites a comparison between the theophany to Moses on Mount Sinai (Gregory of Nyssa's "mountain of the knowledge of God"[4]) and the transfiguration of Jesus on Mount Tabor.[5] As Dale Allison comments, "Jesus' transfiguration moves thoughts both backward and forward in time: it is a replay of Sinai and a foretaste of things to come . . . the mount of transfiguration was, for the evangelists, including Matthew, a second Sinai, where a miracle of old was repeated."[6]

Third, it speaks of light and glory, their relation to the letter and to Christ. Finally, Paul's interpretation of Exodus 33–34 obliges us to specify how Christian interpretations of the Old Testament are christological: are they christocentric, christotelic, christoscopic, or something else? At issue is whether Old Testament authors *intend* to refer to Christ. If not, then must Christian readers import christological presuppositions from elsewhere and read them back onto Old Testament texts, or is there an alternative that avoids what we might call the "nuclear option" of hermeneutics (i.e., eisegesis)? This was the central dilemma of early Christian biblical exegesis: "how to hold together the new revelation of God in Christ with the antecedent revelation of God in Jewish Scripture."[7] As David Dockery and Malcolm Yarnell acknowledge, "It remains difficult to point to one single image, pattern, motif, or theme which can adequately express the apostles' interpretative approach to the Old Testament other than to stress that they grounded their exegesis in . . . Christology."[8] Is it really possible to read the Old Testament *literally* for the light of Christ and, if so, what would this reading look like? The answer is yes, because Jesus' transfiguration is that image and event that encapsulates, grounds, and justifies the apostles' transfigural reading of the Old Testament.

Like physical light, the knowledge of God that shines forth in the economy of light does not always move in a straight line. When physical light travels from

3. Margaret M. Mitchell, *Paul, the Corinthians and the Birth of Christian Hermeneutics* (Cambridge: Cambridge University Press, 2010), 70.

4. See Gregory of Nyssa, *The Life of Moses*, trans. Abraham J. Malherbe and Everett Ferguson, Classics of Western Spirituality (New York: Paulist, 1978), 152.

5. "Relating the Sinai theophany and the transfiguration on Tabor was crucially important for early Christian theology." Bogdan G. Bucur, "Sinai, Zion, and Tabor: An Entry into the Christian Bible," *Journal of Theological Interpretation* 4, no. 1 (2010): 33.

6. Dale C. Allison, *The New Moses: A Matthean Typology* (Minneapolis: Fortress, 1993), 246–47.

7. T. J. Lang, "The Order of Christian Theology: Literal and Ecclesial Senses of the New Testament," *Journal of Theological Interpretation* 14, no. 1 (2020): 120.

8. David S. Dockery and Malcolm B. Yarnell III, *Special Revelation and Scripture* (Brentwood, TN: B&H Academic, 2024), 370.

one medium to another (e.g., from air to water), it changes direction. This is why pencils appear to bend when put into a glass of water, or why a beam of white light splits into different colors after passing through a prism. The technical term in physics is "refraction." In the context of ophthalmology, refraction is the measurement of the eye's focusing characteristics, vital for prescribing the right kind of corrective lenses.[9] Calvin was no ophthalmologist, but he famously described the Scriptures as the "spectacles" or corrective lenses of faith that help readers to perceive what there is to be known of God.[10] The present chapter extends Calvin's image by asking what happens to the light of the Word of God as it passes from one medium to another: from "letter" to "spirit," from "old" to "new" testament/covenant, from the veil covering Moses' face to the veil covering reader's minds. Reading Paul reading Moses will allow us to summarize our proposal concerning the relations of exegesis and theology, New Testament to the Old Testament, and literal to spiritual interpretation. We will put to the exegetical test the five theses set forth in the previous chapter, the better to demonstrate that transfigural interpretation neither changes nor distorts but instead *magnifies* the literal sense, refracting the light of Christ "from one degree of glory to another" (2 Cor 3:18).[11]

"The Prophetic Word Made More Sure": Does Transfiguring Mean Reading Backward?

Cross-cultural tensions between modes of reading—precritical and critical, East and West, exegetical and theological—have loomed large throughout our study, as has the overarching tension between literal and spiritual interpretation. Modern biblical scholars are rightly protective of the literal sense, alert to the ever-present danger of reading one's own biases and beliefs back into the text (eisegesis), thereby forcing words to run in new directions determined no longer by the author but by the reader's interpretive community. I. Howard Marshall mentioned "our modern temptation as Christians" to read the Old Testament Scriptures "as if they had originally been written as a Christian book."[12] For their part, theologians have rightly shown concern for reading for the literal sense of the divine author, in canonical context. Transfigural interpretation

9. A lens is a piece of glass composed of two spherical surfaces, either concave or convex, that by refracting light can focus or magnify objects.

10. John Calvin, *Institutes of the Christian Religion*, 2 vols., ed John T. McNeill (Philadelphia: Westminster, 1960), I.6.1. John McNeil notes that this simile "is probably Calvin's decisive utterance on the role of Scripture as related to the revelation of the Creator in creation" (*Institutes* vol. 1, 70n1).

11. I am using "magnify" in the optic sense of focus and intensify, and in the biblical sense of extol or exalt (2 Sam 7:26; Ps 34:3; Luke 1:46), not in the sense of enlarge or exaggerate.

12. I. Howard Marshall, *1 Peter*, IVP New Testament Commentary (Downers Grove, IL: InterVarsity, 1991), 44.

attempts to honor both concerns by construing the literal sense as grammatical-eschatological (i.e., trans-figural).

Some exegetes may not yet be convinced. It may sound to them as if I am in favor of changing the original meaning, not just its significance, reading something into the text that was not previously there.[13] Is reading backward, from the New Testament to the Old Testament for the light of Christ, legitimate? Many biblical scholars find the practice objectionable on the grounds that it demotes or disregards the discrete witness of the Old Testament, effectively quenching the prophets' own voices. Is reading backward the best way forward for those who want to read the Bible theologically, according to what it really is, the word of God (1 Thess 2:13)?

"Written for Our Instruction": The Old Testament as the Church's Book

The apostle Peter seems to take for granted that the prophets—and indeed the whole Old Testament—were speaking of the future messiah, even if they did not explicitly name him Jesus Christ.[14] The prophets made a concerted effort to determine "what person or time the Spirit of Christ in them was indicating when he predicted the sufferings of Christ and the subsequent glories" (1 Pet 1:11). They knew the *sense* of their words, but not their *referent*. Their vision of how their words would become true in the future was blurry. What was "revealed" (*apekaluphthē*) to them was that "they were serving not themselves but you" (1 Pet 1:12)—not the original but later readers, including those to whom Peter was writing.

Calvin says the prophets "spread the table, that others might afterwards feed on the provisions laid on it."[15] The prophets could not see what is now plain for Christians to see, "a veil as it were being interposed," for it was not fitting,

---

13. The meaning/significance distinction derives from E. D. Hirsch's *Validity in Interpretation* (New Haven, CT: Yale University Press, 1967), a literary critical work that has proved influential among evangelical exegetes. "Meaning" for Hirsch, is fixed: it is what the author intended to communicate. "Significance," by way of contrast, is Hirsch's term for the changing relevance that same meaning has in other contexts. John Farrell works with a similar distinction, between unchanging meaning and changing "impact." John Farrell, *The Varieties of Authorial Intention: Literary Theory beyond the Intentional Fallacy* (London: Palgrave Macmillan, 2017), 56–59. See further my *Is There a Meaning in This Text? The Bible, the Reader, and the Morality of Literary Knowledge* (Grand Rapids: Zondervan, 1998), 259–62.

14. Some scholars (e.g., E. G. Selwyn) contend that Peter is referring to Christian prophets, contemporaries of the apostles. This view faces serious difficulties. See further J. N. D. Kelly, *A Commentary on the Epistles of Peter and Jude* (London: Adam and Charles Black, 1969), 59. Hence it is preferable to adopt the traditional view: these are Old Testament prophets, a rubric that probably encompasses the Law and Writings as well. J. Ramsey Michaels commented that "Christian prophets" and "Old Testament prophets" are not mutually exclusive categories, for there is a sense in which Old Testament prophets are Christian, too, inasmuch as they "bore testimony to Jesus Christ before the fact." *1 Peter*, Word Biblical Commentary vol. 49 (Waco, TX: Word, 1988), 43.

15. Calvin, *Commentary on the Catholic Epistles* (Edinburgh: Calvin Translation Society, 1855), 41.

while Christ was still absent, "that the full light should shine as at mid-day."[16] Nevertheless, that light of the gospel, transfiguration light, is "in accordance with the Scriptures" (1 Cor 15:3–4).

That the prophets' writings were for the benefit of Christian readers occurs frequently in Paul's epistles too.[17] For example, Paul writes: "For whatever was written in former days was written for our instruction, that through endurance and through the encouragement of the Scriptures we might have hope" (Rom 15:4). Similarly: "Now these things happened to them as an example, but they were written down for our instruction, on whom the end of the ages has come" (1 Cor 10:11). What Peter's epistle adds is "the explicit assertion that the prophets themselves knew by revelation that their prophecies were for a later time."[18] All these prophecies are for naught, however, if Brent Strawn's sober diagnosis is right, that the Old Testament is "dying" because contemporary Christians no longer know how to make sense of its language.[19] However, the real question, as we saw in part 2, concerns *frame(s) of reference* and the *grammar of reading*, not the Hebrew language. From Peter's Christian point of view, the Old Testament is not a time-bound book, with messages meant for its original readers only, but a text with a future orientation.[20] Some commentators acknowledge in the Old Testament a tacit "messianic pattern" of suffering followed by glorification that becomes legible only after the Messiah's appearance, suggesting a "retrospective messianic hermeneutic."[21] Others resist any kind of backward interpretive movement, objecting that it sneaks in Christian assumptions through the exegetical back door. John Goldingay expresses this concern in the title of one of his books, *Do We Need the New Testament? Letting the Old Testament Speak for Itself*, and by his exhortation in the last chapter, "Don't Be Christ-Centered."[22] In brief, don't read backward! Many biblical scholars agree. J. R. Daniel Kirk opines, "Being a Trinitarian is all well and good, but since not a single biblical author was Trinitarian, bringing such a lens with you will always obscure more than it illuminates when it comes to understanding what the author was striving to communicate."[23]

---

16. Calvin, 39.

17. See also Peter's similar claims in Acts 2:25–36; 3:18, 24.

18. Michaels, *1 Peter*, 46.

19. Brent A. Strawn, *The Old Testament Is Dying: A Diagnosis and Recommended Treatment* (Grand Rapids: Baker Academic, 2017).

20. Marshall, *1 Peter*, 48.

21. Douglas Harink, *1 & 2 Peter*, Brazos Theological Commentary of the Bible (Grand Rapids: Brazos, 2009), 50–52.

22. John Goldingay, *Do We Need the New Testament? Letting the Old Testament Speak for Itself* (Downers Grove, IL: InterVarsity, 2015).

23. J. R. Daniel Kirk, "Theological Interpretation and the Problem of Whiteness," Patheos, October 4, 2016, http://www.patheos.com/blogs/storiedtheology/2016/10/04/theological-interpretation-and-the-problem-of-whiteness/.

The concern with premature theological articulation is hardly new and is not limited to the Old Testament. Patristic theologians had to fend off charges that the doctrine of the Trinity "imports some strange . . . god" into the New Testament without any scriptural basis. Gregory of Nazianzus rebutted this charge in his *Fifth Theological Oration*, in which he scolded his accusers for their excessive "love for the letter."[24] Are Christian theologians doomed to reading backward, only to be accused of using rather than respecting the letter of the text? Here we may recall Machen's point that though the Old Testament authors did not know the full meaning of what they wrote, they knew part of it, and "the full meaning was in no contradiction with the partial meaning but was its glorious unfolding."[25] Transfigural interpretation *is* the glorious unfolding of the literal sense. What remains to be seen, however, is whether this glorious unfolding involves reading forward and/or backward.

"Do Not Enter: One Way Only": How (Not) to Read Christianly

Think of reading forward as moving progressively from Genesis to Revelation. Conversely, reading backward starts to make sense of the Old Testament from the end, thanks to the "answers" at the back of the book (i.e., the New Testament).[26]

Reading Forward

There is more than one way of reading forward, for the simple reason that not all historical frames of reference are created equal. What they share is a desire to make sense of what the original authors were trying to communicate to their original readers in their original context.

1a. "Hard" Forward ("Jewish")

Call the most extreme examples of this approach "hard forward," in deference to their strict insistence that the only relevant frame of reference is the original historical context. There were forward-looking messianic expectations in Second Temple Judaism and latter Rabbinic Judaism, but also resolute denials that Jesus of Nazareth was the long-awaited Messiah. The operative frame of reference in these cases was the broader faith tradition of Judaism.[27] Even

24. Gregory of Nazianzus, *Fifth Theological Oration: On the Holy Spirit*, in *On God and Christ* (Crestwood, NY: St. Vladimir's University Press, 2002), 31.

25. Machen, "Do We Believe in Verbal Inspiration?," 55.

26. The editors employ the language of "backward" and "forward" in their introduction to *Five Views of Christ in the Old Testament*, ed. Brian J. Tabb and Andrew M. King (Grand Rapids: Zondervan, 2022), 15.

27. See further Jon D. Levenson, *The Hebrew Bible, the Old Testament, and Historical Criticism* (Louisville: Westminster John Knox, 1993), esp. ch. 4, "Theological Consensus or Historicist Evasion? Jews and Christians in Biblical Studies."

though midrashic literature "searched and inquired carefully" after their own fashion, the rabbis never came to the conclusion that Jesus was the Messiah, or that "gospel" replaced the authority of the Torah.[28] This refusal to confess Jesus as the Christ led to the church fathers' and Reformers' pejorative descriptions of Jewish readings as letter-bound.

1b. "Hard" Forward ("Critical")

Modern biblical criticism is arguably more letter-centered than Judaism. Enlightenment historical critics assume that right reading means reading forward, taking into account only what the original author and audience could have known at the time of composition. By bracketing out faith-based presuppositions, modern historical criticism probably represents the purest form of reading forward, in the sense of proceeding strictly according to chronology.

2. "Soft" Forward ("Christian")

Christians, too, read forward, believing it the best way to respect the literal sense, understood as the communicative intent of the human author, and to do justice to the progressive nature of the history of redemption. According to Mark Noll, evangelicals in the late twentieth and early twenty-first centuries successfully negotiated the ugly ditch between faith and criticism with an integrated approach he calls "believing criticism."[29] The strategy, speaking broadly, involves using critical tools while holding to faith-based convictions—reading the Bible in a scholarly manner, with the additional conviction that it is inspired by God. Nigel Cameron wonders, however, whether "believing criticism" is a Trojan horse. Once methodological naturalism is let in the interpreter's house, it tends to take over, insisting that all interpretive decisions be made on historical rather than theological grounds. Although the great Cambridge biblical exegetes J. B. Lightfoot and B. F. Westcott used critical methods to defend conservative conclusions about dates, authorship, and historicity, the net result was to further the viability of the critical method.[30] A century later, the pattern may be repeating itself. A new generation of evangelical biblical scholars wants to be open in principle to revising traditional interpretations in light of historical criticism yet also maintain *"that historical criticism need not imperil any of the fundamental*

---

28. For a study of the history, types, and methods of Jewish midrash, see Michael Fishbane, ed., *The Midrashic Imagination: Jewish Exegesis, Thought, and History* (New York: SUNY Press, 1993) and Jacon Neusner, *The Mishnah: An Introduction* (Lanham, MD: Rowman & Littlefield, 1989).

29. Mark A. Noll, *Between Faith and Criticism: Evangelicals, Scholarship, and the Bible in America* (New York: Harper & Row, 1986), 158.

30. Nigel Cameron, "Inspiration and Criticism: The Nineteenth Century Crisis," *Tyndale Bulletin* 35 (1984): 129–59.

dogmatic tenets of Christianity."[31] The sentiment is laudable, but it is far from clear how to achieve this equilibrium or decide what counts as a fundamental dogmatic tenet. Consider, for example, how believing critics understand Israel's exodus from Egypt. Historical criticism urges them to view any mention of God as belonging to "faith," not history.[32] Thoroughgoing historical critics insist this rules out literal mighty acts of God, such as delivering Israel from Egypt, thus raising questions about the coherence of the "believing criticism" project. To be sure, there is nothing wrong with employing historical frames of reference. The problem comes only when "historical" is combined with an immanent frame of reference, which is often the price of admission into the critical discussion.

A second way Christians read forward is by contending that the Old Testament itself points ahead to Jesus Christ. Benjamin Sargent says the New Testament authors are not reading backward when they read christologically, because Scripture was written not only for but *to* later Christians: "Peter suggests to his readers that as they read the Scriptures of Israel, they are reading things which pertain directly to themselves . . . not because they speak to each generation in the same way [but] because Scripture is *for* them in an exclusive sense."[33]

The Old Testament, Sargent contends, is not typology but kerygma: "a proclamation of the suffering and glories of Christ, in advance, through the Prophets whose words had no meaning other than to refer to this future."[34] This is the "single eschatological reality" prophecy is ultimately about.[35] For Sargent, then, there is no place, or need, for typology, allegory, *sensus plenior*, or transfiguration. Rather, it suffices simply to clarify the single determinate meaning of the prophets, as Jesus does when, for example, in arguing with the religious authorities over the interpretation of David's statement "The Lord says to my Lord . . ." (Ps 110:1), he makes clear that David is speaking of no earthly king but of Jesus himself.[36] The single determinate meaning of prophetic discourse relates directly to Jesus Christ.

---

31. Christopher M. Hays, "Toward a Faithful Criticism," in *Evangelical Faith and the Challenge of Historical Criticism*, ed. Christopher B. Ansberry and Christopher M. Hays (Grand Rapids: Baker Academic, 2013), 5 (emphasis original).

32. Christopher B. Ansberry, "The Exodus: Fact, Fiction, or Both?," in *Evangelical Faith and the Challenge of Historical Criticism*, 72. For a critical response to these believing critics, see Robert Yarbrough, "Should Evangelicals Embrace Historical Criticism? The Hays-Ansberry Proposal," *Themelios* 39 (2014): 37–52.

33. Benjamin Sargent, *Written to Serve: The Use of Scripture in 1 Peter* (London: Bloomsbury T&T Clark, 2015), 33.

34. Sargent, *Written to Serve*, 48.

35. Sargent, *Written to Serve*, 93.

36. Benjamin Sargent, "One Meaning of Many? A Study in New Testament Interpretation of Old Testament Texts," *Churchman* 124, no. 4 (2010): 358. See also Benjamin Sargent, *Written for Our Learning: The Single Meaning of Scripture in Christian Theology* (Eugene, OR: Cascade, 2016).

The main concern of this approach is to insist that the New Testament authors are not reading something back into the Old Testament; rather, they are receiving, or making explicit, something already present in the Old Testament texts themselves. Interestingly, Sargent identifies his own approach with Antiochene *theoria*: "It is an insight built upon the historical and grammatical meaning of the text, rather than a meaning imposed upon the text [à la] Alexandrian allegorical reading."[37] Equally interesting is his description of the single determinate meaning as "both eschatological and ecclesiological."[38] What distinguishes Sargent from others who read the Old Testament forward is his insistence that the prophetic writings "lacked meaning in their own time."[39] It is an odd but consistent result of insisting on reading the Old Testament forward while also insisting it is literally about Christ. What Sargent wants to avoid is the notion that Scripture has two referents (literal and spiritual); what he ought to avoid is the notion that meaning is identical to reference. For the prophets' words had *sense* even when they did not know to whom or what they would eventually *refer*.

Reading Backward

To read backward is to interpret Old Testament passages with a later frame of reference, unavailable to the original authors. Many modern biblical scholars fear that *backward* may be a euphemism for *into*, hence a smokescreen for eisegesis. However, it is important not to generalize too hastily; there is more than one way to read backward.

1. "Hard" Backward ("Greek")

Hard backward reading is the modern biblical scholar's nemesis. It is a stratagem for imposing later ideas onto hapless Old Testament texts, an imposition that, at the limit, violently suppresses the voices of the Old Testament authors themselves. "Greek" serves here as shorthand for any kind of backward reading that results in the text meaning something other than it says. The result: the literal sense is either demeaned or discarded.

2. "Soft" Backward ("Christian")

The New Testament reading of the Old Testament is different. The New Testament authors are not imposing philosophical frames of reference back onto the text; rather, they are . . . doing what, exactly? Richard Hays thinks the New Testament authors are giving retrospective interpretations of Israel's

37. Sargent, *Written to Serve*, 180.
38. Sargent, *Written to Serve*, 187.
39. Sargent, *Written to Serve*, 193.

Scriptures in light of new revelatory events, in particular, the cross and resurrection of Jesus Christ. The apostles' frame of reference is informed by faith, not philosophy.[40] Hays is interested in understanding, and retrieving, the ways in which the Evangelists and Paul read Scripture (i.e., the Old Testament), on the grounds that their Christian hermeneutical assumptions should be ours as well. "A Gospel-shaped hermeneutic necessarily entails *reading backward*, reinterpreting Israel's Scripture in light of the story of Jesus."[41]

Theological interpretation is the result of reading the Old Testament Scriptures and the story of Jesus together. The Old Testament provides the pieces for understanding who Jesus is; Jesus provides the key for putting the Old Testament pieces together. Paul and the Evangelists "do theology" by making sense of the Old Testament and Jesus' story together, and their interpretive methods "are paradigmatic for Christian hermeneutics."[42] According to Hays, it was Paul's Christian experience that led him to read the Old Testament Scriptures rightly. Paul owed his key insight not to his creative genius, but to his having been made a competent reader by the Holy Spirit.

Hays notes the implications for literal interpretation of his reading strategy: "For the Evangelists the 'meaning' of the Old Testament texts was not confined to the human author's original historical setting or to the meaning that could have been grasped by the original readers."[43] Either the New Testament authors were wrong about the meaning of the Old Testament, or the Old Testament authors "actually did intentionally forecast the details of Jesus' life"[44]—a contrast Hays likens to painting oneself into a hermeneutical corner. There *is* a correspondence between what the Old Testament authors wrote and its fulfillment in Christ, but Hays attributes this to divine rather than human intentionality—providence, not prediction. He eventually admits to reading backward and forward, in accordance with the New Testament authors' own dialectical practice: "Paul's proclamation needs the blessing of Scripture, and Scripture's witness . . . stands in judgment of all formulations of the gospel. On the other hand, Scripture's witness gains its eschatological coherence only in light of the gospel."[45] In the final analysis, however, what enables Christian reading backward "depends neither on historical inquiry nor on erudite literary

40. Though the primary contrast here is hermeneutical (viz., forward/backward), it relates to the methodological contrast in Christology: "from above" (from the perspective of later believers, the Christ of faith) versus "from below" (from the historical perspective of the original authors, the Jesus of history).

41. Richard B. Hays, *Echoes of Scripture in the Gospels* (Waco, TX: Baylor University Press, 2016), 358.

42. Hays, *Echoes of Scripture in the Letters of Paul* (New Haven, CT: Yale University Press, 1989), 183.

43. Hays, *Echoes of Scripture in the Gospels*, 358.

44. Hays, *Echoes of Scripture in the Gospels*, 359.

45. Hays, *Echoes of Scripture in the Letters of Paul*, 176–77. See also this statement: "*The Gospels teach us how to read the Old Testament, and—at the same time—the Old Testament teaches us how to read the Gospels.*" Hays, *Reading Backwards*, 4 (emphasis original).

analysis but on attentiveness to the promptings of the Spirit, who reveals the gospel through Scripture in surprising ways."[46]

Peter's Hermeneutic Confession: "We Have the Prophetic Word Made More Sure" (2 Pet 1:19 RSV)

We began by citing Peter's comment that the prophets were serving not themselves but Christian readers when they "testified in advance" (*prophēteusantes*) to the passion and parousia of Christ (1 Pet 1:12). How does this prophetic "speaking forward" connect to what Peter says later in the context of discussing his own experience of Jesus' transfiguration: "We have the prophetic word made more sure" (2 Pet 1:19 RSV)? What does Peter mean, and what is the connection to the transfiguration? Peter urges his readers to pay attention to the prophetic word "as to a light shining in a dark place" (2 Pet 1:19 NIV), and the best way to do that is to recall the role of the transfiguration in the economy of light.

"We ourselves heard this very voice borne from heaven, for we were with him on the holy mountain" (2 Pet 1:18). Peter's eyewitness account of the transfiguration (1:16–18) stresses the glory Jesus receives, the voice from heaven, and the mountaintop location. These are the three elements on which he stakes his claim regarding Jesus' majesty and his claim about the prophetic word attesting Jesus being "more fully confirmed" (*bebaioteron*) as a result of the event of transfiguration. Peter had already confessed that Jesus was the Christ (Matt 16:16). Here he appeals to the historicity of the transfiguration as grounds for his confidence that Jesus will come again (a central theme throughout his epistle), rebutting the charge that the apostolic proclamation of the second coming (Peter uses the usual term *parousia* in 2 Pet 1:16) is nothing but a "cleverly devised myth" (2 Pet 1:16).[47] For Peter, the transfiguration afforded "a view into the future of the coming exaltation of Jesus, a view of his second coming with power and glory."[48]

Peter does not mention Jesus' shining face, preferring to accent the "honor and glory" he receives from God the Father (2 Pet 1:17). Instead, he highlights the voice that comes from the "Majestic Glory" and the location ("the holy mountain"), possibly alluding to the holy hill (Mount Zion) of Psalm 2:6–7,

46. Hays, *Echoes of Scripture in the Letters of Paul*, 156.

47. For a rebuttal of the claim that Peter is referring to Jesus' first coming, see Kelly, who noted that the scoffers to which Peter alluded asked (2 Pet 3:4), "Where is the promise of his coming [*parousia*]?" Kelly, *Commentary on the Epistles of Peter and Jude*, 317–18.

48. Peter H. Davids, *The Letters of 2 Peter and Jude*, Pillar New Testament Commentary (Grand Rapids: Eerdmans, 2006), 202. Cf. Ruth Anne Reese, who says that the transfiguration "functions as a reason for expecting the return of Jesus." Ruth Anne Reese, *2 Peter and Jude*, Two Horizons Commentary (Grand Rapids: Eerdmans, 2007), 142.

an enthronement psalm.[49] In Peter's narrative, the transfiguration becomes "a scene of investiture."[50] Peter's frame of reference for reading the Old Testament is decidedly eschatological: "[Jesus'] sublime identity is itself the pledge of God's promise. Thus everything in this brief story serves to bolster the message ('prophecy') of the parousia, grounded in Jesus' identity."[51] Peter is less interested in the transfiguration as an epiphany of Jesus' hidden divine nature than he is its being a heavenly revelation of God's appointing his "eschatological viceregent."[52] The transfiguration is, for Peter, not an odd one-off event, but an integral and emblematic confirmation of Jesus' person and work. As Douglas Harink succinctly summarizes, "The transfiguration is a prophetic apocalypse of the eschatological enthronement of Jesus Christ as Lord."[53]

Why do I refer to this passage as Peter's *hermeneutic* confession? As Hays and others have shown, the Gospels give ample documentation of how the Old Testament bears witness to Jesus. Peter's account of the transfiguration matters because it does the opposite: it shows "that the Transfiguration bears witness to the permanent validity of the Old Testament."[54] Of particular interest is Peter's mentioning light, our operative concept, in connection not to Jesus' face but to the prophetic word, "a lamp shining in a dark place" (2 Pet 1:19). The prophetic word is more sure because Peter *saw* its light in the bright shining promise of Jesus' once and future glory. He also *heard* the divine voice corroborating and interpreting the Old Testament prophecies about the Messiah (2 Pet 1:18). Harink draws a stunning inference: "*The transfiguration is God's own exegesis of the prophetic word of Ps. 2,* as God himself declares Jesus to be the one about whom the words of the psalms and the prophets are written."[55] This is why Peter has a "surer" or more definite grasp of the prophetic word—and of the plot of the drama of redemption. In light of the transfiguration, Peter now knows, for sure, what the Old Testament prophets were talking about.

Peter's epistle adds yet another layer to the transfiguration's hermeneutical import. In an interesting reversal, it is not prophecy that explains the transfiguration but the transfiguration that confirms prophecy and, indeed, the whole Old Testament, as a word, now made more certain, about the glorious first and second comings of Jesus Christ. It is hardly an exaggeration then, to say, "*The transfiguration reveals to us the proper understanding of the origin and interpretation*

49. "Holy mountain" in the Old Testament always designates Zion (see, e.g., Ps 48; Isa 66:20; Joel 2:1; Zech 8:3).

50. Davids, *Letters of 2 Peter and Jude*, 204.

51. Dorothy Lee, *Transfiguration* (New York: Continuum, 2004), 95.

52. Richard J. Bauckham, *Jude, 2 Peter*, Word Biblical Commentary (Waco, TX: Word, 1983), 212.

53. Harink, *1 & 2 Peter*, 156.

54. Arthur Michael Ramsey, *The Glory of God and the Transfiguration of Christ* (London: Longmans, Green and Co.,1949), 126.

55. Harink, *1 & 2 Peter*, 159 (emphasis original).

of holy scripture."[56] Jesus' transfiguration is God's own spiritual interpretation of the story of Scripture, as it were: *God's own unveiling of the glory of the Old Testament's literal sense.*

The mention of "unveiling" directs us to ascend a final mountaintop. We have just seen how, in Peter's hands, Mount Tabor stands in for Mount Zion. But it was on Mount Sinai that Moses, who spoke with Jesus at his transfiguration, was himself "transfigured," so much so that he had to veil his face: "The typological linking between the transfiguration on the 'holy mountain' (1:18) and the giving of the law at Sinai, so popular in the early and medieval church, is difficult to rule out as a possible intended meaning here in [2] Peter, especially when he says that, in addition to these eye- and ear-witness memories, 'we have the prophetic word made more sure' (v. 19)."[57]

A Tale of Two Mountains: Sinai and Tabor

The story of Moses' "transfiguration" (Exod 34:29–35) provides a fascinating case study in the relative merits of reading backward and forward. Moses' appearing at Jesus' transfiguration could be seen as God's delayed response to Moses' request, "Please show me your glory" (Exod 33:18).[58] Yet the similarity between the two shining faces, Moses' and Jesus', prompts the question: Should we read Mount Sinai in light of Mount Tabor or vice versa? Before examining the apostle Paul's approach, we listen first to contemporary Old Testament scholars.

The episode of Moses' shining face occurs at a key turning point in the biblical story of God's plan to form "a kingdom of priests and a holy nation" (Exod 19:6). God's chosen people were on the verge of becoming "not God's people" due to their idolatrous worship of a golden calf (Exod 32:8). Their timing was terrible: they violated the first commandment just before Moses descended the mountain with the two tablets of the newly minted covenant law (vv. 1–6), a sin Walter Moberly compares to "committing adultery on one's wedding night."[59] When God vents his wrath, Moses comes into his own as covenant mediator, no longer delivering the law but pleading for mercy. He then descends the mountain, throws the tablets to the ground, and punishes Israel himself by melting the calf and making the people drink the dregs (vv. 19–20).

56. Harink, 160 (emphasis added).

57. Kathryn Greene-McCreight, "He Spoke through the Prophets," in *Nicene Christianity: The Future for a New Ecumenism*, ed. Christopher R. Seitz (Grand Rapids: Brazos, 2001), 169.

58. See further Bogdan G. Bucur, who says, "Relating the Sinai theophany and the transfiguration on Tabor was crucially important for early Christian theology." "Sinai, Zion, and Tabor," 33.

59. R. W. L. Moberly, "Exodus," in *Dictionary for Theological Interpretation of the Bible*, ed. Kevin J. Vanhoozer (Grand Rapids: Baker, 2005), 214.

The Lord informs Moses of the consequence of Israel's sin: though the people can continue on to the promised land, God will not go with them, for his holiness would consume them (Exod 33:3). Again, Moses intercedes for Israel, and the Lord grants Moses' request that his presence not depart. Moses then presses his advantage and asks the Lord, "Please show me your glory" (v. 18). God accedes to the request, promising to make his "goodness" pass before Moses, adding an important qualification: "You cannot see my face, for man shall not see me and live" (v. 20). It is at this point in the narrative that the Lord instructs Moses to ascend Mount Sinai again to receive a second copy of the Ten Commandments. God there renews the covenant and proclaims his name, proving himself the God indicated by his name: "merciful and gracious, slow to anger, and abounding in steadfast love and faithfulness" (34:6). Moses was with God on Mount Sinai for forty days. When he came down, he "did not know that the skin of his face shone because he had been talking with God" (v. 29).

Exodus 32–34 is a crucial theological load-bearing narrative.[60] Israel's sin and God's holiness make for a combustible combination, echoing the fall of Adam and anticipating the urgent need for atoning sacrifice and, eventually, the cross of Christ. Perhaps the one theological theme that most stands out is God's glorious presence. It is the tangible sign of the ultimate covenant blessing—or, in the case of a sinful nation, the ultimate curse (divine wrath). Bible readers need to know certain things about God and Israel to make sense of the gospel of Jesus Christ, and this passage plays a pivotal role in helping us understand what is going on as we read forward.

What should we make of Moses' shining face? What is its theological significance, and how does it relate to Jesus' transfiguration? In his study of Exodus 32–34, Moberly provides a helpful double caution: "Theological exegesis naturally runs the same risk as literary exegesis of finding significance where none should be found. But this is no less than the risk of denying significance when it is present."[61] Fred Sanders provides an important criterion for discerning theological significance and a guideline for reading the whole Old Testament theologically: "The one premodern interpretive practice that is crucial for the doctrine of the Trinity is attention to the economy of salvation as a coherent whole."[62] With these cautions and criterion in mind, let us approach Moses' transfiguration as an episode in the broader, indeed all-encompassing, economy

60. Moberly notes that the book of Exodus "is foundational for the biblical understanding both of God . . . and of the people of God" ("Exodus," 211).

61. R. W. L. Moberly, *At the Mountain of God: Story and Theology in Exodus 32–34*, JSOTSup 22 (Sheffield: JSOT, 1983), 39–40.

62. Fred Sanders, *The Triune God* (Grand Rapids: Zondervan, 2016), 180.

of light. As we do so, we do well to remember B. B. Warfield's apt description of the Old Testament as "a chamber richly furnished *but dimly lit*."[63]

Like Jesus' transfiguration, the narrative of Moses ascending the mountain to receive the law and meet God represents a key moment in the economy of light and Israel's covenant history. "The episode of Moses' shining face is the conclusion to the whole Sinai event."[64] But is there adequate textual warrant for seeing a connection between what happens on Mount Sinai (God's proclaiming his name, resulting in Moses' shining face) and Mount Tabor (the voice from heaven that accompanies Jesus' shining face)? Can we connect the canonical dots and, if so, is it by moving from Moses' face to Jesus', or by reading in the opposite direction? The process, if not the proof, of transfigural interpretation is ultimately in the reading.

Moses' Shining Face

The text in question (Exod 34:29–35) mentions Moses' face five times and on three occasions adds the detail of his "shining" face (vv. 29, 30, 35). Is there a meaning in this face? Stephen Barton thinks so: "More than any other part of the body, the face is the place, and facing is the action, where the self receives and expresses its identity, character, and values, especially in *relations of the face*, including relations which, as we say are 'face-to-face.'"[65]

Whatever was going on led to the people being "afraid to come near him" (Exod 34:30). Scholars debate what they must have seen to provoke such a reaction. One suggestion, drawing on an ancient Near Eastern cultural frame of reference, is that Moses had on a frightening ritual mask. But in that case, why put on a veil rather than remove the mask? Another suggestion draws on philology to argue that *qrn* means not "shine" but "horn." Some older translations (e.g., the Vulgate) say Moses did not know that the skin of his face "was horned" (Exod 34:29), an interpretation that led several artists, like Michelangelo, to add horns to his famous sculpture of Moses.

Problematic for both mask and horns theories is the text's insistence that the change occurred on "the skin of his face" (Exod 34:30, 35). Accordingly, William Propp suggests that Moses' proximity to Yahweh, a consuming fire (Deut 4:24), resulted in injurious side-effects and hideous disfigurement: "Presumably, this was some kind of light or heat burn . . . [perhaps] keratosis, a

63. B. B. Warfield, "The Biblical Doctrine of the Trinity," in *Biblical and Theological Studies* (Philadelphia: Presbyterian and Reformed, 1952), 22 (emphasis added).

64. Joshua M. Philpot, "Exodus 34:29–35 and Moses' Shining Face," *Bulletin for Biblical Research* 23, no. 1 (2013): 2.

65. Stephen C. Barton, "The Metaphor of the Face in Paul," in *Conception, Receptions, and the Spirit: Essays in Honor of Andrew T. Lincoln*, ed. J. Gordon McConville and Lloyd K. Pietersen (Eugene, OR: Cascade, 2015), 136–37.

toughening of the layer of skin called keratin (Greek *keras*, 'horn') that can be caused by drastic overexposure to sunlight."[66] On this view, the literal interpretation is that Moses' skin developed small bumps (i.e., little "horns"), comparable to heat rash. Moses' shining face is thus a sign not of his increasing glory but of his increasing immunity to the divine radiance: "Like Achilles and Siegfried, Moses has unnaturally thick skin, but its virtue is apparent in the cult, not on the battlefield."[67] Such a reading might be interesting to present at a medical conference, but its hyper-literal frame of reference does not accord well with the larger narrative context of Exodus.

Seth Sanders is another commentator who employs an ancient Near Eastern frame of reference in an attempt to have his light and horn it too, arguing that Mesopotamian astronomers would be quite familiar with the phenomenon of what looked like horns of light appearing, say, when there was a solar eclipse: "Moses' face could, quite literally, *radiate* horns."[68] These conflicting granular interpretations are intriguing, but they can take readers only so far: "Whatever the ancient Near Eastern parallels, there can be little dispute that the text as it now stands is not describing either a priestly mask or horns."[69] Readers stand a better chance of zeroing in on the literal meaning by practicing close canonical reading, paying attention to the details, yes, but also employing wider frames of reference that set these textual details in a larger literary context.

The broader story, of which the episode of Moses' transfiguration is an integral part, concerns the Lord's preparing Israel to be "a kingdom of priests and a holy nation" (Exod 19:6), fit to dwell in God's holy "house" and before his divine presence.[70] The complication in this story, which runs through the entire Old Testament, is that the people are "stiff-necked" (Exod 32:9; 33:3, 5; 34:9). In the context of the broader biblical narrative, the reader understands that the giving of the Sinaitic law is a gracious provision that makes it possible for a sinful people to live in God's presence (i.e., before his "face"). Scripture singles out Moses as the only prophet "whom the LORD knew face to face" (Deut 34:10). Conversing with God face-to-face ("as a man speaks to his friend"; Exod 33:11) was the supreme privilege of the covenant mediator, not a punishment. Moses' intercession for Israel on Mount Sinai is arguably the high point, geographically

66. William H. Propp, "The Skin of Moses' Face—Transfigured or Disfigured?," *Catholic Biblical Quarterly* 49 (1987): 385.

67. Propp, 386.

68. Seth L. Sanders, "Old Light on Moses' Shining Face," *Vetus Testamentum* 52, no. 3 (2002): 405.

69. Moberly, *At the Mountain of God*, 107.

70. So L. Michael Morales, *Who Shall Ascend the Mountain of the Lord? A Biblical Theology of the Book of Leviticus* (Downers Grove, IL: InterVarsity, 2015), 23. Cf. Peter Enns: "The whole purpose of the Exodus was for God and his people to be together." Peter Enns, *Exodus*, NIV Application Commentary (Grand Rapids: Zondervan, 2000), 578.

and dramatically, of the book of Exodus. Without Moses' mountaintop mediation, there would be no dwelling in God's presence, no tent of meeting, no tabernacle.[71] Michael Morales makes a compelling case for viewing the tabernacle as an extension of Mount Sinai, the place where God meets and speaks with his chosen people: "The purpose of the tabernacle, then, will be to perpetuate the Sinai experience of engagement with God—YHWH's dwelling in the midst of Israel being the very essence of the covenant."[72]

This biblical-theological narrative frame of reference casts a different light on Moses' shining face. It is the result of Moses' successful covenant mediation and of his surviving God's holy presence: "It brought the glory of God back into Israel's midst in a human countenance. It was a visible sign of the Lord's forgiveness, presence, and restored communication with Israel through Moses."[73] Walter Brueggemann points out that Moses' shining face stands midway between two other texts that feature God's glory, the earlier one describing Moses' communion with God in the glory cloud (Exod 24:15–18), the other one having to do with God's glory entering the tabernacle (Exod 40:34–38): "So the glory moves from the mountain to the tabernacle via Moses. So, Moses' descent from the mountain is a device for the awesome coming of heavenly glory to dwell in the midst of Israel."[74]

Moses' Sinai transfiguration is a pivotal moment in the economy of light, a key event in the bigger story of how the God who is glorious light can dwell peaceably with those who dwell in inglorious darkness. Perhaps this is why we read that the refracted glory of God on Moses' face was as intimidating and fearful to the people as was the thunder and lightning that followed Moses' first ascent (Exod 20:18–19). Might this be why Moses, in contrast to Jesus, hides his shining face under a veil?

Moses' Veiled Face

No less a commentator than Calvin found the passage about Moses' veiling and unveiling "confusing."[75] The text in question, Exodus 34:33–35, appears to describe not a onetime event but a continuing practice of veiling and unveiling whenever Moses "went in before the Lord to speak with him" (34:34), presumably the tent of meeting (Exod 33:11). Moses took the veil off when he spoke to

71. Morales, 92.

72. Morales, 96.

73. James K. Bruckner, *Exodus*, Understanding the Bible Commentary (Grand Rapids: Baker, 2008), 311.

74. Walter Brueggemann, "Exodus," in *Genesis to Leviticus*, ed. Terence E. Fretheim, Walter C. Kaiser, and Leander E. Keck, *The New Interpreter's Bible*, 12 vols. (Nashville: Abingdon, 1994), 2:954.

75. John Calvin, *Harmony of the Four Last Books of Moses*, vol. 3, trans. Charles William Bingham (Edinburgh: Calvin Translation Society, 1854), 393.

God, then put it back on after he had finished relaying to the people what God told him (34:33, 35).[76] What are we to make of this?

Brevard Childs stated the interpretive challenge: "What was the purpose of the mask if it was not to cover Moses' shining face which continued to cause the people's anxiety?"[77] Commentators have not been short on suggestions. Although the terms for Moses' veil and the curtain in the temple are not the same, some interpreters see a connection. As the temple curtain kept the Israelites from gazing upon God's glory in the holy of holies, so the veil prevented them from seeing the glory of God shining on Moses' face. "[Moses] has, therefore, become the embodiment of the tabernacle; his role as mediator has reached a level and depth not yet attained."[78] Others disagree, preferring instead to see the shining as a confirmation "that it is God's word that is being spoken to the people when they see the light radiating from Moses' face."[79] The veil was a means Moses used "to keep his own words from being confused with the Lord's revelation."[80] Both suggestions are interesting; both lack explicit textual support.

Thomas White, reading forward, sees Moses functioning throughout Exodus 33–34 as a type or figure of Christ. Moses mediates the covenant, intercedes for Israel, enjoys "face to face" conversation with God (33:11), and eventually experiences a kind of beatific vision of God's "back" (33:20–23).[81] Moses' close encounter with the glory of God causes his face to shine, which White interprets literally as "a mysterious quality of light" that irradiates Moses' face.[82] The light is good, a sign of God's mercy. Why, then, the veil? White's answer: "to conceal the exceptional grace that is given to him [Moses] alone."[83] But why conceal something whose purpose is to reveal (viz., a sign)?

Each of these interpretations tries to make sense of the veil by reading forward. There is a broad consensus that Exodus 33–34 depicts Moses as a covenant mediator of God's glorious presence, but few biblical commentators relate Moses' shining face to Jesus' transfiguration. At least one says,

76. For an overview of its interpretation, see Mariah Case, "A Brief Reception History of Exodus 34:29–35," *Journal of Theta Alpha Kappa* 44, no. 1 (2020): 37–56.

77. Childs, *The Book of Exodus: A Critical, Theological Commentary*, Old Testament Library (Louisville: Westminster John Knox, 1974), 618.

78. Enns, *Exodus*, 587.

79. Menehem Haran, "The Shining of Moses' Face: A Case Study in Biblical and Ancient Near Eastern Iconography," in *In the Shelter of Elyon: Essays on Ancient Palestinian Life and Literature, in Honor of G. W. Ahlstrom*, ed. W. Barrick and John R. Spencer, JSOTSup 31 (Sheffield: JSOT, 1983), 162.

80. Bruckner, *Exodus*, 312.

81. Thomas Aquinas thought "back" symbolized a momentary beatific vision (*Summa Theologica* 1–2.98.3, ad. 2.

82. Thomas Joseph White, *Exodus*, Brazos Theological Commentary on the Bible (Grand Rapids: Brazos, 2016), 284.

83. White, 284.

"Moses' transfiguration was the basis for understanding the transfiguration of Jesus."[84] Others speak of the passage's deeper typological significance: "The radiance of splendor that shines out from the body of Moses is a prefiguration of the eschatological glory of the risen human body in the eschaton."[85] It was the apostle Paul, however, who best read the account of Moses' transfiguration *transfigurally*.

Letter and Spirit: Paul's Reading of Moses' Veiled Glory

Exodus 34:29–35 has one of the most fascinating "echoes" of Scripture in the letters of Paul, 2 Corinthians 3:6–16, one of Paul's most difficult texts—"the only text in which Paul's hermeneutical reflection on reading the old covenant comes to the fore."[86] One commentator on 2 Corinthians notes, "Chapter 3 has been especially knotty for interpreters."[87] Another calls it "the student's nightmare and the exegete's playground."[88] Still another calls it (speaking of ascending mountains) "the Mount Everest of Pauline texts as far as difficulty is concerned."[89] Morna Hooker agrees, noting that the chapter "is full of problems, ambiguities and pitfalls."[90] She also admits that after seeing how New Testament authors read earlier biblical texts, she is often tempted to exclaim, "Whatever the passage from the Old Testament originally meant, it certainly was not this!"[91] Making sense of Paul's interpretation of Moses' veil in Exodus 34, then, is tough going, leading Richard Hays to lament, with tongue in cheek, "It is hard to escape the impression that, to this day, when 2 Corinthians 3 is read a veil lies over our minds."[92]

Despite its high degree of difficulty, Christian interpreters cannot avoid making the dive into the deep end of Paul's interpretation of Moses' veil, and not only because of its possible connections to Jesus' transfiguration. Margaret Mitchell contends that Paul's Corinthian correspondence had a profound

84. Bruckner, *Exodus*, 312. See also R. Alan Cole, who used the term in connection with Moses and Jesus both serving as covenant mediators. *Exodus*, Tyndale Old Testament Commentary (Downers Grove: IVP Academic, 1974), 243.

85. White, *Exodus*, 285.

86. Scott J. Hafemann, *Paul, Moses, and the History of Israel: The Letter/Spirit Contrast and the Argument from Scripture in 2 Corinthians 3* (Peabody, MA: Hendrickson, 1996), 459.

87. George H. Guthrie, *2 Corinthians*, Baker Exegetical Commentary (Grand Rapids: Baker Academic, 2015), 153.

88. Edith Humphrey, "2 Corinthians," in *Dictionary for Theological Interpretation of the Bible*, 138.

89. A. T. Hanson, "The Midrash in II Corinthians 3: A Reconsideration," *Journal for the Study of the New Testament* 9 (1980): 19.

90. Morna D. Hooker, "Beyond the Things That Are Written? St. Paul's Use of Scripture," *New Testament Studies* 27 (1981): 296.

91. Hooker, 295.

92. Hays, *Echoes of Scripture in the Letters of Paul*, 123.

impact on early Christian exegesis, possibly giving birth to a distinctly Christian hermeneutics.[93] She argues that Paul charts a middle course between literal and allegorical exegesis, a claim we will explore, and amend, as our chapter progresses. Mitchell also claims, less compellingly, that Paul, by his example in Corinthians and elsewhere, encouraged early Christians to read rhetorically: to *use* the text for pastorally expedient *strategic* purposes rather than for the properly *communicative* purpose of trying to determine what the author was saying.[94] In short, Mitchell thinks Paul was less interested in describing what the Old Testament authors were doing with their words than with doing new things with their words himself.[95]

To view Paul as one who uses the Old Testament Scriptures for his own pastoral purposes is to confirm the biblical scholars' fear that, in reading backward, Paul foists his own Christian concerns onto a reluctant Jewish text—just like other theological interpreters, contemporary systematicians in particular.[96] This is not a charitable interpretation, nor is it how I read Paul. For, as we shall see, Paul does justice to the literal sense, thanks to an interpretive framework that enables him to perceive its deeper glory.[97]

Letter/Spirit (2 Cor 3:6): What Kind of Contrast?

Paul prefaces his engagement with Exodus 34:29–35 with an adage that has launched a thousand hermeneutical ships: "For the letter kills, but the Spirit gives life" (2 Cor 3:6; cf. Rom 2:29).[98] Paul says this in the context of defending his apostolic credentials. While his Corinthian detractors boast impressive letters of recommendation, Paul counters that the Corinthians themselves are his "letter of recommendation," a letter (Gk. *epistole*) from Christ written by the Spirit of the living God on hearts, not the kind of letter (Gk. *gramma*) engraved on tablets of stone like the Mosaic law (2 Cor 3:1–3).

---

93. Margaret M. Mitchell, *Paul, the Corinthians and the Birth of Christian Hermeneutics* (Cambridge: Cambridge University Press, 2010). I am grateful to Dan Treier for calling this book to my attention.

94. Paul was "a tactically and pastorally variable interpreter." Mitchell, 3.

95. Mitchell herself contrasts *commenting on* and *commenting with* a text and describes her own approach as "reading Paul backwards and forwards." Mitchell, ix.

96. Matthew L. Halsted contends that Paul "dialogically re-authors" Old Testament texts, altering the original meaning: "Paul's Christological horizon fused with the text's original horizon, creating a fresh and radically new meaning." *Paul and the Meaning of Scripture: A Philosophical-Hermeneutic Approach to Paul's Use of the Old Testament* (Eugene, OR: Pickwick, 2022), 105.

97. While many modern scholars compare Paul's interpretative strategies to those of his Jewish contemporaries, Matthew Bates proposes to "situate Paul's exegesis in the context of early Christian hermeneutics." *The Hermeneutics of Apostolic Proclamation: The Center of Paul's Method of Scripture Interpretation* (Waco, TX: Baylor University Press, 2012), 330. I am grateful to Josh Jipp for calling my attention to Bates's important work.

98. Scott Hafemann comments that this letter/spirit contrast "is one of the most difficult passages to understand within the Pauline corpus." Hafemann, *Paul, Moses, and the History of Israel*, 1.

Principles of Salvation or Interpretation?

We have already examined the literal sense of light. What is the literal sense of "letter"? Paul is not referring to Scripture, for *gramma* is not the same as *graphe* (the usual New Testament word for the scriptural writings). Nor is Paul contrasting the Torah itself, the Jewish law, with the Spirit of Christ, for elsewhere he says "the law is spiritual" (Rom 7:14). One possibility is that "letter" stands for the law as a defining element of the old covenant, whereas "Spirit" stands for the life-giving aspect of the new covenant. This *soteriological* view of the letter/spirit distinction focuses on law and Spirit as contrasting principles of covenant administration, with special emphasis on the relative impotence of the old covenant to ensure obedience in contrast to the vivifying power of the new.[99] The focus of this soteriological interpretation is on the progressive outworking of this contrast in the history of redemption.

Origen popularized an alternative *hermeneutic* interpretation of the *gramma/pneuma* contrast, claiming that Paul is distinguishing not law and gospel but, rather, two senses of Scripture: the literal and the spiritual.[100] This reading develops Paul's contrast into "the Magna Carta of allegorical interpretation," a license not to kill but to give the kiss of life to lifeless "lettered" interpretations.[101] Origen's alternative led Calvin to protest strenuously what he took to be the obvious implication, namely, that the biblical text would be useless—a dead letter, as it were—unless allegorized: "This error was the source of many evils."[102]

A Middle Course?

In this section, I want to engage, perchance to mediate, two contrasting approaches to Paul as an interpreter of the Old Testament, and to do so with a view to clarifying the concept and the practice of transfiguring biblical

99. Bernardin Schneider terms what I am calling soteriological the "realistic" view, and contrasts it with the "formalistic" interpretation common among the church fathers, what I call here the "hermeneutic" alternative. "The Meaning of St. Paul's Antithesis 'The Letter and the Spirit'" *Catholic Biblical Quarterly* 15 (1953): 164. Cf. Michael Wolters, who draws a contrast between the "theological" and "hermeneutical" understandings. "'Spirit' and 'Letter' in the New Testament," in *The Spirit and the Letter: A Tradition and a Reversal*, ed. Paul S. Fiddes (London: Bloomsbury, 2013), 34.

100. The picture is actually more complex. As Morwenna Ludlow points out, Origen worked with a subtle but significant distinction between reading "according to the letter" and reading "according to the mere letter." "Spirit and Letter in Origen and Augustine," in Fiddes, ed., *Spirit and the Letter*, 91–92. See also Wai-Shing Chau, *The Letter and the Spirit: A History of Interpretation from Origen to Luther* (New York: Peter Lang, 1995); and Mark A. Seifrid's excursus on "letter and spirit in recent interpretation," in *The Second Letter to the Corinthians* (Grand Rapids: Eerdmans, 2014), 130–50.

101. Mitchell, *Paul, the Corinthians and the Birth of Christian Hermeneutics*, 70. For a book-length history of reception of 2 Corinthians 3:6 from ancient to modern and postmodern times, see the essays in Fiddes, ed., *Spirit and the Letter.*

102. John Calvin, *Commentary on the Epistles of Paul the Apostle to the Corinthians* (Edinburgh: Calvin Translation Society, 1848), 174.

interpretation: the project of reading Scripture as the word of God for the knowledge of God (viz., the light of Christ) with a grammatical-eschatological frame of reference in canonical context.

There is, on the one hand, an emerging consensus that Paul interprets the Old Testament with the zeal of a new convert, "with little regard for its original context and contrary to its canonical meaning."[103] Richard Hays is a good representative of this approach, claiming that "a new reader-competence is born in the Christian convert."[104] However, Hays's critics protest that this scenario has Paul running roughshod over the literal meaning of the text in his haste to read it with a Christian hermeneutic. He thereby comes to resemble the worst kind of theological interpreter. By way of contrast, Scott Hafemann insists that Paul *is* a competent reader who, contra Hays, reads Exodus 34 (and the rest of the Old Testament) in context, in accordance with its canonical intention.[105] Hafemann likewise insists that we must derive our understanding of the letter/spirit contrast from what Paul actually does with it in the context of 2 Corinthians 3.[106] Hays therefore represents those who read Paul reading the Old Testament primarily backward (i.e., from the perspective of the story of Christ and Christian faith), whereas Hafemann represents those who read Paul as one who reads the Old Testament primarily forward, in step with the letter of the Exodus text.

What, then, does Paul literally mean by "the letter kills" (2 Cor 3:6)? One thing is sure: the phrase has negative connotations, for Paul contrasts it with "life-giving." C. K. Barrett associated "letter" with "man-made religion in general."[107] That the letter "kills" may be a metaphorical way of saying that humans' efforts to make themselves right with God (which is what religion is) ultimately fail. This is similar to Augustine's notion of "letter" as "law without grace."[108] The "letter that kills" thus pertains to *reading and using the law with a "religious" frame of reference only*, under the mistaken assumption that we can by our works make ourselves acceptable to God.[109] To read the law "religiously" is to distort its true intent: "'Letter' is rather what the legalist is left with as a result of his misunderstanding and misuse of the law. It is the letter of the law in separation from the Spirit."[110]

103. Hafemann, *Paul, Moses, and the History of Israel*, 452 (describing a trend with which he disagrees).
104. Hays, *Echoes of Scripture in the Letters of Paul*, 124.
105. Hafemann, *Paul, Moses, and the History of Israel*, 453.
106. Hafemann, *Paul, Moses, and the History of Israel*, 33.
107. C. K. Barrett, *The Second Epistle to the Corinthians* (Grand Rapids: Baker Academic, 1993), 113.
108. See Augustine, *On the Spirit and the Letter*.
109. Cf. Guthrie, who says the "letter" refers "to an attempt to minister or engage the Scriptures apart from the new-covenant work of the Spirit" (*2 Corinthians*, 199).
110. C. E. B. Cranfield, *The Epistle to the Romans*, International Critical Commentary (Edinburgh: T&T Clark, 1975), 339–40.

Recall that Paul is engaged in a dispute about the credentials of his apostolic ministry. His bold claim is that his "sufficiency"—the ability to carry out his mission—is not self-sufficiency but "from God" (2 Cor 3:5). Paul declares himself the minister of a new, life-giving covenant, empowered by the life-giving Spirit. That the Spirit has given life to the Corinthians is, for Paul, proof that his new covenant ministry is the fulfillment of Old Testament prophecy (Ezek 11:19–20; 36:26). Paul's ministry is not simply "new and improved," but *eschatologically* new and *pneumatically* improved. Paul therefore presents himself as mediator of a new, supercharged covenant, "the eschatological counterpart to the role of Moses."[111]

Second Corinthians 3 is first and foremost an apology for Paul's new covenant ministry, not a manual on how to do exegesis. It nevertheless remains "a discussion of hermeneutics because the basis of doubts about Paul's apostleship was questions about the status of his *logos*."[112] Paul's apostolic ministry has a hermeneutical dimension, such that the letter/spirit contrast hovers over the whole of Paul's reading of Exodus 34. Hays therefore quips that Stephen Westerholm, in describing the letter/spirit contrast as "the key to Pauline ethics, not Pauline hermeneutics,"[113] is right in what he affirms, but not in what he denies.

Robert Morgan's "new hermeneutical application" of Paul's letter/spirit contrast is also worth mentioning, not least because it reverses the hermeneutical polarities. Unlike those who equate "letter" with the *religious* readings of the Old Testament, Morgan equates it with *nonreligious* interpretations, in contrast to "spirit," which he says refers to explicitly *religious* (i.e., confessional, theological) interpretations. As a modern biblical scholar, Morgan is a proponent of literal interpretation. However, he thinks Paul's letter/spirit contrast brings to light a division in modern biblical studies that dares not speak its name, between those who read with religious faith and those who do not. "A biblical scholarship marked by 'letter' that is *closed* in principle to theological meanings ('spirit') is problematic to Christians."[114] At the same time, Morgan insists that "'Letter' work is a necessary prerequisite of 'spirit' interpretation."[115] He therefore champions the letter insofar as it can remain "open to spirit."

111. Hafemann, *Paul, Moses and the History of Israel*, 33.

112. Mitchell, *Paul, the Corinthians, and the Birth of Christian Hermeneutics*, 145n49. Seifrid agreed: "Although 'letter' and 'Spirit' are material, theological terms for Paul, they have hermeneutical implications." *Second Letter to the Corinthians*, 128. See also Matthew W. Bates, who agrees that 2 Corinthians 3:6b is "hermeneutically crucial." *Hermeneutics of the Apostolic Proclamation: The Center of Paul's Method of Scriptural Interpretation* (Waco, TX: Baylor University Press, 2019), 162.

113. Cited in Hays, *Echoes of Scripture in the Letters of Paul*, 131. See Stephen Westerholm, "Letter and Spirit: The Foundation of Pauline Ethics," *New Testament Studies* 30 (1984): 220–48.

114. Robert Morgan, "Spirit and Letter: Mapping Modern Biblical Interpretation," in *Spirit and the Letter*, ed. Fiddes, 49.

115. Morgan, 55.

With some biblical scholars identifying the letter that kills with "religious" readings of the Old Testament and others with "nonreligious," we now find ourselves in what those great biblical interpreters Laurel and Hardy might describe as "another fine exegetical mess." As to Morgan's proposal, everything depends on what he means by the letter being "open" to the spirit. "Spiritual" interpretation must do more than sneak doctrinal systems through the textual back door. John's caution remains salutary: "Beloved, do not believe every spirit, but test the spirits to see whether they are from God, for many false prophets have gone out into the world" (1 John 4:1). Of course, there is only one true spirit of God: the Spirit of Jesus Christ. Ernst Käsemann was therefore on the right track in suggesting that "spirit" in 2 Corinthians 3:6 refers to a christological reading of the Old Testament that goes beyond the *gramma* of the law in order to retrieve "its original divine intention."[116]

"Letter" and "spirit" represent first and foremost "two different covenants with different descriptions, demands, and results"[117]—and perhaps interpretive significance as well. Hays is thinking about the latter when he asks, "Does this new-covenant ministry-competence entail a new form of reader-competence?"[118] Stated differently, does the new covenant entail a new hermeneutic? This of course raises a prior question: What, exactly, is *new* about the new covenant? Elsewhere, Paul insists that the law is not opposed to the promises of God (Gal 3:21), likening the law to a tutor or teacher (Gk. *paidagogos*) "until Christ came" (v. 24), which suggests that the difference between old and new may not be one of content. After all, Jesus himself insists that the Law and the Prophets were about him (Luke 24:27; John 5:46).

Calvin thought the difference between the two covenants has less to do with content than *form*: the old and new covenants are one in substance—both participate in the one covenant of grace—yet "they differ in mode of dispensation."[119] This idea that the difference between the two covenants, and the letter/spirit contrast, may pertain to form rather than content will be important to keep in mind in what follows. Calvin believed that Christ was known to the Old Testament people of God "under the Law."[120] Israel had light, but it was not as bright as light incarnate. To think theologically about biblical interpretation, I have argued, is to employ a theological framework of understanding that traces

116. Ernst Käsemann, "The Spirit and the Letter," in *Perspectives on Paul*, ed. Ernst Käsemann (London: SCM, 1971), 155.

117. Christopher W. Morgan and Robert A. Peterson, *The Glory of God and Paul: Texts, Themes, and Theology* (Downers Grove, IL: IVP Academic, 2022), 104.

118. Hays, *Echoes of Scripture in the Letters of Paul*, 123.

119. Calvin, *Institutes* II.10.2. Calvin added a chapter to his 1559 edition, where he underlined the point: Christ was known under the law but was clearly revealed only in the gospel (*Institutes* II.9). Calvin went on to elaborate the differences between the testaments under four headings (*Institutes* II.11).

120. Calvin, *Institutes* II.9.

the work of the triune God in communicating light. There is one light yet different degrees of brightness. Recall that light refracts as it passes from one medium (e.g., the old covenant) to another (e.g., the new covenant).

With Veiled Face: Reading Commentators Reading Paul Reading Moses (2 Cor 3:7–13)

We have already examined some of the ways commentators read Exodus 34:29–35 forward, with only that knowledge and frame of reference that would have been available to readers at the time of composition. We now turn our attention to construing the apostle Paul's interpretation of Exodus 34, particularly the light and glory associated with Moses' face. That older "ministry of death, carved in letters on stone" (2 Cor 3:7), though glorious, says Paul, is coming to an end, in contrast to his own ministry "of the Spirit" (v. 8), which is permanent and has surpassing glory (vv. 10–11).[121] He then contrasts the boldness of his own ministry with Moses' practice of veiling his face.

In his retelling the story of Moses' transfiguration and its aftermath, is Paul reading forward or backward? Does his reading count as textual interpretation, or is he simply using the Old Testament for his own strategic purposes? Is he perhaps telling us what *he* would have meant had he written Exodus 34, now that he knows the story ends with the risen Christ? We shall explore both options, represented by Hafemann and Hays respectively, as well as the possibility that Paul is reading transfigurally, with a framework of understanding informed by the economy of light, enabling him to see "how much more" of what there already is in the letter of the text. Paul's comments on veiling and unveiling serve as the touchstone for these diverse interpretations. In particular, we need to know two things: (1) What does Paul make of Moses' veil, to which he refers twice: first, in regard to the glory on Moses' face (2 Cor 3:13) and, second, in regard to the veil over readers' hearts that obscures the meaning of Moses' text (v. 15)? (2) What does Paul say is the reason behind Moses' veiling and unveiling?

Recessive Glory: A Glory That Is Ending

Paul introduces two bits of information missing from Exodus 34 itself: (1) that the glory on Moses' face was "fading" or "being brought to an end" (2 Cor 3:7); and (2) that Moses put a veil over his face to prevent the Israelites from staring at what was fading (2 Cor 3:13). Childs says these details have "no basis at all in the Old Testament."[122] If Childs was correct, can we continue to

121. Garland outlines 2 Corinthians 3:12–18 in a way that clearly shows that Paul was citing from Exodus 34 in verses 13a, 16, and 18 and providing commentary in 13b–15, 17, and 18. David E. Garland, *2 Corinthians*, New American Commentary (Nashville: Broadman and Holman, 1999), 179.

122. Childs, *Exodus*, 621.

describe Paul as reading forward, or do these two insertions prove that he reads backward, asserting his privileged position as a Christian reader, perhaps lifting a veil of ignorance to discover an allegorical truth?

To read modern commentaries on 2 Corinthians 3 is to join a conflict of interpretations about Paul's interpretation. The controversy is partly philological. An exegetical cottage industry has busied itself clarifying the meaning of *katargeō* (2 Cor 3:7), arguably the key term in the passage. The still popular traditional idea that the glory of the old covenant is "fading" away is itself fading. Biblical scholars and translations typically understand this as speaking of Moses' glory being only temporary, in which case the purpose of the veil is to hide from Israel the truth about the old covenant's disappearing glory. Counting against this view is evidence in postbiblical Jewish literature that the glory on Moses' face was thought to be permanent, not fading.[123]

Philology matters. Paul uses the term *katargeō* four times (2 Cor 3:7, 11, 13, 14); it is the key to understanding the distinction he is making between Moses' ministry and his own. Although some translations continue to say "fading" or "passing away," many have now rejected this expression, insisting that there is no lexical evidence for it. Alternate translations are "rendered ineffective," "made inoperative," or "nullified."[124] Hafemann notes that Paul uses the term in contexts having to do with the discontinuity between this age and the age to come: "Its context is consistently eschatological."[125] Paul is saying that the glory on Moses' face, which was so glorious "that the Israelites could not gaze at" it (3:7), was already in the process of being rendered null *before* Moses put on the veil.

Paul seizes on Moses' veil as both symbol and symptom of the distinction between the old and new covenants, and as the reason for the inferiority of Moses' ministry as opposed to Paul's. The veil clearly has something to do with glory—but what, and whose? As to whose, there can be only one answer, for there is only one source: "It is the glory of the Lord on the face of Moses."[126] Paul is saying that Moses put the veil over his face so that the Israelites might not gaze at the "end" of the glory being set aside or rendered inoperative (3:13). "End" (Gk. *telos*) is the other key term that Paul introduces. It also marks another fork

123. For documentation of this point, see Linda Belleville, "Tradition or Creation? Paul's Use of the Exodus 34 tradition in 2 Corinthians 3:7–18," in *Paul and the Scriptures of Israel*, ed. Craig A. Evans and James A. Sanders, JSNTSup 83 (Sheffield: Sheffield Academic, 1993), 165–86.

124. See esp. William R. Baker, "Did the Glory of Moses' Face Fade? A Reexamination of καταργέω in 2 Corinthians 3:7–18," *Bulletin for Biblical Research* 10, no. 1 (2000): 3–5; Duane E. Garrett, "Veiled Hearts: The Translation and Interpretation of 2 Corinthians 3," *JETS* 53, no. 4 (2010): 729–72; George H. Guthrie, "*Katargeo* and the People of the Shining Face (2 Corinthians 3:7–18)," *Southern Baptist Journal of Theology* 19, no. 3 (2015): 41–60.

125. Scott J. Hafemann, "Paul's Argument from the Old Testament and Christology in 2 Corinthians 1–9," in *The Corinthian Correspondence*, ed. R. Bieringer (Louvain: Leuven University Press, 1996), 288.

126. Baker, "Did the Glory of Moses' Face Fade?," 8.

in the interpretive road where commentators diverge. Does the veil conceal the expiration (i.e., a *temporal* end) or the culmination (i.e., a *purposive* end) of the glory of the old covenant that was being annulled? How one answers that also affects one's understanding of Moses' motive for veiling his face, for the veil and its veiling function lie at the heart of the interpretive dispute.

Those who see *telos* as purposive view the veil as representing Israel's inability to see how the law points to Christ as its ultimate goal (cf. Rom 10:4: "For Christ is the end [*telos*] of the law"). For example, Cyril of Alexandria said that by veiling himself, Moses was teaching Israel "that they were not strong enough to see the true face of the law (that is, Christ). Rather, they were attending to what amounts to its second face, the shadow that has no glory. . . . And so Christ, the veiled glory of Moses, was 'the end of the law' that was set aside."[127] In contrast, those who see *telos* as temporal say Moses veiled himself to prevent the people from seeing the fading glory and fragile nature of the old covenant. Moses was reticent to let Israel see the transitory glory for fear that they would see him, too, "as being of no more than temporary importance."[128] It is as if Moses' day and dispensation were coming to an (embarrassing) end: "What the veil hides from Jewish eyes is the temporary character—not of scripture, but of the Mosaic covenant."[129] Ralph Martin calls attention to Israel's intense *gazing* at Moses' shining face (2 Cor 3:13), a symptom of their unwillingness to acknowledge that the old covenant was on its way out.[130]

Hays sees Paul as giving not an exegesis of Exodus 34 as much as "an allusive homily based on biblical incidents."[131] He takes seriously Paul's comment about what happened to Israel being "written down for our instruction, on whom the end of the ages has come" (1 Cor 10:11), claiming that "Israel's story is a metaphor for Christian experience."[132] Paul is for Hays an exemplar of the new reader competence that is part and parcel of being a new covenant member, and 2 Corinthians 3:7–18 provides the ultimate warrant for Paul's Christian reading of the Old Testament inasmuch as it touches on his interpretive aims and methods, as well as providing a concrete example of his hermeneutic.

According to Hays, Paul reads Exodus 34 as a veiled message (so to speak) about the future covenant people of God: the church. That the glory on Moses' face was fading or inoperative (Hays prefers "transitory") is Paul's *retrospective*

---

127. Cyril of Alexandria, *Commentaries on Romans, 1–2 Corinthians, and Hebrews*, Ancient Christian Texts, ed. Joel C. Elowsky (IVP Academic, 2022), 92.

128. Barrett, *Second Epistle to the Corinthians*, 119. Thiselton and Belleville say something similar in their respective commentaries.

129. Hooker, "Beyond the Things That Are Written?," 304.

130. Ralph Martin, *2 Corinthians*, Word Bible Commentary, 2nd ed. (Grand Rapids: Zondervan, 2014), 211.

131. Hays, *Echoes of Scripture in the Letters of Paul*, 132.

132. Hays, 95.

judgment on its meaning.[133] Moses himself understood the true purpose of the law and enjoyed, albeit temporarily, "*the eschatological knowledge of God through personal encounter*,"[134] hence his radiant face. However, the veil that hides the glory is for Hays the key to the whole passage. The Israelites' intense focus on the veil itself—the "letter" or script of the covenant rather than its substance—prevented them from seeing the *telos* of the covenant represented by Moses' shining face: fellowship with God in Christ. Moses caught a glimpse of this during his unveiled encounters; hence he "is both the paradigm for the Christian's direct experience of the Spirit and the symbol for the old covenant to which that experience is set in antithesis."[135]

In contrast to Hays's overtly Christian (backward) reading, Hafemann argues that Paul is indeed reading *forward*, "in accordance with the Scriptures," drawing on distinctive Christian presuppositions, yes, but also reading the text in line with the original context. Hafemann believes the radiance on Moses' face is proof that God's glorious presence is still with the people, mediated by Moses.[136] This is no tame glory, however, but potentially destructive; a people of unclean body parts, whether lips or hearts, cannot withstand being in the presence of an all-holy, righteous God (cf. Isa 6:5). Moses' veil thus *protects* the people from the potentially destructive effects of the glory of the Lord. When Moses veils himself, it is not to hide his "fading" glory; rather, it is to shield the people from being destroyed by the refracted incandescence of a thrice-holy God.[137] The veil is hiding neither the termination of the old covenant nor its fulfillment in Christ (things the author of Exodus could not have known); rather, the veil is "rendering inoperative" what would have been that glory's inevitable end or negative result: destruction. Hafemann thinks this makes better sense of the contrast Paul is making between Moses' and his own ministry: "Paul is consequently bold in his ministry because he knows that God's glory can now reach his people without the fear of judgment."[138] On Hafemann's reading, Paul's insertions are not impositions; they simply serve to make explicit

---

133. Hays underlines the importance throughout his work of "the retrospectively discerned figural coherence between Old Testament and the New," in Hays, *Reading with the Grain of Scripture* (Grand Rapids: Eerdmans, 2020).

134. Barton, "Metaphor of the Face in Paul," 138 (emphasis original).

135. Hays, *Echoes of Scripture in the Letters of Paul*, 143.

136. In this second giving of the law, only Moses experiences God's glory, unlike the first time, when "all the people saw the thunder and the flames of lightning" (Exod 20:18), for now the Israelites had become idolaters.

137. See Hafemann, *Paul, Moses, and the History of Israel*, 223.

138. Hafemann, *Paul, Moses, and the History of Israel*, 361. Hafemann's critics point out that this does not explain why the people were *sometimes* able to look upon Moses' unveiled face without being destroyed. Nor is it clear that Paul actually makes this purpose explicit. See Sigurd Grindheim, "The Law Kills but the Gospel Gives Life: The Letter-Spirit Dualism in 2 Corinthians 3:5–18," *Journal for the Study of the New Testament* 84 (2001): 100.

an unexpressed presupposition that makes sense of Exodus 34 in its original context.[139]

Here ends the backward and forward readings of God's word. We turn now to my transfigural alternative. Tim Savage astutely observes that many commentators "tend to get bogged down in the perplexing details of the text and seldom focus on the broader contours of Paul's thought."[140] The big picture in 2 Corinthians concerns the nature of Paul's ministry, which he contrasts with Moses'. Why refer to Moses, particularly to a Gentile audience? Did Paul expect them to follow his argument, or was he referring to the veil for strategic (i.e., rhetorical) rather than properly interpretive purposes?[141] Savage contends that Moses was the best-known and most-respected Jewish figure in Greco-Roman antiquity and in Palestinian Judaism, largely because of his meeting with Yahweh on Mount Sinai and his resultant shining face. According to one rabbinic text, "If an opening were to be made in the grave of Moses, the entire world could not endure the light."[142]

To read Paul reading Moses, it helps to keep in mind that Paul is essentially "an *interpreter* of the gospel"[143] and that the gospel advance of God's glory—its illuminative progress in the economy of light—is the central theme of 2 Corinthians 3. Keeping in mind Savage's call to keep the big Pauline picture in mind, I believe Paul reads Moses with a concern for the knowledge of God and the light of Christ. It stands to reason that Paul would be preoccupied with the light of Christ given his own conversion experience, suffused with "a light from heaven, brighter than the sun" (Acts 26:13; cf. 9:3; 22:6, 9, 11).[144] Elsewhere, Paul uses the creation of light as a model for the proclamation of the gospel to a world in darkness.[145] It would therefore be a surprise if Paul did *not* parse the letter/spirit contrast in terms of the economy of light. And this is precisely what we find him doing in 2 Corinthians 3.

Both Moses and Paul are ministers of God's glory, yet "Paul's ministry is

---

139. For a shorter version of Hafemann's argument, see his "The Glory and Veil of Moses in 2 Cor 3:7–14: An Example of Paul's Contextual Exegesis of the Old Testament: A Proposal," *Horizons in Biblical Theology* 14, no. 1 (1992): 31–49.

140. Timothy B. Savage, *Power through Weakness: Paul's Understanding of the Christian Ministry in 2 Corinthians*, Society for New Testament Studies Monograph Series (Cambridge: Cambridge University Press, 1996), 105.

141. See Mitchell, "The Mirror and the Veil: Hermeneutics of Occlusion," ch. 4 in *Paul, the Corinthians and the Birth of Christian Hermeneutics*.

142. Cited in Savage, *Power through Weakness*, 109n38.

143. J. Christiaan Beker, *The Triumph of God: The Essence of Paul's Thought* (Minneapolis: Fortress, 1990), 118.

144. Paul uses light imagery to describe both his experience of encountering Christ and the transformative power of the gospel (Eph 5:8), which suggests he sees a connection between light as a divine revelation of truth and the eschatological nature of this light.

145. See further G. L. Borchert, "Light and Darkness," in *Dictionary of Paul and His Letters*, ed. Gerald F. Hawthorne, Ralph P. Martin, Daniel G. Reid (Downers Grove, IL: InterVarsity, 1993), 555–57.

much more glorious than Moses'"[146]—but not because Paul had a different light. On the contrary: the same divine light that streamed from Jesus' face shone on Moses'. However, Moses' glory was but a reflection of the God who is light itself, whereas the light on Jesus' face came from within. Moreover, the old covenant, represented by Moses, though it was lit by the same light, had but a *recessive* glory, a glory that was inoperative the way a recessive gene is inoperative, unable to produce its intended phenotypic effect. The old covenant ("letter") was recessive because, absent the presence and ministry of the Spirit on sinful hearts, it was unable to produce its intended effect the way the new covenant can and does. A better description might be to describe the glory of the old covenant as *eschatologically recessive*, "for as yet [in Moses' time] the Spirit had not been given" (John 7:39).

Because of the people's sin, the old covenant arrangement was doomed as soon as it began. The glory that was Moses'—the glory of the old covenant that Moses embodied and mediated—was being annulled by God himself. "God removes and displaces what is transient to make way for better and abiding things."[147] Paul contrasts the glorious ministry of the law with his own "ministry of righteousness," a term he echoes from Isaiah 58:8, "where 'righteousness' is associated with 'light,' namely, the radiance of the Lord's saving work."[148] It thus appears that Paul is contrasting two stages in the divine economy of light. His apostolic ministry outshines Moses' as the sun outshines the moon, a contrast Paul deploys elsewhere to contrast the relative glory of natural and spiritual bodies (1 Cor 15:40–44).[149] Moses' "ministry of condemnation" (2 Cor 3:9) has only the glory of the "lesser light" that ruled the night of Israel's covenant unfaithfulness.

Back to the meaning of the veil and its function. For Hays, Israel's gazing at the veil represents the people's focus on the letter, rather than that to which it points. For Hafemann, the veil symbolizes God's grace in sparing Israel from the full blast of his holy glory. I am proposing that we situate the veil in the economy of light, where it marks a particular stage in the progress of divine illumination. The veil has redemptive-historical significance, I submit, serving as a permeable barrier as it were between old and new covenants. Paul capitalizes on what Moses *does* with the veil, effectively turning it into symbolic prophetic action similar to Ezekiel's use of a brick to pantomime Babylon's siege of Jerusalem

---

146. Savage, *Power through Weakness*, 110.

147. Moises Silva, "καταργέω," in *New International Dictionary of New Testament Theology and Exegesis*, 2nd ed., vol. 2 (Grand Rapids: Zondervan, 2014), 641.

148. Seifrid, *Second Letter to the Corinthians*, 158.

149. Cf. Wolfgang Musculus: "What else was the letter of the law in the old covenant than what the brightness of the moon is in the night." Cited in 2 *Corinthians*, Reformation Commentary on Scripture, ed. Scott M. Manetsch (Downers Grove, IL: InterVarsity, 2022), 88.

(Ezek 4:1–5:4): "For Paul, the veiling was designed to sift the Israelites into two groups, those who understood the deeper parabolic intent behind 'the letter' (2 Cor 3:6b)—that is, behind the 'literal sense' . . . —and those who did not."[150] In Paul's view, those who understood what Moses was doing would also understand that the old covenant was being annulled, encouraging them to look forward to an even more glorious arrangement. The letter "kills" because the Israelites failed to discern what Moses was doing with the veil: pointing, like John the Baptist, to the necessity of his "decrease" to make room for the increase of Christ's glory to come (cf. John 3:30).

Some kind of veil always separates sinners from the thrice-holy God (Rev 4:8). Paul sees Moses' veil as signifying the barrier that stands between the covenant people and the glorious covenant promise that God will dwell in their midst (cf. Exod 25:8). That Moses veils himself demonstrates that the old covenant has not come to completion, which will include the glorification not of Moses only but also of the people (cf. Exod 33:16). It was because of Israel's sin that this end "was cut short and not brought to completion."[151] The veil therefore indicates the *limited access to God's glorious presence* that marks the Mosaic stage of the economy of light. In this respect, the veil over Moses' face served the same purpose as the curtain in the temple that cordoned off the holy of holies.[152] The thrust of Paul's comparison is that the "letter"—the law before the coming of Christ—glorious as it was, could not fulfill the promise of the covenant. The peculiar glory of the letter of the law was, in Melanchthon's words, only "the power to kill."[153]

Excessive Glory: A Glory That Is Greater

Regardless of other exegetical uncertainties, everyone agrees that Paul is contrasting the lesser glory of Moses' ministry of the old covenant with the greater glory of Paul's ministry of the new.[154] The glory of the life-giving Spirit far exceeds the glory of the life-snuffing power of the bare letter that has become null and void. The real contrast between letter and spirit plays out in terms of their differing degrees of glory (*doxa*), a term Paul uses eight times in the span of just five verses (2 Cor 3:7–11).[155] Paul employs the familiar Jewish *qal wahomer*

150. Bates, *Hermeneutics of the Apostolic Proclamation*, 169.

151. Guthrie, *2 Corinthians*, 221.

152. Seifrid, *Second Letter to the Corinthians*, 164. I am aware that the Greek terms for the curtain used in the temple and the veil that covered Moses' face are different; nevertheless, their functions are similar.

153. Cited in Manetsch, *2 Corinthians*, 83.

154. Thomas Schreiner believes that the center of Paul's theology is the desire to "magnify" God in Christ, and to "enlighten" (*photisai*) everyone concerning the mystery he proclaims (Eph 3:9) that, in Christ, God has fulfilled his plan of salvation to the praise of God's glory. *Paul, Apostle of God's Glory in Christ: A Pauline Theology*, 2nd ed. (Downers Grove, IL: IVP Academic, 2020).

155. Following Garland, *2 Corinthians*, 167–69.

(lit. "light and heavy"; from lesser to greater) to construct a "how much more" argument. The old covenant was indeed glorious, reflecting God's goodness, holiness, and other perfections. Yet, in and of itself, it could only expose Israel's shortcomings, not transform them. Paul's ministry is more glorious because it is life-giving (3:6), communicates righteousness rather than condemnation (3:9), is permanent (3:11), and bolder (3:12): "In these conclusions 'a minori ad maius' ["from lesser to greater"] Paul concludes that the glory of this new covenant must far exceed that of the old."[156] Morna Hooker agrees: "If one could measure the strength of glory with the appropriate instrument—a doxameter perhaps?—the glory seen on Moses' face is nothing by comparison."[157]

Comparative glory was precisely the issue between Paul and his Corinthian opponents. The Corinthians were thinking of Moses' glory in terms of worldly frames of reference—the glory that was Rome. Paul's countercultural claim, that his ministry of the Spirit has "even more glory" (3:8), makes sense only in the context of Moses' place in the economy of light. As we have seen, the light on Moses' face is refracted, filtered through the old covenant and the medium of the veil. In contrast, Paul ministers with unveiled face (3:16). This is what lies behind Paul's boldness (3:12): it is the *greater glory* of the new covenant that gives him hope and empowers his speech. Paul's boldness is therefore "not like Moses, who would put a veil over his face" (3:13).[158] Moses saw only the back of God; Paul met the risen Christ, God's very image, and "only through Christ is [the veil] taken away" (3:14).

Paul knows that what happened to Israel, including the events of Exodus 34, was written for his readers' instruction, "on whom the end of the ages has come" (1 Cor 10:11). Paul believed both that Christ's death and resurrection was "according to the Scriptures" (1 Cor 15:3–4), and that the Scriptures represent God's divine address to the present.[159] The excessive glory of the new covenant has everything to do with the new frame of reference that is part of Pauline already/not-yet eschatology. Paul's "spirited" frame of reference—his awareness that the resurrection of Jesus ushers in a new age—allows him to see the old covenant for what it truly was: a letter that cannot practice what it preaches, a letter without the life-giving Spirit. The crucial difference between Moses' ministry and Paul's finally amounts to "the activity, or lack of activity, of the

---

156. W. C. Van Unnik, "'With Unveiled Face,' An Exegesis of 2 Corinthians iii:12–18," *Novum Testamentum* 6 (1963): 158.

157. Hooker, "Beyond the Things That Are Written?," 297.

158. Van Unnik says that Paul was thinking in Aramaic and made an unconscious connection between the Aramaic idiom for boldness, which is "to uncover one's face." Van Unnik, "'With Unveiled Face,'" 161.

159. See David Lincicum, "How Did Paul Read Scripture?," in *The New Cambridge Companion to St. Paul*, ed. Bruce W. Longenecker (Cambridge: Cambridge University Press, 2020), 231.

Holy Spirit within the human heart."[160] It is a difference in the economy of light: Paul is writing to those upon whom the illumining Spirit has been poured. His similarity to Moses, the mediator of the glorious old covenant, is thereby qualified by an even greater dissimilarity, the "how much more" glorious ministry of the new covenant, a function of the eschatological gift of the Holy Spirit.

Israel's Veiled Hearts: A Glory That Is Obscured (2 Cor 3:14–16)

Paul's decision to use Exodus 34 to stave off Corinthian objections to his apostolic ministry was hardly arbitrary. The previous section explained Paul's letter/spirit contrast in terms of the difference between a recessive and excessive glory, a difference that signals an eschatological changing of the guard (i.e., from the old age of the law to the new age of the Spirit) and a new stage in the economy of light. In this section, we tease out the hermeneutical significance of the contrast by considering Paul's theological interpretation of Moses' veil.[161]

In the world behind the text (i.e., the original historical context), the veil is a physical object that prevents the Israelites from seeing Moses' shining face. In Paul's hands, however, "that same veil" (2 Cor 3:14) shifts registers; its light refracts "from the concrete to the symbolic."[162] It is not simply a physical object but "a spiritual condition."[163] The veil that once obscured Moses from Israel's physical sight is now a "barrier that still hides the truth from the Jewish reader of the Old Testament."[164] Moses' self-veiling remains a prophetic symbolic action, but now on a metaphorical level: "The veil—the barrier which prevents something from being seen—goes hand-in-hand with a refusal to see the truth."[165] For Paul, "not seeing the goal of the fading Old Covenant and having a hardened mind are two sides of the same idea."[166] The failing is spiritual and moral: "The problem signified by the veil is thus not a *cognitive* ability . . . but an inescapable *volitional* inability as a result of a hardened heart untouched by the Spirit's transforming power."[167] The hermeneutical consequence of veiled reading is an inability to see the glorious promissory note of the letter, the "end" of the law.

The link between the literal veil Moses wore and the spiritual veil that clouds understanding is more than arbitrary. Paul explicitly states, it is "the same veil" (3:14). The literal veil hid Moses' face; in Paul's time the spiritual

160. Thomas E. Provence, "'Who Is Sufficient for These Things?,' An Exegesis of 2 Corinthians ii.14-iii.18," *Novum Testamentum* 24, no. 1 (1982): 77.

161. Seifrid, *Second Letter to the Corinthians*, 165.

162. Hafemann, *Paul, Moses, and the History of Israel*, 371.

163. Provence, "Who Is Sufficient for These Things?," 77.

164. Martin, *2 Corinthians*, 217.

165. Hooker, "Beyond the Things That Are Written?," 300.

166. Provence, "Who Is Sufficient for These Things?," 76.

167. Hafemann, *Paul, Moses, and the History of Israel*, 374.

veil hides Moses' meaning. Paul "equates the inability of the Israelites to come to terms with Moses' glowing face with his opponents' inability to comprehend the significance of the new covenant."[168] The problem is not philological but psychological: a denial of truth. First the Israelites and now Paul's opponents fail to understand the "grammar" of glory, in particular, its tense. Both are looking at the glory of God with the wrong (time)frame of reference, thinking that what is past (an earlier stage in the economy of light) is still present. This is the "hardening" that Paul says remains to the present: it is a matter of being in the wrong place, spiritually and intellectually, to interpret Scripture rightly.[169]

What, then, is Moses' veil? Paul's "spiritual" interpretation of the veil is an extension of its literal sense: an impediment to right seeing/understanding. The veil—*the way in which a stubborn attachment to an obsolete frame of reference and earlier stage in the economy of light limits one's access to the transformative power of God's glory*—is what Christ removes or renders inoperative.[170] The law proved unable to make good on the covenant promise for God to dwell with all Israel because it was unable to transform hearts of stone to hearts of flesh. The veil represents the barrier—visual, spiritual, and interpretive—that prevents people from grasping the true end of the law: "In the veiling of Moses, the Israelites' carnal minds were left without spiritual understanding; when Moses put a veil over his face . . . they were kept from perceiving the true import of the glory on Moses' face—that God's ultimate goal was for his covenant people to experience his presence and thus his glory."[171] In Heinrich Bullinger's words, "The veil is the letter, indeed, that dullness of mind, disbelief, and ignorance of Christ."[172]

Paul's case for the superiority of his apostolic ministry concludes with the claim that only "when one turns to the Lord" is the veil removed (3:16). Paul is alluding to Moses' practice of taking off the veil when he went in to speak to the Lord, as well as to Christian conversion: "Paul's own experience was living proof of the validity and force of this 'eschatological exegesis' of the Old Testament, which, through Christian eyes, takes on an added dimension."[173] In an interesting wordplay, Paul says the veil that annulled the glory of the old covenant is itself "annulled" (*katargeō*, again) in Christ (3:14). The negation is negated thanks to the progress of redemption in the economy of light: "The veil is real for those who are *not* 'in Christ,' but the veil has been abolished for those . . . who have embraced . . . the 'unveiled' hermeneutical *guidance* supplied

168. Garrett, "Veiled Hearts," 771.

169. See further the discussion in Bates, *Hermeneutics of the Apostolic Proclamation*, 173–79.

170. Cf. Garland: "The veil comes to stand for this hardened condition that prevents those who may treasure, defend, and diligently study the law from apprehending God's true glory." *2 Corinthians*, 191.

171. Guthrie, *2 Corinthians*, 224.

172. Heinrich Bullinger, commentary on 2 Cor 3:12–13. Cited in Manetsch, *2 Corinthians*, 91.

173. Martin, *2 Corinthians*, 217. Paul made it clear that, unlike Moses, Christians cannot unveil themselves. Conversion requires the grace of the Spirit working through faith.

by the apostolic preaching."[174] That the veil is removed by Christ at conversion demonstrates that Paul has not been reading backward after all: "The veiled reader fails hermeneutically, because he or she does not see that the literal text of the Mosaic scriptures *themselves* testify to the transitory nature of the Mosaic covenant."[175] This is the thesis—that we can read the Old Testament literally in the light of Christ for the light of Christ—at the heart of transfiguring interpretation.[176]

The Letter Unveiled: Transfiguring Interpretation Glorifies the Literal Sense

According to Robert Wilken, the church fathers did not need to allegorize the New Testament because "it speaks directly about Christ. . . . The spiritual meaning of the New Testament events is the literal meaning."[177] According to de Lubac, the situation with the Old Testament is different: "The Old Testament is the 'letter' for which the New Testament is its complementary allegorical 'Spirit.'"[178] Some describe de Lubac's approach as "theological interpretation of Scripture," in which Christian presuppositions deriving from the new reality of the risen Christ are retrospectively imposed onto the Old Testament, effectively "Christianizing" it. From the standpoint of Old Testament scholarship, however, such allegorizing (which is what "Christianizing" amounts to) is in fact a kind of coercive evangelism, a violent takeover that neglects or suppresses the discrete testimony and voices of the people of ancient Israel.

In this chapter, we have been asking whether Paul's interpretation of Exodus exemplifies reading forward or backward and, if backward, whether it goes with or against the grain of literal interpretation.[179] We have already established that the Old Testament *does* speak about Christ. It suffices here to relate what I said earlier about frames of reference to what I now want to say about reading transfigurally, in its dual sense: (1) reading *across* biblical figures in canonical

---

174. Bates, *Hermeneutics of the Apostolic Proclamation*, 182 (emphasis original).

175. Bates, 175.

176. Recall that light can be a source, medium, and result of illumination (i.e., coming to know truth), as can Christ, the illumining Word of God.

177. Robert Louis Wilken, "In Defense of Allegory," *Modern Theology* 14 (1998): 201.

178. Lang, "Order of Christian Theology," 122 (describing de Lubac's position).

179. Richard Hays, my chosen paradigm of one who reads backward, resists the implication that he is reading against the grain (see his book title at the end of this note). If we are to continue using this metaphor, then, it would be useful to clarify what the "grain" in question is. Hays identifies one of his recurring themes as "the *retrospectively discerned* figural coherence between the Old Testament and the New Testament." Hays, "Introduction: Gathering the Wheat," *Reading with the Grain of Scripture* (Grand Rapids: Eerdmans, 2020), emphasis added. It is one thing to discern something retrospectively, another to create it. A charitable reading of Hays is to be preferred: what one sees in reading backward, with veil removed, is a meaning that was already there, though veiled.

context as we did in part 2 (i.e., *trans-figurally*), following the way the figures run (e.g., from Mount Sinai to Mount Tabor) in accordance with divine authorial intent; and (2) reading *from* the Mount of Transfiguration in the economy of light (i.e., *transfigurally*), now knowing what Scripture is ultimately about (the light of Christ) and for (communicating the light of Christ). I have claimed that to read Exodus 34, and the rest of the Old Testament, transfigurally is *to read for the glory of Christ in the letter of the text, a glory that was always there, though veiled.*[180] We are now in a position to say that what is ultimately at stake in Paul's letter/spirit dichotomy is transfigural interpretation. The "letter" that kills is the *untransfigured* literal sense, which veils the light of Christ. The "spirit" that gives life is the *transfigured* literal sense, the sense unveiled by the Spirit, which the light of Christ illumines.[181]

Glorifying the Literal Sense (Part 1): Exalting the Christological Referent

Transfiguring biblical interpretation is the solution to the early Christian dilemma of knowing how the new revelation of God in Christ coheres with the antecedent revelation of God in the Jewish Scriptures. Faced with the prospect of either a Jewish literalism that refused to recognize Christ or a Marcionite literalism that refused to recognize the validity of the Old Testament, patristic and medieval Christian interpreters, while not abandoning the literal sense, gave their blessing to various modes of figural and spiritual interpretation.[182]

Jesus claims the earlier Scriptures "bear witness about me" (John 5:39), adding "[Moses] wrote of me" (v. 46). How should we understand this? Perhaps the Old Testament authors were giving literal pre-dictions of Christ (i.e., speaking of something before it happens). Another possibility is that Christ fulfills Scripture, though this can be known only retrospectively. Yet another approach starts from the other end, viewing Christ as the archetype and the Mosaic law as his witness: "Though Christ followed the Law in time he is understood to have preceded it and ordered it."[183] John Behr says, "For Irenaeus, the crucified Jesus Christ . . . was present prior to the Passion as the veiled content of

180. Note that "letter" here is a cipher for the literal sense, rightly understood, which is different from the "letter" in Paul's letter/spirit contrast. The final chapter will pursue a third sense of transfigural, according to which reading for the light of Christ in the letter of the text has as its ultimate aim the transfiguration of the reader.

181. As we shall see in the next chapter, the light of Christ is transformative in a way that the "letter," the untransfigured law of Moses, was not.

182. This is a broad generalization. Some, like Thomas Aquinas, think that Old Testament prophets can use figurative language to refer literally to Christ (e.g., "There shall come forth a shoot from the stump of Jesse"; Isa 11:1): "The principle is important to St. Thomas: Christ can be spoken of literally in the Old Testament." John Boyle, *Aquinas on Scripture* (Steubenville, OH: Emmaus Road Academic, 2022), 134.

183. Hooker, "Beyond the Things That Are Written?," 306–7.

the Scripture."[184] Christ is before all things, and in him all biblical books hold together (cf. Col 1:17), which is why, on this view, reading christologically does not go "beyond what is written" (1 Cor 4:6). Each of these views is, in one way or another, "Christ-centered." This forces the question, *how* exactly are the Old Testament texts "about" Christ?

The Romanian patristic scholar Bogdan Bucur sheds light on the question when he describes the two transfigurations we have here been considering—Moses' on Mount Sinai and Jesus' on Mount Tabor—as an "entryway" into the Christian Bible.[185] He takes his cue from church fathers who saw Jesus' transfiguration as the fulfillment of Moses' request to the Lord, "Please show me your glory" (Exod 33:18). Moses saw only the Lord's back, leading Irenaeus to suggest that the face-to-face vision had been postponed until later.[186] Of course, this makes sense only if it was the Son who promised Moses in the first place: "the 'face of God' that Moses desires to see is, in fact, the Son."[187] If this is right, we can perhaps imagine the transfigured Jesus greeting Moses with the words, "We meet again!" In any case, Pseudo-Ephrem's comment about the significance of Moses' and Elijah's presence with Jesus and his three disciples at the transfiguration is worth pondering: "There the authors of the old covenant saw the authors of the new."[188]

Bucur has expanded his insight into a book on "christophanic" exegesis.[189] He thinks modern biblical scholarship has failed to appreciate the significance of the early Christians' belief that Christ was "really present" in events narrated in the Old Testament. Bucur has a textual basis for what may initially appear to be a counterintuitive idea: the better manuscripts explicitly identify not Yahweh but Jesus as the agent "who saved a people out of the land of Egypt" (Jude 5).[190] What other scholars term "theophanies" (appearances of God) the church fathers regarded as appearances of the Son: "christophanies." It follows that the Son is not simply the telos to which the old covenant points (the Omega Point), but the one who was there from the beginning: "the Alpha and the Omega" (Rev 1:8; 21:6; 22:13).[191] If this hypothesis is correct, then typology and allegory alike fall short as categories to explain the New Testament use of

184. John Behr, *Way to Nicaea* (New York: St. Vladimir's Seminary Press, 2001), 119–20.

185. Bucur, "Sinai, Zion, and Tabor," 33–52.

186. Irenaeus, *Against Heresies* 4.20.9.

187. Bucur, "Sinai, Zion, and Tabor," 35.

188. Ephrem the Syrian, "Sermon on the Transfiguration of our Lord." Cited in Bucur, "Sinai, Zion, and Tabor," 37; see also "Of Our Venerable Father Ephrem the Syrian."

189. Bogdan Bucur, *Scripture Re-Envisioned: Christophanic Exegesis and the Making of a Christian Bible* (Leiden: Brill, 2018).

190. Insisting that it was indeed the Son who appeared to the patriarchs and Moses was an important plank in the church fathers' anti-Arian polemic.

191. Athanasius said explicitly, "Moses beheld God," and then specified the Logos. *Contra Arianos* 3.24.13–14.

the Old Testament. Strictly speaking, the Old Testament does not foreshadow Christ with "veiled" types; rather, the Old Testament directly *refers* to the Son as a personal speaking presence.[192] Consider: if the Logos-to-be-incarnate really appeared to Moses on Sinai, then there is no need to allegorize the text in order to find Christ. The Son is directly present in a number of preincarnate, divinely accommodated forms, be it a burning bush, a pillar of fire, or a cloud of glory. Paul in 2 Corinthians 3 may therefore be providing a literal-*cum*-christological interpretation of the Sinai theophany.

The appropriateness of using the economy of light as a framework for understanding the process of biblical interpretation should now be evident. That Christ was the author/revealer/speaker of the Old Testament may have been a new idea to early Christians, but that does not count against its reality. Paul Blowers explains the significance of Bucur's work for understanding early Christian hermeneutics: "Interpretation entailed an encounter with the Divine Author present in and behind the texts, something that could happen not simply by mechanically or scholastically extracting meaning from those texts but engaging them 'performatively' within the life and worship of the Church."[193]

What is true of patristic interpretation applies "how much more" to Pauline hermeneutics. Paul, too, believed that Old Testament narrative recounts the literal action of Jesus Christ as a literal agent, as is evident in his remarkable claim about Israel's wilderness wandering: "For they drank from the spiritual Rock that followed them, and the Rock was Christ" (1 Cor 10:4).

If Christ is in some respect identical with Yahweh, such that theophanies are christophanies, then there is no reason to read Christ "back" into the Old Testament: he is already there. Paul may very well be interpreting Old Testament accounts of theophanies "as manifestations of the pre-incarnate Son of God."[194] The burning bush is on this view not a *type* of the radiance on Jesus' transfigured face as a *form* of the Son's glory, for Christ is "straightforwardly *identified* with the 'Lord' in the Old Testament narrative."[195] Christ's manifestation to Moses on Mount Tabor echoes or completes his earlier appearance to Moses on Mount Sinai: "What Moses once saw in darkness, he now sees, on Tabor, in the blazing light of the Transfiguration."[196] Bucur is hardly alone in his claim that many Old Testament passages are *literally* about Jesus Christ. The

192. Kelly, commenting on 1 Peter 1:11, said it was the preexistent Christ himself who spoke through the prophets. *Commentary on the Epistles of Peter and Jude*, 61.

193. Paul Blowers, "Foreword" to Bucur, *Scripture Re-Envisioned*, viii.

194. Larry Hurtado, *Lord Jesus Christ: Devotion to Jesus in Earliest Christianity* (Grand Rapids: Eerdmans, 2005), 565–66.

195. Bucur, *Scripture Re-Envisioned*, 137.

196. Bucur, "Christological Exegesis of Theophanies and the Making of Early Christian Theology," *Concordia Theological Quarterly* 86 (2022): 113.

Old Testament clearly attests to the reality of one God (Deut 6:4) but leaves somewhat open the crucial question about the referent of "the *God outside of the text* to whom these words direct us."[197]

Can we say that the Old Testament is about the triune God, or do we chalk it up to the import/export business of systematic theology? C. Kavin Rowe speaks of "biblical pressure" moving us "to the conclusion that YHWH is not the Father alone."[198] The name YHWH revealed to Moses out of the burning bush (Exod 3:13–15) "enables the reader to perceive the ascriptive subject of the Old Testament as the one God, known to Christians as Father, Son, and Holy Spirit."[199] It matters that the Old Testament is about the same God as the New Testament. So Childs: "The church's struggle with the Trinity was not a battle *against* the Old Testament, but rather a battle *for* the Old Testament."[200] There is no need to allegorize the Old Testament if it is already about Christ. We can therefore say that YHWH *always* referred to the one God who is Father, Son, and Spirit, even if the authors of the Old Testament did not yet have a developed concept of the Trinity. The overlapping biblical uses of "light" for the one God (1 John 1:5, "God is light"), for the "Father" of lights (James 1:17), for the Son who is the light of the world (John 8:12), and for the Spirit who shines the light of Christ in our hearts (2 Cor 4:6) all attest the triune identity of the divine referent.

Glorifying the Literal Sense (Part 2): Illuminating the Letter

All serious interpreters of the Bible have to grapple with the literal sense—and with its transfiguration. The editors of *A Manifesto for Theological Interpretation* rightly encourage readers "to press through the verbal/grammatical sense of the text to its theological subject matter," adding, "Ideally, theological commentary reveals the organic relationship between the literal sense of Scripture and its figural sense."[201] Perhaps, but unpacking "organic hermeneutics" is every bit as challenging as explaining organic chemistry.

Let us return for a moment to the veil that complicates our reading. Ralph Martin says removing the veil from our reading of Scripture (the result of turning to the Lord; 2 Cor 3:16), enables an "eschatological exegesis" of the Old

197. C. Kavin Rowe, "Biblical Pressure and Trinitarian Hermeneutics," *Pro Ecclesia* 11 no. 3 (2002): 311.
198. Rowe, 303.
199. Andrea D. Saner, *"Too Much to Grasp": Exodus 3:13–16 and the Reality of God*. Journal of Theological Interpretation Supplements 11 (Winona Lake, IN: Eisenbrauns, 2015), 229.
200. Brevard Childs, *Biblical Theology of the Old and New Testaments: Theological Reflections on the Christian Bible* (Minneapolis: Fortress, 1992), 376 (emphasis original).
201. Craig G. Bartholomew and Heath A. Thomas, "A Manifesto for Theological Interpretation," in *A Manifesto for Theological Interpretation* (Grand Rapids: Baker Academic, 2016), 23–24.

Testament, thanks to which "Christ in all the Scriptures" is made known.[202] Eschatological exegesis reads for what we might call the eschatological *is*, where *is* identifies not something fully present or actual but, rather, something that *is coming to be in Christ*, an already/not-yet state of affairs. Of course, to do this, you need an eschatological frame of reference. This is precisely what I have argued the transfiguration provides: an eschatological frame of reference for relating the Old Testament and New Testament in terms of *how much more glorious*. The transfiguration is *literally* (i.e., historically) a tasting and seeing of an "end of the ages" event, one that enables those upon whom the end of the ages has come—which is to say everyone after the apostles, including readers today—to understand in a deeper way what happened beforehand to those who were awaiting the end.[203] Paul says these things (Old Testament stories) were written down for the sake of instructing those "on whom the end of the ages has come" (1 Cor 10:11), a set whose members include Paul and all subsequent interpreters, including contemporary Christians. Not all Christians share the same historical context, but we all share the same eschatological context: between the times of Christ's first and second comings.

The transfiguration fixes our attention on the precise moment when the frame of reference shifts: from "letter" to "spirit"; old to new age. *It does so by illumining, not canceling, the Old Testament letter, uncovering the glory of the Old Testament's literal sense.* What makes the transfiguration a Christianly apt framework of understanding is its combination of narrative continuity (Christ's story is "in accordance with the scriptures," represented by Moses and Elijah) and apocalyptic discontinuity (Christ's resurrection and ascension, together with the coming of the Holy Spirit, usher in a new age, symbolized by even more glorious light). Recall, too, that Moses and Elijah are talking about Jesus' death (his "departure"; Luke 9:31), even as his divinity is being revealed and his exaltation anticipated. It is as if the transfiguration serves as a synopsis of the whole story of creation, fall, redemption, and consummation. In Vern Poythress's words, "The first heaven and earth does not contain its full meaning in itself. It is destined for transfiguration. That transfiguration shows openly and climactically what it was meant for all along. So, in terms of purpose, the goal is more 'ontologically basic' than the incomplete starting point."[204]

So how hermeneutically central is the transfiguration, and does reading the Old Testament in its light involve reading forward or backward? I want to tackle

202. Ralph Martin, *2 Corinthians*, 217.

203. I agree with Bates that the plural "ends of the ages" is best understood as "the solitary eschatological age in which all the preceding ages find their termination" (Bates, *Hermeneutics of the Apostolic Proclamation*, 132).

204. Vern Poythress, *The Mystery of the Trinity: A Trinitarian Approach to the Attributes of God* (Phillipsburg, NJ: P&R, 2020), 240.

these questions in dialogue with Matthew Bates's study of apostolic hermeneutics. According to Bates, what governs Paul's use of Scripture is a "christocentric protocreedal narrative" that is kerygmatic (i.e., a core Christian proclamation), apostolic (i.e., held in common by all the apostles), and economic (i.e., the result of God's "administrative providence"). Bates identifies two protocreeds (Rom 1:1–6 and 1 Cor 15:3–11), in which Paul states that Christ's death and resurrection are "according to the scriptures" and "promised in advance."[205] Only those familiar with the "eight-stage master kerygmatic narrative," however, have the interpretive key that unlocks the true meaning of the Old Testament.[206] Bates's thesis is that Paul uses the apostolic kerygma as his interpretive framework for reading the Old Testament.

Bates's approach is preferable to those who locate the interpretive key in the believing community's experience, particularly when some insist that the Spirit *continues* to lead the church in ways that go *beyond* the New Testament, as the New Testament goes beyond the Old Testament.[207] Such approaches give rise to the "ecclesial sense" of the New Testament, namely, the way the church's present experience of the Spirit leads it to "refract" Scripture. David Ford describes this as a "Spirit-led 'reading forwards'" into the life of the church.[208] On Bates's view, however, the criterion for right backward reading is not contemporary Christian experience (something postcanonical) but the apostolic kerygma. The story of Christ serves as Paul's primary lens for interpreting the unified divine economy, including the Old Testament. It is the story of Christ, not adherence to typological or allegorical interpretation, that governs Paul's reading of the Old Testament: "Paul does not reason forward from scriptural type to present application, but rather backward from presently known realities to text."[209] According to Bates, it is not Paul's hermeneutic but his *rhetoric* that is typological: "For Paul . . . the selection of a suitable trope [e.g., "type"] . . . occurs *subsequent* to the linking of the mental images."[210]

There is much to admire in Bates's account of Paul's approach to biblical interpretation, particularly its emphasis on the normative role of the apostolic kerygma. With Hafemann, Bates affirms Paul's "respect for context." However, contra Hafemann, Bates contends that "the first hermeneutical move for Paul is not a sequential engagement with the Pentateuch, but a story about Christ

205. Bates, *Hermeneutics of the Apostolic Proclamation*, 107.

206. The eight stages include creation, sin, covenant with Israel, birth of the Messiah, Jesus' ministry, death, resurrection, and commission of the apostles to spread the gospel.

207. E.g., Luke Timothy Johnson, *Scripture and Discernment: Decision Making in the Church* (Nashville: Abingdon, 1996).

208. See the discussion in Lang, "Order of Christian Theology," esp. 123 and 137.

209. Bates, *Hermeneutics of Apostolic Proclamation*, 332.

210. Bates, 340.

that has already been judged to be in accordance with the scriptures."[211] Paul's hermeneutical reasoning travels primarily from the apostolic proclamation of the Christ event to Old Testament text, not from Old Testament text to Christ event.[212] This leads Bates to champion, with Hays, reading backward: "Paul reads the scriptures from his post-Christ event location."[213] At the same time, Bates disagrees with Hays's claim that what ensures reader competence is the presence of the Spirit. On the contrary, what matters most is reading the story of Israel, and the story of our own lives, in light of the apostolically proclaimed story of Christ. The stakes are high, for Bates describes Paul as "the foundation of subsequent Christian hermeneutics," a norm for all Christian reading.[214] If Paul is indeed the father of mere Christian hermeneutics, how do things stand with literal interpretation?

Let me make three points in response. First, the transfiguration is conspicuous by its absence from Bates's summary of the kerygma; it does not figure in his reconstructed apostolic narrative or in its built-in hermeneutic. As we have seen, however, all three Synoptic Gospels include it, and the fourth gospel is arguably an extended transfiguration narrative. I am not saying that the transfiguration is a saving event, an essential of the gospel; rather, I am suggesting that the transfiguration is an event of hermeneutical significance inasmuch as it reveals the Son's divine nature, explains the Son's mission (via the coordinates of the Law and the Prophets), and discloses the final purpose of his person and work (viz., basking in the glorious presence of God). *The transfiguration boasts a built-in hermeneutic.*

The second point concerns Bates's claim that although God authored the "internal meaning" or *res* of the Scriptures (i.e., the history of salvation that it recounts), Paul chooses the rhetorical tropes or *verba* that express the "natural correspondence" between the Old Testament and the Christ-event and post-Christ events. Bates says Paul "does not reason forward from scripture type to present application, but rather backward from presently known realities to text."[215] The denial of forward reasoning calls into question the *truth* of the typological correspondences Paul discerns between the Old Testament and the story of Christ: are they *discovered* or *invented?* On the one hand, Bates wants to say they are really there, inscribed into history by the divine author of the economy; on the other hand, he wants to say that these correspondences are invented, a product of Paul's rhetoric. For example, in connection with Paul's allegory of

211. Bates, 351. Bates is here responding to Francis Watson, but the point he makes applies to Hafemann too.

212. Bates, 352.

213. Bates, 353.

214. Bates, 353–54.

215. Bates, 353–54.

Sarah and Hagar in Galatians 4, Bates writes, "God has orchestrated . . . the deeper metatextual reality, but not the precise linguistic housing."[216] By way of contrast, I have argued that God is the author of both (salvation) history and the (biblical) discourse that recounts it. If God is author and rhetor, then Paul is merely figuring out God's figures after him.

Third, Bates misconstrues Paul's hermeneutics when he identifies it as a species of reading backward. The reality is more complex. For the events of the Old Testament are, in themselves, forward-looking—this is the thrust of the claim that they *deliberately anticipate* the Christ event. Clearly, the divine economy is future-oriented.[217] Old Testament persons, things, and events *really* figure their fulfillment in Christ: they may be discovered retrospectively, but they are not invented. Paul's use of typological figures is less a rhetorical than an epistemological invention, an instrument (like the telescope) without which he could not see what is really there in the divine discourse of the Old Testament. When it comes to typology, the correct formula is "ontology determines epistemology." To call Jesus "the last Adam" (1 Cor 15:45) is more than a clever turn of phrase. It is a piece of theological grammar, a way of saying what something *is*.[218] Here, too, the transfiguration makes straight our interpretive way, enabling us to think correctly about Scripture's literal sense in the light of Christ. As we have seen, Jesus' transfiguration did not change what he was ("the whole fullness of deity"—Col 2:9) but more clearly disclosed it. Similarly, to read transfigurally does not change the meaning of the Old Testament by reading back something that was not originally in it, but discerns more of what was already there.

We can no longer postpone answering the question: Should Christians read the Old Testament forward or backward? Yes! Understanding Paul's hermeneutic requires a back *and* forth movement "from the earliest days, in which Christ was viewed through the lens of the scriptures, to the conviction that the scriptures must be viewed through the lens of Christ."[219] Richard Gaffin rightly remarks, "There is a difference between reading the New Testament back into the Old Testament and reading the Old Testament in light of the New. The former is wrong; the latter is not only legitimate but also requisite."[220] In the

216. Bates, 353–54.

217. There is a real sense in which the eschatology of the New Testament has its basis in the protology of the creation narrative. See Geerhardus Vos, *The Eschatology of the Old Testament* (Phillipsburg, NJ: P&R, 2001).

218. Cf. Ludwig Wittgenstein: "Grammar tells what kind of object anything is. (Theology as grammar)." In *Philosophical Investigations*, trans. G. E. M. Anscombe (New York: Macmillan, 1953), part 1, section 371.

219. Morna Hooker, review of Bates's *Hermeneutics of the Apostolic Proclamation*, in *Journal of Theological Studies* 67, no. 1 (2016): 250.

220. Richard B. Gaffin Jr., "Biblical Theology at Westminster Theological Seminary," in *Seeing Christ in All of Scripture: Hermeneutics at Westminster Theological Seminary*, ed. Peter A. Lillback (Philadelphia: Westminster Seminary Press, 2016), 84.

"New Testament Context" section of his commentary on Exodus 34, Brevard Childs says Paul comes to the text from the perspective of the Christian gospel, yet he also reads Paul as insisting "that already the Old Testament witnesses to the coming of the new."[221] Paul is reading forward as well as backward. Yes, Paul brings "a framework of Christian theology" to the text, but he also "gives evidence of a serious wrestling with the biblical text in an effort to penetrate the content of the witness."[222] There is, says Childs, a genuine interpretive to-and-fro: "[Paul] brings *to* the text the perspective of faith which had learned to hope in Christ, but he brings *from* the text a witness which conversely forms his understanding."[223]

Paul reads the story of Moses' transfiguration both forward and backward—much like the transfiguration itself, which looks back (to Moses and Elijah) to see forward (to Christ's exaltation). Paul is not allegorizing or otherwise forcing Christian presuppositions onto Exodus 34. Rather, he is interpreting the figures—the currency of divine discourse—with a frame of reference that lets them come into their own, as witnesses to the light of Christ. *Paul provides a transfiguring interpretation of what those figures originally meant, putting them in a frame of reference that renders more explicit the intrinsic, though veiled, glory they had all along.* Paul reads back, from the Mount of Transfiguration, as it were, in order to read forward rightly. He looks back with unveiled face to see where the words had been running all along. Think of reading backward, in the transfigural way I am suggesting here, as a way of reading forward that *glorifies* the letter. Of course, only readers whom the Spirit unveils perceive the light of Christ in the letter of the Mosaic law.[224] If we would read the Bible as Christians, with Paul, we must read with unveiled faces, hearts, and minds—in a word, *transfigurally*.[225]

Glorifying the Literal Sense (Part 3): "Sensing" Christ in All the Scriptures

Misunderstanding happens. Interpreters sometimes see things in the text that are not there. However, those who find Christ "in all the Scriptures" (Luke 24:27) are not suffering from hermeneutical hallucinations. It only remains to specify in what manner transfiguring interpretation "senses" Christ in all the Scriptures. Is it christocentric, christotelic, christophanic, something else?

221. Childs, *Exodus*, 624.

222. Childs, *Exodus*, 624.

223. Childs, *Exodus*, 624.

224. So Peter Balla: "The Old Testament 'letter' does not kill if it is read through the Spirit, who leads us to Christ and to a christological reading of the Old Testament." "2 Corinthians," in *Commentary on the New Testament Use of the Old Testament*, ed. G. K. Beale and D. A. Carson (Grand Rapids: Baker Academic, 2007), 761.

225. I will say more about what is involved in transfigural reading in the next chapter.

The terminology used for distinguishing different views is muddled: *christocentric* and *christotelic* are often used interchangeably, and there is more than one variety of the latter. For example, Daniel Block uses *christotelic* to indicate that we understand Scripture only in light of its end/goal (*telos*): "Not every text points to Jesus Christ as Messiah, but every text presents a vital part of that story of Jesus."[226] In contrast, Peter Enns does not think the Old Testament authors "predict" Jesus; rather, Jesus and his resurrection were a "surprise ending" that the Old Testament authors could not have foreseen. According to Enns, the New Testament authors take Old Testament texts out of their original context, reading them not on their own terms, but creatively, so that they correspond to the gospel.[227]

Bucur's emphasis on the "Christophanic" nature of the Old Testament is intriguing but relatively recent and, as yet, exegetically unproven. I therefore prefer to associate the transfigural interpretation I have identified as apostolic, Johannine, and Pauline with Oecolampadius's "christoscopic" reading, with its emphasis on Christ as the *scopus* ("aim; goal") of all the Scriptures and its concern to preserve both the letter (history) and spirit (mystery) of the text.[228] Christoscopic interpretation does not look for Christ in every detail of Scripture (in contrast to some forms of Christocentric preaching); rather, it situates every passage in relation to the overarching story of Christ, his suffering, and his glorious kingdom, which, as we have seen, is the climax to the all-encompassing story of the triune communication of divine and supernatural light.[229]

We are now in a better position to appreciate the truth of Warfield's wry comment on Scripture's interior decorating: the Old Testament is "a chamber richly furnished *but dimly lit*."[230] Thanks to the illumining Spirit, Paul sees more of these Old Testament furnishings when he reads with his unveiled Christian face in transfiguration light. His contrast between letter and spirit is not a derogatory put down of the Old Testament's literal sense. On the contrary, spiritual interpretation—reading theologically with unveiled face—is another

---

226. Daniel I. Block, "Christotelic Preaching: A Plea for Hermeneutical Integrity and Missional Passion," *Southern Baptist Journal of Theology* 22, no. 3 (2018): 14.

227. Enns says of the New Testament authors: "These writers did not fret about sticking to the biblical script." *The Bible Tells Me So . . . Why Defending Scripture Has Made Us Unable to Read It* (New York: HarperOne, 2015), 199. See also Kyle Dunham, "Challenges to Intertextuality and Christotelism: A New Model of Canonical-Linguistic Priming," *Journal of the Evangelical Theological Society* 64, no. 2 (2021): 287–301.

228. See the discussion in chapter 5 above.

229. Cf. Iain M. Duguid: "That does not mean that every verse taken by itself contains a hidden allusion to Christ, but that the central thrust of every passage leads us in some way to the central message of the gospel" ("Old Testament Hermeneutics," in *Seeing Christ in All of Scripture*, 19).

230. Warfield, "The Biblical Doctrine of the Trinity," 22 (emphasis added).

way of saying *reading for the glory of the literal*. In the words of de Lubac, "The Old Testament lives on, transfigured, in the New."[231]

As the transfiguration of Jesus reveals his true nature and identity, so the New Testament reveals what the Old Testament authors were ultimately talking about in their veiled references to God's wisdom and Israel's future. The New Testament's transfigural interpretation of the Old Testament does not distort but, rather, *glorifies* the literal meaning, extolling the letter by intensifying its brightness. Something like transfigural interpretation—reading with a grammatical-eschatological frame of reference in canonical context with unveiled face turned to Christ—is necessary if we are to do full justice to the Bible's literal meaning. For Paul, "the letter kills" only "when it is not accompanied by an understanding of the deeper divine intent behind the letter."[232] This is precisely what my proposal brings into focus: trans-figuring interpreters read *forward* as they trace the economy of light across the biblical figures to its ultimate referent; transfiguring interpreters read *backward* as they employ their unveiled referent, Christ, to light up the chamber dimly lit. No matter the direction, transfigural reading attends to the divine discourse that makes of the many texts a unified canonical Scripture. In so doing, it "senses" Christ and hears the voice of God shining through the letter, commanding us, "Listen to him," the light of the world, bedazzling in the canonical fabric of the text.

231. Henri de Lubac, *Scripture in the Tradition* (New York: Crossroad, 2000), 175.
232. Bates, *Hermeneutics of the Apostolic Proclamation*, 333.

CHAPTER 9

Transfiguring the Reader

Light Reflected

Let us climb the mountain, and join in contemplation, and let us be changed along with him, and radiate light along with him.

—Leo the Wise[1]

How we choose to read, how we submit to or question or resist the terms set by the writer, are choices that shape the habits of our minds and the habits of our hearts.

—Marilyn McEntyre[2]

Transfigural interpretation glorifies rather than distorts the literal sense. But what is the role of the readers and the reading cultures that form them in a transfigural framework of understanding? How should Bible readers answer the divine address that bespeaks the glorified literal sense? What should readers do when face-to-face before the glory of God in the face of Jesus Christ that irradiates the text?

You could maintain your distance and look *at* the light, like the critic in Lewis's toolshed. Readers who take this approach remain outside the light, in the dark, aware of the letters floating in the text but unable to follow them to their ultimate referent. Readers content to keep their critical distance, only looking at the light, can follow the literal *historia* but not the spiritual *theoria*, to

1. Emperor Leo VI, "Homily 10." Cited in Brian E. Daley, trans., *Light on the Mountain: Greek Patristic and Byzantine Homilies on the Transfiguration of the Lord* (Yonkers, NY: St. Vladimir's Seminary Press, 2013), 238.

2. Marilyn McEntyre, *Caring for Words in a Culture of Lies*, 2nd ed. (Grand Rapids: Eerdmans, 2021), 69.

use the traditional patristic distinction.[3] Alternately, readers could step into the light and look *along* it in order to gaze at the dazzling referent of the text. Both kinds of reading can expand our knowledge, but not in the same way and not of the same thing. Other readers may be tempted to hide their faces, as Moses did when he was afraid to look at God (Exod 3:6). The point is that biblical interpretation is a self-involving practice. There is something existentially at stake, namely, our sense of self in the world—and in relation to God. All biblical interpretation is spiritual in the sense that it is deeply personal, stretching and testing our human spirits (cf. 1 John 4:1).

Guigo II, a twelfth-century monk, commended a "spiritual" reading of Scripture, the aim of which was knowing God.[4] Gregory of Nyssa, in his *Life of Moses*, commented that the "knowledge of God is a mountain steep indeed and difficult to climb—the majority of people scarcely reach its base."[5] Can we by climbing—reading—find out God? René van Woudenberg argues that reading is a genuine source of knowledge, distinct from other sources, such as reason, perception, or memory.[6] Reading yields three different types of knowledge: propositional, procedural, and personal. We can come to know certain facts (knowledge *that*), learn certain skills (knowledge *how*), or become acquainted with things or persons (knowledge *of*). Of particular interest is how, in ascending the mountain of the biblical text, readers come to see "the light of the knowledge of the glory of God in the face of Jesus Christ" (2 Cor 4:6). What kind of textually mediated knowing is *that*? What are the conditions for this knowing, and its effects?

This chapter focuses on the reader in the economy of light, in that eschatological space in which readers come face-to-face as it were with the figure of Christ, shining behind, in, and in front of the world of the text. Here, too, the transfiguration has hermeneutical significance. Leo the Great provided a clue to what that is in noting that what happened on Mount Tabor laid a foundation for the church's hope that all Christians would have "a share in that honor which had already shone forth in their Head."[7] In the words of the apostle Paul, "We shall all be changed" (1 Cor 15:51). Hence the present chapter's thesis: *transfig-*

---

3. To restate the distinction in terms of the present work, critical readers can know the grammatical-historical sense but not the grammatical-eschatological referent. I am working with the Antiochian rather than Alexandrian sense of *theoria*, according to which the "other" meaning is a function of future typological fulfillment, or what in this work I am calling the transfigural sense.

4. Guigo II, *The Ladder of Monks*, trans. Edmund Colledge and James Walsh (Kalmazoo, MI: Cistercian, 1979).

5. Gregory of Nyssa, *The Life of Moses*, trans. Abraham J. Malherbe and Everett Ferguson, Classics of Western Spirituality (New York: Paulist, 1978), 93.

6. René van Woudenberg, *The Epistemology of Reading and Interpretation* (Cambridge: Cambridge University Press, 2021).

7. Leo the Great, Sermon 51.

ural interpretation transfigures the interpreter. To read the Bible theologically, in the economy of light, is to behold the glory of God in a transformative manner, such that attentive readers come to reflect the very light they see: "We become like what we behold."[8]

To read the Bible theologically involves ascending, beholding, and reflecting the light we see. In ascending and beholding, readers open themselves up to the divine address. In Ephraim Radner's words, "Theological interpretation . . . [is] a posture of receptivity."[9] It recalls Anselm's "faith seeking understanding" approach to theology, a search he conducted *as* prayer: "I seek thy face; thy face, Lord, do I desire."[10] Reading the Bible theologically—attending to the divine address for the purpose of knowing God in the face of Christ—is similarly a form of prayer. Theological interpretation of Scripture more closely resembles dialogue with its living divine author than it does an operation performed on dead letters. To read the Bible theologically is to approach the text in the expectation of entering into the communicative presence of the living God. To read theologically is to enter into the domain of the word of God, to stand with others on holy ground—a mountaintop engulfed by a glory cloud.

John Webster calls biblical interpreters to concentrate less on what interpretive methods they should use and more on what sort of persons they should be: "It is more important to lay out an anthropology of the reader than to establish a set of methodological directives for reading."[11] This thought returns us to my opening experiment in biblical-theological criticism. Transfiguring interpretation is not a discrete method but a set of sensibilities that, taken together, foster a certain type of reading culture (and reader). Whereas secular reader-response criticism construes the text as a playground for the reader's creativity, this distinctly theological reader-response criticism is more like a proving ground that tests the reader's readiness and aptness. Because the Bible is divine address, biblical interpretation is best viewed as the reader's "answering speech," Eugene Peterson's pithy description of prayer.[12] This suggests that transfigural interpretation is a species of "reader-response" criticism, where the response is not constitutive of textual meaning but symptomatic of the reader's spiritual condition.

Like the characters in the biblical stories they interpret, readers participate

8. Jeremy M. Kimble, *Behold and Become: Reading Scripture for Transformation* (Grand Rapids: Kregel Academic, 2023), 36.

9. Ephraim Radner, "'I Contain Multitudes': The Divine Basis for the Theological Interpretation of Scripture," *Pro Ecclesia* 31, no. 2 (2022): 145.

10. Anselm, *An Address (Proslogion)*, ch. 1, in *A Scholastic Miscellany: Anselm to Ockham*, ed. Eugene R. Fairweather (Philadelphia: Westminster, 1956), 70.

11. John Webster, *The Culture of Theology* (Grand Rapids: Baker Academic, 2019), 73.

12. See Eugene H. Peterson, *Answering God: The Psalms as Tools for Prayer* (San Francisco: Harper & Row, 1989), 6.

in the economy of light: "We, too, can and ought to pray with awareness of our place in the biblical storyline, in accord with our 'act' in God's drama."[13] This chapter therefore contrasts the reader as *sovereign subject*—one who operates on the biblical text as a surgeon on a helpless patient—with the reader as *sanctified servant*: "The differences between 'Here I am' and 'I see' are obvious. In the one, I place myself at the disposal of the covenant Lord . . . in the other, I am in possession."[14]

Like prayer, biblical interpretation is a form of answering speech. Like prayer, biblical interpretation can be a struggle—a struggle to be honest to God. Readers struggle with texts and other readers but ultimately with themselves before God. In the final analysis, the most important context for spiritual interpretation is the reader's context of being addressed by the living God. It follows that the greatest hindrance to understanding the Bible is not historical but spiritual distance. This leads us to examine the relationship of spiritual interpretation and spiritual formation, and the role of the Holy Spirit in fostering right-minded and right-hearted readers. The latter read with unveiled faces and, by fixing their gaze on the light of Christ, begin to reflect it.

Wrestling with Texts (and Other Readers): The Struggle for Understanding

As mentioned in chapter 5 above, the hermeneutic philosopher Paul Ricoeur described reading as first and foremost "a struggle with the text."[15] Standing "in front of" the text, readers struggle with historical and cultural distance, different frames of reference, and difficulties of translation. Readers of the Bible struggle with an additional difficulty: a summons to be doers and not hearers only, perchance to die to self. According to Ricoeur, texts often call for the "dispossession" of the ego: stories seek to "refigure" our existence, to effect a change in our beliefs, values, or behavior.[16] To wrestle with the text and its proposed way of being in the world is often to engage in a life-or-death conflict or, minimally, a struggle to preserve one's former identity and way of life.

If texts in general hold up a mirror to our human condition, how much more do the Scriptures. Søren Kierkegaard, recalling the image of the biblical text as a mirror (James 1:23), said, "*You must not look at the mirror . . . but must*

13. Daniel J. Brendsel, *Answering Speech: The Life of Prayer as Response to God* (Wheaton, IL: Crossway, 2023), 105.

14. Michael Horton, *The Christian Faith: A Systematic Theology for Pilgrims on the Way* (Grand Rapids: Zondervan, 2011), 85.

15. Paul Ricoeur, *A Ricoeur Reader: Reflection and Imagination*, ed. Mario J. Valdés (New York: Harvester Wheatsheaf, 1991), 494.

16. See further Paul Ricoeur, *Time and Narrative*, vol. 3, trans. Kathleen Blamey and David Pellauer (Chicago: University of Chicago Press, 1988).

see yourself in the mirror."[17] This is indeed the existential challenge of biblical interpretation. For we are reading not simply about actions of people now long gone; we are looking at people like us. Nay, we are looking at types of ourselves in relation to God. It is not always a pretty sight. Kierkegaard was acutely aware of our tendency to read the Bible in order "to defend [the reader] against God's Word."[18] A desire to snuff out the light of Christ and its fearsome brightness is hardly a modern invention, of course. The history of Israel was largely that of resistance to God's word: "To whom shall I speak and give warning, that they may hear? Behold, their ears are uncircumcised, they cannot listen" (Jer 6:10).

The story of Jacob wrestling through the night with a mysterious figure (Gen 32:22–32) is an apt illustration of the struggle of reading the Bible. It suggests that understanding (the blessing sought) is often had only through some kind of existential struggle with the text. It also raises the question: With whom/what exactly are readers struggling? The struggle involves more than grammatical infelicities or *hapax legomena*. To paraphrase the apostle Paul, "For we wrestle not against verb and noun, but against the authors, against the varied frames of reference, against spiritual readers in their contextual places." This section begins, then, with a survey of the various struggles Bible readers have, but then goes on to argue that the greatest struggle is internal, between facing the light of Christ and the sinful desire to hide in the dark (Matt 6:23; John 3:19).

Wrestling with Texts (and Their Difficulties)

How are biblical texts "difficult"?[19] Let me count the ways! In the first place, their historical and cultural distance often makes it hard for contemporary readers to forge meaningful connections. Second, apocalyptic texts are equally foreign, using imagery that often boggles the mind. Third, some readers find the content of certain texts either ethically questionable or intellectually suspect. Tremper Longman identifies several such areas in the Old Testament, including evolution and the apparent conflict between the Bible and science, God's commanding Israel to wreak violence on Canaan in the conquest narratives, and the exclusivity of heterosexual marriage and the condemnation of homosexuality.[20]

---

17. Søren Kierkegaard, "What Is Required in Order to Look at Oneself with True Blessing in the Mirror of the Word," in Søren Kierkegaard, *For Self-Examination* and *Judge for Yourself!*, ed. and trans. Howard V. Hong and Edna H. Hong (Princeton, NJ: Princeton University Press, 1990), 25 (emphasis original).

18. Kierkegaard, 34. For more on Kierkegaard himself as a reader of Scripture, see Timothy Polk, *The Biblical Kierkegaard* (Macon, GA: Mercer University Press, 1997), and Kevin Storer, *Reading Scripture with Kierkegaard: Kierkegaard's Upbuilding Hermeneutic of Scripture in the Discourses* (Frankfurt: Peter Lang, 2022).

19. Cf. George Steiner, *On Difficulty and Other Essays* (Oxford: Oxford University Press, 1978).

20. Tremper Longman III, *Confronting Old Testament Controversies: Pressing Questions about Evolution, Sexuality, History, and Violence* (Grand Rapids: Baker, 2019).

The real wrestling match in these latter cases is between the text and the reader's moral sensibilities, as one modern biblical scholar makes abundantly clear: "If we follow biblical writers' descriptions of God in the ancient world, only one reasonable conclusion remains: God is sexist and racist."[21]

Phyllis Trible calls attention to "texts of terror," her name for the underside of biblical texts that document the abuse of women. Ezekiel 16:35–42 is one such text of terror, for it depicts God as a devoted yet exasperated husband who exposes the nakedness of unfaithful Jerusalem and abandons her to the madness of a mob who cuts her to pieces. One commentator opines, "According to this image, God's key attributes are male dominance, power, and control."[22] Trible compares reading such texts to the story of Jacob's wrestling, though she imagines herself in the grip not of angels, but of something more sinister: "To tell and hear tales of terror is to wrestle with demons in the night, without a compassionate God to save us."[23]

These and other "toxic texts" of Scripture "function as a mirror that reveals . . . our habit of projecting our own un-Christlike images onto God, especially in the form of religious violence."[24] Of course, Jesus can be "difficult" too—and occasionally terrifying. His indignant overturning of the money-changers' tables in the temple (John 2:14–17) was no spring cleaning, and neither do his condemnation of the Pharisees (Matt 23) nor his teaching about hell (Matt 5:22, 29; 10:28) betoken a tolerant inclusivism.

Underlying these difficulties, as well as those that touch on issues of sexuality and gender, is the tension between contemporary readers' moral frames of reference (and social imaginary) and the frames of reference we encounter in Scripture. Consider, for example, the most difficult issue of all: the problem of evil. How can readers reconcile the all-good and all-powerful God of the biblical text with the undeniable reality of unjust suffering in the world, and their own experience? The father-son authorial team Bill and Will Kynes confront precisely this dilemma in their aptly titled book, *Wrestling with Job*: "The book of Job is, in many ways, a hard book. . . . Because it doesn't give us the answers we want."[25] Readers identify with Job, who himself wrestles with the problem. Each of Job's friends represents a different moral frame of reference, none of

21. Jonathan L. Walton, *A Lens of Love: Reading the Bible from Its World for Our World* (Louisville: Westminster John Knox, 2018), 96.

22. Walton, *A Lens of Love*, 108.

23. Phyllis Trible, *Texts of Terror: Literary-Feminist Readings of Biblical Narratives*, 40th anniversary ed. (Minneapolis: Fortress, 2022), 4.

24. Bradley Jersak, *A More Christlike Word: Reading Scripture the Emmaus Way* (New Kensington, PA: Whitaker House, 2021), 58.

25. Will Kynes and Bill Kynes, *Wrestling with Job: Defiant Faith in the Face of Suffering* (Downers Grove, IL: IVP Academic, 2022), 1.

which is able to meet the difficulty, proposing instead that Job's suffering must be deserved.

The core issue is whether Job, and his readers, will trust God come what may.[26] To believe that God is worthy of worship, even in the face of suffering, is to adopt an eschatological frame of reference that turns our typical moral calculations upside down. The book of Job does not provide an "answer"; instead, it asks readers to respond to the God who speaks out of the whirlwind with a faith that endures its fiery trial. The "solution" requires readers to reject the frame of reference that gives rise to the problem in the first place. Readers come to "know" God as trustworthy through reading Job, but not in the mode of theoretical explanation. Rather, they come to know only by having their hip—their moral frame of reference—put out of joint. The blessing Job receives is a new frame of reference that shows God to be both sovereign and trustworthy, even when appearances are to the contrary.

Wrestling with Authors (and Their Intentions)

Another source of difficulty are authors with whom we may disagree or who resist saying what we would like them to say. Whose text is it anyway? Copyright protects the legal rights of modern authors as originators of their works, but it does not give them the exclusive right to say what their works mean. That privilege has been appropriated by a priestly professional caste: the literary (and later biblical) critic. Matthew Arnold's famous 1869 essay "Culture and Anarchy" depicts the critic as a disinterested observer of literary works and of culture as a whole. Literary criticism was, for Arnold, a qualification for the criticism of society itself.[27] Whereas earlier readers were philologists whose chief aim was simply to follow the way the words go, these later, professional readers often presume to know *better* or *more* than the authors. A few biblical critics even think that we can dispense with authors altogether.[28]

John Guillory's *Professing Criticism* is a searching (and scathing) analysis of the role of literary study in the contemporary university. It is relevant to the present discussion for two reasons: first, because of the significant parallels between literary and biblical criticism; second, because of his overarching concern for how educational institutions, and literary criticism in particular, shape reading cultures. Guillory notes the irony of our situation: while literature "is *studied*

26. Kynes and Kynes, 3–4.

27. Matthew Arnold, *Culture and Anarchy and Other Writings*, ed. Stefan Collini (Cambridge: Cambridge University Press, 1993), 53–211.

28. See the essays by Clar, Dinkler, Strømmen, and Moore in *Biblical Exegesis without Authorial Intention? Interdisciplinary Approaches to Authorship and Meaning*, ed. Clarissa Breu (Leiden: Brill, 2019).

in the university, it is criticism that is *professed*."[29] He laments that English literature students are learning not literature but *criticism*, a particular way of viewing and talking about literature. Moreover, criticism today has become the domain of professionals, even though "for most of its history, literary study was a set of practices with many different sites, both within and outside the university."[30] The net result, both in literary and, arguably, biblical studies alike, is the supremacy of secondary (i.e., critical) over primary (i.e., authorial) discourse. Seminary faculty, take note: are you teaching students to be readers or critics?

In the current cultural climate, the humanities have become a hard sell, a not-for-profit option for a mere fraction of the population. One social commentator says that we now live in "a doubly secularized age, post-religious and postcanonical": we have lost faith in religion and the humanities largely because criticism has become a tool for exposing and deconstructing the values, both explicit and implicit, in literature that serve special interests groups.[31] Professing to study literature, we instead place faith in forms of criticism, methods that have as their mission the criticism of texts and society alike, often with an aim toward the redistribution of political power. "Professing" readers today are in fact likely to be ideology critics, intent less on interpreting the world of the text than on transforming the world in front of it.

This is not the place for a comprehensive review of the myriad forms of biblical criticism.[32] However, the status of authorial intention in biblical studies deserves special mention in light of the tendency of professional readers to profess types of criticism that either read against the grain of or overrule the author's communicative intentions. It is an urgent question: To what extent is biblical exegesis without authorial intention possible? The question is more than hermeneutical; it ultimately has to do with whether readers are willing to face the authors whose works they read—and whether they are willing to let the (author's) face speak.

It is a foregone conclusion in much postmodern literary theory that the author is dead, no longer there to determine or clarify textual meaning.[33] At best, many critics treat the author's voice, insofar as it can be recovered, as but one witness to textual meaning, not an authority. At worst, they regard the author as a mere mouthpiece for the cultural ideologies of the day, in which case

29. John Guillory, *Professing Criticism: Essays on the Organization of Literary Study* (Chicago and London: University of Chicago Press, 2022), vii (emphasis original).

30. Guillory, ix.

31. Simon During, "Losing Faith in the Humanities," in *The Chronicle of Higher Education*, December 18, 2019, http://www.chronicle.com/article/losing-faith-in-the-humanities/.

32. For a survey of types of biblical criticism, see Stanley E. Porter, ed., *Dictionary of Biblical Criticism and Interpretation* (New York: Routledge, 2007).

33. For the long version, see my *Is There a Meaning in This Text? The Bible, the Reader, and the Morality of Literary Knowledge* (Grand Rapids: Zondervan, 1998), chs. 1–3.

the critic's task is to uncover what lay *behind* the author's apparent intention. In the words of one New Testament scholar, "It is impossible to recover the original intent of an author who died long ago (and therefore cannot corroborate or contradict our perceptions), and even if we could speak with ancient authors, they might not know their own motivations and intentions fully."[34] Moreover, the author's original historical context is no more privileged than any other because, once written, texts have a nomadic existence, "veering" here and there, in and out of various reading communities where, like erstwhile hippies, they may "discover" themselves.[35] If exegesis is a "leading out" of textual meaning, biblical critics who question the utility of authorial intention want people to know that it is the reader, not the author, who does the leading.[36]

Rumors of the author's death have nevertheless been greatly exaggerated. A remnant of author-oriented interpreters remains. It is incontrovertible that the biblical texts were produced by historical persons, and, if nothing else, knowing who these persons were—where and when they lived—helps us locate their texts as concerns language, culture, and history. "Authors are persons . . . and in understanding their intentions by reading their texts, we meet human beings . . . these encounters with authors are one of the prime benefits of the humanities."[37] Note, too, that the very notion of authorship, even if underdeveloped, was tied to apostolic authority in the early church: "The abiding importance of a text depended on its authorship."[38]

Reading with a suspicion that authors are merely instruments of the prevailing ideologies of their day implies that critics know better: "Critique glorifies its own agency but occludes the agency of the author."[39] To ignore what an author said/did in expressing certain communicative intentions in the publicly accessible arena of writing either negates or attempts to rewrite the past. "Once the author is gone, the context goes with him and the reader is entirely on her own."[40] This cannot be, for "actions taken in the past, including artistic utterances, cannot change, however much our understanding of them [may]."[41] The ethics of interpretation obliges readers to recognize an author's communica-

34. Michal Beth Dinkler, "Between Intention and Reception: Textual Meaning-Making in Intersubjective Perspective," in Breu, *Biblical Exegesis without Authorial Intention?*, 75.

35. Brennan Breed, *Nomadic Text: A Theory of Biblical Reception History* (Bloomington: Indiana University Press, 2014).

36. "Traditional exegesis wants to disavow readerly influences over textual meaning in pursuit of scholarly objectivity" (Dinkler, "Between Intention and Reception," 77).

37. Oda Wishmeyer, "Author–Text–Intention: A Case Study on the Letter of James," in Breu, *Biblical Exegesis without Authorial Intention?*, 37.

38. Wishmeyer, 26.

39. John Farrell, *The Varieties of Authorial Intention: Literary Theory beyond the Intentional Fallacy* (London: Palgrave Macmillan, 2017), ix.

40. Farrell, 81.

41. Farrell, 241.

tive intentions, even if they do not agree with them. "We can listen but still disagree."[42] Moreover, if we do not even try to recover the author's intention and respect its own communicative integrity, "we will only hear the echo of our own voices or, like Narcissus, see our own faces in the mirror of the text."[43] Alas, there is neither blessing nor understanding to be had in regarding one's own reflection in the mirror of the biblical text. A haughty hermeneutical spirit goes before interpretive de(con)struction.

Wrestling with Readers (and Their Contexts)

The reader's most painful interpretive struggles are not with the text or with the author but with other readers and reading communities. Stanley Fish speaks of the "authority" of interpretive communities, groups of people who share the same context or interpretive interest—that is, *frame of reference* and *reading culture*.[44] Typical frames of reference that distinguish one interpretive community from another could be disciplinary, denominational, ethical, or sociopolitical. Because meaning is context dependent, Fish claims that a text's meaning changes as it enters into different contexts of reading.[45] The conflict of interpretations boils down to differences between interpretive communities, each with its own interpretive interest and corresponding method. The conflict of interpretations quickly becomes a conflict of interpretive authority between rival interpretive communities, a conflict that eventually escalates into the full-scale reading-culture wars that are a distinguishing feature of the contemporary context.

It is one thing to view reading as a source of knowledge, and quite another to decide *whose* reading is justified and whose is not. Jean-François Lyotard's seminal work, *The Postmodern Condition: A Report on Knowledge*, rightly identifies the main challenge for Western readers of the Bible or of any other text: how to respond to the legitimation crisis in interpretation.[46] Whose understanding counts, and why? Which reading counts as knowledge rather than a hostile takeover, a meaning grab for political power? Readings that employ frames of reference other than those used by the author may be described as *extratextual*.[47]

---

42. Farrell, 241. Indeed, Farrell speaks of the "varieties" of authorial intention precisely to distinguish the task of *understanding* a text from *evaluating* it, where the latter involves judging the goodness of what the author hoped to achieve, namely, the "practical effects of the work which constitute its impact" (*Varieties of Authorial Intention*, 239).

43. Wishmeyer, "Author–Text–Intention," 38.

44. Stanley Fish, *Is There a Text in This Class? The Authority of Interpretive Communities* (Cambridge, MA: Harvard University Press, 1980).

45. Of course, it is a disputed question as to which context(s) determine meaning, that of the author only or also that of subsequent readers.

46. Jean-François Lyotard, *The Postmodern Condition: A Report on Knowledge* (Minneapolis: University of Minnesota Press, 1984), 6–8.

47. Woudenberg employs a similar term, describing interpretations that use a different frame of reference than that of the author *externalist* (*Epistemology of Reading and Interpretation*, 210).

Such readings typically seek answers to questions the text does not address and are thus examples of *overstanding*. Such exercises would be fine if interpretation were about opinion only rather than knowledge. Christian readers of the Bible want more than opinion, however: "We want our interpretations to be explanatory. We want them to tell us how the text actually acquired the features that it has and what they were intended to mean."[48] The alternative to right understanding is every reader doing what is right in her own eyes. Subjectivity happens, and Bible readers are no exception. As Rhyne Putman says, "There is evidence of confirmation bias in routine theological procedures like exegesis and proof-texting."[49]

The interpreter's cultural context weighs heavily in the choice of which frame of reference to privilege. Even the vaunted historical-critical method is a product of its time and place: "Far from being an objective, neutral method, the practice of historical criticism was always bound up with ideological, religious, and political concerns, especially those prioritized in the European Enlightenment."[50] Readers today are keenly aware that "the historical and cultural location as well as the agenda of a given interpreter [are] just as consequential as that of the work being interpreted."[51] This hyper-awareness of the contextually contingent nature of historical criticism, along with other interpretive frameworks, undermines any and all claims to superiority, further fueling the legitimation crisis.

At present, "contextual biblical interpretation" serves as a catchall term describing approaches that prioritize the interpreter's ethnic or sociocultural location over other locations and contexts, including the original historical context insofar as it contributed to the suppression of minority voices. Contextual exegesis "explicitly integrates thinking about the contextual situatedness of the reader."[52] For example, postcolonial biblical criticism is written from the perspective of the colonized—those who, like the Canaanites, lost their land to European conquerors or remain under the influence of former colonial powers that used biblical texts to justify their land possession.[53] This is but one example

48. Farrell, *Varieties of Authorial Intention*, 79.

49. Rhyne R. Putman, *When Doctrine Divides: An Evangelical Approach to Theological Diversity* (Wheaton, IL: Crossway, 2020), 155.

50. Ian Boxall and Bradley C. Gregory, "Introduction," *The New Cambridge Companion to Biblical Interpretation* (Cambridge: Cambridge University Press, 2023), 2.

51. Boxall and Gregory, 3.

52. Peter-Ben Smit and Klaas Spronk, "Contextual Biblical Interpretation: A Theological Necessity," *Concilium* 58, no. 3 (2022): 15. For an impassioned plea not to impose Western reading methods on the rest of the world, see Larry W. Caldwell, "Towards the New Discipline of Ethnohermeneutics: Questioning the Relevance of Western Hermeneutical Methods in the Asian Context," *Journal of Asian Mission* 1, no. 1 (1999): 21–43.

53. See further, Jin Young Choi, "Postcolonial Interpretation," in *New Cambridge Companion to Biblical Interpretation*, 210–27.

of the myriad interpretive frameworks now on offer, including geographic (e.g., various types of Asian and African theology), gender-based (e.g., feminist, womanist), ethnic/liberationist (e.g., mujerista, minjung), and more. William Blake anticipated this variety in his poem "The Everlasting Gospel," in which he vividly depicted the conflict of Jewish and Christian interpretive frameworks:

> The Vision of Christ that thou dost see
> Is my Visions Greatest Enemy
> Thine has a great hook nose like thine
> Mine has a snub nose like to mine
> . . .
> Both read the Bible day & night
> But thou readst black where I read white.[54]

Blake was inadvertently ahead of his time in speaking of "reading black" and "reading white." Mark Noll describes the Civil War as a theological crisis, but it was equally hermeneutical: anti-abolitionists read the Bible as supporting slavery; abolitionists protested that slavery was an evil that the gospel opposed.[55] To paraphrase Noll's tragic conclusion: it was left to those consummate biblical interpreters, the Generals Ulysses S. Grant and William Sherman, to decide how the Bible would henceforth be read. To the victors go the interpretive spoils!

Esau McCaulley's *Reading While Black* is an important *cri de coeur* from one who inhabits the African American ecclesial context. He draws on the experience of the Black church to foreground certain questions (e.g., about policing and politics) that white interpreters typically do not raise.[56] However, unlike many contextual interpreters, McCaulley does not fall into the trap of simply asserting the superiority of his frame of reference, nor does he allow his own context to trump the biblical text: "I propose instead that we adopt the posture of Jacob and refuse to let go of the text until it blesses us."[57] McCaulley does what I wish all readers who inhabit their particular contexts would do. He realizes there is "a difference between acknowledging the social location of interpretation and letting said location eclipse the text itself."[58] In short, he realizes that interpretive communities must not pursue their own narrow interpretive interests only. "The Dwarfs are for the Dwarfs,"[59] as C. S. Lewis stated

54. William Blake, *The Complete Poems*, ed. Alicia Ostriker (London: Penguin Classics, 1978), 851.

55. See Mark A. Noll, *The Bible Civil War as a Theological Crisis* (Chapel Hill: University of North Carolina Press, 2006), 31–50.

56. Esau McCaulley, *Reading While Black: African American Biblical Interpretation as an Exercise in Hope* (Downers Grove, IL: IVP Academic, 2020).

57. McCaulley, 21.

58. McCaulley, 182.

59. C. S. Lewis, *The Last Battle* (New York: Puffin, 1964), 111.

in *The Last Battle*, but in the church of Jesus Christ, it must not be the case that the Blacks are for the Blacks, or the whites for the whites, and so forth. Hence McCaulley rightly calls for the varied interpretive communities to turn "to the text in dialogue with one another to discern the mind of Christ."[60]

Differences can be threatening, especially to readers who are either too sure or insecure in their identities. Perfect love for the biblical text must cast out interpretive fear. Not every difference need be divisive. Some differences are salutary, allowing us to see more colors in the white light of Christ that shines forth from the text. Wise readers will honestly acknowledge the limitations of their own contexts: "Some of the habits that we readers from the West . . . bring to the Bible can blind us to interpretations that the original audience and readers in other cultures see quite naturally."[61] Church history is similarly replete with diverse contexts: "Paying attention to the history of reception is, therefore, also a form of contextual exegesis."[62] The way forward, then, beyond the conflict of contexts and interpretive communities, is to retrieve a *contextual catholicity and catholic contextuality*—the breadth of Christian readers across time and space—while simultaneously acknowledging the primacy of the canonical context. Mere Christian interpreters must strive to become the kind of readers who listen to what other readers who inhabit different contexts than one's own have heard in the Scriptures: "Understanding how other people, across different eras, cultures, and locations, have received and used the Bible can make interpreters more self-aware of their own contingency and foster understanding between reading communities."[63] There is no one privileged context, only a reading community—the one, holy, catholic, and apostolic church—in its many local expressions.[64]

Wrestling with God? Reading Jacob at Jabbok

The ultimate struggle that impedes reading the Bible theologically and reflecting the light of Christ that such reading perceives is the reader's struggle with

60. McCaulley, 22.

61. E. Randolph Richards and Brandon J. O'Brien, *Misreading Scripture with Western Eyes: Removing Cultural Blinders to Better Understand the Bible* (Downers Grove, IL: IVP Books, 2012), 15.

62. Smit and Spronk, "Contextual Biblical Interpretation," 18.

63. Boxall and Gregory, "Introduction," *New Cambridge Companion to Biblical Interpretation*, 10.

64. For two recent examples of what this canonical catholicity looks like (both doctoral dissertations written under my supervision), see Isuwa Y. Atsen, *A Tapestry of Global Christology: Weaving a Three-Stranded Theological Cord* (Carlisle, UK: Langham Monographs, 2022); and Taimaya Ragui, *Confessing Community: An Entryway to Theological Interpretation in North East India* (Minneapolis: Fortress, 2023). See also Stephen T. Pardue's five theses in his *Why Evangelical Theology Needs the Global Church* (Grand Rapids: Baker, 2023).

God, or rather, with oneself before God's word. To paraphrase Calvin: the sum of hermeneutical wisdom consists of two parts, the reading of God's Word and of ourselves. Without knowledge of self, there is no reading of God; without knowledge of God, there is no reading of self. However, many readers, like Adam and Eve, may be tempted to hide themselves from the voice—the speaking presence—of the Lord. Reading theologically involves more than methodological procedures; it also concerns our spiritual posture, that is, our relation to the Holy Spirit.[65]

The struggle between Jacob and the *ish* ("man") that Genesis 32:22–32 records does not at first glance seem to be about reading, although modern commentators are quick to confess that it *occasions* some wrestling—with the text—to understand it.[66] On the literal level, the story, though strange, is not hard to follow: Jacob spends the night by a stream called Jabbok, wrestles with a stranger, asks the stranger for his name and a blessing, loses the wrestling match, yet receives a blessing and new name all the same. Who was Jacob's opponent? Was it Esau's guardian angel, Esau himself, an angel of the Lord, Jacob's alter-ego, or God himself? Why was Jacob so insistent on learning his name? Identifying this stranger both requires and provides a frame of reference and is key to understanding. The story is relevant for present purposes, both because Jacob, or at least his name, is "transfigured," and because a number of interpreters, past and present, relate the story to hearing and/or seeing God, the very goal of transfiguring interpretation.[67]

Philo's depiction of Jacob as "a mind in training," a seeker of wisdom who underwent a variety of spiritual exercises in his pursuit of virtue, influenced early Christian readers.[68] Philo contrasted Jacob, one who engages in ascetic practices that lead to wisdom, with Esau, the personification of passion and foolishness.[69] Jacob's experiences were a form of *paideia*, an educational process aiming at "the light of the soul."[70] Philo thought the Jacob stories are about the good of spiritual exercises, in particular the good of seeing God, which Philo

65. Gordon D. Fee made a passionate and compelling case for translating New Testament references to "spiritual" (*pneumatikos*) as having to do with the presence and activity of the Holy Spirit, thus providing a fresh theological understanding of what is meant by *spiritual* sense and *spiritual* interpretation. "On Getting the Spirit Back into Spirituality," in *Life in the Spirit: Spiritual Formation in Theological Perspective*, ed. Jeffrey P. Greenman and George Kalantzis (Downers Grove, IL: IVP Academic, 2010), 36–44.

66. See, e.g., Henry F. Knight, "Meeting Jacob at the Jabbok: Wrestling with a Text; A Midrash on Genesis 32:22–32," *Journal of Ecumenical Studies* 29, no. 3–4 (1992): 451–60.

67. See further Frederick C. Holmgren, "Holding Your Own against God! Genesis 32:22–32 (in the Context of Genesis 31–33)," *Interpretation* 44, no. 1 (1990): 5–17.

68. Elisa Uusimäki, "A Mind in Training: Philo of Alexandria on Jacob's Spiritual Exercises," *Journal for the Study of the Pseudepigrapha* 27, no. 4 (2018): 265–88.

69. See Philo, "Who Is the Heir of Divine Things," in *The Works of Philo Judaeus*, vol. 1, trans. Charles Duke Yonge (London: Bohn, 1854–90), 252–53.

70. Philo, *Allegorical Interpretation*, in *The Works of Philo Judaeus*, 3.167.

thinks explained Jacob's name change in verse 28: the "supplanter" (Jacob), through his pursuit of wisdom, becomes "he who sees God," Philo's typical rendering of "Israel."[71] This picture of Jacob as one who is in training to see God, made perfect sense to the church fathers, who also associated Jacob's change of name with his spiritual growth.[72] Genesis 32:22–32 thus became in the early church "a vehicle for the transmission of a theory of the spiritual life."[73] "One who sees God" is an apt description of those who want to read the Bible theologically for a blessing.

Augustine thought Jacob's new name, with its allusion to seeing God, "will be the reward of all the saints at the end of the world."[74] What commends Jacob as an exemplar of spiritual discipline is his refusal to let go of his opponent, even after he was injured. As Ambrose said, "What is it to wrestle with God other than to enter upon the struggle for virtue?"[75] Jacob clearly suspects that his sparring partner is no mere human; he wants to know his adversary's name (as Moses wanted to see God's face) and refuses to let go until he receives a blessing.[76] Clement of Alexandria identified the "man" with whom Jacob struggles as the master Pedagogue, God's Logos, who trains Jacob in the struggle against evil and vice.[77] No blessing or new name is given, however, until Jacob comes clean and reveals his old name/nature—the supplanter/deceiver. Jacob must struggle, not least with himself, for his blessing: the privilege of seeing God.

As Gordon Wenham rightly notes, the key to understanding the account has everything to do with Jacob's new name and his renaming of the place: "The emphasis of the story is on the names Israel and Peniel."[78] One complication in the patristic interpretation, however, is that biblical scholars now agree that "Israel" does not mean "he who sees God" but, rather, "he who strives with God" (or "God strives"). That Jacob's opponent was indeed God is made explicit

---

71. See Philo, *De Mutatione Nominum*, 81, in *Philo* 5, trans. F. H. Colson (Cambridge, MA: Loeb Classical Library, 1945), 183. Modern commentators reject this translation of the Hebrew. Philo seems to have taken it from verse 31, and from his conviction that Israel symbolizes those who seek to see or contemplate God. See further C. T. R. Hayward, "Philo, the Septuagint of Genesis 32:24–32 and the Name 'Israel': Fighting the Passions, Inspiration, and the Vision of God," *Journal of Jewish Studies* 51, no. 2 (2000): 209–26.

72. See further Mark Sheridan, "Jacob and Israel: A Contribution to the History of an Interpretation," in *From Nile to the Rhone and Beyond: Studies in Early Monastic Literature and Scriptural Interpretation* (Rome: Pontificio Ateneo Sant'Anselmo, 2012), 315–34.

73. Sheridan, "Jacob and Israel," 317.

74. Augustine, *City of God* 16:39. Cited in *Ancient Christian Commentary on Genesis 12–50*, ed. Mark Sheridan (Downers Grove, IL: InterVarsity, 2002), 222.

75. Ambrose, *Jacob and the Happy Life* 7.30. Cited in *Ancient Christian Commentary on Genesis 12–50*, 219.

76. James McKeown notes the comparison with the story of Moses. *Genesis*, Two Horizons Old Testament Commentary (Grand Rapids: Eerdmans, 2008), 154.

77. Clement, *The Pedagogue* I.7.57.1.

78. Gordon J. Wenham, *Genesis 16–50*, Word Biblical Commentary (Grand Rapids: Zondervan, 2015), 295.

in Hosea 12:3: "In his manhood he [Jacob] strove with God [*elohim*.]" Jacob confirms that he knew who his opponent was by calling the place "Peniel" ("face of El [God]"), adding "For I have seen God face to face, and yet my life has been delivered" (Gen 32:30). Although Philo and the Fathers misinterpreted the Hebrew meaning of Jacob's new name, they nevertheless correctly identified him as seeing, or at least coming "face to face" with, God. Their interpretation may not be philologically up to date, but it *is* text-based. Like Jacob, then, those who read the Bible theologically may find themselves face-to-face with God, perchance to struggle.

According to Hosea 12:4, Jacob "strove with the angel [God] and prevailed." God turns out to be both opponent and ally, one who wounds and blesses. For it is only through his struggle with God that Jacob makes spiritual progress. Derek Kidner rightly comments, "It was against Him, not Esau or Laban, that he had been putting his strength, as he now discovered; yet the initiative had been God's, as it was this night, to chasten his pride and challenge his tenacity."[79] Jacob is struggling not only against God, then, but against himself before God. Jacob's struggle is to acknowledge, before God, who he (Jacob) is—one who has relied on his own deceit to obtain his father's blessing and his brother's birthright—while simultaneously holding on to God's promise to make of his seed a great nation. Jacob's struggle is to face his true self before the face of God.

Is there any textual evidence to support the claim that Jacob has changed, repented, and made spiritual progress as a result of his struggle? After all, "When Moses saw God face to face, his face shone.... When Jacob meets God, he comes away with a limp."[80] Interestingly, Bruce Waltke says that the formula in Genesis 32:28 preceding Jacob's new name ("shall no longer be called") indicates a "spiritual metamorphosis."[81] "Metamorphosis," we may recall, is the Greek term Matthew uses for Jesus' transfiguration (Matt 17:2). In the Jabbok narrative, however, Jacob does not come away with a shining face; the physical result of his encounter with God is a hip put out of joint. Yet the text *does* mention light. As Cyril of Alexandria noted, the struggle ceases at daybreak (Gen 32:26) because "there is no fight for those who already live in the light."[82]

Kierkegaard thought the story of Jacob is indirectly about the reader's struggle to understand herself before Scripture. On a formal level, it resembles the situation in James 1:23–25 when readers look into the mirror of the biblical

79. Derek Kidner, *Genesis*, Tyndale Old Testament Commentary (Downers Grove, IL: InterVarsity, 1967), 169.

80. James McKeon, *Genesis*, Two Horizons Old Testament Commentary (Grand Rapids: Eerdmans, 2008), 156.

81. Bruce K. Waltke, *Genesis: A Commentary* (Grand Rapids: Zondervan, 2001), 446. Waltke takes the idea of a spiritual metamorphosis from Moshe Weinfeld, "Jeremiah and the Spiritual Metamorphosis of Israel," *Zeitschrift für die alttertestamentliche Wissenschaft* 88, no. 1 (1976): 17–56.

82. *Galphyra on Genesis* 5.3. Cited in *Ancient Christian Commentary on Genesis 12–50*, 220.

text. Looking into the mirror of Scripture can become a kind of wrestling match, a spiritual struggle in which the reader strives to keep not the divine face but *voice* at a critical distance. Yet it may also become the kind of struggle that yields understanding and results in the reader's transfiguration, as I suggest below.[83] Kierkegaard knows that Bible readers are answerable subjects who do more than respond intellectually to impersonal messages: "To interpret Scripture *in truth*, the Christian must interpret it *before God* as a message *from God*."[84] Like Jacob, readers of the Bible invariably struggle with themselves before God, grasped as they are by his living, active, and hip-dislocating discourse.

To read the Bible well is ultimately to have oneself—one's false self and idolatrous ideologies—called into question. Engaging the text places every reader into vigorous training, like Jacob, striving for wisdom. To confess the Bible as God's word is to acknowledge it as the divinely appointed means whereby God shapes and sanctifies a motley collection of supplanter-deceivers into a holy nation. It is in reading and wrestling with Scripture that readers learn to grapple with their true names, faces, and identities. It is therefore important to resist the twin temptations of unfaithful reading: either to overstand God's word, bending it to our own purposes, or to abandon the attempt to make sense of it altogether. By way of contrast, faithful reading involves both discerning *what the text means* (our interpretation) and the more difficult task of discerning *ourselves in relation to the text* (our lived response). It is one thing to read about Jacob, quite another to read the story of Jacob as our own. Mere Christian hermeneutics requires interpreters to do more than shine their methodological flashlights on the text. It requires a willingness to expose oneself to the white-hot light that streams from the majestic divine voice. To read Scripture rightly, we need to ask not only what the text means, but rather, who am I, and what does my situation mean, when seen in Scripture's own frame of reference, in the all-disclosing light of the divine address?

Varieties of Spiritual Interpretation

We struggle to understand the biblical text, then, not only because the material is hard, but because our hearts are too. Critics sometimes murder to dissect, but at other times they shudder to inspect, for fear that they may become accountable to what they find. Jane Austen's *Pride and Prejudice* is not simply evidence for its opening proposition ("It is a truth universally acknowledged,

83. Iben Damgaard, "Kierkegaard's Rewriting of Biblical Narratives: The Mirror of the Text," in *Kierkegaard and the Bible. Tome I: The Old Testament*, ed. Lee. C. Barrett and Jon Stewart (London: Routledge, 2016), 209 (essay pp. 207–30).

84. Andrew Torrance, "A Kierkegaardian Guide to Reading Scripture," *New Blackfriars* 97, no. 1071 (September 2016): 630.

that a young man with a fortune, must be in want of a wife"[85]) but a challenge to the reader's own lingering pride and/or prejudice, namely, the tendency to judge others too harshly and hastily. Even nonbiblical books can occasion what Paul Ricoeur called a "dispossession of the ego,"[86] that is, a surrender of one's previous self-understanding or, in biblical terms, a dying to self (Col 3:3).

Reading Scripture rightly is a spiritual struggle that cuts to the joints and marrow of personal identity. The church fathers rightly understood that the goal of biblical interpretation is the reader's spiritual formation—the ability to see and live to God thanks to the presence and activity of the Spirit in one's life. In his letter to Marcellinus, Athanasius recommended daily reading of the Psalter, well aware of the crucial function of the Psalms in the reformation of the self.[87] If what readers see in texts is partly a function of what kind of people they are, then we must do some honest soul searching: Are we the kind of people who walk in the counsel of the cynic, stand in the way of skeptics, and sit in the seat of critics (cf. Ps 1:1)? If so, we will not delight in the law of the Lord or the gospel. This puts a fresh spin on the hermeneutic circle. The older hermeneutical circle concerned the way the parts of a text affect one's understanding of the whole (and vice versa). Spiritual interpretation has rather to do with the *special* hermeneutical circle that acknowledges the necessity of sanctification for reading Scripture rightly and the way in which reading Scripture rightly contributes to our sanctification.

The process of becoming the right kind of reader is not something readers can do for themselves, however. Reading the Bible on a daily basis may be salutary, but coming to understand is not achieved *ex opere operato*—simply by reading itself. It is tempting to read the text in ways that promote self-interest. Billy Collins imagines some less than sanctified readers tying the text to a chair with a rope in order to "torture a confession out of it."[88] The academy sometimes forms such critics. In contrast, the formation of right-minded, right-hearted readers is a theological phenomenon, a process by which the Holy Spirit takes away the veil, giving sight to the blind.[89]

---

85. Jane Austen, *The Oxford Illustrated Jane Austen*, vol. 2, *Pride and Prejudice*, ed. R. W. Chapman (Oxford: Oxford University Press, 1988), 3.

86. Paul Ricoeur, *Interpretation Theory: Discourse and the Surplus of Meaning* (Fort Worth: Texas Christian University Press, 1976), 94.

87. See Athanasius, "A Letter to Marcellinus," in *The Life of Antony and The Letter to Marcellinus*, trans. Robert C. Gregg (New York: Paulist, 1980), 101–30. See also Paul R Kolbet, "Athanasius, the Psalms, and the Reformation of the Self," *Harvard Theological Review* 99, no. 1 (2006): 85–101.

88. Billy Collins, "Introduction to Poetry," *The Apple That Astonished Paris* (Fayetteville: University of Arkansas Press, 1988), 58.

89. See further Angela Harvey, *Spiritual Reading: A Study of the Christian Practice of Reading Scripture* (Eugene, OR: Cascade, 2015); and Chris E. W. Green, *Sanctifying Interpretation: Vocation, Holiness, and Scripture* (Cleveland, TN: CPT, 2015). Green worries that Protestant evangelicals focus on knowing the objective content of Scripture as divine revelation. His counterproposal is to attend to the usefulness of

Earlier Christians took it for granted that reading the Bible was a spiritual exercise, a struggle with oneself before God. They knew that in engaging the Scriptures "it is not just the text but also the Christian who gets interpreted."[90] Again, at the core of reading theologically is a dialogical encounter with God: divine address, human response.[91] The prevailing reading cultures in the post-Enlightenment West have turned what ought to be a house of prayer into an academic common room. One of the encouraging recent developments in biblical hermeneutics has been the attempt to recover, and reintegrate, a spiritual concern—for the spiritual sense of the text, the spiritual condition of the reader (the two go together), and the work of the Holy Spirit. It will be helpful to discuss some of these approaches to spiritual interpretation before setting out my own thoughts on the transfiguration of the reader.

Reading Virtuously

Anyone familiar with Aesop's fables knows that stories teach children (and adults) the difference between right and wrong, foolishness and wisdom. For example, we learn by reading "The Hare and the Tortoise" that it is better to persevere at a slow speed than to proceed in fits and starts. Stories with such morals form character.[92] Reading not only depicts and teaches virtues but also requires them. It takes endurance to get to the end of Tolstoy's *War and Peace*, patience to appreciate poetry, and attentiveness to follow James Joyce's complex narrative and multilayered allusions. These and similar interpretive virtues are useful when reading anything, including the Bible.

Reading Scripture rightly requires not only the proper methodological procedures but also the interpretive virtues that characterize right-headed and right-hearted readers who want to be hearers and doers of God's word, not simply purveyors of their own ideas and agendas. In periods of legitimation crisis, such as the present, when it is difficult to know whose interpretation counts, and why, the interpretive virtues become indispensable. An interpretive virtue is a characteristic, disposition, or habit of the reader that is conducive to textual understanding.[93]

Scripture for sanctification, how it is divinely fitted "to work *our transfiguration* into God's divine human life" (*Sanctifying Interpretation*, 161). As I hope has or will become clear, my own proposal tries to have it both ways, attending to both letter and Spirit.

90. Hans Boersma, *Scripture as Real Presence: Sacramental Exegesis in the Early Church* (Grand Rapids: Baker Academic, 2017), 251.

91. "The reading of Scripture is one of the most tangible ways that this cooperation between God and the believer may take place, as in the human effort of reading the Bible . . . both the individual's work and the work of God are operative" (Harvey, *Spiritual Reading*, 9).

92. For an excellent discussion of how literature can be formative of virtue, see Karen Swallow Prior, *On Reading Well: Finding the Good Life through the Great Books* (Grand Rapids: Brazos, 2018).

93. "*An interpretive virtue is a disposition of the mind and heart that arises from the motivation for understanding, for cognitive contact with the meaning of the text*" (Vanhoozer, *Is There a Meaning in This Text?*, 376 (emphasis original).

To acknowledge the necessity of interpretive virtues is to realize that the reader's sanctification may be as or more important than competence in literary or biblical criticism. Interpretive virtues such as honesty, patience, charity, and humility aid readers in their struggle to understand the text and to understand themselves in front of the text. Many biblical stories either feature, or call for, various interpretive virtues.[94] To read as a person of interpretive virtue is to acquire wisdom, "the ability to see the world as God would have us see it."[95] In contrast, without virtues like faith, honesty, and humility, sinful readers who are turned in upon themselves will resist seeing the world, and themselves, in God's perspective, thereby failing to see or live along the grain of reality.[96] Readers cannot will their blindness away, much less muster faith, simply by trying hard. Practice may make perfect when learning scales on the piano, but it cannot lift the veil of misunderstanding. Only the Spirit's illumination can do that. The point is that becoming a person of interpretive virtue is yet another way that readers participate in the economy of light. What you see and understand depends on the kind of person you are and how you are participating in the economy of light. To read the Bible theologically requires resources beyond those of general hermeneutics, beyond even the secular interpretive virtues. In the final analysis, reading the Bible rightly requires the *theological* interpretive virtues—faith, hope, and love—and a theological frame of reference. The particular interpretive virtues commensurate with reading for the spiritual sense require spiritual formation, which is to say, the sanctifying work of the Holy Spirit.[97]

Reading Pneumatically

There is an obvious and important connection between the spiritual sense, spiritual interpretation, spiritual formation, and the Holy Spirit. Specifying what that relation consists in, however, is less than obvious. Protestant accounts of the Spirit's illumination focus on the Spirit's work in the reader, not the text: "The Holy Spirit's role in interpretation does not consist in giving the interpreter cognition of what the Bible is saying, which would involve dispensing additional information, beyond the historical-grammatical data. . . . Rather, the

94. Richard S. Briggs, *The Virtuous Reader: Old Testament Narrative and Interpretive Virtue* (Grand Rapids: Baker Academic, 2010).

95. Richard S. Briggs, *Reading the Bible Wisely* (Grand Rapids: Baker Academic, 2003), 111.

96. See further J. De Waal Dryden, *A Hermeneutic of Wisdom: Recovering the Formative Agency of Scripture* (Grand Rapids: Baker Academic, 2018).

97. So Robert Eby, *Virtue Hermeneutics: New Horizons in Textual Understanding* (Eugene, OR: Pickwick, 2022). In addition to the interpretive virtues already mentioned, Radner calls for an interpretive posture that befits responding to divine speech, a posture that includes absolute attention and utter openness ("'I Contain Multitudes,'" 151–53).

Holy Spirit's role is to change the heart of the interpreter, so that he loves the message that is conveyed by the historical-grammatical data."[98]

Many Pentecostal scholars in the mid-twentieth century signed on to this understanding of the Spirit's role in biblical interpretation. More recently, however, some have worried this subordinates the Spirit to the written word.[99]

"Pneumatic reading" describes newer Pentecostal approaches that attempt to break from their "captivity to evangelical hermeneutical principles."[100] They share a special interest in "a tridactic negotiation for meaning between the biblical text, Pentecostal community and the Holy Spirit."[101] Several recent works explore this three-way interpretive traffic, most notably Amos Yong's *Spirit-Word-Community: Theological Hermeneutics in Trinitarian Perspective*.[102] According to this "trialectic," the Spirit who inspired the Scriptures is active in shaping the whole interpretive community. "The Pentecostal interpreter has been formed in such a way that the expectancy of the Spirit's intervention is part of the interpretive worldview or framework."[103] Pneumatic hermeneutics adds a distinctly theological note to what otherwise might amount to run-of-the-mill reader-response criticism. "The community has a role within the interpretive process and the Holy Spirit works through that community by *inspiring* it to make right decisions (Acts 15)."[104]

Acts 15 plays a central role in pneumatic hermeneutics in recording an important precedent: "Inspiration to interpret Scripture is the primary consequence of being filled with the Holy Spirit in Acts."[105] As the Spirit helped the Jerusalem church to navigate uncharted paths, so the Spirit is active today. "Experience of the Spirit shapes the community's understanding of Scripture, while the Spirit's work in the community is interpreted through the scriptural

98. Daniel P. Fuller, "The Holy Spirit's Role in Biblical Interpretation," in *Scripture, Tradition, and Interpretation*, ed. W. Ward Gasque and William S. LaSor (Grand Rapids: Eerdmans, 1978), 189.

99. See esp. Kenneth J. Archer, *A Pentecostal Hermeneutic: Spirit, Scripture, and Community* (Cleveland, TN: CPT, 2005), 209–11.

100. Leulseged Philemon, *Pneumatic Hermeneutics: The Role of the Holy Spirit in the Theological Interpretation of Scripture* (Cleveland, TN: CPT, 2019), 208.

101. Archer, *Pentecostal Hermeneutic*, 6.

102. Amos Yong, *Spirit-Word-Community: Theological Hermeneutics in Trinitarian Perspective* (Burlington, VT: Ashgate, 2002). See also Amos Yong, "The Hermeneutical Trialectic: Notes toward a Consensual Hermeneutic and Theological Method," *Heythrop Journal* 45 (2004): 22–39; and the essays in *Spirit and Scripture: Examining a Pneumatic Hermeneutic*, ed. Kevin L. Spawn and Archie T. Wright (London: T&T Clark, 2012).

103. John Christopher Thomas, "'What the Spirit Is Saying to the Church'—the Testimony of a Pentecostal in New Testament Studies," in Spawn and Wright, *Spirit and Scripture*, 129.

104. Mark J. Cartledge, "Text–Community–Spirit: The Challenges Posed by Pentecostal Theology to Evangelical Theology," in Spawn and Wright, *Spirit and Scripture*, 133 (emphasis added).

105. Philemon, *Pneumatic Hermeneutics*, 191–92. Philemon also examines Peter's "inspired" sermon on the Day of Pentecost in Acts 2:14–41 and Philip's "inspired" interpretation of Isaiah 53 for the Ethiopian eunuch in Acts 8:26–39 (190–94).

framework."[106] The aim of pneumatic hermeneutics is not to recover the original "once for all" meaning of the inspired text. Rather, all three parties, "the community, the Scripture, and the Spirit must negotiate the meaning in the context of faithful praxis."[107] As another Pentecostal author puts it, "The Spirit who inspired the ancient texts, and continues to inspire reading traditions, allows 'meaning and application' to emerge in the dynamic between them."[108]

To be sure, the church is not like other reading communities. Rather, it is "a pneumatological interpretive community"[109]—a "fellowship of the Holy Spirit" (2 Cor 13:14). It is also the context "in which meaning takes place through the reading of Scripture in light of experience and testimony and work of the Holy Spirit."[110] What precisely does the Holy Spirit *do* in the community that contributes to biblical interpretation? The answer pneumatic readers give, as far as I am able to discern it, has more to do with the Spirit speaking in and through the *community* than it does with the Spirit speaking in and through the *Scriptures*.[111] Is the Spirit's inspirational activity a kind of *authorial* activity, in which meaning is generated through human reading? If not, what is the nature of the Spirit's activity? And finally, to raise once more one of the key issues of the present work: What is the Spirit's relation to Scripture's literal sense?

Walter Moberly affirms the concern of pneumatic hermeneutics to clarify the role of the Spirit but believes the crucial issue—saying how the Spirit mediates a contemporary meaning from the ancient text of Scripture—is left hanging: "It is important to know that word and Spirit should be combined . . . but this leaves me at least little wiser as to *how* they should be combined."[112] The other question left hanging is knowing *which* community the Spirit is currently inspiring. Whose pneumatic interpretation counts, and how can we recognize it as genuinely pneumatic? The question is difficult, but unavoidable, for although the church is one, it presently appears as many: a smorgasbord of differing, often divided, interpretive communities.[113]

---

106. Philemon, 167.

107. Archer, *Pentecostal Hermeneutic*, 260.

108. Mark J. Cartledge, "Pneumatic Hermeneutics: A Reply to Respondents," in Spawn and Wright, *Spirit and Scripture*, 186.

109. Philemon, *Pneumatic Hermeneutics*, 208.

110. Philemon, 167.

111. Archer's constructive final chapter devotes seven pages to "Word," five and a half pages to "Spirit," and twenty-three pages to "Community" (see Archer, *Pentecostal Hermeneutic*, 212–60).

112. R. W. L. Moberly, "Pneumatic Biblical Hermeneutics: A Response," in Spawn and Wright, *Spirit and Scripture*, 165.

113. For more on pneumatic hermeneutics, see my "The Spirit of Light after the Age of Enlightenment: Renewing/Reforming Pneumatic Hermeneutics via the Economy of Illumination," in *Spirit of God: Christian Renewal in the Community of Faith*, ed. Jeffrey Barbeau and Beth Felker Jones (Downers Grove, IL: InterVarsity, 2015), 149–67.

Reading Supernaturally

John Piper's proposal for reading "supernaturally" represents another type of spiritual interpretation, even if he does not use the term. The book begins with a quotation from his beloved Jonathan Edwards about what it is "spiritually to understand the Scriptures."[114] Edwards's view anticipates much of what I want to say about transfigural interpretation. We agree that the letter of the text radiates the "excellency" of Christ. The light of Christ is, and has always been, in the Bible, "and would have been seen before, if it had not been for blindness."[115] To understand Scripture spiritually, said Edwards, is to behold the light of Christ—and one can do this without changing the sense, or adding a new sense, to the words of Scripture. A new "sense" is added, yes, but to the *reader*: sight.

Piper's working assumption is that the glorious perfections are as plain to see in Scripture as they are in nature, though in both cases one needs the eyes of the heart to be open in order to see them, lest we remain "darkened in [our] understanding" (Eph 4:18). The brightness of God's glory "shines through the whole Bible but finds its most beautiful radiance in the person and work of Jesus Christ."[116] Scripture is a human book (letter) luminous with divine glory (the light of Christ). It therefore calls for natural and supernatural reading: "God's glory does not float over the Bible like a gas. . . . *It is seen in and through the meaning of texts.*"[117]

Piper's approach accords well with the present argument, as does what he takes to be the telos of biblical interpretation. We read the Bible to perceive God's infinite worth and beauty, the better to exalt him. This doxological goal calls for a supernatural reading "since seeing divine glory in human words is not your ordinary way of reading a book."[118] Like Edwards, Piper wants readers of the Bible not simply to comprehend the sense of the words, but to *sense* (spiritually) the excellence of their referent. The point is "to be *transformed* by this seeing and savoring."[119] In terms of the present work, the purpose of reading for the transfigured literal (i.e., spiritual) sense is the transfiguration of the reader (see below).

Piper's thesis is that "*a proper reading of the Bible is a supernatural act.*"[120] The phrasing is intriguing. Does he mean that reading is an act of God, like an

---

114. John Piper, *Reading the Bible Supernaturally: Seeing and Savoring the Glory of God in Scripture* (Wheaton, IL: Crossway, 2017), 154.

115. From Jonathan Edwards, *Religious Affections*, ed. John E. Smith and Harry S. Stout, vol. 2 of *The Works of Jonathan Edwards*, rev ed. (New Haven, CT: Yale University Press, 2009), 281.

116. Piper, *Reading the Bible Supernaturally*, 26.

117. Edwards, *Religious Affections*, 299 (emphasis original).

118. Piper, *Reading the Bible Supernaturally*, 38.

119. Piper, 39.

120. Piper, 179 (emphasis original).

earthquake or a tsunami? No. He means that reading the Bible is no ordinary human activity but requires the action of the Holy Spirit. He is careful to insist that the supernatural act of seeing the light of Christ does not happen *apart from* the "natural" act of reading the letter. The letter of the text is the *natural* means God appoints to serve his *supernatural* purpose: communicating his glory, the brilliant concentration of the divine perfections, through the light that streams from the face of Christ. Spiritual reading is not "against nature," then, but employs the reader's natural powers in a supernatural way (illumination) for a supernatural end (transformation).[121]

With Unveiled Faces: Reading by Lamb-Light

> And the city has no need of sun or moon to shine on it, for the glory of God gives it light, and its lamp is the Lamb. (Rev 21:23)

The present section completes our case for transfiguring biblical interpretation by showing how it explains what it is to read Scripture spiritually or theologically, for the *glory* of the literal sense. As we have seen, biblical interpretation involves a struggle not only to make sense of, say, Paul's letter/spirit contrast, but also of one's sense of self in relation to God. Accordingly, we shall return to Paul's discussion in 2 Corinthians 3–4 to complete our account of readers in the triune economy of light, with special attention to the new eschatological context that corresponds to the gift of the Spirit. The Spirit's work in and on readers enables them to read with a grammatical-eschatological frame of reference for the trans-figural sense, and eventually to reflect the light of Christ in a transfiguration of their own. We begin with some comments on reading in the economy of light. Next we consider how the Spirit enables an illumined reading. Finally, we examine the effect on the reader of reading in eschatological context, face-to-face with the divine voice speaking in Scripture.

Reading in the Economy of Light

The economy of light refers to the missions of the Son and Spirit in making known the God of the gospel and the gospel of God. A theological account of the Bible and biblical interpretation belongs in this economy, for both Scripture and its reading are elements in the communication of the light the Father is

121. Craig Bartholomew makes a similar point but with different terms: "In devotional reading of the Bible . . . the heart dominates while the head remains engaged. In academic biblical study, the head dominates while the heart remains—or should remain—engaged." Craig G. Bartholomew, *Listening to God: An Introduction to Interpreting the Bible* (Grand Rapids: Baker Academic, 2023), 8. Bartholomew goes on to say that if he had to privilege one approach, it would be the devotional or spiritual "because it specializes in receiving the Bible as what it is: God's Word, his address to us in our hearts" (9).

through the light the Son shines by the Spirit who opens our eyes to see the "the light of the knowledge of the glory of God" (2 Cor 4:6).[122] We saw how God's speaking creation into being ("Let there be light") was but the opening salvo in an ongoing light show that culminates in Jesus' transfiguration. That Jesus' face "shone like the sun" (Matt 17:2) anticipates the consummation of redemption, when Jesus will be revealed as the Alpha and Omega, with his face again "like the sun shining in full strength" (Rev 1:16). It is surely significant that the Bible ends, as it begins, with a reference to God and light. The new Jerusalem, God's dwelling place with humanity on the new earth, "has no need of sun or moon to shine on it, for the glory of God gives it light, and its lamp is the Lamb" (Rev 21:23). There will be no darkness, for night will be no more. Those who dwell with God "will need no light of lamp or sun, for the Lord God will be their light" (Rev 22:5).

The whole Bible is about God's revealing the light he is in himself to creation and his covenant people, old and new, which is why Jesus' transfiguration represents a climactic point in the story. As we saw in chapter 7, the transfiguration both recalls God's cloudy revelation to Israel at Sinai and anticipates the bright resplendence to come in the new Jerusalem. Light, remarkably, is both what is made known (God's glory, the sum total of all the divine perfections) and the process of making known (God's self-communication): it is "a power that manifests and that, in manifesting, manifests itself."[123] The transfiguration compels us to think about Jesus' identity in relation to, on the one hand, the Law and the Prophets (represented by Moses and Elijah), and on the other, the Father and Spirit (represented by the voice and the cloud). The economy of light is thus a fitting mere Christian hermeneutical framework in which to think theologically about transfigural interpretation, both the action of the reader on the text and its corresponding effect on the reader.

Reading the Bible theologically requires thinking about the author, text, and readers of Scripture in theological terms, in particular, in relation to the economy of light. *God's illumining and illuminating presence and activity—the light of Christ; in a word, transfiguration—is an essential factor in the context of both text and reader.* God illuminates the letter of the text by directing its words to reveal Christ; God illumines readers by opening their eyes to the text's illumination. God enables readers to pierce beyond the letter to its subject matter—what Piper describes as God's "supernatural help in the natural act of reading."[124] This enlightening is altogether different from what Spinoza had in mind when

122. As such, my account complements John Webster's descriptions of reading Scripture in the economy of grace. See esp. his "Reading in the Economy of Grace," ch. 3 of *Holy Scripture: A Dogmatic Sketch* (Cambridge: Cambridge University Press, 2003).

123. Chrétien, *Under the Gaze of the Bible*, 87.

124. Piper, *Reading the Bible Supernaturally*, 392.

he claimed that the true method for interpreting Scripture "requires no other light than that of natural reason."[125] Critical reason would be appropriate if the biblical text were only a natural object, like any other text: "If the goal is to grasp the original meaning of the text, pneumatology is dispensable."[126] The Spirit is indispensable, however, if the goal is to remove the veil that prevents readers from discerning the light of Christ in the letter of the text (cf. 2 Cor 3:14–16). The Bible is more than a natural object; it is a divinely inspired creaturely component in the divine economy of light, a natural means by which God makes known his supernatural reality.

Both text and reader are thus caught up in the revelatory and redemptive activity of the triune God. Those who are dark-minded, hard-hearted, and strong-willed—who have not turned to the Lord and received the Spirit—may be able to make sense of the letter, but they cannot see its glory, the light of Christ. The Spirit enables a transfigural reading that corresponds to the transfigured literal (i.e., grammatical-eschatological) sense. The transfigured biblical interpretation sees that the history of salvation recounted in Scripture has been recapitulated in the reader's own personal history: "To read Holy Scripture is to participate in the history of sin and its overcoming."[127]

Reading Eschatologically: The Illumination of the Spirit

To read with unveiled faces is to enjoy with other reconciled sinners a prime benefit of the Spirit's regenerative and reparative work. It is to inhabit a new, thoroughly eschatological, interpretive condition, new because it represents a distinct new stage in the economy of light, inaugurated by Christ's gift of the Spirit. "Metaphysics, ethics and hermeneutics all stand under the same rule: 'the old has passed away, behold, the new has come' (2 Cor. 5:17)."[128] This new eschatological situation calls for an eschatological exegesis that discerns the light of the new *in* the letter of the old.[129]

The objective light of God and the gospel shines forth in Christ, and the Old Testament Scriptures that bear witness to him; however, this light cannot be seen until the veil is lifted from fallen hearts and minds.[130] The veil—the

125. Baruch Spinoza, *Theological-Political Treatise* (Cambridge: Cambridge University Press, 2007), 111.

126. Darren Sarisky, *Scriptural Interpretation: A Theological Exploration* (Malden, MA: Wiley-Blackwell, 2012), 221.

127. Webster, *Holy Scripture*, 87.

128. John Webster, "Reading Scripture Eschatologically (1)," in *Reading Texts, Seeking Wisdom: Scripture and Theology*, ed. David F. Ford and Graham Stanton (Grand Rapids: Eerdmans, 2003), 248.

129. Ralph Martin speaks of the "eschatological exegesis" that results from reading the Old Testament, like Paul, with unveiled faces. Ralph Martin, *2 Corinthians*, Word Bible Commentary, 2nd ed. (Grand Rapids: Zondervan, 2014), 217.

130. David Whidden has the objective aspect in mind when he says, "The illumination of our minds is primarily the mission of the Son." David L. Whidden III, *Christ the Light: The Theology of Light and Illumination in Thomas Aquinas* (Minneapolis: Fortress, 2014), 8.

sinful resistance to and refusal of the divine address and its implications—leads readers to wrestle with the text. It prompts readers anxious to secure their own fleshly identities to compel and sometimes violate the text to make it serve their own egoistic, ethnic, or ideological interests. That veil of misunderstanding is removed by the Spirit, who has "delivered us from the domain of darkness and transferred us to the kingdom of his beloved Son" (Col 1:13). The Spirit's ministry of new life comes with hermeneutic benefits: to read with unveiled face is to come face-to-face with the shining face of Christ.

The concept of "economy" calls attention to the inseparable operations of the God who is light in communicating the light that he is to the world. The Father lives "in unapproachable light" (1 Tim 6:16); the Son shines forth (reveals) this light into the world as "the radiance of God's glory" (Heb 1:3 NIV). The Spirit is not an independent source of light but nevertheless plays an essential role in the economy. The illumination of the Spirit is a theological description of what happens in Bible reading when, like the apostle Paul on the road to Damascus, one suddenly "sees" beyond the letter to the glorious referent to which the literal sense bears witness.

Several theologians have sought to describe this invisible yet enlightening work of the Spirit and its relation to the light of Christ. In his seminal treatise *On the Holy Spirit*, Basil the Great described Christ, the image of the invisible God, as a light that mediates the knowledge of God which can be seen only when the Spirit "supplies to those who love to see the truth the power to see the image in himself."[131] Divine revelation proceeds from the Father through the Son by the Spirit, but the way back to God via human knowing "is from the one Spirit, through the one Son, to the one Father."[132] For Basil, reading Scripture spiritually is comparable to Moses' speaking face-to-face with God. As Sarisky explains, "Turning to the Lord while reading means following the text's ultimate, though indirect, reference to God."[133] The Spirit opens readers' eyes to the truth of the Mosaic law, enabling them to see past its letter to discern what it is about, the mystery of Christ.[134] The Spirit's illumination is no excuse for not parsing verbs or ignoring literary genre. The Spirit does not miraculously give insight either into philology or the original historical context. Rather, the Spirit enables readers to attend to what God is speaking by means of the text:

131. Basil, *On the Holy Spirit*, trans. Stephen Hildebrand (Yonkers, NY: St. Vladimir's Seminary Press, 2011), 18.47. Basil is assuming the optical theory of his day, according to which there must be a likeness between the light one sees and the eyes doing the seeing, which would explain why one must be spiritual to know the thoughts of God, who is Spirit (see 1 Cor 2:10–14).

132. Basil, *On the Holy Spirit* 18.47.

133. Sarisky, *Scriptural Interpretation*, 97.

134. Basil, *On the Holy Spirit* 18.47.

"Just as the Father is seen in the Son, so the Son is seen in the Spirit."[135] This is the context in which Basil cited Psalm 36:9: "In your light do we see light."

Scripture, too, is part of the economy of light because, as Calvin said, in testifying to Christ it presents the light of the gospel. Word and Spirit are twin pillars in the economy, light's objective and subjective moments, respectively. Accordingly, Calvin insisted that the Spirit adds no new substance to what has been written, appealing to Jesus' own teaching: "He will not speak on his own; he will speak only what he hears" (John 16:13 NIV). The economy of light follows the general pattern representing the inseparable operations of the Trinity: the Father initiates, the Son enacts, "but to the Spirit is assigned the power and efficacy of that activity."[136] The Spirit, we might say, is the efficacy of the word, which is to say, *the efficacy of the light of Christ in the letter of the text*. Calvin, commenting on 2 Corinthians 4:6, said, "God has, by His Spirit, opened the eyes of our understandings, so as to make them capable of receiving the light of the gospel."[137] The Spirit restores us to our proper senses so that we can see the light of Christ in the letter of the text—call it the *glorified* literal sense.

John Owen similarly viewed Scripture as "a lamp shining in a dark place" (2 Pet 1:19), adding that it is no criticism of the light that the blind cannot see it. Given the Spirit's ability to open what Paul describes as "the eyes of your heart" (Eph 1:18), Owen designated the Spirit as the "principal efficient cause" of understanding: "Men may have a knowledge of *words*, and the *meaning* of propositions in the Scripture, who have no knowledge of the *things themselves* designed in them."[138] Illumination involves restoring readers to their right senses, not dispensing new information: "[The Spirit] irradiates the mind with a spiritual light, whereby it is enabled to discern the glory of spiritual things."[139] Although the Spirit is the "cause" of understanding, natural reading (as Piper calls it) was for Owen the "means" of understanding. Illumination is therefore no excuse for shirking the hard work of exegesis. It belongs rather to the *harder* part of understanding, namely, responding rightly to what one reads in Scripture with all one's mind, heart, and soul.[140]

John Webster's essay on illumination picks up where Owen left off,

135. Basil, *On the Holy Spirit* 26.64.

136. John Calvin, *Institutes* I.xiii.18.

137. John Calvin, *Commentary on the Epistles of Paul the Apostle to the Corinthians* (Edinburgh: Calvin Translation Society, 1848), 200.

138. See Owen, "Causes, Ways, and Means of Understanding the Mind of God," in *The Reason of Faith* (Glasgow: Falconer, 1801), 215 (emphasis mine).

139. John Owen, *The Works of John Owen*, ed. William H. Goold, vol. 4 (Edinburgh: T&T Clark, n.d.), 57.

140. J. I. Packer, himself a student of Owen, put it well: "The Spirit is not given to make Bible study needless, but to make it effective." J. I. Packer, *Fundamentalism and the Word of God* (Grand Rapids: Eerdmans, 1958), 112.

reminding us that "the end of reading Holy Scripture is to know the mind of God."[141] The term *illumination* reminds us that the Spirit's work serves the purpose of divine light: to make known God's mind. The Spirit is the giver of light and life; his ministry does not do violence to but restores human nature, putting sinners in their right minds, quickening their created intellects.[142] God is the primary cause of our understanding, then, and illumination is shorthand for the Spirit's work of interpretive grace whereby he grants us what we need to understand what we are reading: the eyes to discern the light of Christ (the divine *res*) in the letter of the text (the textual *signum*). Once we understand the proper place of illumination in the economy of light, we see that it avoids "both hermeneutical naturalism in which the actings of the mind, unmoved from outside, claim sufficiency for themselves, and hermeneutical immediacy in which seizure by the Spirit breaks off the exercise of intelligence and interpretation becomes rapture."[143]

It was Edwards, however, who came closest to what I want to say about transfiguring biblical interpretation. He did not use the term "economy of light," but he had much to say about it, especially in his sermon "A Divine and Supernatural Light."[144] Edwards first stated what the divine light of illumination is not: it is not mere conviction of sin or emotional affect, much less new revelation. Rather, it is "a true sense of the divine excellency of the things revealed in the word of God."[145] It is as if the Spirit opens up a sixth sense, a spiritual sense: the ability to perceive the glory of God. Natural reason neither sees nor appreciates the beauty and wisdom of Christ crucified; on the contrary, the unillumined cross appears ugly and tragic—*senseless*. Nor can the Bible's words alone illumine: words bring things to mind, but words cannot bestow the sense of their divine excellency. There is a difference between having an opinion of God's holiness and having a spiritual *sense* of that holiness: "There is a difference between having a rational judgment that honey is sweet, and having a sense of its sweetness."[146] The Spirit's illumination bestows not only spiritual sight, but spiritual *taste*: "Oh, taste and see that the Lord is good!" (Ps 34:8). The spiritual interpretation of Scripture reads for this spiritual sense, the sense that what the text is saying is excellent. To *transfigure* biblical interpretation is to sense the *spiritual excellency* of the literal sense.

As we have seen, thanks to the gift of the Holy Spirit, illumined readers

141. John Webster, "Illumination," in *The Domain of the Word: Scripture and Theological Reason* (London: T&T Clark, 2012), 61.

142. Webster, 55.

143. Webster, 61.

144. In *The Sermons of Jonathan Edwards: A Reader*, ed. Wilson J. Kimnach, Kenneth P. Minkema, and Douglas A. Sweeney (New Haven, CT: Yale University Press, 1999).

145. *Sermons of Jonathan Edwards*, 126.

146. *Sermons of Jonathan Edwards*, 126.

find themselves in a new, eschatologically charged situation. The light of the gospel that the Spirit shines in our hearts and minds "is the long awaited light of the eschaton."[147] As the transfiguration of Jesus reveals the Son and anticipates his future glory, so the quickening of the Spirit renews our minds (Rom 12:2) and anticipates our own glorification: "Illumination is a new-creation metaphor, expressing how readers align themselves with God's renewal of creation through Christ."[148] Illumination is therefore shorthand for the whole eschatologically charged framework of understanding by which those with unveiled faces read Scripture. We have been exploring the nature of such reading, but there is more light yet to come. We turn now to discuss the consequences of transfiguring interpretation.[149]

Reading That Reflects the Light: The Glory of Biblical Interpretation

Basil described the aim of reading the Bible theologically, with unveiled face, as "spiritual contemplation" (*pneumatike theoria*).[150] He was commenting on 2 Corinthians 3:18: "And we all, with unveiled face, beholding the glory of the Lord, are being transformed into the same image from one degree of glory to another." When Christians read the Old Testament, they, like Moses, behold something that transforms them: "He who clearly fixes his eye on the Spirit is somehow transformed by the Spirit's glory into something brighter as his heart is illuminated by the truth of the Spirit, as if by a light."[151] Paul's text, along with Basil's commentary, raises two important issues, both pertaining to the transfiguration of the reader. The first pertains to *beholding*: its cause, object, and nature. The second pertains to the intended result of that beholding: *being transformed*.

Beholding the Glory

The previous section treated the cause of what we behold in Scripture. Thanks to the Spirit's illumination, readers are able to understand not simply the words but what the words are ultimately about: their transfigured literal sense and referent. The apostle Paul describes the object of our beholding, what we see when we read with unveiled face, in several striking and increasingly

147. Timothy B. Savage, *Power through Weakness: Paul's Understanding of the Christian Ministry in 2 Corinthians*, Society for New Testament Studies Monograph Series (Cambridge: Cambridge University Press, 1996), 126.

148. Sarisky, *Scriptural Interpretation*, 219.

149. See also John Feinberg's detailed analysis of the various conceptual nuances of and biblical grounding for the doctrine of illumination in his *Light in a Dark Place: The Doctrine of Scripture* (Wheaton, IL: Crossway, 2018), 576–608.

150. Basil, *On the Holy Spirit* 21.52.

151. Basil, *On the Holy Spirit* 21.52.

expansive phrases—"the glory of the Lord" (2 Cor 3:18); "the light of the gospel of the glory of Christ" (2 Cor 4:4); "the light of the knowledge of the glory of God in the face of Jesus Christ" (2 Cor 4:6)—each of which merits further comment.

"The glory of the Lord." It should come as no surprise that the content of the Bible's divine discourse is the divine glory, for God has been shining—lighting and enlightening the world—from the beginning. The divine author has published two books—creation and Scripture—in and through which he makes himself known, communicating the light that he is in himself to his human creatures through more light. Like the sun, the light that God is cannot be looked at directly; it is blindingly bright. Yet, again like the sun, the light God radiates is that by which we see everything else. God's glory is the outward display of the divine perfections, his "visible splendor."[152] According to Edwards, displaying his glory is the end for which God created the world in the first place.[153] There is arguably nothing more theological than "light from light"! The whole story of the Bible, particularly the economy of light, "is, in large part, the drama of God's glory."[154] To read the Bible theologically, then, is to behold the glory of the Lord in and through the letter of the text.

"The light of the gospel of the glory of Christ." The superiority of Paul's ministry derives from the eminence of its object. The glory of Christ is God's own glory, as Paul shows by identifying Christ as "the image of God" (2 Cor 4:4) and by referring to "the glory of God in the face of Jesus Christ" (2 Cor 4:6). The glory of Christ is his mirror-like reflection of God's glory. Paul speaks of the *light* of the gospel because Jesus' death and resurrection are the events by which God makes his cruciform glory known (Rom 6:4; Heb 2:9). The light of the gospel is the light of the new creation inaugurated by Christ's work, and it is a gospel of glory because both the means (the cross) and the end (bodies of the faithful raised in power—1 Cor 15:42–44) display God's unsurpassed brilliance: "It is the long awaited light of the eschaton, heralding a new creation and commencing the day of salvation."[155] What the spiritual reader beholds in the letter of the text is thus a glimpse of the already/not-yet eschatological reality of the age to come—a glory, and a fate, briefly unveiled at Jesus' transfiguration. When Paul speaks, then, of "the light of the gospel of the glory of Christ," he is saying "the gospel's content is the glorious Christ himself."[156]

152. Richard Bauckham, *Gospel of Glory: Major Themes in Johannine Theology* (Grand Rapids: Baker Academic, 2015), 44.

153. Jonathan Edwards, *The End for Which God Created the World*, in *The Works of Jonathan Edwards*, vol. 8, *Ethical Writings* (New Haven, CT: Yale University Press, 1989).

154. See further Christopher W. Morgan and Robert A. Peterson, *The Glory of God and Paul: Texts, Themes, and Theology* (Downers Grove, IL: IVP Academic, 2022), 31.

155. Savage, *Power through Weakness*, 126.

156. Morgan and Peterson, *Glory of God and Paul*, 120.

"The light of the knowledge of the glory of God in the face of Christ." This is as good a description of Jesus' transfiguration as one can make. In context, however, Paul is referring to the result of the Spirit's illumination, what the Spirit "has shone in our hearts" (2 Cor 4:6). Paul may also be thinking of his own conversion experience of the light of Christ (Acts 9:3; 22:6; 26:13), and of the blessing given to the Israelites: "The Lord make his face to shine upon you and be gracious to you" (Num 6:25). The point is this: what illumined readers behold and come to know in reading Scripture is the glory of God in the face of Christ.[157] This is a personal knowledge than which nothing greater or better can be conceived. It is the knowledge that results from encountering a person, or at least that person's speaking presence, as Paul did at his conversion ("Saul, Saul, why are you persecuting me?"; Acts 9:4; 22:7; 26:14). The face of Jesus Christ is the speaking presence of God. The face speaks light/knowledge, a resplendent personal address.

This brings us to the reader's response and the nature of the reader's beholding. This too is part of transfiguring interpretation. Even unveiled readers see the glorious face of Christ in the mirror of the gospel only dimly, as Paul says in 1 Corinthians 13:12, in comparison to the *unmediated* "face to face" seeing to be enjoyed at the end of the age.[158] Present beholding must be confused neither with past conversion or future "face to face" seeing. What, then, is it for readers to behold the glory of God in the face of Christ? How can *reading* be a kind of *beholding*?

In the first place, a beholding reading "is decidedly more than a visual or intellectual activity. It must be related with that existential confrontation that is contained in the preaching of the gospel"[159]—and with Jacob's wrestling with God. Beholding is one dimension of the reader's response to the divine address in Scripture. Recall that God gives himself, as light, to behold in speaking.[160] Paul says in 2 Corinthians 4:6 that the God who in the beginning said, "Let light shine out of darkness," has now shone light in our hearts to communicate knowledge. Paul strikingly compares God's speaking physical light into existence with his shining light into darkened human hearts: "The spoken word of God creates light. . . . The light of the Gospel and of God's glory in Christ comes

157. For a book-length study of this theme, see David H. Wenkel, *Shining Like the Sun: A Biblical Theology of Meeting God Face to Face* (Wooster, OH: Weaver, 2016).

158. N. T. Wright suggests that the mirror in question is not the text or the gospel, but fellow Christians who are being transformed into the glorious image of Christ: "It is the peculiar glory of the Spirit that is seen when one looks at one's fellow Christians." "Reflected Glory: 2 Corinthians 3:18," in *The Glory of Christ in the New Testament: Studies in Christology*, ed. L. D. Hurst and N. T. Wright (Eugene, OR: Wipf & Stock, 2015), 145.

159. Jan Lambrecht, "Transformation in 2 Cor 3:18," *Biblica* 64, no. 2 (1983): 250–51.

160. See further Jeremy M. Kimble, *Behold and Become: Reading Scripture for Transformation* (Grand Rapids: Kregel Academic, 2023), ch. 1.

to us through our ears."[161] The Bible's literal sense is the luminous medium through which God communicates his name and nature.

Commentators are right to highlight the *verbal* aspect of this beholding. Moses' meeting with the Lord—the episode on which Paul has been commenting—"is presented in Exodus fundamentally as a *verbal exchange*, even if it includes a visual encounter."[162] Recall, too, that Paul employs the veil metaphor to describe Israel's inability to *read* the old covenant rightly. When Paul mentions "beholding the glory of the Lord," then, he is using "seeing" as a synthetic metaphor for physical and spiritual sensing: "our present 'seeing' is 'hearing.'"[163] Satan's "blinding" the mind of unbelievers describes those who read the biblical text but cannot "hear" the light shining in the letter of the biblical text.

The knowledge of the glory of God's gospel is what Paul's apostolic ministry and, arguably, mere Christian hermeneutics, is all about. C. K. Barrett noted that Paul's apostolic ministry "resembles the creation of light"[164] inasmuch as it, too, is part of the economy of light—part of God's plan to shed abroad his light to the nations (cf. Isa 9:2; 42:6; 60:3; Rev 21:24). The focus of this plan, and the linchpin of the economy, is the light streaming from the face of Christ. To read the Scriptures with unveiled face is thus to come face-to-face with God, as Jacob did at Jabbok, as Moses did at Sinai, and as the three disciples did on Mount Tabor. According to Paul, those who are beholding the glory of Christ, including readers of his gospel, are "being transformed into the same image from one degree of glory to another" (2 Cor 3:18). The final end of the economy of light is the transfiguration of the reader: "Because we are free, we have no veil, we are bold to reflect the splendor of Christ and are thus transfigured by his Spirit."[165]

Reflecting the Glory

Some translations of 2 Corinthians 3:18 (e.g., NIV) have Paul saying that Christians "reflect" rather than "behold" the glory of the Lord. On this view, the readers' faces, not Christ's, are what mirror God's glory. For present purposes, it is a moot point, for Paul goes on to say explicitly that Christian readers "are being transformed into the same image" that they are beholding. The verb *katoptrizomenoi* may not mean "reflecting as a mirror does," but reflection (becoming like the image one is beholding) is still the end result of Paul's way of reading

161. Mark A. Seifrid, *The Second Letter to the Corinthians* (Grand Rapids: Eerdmans, 2014), 200, 204.
162. Seifrid, 178.
163. Seifrid, 182.
164. C. K. Barrett, *The Second Epistle to the Corinthians* (Grand Rapids: Baker Academic, 1993), 135.
165. Brevard Childs, *The Book of Exodus: A Critical, Theological Commentary*, Old Testament Library (Louisville: Westminster John Knox, 1974), 624.

Moses, which is what 2 Corinthians 3 is all about.[166] And the verb Paul chooses to signify what happens to those who read Scripture rightly has everything to do with transfiguring the reader.

Those who read the Bible with unveiled faces, says Paul, "are being transformed [*metamorphoumetha*]" into the image of Christ. It is by beholding a reflected image (the glory of God in the face of Christ) that one comes gradually to reflect that image oneself ("transformed into the same image from one degree . . . to another"). We have come across this verb for transformation (*metamorphoō*) before. Matthew and Mark use it in their accounts of Jesus' transfiguration (Matt 17:2; Mark 9:2). Its only other appearance in the New Testament is in Romans 12:2: "Do not be conformed to this world, but be *transformed* by the renewal of your mind" (emphasis added). Both uses raise the question: Who is the agent of this transformation? The answer in both cases is "the Spirit," though, as Cranfield observed, Christians "nevertheless have a real responsibility in the matter—to let themselves be transformed, to respond to the leading and pressure of God's Spirit."[167] For present purposes, however, the more pressing question is: What does it mean to be "metamorphosed"?

Biblical scholars note that the LXX does not use the term *metamorphoō*. Some say Paul borrowed it from Greco-Roman metamorphosis literature (e.g., Ovid). However, Paul does not say we are transformed *into* Christ; rather, we are transformed into his image, by degrees.[168] While not excluding the possibility that Paul may have had Jesus' transfiguration in mind, the context suggests that he is more likely thinking of the change that led to Moses' shining face, an auditory rather than visual experience. Although Moses encountered God's presence in the form of a voice, the mention of his unveiled face suggests that he was indeed in God's presence, and that this was the cause of his transformation. Something similar happens to readers who, with unveiled faces, encounter the glory of the face of Christ in the letter of the text. They, too, expose themselves to the sheer luminosity of the divine address, for the God who created light "has shone in our hearts to give the light of the knowledge of the glory of God in the face of Jesus Christ" (2 Cor 4:6). It is this shining—the result of hearing the gospel and the Spirit's illumination—that transforms.

Paul's argument for the superiority of his apostolic ministry of the life-giving Spirit comes to a climax in the claim that the Corinthians are his letter of

166. "The context of our passage is the reason many commentators continue to prefer 'reflect.'" Lambrecht, "Transformation in 2 Cor 3:18," 247.

167. C. E. B. Cranfield, *The Epistle to the Romans*, vol. 2 (Edinburgh: T&T Clark: 1979), 607.

168. Joseph A. Fitzmyer agreed that *metamorphoō* is a Greco-Roman motif but argued that Paul infused it with a nuance he derived from the Palestinian Judaism found at Qumran. See his "Glory Reflected on the Face of Christ (2 Cor 3:7–4:6) and a Palestinian Jewish Motif," *Theological Studies* 42, no. 4 (1981): 638–39.

recommendation (2 Cor 3:2) precisely because they are being transformed from one degree of glory to another. How ought we to understand this remarkable phenomenon? What actually happens to the Corinthians, and to us, readers of Paul's texts, when we read the gospel with unveiled faces? To read the Bible theologically is to expose oneself to supernatural light, the self-publication of the God who is light itself, through the medium of a lesser light, the letters of the biblical text. Like Jacob, Moses, and Paul himself, those who come face-to-face with God and hear his voice will not come away unchanged. To behold God's glory in the face of Christ *is* to be transformed, for it is through beholding that God shines his light into our hearts (2 Cor 4:6). J. I. Packer said, "Through the Holy Spirit's agency, we become like the One we look at as we absorb the gospel word."[169] Paul's ministry surpassed Moses' because it issued in a transformation of his hearers, while Moses' did not.

Can we view this transformation from glory to glory as a transfiguration? Michael Kibbe thinks so, and I am inclined to agree. All the ingredients are present: Moses' shining face; unveiled faces; beholding God's glory; the light of the glory of God in the face of Jesus Christ; and of course the key term, *metamorphoō*. Kibbe also notes Luke's allusion to Moses' glory (Luke 9:30–31), the tendency of the Synoptics "to depict the transfiguration in Sinaiesque terms," and of course the phrase "glory of God in the face of Christ," an obvious allusion to Jesus' transfiguration.[170] Paul expands on Matthew's hint that Jesus' transfigural glory will also be ours, connecting the shared phrasing of Matthew 17:2 (Jesus' face shone "like the sun") and 13:43 (the righteous will shine "like the sun" in the kingdom of their Father). Kibbe rightly notes the difference between Jesus' transfiguration and the Christian's: his glory is innate; ours is reflected.

Paul's claim should give us pause. It is a stunning idea that biblical interpretation—reading for the light of Christ in the letter of the text—"is a vehicle by which human beings approach their telos, a means by which they become their true selves."[171] Jesus' transfiguration—and the knowledge that comes from beholding the glory streaming from his shining face—brings to fulfillment the veiled promise of Moses' face and anticipates the glorious feature awaiting all Christians. Glorification is the blessing mentioned in Revelation 1:3, which is for those who read, hear, and keep the prophetic word. Perhaps the idea that biblical interpretation is transformative should not be surprising. For we are reading Holy Scripture, human words set apart for a divine purpose,

169. J. I. Packer, *Rediscovering Holiness* (Ann Arbor, MI: Servant, 1992), 171.

170. Michael Kibbe, "From Glory to Glory: Transfiguration and New Creation in 2 Corinthians 2:14–4:6," in *Christian Origins and the Formation of the Early Church*, ed. Stanley E. Porter (Leiden, Brill, forthcoming).

171. Sarisky, *Scriptural Interpretation*, 98. See also Howell R. Jones, *Transfiguration and Transformation* (Edinburgh: Banner of Truth Trust, 2021).

words that mediate God's personal presence and create the eschatological culture that characterizes the domain of God's word.

In the opening pages of this book, I asked, "Can biblical interpretation change the world?" Yes it can, for it is the God-appointed means of revealing, refracting, and reflecting divine supernatural light, light with the ability to enlighten and transform. Transfiguring interpretation culminates in the transformation of the reader effected by beholding the glory of God in the face of Christ. To behold this face is the privilege and responsibility of all those who read the Bible as Christian Scripture. Moreover, all readers who care about literal interpretation should also care about spiritual or transfigural interpretation—reading for the *glory* of the literal sense—for it is a means to the knowledge of God and the key to the meaning of the whole Bible, indeed, the whole of history.

Almost everything I want to say about transfiguring the reader may be found in 2 Corinthians 3:18. According to Paul, the Spirit enables *spiritual* interpretation, namely, the ability to behold the glory of the Lord in the face of Christ, a beholding that has a *transfigurative* effect inasmuch as it transforms the reader, by degrees, into the same glorious image: "We become like what we behold; what captivates us shapes us."[172] To paraphrase C. S. Lewis's character Digory: "It's all in Paul, all in Paul. Bless me, what do they teach them at these theological schools?"[173] Reading the Bible theologically involves considerably more than moving the eyes from left to right, for in looking into and along the text, we step into its light, there to commune with the enlightening, enlivening triune God. God's glorious beauty calls us to respond with glory hallelujahs.

The Spirit's illumination concerns more than cognition. For Paul, the becoming that follows beholding involves a change not in outward appearance but inner being. Richard Sibbes declared, "The very beholding of Christ is a transforming sight. . . . A man cannot look upon the love of God and of Christ in the gospel, but it will change him to be like God and Christ."[174] Edwards agreed, saying, "This light is such as effectually influences the inclination, and changes the nature of the soul. It assimilates the nature to the divine nature, and changes the soul into an image of the same glory that is beheld."[175] Piper says similarly that Spirit-enabled beholding of Christ in the letter of the text is "a seeing with savoring."[176] Transfiguring reading speaks to the efficacy of the economy of light: "God creates the Christian believer by showing a person God's

---

172. Kimble, *Behold and Become*, 36.

173. The original: "It's all in Plato, all in Plato: bless me, what *do* they teach them at these schools!" (from Lewis, *The Last Battle*, 154).

174. Richard Sibbes, "A Description of Christ," in *The Works of Richard Sibbes* (Edinburgh: James Nichol, 1862–64), 1:14.

175. Jonathan Edwards, "Divine and Supernatural Light," *WJE* 19:405–26.

176. Piper, *Reading the Bible Supernaturally*, 145.

glory on Christ's face."[177] We may recall the Spirit's special role in the triune economy: to complete and perfect God's works *ad extra*, in this case, God's luminous self-communication. The Spirit enables us to sense—not simply to see but to be transfixed and transfigured by—the light of Christ in the letter of the text. Readers who discern the glory of the Lord in the face of Christ come both to understand and delight in the truth of the gospel.

Philology and exegesis play an important role, to be sure, but they are not transformative on their own. The Bible is a lamp, but we need the Spirit to see by its light: "The Spirit's role—or goal—in interpretation is to allow the interpreter to understand the text in such a way that the text transforms the interpreter into the image of Christ."[178] The Spirit shines the light of Christ into our hearts so thoroughly that it begins to characterize what is in us too. To enlighten the eyes of his readers' hearts (Eph 1:18) is Paul's burden too: he tells the Galatians that he is "in the anguish of childbirth until Christ is formed in you" (Gal 4:19). The term for "is formed" is *morphothe*, and it is related to the "being transformed" (*metamorphoumetha*) of 2 Corinthians 3:18. To read the Bible theologically, with Paul, is ultimately a means of spiritual formation and transformation unto Christlikeness: in a word, *transfiguration*.[179]

The peculiar metamorphosis of which Paul speaks is transfigurative because what the readers come to know in Scripture causes them to reflect the light of Christ. An illumined reader "begins to reflect that to which he has been exposed, and its likeness begins to be formed in him."[180] In becoming more like Christ, we do not lose but rather become our true selves—the image of God in which we were originally created: "God created humans to be imaging beings who reflect his glory."[181] The fall of Adam temporarily impeded this authorial intention, but a promise of salvation was made, and "the gospel is the news about that intervention and that restoration."[182] The economy of light reveals and redeems: in Christ was life, "and the life was the light of men" (John 1:4). In Jonathan Edwards's words, "The beams of glory come from God, and are something of God, and are refunded back again to their original. So that the

177. Peter Balla, "2 Corinthians," in *Commentary on the New Testament Use of the Old Testament*, ed. G. K. Beale and D. A. Carson (Grand Rapids: Baker Academic, 2007), 764.

178. Gary L. Nebeker, "The Holy Spirit, Hermeneutics, and Transformation: From Present to Future Glory," *Evangelical Review of Theology* 27 (2003): 47.

179. Cf. C. S. Lewis's depiction of saints in heaven as "bright people." *The Great Divorce* (New York: HarperCollins, 2001), 59.

180. Thomas A. Smail, *Reflected Glory: The Spirit in Christ and Christians* (London: Hodder and Stoughton, 1975), 26.

181. G. K. Beale, *We Become What We Worship: A Biblical Theology of Idolatry* (Downers Grove, IL: InterVarsity, 2008), 16.

182. Graham A. Cole, *Glorification: An Introduction* (Wheaton, IL: Crossway, 2022), 45. See also Haley Goranson Jacob, *Conformed to the Image of His Son: Reconsidering Paul's Theology of Glory in Romans* (Downers Grove, IL: IVP Academic, 2018).

whole is *of God*, and *in* God, and *to* God; and God is the beginning, middle and end in this affair."[183]

To behold the glory of the Lord so as to be transfigured into that same image is the human creature's supreme vocation and destiny: "Our future is revealed in the face of Jesus."[184] Those who, thanks to the Spirit's illumination, behold the splendor of God's truth made flesh, the scintillating brilliance of the love of God poured out in Christ, cannot but be affected. The locus of the reader's own transfiguration, however, is not the face but the heart and mind. Readers who behold the light of Christ in the letter of the text begin to experience *"a participation in the Son's knowledge of the Father by the power of the Holy Spirit."*[185] This is the ultimate blessing of reading with a mere Christian hermeneutic: basking before the glory of the Lord and, by so keeping company with him, becoming ever more like him. Reading the Bible as the two-testament Christian Scripture is thus a thoroughly theological affair, a means of coming to know God as he shines forth in Christ through the Spirit to cultivate godliness, which is to say, Christlikeness.

Transfiguring biblical interpretation—the Spirit-enabled ability to sense the light of Christ in the letter of the text—calls attention to yet another variation of the celebrated hermeneutical circle. For there is a hermeneutical dimension to sanctification and a sanctifying dimension to hermeneutics, each having to do with beholding the glory of the Lord. Like sanctification, the transfiguration of the reader is similarly progressive, "from one degree of glory to another" (2 Cor 3:18). Conversely, those who persist in reading the Bible with veiled faces (and forms of criticism) will fail to see the glory of Christ, which is to say, the true subject matter of Scripture, a failure that is spiritual and hermeneutical.[186] Make no mistake: to fail to behold the glory of Christ falls short not only of spiritual interpretation *but of literal interpretation* as well, inasmuch as such readings fail to discern the *glory* of the literal sense. The divine address in Scripture falls on deaf ears in such dimness, short-circuiting the economy of light, and missing the raison d'être of the Scriptures themselves. For as Webster reminds us, "Scripture is not a self-enclosed, wholly achieved communicative event, but an instrument in the fellowship between the revelatory Word and its addressees."[187]

---

183. Edwards, *Ethical Writings*, 531.

184. Patrick Schreiner, *The Transfiguration of Christ: An Exegetical and Theological Reading* (Grand Rapids: Baker Academic, 2024), 124.

185. Ike Miller, *Seeing by the Light: Illumination in Augustine's and Barth's Readings of John* (Downers Grove, IL: IVP Academic, 2020), 5 (emphasis original).

186. Cf. Samuel E. Parkison: "For Paul, there is an absolute antithesis: either readers of Moses read in light of the glory of Christ, and thus read truly and with 'unveiled face,' or they read with minds and hearts draped with a veil that obscures the glory of Christ, and thus read wrongly." *Irresistible Beauty: Beholding Triune Glory in the Face of Jesus Christ* (Ross-shire, UK: Mentor, 2022), 192.

187. Webster, *Domain of the Word*, 24.

The economy of light begins and ends in glory. The light God spoke into being at creation shines again from the face of Christ into the hearts of those who read with unveiled faces. God brings these readers to glory (Heb 2:10), constituting them "children of light" (Eph 5:8; 1 Thess 5:5) as they are progressively transfigured into the image of Christ (Rom 8:29; 1 Cor 15:49; Col 3:10). Biblical interpreters must take great care, however, lest they begin to glorify themselves and their own readings. Mere Christian hermeneutics helps readers find glory in the letter of the text, *not* in their own vainglorious interpretations. To elevate one's interpretive interest, or interpretive method, or particular interpretation over the text is to profess some kind of criticism, not Christ.[188]

The true vocation of Christian readers, and of human beings in general, is to reflect the glory of Christ, not a glory of their own. Peter explicitly tells his readers they have been called "out of darkness into [God's] marvelous light" so that they "may proclaim the excellencies of him who called you" (1 Pet 2:9). This, finally, is how biblical interpretation changes the world: it is the divinely appointed means to call people into the light and, in living as children of light (Eph 5:8), to spread it further. What could well serve as Paul's mission statement for his apostolic ministry is also the watchword for mere Christian hermeneutics: "For what we proclaim is not ourselves, but Jesus Christ as Lord" (2 Cor 4:5). Transfigured interpreters of the Bible must go and do likewise, not as sovereign subjects but as sanctified servants of the word.

188. For a critique of "professing criticism," see John Goldingay, "Reading Rahab: How Criticism Serves Itself or Eats Itself," *Scottish Journal of Theology* 76, no. 1 (2023): 24–30. Goldingay uses the Rahab story to illustrate how interpreters can read their own interests into a text while turning a deaf ear to the communicative interests of the text itself. Such critics are not reading so much as using the text, finding confirmation in it of their own biases.

Conclusion: Beatific Lection

Transfiguring Christian Reading Cultures

The splendor of the divine countenance, which even the apostle calls "unapproachable" [1 Tim 6:16], is for us like an inexplicable labyrinth unless we are conducted into it by the thread of the Word; so that it is better to limp along this path than to dash with all speed outside it.

—Calvin, *Institutes* I.6.3

For we are only creatures; our role must be that of patient to agent . . . mirror to light, echo to voice. Our highest activity must be response, not initiative.

—C. S. Lewis, *The Problem of Pain*

Our climb is nearly complete. It is time to retrace our journey, assess its significance, respond to a possible objection, and indicate a way forward.

The Experiment's Results: A Summary Mountaintop Report

Throughout this book, I have adopted the patristic trope of viewing biblical interpretation as an ascent up what Gregory of Nyssa referred to in his *Life of Moses* as "the mountain of the knowledge of God."[1] Gregory acknowledged that the knowledge of God "is a mountain steep indeed and difficult to climb—the majority of people scarcely reach its base."[2] We began in part 1 setting up camp, surveying the terrain, and taking the measure of the mountain before us, namely, the challenge of reading the Bible to hear and meet God in an age of disordered and divided reading cultures. I there argued that successful ascents

1. Gregory of Nyssa, *The Life of Moses*, 15.
2. Gregory of Nyssa, 158.

require the services of both exegetes and theologians. The two subsequent parts, constituting the bulk of the present book, parallel the two ways in which Gregory examined the life of Moses, first the *historia* (what happened), then the *theoria* ("the spiritual understanding which corresponds to the history").[3]

Part 2, our first ascent, focused on the formal principle of mere Christian hermeneutics: the letter of the text; the literal sense and its interpretation. The challenge here was to give the letter due diligence—and an appropriately thick theological description, which I said required multiple frames of reference and a canonical context, not simply literal-grammatical exegesis in the original historical context. To read the Bible as divine discourse, I argued, is to follow the way the divinely directed words run from one figure to another through redemptive history (hence "trans-figural") to what they are ultimately about—their fully-figured christological referent. In spite of the diverse concepts of literality we surveyed, I claimed that we could discern a consensus, in all periods of church tradition and in all sections of the church, about Scripture's literal meaning, including events in the immediate present of the human author (the historical occasion) and their future fulfillment (the eschatological realization). To transfigure the letter, I said, is to read with an eschatological frame of reference and trans-figural hermeneutical strategy, in canonical context, with christoscopic vision. Trans-figuring interpretation thus gives rise to a reading practice characterized by close canonical reading, following the way its figures run across the Scriptures toward Jesus Christ, their North Star.

Part 3 followed a different path up the mountain, focusing on the material principle of mere Christian hermeneutics: the light of Christ or, more expansively, the knowledge of God in the face of Christ. It is the material principle of mere Christian hermeneutics because it is what the Bible, when interpreted literally (which is to say, trans-figurally), is ultimately about. Here, too, transfiguring did heavy lifting, referring not simply to trans-figural interpretation but, rather, to the historical event ultimately justifying figuration: Jesus' transfiguration. The main proposition I demonstrated here was that Jesus' transfiguration displays, rather than distorts, who he is. Transfigural interpretation, analogously, neither distorts nor changes the literal sense but, instead, like Jesus' transfiguration, magnifies and glorifies the body of the text, enabling readers to discern therein the light of Christ (shorthand for what God makes known).

Each ascent up the mountain constituted a stage in my biblical-theological experiment in criticism, according to which we judge the rightness of an interpretation not on the basis of the critical method it employs, but on what kind of theological reading, reading culture, and reader it produces. Unlike in the

3. Gregory of Nyssa, 15.

academy, where critical methods serve a variety of interpretive interests, our experiment proposed measuring the appropriateness of a critical approach by determining whether, and to what extent, it enables readers to perceive the light of Christ: "Exegetical practices are subordinate to the nature of the text, and their end is attention to the text's direction."[4] The result of the experiment was a newfound appreciation for a reformed catholic way of reading the Bible that discerns the depths of the literal sense.

The motive behind wanting to read the Bible theologically, for a blessing, should be clear. (1) We benefit most from Scripture's light when we read it not in the solitary disciplinary silos of academia, or in the relative comfort of our ethnic or denominational ghettoes, but with all the saints, including exegetes, theologians, and church historians from premodern and modern times, East and West, industrial North and global South. (2) We do most justice to the Bible's literal sense when we read it spiritually, for its glorious referent, with a grammatical-eschatological frame of reference in canonical context. Hermeneutic approaches that fail to see the light of Christ in the letter of the text short-circuit the divine authorial intent, ignore the canonical context, and miss the redemptive-historical-eschatological frame of reference. To fail to see the light of Christ in the letter of the text is to do the letter an injustice.

In sum, "transfiguring" biblical interpretation refers both to *a transfiguration of the process* of biblical interpretation (i.e., a rethinking of what is involved in reading theologically) and to *an interpretative process that transfigures*. We transfigure the process by rethinking the means and ends of biblical interpretation in terms of the economy of light. That interpretive process then transfigures by reading in and for the light of Christ, glorifying both the literal sense and the reader. Indeed, readers are "figured" in two ways: first, by seeing themselves as the divine addressees, part of the people of God whose story the Bible narrates or *con*figures; second, by gazing into the face of Christ and reflecting the light that the Spirit shines into their hearts, part of their *trans*figuration into the likeness of Christ. The church, likewise, should be a figure of Christ shining in ten thousand places and a transfiguring reading culture that forms readers to read transfigurally.

Why call it "mere Christian hermeneutics"? Here are four reasons: (1) Transfiguring biblical interpretation practices a manner of literal reading that the whole church has agreed is basic to the faith. (2) This ecclesial reading culture neither privileges nor excludes any particular critical method, though it cautions against reducing textual meaning to any single frame of reference. (3) This ecclesial reading culture neither privileges nor excludes any particular

4. John Webster, "Resurrection and Scripture," in *The Domain of the Word: Scripture and Theological Reason* (London: T&T Clark, 2012), 47.

theological community, though it critiques those who fail to respect the literal sense or attempt to reduce it to a single frame of reference. (4) This ecclesial reading culture forms its members to be right-minded and right-hearted answerable subjects, responsible for and responsive to the divine address of the biblical text.

"Listen to Him": Attending to (and Answering) Light

For modern readers trained to think about biblical interpretation in terms of exegetical methods and types of criticism, the most surprising feature of the present book is probably its emphasis on the *why* rather than the *how* question: Why read the Bible as Christian *Scripture?* What is Bible reading *for?* With Gregory, I have argued that readers ought to follow Moses up the mountain to hear the voice of God, learn virtue, gain wisdom, and become Christlike.

Gregory views Moses' entire life as an ascent up the mount of perfection and sees him as a paragon of virtue to be imitated: "The Lord used to speak to Moses face to face, as a man speaks to his friend" (Exod 33:11). Similarly, I have proposed that the Christian life is largely a response to the divine address in Scripture, and that Christians ought to read the Bible to see therein the face of Christ and, in so seeing, to become more like him, knowing God as their Father. From this height, exegesis appears to be less about reconstructing the original historical situation and more about restoring the original Adamic vocation: "Scripture is instrumental in restoring human life to its proper form."[5] The chief purpose of reading the Bible theologically is to learn Christ—which involves much more than learning *about* Christ. Reading the Bible transfigurally is an important means for fulfilling our creaturely vocation as men and women created in God's image (Gen 1:28) to be conformed to the consummate image of Jesus Christ.

It is worth pausing at the end of our journey to reflect on a paradox I mentioned in passing but did not examine. Light is something to be seen, not read, and the transfiguration itself was something the disciples did not read about but saw. What is a book on biblical interpretation doing employing metaphors pertaining to vision and light? The paradox is most acute, and ironic, in the transfiguration narrative itself, for though Jesus elsewhere identifies himself as the light of the world (John 8:12), at the very moment when his face is shining like the sun, he says almost nothing.[6] The passage concludes, however, with the

5. Darren Sarisky, *Scriptural Interpretation: A Theological Exploration* (Malden, MA: Wiley-Blackwell, 2012), 34.

6. In Matthew 17:7, Jesus says, "Rise, and have no fear," to the disciples after they had fallen on their faces in fear at the divine voice.

divine voice that speaks out of the cloud, which says, "Listen to him" (Matt 17:5; Mark 9:7; Luke 9:35). How does one listen to, or read for, the light of Christ? How can a visual address elicit an auditory response? The answer lies in plain sight: "seeing the light" is a figure of speech, a metaphor for gaining knowledge, often by hearing or reading. Throughout this work, I have argued that light and enlightening are key biblical figures for God in his self-revelation and manifest presence. Light lights, and in doing so, shows itself and other things. God speaks light, and light "speaks."

Accounts of God's audible voice are extremely rare in the New Testament. It is noteworthy, then, that the voice that speaks from the cloud at Jesus' transfiguration says, "Listen to him." The disciples surely understood the voice to be instructing them to attend to Jesus rather than Moses or Elijah (which may be why the voice interrupted Peter's plan to make *three* tents).[7] The voice from heaven also suggests how seeing and hearing relate: it is because Christ alone is the visible manifestation of God, God's glory in the flesh, that disciples ought to listen to him alone. Indeed, as Pierre-Yves Brandt observes, the transfiguration narratives identify not only Jesus but also his disciples. For it becomes clear on the Mount of Transfiguration that the true disciple is the one who listens to Jesus only.[8] Those who attend to Jesus only behold the glory of the Lord and are themselves transfigured into his glorious likeness. Paul's description of these enlightened Bible readers is striking: they "are light in the Lord" (Eph 5:8), citizens of light who produce the "fruit of light" (Eph 5:9).[9] The transfigured reader is a conduit of light because Christ has shone upon them, in and through the letter of the texts that bear witness to him (John 5:39).

The voice from heaven directs reader-disciples to listen to the one who is the light of the world. Christ Jesus' shining face speaks volumes, far more than any single interpreter can comprehend. We are the mastered, not the masters, of this shining face. It is his manifest presence, his speaking voice, who addresses us in and through the Scriptures, as he did the apostle Paul on the road to Damascus: "I am Jesus" (Acts 9:5). The Word's words are "living and active" (Heb 4:12), revelatory photons in the economy of light, a luminous

7. Thorvald B. Madsen says the context suggests that the disciples are to trust in particular what Jesus says about the necessity of his impending death, a hard saying: "The command, 'listen to him,' is . . . likely to have the passion predictions in view." "Listen to Him: The Exhortation of Matthew 17:5 in the Context of the Transfiguration Narrative," *Midwestern Journal of Theology* 15, no. 2 (2016): 129.

8. See Pierre-Yves Brandt, *L'identité de Jésus et l'identité de son disciple. Le récit de la transfiguration comme clef de lecture de l'Évangile de Marc* (Göttingen: Vandenhoeck & Ruprecht, 2002), pt. 4. Oecolampadius similarly stated that the main theme of Hebrews is the importance of listening to Christ: "For we considered that the scope of the epistle was that the Hebrews—to this point, hearers of the law and the prophets—not listen to their Moses more than Christ." Cited in Jeff Fisher, *A Christoscopic Reading of Scripture: Johannes Oecolampadius on Hebrews* (Göttingen: Vandenhoeck & Ruprecht, 2016), 93.

9. "Those whom God has called out of darkness are now themselves 'luminaries.'" S. M. Baugh, *Ephesians: Evangelical Exegetical Commentary* (Bellingham, WA: Lexham, 2016), 429.

communicative medium of the one who is himself resplendent and eloquent. As Webster rightly reminds us, nothing is more foundational in biblical interpretation than this: "Christ is God, and he is speaking."[10] The voice and face of Christ that speak and shine from the biblical texts are the bright focus of the triune economy of light, the locus and fulcrum where and by which the Father has shone and continues to shine the Son's knowledge of God into readers' hearts by the Spirit. Transfiguring biblical interpretation is ultimately a theological "account of the being of texts and interpreters in the domain of the revelatory presence of Christ."[11]

The face speaks; the voice shines. For much of Christian tradition, seeing God—the beatific vision—was thought to be our chief end, the ultimate blessing reserved for heaven. This was Gregory's conclusion as he contemplated Moses' ascent up the mountain of the knowledge of God. The glory Moses asked to see, and the glory he progressively experienced, was the firstfruit of beatific vision. As we saw in chapter 9, beholding the glory of the Lord in the face of Christ is an important means of sanctification. John Owen was therefore right to highlight the centrality of Christ in the beatific vision, for it is in the human form of Christ that we most fully see the glory of the Lord: "Therefore the blessed and blessing sight which we shall have of God will always be 'in the face of Jesus Christ.'"[12] More specifically, as Suzanne McDonald points out, it is for Owen "*the person of Jesus Christ, in his ascended, glorified humanity*, who is at the heart of the beatific vision."[13] The beatific vision is thoroughly transfigural inasmuch as the transfiguration is both the revelation of Jesus' deity and an anticipation of his exaltation, itself a promissory note of the believer's future glorification. Of course, this side of glory, we, like Moses, can only look into the promised land of beatific vision from a distance: "What we will be has not yet appeared; but we know that when he appears we shall be like him, because we shall see him as he is" (1 John 3:2).

Theologians sometimes debate the "how" of beatific vision: will it involve an intellectual vision, the eyes of the heart, a glorified physical vision?[14] This is not the place to stake out a position. Instead, let me suggest that apprehending the glory of God in the face of Christ, whatever this may involve, is the true end of transfiguring biblical interpretation. To read theologically is therefore

10. Webster, "Resurrection and Scripture," 49.

11. Webster, 38.

12. John Owen, "Meditations and Discourses on the Glory of Christ in His Person, Office, and Grace," in *The Works of John Owen*, ed. William H. Goold, vol. 1 (London: Johnstone and Hunter, 1850), 292–93.

13. Suzanne McDonald, "Beholding the Glory of God in the Face of Jesus Christ: John Owen and the 'Reforming' of the Beatific Vision," in *The Ashgate Research Companion to John Owen's Theology*, ed. Kelly M. Kapic and Mark Jones (Burlington, VT: Ashgate, 2012), 153 (emphasis original).

14. See further Peter Anthony, *Patristic Perspectives on Luke's Transfiguration: Interpreting Vision*, The Library of New Testament Studies (London: T&T Clark, 2022).

to aim for a beatific *lection*: a beholding, through reading, of the radiant face of Christ in the letter of the text and, in the human face of Christ, the very face of God.[15] It is *lection* because it involves seeing, hearing, and knowing through reading ("Listen to him"); it is *beatific* because through reading we attend to the self-presentation of the luminous Christ and open ourselves up to the blessing of beholding his face and becoming like him.[16] John Owen said something similar in his *Meditations and Discourse on the Glory of Christ*, in which he exhorted Christians to read Scripture contemplating the glory of Christ—who he is; what he did; what he continues to do—that we know now by faith in hearing his word, a foretaste of the beatific vision.[17]

To speak of beatific lection reminds us that answerable readers will feel awe in the manifest speaking presence of Christ, the voice and face of God. This awe is "the feeling of being diminished in the presence of something greater than the self,"[18] a perception of a transcendence "that dramatically expands the observer's usual frame of reference."[19] Indeed. To attend to Christ speaking in the Scriptures requires a special frame of reference, one that I have described as eschatological, christoscopic, trans-figural, and transfiguring. Each term conveys a slightly different nuance, but they have in common a resistance to reading within narrow frames of reference only that are curved in upon themselves, immanent and self-enclosed. In contrast, what my description of the frames of reference that render Bible reading theological highlight is their openness to transcendence—to the divine address by which God shows and communicates his glory.

In reading the Bible in the trans-figural/transfiguring way I am here commending, we do not suppress the voice of the human authors; rather, we listen first and foremost to the living and active voice of Christ in Scripture, shining through the letter of the text. This is what qualifies Jesus' transfiguration to serve as the proper framework of theological understanding: "Being spiritually minded and viewing the glorious Christ is not to be myopic . . . but to view all things in transfigured light."[20] It is a grand claim, to be sure, one that raises

15. We can also speak of a beatific *audition* in relation to oral or preliterate cultures. For a comprehensive survey of the beatific vision, see Hans Boersma, *Seeing God: The Beatific Vision in Christian Tradition* (Grand Rapids: Eerdmans, 2018).

16. "Reading the light" is no stranger a locution than "seeing the voice" (Rev 1:12). Both are attempts to describe the experience of being in Christ's self-communicative presence.

17. See further Suzanne McDonald, "John Owen on the Beatific Vision: Historic Reformed 'Spirituality' in Action," *Theology Matters*, May 30, 2023, https://www.theologymatters.com/articles/theology/2023/john-owen-on-the-beatific-vision-historic-reformed-spirituality-in-action/.

18. Paul K. Piff, Pia Dietze, Matthew Feinberg, Daniel M. Stancato, and Dacher Keltner, "Awe, the Small Self, and Prosocial Behavior," *Journal of Personality and Social Psychology* 108, no. 6 (2015): 883.

19. Piff et al., 884.

20. Michael Allen, *Grounded in Heaven: Recentering Christian Hope and Life on God* (Grand Rapids: Eerdmans, 2018), 98.

a possible objection: Is not the beatific lection I have identified as the goal of theological interpretation an instance of overstanding, not understanding, the biblical text? Is it really the case that Christian readers should look into the mirror of the biblical text to see Jesus' face, to listen only to him?

Whose Song Is It? On Seeking (and Finding) Christ in the "Wrong" Places

Isaiah encourages readers to "Seek the Lord while he may be found" (Isa 55:6), and Jesus says, "Seek, and you will find" (Matt 7:7), but some exegetes may still be wary of searching for the face of Christ in every Old Testament text. John Goldingay expresses the concern as follows: "The Old Testament is about God; it is not about Christ. . . . The Old Testament's spiritual meaning is its surface meaning. Its surface meaning is its spiritual meaning."[21] He worries that readers who expect to find Christ on every page will miss what the text actually says. It is a valid concern. In discussing spiritual interpretation of the Old Testament, it is important to distinguish large-scale typological trajectories from detailed allegorical inventories.[22] It is one thing to follow figures across the canon with a grammatical-eschatological frame of reference toward their christological referent, quite another to compile an elaborate list of correspondences between figures and that to which they supposedly refer, according to some extracanonical scheme. Frederic Farrar rightly feared that by allegorizing one can "make anything of anything."[23] However, I have taken pains to distinguish that kind of arbitrary allegorizing with the biblically disciplined, Christ-focused approach to figural reading. Here I simply specify what it means to seek and see Christ by interpreting transfigurally.

To state the issue bluntly, are readers wrong to find Christ in the Song of Songs? After all, the Song of Songs is one of only two books in the Bible in which there is no explicit reference to God (the other is Esther). This did not stop premodern interpreters from reading the Song figurally, as an ode to Christ's love for the church. Indeed, there was an unbroken consensus for nearly nineteen centuries, so much so that one might say the "mere Christian" interpretation of the Song was christological. In stark contrast, most modern interpreters view the Song as an ode to erotic love, an approach that may be symptomatic of modern reading cultures that train students to employ immanent frames

21. John Goldingay, "Review Article: What Theologians and Biblical Scholars Wish the Others Knew," *Journal of Theological Interpretation* 16, no. 1 (2022): 139.

22. Kevin J. Vanhoozer, "Ascending the Mountain, Singing the Rock: Biblical Interpretation Earthed, Typed, and Transfigured," *Modern Theology* 20, no. 4 (2012): 789–90.

23. Frederic W. Farrar, *History of Interpretation: Eight Lectures Preached before the University of Oxford in the Year MDCCCLXXXV on the Foundation of the Late Rev. John Bampton* (London: Macmillan, 1886), 32.

of reference only.[24] Note well: the disagreement is not about what the Song *says* (i.e., sense, semantic content) but, rather, what it is *about* (i.e., reference, subject matter). Marvin Pope spoke for many modern commentators in suggesting that premodern commentators allegorized the Song because they could not bring themselves to acknowledge that it is patently about human sexuality: "Interpreters who dared acknowledge the plain sense of the Song were assailed as enemies of truth and decency."[25]

Once again, the real dispute is over which frames of reference are legitimate and appropriate, and why. I understand and sympathize with biblical scholars' frustration over far-fetched allegorical interpretations that find significance in every textual detail, such as Hippolytus's claim that "your two breasts are like two fawns" (Song 4:5) refers to the Old Testament and New Testament.[26] Why two Testaments rather than other pairs, like baptism and the Lord's Supper, law and grace, or elders and deacons, all of which could be broadly construed in terms of spiritual mammary glands? Modern biblical scholars insist on interpreting the Song in its original frame of reference, ancient Near Eastern love poetry.[27] Let me make two comments in response to this concern that will hopefully clarify what it means to read the Song transfigurally.

In the first place, the Song is love poetry, a celebration of marital love and sexual intimacy, and readers must honor the communicative intent of its human author (i.e., its literal sense). Yet as Chloe Sun has argued, there are a number of intriguing textual details that suggest something more is going on: "The major setting of the Song is a garden, which alludes to the Garden of Eden as the temple of God."[28] Moreover, the Song is told from the point of view of the woman, and one of its leading themes is her fervent desire for union with her beloved. Her yearning only increases when she notes her beloved's absence: "It is she who searches for him, and desires him."[29] Sun notes that this "bears astounding similarities to the theology of divine absence in lament psalms where one party yearns and searches for the presence of the other in his absence."[30] God is thus conspicuous by his absence: "Song of

24. See further Annette Schellenberg and Ludger Schwienhorst-Schönberger, eds., *Interpreting the Song of Songs: Literal or Allegorical?* (Leuven: Peeters, 2016).

25. Marvin H. Pope, *Song of Songs: A New Translation with Introduction and Commentary*, Anchor Bible 7C (Garden City, NY: Doubleday, 1977), 17.

26. See Tremper Longman, *Song of Songs*, New International Commentary on the Old Testament (Grand Rapids: Eerdmans, 2001), 28.

27. See further Arthur Holder, "Christian Reception of the Song of Songs Since 1800," in *A Companion to the Song of Songs in the History of Spirituality*, ed. Timothy H. Robinson (Leiden: Brill, 2021), 359–60.

28. Chloe T. Sun, *Conspicuous in His Absence: Studies in the Song of Songs and Esther* (Downers Grove, IL: IVP Academic, 2021), 10. See also Tim Chester, "Introduction," *Meeting Christ in the Garden: A Devotional of Classic Writing on the Song of Song* (Ross-shire, UK: Christian Focus, 2023), 12.

29. Sun, 232.

30. Sun, 52.

Songs presents an absent male lover (God) . . . a hidden God in the guise of a fierce love and an ascetic garden."[31]

Still, if we had to make sense of the Song on its own, there is little to stop us from reading it as about "sexual love or unrestrained free love or even soft pornography."[32] However, there are also interbiblical and canonical grounds for thinking that the Song symbolically depicts God's relationship to Israel. We know, for example, that other biblical books describe the nation of Israel as an often faithless bride and YHWH as an always faithful husband (Hos 2:16–20). Moreover, the Song's depiction of the woman with vineyard imagery (Song 1:6) recalls canonical representations of Israel as God's vineyard (e.g., Isa 5:1, 7). Sun also observes numerous allusions to the Exodus story, beginning with the lover comparing the woman to "a mare among Pharaoh's chariots" (Song 1:9) and, later, to frankincense and myrrh (Song 4:6), both found in the tabernacle: "No wonder Jewish commentators thought of the women in the Song metaphorically as the embodiment of Israel."[33] Ellen Davis believes the Song, despite its lack of mention of God, is the "most biblical" of all biblical texts because it deals with biblical themes that speak of God's troubled relationship with Israel, his inconstant bride, and because its garden love scenes depict "the reversal of that primordial exile from Eden."[34] In light of these textual indications, there is no need to resort to extravagant allegorical schemes in order to read the Song theologically.

Second, the Song is biblical discourse, and thus part of God's address to his covenant people. Richard Swinburne argues that if God is indeed the ultimate author, and if he is addressing future generations as well as the original recipients, then later contexts, including those of the New Testament, are relevant to determining the Song's meaning.[35] To read the Song transfigurally, then, is to pursue a literalism at the level of the whole canon, asking what the *divine* author was doing inserting human love poetry into the collection of Israel's sacred writings. A transfiguring interpretation of the Song thus engages in a *spiritual literalism* that attends to the intention of the Holy Spirit, its ultimate author. When read in canonical context, there is every reason to believe that the divinely intended literal sense is the figural sense, in which the bride stands for Israel, particularly in those moments when she felt God was absent or had

31. Sun, 81.

32. Sun, 265.

33. Sun, 237.

34. Ellen F. Davis, *Proverbs, Ecclesiastes, and the Song of Songs* (Louisville: Westminster John Knox, 2000), 232.

35. Richard Swinburne, *Revelation: From Metaphor to Analogy*, 2nd ed. (Oxford: Oxford University Press, 2007), 266.

abandoned her.[36] The Song is meant to be read on more than one level, with more than one frame of reference.

The Protestant Reformers prove themselves exemplary mere Christian interpreters in their own christological readings of the Song. Without reneging on their commitment to the priority of the literal sense, they were able, in good interpretive conscience, to read the Song in its plain canonical sense, that is, transfigurally, as pointing typologically to God's love for his people and, by extension, Christ's love for the church. Theodore Beza's opinion is representative: "The Holy Spirit thus wishing to represent to us what is in itself incomprehensible to us namely, the closest possible spiritual bond of Jesus Christ with the faithful soul . . . could have chosen neither a better similitude, nor a more vivid pattern and model, of this communion."[37] Marriage, viewed typologically, is for Beza the perfect figure of the indissoluble bond of covenant love: "For in truth it can and must be said that the Son of God has kissed us . . . when he so closely joined himself to our nature."[38] Charles Spurgeon described the Song as "the Most Holy Place," the inner sanctum of the canon, because in it we meet Christ.[39] This is the crucial claim, and the point of contention with modern biblical scholars who say that, with respect to the Song, the Son is nowhere to be found.

It should by now be clear how everything in biblical interpretation turns on one's frame of reference, and on the criteria one gives for preferring one frame of reference rather than another. These criteria, I have argued, are based on what the Bible is (ontology) and is for (teleology). Exegetes establish the legitimacy of a particular frame of reference by showing how, without it, we are unable to do justice to some aspect of biblical discourse. Accordingly, we justify reading transfigurally by demonstrating that interpretation of the Old Testament as Christian Scripture is incomplete unless and until we read it christoscopically, aware that the Bible's historical meaning is oriented toward an eschatological goal: "Everything written in Scripture was about [Christ] and for the benefit of his church."[40] Transfiguring interpretation is not about contorting individual verses so that they somehow correspond to particular aspects or moments of Jesus' person and work. On the contrary, it is about being aware that all

36. Sun writes, "When the two texts [Jeremiah and the Song] are read together, they form a dialogue of love, loss, and longing. It is as if the woman in the Song is responding to her God/husband in Jeremiah 31:20, 'Your heart churns for me. My heart churns for you too." *Conspicuous in His Absence*, 253.

37. Theodore Beza, *Sermons sur les trois premiers chapitres du Cantique des Cantiques, de Salomon* (Geneva: Jehan le Preux, 1586), 10 (my translation). See also the examples in David Fink, ed., *Proverbs, Ecclesiastes, Song of Songs*, Reformation Commentary on Scripture (Downers Grove, IL: IVP Academic, 2023).

38. Beza, 37 (my translation).

39. C. H. Spurgeon, *The Most Holy Place: Sermons on the Song of Solomon* (Ross-shire, Scotland: Christian Focus, 1996).

40. Fisher, *Christoscopic Reading of Scripture*, 53.

of Scripture is ultimately about some aspect or other of God's glorious reign for the sake of forming a people to be God's treasured possession, the body of Christ. As Arnold Huijgen explains, Jesus is not the center of each biblical text, for "he himself is not a text but a person . . . the external center of scripture, to which all of scripture refers, which affects all of its parts."[41]

Back to the Song. We know from Ephesians 5:32 that God intended human marriage to figure Christ's love for the church, a figure that continues into the book of Revelation, with its several references to the marriage supper of the Lamb (Rev 19:7–9; 21:2, 9; 22:17). This corroborates my working hypothesis: the details of the Song are not meant to be interpreted either literalistically or allegorically. Rather, they are meant to be taken together as a figurative description of Christ's love for church and the church's desire for union with Christ. Far from being a fanciful interpretation, beholding Christ in the Song simply acknowledges that it is toward Christ—the fulfillment of God's covenant love for his people—that the letters have been running all along. To focus only on the letter, and not see the light of Christ, is to fail to do justice to the letter. In the words of Gregory the Great, "He is dumber than dumb who pays such close attention to the colors of the picture that he ignores the subject depicted."[42]

An Ongoing Ascent: Mere Christian Hermeneutics as Witness and Worship

How then shall we—biblical scholars, theologians, clergy, and laypeople—read? The answer involves more than following a step-by-step how-to manual. Exegetical procedures are helpful, but they can also give readers the impression that they are in control of the process. Not so. The most important qualification for biblical interpretation, and the Christian reader's primary vocation, is to be "canonically aware and redemptively responsible"[43]—alert to the purpose of Scripture as a whole and prepared to answer the divine summons to follow the words where they lead. More than knowing exegetical procedures (or even the original languages), readers must stand in front of the text as certain kinds of

41. Arnold Huijgen, Koert van Bekkum, and Hans Burger, "Biblical Exegesis and Systematic Theology: Toward Mutual Benefit," *Journal of Reformed Theology* 16 (2022): 190. Huijgen also notes, "It is remarkable that no elaborate methodology for cooperation between biblical studies and systematic theology exists to date" (187).

42. Gregory the Great, *On the Song of Songs*, trans. Mark DelCogliano (Collegeville, MN: Liturgical, 2012), 110–11.

43. This is my Christian take on Henry James's formula for good reading: being "finely aware and richly responsible." See Martha C. Nussbaum, "'Finely Aware and Richly Responsible': Literature and the Moral Imagination," in *Love's Knowledge: Essays on Philosophy and Literature* (Oxford: Oxford University Press, 1990), 148–67.

persons: illumined listeners.[44] To stand before the text, which is to say, before the manifest presence of God, is often a struggle, with the text and with oneself before God, which is why theologians through the centuries have compared the Christian life and biblical interpretation to an ascent up the mountain. It takes effort to read the Bible theologically, in particular the effort of letting go of our self-serving veils and masks. Many of us in the interpretive lowlands may not yet be ready or fit to hear God's word.

Kierkegaard is known for his concern "that 'objective' biblical scholarship was undermining the possibility of a reader's subjective life being affected, challenged and provoked by its message."[45] Theology, too, can stifle Scripture's ability to challenge us if it encourages readers simply to assume a particular doctrinal framework rather than being open to have their biases questioned rather than confirmed. Overcoming the potential pathologies of the theological disciplines, as well as the disciplinary divide that too often keeps exegesis and theology separate, has been one of my chief preoccupations, not least in this book. I have argued that both exegesis and theology are necessary—and that both, on their own, have limitations. The way up the mountain of biblical interpretation is for biblical exegesis and systematic theology to work in tandem, reading for the glory of the literal sense with both historical and eschatological frames of reference, at once fully philological and fully christological as befits theological figuration: in a word, *trans-figural and transfiguring*.

In addition to calling for a renewed partnership between exegetes and theologians, transfiguring biblical interpretation is a plea for reforming church and seminary reading cultures, communities whose very existence is inextricably linked to reading the Bible. The way out of modern and postmodern impasses in biblical interpretation involves a retrieval of earlier theological practices of reading the Bible—ways of reading to hear, know, and meet God, and to know oneself before God. "Mere Christian hermeneutics" is my chosen designation for the set of such practices.[46] This set includes interpretive assumptions that have characterized large swaths of the historic Christian tradition—from premodern to modern, East to West, and Protestant to Roman Catholic. The transfiguration of Jesus grounds and exemplifies what these reading practices

44. On listening and biblical interpretation, see Craig G. Bartholomew, *Introducing Biblical Hermeneutics: A Comprehensive Framework for Hearing God in Scripture* (Grand Rapids: Baker Academic, 2015), 17–50.

45. Andrew Torrance, "A Kierkegaardian Guide to Reading Scripture," *New Blackfriars* 97, no. 1071 (September 2016): 624.

46. For examples and surveys of such practices, see Daniel J. Treier, *Introducing Theological Interpretation of Scripture: Recovering a Christian Practice* (Grand Rapids: Baker Academic, 2008); J. Todd Billings, *The Word of God for the People of God: An Entryway to the Theological Interpretation of Scripture* (Grand Rapids: Eerdmans, 2010); Eugene Peterson, *Eat This Book: A Conversation in the Art of Spiritual Reading* (Grand Rapids: Eerdmans, 2006).

have in common: the conviction that by attending to the body of the biblical text (the letter), readers who have been illumined by the Spirit with unveiled faces will behold the glory of the knowledge of God in Jesus' face (the light of Christ).

Culture cultivates, and reading cultures cultivate certain kinds of readers. The question, then, is what kind of readers and what kind of literacy our interpretive communities are producing. Each of us belongs to one or more reading cultures, be they disciplinary, denominational, or ideological. Into what kind of reading community are we socializing seminary students and churchgoers, and with which frames of reference? Are we teaching students to read for the plain canonical sense? Are we helping congregants to become canonically aware and redemptively responsible? Are we helping disciples to read for the blessing of transfiguration, becoming little Christs?

I have argued that historical, literary, and eschatological frames of reference are all necessary, for the Bible's words are as fully human as Jesus' face, and that the transfiguration does not distort but glorifies them both. Still, a Christian reading culture must be deemed a failure if the readers it begets are not able to walk and read as children of light (Eph 5:8; 1 Thess 5:5). For God, the Father of lights, is seeking readers who will witness to and worship him in Spirit and truth (John 4:24), in the light of Christ and in accordance with the letter.[47] As we have seen, Christ's coming into the world was a high point in the economy of light, not least because Christ's light "gives light to everyone" (John 1:9). Bible readers, too, have been given the privilege and responsibility of participating in this economy of light, the God-appointed means of diffusing the knowledge of God "to those who sit in darkness" (Luke 1:79). The vocation of biblical interpreters parallels that of John the Baptist: "He came as a witness, to bear witness about the light. . . . He was not the light, but came to bear witness about the light" (John 1:6–8). To read the Bible theologically is to bear witness to the light of Christ in the letter of the text.

No single exegetical method catches everything there is in biblical discourse. Something similar may be said about reading cultures themselves. No one reading culture, whether premodern or modern, Western or non-Western, sees everything there is to see. It takes many bands on the spectrum of reading cultures to see the white light of Christ. To think that one's own "color"—exegetical approach, ethnic or social location, interpretive aim or interest—is the whole of light is as foolish as paying attention only to the colors in a picture, and not what they depict. Scripture is a unity in diversity, a coat of many canonical colors; so is the church community that reads it. We can adapt Andrew Walls's wise comment about missiology to hermeneutics. According to Walls, every

47. Webster reminds us that God has appointed Scripture for a holy function, to serve "as herald of the self-communicative presence of the risen one." "Resurrection and Scripture," 32.

faithful reception or cross-cultural contextualization of the gospel is a gift to the whole church, enlarging its understanding of their shared text: "It is as though Christ himself actually grows through the work of mission."[48] Likewise, every Christian reading practice should contribute to our understanding Scripture, so that we might say, "It is as though Christ himself actually grows brighter through the work of biblical interpretation." Every local reading culture has a role to play in the economy of light. Stephen Pardue puts it well: "Evangelical contextual theologies should seek to discern the plenitude of the riches of Christ through the cultivation of authentic Christian witness in every culture while seeking the unity of the Spirit by rejecting local theologies that fail to engage the worldwide church."[49]

Paul describes his Corinthian readers as themselves letters from Christ, written with the Spirit (2 Cor 3:2–3). If we combine this Pauline image with his other of Christians as children of light (Eph 5:8; 1 Thess 5:5; cf. Phil 2:15), the result is a picture of the church comprised of a host of bright letters. The readers' own transfiguration is also a part of their witness. The church is not like other reading communities or other peoples of the book; rather, in reading to behold and reflect the light of Christ, the church itself becomes a kind of illuminated manuscript—a lived liturgical interpretation, a beatific lectionary.

We can go further. The church is both an illuminated and illuminating manuscript to the extent that its reading culture begets children of light. The metaphor is neither far-fetched nor unbiblical. Jesus likens his disciples to a city of light set on a mountaintop whose vocation is to provide lamplight to the world (Matt 5:14–16). "Your word is lamp to my feet and a light to my path" (Ps 119:105). Amen, and this is also the calling of the church vis-à-vis the world. It is a reading community's entire way of life that is the index of the depth of their textual understanding. If light by its very nature communicates light, then the church, a reading culture that participates in the economy of light, is a means by which God's word and Spirit are even now overcoming the darkness, transfiguring the world.[50] Every local church is called to bear witness to the light of Christ in its own place so that what was said of Jesus could, ideally, be said of communities of his disciples: "The people dwelling in darkness have seen a great light" (Matt 4:16). The book of Revelation depicts local churches as lampstands set up in God's holy temple, a fitting image for reading communities with light-bearing

---

48. Andrew F. Walls, *The Missionary Movement in Christian History: Studies in the Transmission of Faith* (Maryknoll, NY: Orbis, 1996), xvii.

49. Stephen T. Pardue, *Why Evangelical Theology Needs the Global Church* (Grand Rapids: Baker, 2023). This is the fourth of his five basic theses on evangelical contextual theology.

50. Evangelization and prophetic witness are two lights the church uses to banish darkness. See further Michael H. Kibbe, "Light that Conquers the Darkness: Oscar Romero on the Transfiguration of Jesus," *Theology Today* 75, no. 4 (2019): 447–57.

vocations.[51] "In your light do we see light" (Ps 36:9). In his light do we read and reflect light. May it be so.

Mere Christian hermeneutics is ultimately a vision for forming reading cultures that, in turn, form readers who can bear witness to the light by proclaiming the excellencies of him who called us into his marvelous light (1 Pet 2:9). Such witness continues until that day, anticipated by Jesus' transfiguration, when the city of light "will need no light of lamp or sun, for the Lord God will be their light" (Rev 22:5). In the enthralling words of Augustine,

> When such a day is at hand, lamps will not be necessary. A prophet will not be read to us, the book of the Apostle will not be opened; we shall not seek the testimony of John, we shall not need the Gospel itself. Therefore, all the Scriptures will be taken from our midst which were burning as lamps for us in the night of this world that we might not remain in the darkness. With all these taken away . . . what shall we see? . . . You will see the naked light itself.[52]

In the meantime, churches and seminaries must do everything they can to create theological reading cultures while it is still *today*—when we can still read, hear, and respond to God's voice (Heb 3:15). Mere Christian hermeneutics invites such reading cultures from across the whole communion of saints and scholars to pool their resources, resolving to form competent interpreters and faithful witnesses who read Scripture *today* for the grace of the Lord Jesus Christ, the love of God, and the fellowship of the Holy Spirit, in the hope of the great transfiguration yet to come.

---

51. See Brian H. Tabb, *All Things New: Revelation as Canonical Capstone* (Downers Grove, IL: IVP Academic, 2019), 95–97, 110.

52. Augustine, *Tractates on the Gospel of John 28–54*, 35.9, in *The Fathers of the Church*, trans. John W. Rettig (Washington, DC: Catholic University of America Press, 1993), 79.

Select Bibliography

Abelard, Peter. *Sic et Non: A Critical Edition*. Edited by Blanche Beatrice Boyer and Richer Peter McKeon. Chicago: University of Chicago Press, 1978.

Abernethy, Andrew T., ed. *Interpreting the Old Testament Theologically: Essays in Honor of Willem A. VanGemeren*. Grand Rapids: Zondervan, 2018.

Akin, Daniel L. *1, 2, 3 John*. New American Commentary. Nashville: B&H, 2001.

Allen, John J. "'Go up onto a High Mountain' (Is. 40:9): Theophanic Exegesis as Mystical Ascent in *On First Principles*." *Pro Ecclesia* 29, no. 1 (2020): 104–15.

Allen, Michael, and Scott R. Swain. *Reformed Catholicity: The Promise of Retrieval for Theology and Biblical Interpretation*. Grand Rapids: Baker Academic, 2015.

Allen, Michael, and Jonathan A. Linebaugh, eds. *Reformation Readings of Paul: Explorations in History and Exegesis*. Downers Grove, IL: IVP Academic, 2015.

Allen, Michael. "Dogmatics as Ascetics." In *The Task of Dogmatics*, edited by Oliver D. Crisp and Fred Sanders, 189–209. Grand Rapids: Zondervan, 2017.

———. *Grounded in Heaven: Recentering Christian Hope and Life on God*. Grand Rapids: Eerdmans, 2018.

Allert, Craig. *Early Christian Readings of Genesis One: Patristic Exegesis and Literal Interpretation*. Downers Grove, IL: IVP Academic, 2018.

Allison, Dale C. *The New Moses: A Matthean Typology*. Minneapolis: Fortress, 1993.

Alston, William. *Divine Nature and Human Language: Essays in Philosophical Theology*. Ithaca, NY: Cornell University Press, 1989.

Alter, Robert. *The Art of Biblical Narrative*. New York: Basic, 1981.

———. *The Art of Bible Translation*. Princeton, NJ: Princeton University Press, 2019.

Altieri, Charles. *Act and Quality: A Theory of Literary Meaning and Humanistic Understanding*. Amherst: University of Massachusetts Press, 1981.

Amos, N. Scott. *Bucer, Ephesians and Biblical Humanism: The Exegete as Theologian*. Cham, Switzerland: Springer, 2015.

Andrews, James A. *Hermeneutics and the Church: In Dialogue with Augustine*. Notre Dame, IN: Notre Dame University Press, 2012.

Andreopoulos, Andre. *This Is My Beloved Son: The Transfiguration of Christ*. Brewster, MA: Paraclete, 2012.

Ansberry, Christopher B., and Christopher M. Hays, eds. *Evangelical Faith and the Challenge of Historical Criticism*. Grand Rapids: Baker Academic, 2013.

Anselm. *An Address (Proslogion)*. In *A Scholastic Miscellany: Anselm to Ockham*. Edited by Eugene R. Fairweather. Philadelphia: Westminster, 1956.

Anthony, Peter. *Patristic Perspectives on Luke's Transfiguration: Interpreting Vision*. New York: T&T Clark, 2022.

Aquinas, Thomas. *Summa Theologica*. 5 vols. Notre Dame, IN: Christian Classics, 1981.

———. *The Literal Exposition on Job*. Translated by Anthony Damico. Atlanta: Scholars, 1989.

Archer, Kenneth J. *A Pentecostal Hermeneutic: Spirit, Scripture, and Community*. Cleveland, TN: CPT, 2005.

Arnold, Matthew. *Culture and Anarchy and Other Writings*. Edited by Stefan Collini. Cambridge: Cambridge University Press, 1993.

Athanasius. *The Life of Antony and the Letter to Marcellinus*. Translated by Robert C. Gregg. New York: Paulist, 1980.

Atsen, Isuwa Y. *A Tapestry of Global Christology: Weaving a Three-Stranded Theological Cord*. Carlisle, UK: Langham Monographs, 2022.
Atwell, James E. *The Sources of the Old Testament: A Guide to the Religious Thought of the Hebrew Bible*. London: T&T Clark, 2004.
Auerbach, Erich. "Figura." In *Scenes from the Drama of European Literature*, 11–76. Gloucester, MA: Peter Smith, 1973.
———. *Mimesis: The Representation of Reality in Western Literature*. Princeton, NJ: Princeton University Press, 1968.
Augustine. *Confessions*. Translated by Maria Boulding. New York: New City, 1997.
———. *Expositions of the Psalms: 1–32*. Translated by Maria Boulding. New York: New City, 2000.
———. *The Retractions*. Translated by M. Inez Bogan. Fathers of the Church 60. Washington, DC: Catholic University of America Press, 1968.
———. *Sermons*. Vol. 2. Translated by Edmund Hill. Hyde Park, NY: New City, 2009.
———. *Sermon* 78. In *The Works of St. Augustine*. Translated by Edmund Hill. Vol. 3. Part 3. New York: New City, 1991.
———. *Teaching Christianity: De Doctrina Christiana*. Translated by Edmund Hill. New York: New City, 2014.
———. *Tractates on the Gospel of John, 28–54*. Translated by John W. Rettig. Washington, DC: Catholic University Press of America, 1993.
———.*The City of God against the Pagans*. Translated by R.W. Dyson. Cambridge: Cambridge University Press, 1998.
———. *The Literal Meaning of Genesis*. Translated by John Hammond Taylor. Vol. 1. New York: Paulist, 1982.
Ayres, Lewis. *Nicaea and its Legacy: An Approach to Fourth-Century Trinitarian Theology*. Oxford: Oxford University Press, 2004.
———. "The Soul and the Reading of Scripture: A Note on Henri de Lubac." *Scottish Journal of Theology* 61, no. 2 (2008): 173–90.
———. "'There's Fire in That Rain': On Reading the Letter and Reading Allegorically." *Modern Theology* 28, no. 4 (2012): 616–34.
———. "The Word Answering the Word: Opening the Space of Catholic Biblical Interpretation." In *Theological Theology: Essays in Honour of John Webster*, edited by R. David Nelson, Darren Sarisky, and Justin Stratis, 37–53. London: Bloomsbury T&T Clark, 2015.
———. "Seven Theses on Dogmatics and Patristics in Catholic Theology." *Modern Theology* 38, no. 1 (2022): 36–62.
Baker, David L. *Two Testaments, One Bible: The Theological Relationship Between the Old and New Testaments*. 3rd ed. Downers Grove, IL: IVP Academic, 2010.
Baker, William R. "Did the Glory of Moses' Face Fade? A Reexamination of καταργέω in 2 Corinthians 3:7–18." *Bulletin for Biblical Research* 10, no. 1 (2000): 1–15.
Barnett, Randy E. *Our Republican Constitution: Securing the Liberty and Sovereignty of We the People*. New York: HarperCollins, 2016.
Barr, James. *The Bible in the Modern World*. London: SCM, 1973.
———. *Fundamentalism*. Philadelphia: Westminster, 1978.
———. *Holy Scripture: Canon, Authority, Criticism*. Philadelphia: Westminster John Knox, 1983.
———. *Escaping from Fundamentalism*. London: SCM, 1984.
———. "Literality." *Faith and Philosophy* 6 (1989): 412–28.
Barrett, C. K. "The Eschatology of the Epistle to the Hebrews." In *The Background of the NT and Its Eschatology*, edited by W. D. Davies and D. Daube, 363–93. Cambridge: Cambridge University Press, 1956.
———. *The Second Epistle to the Corinthians*. Grand Rapids: Baker Academic, 1993.
Barrett, Matthew. *The Reformation as Renewal: Retrieving the One, Holy, Catholic, and Apostolic Church*. Grand Rapids: Zondervan, 2023.
Barth, Karl. *Church Dogmatics*. Edited by G. W. Bromiley and T. F. Torrance. Translated by Geoffrey Bromiley et al. 4 vols. Edinburgh: T&T Clark, 1937–77.
———. *Dogmatics in Outline*. London: SCM, 1949.
———. *Witness to the Word: A Commentary on John*. Eugene, OR: Wipf & Stock, 1986.

Bartholomew, Craig G. *Introducing Biblical Hermeneutics: A Comprehensive Framework for Hearing God in Scripture*. Grand Rapids: Baker Academic, 2015.

———. *Listening to Scripture: An Introduction to Interpreting the Bible*. Grand Rapids: Baker Academic, 2023.

Bartholomew, Craig G., and Heath A. Thomas, eds. *A Manifesto for Theological Interpretation*. Grand Rapids: Baker Academic, 2016.

Barton, John. *The Nature of Biblical Criticism*. Louisville: Westminster John Knox, 2007.

———. *The Old Testament: Canon, Literature, and Theology; Collected Essays of John Barton*. New York: Routledge, 2016.

Barton, Stephen C., and David Wilkinson, eds. *Reading Genesis after Darwin*. Oxford: Oxford University Press, 2009.

———. "The Transfiguration of Christ according to Mark and Matthew: Christology and Anthropology." In *Auferstehung–Resurrection*, edited by Friedrich Avemarie and Hermann Lichtenberger, 231–46. Tübingen: Mohr Siebeck, 2001.

———. "The Metaphor of the Face in Paul." In *Conception, Receptions, and the Spirit: Essays in Honor of Andrew T. Lincoln*, edited by J. Gordon McConville and Lloyd K. Pietersen, 136–53. Eugene, OR: Cascade, 2015.

Basil of Caesarea. *Hexaëmeron* 1–9. In *St Basil: Exegetic Homilies*. Fathers of the Church 46. Translated by Agnes Clare Way. Washington, DC: Catholic University of America Press, 1963.

Basil the Great. *On the Holy Spirit*. Translated by Stephen Hildebrand. Yonkers, NY: St. Vladimir's Seminary Press, 2011.

Bates, Matthew W. *The Hermeneutics of Apostolic Proclamation: The Center of Paul's Method of Scripture Interpretation*. Waco, TX: Baylor University Press, 2012.

Bauckham, Richard J. *Jude, 2 Peter*. Word Biblical Commentary. Waco, TX: Word, 1983.

———. *Gospel of Glory: Major Themes in Johannine Theology*. Grand Rapids: Baker Academic, 2015.

Bauckham, Richard J., and Carl Mosser, eds. *The Gospel of John and Christian Theology*. Grand Rapids: Eerdmans, 2008.

Bauckham, Richard J., Daniel R. Driver, Trevor A. Hart, and Nathan MacDonald, eds. *The Epistle to the Hebrews and Christian Theology*. Grand Rapids: Eerdmans, 2009.

Baugh, S. M. *Ephesians: Evangelical Exegetical Commentary*. Bellingham, WA: Lexham, 2016.

Bayer, Oswald. *Martin Luther's Theology: A Contemporary Interpretation*. Grand Rapids: Eerdmans, 2008.

Beale, G. K. *We Become What We Worship: A Biblical Theology of Idolatry*. Downers Grove, IL: InterVarsity Press, 2008.

Beale, G. K., and D. A. Carson, eds. *Commentary on the New Testament Use of the Old Testament*. Grand Rapids: Baker Academic, 2007.

Beare, F. W. *The Earliest Records of Jesus*. Nashville: Abingdon, 1962.

Bede. *Opera Exegetica 3. In Lucae Evangelism Expositio*. Turnhout: Brepols, 1960.

Behr, John. *The Way to Nicaea: The Formation of Christian Theology*. Vol. 1. New York: St. Vladimir's Seminary Press, 2001.

Beker, J. Christiaan. *The Triumph of God: The Essence of Paul's Thought*. Minneapolis: Fortress, 1990.

Belleville, Linda. "Tradition or Creation? Paul's Use of the Exodus 34 Tradition in 2 Corinthians 3:7–18." In *Paul and the Scriptures of Israel*, edited by Craig A. Evans and James A. Sanders, 165–86. JSNTSup 83. Sheffield: Sheffield Academic Press, 1993.

Bender, Kimlyn J. *1 Corinthians*. Grand Rapids: Brazos, 2022.

Berger, Peter, and Thomas Luckmann. *The Social Construction of Reality: A Treatise in the Sociology of Knowledge*. New York: Anchor, 1967.

Bernardin, J. B. "The Transfiguration." *Journal of Biblical Literature* 52 (1933): 181–89.

Best, Thomas F. "The Transfiguration: A Select Bibliography." *Journal of the Evangelical Theological Society* 24, no. 2 (June 1981): 157–61.

Beza, Theodore. *Sermons sur les trois premiers chapitres du Cantique des Cantiques, de Salomon*. Geneva: Jehan le Preux, 1586.

Billings, J. Todd. *The Word of God for the People of God: An Entryway to the Theological Interpretation of Scripture*. Grand Rapids: Eerdmans, 2010.

Black, C. Clifton. "Transfigured Exegesis." In *Crisis, Call, and Leadership in the Abrahamic Traditions*, edited by Peter Ochs and William State Johnson, 243–58. New York: Palgrave Macmillan, 2009.

Blocher, Henri. *In the Beginning: The Opening Chapters of Genesis*. Downers Grove, IL: IVP, 1984.
Block, Daniel I. "Christotelic Preaching: A Plea for Hermeneutical Integrity and Missional Passion." *Southern Baptist Journal of Theology* 22, no. 3 (2018): 7–34.
Blomberg, Craig. *Interpreting the Parables*. Downers Grove, IL: InterVarsity, 1990.
Bloom, Lackland H. *Methods of Interpretation: How the Supreme Court Reads the Constitution*. Oxford: Oxford University Press, 2009.
Blowers, Paul M. "Mystics and Mountains: Comparing Origen's Exegesis of the Transfiguration and Gregory of Nyssa's Exposition of the Sinai Theophany." *Phronema* 30, no. 2 (2015): 1–18.
———. *Maximus the Confessor: Jesus Christ and the Transfiguration of the World*. Oxford: Oxford University Press, 2016.
———. *Drama of the Divine Economy: Creator and Creation in Early Christian Theology and Piety*. Oxford: Oxford University Press, 2012.
———. "The Transfiguration of Jesus Christ as 'Saturated Phenomenon' and as a Key to the Dynamics of Biblical Revelation in Saint Maximus the Confessor." In *What is the Bible? The Patristic Doctrine of Scripture*, edited by Matthew Baker and Mark Mourachian, 83–102. Minneapolis: Fortress, 2016.
Blowers, Paul M., and Peter W. Martens, eds. *Oxford Handbook of Early Christian Biblical Interpretation*. Oxford: Oxford University Press, 2019.
Bock, Darrell L. "Single Meaning, Multiple Contexts and Referents." In *Three Views on the New Testament Use of the Old Testament*, edited by Kenneth Berding and Jonathan Lunde, 105–51. Grand Rapids: Zondervan, 2007.
Bockmuehl, Marcus. *Seeing the Word: Refocusing New Testament Study*. Grand Rapids: Baker, 2006.
Boersma, Hans. *Five Things Theologians Wish Biblical Scholars Knew*. Downers Grove, IL: InterVarsity Press, 2021.
———. *Heavenly Participation: The Weaving of a Sacramental Tapestry*. Grand Rapids: Eerdmans, 2011.
———. *Nouvelle Théologie and Sacramental Ontology: A Return to Mystery*. Oxford: Oxford University Press, 2009.
———. *Scripture as Real Presence: Sacramental Exegesis in the Early Church*. Grand Rapids: Baker Academic, 2017.
———. *Seeing God: The Beatific Vision in Christian Tradition*. Grand Rapids: Eerdmans, 2018.
Boersma, Hans, and Matthew Levering, eds. *Heaven on Earth? Theological Interpretation in Ecumenical Dialogue*. Oxford: Blackwell, 2013.
Bogataj, Jan Dominik. "Jerome's Interpretation of the Transfiguration in Light of Some Recent Patristic Discoveries." *Bogoslovni Vestnik/Theological Quarterly* 81 (2021): 309–23.
Bokedal, Tomas, Ludger Jansen, and Michael Borowski, eds. *Scripture and Theology: Historical and Systematic Perspectives*. Berlin: De Gruyter, 2023.
Bonhoeffer, Dietrich. *Theological Education at Finkenwalde: 1935–1937*. Edited by Mark Brocker and H. Gaylon Barker. Minneapolis: Fortress, 2013.
Bornkamm, Heinrich. *Luther and the Old Testament*. Minneapolis: Fortress, 1969.
Bovon, Francois. *A Commentary on the Gospel of Luke 1:1–9:50*. Minneapolis: Fortress, 2002.
Bowald, Mark Allan. *Rendering the Word in Theological Hermeneutics: Mapping Divine and Human Agency*. Burlington, VT: Ashgate, 2007.
Boxall, Ian, and Bradley C. Gregory. *The New Cambridge Companion to Biblical Interpretation*. Cambridge: Cambridge University Press, 2023.
Boyarin, Daniel. "Origen as Theorist of Allegory: Alexandrian Contexts." In *The Cambridge Companion to Allegory*, edited by Rita Copeland and Peter T. Struck, 39–54. Cambridge: Cambridge University Press, 2010.
Boyle, John. *Aquinas on Scripture*. Steubenville, OH: Emmaus Road Academic, 2022.
Bradley, W. P. "The Transfiguration: Credential or Answer?" *CrozQ* 12 (1935): 57–76.
Brandt, Pierre-Yves. *L'identité de Jésus et l'identité de son disciple. Le récit de la transfiguration comme clef de lecture de l'Évangile de Marc*. Göttingen: Vandenhoeck & Ruprecht, 2002.
Brandt, Ryan A., and John Frederick. *Theological Interpretation of Scripture as Spiritual Formation*. Leiden: Brill, 2022.
Breed, Brennan. *Nomadic Text: A Theory of Biblical Reception History*. Bloomington, IN: Indiana University Press, 2014.
Brendsel, Daniel J. *Answering Speech: The Life of Prayer as Response to God*. Wheaton, IL: Crossway, 2023.

Breu, Clarissa, ed. *Biblical Exegesis without Authorial Intention? Interdisciplinary Approaches to Authorship and Meaning*. Leiden: Brill, 2019.
Briggs, Richard S. *Reading the Bible Wisely*. Grand Rapids: Baker Academic, 2003.
———. *The Virtuous Reader: Old Testament Narrative and Interpretive Virtue*. Grand Rapids: Baker, 2010.
———. *Theological Hermeneutics and the Book of Numbers as Christian Scripture*. Notre Dame, IN: University of Notre Dame Press, 2018.
———. "Premodern Interpretation and Contemporary Exegesis." In *The New Cambridge Companion to Biblical Interpretation*, edited by Ian Boxall and Bradley C. Gregory, 301–17. Cambridge: Cambridge University Press, 2023.
Brown, Andrew J. *The Days of Creation: A History of Christian Interpretation of Genesis 1:1–2:3*. Dorset, UK: Deo, 2014.
Brown, Raymond E., Joseph A. Fitzmyer, and Roland E. Murphy, eds. *The New Jerome Biblical Commentary*. Englewood Cliffs, NJ: Prentice Hall, 1990.
Bruce, F. F. "The Transfiguration." *Inter-Varsity* (Summer Term 1961): 19–21.
Bruckner, James K. *Exodus*. Understanding the Bible Commentary. Grand Rapids: Baker, 2008.
Brueggemann, Walter. "Exodus." In *Genesis to Leviticus NIB* 2. Edited by Terence E. Fretheim, Walter C. Kaiser, and Leander E. Keck. Nashville: Abingdon, 1994.
———. *Theology of the Old Testament: Testimony, Dispute, Advocacy*. Minneapolis: Augsburg, 1997.
Brümmer, Vincent. *What Are We Doing When We Pray?* Aldershot, UK: Ashgate, 2008.
Bruner, Frederick Dale. *Matthew: A Commentary*. Vol. 2. *The Churchbook*. Rev. ed. Grand Rapids: Eerdmans, 2004.
Bruno, Clifton. "Discerning the Literal Sense: Bringing together Biblical Scholarship and Dogmatic Theology." *Nova et Vetera* 19 no. 1 (2021): 251–67.
Buber, Martin. *I and Thou*. New York: Scribner's, 1970.
Buckley, Michael J. *At the Origins of Modern Atheism*. New Haven, CT: Yale University Press, 1987.
Bucur, Bogdan G. "Christological Exegesis of Theophanies and the Making of Early Christian Theology." *Concordia Theological Quarterly* 86 (2022): 97–124.
———. *Scripture Re-Envisioned: Christophanic Exegesis and the Making of a Christian Bible*. Leiden: Brill, 2018.
———. "Sinai, Zion, and Tabor: An Entry into the Christian Bible." *Journal of Theological Interpretation* 4, no. 1 (2010): 33–52.
Bultmann, Rudolf. "Is Exegesis without Presuppositions Possible?" In *Existence and Faith*, 289–96. London: Hodder and Stoughton, 1961.
Burger, Hans. "Quadriga without Platonism." In *Scripture and Theology: Historical and Systematic Perspectives*, edited by Tomas Bokedal, Ludger Jansen, and Michael Borowski, 375–96. Berlin: De Gruyter, 2023.
Burkett, Delbert. "The Transfiguration of Jesus (Mark 9:2–8): Epiphany or Apotheosis?" *Journal of Biblical Literature* 138, no. 2 (2019): 413–32.
Burnett, Richard. "John Calvin and the *Sensus Literalis*." *Scottish Journal of Theology* 57, no. 1 (2004): 1–13.
Byassee, Jason. *Praise Seeking Understanding: Reading the Psalms with Augustine*. Grand Rapids: Eerdmans, 2007.
Caird, G. B. "The Transfiguration." *Expository Times* 67 no. 10 (1956): 291–94.
Calvin, John. *Institutes of the Christian Religion*. 2 vols. Edited by John T. McNeill. Philadelphia: Westminster, 1960.
———. *Gospel according to John 1–10*. Calvin's New Testament Commentaries. Vol. 4. Grand Rapids: Eerdmans, 1995.
———. *Harmony of the Four Last Books of Moses*. Vol. 3. Translated by Charles William Bingham. Edinburgh: Calvin Translation Society, 1854.
———. *Calvin's Commentaries: A Harmony of the Gospels; Matthew, Mark, and Luke*. Vol. 2. Translated by T. H. L. Parker. Grand Rapids: Eerdmans, 1972.
———. *Commentary on the Catholic Epistles*. Edinburgh: Calvin Translation Society, 1855.
———. *Commentary on the Epistles of Paul the Apostle to the Corinthians*. Edinburgh: Calvin Translation Society, 1848.
———. *Commentary on the Epistles of Paul to the Galatians and Ephesians*. Translated by William Pringle. Edinburgh: Thomas Clark, 1856.

———. *The Epistles of the Apostle Paul to the Galatians, Ephesians, Philippians, and Colossians.* Translated by T. H. L. Parker. Grand Rapids: Eerdmans, 1965.

Cameron, Michael. "Transfiguration: Christology and the Roots of Figurative Exegesis in St. Augustine." *Studia Patristica* 33, edited by A. Livingstone, 40–47. Leuven: Peeters, 1997.

Canlis, Julie. *Calvin's Ladder: A Spiritual Theology of Ascent and Ascension.* Grand Rapids: Eerdmans, 2010.

Canty, Aaron. *Light and Glory: The Transfiguration of Christ in Early Franciscan and Dominican Theology.* Washington, DC: Catholic University of America Press, 2011.

Carson, D. A. "Understanding Misunderstanding in the Fourth Gospel." *Tyndale Bulletin* 33 (1982): 59–91.

———. "Theological Interpretation of Scripture: Yes, But . . ." In *Theological Commentary: Evangelical Perspectives,* edited by R. Michael Allen, 187–207. New York: T&T Clark International, 2011.

Carter, Craig. *Interpreting Scripture with the Great Tradition: Recovering the Genius of Premodern Exegesis.* Grand Rapids: Baker Academic, 2018.

Case, Mariah. "A Brief Reception History of Exodus 34:29–35." *Journal of Theta Alpha Kappa* 44, no. 1 (2020): 37–56.

Cassedy, Steven. *What Do We Mean When We Talk about Meaning?* Oxford: Oxford University Press, 2022.

Certeau, Michel de. *The Practice of Everyday Life.* 3rd ed. Berkeley: University of California Press, 1984.

Chamberas, Peter A. "The Transfiguration of Christ: A Study in the Patristic Exegesis of Scripture." *St. Vladimir's Theological Quarterly* 14 no. 1–2 (1970): 48–65.

Chambers, Nathan J. *Reconsidering Creation Ex Nihilo in Genesis 1.* Winona Lake, IN: Eisenbrauns, 2020.

Charles, J. Daryl, ed. *Reading Genesis 1–2: An Evangelical Conversation.* Peabody, MA: Hendrickson, 2013.

Chase, Mitchell L. *40 Questions about Typology and Allegory.* Grand Rapids: Kregel, 2020.

Chau, Wai-Shing. *The Letter and the Spirit: A History of Interpretation from Origen to Luther.* New York: Peter Lang, 1995.

Chenu, Marie-Dominique. *Towards Understanding Saint Thomas.* Chicago: Regency, 1953.

Chester, Tim. Introduction to *Meeting Christ in the Garden: A Devotional of Classic Writing on the Song of Song.* Ross-shire, UK: Christian Focus, 2023.

Childs, Brevard S. "Allegory and Typology in Biblical Interpretation." In *The Bible as Christian Scripture,* edited by Christopher R. and Kent Harold Richards, 299–311. Atlanta: Society of Biblical Literature, 2013.

———. *Biblical Theology in Crisis.* Philadelphia: Westminster, 1970.

———. *Biblical Theology of the Old and New Testaments: Theological Reflections on the Christian Bible.* Minneapolis: Fortress, 1992.

———. *The Book of Exodus: A Critical, Theological Commentary.* Old Testament Library. Louisville: Westminster John Knox, 1974.

———. *Isaiah.* Louisville: Westminster John Knox, 2001.

———. "The Old Testament as Scripture of the Church." *Concordia Theological Monthly* 43 (1972): 709–22.

———. "The *Sensus Literalis* of Scripture: An Ancient and Modern Problem." In *Beiträge zur alttestamentlich Theologie,* edited by H. Donner, 80–93. Göttingen: Vandenhoeck & Ruprecht, 1977.

———. *The Struggle to Understand Isaiah as Christian Scripture.* Grand Rapids: Eerdmans, 2004.

———. "Toward Recovering Theological Exegesis." *Ex Auditu* 16 (2000): 121–29.

Chirila, Ioan. "*Let There Be Light!* Gen. 1:3 in the Interpretation of the Primordial Light." *SUBBTO* 65, no. 1 (2020): 5–22.

Chrétien, Jean-Louis. *Under the Gaze of the Bible.* New York: Fordham University Press, 2015.

Clarke, Bridget. "Iris Murdoch and the Prospects for Critical Moral Perception." In *Iris Murdoch, Philosopher,* edited by Justin Broackes, 227–54. Oxford: Oxford University Press, 2012.

Clausewitz, Carl von. *On War.* Edited and translated by Michael Howard and Peter Paret. Princeton, NJ: Princeton University Press, 1984.

Clifford, W. K. *Lectures and Essays.* London: Macmillan, 1886.

Cockayne, Joshua. *Contemporary with Christ: Kierkegaard and Second-Personal Spirituality.* Waco, TX: Baylor University Press, 2020.

Cole, R. Alan. *Exodus: An Introduction and Commentary.* Tyndale Old Testament Commentaries; Downers Grove, IL: 2008.

Cole, Graham A. *Glorification: An Introduction*. Wheaton, IL: Crossway, 2022.
Collett, Don C. *Figural Reading and the Old Testament: Theology and Practice*. Grand Rapids: Baker Academic, 2020.
Collins, Billy. "Introduction to Poetry." *The Apple that Astonished Paris*. Fayetteville: University of Arkansas Press, 1988.
Collins, John C. *Genesis 1–4: A Linguistic, Literary, and Theological Commentary*. Phillipsburg, NJ: P&R, 2006.
———. *Reading Genesis Well: Navigating History, Poetry, Science, and Truth in Genesis 1–11*. Grand Rapids: Zondervan, 2018.
Collins, John J. *The Apocalyptic Imagination: An Introduction to Jewish Apocalyptic Literature*. 3rd ed. Grand Rapids: Eerdmans, 2016.
Coolman, Boyd Taylor. *The Theology of Hugh of St. Victor: An Interpretation*. Cambridge: Cambridge University Press, 2010.
Copeland, Rita, and Peter T. Struck, eds. *The Cambridge Companion to Allegory*. Cambridge: Cambridge University Press, 2010.
Cranfield, C. E. B. *The Epistle to the Romans*. International Critical Commentary. Edinburgh: T&T Clark, 1975.
Crapanzano, Vincent. *Serving the Word: Literalism in America from the Pulpit to the Bench*. New York: New Press, 2000.
Crisp, Oliver D. *Analyzing Doctrine: Toward a Systematic Theology*. Waco, TX: Baylor University Press, 2019.
Crisp, Oliver D., and Michael C. Rea, eds. *Analytic Theology: New Essays in the Philosophy of Theology*. Oxford: Oxford University Press, 2009.
Culpepper, R. Alan. *Anatomy of the Fourth Gospel: A Study in Literary Design*. Philadelphia: Fortress, 1983.
Cummings, Brian. "Literally Speaking, or, the Literal Sense from Augustine to Lacan." *Paragraph* 21, no. 2 (1998): 200–226.
———. *The Literary Culture of the Reformation: Grammar and Grace*. Oxford: Oxford University Press, 2002.
Curran, Ian. "Transformed." *Christian Century*, July 15, 2008, 26–31.
Cyril of Alexandria. *Commentaries on Romans, 1–2 Corinthians, and Hebrews*. Edited by Joel C. Elowsky. Ancient Christian Texts. Downers Grove, IL: IVP Academic, 2022.
Daley, Brian E. *God Visible: Patristic Christology Reconsidered*. Oxford: Oxford University Press, 2020.
Daley, Brian E., ed. and trans. *Light on the Mountain: Greek Patristic and Byzantine Homilies on the Transfiguration of the Lord*. Yonkers, NY: St Vladimir's Seminary Press, 2013.
Daley, Brian E., and Paul R. Kolbet, eds. *The Harp of Prophecy: Early Christian Interpretation of the Psalms*. Notre Dame, IN: University of Notre Dame Press, 2015.
Dalferth, Ingolf. "Die Mitte ist außen: Anmerkungen zum Wirklichkeitsbezug evangelischer Schriftauslegung." In *Jesus Christus als die Mitte der Schrift: Studien zur Hermeneutik des Evangeliums*, edited by Christof Landmesser, 173–98. Berlin: Walter de Gruyter, 1997.
Damgaard, Iben. "Kierkegaard's Rewriting of Biblical Narratives: The Mirror of the Text." In *Kierkegaard and the Bible. Tome I: The Old Testament*, edited by Lee. C. Barrett and Jon Stewart, 207–30. New York: Routledge, 2016.
Daniélou, Jean. *The Bible and the Liturgy*. Notre Dame, IN: University of Notre Dame Press, 1956.
———. *From Shadows to Reality: Studies in the Biblical Typology of the Fathers*. London: Burns & Oates, 1960.
———. "Les orientations présentes de la pensée religieuse." *Études* 249 (1946): 5–21.
———. *Origen*. London: Sheed and Ward, 1955.
Davids, Peter H. *The Letters of 2 Peter and Jude*. Pillar New Testament Commentary. Grand Rapids: Eerdmans, 2006.
Davidson, A. B. "The Book of Isaiah Ch. XLff." *The Expositor*, series 2, vol. 8, 358–59. London: Hodder and Stoughton, 1884.
Davidson, Ivor. "Divine Light: Some Reflections after Barth." In *Trinitarian Theology After Barth*, edited by Myk Habets and Phillip Tolliday, 48–69. Eugene, OR: Pickwick, 2011.
Davies, Jamie. *The Apocalyptic Paul: Retrospect and Prospect*. Eugene, OR: Cascade, 2022.

Davis, Ellen F. *Proverbs, Ecclesiastes, and the Song of Songs*. Louisville: Westminster John Knox, 2000.
Dawson, David. *Christian Figural Reading and the Fashioning of Identity*. Berkeley: University of California Press, 2001.
Dever, William G. *What Did the Biblical Writers Know and When Did They Know It? What Archaeology Can Tell Us about the Reality of Ancient Israel*. Grand Rapids: Eerdmans, 2001.
Diodore of Tarsus. *Commentary on Psalms 1–51*. Translated by Robert C. Hill. Atlanta: SBL, 2005.
Dilley, Frank B. "Does the 'God Who Acts' Really Act?" In *God's Activity in the World: The Contemporary Problem*, edited by Owen C. Thomas, 45–60. Chico, CA: Scholars, 1983.
Dockery, David S., and Malcolm B. Yarnell III. *Special Revelation and Scripture*. Brentwood, TN: B&H Academic, 2024.
Dodd, C. H. *According to the Scriptures: The Substructure of New Testament Theology*. London: Nisbet, 1952.
———. *The Interpretation of the Fourth Gospel*. Cambridge: Cambridge University Press, 1953.
———. *The Parables of the Kingdom*. London: Nisbet, 1935.
Donaldson, Terence L. *Jesus on the Mountain: A Study in Matthean Theology*. Sheffield: JSOT Press, 1985.
Driver, Daniel R. *Brevard Childs, Biblical Theologian: For the Church's One Bible*. Grand Rapids: Baker Academic, 2010.
Dryden, J. De Waal. *A Hermeneutic of Wisdom: Recovering the Formative Agency of Scripture*. Grand Rapids: Baker Academic, 2018.
Duckworth, Alistair M., ed. *Emma: A Case Study in Contemporary Criticism*. Boston/New York: Bedford/St. Martin's, 2002.
Dunham, Kyle. "Challenges to Intertextuality and Christotelism: A New Model of Canonical-Linguistic Priming." *Journal of the Evangelical Theological Society* 64, no. 2 (2021): 287–301.
During, Simon. "Losing Faith in the Humanities." *The Chronicle of Higher Education*, December 18, 2019.
Dykstra, Craig. *Vision and Character: A Christian Educator's Alternative to Kohlberg*. New York: Paulist, 1981.
Earnshaw, Rebekah. *Creator and Creation according to Calvin on Genesis*. Göttingen: Vandenhoeck & Ruprecht, 2020.
East, Brad. "The Hermeneutics of Theological Interpretation: Holy Scripture, Biblical Scholarship and Historical Criticism." *International Journal of Systematic Theology* 19, no. 1 (2017): 30–52.
Eby, Robert. *Virtue Hermeneutics: New Horizons in Textual Understanding*. Eugene, OR: Pickwick, 2022.
Eco, Umberto. *The Limits of Interpretation*. Bloomington: Indiana University Press, 1990.
Edmondson, Stephen. *Calvin's Christology*. Cambridge: Cambridge University Press, 2004.
———. "Christ and History: Hermeneutical Convergence in Calvin and Its Challenge to Biblical Theology." *Modern Theology* 21, no. 1 (2005): 3–35.
Edwards, Jonathan. *Religious Affections*. Edited by John E. Smith and Harry S. Stout. In *The Works of Jonathan Edwards*. Vol. 2. New Haven, CT: Yale University Press, 2009.
———. *The End for which God Created the World*. In *The Works of Jonathan Edwards*. Vol. 8. *Ethical Writings*. New Haven, CT: Yale University Press, 1989.
Ehrman, Bart. *Lost Christianities: The Battles for Scripture and the Faiths We Never Knew*. Oxford: Oxford University Press, 2003.
———. *Lost Scriptures: Books That Did Not Make It Into the New Testament*. Oxford: Oxford University Press, 2003.
Eklund, Rebekah Ann. "The Goods of Reading: Theological Interpretation and Scripture Reasoning." *Journal of Scriptural Reasoning* 9, no. 1 (2010), https://jsr.shanti.virginia.edu/back-issues/vol-9-no-1-december-2010-the-fruits-of-scriptural-reasoning/the-goods-of-reading-theological-interpretation-and-scriptural-reasoning/.
Ellis, E. Earle. *The Old Testament in Early Christianity: Canon and Interpretation in the Light of Modern Research*. Grand Rapids: Baker, 1992.
Enns, Peter. *The Bible Tells Me So: Why Defending Scripture Has Made Us Unable to Read It*. New York: HarperOne, 2015.
———. *How the Bible Actually Works*. New York: HarperOne, 2019.
Evans, G. R. *Old Arts and New Theology: The Beginnings of Theology as an Academic Discipline*. Oxford: Oxford University Press, 1980.
———. *The Language and Logic of the Bible: The Earlier Middle Ages*. Cambridge: Cambridge University Press, 1984.

Evans, G. R., ed. *The First Theologians: An Introduction to Theology in the Early Church*. Oxford: Blackwell, 2004.
Fabiny, Tibor. *Figura and Fulfillment: Typology in the Bible, Art, and Literature*. Eugene, OR: Wipf & Stock, 2016.
Farley, Edward. *Theologia: The Fragmentation and Unity of Theological Education*. Minneapolis: Augsburg Fortress, 1994.
Farrell, John. *The Varieties of Authorial Intention: Literary Theory beyond the Intentional Fallacy*. London: Palgrave Macmillan, 2017.
Farrar, Frederic W. *History of Interpretation: Eight Lectures Preached Before the University of Oxford in the Year MDCCCLXXXV on the Foundation of the Late Rev. John Bampton*. London: Macmillan, 1886.
Fee, Gordon D. "On Getting the Spirit Back into Spirituality." In *Life in the Spirit: Spiritual Formation in Theological Perspective*, edited by Jeffrey P. Greenman and George Kalantzis, 36–44. Downers Grove, IL: IVP Academic, 2010.
Feinberg, John S. *Light in a Dark Place: The Doctrine of Scripture*. Wheaton, IL: Crossway, 2018.
Felski, Rita. *The Limits of Critique*. Chicago: University of Chicago Press, 2015.
Ferguson, Everett. *The Rule of Faith: A Guide*. Eugene, OR: Cascade, 2015.
Feuerbach, Ludwig. *The Essence of Christianity*. Translated by George Eliot. Buffalo: Prometheus, 1989.
Fiddes, Paul S., and Günter Bader, eds. *The Spirit and the Letter: A Tradition and a Reversal*. New York: Bloomsbury T&T Clark, 2013.
Fink, David, ed. *Proverbs, Ecclesiastes, Song of Songs*. Reformation Commentary on Scripture. Downers Grove, IL: IVP Academic, 2023.
Finkelstein, Israel, and Amihai Mazar. *The Quest for the Historical Israel: Debating Archaeology and the History of Early Israel*. Atlanta: Society of Biblical Literature, 2007.
Fish, Stanley. *Is There a Text in This Class? The Authority of Interpretive Communities*. Cambridge, MA: Harvard University Press, 1980.
Fishbane, Michael, ed. *The Midrashic Imagination: Jewish Exegesis, Thought, and History*. Albany, NY: SUNY Press, 1993.
Fiorenza, Elisabeth Schüssler. *Bread Not Stone: The Challenge of Feminist Biblical Interpretation*. Rev. ed. Boston: Beacon, 1995.
———. "The Ethics of Interpretation: Decentering Biblical Scholarship." *Journal of Biblical Literature* 107 (1988): 101–15.
Fisher, Jeff. *A Christotopic Reading of Scripture: Johannes Oecolampadius on Hebrews*. Göttingen: Vandenhoeck & Ruprecht, 2016.
Fitzgerald, Allan D., ed. *Augustine through the Ages: An Encyclopedia*. Grand Rapids: Eerdmans, 1999.
Fitzmeyer, Joseph A. "Glory Reflected on the Face of Christ (2 Cor 3:7–4:6) and a Palestinian Jewish Motif." *Theological Studies* 42, no. 4 (1981): 630–44.
Fowl, Stephen. *Engaging Scripture: A Model for Theological Interpretation*. Oxford: Blackwell, 1998.
———. "Christian Theological Interpretation." In *The New Cambridge Companion to Biblical Interpretation*, edited by Ian Boxall and Bradley C. Gregory, 173–90. Cambridge: Cambridge University Press, 2023.
Frege, Gottlob. "On Sense and Reference." In *Translations from the Philosophical Writings of Gottlob Frege*, edited by Peter Geach and Max Black, 3rd ed., 56–78. Oxford: Blackwell, 1980.
Frei, Hans. *The Eclipse of Biblical Narrative: A Study in Eighteenth and Nineteenth Century Hermeneutics*. New Haven, CT: Yale University Press, 1974.
———. "The 'Literal Reading' of Biblical Narrative in the Christian Tradition: Does It Stretch or Will It Break?" In *The Bible and the Narrative Tradition*, edited by Frank McConnell, 36–77. Oxford: Oxford University Press, 1986.
———. *Types of Christian Theology*. New Haven, CT: Yale University Press, 1992.
Frey, Jörg. *The Glory of the Crucified One: Christology and Theology in the Gospel of John*. Waco, TX: Baylor University Press, 2019.
Froelich, Karlfried. *Biblical Interpretation in the Early Church*. Philadelphia: Fortress, 1984.
———. "'Always to Keep the Literal Sense in Holy Scripture Means to Kill One's Soul': The State of Biblical Hermeneutics at the Beginning of the Fifteenth Century." In *Literary Uses of Typology from the Late Middle Ages to the Present*, edited by Earl Miner, 20–48. Princeton, NJ: Princeton University Press, 1977.

Gadamer, Hans-Georg. "The Universality of the Hermeneutical Problem." In *Philosophical Hermeneutics*, 3–17. Berkeley: University of California Press, 1976.

———. *Truth and Method*. Translated by Joel Weinsheimer and Donald G. Marshall. London: Sheed and Ward, 1989.

Gallie, W. B. "Essentially Contested Concepts." *Proceedings of the Aristotelian Society* 54 (1956): 167–98.

Garland, David. E. *2 Corinthians: An Exegetical and Theological Exposition of Holy Scripture*. Nashville: Holman Reference, 1999.

Garrett, Duane E. "Veiled Hearts: The Translation and Interpretation of 2 Corinthians 3." *JETS* 53, no. 4 (2010): 729–72.

Gasque, W. Ward, and William S. LaSor, eds. *Scripture, Tradition, and Interpretation*. Grand Rapids: Eerdmans, 1978.

George, Timothy. *Reading Scripture with the Reformers*. Downers Grove, IL: IVP Academic, 2011.

Gentry, Kenneth L. *As It Is Written: The Genesis Account Literal or Literary? Dismantling the Framework Hypothesis*. Green Forest, AR: Master, 2016.

Gignilliat, Mark. "Paul, Allegory, and the Plain sense of Scripture: Galatians 4:21–31." *Journal of Theological Interpretation* 2, no. 1 (2008): 135–46.

———. *Reading Scripture Canonically: Theological Instincts for Old Testament Interpretation*. Grand Rapids: Baker Academic, 2019.

Goldingay, John. *Do We Need the New Testament? Letting the Old Testament Speak for Itself*. Downers Grove, IL: InterVarsity Press, 2015.

———. "Review Article: What Theologians and Biblical Scholars Wish the Others Knew." *Journal of Theological Interpretation* 16, no. 1 (2022): 132–47.

———. "Reading Rahab: How Criticism Serves Itself or Eats Itself." *Scottish Journal of Theology* 76, no. 1 (2023): 24–30.

Goppelt, Leonhard. *Typos: The Typological Interpretation of the Old Testament in the New Testament*. Grand Rapids: Eerdmans, 1982.

Gordon, Bruce. *Calvin*. New Haven: Yale University Press, 2009.

Gorman, Michael. *Elements of Biblical Exegesis: A Basic Guide for Students and Ministers*. 3rd ed. Grand Rapids: Baker Academic, 2020.

Graham, David. "Defending Biblical Literalism: Augustine on the Literal Sense." *Pro Ecclesia* 25, no. 2 (2016): 173–99.

Green, Chris E. W. *Sanctifying Interpretation: Vocation, Holiness, and Scripture*. Cleveland, TN: CPT, 2015.

Greene, Colin J. D. *Christology in Cultural Perspective: Marking Out the Horizons*. Grand Rapids: Eerdmans, 2003.

Greene-McCreight, Kathryn. *Ad Litteram: How Augustine, Calvin, and Barth Read the "Plain Sense" of Genesis 1–3*. New York: Peter Lang, 1999.

———. "He Spoke through the Prophets." In *Nicene Christianity: The Future for a New Ecumenism*, edited by Christopher R. Seitz, 167–75. Grand Rapids: Brazos, 2001.

Greenwood, Kyle R., ed. *Since the Beginning: Interpreting Genesis 1 and 2 through the Ages*. Grand Rapids: Baker Academic, 2018.

Gregory, Brad S. *The Unintended Reformation: How a Religious Revolution Secularized Society*. Cambridge, MA: Belknap Press of Harvard University Press, 2012.

Gregory of Nazianzus. *On God and Christ*. Crestwood, NY: St. Vladimir's University Press, 2002.

Gregory of Nyssa. *The Life of Moses*. Translated by Abraham J. Malherbe and Everett Ferguson. New York: Paulist, 1978.

Gregory the Great. *On the Song of Songs*. Translated by Mark DelCogliano. Collegeville, MN: Liturgical, 2012.

Greschat, Martin. *Martin Bucer: A Reformer and His Times*. Louisville: Westminster John Knox, 2004.

Grey, Thomas C. "The Constitution as Scripture." *Stanford Law Review* 37, no. 1 (1984): 1–25.

Griffiths, Jonathan I. *Hebrews and Divine Speech*. New York: Bloomsbury T&T Clark, 2014.

Grice, H. P. "Logic and Conversation." In *Studies in the Ways of Words*, 22–40. Cambridge, MA: Harvard University Press, 1989.

Griffiths, Jonathan I. *Hebrews and Divine Speech*. New York: Bloomsbury T&T Clark, 2014.

Griffiths, Paul. *Song of Songs*. Brazos Theological Commentary on the Bible. Grand Rapids: Brazos, 2011.

Grindheim, Sigurd. "The Law Kills but the Gospel Gives Life: The Letter-Spirit Dualism in 2 Corinthians 3:5–18." *Journal for the Study of the New Testament* 84 (2001): 97–115.

Grosseteste, Robert. *On the Six Days of Creation*. Translated by C. F. J. Martin. Oxford: Oxford University Press, 1996.

Guigo II. *The Ladder of Monks*. Translated by Edmund Colledge and James Walsh. Kalamazoo, MI: Cistercian, 1979.

Guillory, John. *Professing Criticism: Essays on the Organization of Literary Study*. Chicago: University of Chicago Press, 2022.

Gundry, Robert H. *Mark: A Commentary on His Apology for the Cross*. Grand Rapids: Eerdmans, 1993.

———. *Jesus the Word according to John the Sectarian*. Grand Rapids: Eerdmans, 2002.

———. "To Plato or Not to Plato?" *Books & Culture* 17 (March–April 2011): 25–26.

Guthrie, George. "Boats in the Bay: Reflections on the Use of Linguistics and Literary Studies in Biblical Studies." In *Linguistics and the New Testament: Critical Junctures*, edited by Stanley E. Porter and D. A. Carson, 23–35. Sheffield: Sheffield Academic Press, 1999.

———. "*Katargeo* and the People of the Shining Face (2 Corinthians 3:7–18)." *Southern Baptist Journal of Theology* 19, no. 3 (2015): 41–60.

———. *2 Corinthians*. Baker Exegetical Commentary. Grand Rapids: Baker Academic, 2015.

Habets, Myk. "*Theological* Theological Interpretation of Scripture." *International Journal of Systematic Theology* 23, no. 2 (2021): 235–58.

Hafemann, Scott J. "The Glory and Veil of Moses in 2 Cor 3:7–14: An Example of Paul's Contextual Exegesis of the OT – A Proposal." *Horizons in Biblical Theology* 14, no. 1 (1992): 31–49.

———. *Paul, Moses, and the History of Israel: The Letter/Spirit Contrast and the Argument from Scripture in 2 Corinthians 3*. Peabody, MA: Hendrickson, 1996.

Hahn, Scott W., and Benjamin Wiker. *Politicizing the Bible: The Roots of Historical Criticism and the Secularization of Scripture, 1300–1700*. New York: Crossroad, 2013.

Hahn, Scott W., and Jeffery L. Morrow. *Modern Biblical Criticism as a Tool of Statecraft (1700–1900)*. Steubenville, OH: Emmaus Academic, 2020.

Haidt, Jonathan. *The Righteous Mind: Why Good People Are Divided by Politics and Religion*. New York: Vintage, 2013.

Hains, Todd R. *Martin Luther and the Rule of Faith: Reading God's Word for God's People*. Downers Grove, IL: IVP Academic, 2022.

Hall, Christopher A. *Reading Scripture with the Church Fathers*. Downers Grove, IL: InterVarsity Press, 1988.

Hallo, W. W., and K. L. Younger, eds. *The Context of Scripture*. 3 vols. Leiden: Brill, 1997–2002.

Halsted, Matthew L. *Paul and the Meaning of Scripture: A Philosophical-Hermeneutic Approach to Paul's Use of the Old Testament*. Eugene, OR: Pickwick, 2022.

Hamilton, James M. *What Is Biblical Theology? A Guide to the Bible's Story, Symbolism, and Patterns*. Wheaton, IL: Crossway, 2014.

Hamilton, Victor P. *The Book of Genesis, Chapters 1–17*. NICOT. Grand Rapids: Eerdmans, 1990.

Hanson, R. P. C. *Allegory and Event: A Study of the Sources and Significance of Origen's Interpretation of Scripture*. Richmond: John Knox, 1959.

Hanson, A. T. "The Midrash in II Corinthians 3: A Reconsideration." *Journal for the Study of the New Testament* 9 (1980): 2–28.

Haran, Menahem. "The Shining of Moses' Face: A Case Study in Biblical and Ancient Near Eastern Iconography." In *In the Shelter of Elyon: Essays on Ancient Palestinian Life and Literature, in Honor of G. W. Ahlstrom*, edited by W. Barrick and John R. Spencer, 159–73. JSOTSup 31. Sheffield: JSOT Press, 1983.

Hardy, Nicholas. *Criticism and Confession: The Bible in the Seventeenth Century Republic of Letters*. Oxford: Oxford University Press, 2017.

Harink, Douglas. *1 and 2 Peter*. Brazos Theological Commentary on the Bible. Grand Rapids: Brazos, 2007.

Hart, David Bentley. "Ad Litteram." In *A Splendid Wickedness and Other Essays*, 274–77. Grand Rapids: Eerdmans, 2016.

Harvey, Angela. *Spiritual Reading: A Study of the Christian Practice of Reading Scripture*. Eugene, OR: Cascade, 2015.

Harvey, Van. *Feuerbach and the Interpretation of Religion*. Cambridge: Cambridge University Press, 1995.

Hauser, Alan J., and Duane F. Watson, eds. *A History of Biblical Interpretation*. Vol. 1. *The Ancient Period*. Grand Rapids: Eerdmans, 2003.

Hawthorne, Gerald F., Ralph P. Martin, and Daniel G. Reid, eds. *Dictionary of Paul and His Letters*. Downers Grove, IL: InterVarsity Press, 1993.

Hay, Andrew R. *God's Shining Forth: A Trinitarian Theology of Divine Light*. Eugene, OR: Pickwick, 2017.

Hayes, John H., and Carl R. Holladay. *Biblical Exegesis: A Beginner's Handbook*. 4th ed. Louisville: Westminster John Knox, 2022.

Hays, Richard B. *Echoes of Scripture in the Letters of Paul*. New Haven, CT: Yale University Press, 1989.

———. "Knowing Jesus: Story, History and the Question of Truth." In *Jesus, Paul and the People of God: A Theological Dialogue with N. T. Wright*, edited by Nicholas Perrin and Richard B. Hays, 41–65. Downers Grove, IL: IVP Academic, 2011.

———. *Reading Backwards: Figural Christology and the Fourfold Gospel Witness*. Waco, TX: Baylor University Press, 2014.

———. *Echoes of Scripture in the Gospels*. Waco, TX: Baylor University Press, 2016.

———. "Figural Exegesis and the Retrospective Recognition of Israel's Story." *Bulletin for Biblical Research* 29 (2019): 32–48.

———. *Reading with the Grain of Scripture*. Grand Rapids: Eerdmans, 2020.

Hayward, C. T. R. "Philo, the Septuagint of Genesis 32:24–32 and the Name 'Israel': Fighting the Passions, Inspiration, and the Vision of God." *Journal of Jewish Studies* 51, no. 2 (2000): 209–26.

Heil, John Paul. *The Transfiguration of Jesus: Narrative Meaning and Function of Mark 9:2–8, Matt 17:1–8 and Luke 9:28–36*. Rome: Pontifical Biblical Institute, 2000.

Henry, Carl F. H. *God, Revelation, and Authority*. Vol. 2. Waco, TX: Word, 1976.

Heringer, Seth. "Preparing to Read: Theological Presuppositions and Biblical Interpretation." *Journal of Theological Interpretation* 17, no. 1 (2023): 130–31.

Herrmann, Erik. "Luther's Absorption of Medieval Biblical Interpretation." In *The Oxford Handbook of Martin Luther's Theology*, edited by Robert Kolb, Irene Dingel, and L'Ubomir Batka, 71–90. Oxford: Oxford University Press, 2014.

Hiestand, Gerald, and Todd Wilson. *The Pastor Theologian: Resurrecting an Ancient Vision*. Grand Rapids: Zondervan, 2015.

Hilber, John W. *Old Testament Cosmology and Divine Accommodation: A Relevance Theory Approach*. Eugene, OR: Cascade, 2020.

Hildebrand, Stephen M. *Basil of Caesarea*. Grand Rapids: Baker Academic, 2014.

Hill, Robert C. *Reading the Old Testament in Antioch*. Atlanta: SBL, 2005.

Hirsch, E. D. *Validity in Interpretation*. New Haven, CT: Yale University Press, 1967.

Hodge, Charles. *Systematic Theology*. Vol. 1. Grand Rapids: Eerdmans, 1979.

Hogan, Patrick Colm, ed. *The Cambridge Encyclopedia of Language Sciences*. Cambridge: Cambridge University Press, 2010.

Holder, Arthur. "Christian Reception of the Song of Songs Since 1800." In *A Companion to the Song of Songs in the History of Spirituality*, edited by Timothy H. Robinson, 358–80. Leiden: Brill, 2021.

Holmes, Jeremy. "Aquinas' *Lectura in Matthaeum*." In *Aquinas on Scripture: An Introduction to His Biblical Commentaries*, edited by Thomas G. Weinandy, Daniel A. Keating, and John P. Yocum, 73–98. New York: T&T Clark International, 2005.

Holmgren, Frederick C. "Holding Your Own Against God! Genesis 32:22–32 (in the Context of Genesis 31–33)." *Interpretation* 44, no. 1 (1990): 5–17.

Hooker, Morna. "Beyond the Things That Are Written? St. Paul's Use of Scripture." *New Testament Studies* 27 (1981): 295–309.

———. Review of Matthew Bates, *Hermeneutics of the Apostolic Proclamation*, in *Journal of Theological Studies* 67 no. 1 (2016): 249–50.

———. "'What Doest Thou Here, Elijah?' A Look at St Mark's Account of the Transfiguration." In *The Glory of Christ in the New Testament: Studies in Christology*, edited by L. D. Hurst and N. T. Wright, 59–70. Oxford: Oxford University Press, 1987.

Horton, Michael. *The Christian Faith: A Systematic Theology for Pilgrims on the Way*. Grand Rapids: Zondervan, 2011.

Houlden, J. L., ed. *The Interpretation of the Bible in the Church*. London: SCM, 1995.

Hugh of St. Victor. *The Didascalicon of Hugh of Saint Victor: A Medieval Guide to the Arts.* Translated by Jerome Taylor. New York: Columbia University Press, 1991.

Huijgen, Arnold, Koert van Bekkum, and Hans Burger. "Biblical Exegesis and Systematic Theology: Toward Mutual Benefit." *Journal of Reformed Theology* 16 (2022): 173–93.

———. "Reinventing the Quadriga." In *Scripture and Theology: Historical and Systematic Perspectives,* edited by Tomas Bokedal, Ludger Jansen, and Michael Borowski, 397–414. Berlin: De Gruyter, 2023.

Hurst, L. D. and N. T. Wright, eds. *The Glory of Christ in the New Testament: Studies in Christology.* Oxford: Oxford University Press, 1987.

Hurtado, Larry W. *Lord Jesus Christ: Devotion to Jesus in Earliest Christianity.* Grand Rapids: Eerdmans, 2005.

Illich, Ivan. *In the Vineyard of the Text: A Commentary on Hugh's Didascalicon.* Chicago: University of Chicago Press, 1993.

Ingraffia, Brian D. *Postmodern Theology and Biblical Theology: Vanquishing God's Shadow.* Cambridge: Cambridge University Press, 1996.

Inman, Ross. "Theology in the Second Person: Christian Dogmatics as a Mode of Prayer." In *Analyzing Prayer: Theological and Philosophical Studies,* edited by Oliver D. Crisp, James M. Arcadi, and Jordan Wessling, 116–35. Oxford: Oxford University Press, 2022.

Irenaeus. *On the Apostolic Preaching.* Translated by John Behr. Crestwood, NY: St. Vladimir's Seminary Press, 1997.

Irvine, Martin. *The Making of Textual Culture: "Grammatica" and Literary Theory 350–1100.* Cambridge: Cambridge University Press, 2006.

Irwin, Luke. "Jesus' Body and Divine Glory in John's Gospel." *Presbyterian* 47, no. 2 (2021): 69–72.

Jacob, Haley Goranson. *Conformed to the Image of His Son: Reconsidering Paul's Theology of Glory in Romans.* Downers Grove, IL: IVP Academic, 2018.

Jacobs, A. J. *The Year of Living Biblically: One Man's Humble Quest to Follow the Bible as Literally as Possible.* New York: Simon & Schuster, 2007.

Jamieson, R. B., and Tyler R. Wittman. *Biblical Reasoning: Christological and Trinitarian Rules for Exegesis.* Grand Rapids: Baker Academic, 2022.

Janzen, David. *The Liberation of Method: The Ethics of Emancipatory Biblical Interpretation.* Minneapolis: Fortress, 2021.

Jay, Pierre. "Jerome (ca. 347–419/420)." In *Handbook of Patristic Exegesis: The Bible in Ancient Christianity,* edited by Charles Kannengiesser, vol. 2, 1094–1133. Leiden: Brill, 2004.

Jerome. *Commentarium in Matthaeum* in *Hieonymus: Commentariorum in Matheum libri 4,* Corpus Christianorum Series Latina 77. Edited by David Hurst and Marcus Adriaen. Turnhout: Brepols, 1969.

———. *The Homilies of St. Jerome.* Vol. 2. Translated by Marie Liguori Ewald. Washington, DC: Catholic University Press of America, 1966.

Jersak, Bradley. *A More Christlike Word: Reading Scripture the Emmaus Way.* New Kensington, PA: Whitaker, 2021.

Jipp, Joshua W. *The Messianic Theology of the New Testament.* Grand Rapids: Eerdmans, 2020.

Johnson, Elliot. "Author's Intention and Biblical Interpretation." In *Hermeneutics, Inerrancy, and the Bible,* edited by Earl Radmacher and Robert D. Preus, 409–29. Grand Rapids: Zondervan, 1984.

Johnson, Luke Timothy. *Hebrews: A Commentary.* Louisville: Westminster John Knox, 2006.

———. *Scripture and Discernment: Decision Making in the Church.* Nashville: Abingdon, 1992.

Johnson, Mark F. "Another Look at the Plurality of the Literal Sense." *Medieval Philosophy and Theology* 2 (1992): 117–41.

Jones, Howell R. *Transfiguration and Transformation.* Edinburgh: Banner of Truth Trust, 2021.

Jonge, Martin de. "Nicodemus and Jesus: Some Observation on Misunderstanding and Understanding in the Fourth Gospel." *Bulletin of the John Rylands Library* 53 (1970/71): 337–59.

Jordan, James B. *Creation in Six Days: A Defense of the Traditional Reading of Genesis One.* Moscow, ID: Canon, 1999.

Josephus. *Jewish War.* Loeb Classical Library. Cambridge, MA; Harvard University Press, 1927.

Jowett, Benjamin. *The Interpretation of Scripture and Other Essays.* London: George Routledge, 1907.

Kant, Immanuel. *Critique of Pure Reason.* 2nd ed. Translated by Norman Kemp Smith. London: Macmillan, 1933.

———. *Foundations of the Metaphysics of Morals* and *What Is Enlightenment?* Translated by Lewis White Beck. New York: Liberal Arts, 1959.
———. *Religion and Rational Theology*. Edited and translated by Allen W. Wood and George Di Giovanni. Cambridge: Cambridge University Press, 1996.
Kapic, Kelly M. *Communion with God: The Divine and the Human in the Theology of John Owen*. Grand Rapids: Baker Academic, 2007.
Käsemann, Ernst, ed. *Perspectives on Paul*. London: SCM, 1971.
Kee, Howard Clark. "'The Transfiguration in Mark': Epiphany or Apocalyptic Vision?" In *Understanding the Sacred Text: Essays in Honor of Morton S. Enslin on the Hebrew Bible and Christian Beginnings*, edited by J. Reumann, 135–52. Valley Forge, PA: Judson, 1972.
Kelly, J. N. D. *A Commentary on the Epistles of Peter and Jude*. London: Black, 1969.
Kelsey, David. *The Fabric of Paul Tillich's Theology*. New Haven, CT: Yale University Press, 1967.
Kibbe, Michael H. "Light That Conquers the Darkness: Oscar Romero on the Transfiguration of Jesus." *Theology Today* 75, no. 4 (2019): 447–57.
———. "From Glory to Glory: Transfiguration and New Creation in 2 Corinthians 2:14–4:6." In *Christian Origins and the Formation of the Early Church*. Edited by Stanley E. Porter. Leiden: Brill, 2024.
Kidner, Derek. *Genesis*. Downers Grove, IL: Inter-Varsity Press, 1979.
Kierkegaard, Søren. *For Self-Examination* and *Judge for Yourself!* Edited by Howard V. Hong and Edna H. Hong. Princeton, NJ: Princeton University Press, 1990.
Kim, Yoon Kyung. *Augustine's Changing Interpretations of Genesis 1–3: From De Genesi contra Manichaeos to De Genesi ad litteram*. Lewiston, NY: Edwin Mellen, 2006.
Kimble, Jeremy M. *Behold and Become: Reading Scripture for Transformation*. Grand Rapids: Kregel Academic, 2023.
Kimnach, Wilson J., Kenneth P. Minkema, and Douglas A. Sweeney, eds. *The Sermons of Jonathan Edwards: A Reader*. New Haven, CT: Yale University Press, 1999.
Kirk, J. R. Daniel. "Colonizing Biblical Interpretation." *Storied Theology* (blog). April 26, 2016. http://www.patheos.com/blogs/storiedtheology/2016/04/22/colonizing-biblical-interpretation/.
Klein, Elizabeth. *Augustine's Theology of Angels*. Cambridge: Cambridge University Press, 2018.
Klein, Ezra. *Why We're Polarized*. New York: Avid Reader, 2020.
Knight, Henry F. "Meeting Jacob at the Jabbok: Wrestling with a Text; A Midrash on Genesis 32:22–32." *Journal of Ecumenical Studies* 29, no. 3–4 (1992): 451–60.
Knights, Chris. "Metamorphosis and Obedience: An Interpretation of Mark's Account of the Transfiguration of Jesus." *Expository Times* 121, no. 5 (2010): 218–22.
Kolbet, Paul R. "Athanasius, the Psalms, and the Reformation of the Self." *Harvard Theological Review* 99, no. 1 (2006): 85–101.
Kooy, Vernon H. "The Transfiguration Motif in the Gospel of John." In *Saved by Hope: Essays in Honor of Richard C. Oudersluys*, edited by James I. Cook, 64–78. Grand Rapids: Eerdmans, 1978.
Kort, Wesley A. "Calvin's Theory of Reading." *Christianity & Literature* 62, no. 2 (2013): 189–202.
Kugel, James L., and Rowan A. Greer. *Early Biblical Interpretation*. Philadelphia: Westminster, 1986.
Kuhn, Thomas. *The Structure of Scientific Revolutions*. Chicago: University of Chicago Press, 1962.
Kynes, Bill, and Will Kynes. *Wrestling with Job: Defiant Faith in the Face of Suffering*. Downers Grove, IL: IVP Academic, 2022.
Laansma, Jon, and Daniel J. Treier, eds. *Christology, Hermeneutics, and Hebrews: Profiles from the History of Interpretation*. London: Bloomsbury T&T Clark, 2012.
Ladd, George. *A Theology of the New Testament*. Grand Rapids; Eerdmans, 1993.
Lambrecht, Jan. "Transformation in 2 Cor 3:18." *Biblica* 64, no. 2 (1983): 243–54.
Lang, T. J. "The Order of Christian Theology: Literal and Ecclesial Senses of the New Testament." *Journal of Theological Interpretation* 14, no. 1 (2020): 129–39.
Larsen, Timothy. *Every Leaf, Line, and Letter: Evangelicals and the Bible from the 1730s to the Present*. Downers Grove, IL: IVP Academic, 2021.
Lash, Nicholas. *The Beginning and End of "Religion."* Cambridge: Cambridge University Press, 1996.
Leclercq, Jean. *The Love of Learning and the Desire for God: A Study of Monastic Culture*. New York: Fordham University Press, 1982.
Lee, Dorothy. *Transfiguration*. London and New York: Continuum, 2004.

Lee, Gregory W. *Today When You Hear His Voice: Scripture, the Covenants, and the People of God*. Grand Rapids: Eerdmans, 2016.
Lee, Jihye. *A Jewish Apocalyptic Framework of Eschatology in the Epistle to the Hebrews*. London: Bloomsbury T&T Clark, 2021.
Lee, Simon S. *Jesus' Transfiguration and the Believers' Transformation*. WUNT 2. No. 265. Tübingen: Mohr Siebeck, 2009.
Legaspi, Michael. *The Death of Scripture and the Rise of Biblical Studies*. Oxford: Oxford University Press, 2011.
———. "The Consolation of Philology." *First Things*. October 2015. 66.
Leinsle, Ulrich G. *Introduction to Scholastic Theology*. Washington, DC: Catholic University of America Press, 2010.
Leithart, Peter J. *Creator: A Theological Interpretation of Genesis 1*. Downers Grove, IL: IVP Academic, 2023.
———. *Deep Exegesis: The Mystery of Reading Scripture*. Waco, TX: Baylor University Press, 2009.
———. "The Quadriga or Something Like It: A Biblical and Pastoral Defense." In *Ancient Faith for the Church's Future*, edited by Mark Husbands and Jeffrey P. Greenman, 110–25. Downers Grove, IL: IVP Academic, 2012.
———. *Theopolitical Reading*. West Monroe, LA: Theopolis, 2020.
Lennox, John. *Seven Days that Divide the World: The Beginning according to Genesis and Science*. Grand Rapids: Zondervan, 2011.
Lentricchia, Frank, and Andrew Dubois, eds. *Close Reading: The Reader*. Durham, NC: Duke University Press, 2003.
Letham, Robert. "'In the Space of Six Days': The Days of Creation from Origen to the Westminster Assembly." *Westminster Theological Journal* 61 (1999): 175–207.
———. *Through Western Eyes. Eastern Orthodoxy: A Reformed Perspective*. Ross-shire, UK: Mentor, 2010.
Levenson, Jon D. *The Hebrew Bible, the Old Testament, and Historical Criticism: Jews and Christians in Biblical Studies*. Louisville: Westminster John Knox, 1993.
Levering, Matthew. *Participatory Biblical Exegesis: A Theology of Biblical Interpretation*. Notre Dame, IN: University of Notre Dame Press, 2008.
Levin, Yuval. *A Time to Build: From Family and Community to Congress and the Campus, How Recommitting to our Institutions Can Revive the American Dream*. New York: Basic, 2020.
Levinas, Emmanuel. *Totality and Infinity: An Essay on Exteriority*. Dordrecht: Kluwer Academic, 1991.
Levy, Ian Christopher. *Introducing Medieval Biblical Interpretation: The Senses of Scripture in Premodern Exegesis*. Grand Rapids: Baker Academic, 2018.
Lewis, C. S. *Experiment in Criticism*. Cambridge: Cambridge University Press, 1961.
———. *God in the Dock: Essays on Theology and Ethics*. Grand Rapids: Eerdmans, 1970.
———. "Is Theology Poetry?" In *Weight of Glory: And Other Addresses*, 116–40. New York: HarperCollins, 2001.
———. *Mere Christianity*. San Francisco: HarperSanFrancisco, 2001.
———. *Miracles: A Preliminary Study*. New York: Macmillan, 1947.
———. *A Preface to Paradise Lost*. London: Oxford University Press, 1942.
———. *Studies in Words*. 2nd ed. Cambridge: Cambridge University Press, 1967.
Lillback, Peter A., ed. *Seeing Christ in All of Scripture: Hermeneutics at Westminster Theological Seminary*. Philadelphia: Westminster Seminary Press, 2016.
Lincoln, Andrew J., and Angus Paddison, eds. *Christology and Scripture: Interdisciplinary Perspectives*. New York: T&T Clark, 2008.
———. *Truth on Trial: The Lawsuit Motif in the Fourth Gospel*. Peabody, MA: Hendrickson, 2000.
Lindbeck, George A. *The Nature of Doctrine: Religion and Theology in a Postliberal Age*. Philadelphia: Westminster, 1984.
———. "Two Kinds of Ecumenism: Unitive and Interdenominational." *Gregorianum* 70, no. 4 (1989): 647–60.
———. "Postcritical Canonical Interpretation: Three Modes of Retrieval." In *Theological Exegesis: Essays in Honor of Brevard S. Childs*, edited by Christopher Seitz and Kathryn Greene-McCreight, 26–51. Grand Rapids: Eerdmans, 1999.

Loisy, Alfred. *Le Quatrième Évangile*. Paris: Alphonse Picard et Fils, 1903.
Long, V. Philips. "Irenaeus, Scripture, and the 'Rule of Truth': Of Kings, Foxes, and Mosaics." *Crux* 54, no. 2 (2018): 13–25.
Longenecker, Bruce W., ed. *The New Cambridge Companion to St. Paul*. Cambridge: Cambridge University Press, 2020.
Longenecker, Richard. *Biblical Exegesis in the Apostolic Period*. 2nd ed. Grand Rapids: Eerdmans, 1999.
Longman, Tremper. *Song of Songs*. New International Commentary on the Old Testament. Grand Rapids: Eerdmans, 2001.
———. *Confronting Old Testament Controversies: Pressing Questions about Evolution, Sexuality, History, and Violence*. Grand Rapids: Baker, 2019.
Lossky, Vladimir. *In the Image and Likeness of God*. New York: St. Vladimir's Seminary Press, 1974.
Louth, Andrew. *Discerning the Mystery: An Essay on the Nature of Theology*. Oxford: Clarendon, 1983.
———. "St. Augustine's Interpretation of the Transfiguration of Christ." *Studia Ephemeridis Augustinianum* 68, 375–82. Rome: Institutum Patristicum Augustinianum, 2000.
———. *Introducing Eastern Orthodox Theology*. Downers Grove, IL: IVP Academic, 2013.
Lubac, Henri de. *Sources of Revelation*. London: Herder and Herder, 1968.
———. *Medieval Exegesis*. Vol. 1. *The Four Senses of Scripture*. Translated by Marc Sebanc. Grand Rapids: Eerdmans, 1998.
———. *Scripture in the Tradition*. New York: Crossroad, 2000.
———. *History and Spirit: The Understanding of Scripture according to Origen*. San Francisco: Ignatius, 2007.
Lundeen, Erik. "In Search of the Literal Sense: Johannes Oecolampadius (1482–1531) and the Exegetical Tradition on Isaiah." PhD diss., Baylor University, 2022.
Luther, Martin. *Luther's Works*. Vol. 1. *Lectures on Genesis Chapters 1–5*. Edited by Jaroslav Pelikan. Saint Louis: Concordia, 1958.
———. *Luther's Works*. Vol. 8. *Lectures on Genesis Chapters 45–50*. St. Louis: Concordia, 1968.
———. *Luther's Works*. Vol. 35. *Word and Sacrament I*. Edited by E. Theodore Bachmann. Minneapolis: Fortress, 1960.
———. "On the Bondage of the Will." In *Luther and Erasmus: Free Will and Salvation*. Translated by E. Gordon Rupp and Philip S. Watson. Philadelphia: Westminster, 1959.
———. "To the Councilmen of all Cities in Germany That They Establish and Maintain Christian Schools." In *Martin Luther's Basic Theological Writings*, edited by Timothy E. Lull, 704–35. Minneapolis: Fortress, 1989.
Luxon, Thomas, *Literal Figures: Puritan Allegory and the Reformation Crisis in Representation*. Chicago: University of Chicago Press, 1995.
Luz, Ulrich. *Matthew 8–20*. Minneapolis: Fortress, 2001.
Lyotard, Jean-François. *The Postmodern Condition: A Report on Knowledge*. Minneapolis: University of Minnesota Press, 1984.
Machen, J. Gresham. *The Christian Faith in the Modern World*. Grand Rapids: Eerdmans, 1947.
Madsen, Thorvald B. "Listen to Him: The Exhortation of Matthew 17:5 in the Context of the Transfiguration Narrative." *Midwestern Journal of Theology* 15, no. 2 (2016): 119–30.
Malcolm, Matthew. *From Hermeneutics to Exegesis: The Trajectory of Biblical Interpretation*. Nashville: B&H Academic, 2018.
Manetsch, Scott M., ed. *2 Corinthians*. Reformation Commentary on Scripture. Downers Grove, IL: InterVarsity Press, 2022.
Manton, Thomas. *Christ's Temptation and Transfiguration: Practically Explained and Improved in Several Sermons*. London: n.p., 1685.
Mann, Jeremy R. "Sacramental Ontology and Calvin: Toward a Re-enchanted World." *Bulletin of Ecclesial Theology* 4, no. 2 (2017): 19–38.
———. "Is the World Sacramental? Ontology, Language, and Scripture." In *Creation and Doxology: The Beginning and End of God's Good World*, edited by Gerald Hiestand and Todd Wilson, 79–98. Downers Grove, IL: IVP Academic, 2018.
Marsden, George M. *Jonathan Edwards: A Life*. New Haven: Yale University Press, 2003.
Marsh, William. *Martin Luther on Reading the Bible as Christian Scripture: The Messiah in Luther's Biblical Hermeneutic and Theology*. Eugene, OR: Pickwick, 2017.
Marshall, I. Howard. *1 Peter*. IVP NT Commentary Series. Downers Grove, IL: InterVarsity Press, 1991.

Martens, Peter W. "Revisiting the Allegory/Typology Distinction: The Case of Origen." *Journal of Early Christian Studies* 16, no. 3 (2008): 283–317.

———. *Origen and Scripture: The Contours of the Exegetical Life.* Oxford: Oxford University Press, 2012.

———. *Adrian's* Introduction to the Divine Scriptures: *An Antiochene Handbook for Scriptural Interpretation.* Oxford: Oxford University Press, 2017.

Martin, Ralph. *2 Corinthians.* Word Bible Commentary. 2nd ed. Grand Rapids: Zondervan, 2014.

Mattox, Mickey L. "Faith in Creation: Martin Luther's Sermons on Genesis 1." *Trinity Journal* 39 (2018): 199–219.

May, Herbert Gordon. "The Creation of Light in Genesis 1:3–5." *Journal of Biblical Literature* 58, no. 3 (1939): 203–11.

McCall, Thomas H. *An Invitation to Analytic Christian Theology.* Downers Grove, IL: InterVarsity Press, 2015.

McCaulley, Esau. *Reading While Black: African American Biblical Interpretation as an Exercise in Hope.* Downers Grove, IL: IVP Academic, 2020.

McClendon, James W. *Systematic Theology.* Vol. 2. *Doctrine.* Nashville: Abingdon, 1994.

McClymond, Michael J., and Gerald R. McDermott. *The Theology of Jonathan Edwards.* Oxford: Oxford University Press, 2012.

McDonald, Suzanne. "Beholding the Glory of God in the Face of Jesus Christ: John Owen and the 'Reforming' of the Beatific Vision." In *The Ashgate Research Companion to John Owen's Theology,* edited by Kelly M. Kapic and Mark Jones, 141–58. Burlington, VT: Ashgate, 2012.

———. "John Owen on the Beatific Vision: Historic Reformed 'Spirituality' in Action." *Theology Matters.* May 30, 2023.

McEntyre, Marilyn Chandler. *Caring for Words in a Culture of Lies.* Grand Rapids: Eerdmans, 2009.

McGilchrist, Iain. *The Master and his Emissary: The Divided Brain and the Making of the Western World.* Expanded ed. New Haven, CT: Yale University Press, 2019.

McGuckin, John Anthony. *The Transfiguration of Christ in Scripture and Tradition.* Lewiston, New York: Edwin Mellen, 1986.

———. "Patterns of Biblical Exegesis in the Cappadocian Fathers: Basil the Great, Gregory the Theologian, and Gregory of Nyssa." In *Orthodox and Wesleyan Scriptural Understanding and Practice,* edited by S. T. Kimbrough, 37–54. New York: St. Vladimir's Seminary Press, 2005.

McKenzie, Steven L., ed. *Oxford Encyclopedia of Biblical Interpretation.* 2 vols. Oxford: Oxford University Press, 2013.

McKeown, James. *Genesis.* Two Horizons Old Testament Commentary. Grand Rapids: Eerdmans, 2008.

McKim, Donald K., ed. *Dictionary of Major Biblical Interpreters.* Downers Grove, IL: IVP Academic, 2007.

McKnight, Scot. *The King Jesus Gospel: The Original Good News Revisited.* Grand Rapids: Zondervan 2011.

———. *Five Things Biblical Scholars Wish Theologians Knew.* Downers Grove, IL: IVP Academic, 2021.

Michaels, J. Ramsey. *1 Peter.* Word Biblical Commentary 49. Waco, TX: Word, 1988.

Miller, Ike. *Seeing By the Light: Illumination in Augustine's and Barth's Readings of John.* Downers Grove, IL: IVP Academic, 2020.

Mitchell, David C. *The Songs of Ascents: Psalms 120 to 134 in the Worship of Jerusalem's Temples.* Newton Mears, Scotland: Campbell, 2015.

Mitchell, Margaret M. *Paul, the Corinthians and the Birth of Christian Hermeneutics.* Cambridge: Cambridge University Press, 2010.

Moberly, R. W. L. *At the Mountain of God: Story and Theology in Exodus 32–34.* JSOTSuppl22. Sheffield: JSOT, 1983.

———. *The Bible, Theology, and Faith: A Study of Abraham and Jesus.* Cambridge: Cambridge University Press, 2000.

———. "Exodus." In *Dictionary for Theological Interpretation of the Bible,* edited by. Kevin J. Vanhoozer, 211–16. Grand Rapids: Baker, 2005.

———. *The Old Testament of the Old Testament: Patriarchal Narratives and Mosaic Yahwism.* Minneapolis: Fortress, 1992.

———. *Old Testament Theology: Reading the Hebrew Bible as Christian Scripture.* Grand Rapids: Baker Academic, 2013.

———. "What Is Theological Interpretation of Scripture?" *Journal of Theological Interpretation* 3, no. 2 (2009): 161–78.

Monson, John. "Contextual Criticism as a Framework for Biblical Interpretation." In *Israel: Ancient Kingdom or Late Invention?*, edited by Daniel Block, 25–55. Nashville: B&H, 2008.

Morales, Michael L. *Who Shall Ascend the Mountain of the Lord? A Biblical Theology of the Book of Leviticus*. Downers Grove, IL: InterVarsity Press, 2015.

Morgan, Christopher W., and Robert A. Peterson. *The Glory of God and Paul: Texts, Themes, and Theology*. Downers Grove, IL, 2022.

Morgan, Robert, and John Barton. *Biblical Interpretation*. Oxford: Oxford University Press, 1988.

———. "Spirit and Letter: Mapping Modern Biblical Interpretation." In *The Spirit and the Letter*, edited by Paul S. Fiddes, 47–73. New York: Bloomsbury, 2013.

Morrow, Jeffrey L. "The Politics of Biblical Interpretation: A 'Criticism of Criticism.'" *New Blackfriars* 91 (2010): 528–45.

Moscicke, Hans. "The Theological Presuppositions of Ancient Christian Exegesis: G. K. Beale and Henri de Lubac in Conversation." *Journal of Theological Interpretation* 10, no. 1 (2016): 125–43.

Moss, Candida A. "The Transfiguration: An Exercise in Markan Accommodation." *Biblical Interpretation* 12 (2004): 69–89.

Muller, Richard A. *Post-Reformation Reformed Dogmatics: The Rise and Development of Reformed Orthodoxy, ca. 1520 to ca. 1725*. 4 vols. 2nd ed. Grand Rapids: Baker Academic, 2003.

———. "Biblical Interpretation in the Sixteenth and Seventeenth Centuries." In *Dictionary of Major Biblical Interpreters*, edited by Donald K. McKim, 22–44. Downers Grove, IL: IVP Academic, 2007.

Muller, Richard A., and John L. Thompson, eds. *Biblical Interpretation in the Reformation Era*. Grand Rapids: Eerdmans, 1996.

Murdoch, Iris. *The Sovereignty of Good*. London: Routledge & Kegan Paul, 1970.

Nagel, Thomas. *The View from Nowhere*. Oxford: Oxford University Press, 1986.

Nassif, Bradley. "The 'Spiritual Exegesis' of Scripture: The School of Antioch Revisited." *Anglican Theological Review* 75, no. 4 (1993): 437–70.

———. "Antiochene *Theoria* in John Chrysostom's Exegesis." In *Exegesis and Hermeneutics in the Churches of the East*. Edited by Vahan S. Hovhanessian. New York: Peter Lang, 2009.

Nebeker, Gary L. "The Holy Spirit, Hermeneutics, and Transformation: From Present to Future Glory." *Evangelical Review of Theology* 27 (2003): 47–54.

Nes, Solrunn. *The Uncreated Light: An Iconographical Study of the Transfiguration in the Eastern Church*. Grand Rapids: Eerdmans, 2007.

Neusner, Jacob. *The Mishnah: An Introduction*. Lanham, MD: Rowman & Littlefield, 1989.

Nichols, Stephen R. C. "Jonathan Edwards' Principles of Interpreting Scripture." In *Jonathan Edwards and Scripture: Biblical Exegesis in British North America*, edited by David P. Barshinger and Douglas A. Sweeney, 32–50. Oxford: Oxford University Press, 2018.

Noble, Paul. "The *Sensus Literalis*: Jowett, Childs, and Barr." *Journal of Theological Studies* 54 (1993): 1–23.

Noll, Mark A. *Between Faith and Criticism: Evangelicals, Scholarship, and the Bible in America*. New York: Harper & Row, 1986.

———. *The Civil War as a Theological Crisis*. Chapel Hill: The University of North Carolina Press, 2006.

———. *America's Book: The Rise and Decline of a Bible Civilization, 1794–1911*. Oxford: Oxford University Press, 2022.

Nussbaum, Martha C. *Love's Knowledge: Essays on Philosophy and Literature*. Oxford: Oxford University Press, 1990.

Oberman, Heiko. *Forerunners of the Reformation: The Shape of Late Medieval Thought Illustrated by Key Documents*. Philadelphia: Fortress, 1981.

Oecolampadius, Iojannes. *An Exposition of Genesis*. Translated by Mickey L. Mattox. Milwaukee: Marquette University Press, 2013.

Ocker, Christopher. *Biblical Poetics before Humanism and Reformation*. New York: Cambridge University Press, 2002.

O'Collins, Gerald, and Mary Ann Meyers, eds. *Light from Light: Scientists and Theologians in Dialogue*. Grand Rapids: Eerdmans, 2012.

O'Keefe, John J., and R. R. Reno. *Sanctified Vision: An Introduction to Early Christian Interpretation of the Bible*. Baltimore: Johns Hopkins University Press, 2005.

Opitz, Peter. "Exegetical and Hermeneutical Work of Oecolampadius, Zwingli and Calvin." In *Hebrew Bible, Old Testament: The History of Its Interpretation*, edited byMagne Saebø, vol. 2, 407–13. Göttingen: Vandenhoeck & Ruprecht, 2008.
Origen. *Treatise on the Passover; and, Dialogue with Heraclides*. Translated by Robert J. Daly. Mahwah, NJ: Paulist, 1992.
———. *Homilies on Luke*. Translated by Joseph T. Lienhard. Washington, DC: Catholic University of America Press, 1996.
———. *On First Principles*. Translated by G. W. Butterworth. Notre Dame, IN: Ave Maria, 2013.
Ortlund, Dane C. "Christocentrism: An Asymmetrical Trinitarianism?" *Themelios* 34, no. 3 (November 2009): 309–21.
Ortlund, Gavin. *Retrieving Augustine's Doctrine of Creation: Ancient Wisdom for Current Controversy*. Downers Grove, IL: IVP Academic, 2020.
Ott, Craig, and Harold A. Netland, eds. *Globalizing Theology: Belief and Practice in an Era of World Christianity*. Grand Rapids: Baker Academic, 2006.
Overbeck, Franz. *Das Johannesevangelium: Studien zur Kritik seiner Erforschung*. Tübingen: Mohr, 1911.
Ovid. *Metamorphoses*. Translated by Charles Martin. New York: Norton, 2004.
Owen, John. "Meditations and Discourses on the Glory of Christ in His Person, Office, and Grace." In *The Works of John Owen*, vol. 1, edited by William H. Goold, 2–417. London: Johnstone and Hunter, 1850.
———. "The Causes, Ways, and Means of Understanding the Mind of God, as Revealed in His Word." In *The Reason of Faith*, 161–320. Glasgow: Falconer, 1801.
Packer, J. I. *Fundamentalism and the Word of God*. Grand Rapids: Eerdmans, 1958.
———. *The Quest for Godliness: The Puritan Vision of the Christian Life*. Wheaton, IL: Crossway, 1990.
———. *Rediscovering Holiness*. Ann Arbor, MI: Servant, 1992.
Pagels, Elaine. *The Gnostic Gospels*. New York: Random House, 1979.
Pak, G. Sujin. *The Judaizing Calvin: Sixteenth-Century Debates over the Messianic Psalms*. Oxford: Oxford University Press, 2010.
Palamas, Gregory. *The Triads*. Mahwah, NJ: Paulist, 1983.
Pardue, Stephen T. *Why Evangelical Theology Needs the Global Church*. Grand Rapids: Baker, 2023.
Parker, Brent E. "Typology and Allegory: Is There a Distinction? A Brief Examination of Figural Reading." *Southern Baptist Journal of Theology* 21, no. 1 (2017): 57–83.
Parker, T. H. L. *Calvin's Old Testament Commentaries*. Louisville: Westminster John Knox, 1993.
Parkison, Samuel E. *Irresistible Beauty: Beholding Triune Glory in the Face of Christ*. Ross-shire, UK: Mentor, 2022.
Patton, Corrine. "Creation, Fall and Salvation: Lyra's Commentary on Genesis 1–3." In *Nicholas of Lyra: The Senses of Scripture*, edited by Philip D. W. Krey and Lesley Smith, 19–43. Leiden: Brill, 2000.
Payton, James R., Jr. *Light from the Christian East: An Introduction to the Orthodox Tradition*. Downers Grove, IL: IVP Academic, 2007.
Peckham, John C. *Canonical Theology: The Biblical Canon, Sola Scriptura, and Theological Method*. Grand Rapids: Eerdmans, 2016.
Pelikan, Jaroslav. *The Light of the World*. New York: Harper, 1962.
———. *The Preaching of Chrysostom: Homilies on the Sermon on the Mount*. Philadelphia: Fortress, 1967.
———. *Interpreting the Bible and the Constitution*. New Haven, CT: Yale University Press, 2004.
Pennington, Jonathan. *Reading the Gospels Wisely: A Narrative and Theological Introduction*. Grand Rapids: Baker Academic, 2012.
Perhai, Richard J. *Antiochene Theoria in the Writings of Theodore of Mopsuestia and Theodoret of Cyrus*. Minneapolis: Fortress, 2015.
Perry, Tim, ed. *The Theology of Benedict XVI: A Protestant Appreciation*. Bellingham, WA: Lexham, 2019.
Peterson, Eugene H. *Answering God: The Psalms as Tools for Prayer*. San Francisco: Harper & Row, 1989.
———. *Eat This Book: A Conversation in the Art of Spiritual Reading*. Grand Rapids: Eerdmans, 2006.
Philemon, Leulseged. *Pneumatic Hermeneutics: The Role of the Holy Spirit in the Theological Interpretation of Scripture*. Cleveland, TN: CPT, 2019.
Philo. "On the Creation." In *The Works of Philo: Complete and Unabridged*, translated by C. D. Yonge, 1–51. Peabody, MA: Hendrickson, 1993.

Philpot, Joshua M. "Exodus 34:29–35 and Moses' Shining Face." *Bulletin for Biblical Research* 23, no. 1 (2013): 1–17.

Pickstock, Catherine. "What Shines Between: The *Metaxu* of Light." In *Between System and Poetics: William Desmond and Philosophy after Dialectic*, edited by Thomas A. F. Kelley, 107–22. New York: Routledge, 2016.

Piff, Paul K., Pia Dietze, Matthew Feinberg, Daniel M. Stancato, and Dacher Keltner. "Awe, the Small Self, and Prosocial Behavior." *Journal of Personality and Social Psychology* 108 no. 6 (2015): 883–99.

Piper, John. *Reading the Bible Supernaturally: Seeing and Savoring the Glory of God in Scripture*. Wheaton, IL: Crossway, 2017.

Pitkin, Barbara. *Calvin, the Bible, and History: Exegesis and Historical Reflection in the Era of Reform*. Oxford: Oxford University Press, 2020.

Polanyi, Michael. *Personal Knowledge: Towards a Post-Critical Philosophy*. Chicago: University of Chicago Press, 1958.

Polk, Timothy Houston. *The Biblical Kierkegaard: Reading by the Rule of Faith*. Macon, GA: Mercer University Press, 1997.

Pope, Marvin H. *Song of Songs: A New Translation with Introduction and Commentary*. Anchor Bible 7C. Garden City, NY: Doubleday, 1977.

Porter, Stanley E., ed. *Dictionary of Biblical Criticism and Interpretation*. New York: Routledge, 2007.

Porter, Stanley E., and Matthew R. Malcolm, eds. *The Future of Biblical Interpretation: Responsible Plurality in Biblical Hermeneutics*. Downers Grove, IL: IVP Academic, 2013.

Powell, Mark Allen, ed. *Methods for Matthew*. Cambridge: Cambridge University Press, 2009.

Poythress, Vern. "Divine Meaning of Scripture." *Westminster Theological Journal* 48 (1986): 241–79.

———. "Typology and Christocentricity in the Hermeneutics of Johannes Oecolampadius." *Westminster Theological Journal* 81 (2019): 295–304.

———. *Interpreting Eden: A Guide to Faithfully Reading and Understanding Genesis 1–3*. Wheaton, IL: Crossway, 2019.

———. *The Mystery of the Trinity: A Trinitarian Approach to the Attributes of God*. Phillipsburg, NJ: P&R, 2020.

Preus, James Samuel. *From Shadow to Promise: Old Testament Interpretation from Augustine to the Young Luther*. Cambridge, MA: Belknap, 1969.

Principe, Lawrence M. *Scientific Revolution: A Very Short Introduction*. Oxford: Oxford University Press, 2011.

Prior, Karen Swallow. *On Reading Well: Finding the Good Life through the Great Books*. Grand Rapids: Brazos, 2018.

Propp, William H. "The Skin of Moses' Face–Transfigured or Disfigured?" *Catholic Biblical Quarterly* 49 (1987) 375–86.

Provan, Iain. *The Reformation and the Right Reading of Scripture*. Waco, TX: Baylor University Press, 2017.

Provence, Thomas E. "'Who Is Sufficient for These Things?' An Exegesis of 2 Corinthians ii.14-iii.18." *Novum Testamentum* 24, no. 1 (1982): 54–81.

Puckett, David L. *John Calvin's Exegesis of the Old Testament*. Louisville: Westminster John Knox, 1995.

Putman, Rhyne R. *When Doctrine Divides: An Evangelical Approach to Theological Diversity*. Wheaton, IL: Crossway, 2020.

Pyle, William T. "Understanding the Misunderstanding Sequences in the Gospel of John." *Faith & Mission* 11 no. 2 (1994): 26–47.

Pyper, Hugh S. *The Joy of Kierkegaard: Essays on Kierkegaard as a Biblical Reader*. New York: Routledge, 2011.

Rad, Gerhard von. "Typological Interpretation of the Old Testament." *Interpretation* 15 (1961): 174–92.

———. *Genesis: A Commentary*. Old Testament Library. Rev. ed. Louisville: Westminster John Knox, 1973.

Radner, Ephraim. *Time and the Word: Figural Reading of the Christian Scriptures*. Grand Rapids: Eerdmans, 2016.

———. "'I Contain Multitudes': The Divine Basis for the Theological Interpretation of Scripture." *Pro Ecclesia* 31, no. 2 (2022); 142–59.

Radner, Ephraim, and David Ney, eds. *All Thy Lights Combine: Figural Reading in the Anglican Tradition*. Bellingham, WA: Lexham, 2022.

Ragui, Taimaya. *Confessing Community: An Entryway to Theological Interpretation in North East India.* Minneapolis: Fortress, 2023.

Rakove, Jack N. *Original Meanings: Politics and Ideas in the Making of the Constitution.* New York: Vintage, 1996.

Ramm, Bernard. *Protestant Biblical Interpretation.* 3rd ed. Grand Rapids: Baker, 1970.

Ramsey, Arthur Michael. *The Glory of God and the Transfiguration of Christ.* Eugene, OR: Wipf & Stock, 2009.

Rasmussen, Joel D. S. "Kierkegaard the Reader of Scripture." In *T&T Clark Companion to the Theology of Kierkegaard,* edited by Aaron P. Edwards and David J. Gouwens, 111–38. New York: T&T Clark, 2020.

Ratzinger, Joseph. "Biblical Interpretation in Crisis: On the Question of the Foundations and Approaches of Exegesis Today." In *Biblical Interpretation in Crisis: The Ratzinger Conference on Bible and Church,* edited by Richard John Neuhaus, 1–23. Grand Rapids: Eerdmans, 1989.

Reese, Ruth Anne. *2 Peter and Jude.* Two Horizons Commentary. Grand Rapids: Eerdmans, 2007.

Reno, R. R. *The End of Interpretation: Reclaiming the Priority of Ecclesial Exegesis.* Grand Rapids: Baker Academic, 2022.

Reynolds, Benjamin E., and Loren T. Stuckenbruck, eds. *The Jewish Apocalyptic Tradition and the Shape of New Testament Thought.* Minneapolis: Fortress, 2017.

Ribbens, Benjamin J. "Typology of Types: Typology in Dialogue." *Journal of Theological Interpretation* 5, no. 1 (2011): 81–96.

———. "Hebrews as Participatory Exegesis." *Journal of Theological Interpretation* 15, no. 1 (2021): 101–20.

Richards, E. Randolph, and Brandon J. O'Brien. *Misreading Scripture with Western Eyes: Removing Cultural Blinders to Better Understand the Bible.* Downers Grove, IL: IVP Books, 2012.

Ricoeur, Paul. *The Symbolism of Evil.* Boston: Beacon, 1969.

———. *The Conflict of Interpretations: Essays in Hermeneutics.* Edited by D. Ihde. Evanston, IL: Northwestern University Press, 1974.

———. *Hermeneutics and the Human Sciences: Essays on Language, Action, and Interpretation.* Cambridge: Cambridge University Press, 1981.

———. *Time and Narrative.* Vol. 3. Translated by Kathleen Blamey and David Pellauer. Chicago: University of Chicago Press, 1988.

Riga, Peter. "Signs of Glory: The Use of '*Semeion*' in St. John's Gospel." *Interpretation* 17, no. 4 (1963): 402–24.

Robertson, Duncan. *Lectio Divina: The Medieval Experience of Reading.* Collegeville, MN: Liturgical, 2011.

Rogerson, J. W., and Judith M. Lieu, eds. *Oxford Handbook of Biblical Studies.* Oxford: Oxford University Press, 2008.

Rorem, Paul. *Hugh of Saint Victor.* Oxford: Oxford University Press, 2009.

Rosemann, Philipp W. *The Story of a Great Medieval Book: Peter Lombard's Sentences.* University of Toronto Press, 2013.

Ross, Hugh. *Navigating Genesis: A Scientist's Journey through Genesis 1–11.* Covina, CA: RTB Press, 2014.

Rowe, C. Kavin. "Biblical Pressure and Trinitarian Hermeneutics." *Pro Ecclesia* 11, no. 3 (2002): 295–312.

Rowe, C. Kavin, and Richard Hays. "Biblical Studies." In *Oxford Handbook of Systematic Theology,* edited by John Webster, Kathryn Tanner, and Iain Torrance, 435–55. Oxford: Oxford University Press, 2007.

Rowland, Christopher. *The Open Heaven: A Study of Apocalyptic in Judaism and Early Christianity.* New York: Crossroad, 1982.

Ryken, Leland, James C. Wilhoit, and Tremper Longman III, eds. *Dictionary of Biblical Imagery.* Downers Grove, IL: InterVarsity Press, 1998.

Sanders, Seth L. "Old Light on Moses' Shining Face." *Vetus Testamentum* 52, no. 3 (2002): 400–407.

Salkeld, Brett. *Transubstantiation: Theology, History, and Christian Unity.* Grand Rapids: Baker Academic, 2019.

Sandys-Wunsch, John, and Laurence Eldredge. "J. P. Gabler and the Distinction between Biblical and Dogmatic Theology: Translation, Commentary, and Discussion of His Originality." *Scottish Journal of Theology* 33 (1980): 133–58.

Sanders, Fred. *The Triune God.* Grand Rapids: Zondervan, 2016.

Saner, Andrea D. *"Too Much to Grasp": Exodus 3:13–16 and the Reality of God.* Journal of Theological Interpretation Supplements 11. Winona Lake, IN: Eisenbrauns, 2015.

Sargent, Benjamin. "One Meaning or Many? A Study in New Testament Interpretation of Old Testament Texts." *Churchman* 124 no. 4 (2010): 357–65.

———. *Written to Serve: The Use of Scripture in 1 Peter.* New York: Bloomsbury T&T Clark, 2015.

———. *Written for Our Learning: The Single Meaning of Scripture in Christian Theology.* Eugene, OR: Cascade, 2016.

Sarisky, Darren. *Reading the Bible Theologically.* Cambridge: Cambridge University Press, 2019.

———. *Scriptural Interpretation: A Theological Exploration.* Malden, MA: Wiley-Blackwell, 2012.

Savage, Timothy B. *Power through Weakness: Paul's Understanding of the Christian Ministry in 2 Corinthians.* Society for New Testament Studies Monograph Series. Cambridge: Cambridge University Press, 1996.

Scalise, Charles J. *Hermeneutics as Theological Prolegomenon: A Canonical Approach.* Macon, GA: Mercer University Press, 1994.

Schaff, Philip. "Calvin as a Commentator." *Presbyterian and Reformed Review* 3 (1892): 462–69.

Schellenberg, Annette, and Ludger Schwienhorst-Schönberger, eds. *Interpreting the Song of Songs: Literal or Allegorical?* Leuven: Peeters, 2016.

Schneider, Bernardin. "The Meaning of St. Paul's Antithesis 'The Letter and the Spirit.'" *Catholic Biblical Quarterly* 15 (1953): 163–207.

Schneiders, Sandra. *The Revelatory Text: Interpreting the New Testament as Sacred Scripture.* 2nd ed. Collegeville, MN: Liturgical, 1999.

Schenck, Kenneth. *A Brief Guide to Philo.* Louisville: Westminster John Knox, 2005.

Schindler, D. C. *Freedom from Reality: The Diabolical Character of Modern Liberty.* Notre Dame, IN: University of Notre Dame Press, 2017.

Schleiermacher, Friedrich. *The Christian Faith.* Edinburgh: T&T Clark, 1928.

Schreiner, Patrick. *The Transfiguration of Christ: An Exegetical and Theological Reading.* Grand Rapids: Baker Academic, 2024.

Schreiner, Thomas. *Paul, Apostle of God's Glory in Christ: A Pauline Theology.* 2nd ed. Downers Grove, IL: IVP Academic, 2020.

Schumacher, Lydia. *Divine Illumination: The History and Future of Augustine's Theory of Knowledge.* Oxford: Wiley-Blackwell, 2011.

Seifrid, Mark A. *The Second Letter to the Corinthians.* Pillar New Testament Commentary. Grand Rapids: Eerdmans, 2014.

Seitz, Christopher. *Figured Out: Typology and Providence in Christian Scripture.* Louisville: Westminster John Knox, 2001.

———. *Prophecy and Hermeneutics: Toward a New Introduction to the Prophets.* Grand Rapids: Baker, 2007.

———. *Convergences: Canon and Catholicity.* Waco, TX: Baylor University Press, 2020.

———. *The Elder Testament: Canon, Theology, Trinity.* Waco, TX: Baylor University Press, 2021.

Seters, John van. *In Search of History: Historiography in the Ancient World and the Origins of Biblical History.* New Haven, CT: Yale University Press, 1983.

Shead, Andrew H. *A Mouth Full of Fire: The Word of God in the Words of Jeremiah.* Downers Grove, IL: InterVarsity Press, 2012.

Sheridan, Mark. "Jacob and Israel: A Contribution to the History of an Interpretation." In *From Nile to the Rhone and Beyond: Studies in Early Monastic Literature and Scriptural Interpretation,* 315–34. Rome: Pontificio Ateneo Sant'Anselmo, 2012.

Sibbes, Richard. "A Description of Christ." In *The Works of Richard Sibbes.* Edinburgh: James Nichol, 1862–64.

Silva, Moises, ed. *New International Dictionary of New Testament Theology and Exegesis.* 2nd ed. Grand Rapids: Zondervan, 2014.

Skillen, James W. "Reengaging Figural Interpretation: The Impact of Erich Auerbach." *Calvin Theological Journal* 52, no. 2 (2017): 181–203.

Smail, Thomas A. *Reflected Glory: The Spirit in Christ and Christians.* London: Hodder and Stoughton, 1975.

Smalley, Beryl. *The Study of the Bible in the Middle Ages.* Oxford: Basil Blackwell, 1952.

Smit, Peter-Ben, and Klaas Spronk. "Contextual Biblical Interpretation: A Theological Necessity." *Concilium* 58, no. 3 (2022): 15–24.

Smith, Brandon D. *Taught by God: Ancient Hermeneutics for the Modern Church*. Brentwood, TN: B&H Academic, 2024.

Smith, Mark. *The Priestly Vision of Genesis 1*. Minneapolis: Fortress, 2010.

Snow, C. P. *The Two Cultures*. Cambridge: Cambridge University Press, 1993.

Soskice, Janet. "Why *Creatio ex nihilo* for Theology Today?" In *Creation* ex nihilo: *Origins, Development, Contemporary Challenges*, edited by Gary A. Anderson and Markus Bockmuehl, 37–54. Notre Dame, IN: Notre Dame University Press, 2018.

Soulen, Richard N., and R. Kendall Soulen. *Handbook of Biblical Criticism*. 4th ed. Louisville: Westminster John Knox, 2011.

Sparks, Kenton. "Genesis 1–11 as Ancient Historiography." In *Genesis: History, Fiction, or Neither? Three Views on the Bible's Earliest Chapters*, edited by Charles Halton, 110–39. Grand Rapids: Zondervan, 2015.

Spawn, Kevin L., and Archie T. Wright, eds. *Spirit and Scripture: Examining a Pneumatic Hermeneutic*. New York: T&T Clark International, 2012.

Spellman, Ched. *Toward a Canon-Conscious Reading of the Bible: Exploring the History and Hermeneutics of the Canon*. Sheffield: Sheffield Phoenix Press, 2014.

Spellman, Ched, and Jason K. Lee, eds. *The Seminary as a Textual Community: Exploring John Sailhamer's Vision for Theological Education*. Dallas: Fontes, 2021.

Spinks, Christopher D. *The Bible and the Crisis of Meaning: Debates on the Theological Interpretation of Scripture*. New York: T&T Clark, 2007.

Sperber, Dan, and Deirdre Wilson. "Pragmatics." In *The Oxford Handbook of Contemporary Philosophy*, edited by Frank Jackson and Michael Smith, 468–95. Oxford: Oxford University Press, 2007.

Spinoza, Baruch. *Theological-Political Treatise*. Cambridge: Cambridge University Press, 2007.

Springs, Jason A. *Toward a Generous Orthodoxy: Prospects for Hans Frei's Postliberal Theology*. Eugene, OR: Wipf & Stock, 2016.

Spurgeon, C. H. *The Most Holy Place: Sermons on the Song of Solomon*. Ross-shire, Scotland: Christian Focus, 1996.

Stanglin, Keith D. *The Letter and Spirit of Biblical Interpretation: From the Early Church to Modern Practice*. Grand Rapids: Baker Academic, 2018.

Starling, David I. *Hermeneutics as Apprenticeship: How the Bible Shapes our Habits and Practices*. Grand Rapids: Baker Academic, 2016.

Steele, Richard B. "Transfiguring Light: The Moral Beauty of the Christian Life According to Gregory Palamas and Jonathan Edwards." *St. Vladimir's Theological Quarterly* 52 (2008): 403–39.

Steiner, George. *On Difficulty and Other Essays*. Oxford: Oxford University Press, 1978.

Steinmetz, David C. "The Superiority of Pre-Critical Exegesis." *Theology Today* 37 (1980): 27–38.

———. "Divided by a Common Past: The Reshaping of the Christian Exegetical Tradition in the Sixteenth Century." *Journal of Medieval and Early Modern Studies* 27 (Spring 1997): 245–64.

Stendahl, Krister. "Biblical Theology, Contemporary." *Interpreter's Dictionary of the Bible*, edited by George Arthur Buttrick, vol. 1, 418–32. New York: Abingdon, 1962.

Sternberg, Meir. *The Poetics of Biblical Narrative: Ideological Literature and the Drama of Reading*. Bloomington: Indiana University Press, 1985.

Stevenson, Kenneth. "From Hilary of Poitiers to Peter of Blois: A Transfiguration Journey of Biblical Interpretation." *Scottish Journal of Theology* 61 no. 3 (2008): 288–306.

Stock, Brian. *Augustine the Reader: Meditation, Self-Knowledge, and the Ethics of Interpretation*. Cambridge, MA: Belknap, 1996.

Storer, Kevin. "Theological Interpretation and the Spiritual Sense of Scripture: Henri de Lubac's Retrieval of a Christological Hermeneutic of Presence." *Journal of Theological Interpretation* 7, no. 1 (2013): 79–96.

———. *Reading Scripture with Kierkegaard: Kierkegaard's Upbuilding Hermeneutic of Scripture in the Discourses*. Frankfurt: Peter Lang, 2022.

Strawn, Brent A. *The Old Testament Is Dying: A Diagnosis and Recommended Treatment*. Grand Rapids: Baker Academic, 2017.

Sugirtharajah, R. S. *Postcolonial Criticism and Biblical Interpretation*. Oxford: Oxford University Press, 2002.

Sugirtharajah, R. S., ed. *Exploring Postcolonial Biblical Criticism: History, Method, Practice*. Oxford: Wiley-Blackwell, 2011.
Sun, Chloe T. *Conspicuous in His Absence: Studies in the Song of Songs and Esther*. Downers Grove, IL: IVP Academic, 2021.
Swain, Scott R. *Trinity, Revelation, and Reading: A Theological Introduction to the Bible and Its Interpretation*. New York: T&T Clark, 2011.
Sweeney, Douglas A. *Edwards the Exegete: Biblical Interpretation and Anglo-Protestant Culture on the Edge of the Enlightenment*. Oxford: Oxford University Press, 2016.
Swinburne, Richard. *Revelation: From Metaphor to Analogy*. 2nd ed. Oxford: Oxford University Press, 2007.
Tabb, Brian H. *All Things New: Revelation as Canonical Capstone*. Downers Grove, IL: IVP Academic, 2019.
Tabb, Brian H., and Andrew M. King, eds. *Five Views of Christ in the Old Testament*. Grand Rapids: Zondervan, 2022.
Tanner, Kathryn. "Theology and the Plain Sense." In *Scriptural Authority and Narrative Interpretation*, edited by Garrett Green, 59–78. Philadelphia: Fortress, 1987.
Tate, W. Randolph. *Biblical Interpretation: An Integrated Approach*. Rev. ed. Peabody, MA: Hendrickson, 1997.
Taylor, Charles. *A Secular Age*. Cambridge, MA: Belknap, 2007.
———. *The Language Animal: The Full Shape of the Human Linguistic Capacity*. Cambridge, MA: Belknap, 2016.
Taylor, Derek W. *Reading Scripture as the Church: Dietrich Bonhoeffer's Hermeneutic of Discipleship*. Downers Grove, IL: IVP Academic, 2020.
Thatcher, Adrian. "The Literal Sense of Scripture: A Hermeneutical Disaster." *Modern Believing* 53, no. 1 (2012): 5–12.
Theodore of Mopsuestia. *Commentary on the Minor Pauline Epistles*. Translated by Rowan A. Greer. Atlanta: SBL, 2010.
Thiessen, Gerd. *The Miracle Stories of the Early Christian Tradition*. Edinburgh: T&T Clark, 1983.
Thiselton, Anthony C. *Hermeneutics: An Introduction*. Grand Rapids: Eerdmans, 2009.
———. *Promise and Prayer: The Biblical Writings in the Light of Speech-Act Theory*. Eugene, OR: Cascade, 2020.
Thomas, Benjamin. *An Anglican Hermeneutic of the Transfiguration*. New York: Peter Lang, 2013.
Thompson, J. W. *The Beginnings of Christian Philosophy: The Epistle to the Hebrews*. Washington, DC: Catholic Biblical Association of America, 1982.
Thompson, Thomas L. *The Historicity of the Patriarchal Narratives: The Quest for the Historical Adam*. Harrisburg, PA: Trinity Press International, 2002.
Tillich, Paul. *Systematic Theology*. Vol. 1. Chicago: University of Chicago Press, 1951.
———. *Biblical Religion and the Search for Ultimate Reality*. Chicago: University of Chicago Press, 1955.
Torjesen, Karen J. *Hermeneutical Procedure and Theological Method in Origen's Exegesis*. Berlin: de Gruyter, 1985.
Torrance, Andrew. "A Kierkegaardian Guide to Reading Scripture." *New Blackfriars* 97, no. 1071 (September 2016): 624–39.
Torrance, Andrew, and Thomas H. McCall, eds. *Knowing Creation: Perspectives from Theology, Philosophy, and Science*. Grand Rapids; Zondervan, 2018.
Torrance, Thomas F. *Divine Meaning: Studies in Patristic Hermeneutics*. Edinburgh: T&T Clark, 1995.
Tracy, David. "Literary Theory and the Return of the Forms for Naming and Thinking God in Theology." *Journal of Religion* 74 (1994): 302–19.
———. *On Naming the Present: God, Hermeneutics, and Church*. Maryknoll, NY: Orbis, 1994.
Treier, Daniel J. *Introducing Theological Interpretation of Scripture: Recovering a Christian Practice*. Grand Rapids: Baker Academic, 2008.
———. "*Heavenly Participation*: The Weaving of a Sacramental Tapestry—A Review Essay." *Christian Scholar's Review* 41 (2011): 67–71.
———. "Keeping Time: Human Finitude and Figural Interpretation." *Pro Ecclesia* 27, no. 3 (2018): 289–99.
———. "'Christian Platonism' and Christological Interpretation." *Reformed Faith & Practice* 5, no. 3 (2020): 40–54.

Treier, Daniel J., and Douglas A. Sweeney, eds. *Hearing and Doing the Word: The Drama of Evangelical Hermeneutics*. New York: T&T Clark, 2021.
Trigg, Joseph Wilson. *Origen: The Bible and Philosophy in the Third-Century Church*. Atlanta: John Knox, 1983.
Trites, Allison A. "The Transfiguration of Jesus: the Gospel in Microcosm." *Evangelical Quarterly* 51, no. 2 (1979): 67–79.
———. *The Transfiguration of Christ: A Hinge of Holy History*. Hantsport, Nova Scotia: Lancelot, 1994.
Trible, Phyllis. *Texts of Terror: Literary-Feminist Readings of Biblical Narratives*. 40th anniversary ed. Minneapolis: Fortress, 2022.
Troeltsch, Ernst. *The Social Teaching of the Christian Churches*. 2 vols. New York: Harper Row, 1960.
Tsai, Lee-Chen A. "The Development of Luther's Hermeneutics in His Commentaries on the Psalms." PhD diss., University of Aberdeen, 1989.
Turner, James. *Philology: The Forgotten Origins of the Modern Humanities*. Princeton, NJ: Princeton University Press, 2014.
Uusimäki, Elisa. "A Mind in Training: Philo of Alexandria on Jacob's Spiritual Exercises." *Journal for the Study of the Pseudepigrapha* 27, no. 4 (2018): 265–88.
Valdés, Mario J., ed. *A Ricoeur Reader: Reflection & Imagination*. New York: Harvester Wheatsheaf, 1991.
Vanhoozer, Kevin J. "Ascending the Mountain, Singing the Rock: Biblical Interpretation Earthed, Typed, and Transfigured." *Modern Theology* 20, no. 4 (2012): 781–803.
———. "The Apostolic Discourse and its Developments." In *Scripture's Doctrine and Theology's Bible: Studies in the New Testament's Normativity for Christian Dogmatics*, edited by Markus Bockmuehl and Alan Torrance, 191–207. Grand Rapids: Baker, 2008.
———. *Biblical Authority after Babel: Retrieving the Solas in the Spirit of Mere Protestant Christianity*. Grand Rapids: Brazos, 2016.
———. *Biblical Narrative in the Philosophy of Paul Ricoeur: An Essay in Hermeneutics and Theology*. Cambridge: Cambridge University Press, 1990.
———. "Expounding the Word of the Lord: Joseph Ratzinger on Revelation, Tradition, and Biblical Interpretation." In *The Theology of Benedict XVI: A Protestant Appreciation*, edited by Tim Perry, 66–86. Bellingham, WA: Lexham, 2019.
———. "Holy Scripture." In *Christian Dogmatics: Reformed Theology for the Church Catholic*, edited by Scott Swain and Michael Allen, 30–56. Grand Rapids: Zondervan, 2016.
———. "Holy Scripture." In *The New Cambridge Companion to Christian Doctrine*, edited by Michael Allen, 119–38. Cambridge: Cambridge University Press, 2023.
———. *Is There a Meaning in This Text? The Bible, the Reader, and the Morality of Literary Knowledge*. Grand Rapids: Zondervan, 1998.
———. "The Origin of Paul's Soteriology: Election, Incarnation, and Union with Christ in Ephesians 1:4 (with Special Reference to Evangelical Calvinism)." In *Reconsidering the Relationship between Biblical and Systematic Theology in the New Testament*, edited by Benjamin E. Reynolds, Brian Lugioyo, and Kevin J. Vanhoozer, 177–212. Tübingen: Mohr Siebeck, 2014.
———. *Pictures at a Theological Exhibition: Scenes of the Church's Worship, Witness, and Wisdom*. Downers Grove, IL: IVP Academic, 2016.
———. "The Reader in New Testament Study." In *Hearing the New Testament: Strategies for Interpretation*, edited by Joel B. Green, 2nd ed., 301–28. Grand Rapids: Eerdmans, 2010.
———. *Remythologizing Theology: Divine Action, Passion, and Authorship*. Cambridge: Cambridge University Press, 2012.
———. "The Spirit of Light after the Age of Enlightenment: Renewing/Reforming Pneumatic Hermeneutics via the Economy of Illumination." In *Spirit of God: Christian Renewal in the Community of Faith*, edited by Jeffrey Barbeau and Beth Felker Jones, 149–67. Downers Grove, IL: InterVarsity Press, 2015.
———. "Staurology, Ontology, and the Travail of Biblical Narrative: Once More unto the Biblical Theological Breach," *Southern Baptist Journal of Theology* 23, no. 2 (2019): 7–33.
———. "T. F. Torrance: Christ the Key to Creation and Theological Science." In *Science and the Doctrine of Creation*, edited by Geoffrey H. Fulkerson and Joel Thomas Chopp, 121–47. Downers Grove, IL: IVP Academic, 2021.

———. "Theological Commentary and the 'Voice from Heaven': Exegesis, Ontology, and the Travail of Biblical Interpretation." In *On the Writing of New Testament Commentaries*, edited by Stanley E. Porter and Eckhard J. Schnabel, 269–98. Leiden: Brill, 2013.

———. "Triune Discourse: Theological Reflections on the Claim that God Speaks." In *Trinitarian Theology for the Church: Scripture, Community, Worship*, edited by David Lauber and Daniel Treier, 25–78. Downers Grove, IL: InterVarsity, 2009.

Vanhoozer, Kevin J., ed. *Dictionary for Theological Interpretation of the Bible*. Grand Rapids: Baker Academic, 2005.

Vanhoozer, Kevin J., and Daniel J. Treier. *Theology and the Mirror of Scripture: A Mere Evangelical Account*. Downers Grove: IL: IVP Academic, 2015.

Vanhoozer, Kevin J., and Owen Strachan. *The Pastor as Public Theologian: Recovering a Lost Vision*. Grand Rapids: Baker Academic, 2015.

Van Unnik, W. C. "'With Unveiled Face,' An Exegesis of 2 Corinthians iii:12–18," *Novum Testamentum* 6 (1963): 153–69.

Venard, Olivier-Thomas, ed. *Le sens littéral des Écritures*. Paris: Cerf, 2009.

Vincent, Gilbert. *Exigence éthique et interprétation dans l'oeuvre de Calvin*. Geneva: Labor et Fides, 1984.

Volf, Miroslav. *Captive to the Word of God: Engaging the Scriptures for Contemporary Theological Reflection*. Grand Rapids: Eerdmans, 2010.

———. *Exclusion and Embrace: A Theological Exploration of Identity, Otherness, and Reconciliation*. Rev. ed. Nashville: Abingdon, 2019.

Wacker, Grant. "The Demise of Biblical Civilization." In *The Bible in America: Essays in Cultural History*, edited by Nathan O. Hatch and Mark A. Noll, 121–38. Oxford: Oxford University Press, 1982.

Wallace, Daniel B. *Greek Grammar Beyond the Basics: An Exegetical Syntax of the New Testament*. Grand Rapids: Zondervan, 1996.

Walls, Andrew F. *The Missionary Movement in Christian History: Studies in the Transmission of Faith*. Maryknoll, NY: Orbis, 1996.

Waltke, Bruce K. *Genesis: A Commentary*. Grand Rapids: Zondervan, 2001.

Waltke, Bruce K., and Fred Zaspel. *How to Read and Understand the Psalms*. Wheaton, IL: Crossway, 2023.

Walton, John H. *The Lost World of Genesis One: Ancient Cosmology and the Origins Debate*. Downers Grove, IL: IVP Academic, 2009.

———. *Ancient Near Eastern Thought and the Old Testament: Introducing the Conceptual World of the Hebrew Bible*. 2nd ed. Grand Rapids: Baker Academic, 2018.

Walton, Jonathan L. *A Lens of Love: Reading the Bible from Its World for Our World*. Louisville: Westminster John Knox, 2018.

Wand, J. W. C. *Transfiguration*. London: Faith, 1967.

Ward, Timothy. *Words of Life: Scripture as the Living and Active Word of God*. Downers Grove, IL: IVP Academic, 2009.

Warfield, B. B. "Inspiration." In *The International Standard Bible Encyclopedia*, edited by James Orr, vol. 3, 1473–83. Chicago: Howard-Severance, 1915.

———. *Biblical and Theological Studies*. Philadelphia: Presbyterian and Reformed, 1952.

Watson, Bruce. *Light: A Radiant History from Creation to the Quantum Age*. New York: Bloomsbury, 2016.

Watson, Francis. "Hermeneutics and the Doctrine of Scripture: Why They Need Each Other." *International Journal of Systematic Theology* 12, no. 2 (2010): 118–43.

Webster, John. *Confessing God: Essays in Christian Dogmatics II*. London: T&T Clark, 2005.

———. *The Culture of Theology*. Grand Rapids: Baker Academic, 2019.

———. *The Domain of the Word: Scripture and Theological Reason*. London: T&T Clark, 2012.

———. "Editorial." *International Journal of Systematic Theology* 14 no. 4 (2012): 379–80.

———. *Holy Scripture: A Dogmatic Sketch*. Cambridge: Cambridge University Press, 2003.

———. *Word and Church: Essays in Christian Dogmatics*. Edinburgh & New York: T&T Clark, 2001.

Wedderburn, Alexander. *Heaven upon Earth, or, The History of the Transfiguration of Jesus Christ Opened, and Practically Improven in Several Sermons*. Edinburgh: Reid, 1703.

Weinandy, Thomas G. *Jesus Becoming Jesus: A Theological Interpretation of the Synoptic Gospels*. Washington, DC: Catholic University of America Press, 2018.

Weinfeld, Moshe. "Jeremiah and the Spiritual Metamorphosis of Israel." *Zeitschrift für die alttertestamentliche Wissenschaft* 88, no. 1 (1976): 17–56.

Wellhausen, Julius. *Das Evangelium Marci: Übersetzt und erklärt*. 2nd ed. Berlin: Reimer, 1909.
Wengert, Timothy J. *Word of Life: Introducing Lutheran Hermeneutics*. Minneapolis: Fortress, 2019.
Wenham, Gordon J. *Genesis 1–15*. Word Biblical Commentary. Vol. 1 Nashville: Thomas Nelson, 1987.
———. *Genesis 16–50*. Word Biblical Commentary. Grand Rapids: Zondervan, 2015.
Wenkel, David H. *Shining Like the Sun: A Biblical Theology of Meeting God Face to Face*. Wooster, OH: Weaver, 2016.
Wesley, John. *The Works of John Wesley*. Vol. 1. Nashville: Abingdon, 1984.
Westerholm, Stephen. "Letter and Spirit: The Foundation of Pauline Ethics." *New Testament Studies* 30 (1984): 220–48.
Westphal, Merold. "On Reading God the Author." *Religious Studies* 37 (2001): 271–91.
———. "Transfiguration as Saturated Phenomenon." *Journal of Philosophy & Scripture* 1, no. 1 (Fall 2003): 26–35.
White, Thomas Joseph. *Exodus*. Brazos Theological Commentary on the Bible. Grand Rapids: Brazos, 2016.
Williams, Rowan. "The Literal Sense of Scripture." *Modern Theology* 7 (1990): 121–34.
———. *Looking East in Winter: Contemporary Thought and the Eastern Christian Tradition*. New York: Bloomsbury Continuum, 2021.
Williams, Stephen. "The Transfiguration of Jesus Christ (Part 1)." *Themelios* 28, no. 1 (Autumn 2002): 13–25.
———. "The Transfiguration of Jesus Christ (Part 2): Approaching Sonship." *Themelios* 28, no. 2 (Spring 2003): 16–27.
Witherington, Ben, III. "Transfigured Understanding: A Critical Note on Mark 9:2–13 as a Parousia Preview." *Anglican Theological Journal* (1992): 88–91.
Wood, Arthur S. *Luther's Principles of Biblical Interpretation*. London: Tyndale, 1960.
Woudenberg, René van. *The Epistemology of Reading and Interpretation*. Cambridge: Cambridge University Press, 2021.
Wright, William M., IV. "The Literal Sense of Scripture according to Henri de Lubac: Insights from Patristic Exegesis of the Transfiguration." *Modern Theology* 28, no. 2 (2012): 252–77.
Wright. N. T. *Justification: God's Plan & Paul's Vision*. Downers Grove, IL: InterVarsity Press, 2009.
———. "Historical Paul and 'Systematic Theology': To Start a Discussion." In *Biblical Theology: Past, Present, and Future*. Edited by Carey Walsh and Mark W. Elliott. Eugene, OR: Cascade, 2016.
———. "Responding to Exile." In *Exile: A Conversation with N. T. Wright*. Edited by James M. Scott. Downers Grove, IL: IVP Academic, 2017.
Yarbrough, Robert. "Should Evangelicals Embrace Historical Criticism? The Hays-Ansberry Proposal." *Themelios* 39 (2014): 37–52.
Yeago, David S. "The NT and the Nicene Dogma: A Contribution to the Recovery of Theological Exegesis." *Pro Ecclesia* 3 (1994):152–64.
Yeo, Ray S. *Renewing Spiritual Perception with Jonathan Edwards: Contemporary Philosophy and the Theological Psychology of Transforming Grace*. New York: Routledge, 2016.
Yoffie, Adina Miriam. "Biblical Literalism and Scholarship in Protestant Northern Europe, 1630–1700." PhD diss. Harvard University, 2009.
Yong, Amos. *Spirit-Word-Community: Theological Hermeneutics in Trinitarian Perspective*. Burlington, VT: Ashgate, 2002.
———. "The Hermeneutical Trialectic: Notes Toward a Consensual Hermeneutic and Theological Method." *Heythrop Journal* 45 (2004): 22–39.
Yovel, Jonathan. "The Creation of Language and Language without Time: Metaphysics and Metapragmatics in Genesis 1." *Biblical Interpretation* 20 (2012): 205–25.
Young, Frances M. *Biblical Exegesis and the Formation of Christian Culture*. Cambridge: Cambridge University Press, 1997.
Zachmann, Randall C. "Calvin as Analogical Theologian." *Scottish Journal of Theology* 51, no. 2 (1998): 162–87.
———. *John Calvin as Teacher, Pastor, and Theologian: The Shape Of His Writings and Thought*. Grand Rapids: Baker Academic, 2006.
Zinn, Grover. "The Augustinian Tradition of Sacred and Secular Reading Revised." In *Reading and Wisdom: The De doctrina christiana of Augustine in the Middle Ages*, edited by Edward English, 61–83. Notre Dame, IN: University of Notre Dame Press, 1995.

Glossary

allegory: In this work, a figural interpretation that means "other" (Gk. *allos*) than what is said, and which therefore goes beyond the literal sense thanks to reading with a frame of reference taken from somewhere other than the biblical text itself (e.g., Neoplatonism; existentialism)

analogia corporis: the idea that there is an analogy between Christology and the literal sense, specifically, between what happens to Jesus' body in the Transfiguration and what happens to the letter of the biblical text when read theologically

beatific lection: describes a theological reading that beholds Christ (and the glory of God in his radiant face) and begets Christlikeness

christoscopic: shorthand for any approach to interpretation that views the Bible's ultimate aim or purpose (Gk. *skopos*) to be communicating Christ

close canonical reading: an approach to understanding the Bible that reads each text in the context of the entire biblical canon, attending both to the text's distinctive contribution and to its place in the overarching narrative

discourse: what someone says/writes about something to someone at some time, in some way, for some purpose

economy of light: the process by which the triune God shares the light he is in himself (i.e., his self-knowledge) with his covenant people; the ordered way God makes himself known by the Father shining his light (i.e., revealing himself) through the Son by the Spirit

figure: in this work, more than a figure of speech; a means of speaking of one thing in terms of something else; the result of a divine intention to establish a correspondence relation between two or more things, persons or events, such that the earlier thing betokens the later

frame of reference: the set of assumptions—political (e.g., feminist, postcolonial), critical (e.g., source, form, redaction), or confessional (e.g., Lutheran; Reformed; Roman Catholic)—that influences or determines what one thinks the text is about; the set of assumptions that conditions the readers' perception of the literal sense

framework of understanding: a way of ordering and coordinating various frames of reference by privileging a particular story, picture, or conceptual scheme (e.g., naturalism; supernaturalism; Christian Platonism); an interpretive framework; in this book, the economy of light, whose key is Jesus' Transfiguration

grammatical-eschatological exegesis: a way of reading for the trans-figural sense of Scripture, combining a grammatical interest in the way the words go (literal sense) with an eschatological interest in that to which they ultimately refer (Christological subject matter)

hermeneutics: the art or science of discerning the discourse in the text; a theoretical description and justification of what one takes to be best practices in textual interpretation

immanent frame: Charles Taylor's term for the secular picture of a self-enclosed natural world from which all transcendence is shut off; in this book, the frame of reference preferred in the modern study of the "academic" Bible, which tends toward methodological naturalism

literal sense: an oft-used term whose familiarity belies its complexity; in the history of biblical interpretation, the straightforward, surface, or nonfigural level of meaning of the textual letter; in this book, the meaning of the human-divine biblical discourse when read grammatically-eschatologically in canonical context, and the norm of theological interpretation

mere Christian hermeneutics: principles used everywhere and at all times by those who read the Bible as Scripture, whose "formal" principle is the trans-figured literal sense and whose "material" principle is the light of Christ (i.e., knowledge of God in the face of Christ)

methodological naturalism: the limitation of scientific explanation to natural and material causes; in this book, the notion that the Bible ought to be read like any other culturally and historically conditioned book, free from all theological presuppositions

philology: the love of words; also, the integrative discipline or glue that holds together the humanities; in this book, an image for the common interest of biblical studies and systematic theology to make sense of the way the words go in the Bible

plain canonical sense: in this book, a description of the "plain sense" of Scripture when read in canonical context; the thick, trans-figural literal sense

reading culture: the set of values, textual practices, and habits of reading that characterizes an interpretive community and forms its members; a communal place that socializes individuals into certain habits, and postures, of reading

sense/reference: a way to distinguish between two aspects of discourse: "what someone says" (sense) and that about which something is said (reference), both of which comprise literal meaning

social imaginary: Charles Taylor's term for the (secular) story that frames the everyday beliefs and practices of modern men and women; my term for the (scriptural) story that ought to frame the everyday beliefs and practices of Christians in every time and place

tactics vs. strategies, exegetical: in this book, a way of contrasting the means and ends of biblical interpretation; the difference between interpretive processes and techniques ("tactics"; the *how*) and interpretive aims and goals ("strategies"; the *what for*)

trans-figural interpretation: reading that follows the way the biblical words run across or beyond (*trans-*) figures to the realities those figures foreshadow and anticipate

transfigural interpretation: reading attentive to Christ's centrality in the economy of light; reading that discerns the glory of Christ in the letter of the text; also, reading that consciously adopts Jesus' transfiguration as its frame of reference

Scripture Index

Numbers

Deuteronomy

Joshua

Judges

1 Samuel

2 Samuel

1 Kings

1 Chronicles

Nehemiah

Esther

Job

Psalms

Ecclesiastes

Song of Songs

Isaiah

John

Acts

Romans

1 Corinthians

2 Corinthians

Galatians

Ephesians

Philippians

Colossians

1 Thessalonians

2 Thessalonians

1 Timothy

2 Timothy

Hebrews

James

1 Peter

2 Peter

1 John

2 John

Jude

Revelation

Proper-Name Index

Subject Index